THE ECONOMICS OF PUBLIC SERVICES

OTHER INTERNATIONAL ECONOMIC ASSOCIATION PUBLICATIONS

MONOPOLY AND COMPETITION AND THEIR REGULATION
THE BUSINESS CYCLE IN THE POST-WAR WORLD
THE THEORY OF WAGE DETERMINATION
THE ECONOMICS OF INTERNATIONAL MIGRATION
STABILITY AND PROGRESS IN THE WORLD ECONOMY
THE ECONOMIC CONSEQUENCES OF THE SIZE OF NATIONS
ECONOMIC DEVELOPMENT OF LATIN AMERICA
INFLATION
THE ECONOMICS OF TAKE-OFF INTO SUSTAINED GROWTH
INTERNATIONAL TRADE THEORY IN A DEVELOPING WORLD
ECONOMIC DEVELOPMENT WITH SPECIAL REFERENCE TO EAST ASIA
THE THEORY OF INTEREST RATES
THE ECONOMICS OF EDUCATION
PROBLEMS IN ECONOMIC DEVELOPMENT
THE ECONOMIC PROBLEMS OF HOUSING
PRICE FORMATION IN VARIOUS ECONOMIES
THE DISTRIBUTION OF NATIONAL INCOME
ECONOMIC DEVELOPMENT FOR EASTERN EUROPE
ECONOMIC PROBLEMS OF AGRICULTURE IN INDUSTRIAL SOCIETIES
INTERNATIONAL ECONOMIC RELATIONS
PUBLIC ECONOMICS
ECONOMIC DEVELOPMENT IN SOUTH ASIA
NORTH AMERICAN AND WESTERN EUROPEAN ECONOMIC POLICIES
PLANNING AND MARKET RELATIONS
THE GAP BETWEEN RICH AND POOR NATIONS
LATIN AMERICA IN THE INTERNATIONAL ECONOMY
MODELS OF ECONOMIC GROWTH
SCIENCE AND TECHNOLOGY IN ECONOMIC GROWTH
ALLOCATION UNDER UNCERTAINTY
TRANSPORT AND THE URBAN ENVIRONMENT
THE ECONOMICS OF HEALTH AND MEDICAL CARE
THE MANAGEMENT OF WATER QUALITY AND THE ENVIRONMENT
THE ECONOMIC DEVELOPMENT OF BANGLADESH
AGRICULTURAL POLICY IN DEVELOPING COUNTRIES
METHODS OF LONG-TERM PLANNING AND FORECASTING
ECONOMIC FACTORS IN POPULATION GROWTH
ECONOMIC INTEGRATION
CLASSICS IN THE THEORY OF PUBLIC FINANCE

The Economics of Public Services

Proceedings
of a Conference held by the
International Economic Association
at Turin, Italy

EDITED BY
MARTIN S. FELDSTEIN
ROBERT P. INMAN

M

First published 1977 by
THE MACMILLAN PRESS LTD
London and Basingstoke
Associated companies in New York
Dublin Melbourne Johannesburg and Madras

Distributed in the United States
by Halsted Press, a Division of
John Wiley & Sons, Inc., New York

ISBN 0 333 19543 4

Text set in 10/11pt IBM Press Roman, printed by photolithography, and bound in Great Britain at The Pitman Press, Bath

Library of Congress Cataloging in Publication Data
Main entry under title:

The Economics of public services.

(International Economic Association series)
Includes index.
1. Finance, Public–Congresses. 2. Expenditures, Public–Congresses. I. Feldstein, Martin S. II. Inman, Robert P. III. International Economic Association. IV. Series: International Economic Association. International Economic Association series.
HJ113.E35 336 75–37750
ISBN 0–470–01374–5

Contents

Acknowledgements

The Agnelli Foundation of Turin, Italy, were the sponsors and hosts for the conference. The success and pleasure of the conference was due in no small part to the excellent facilities and services that they provided. Mr Giovanni Granaglia represented the Agnelli Foundation and was responsible for all local arrangements. All participants were grateful for his careful planning and for his efficient management of the conference activities.

Professor Fritz Machlup, President of the International Economic Association from 1971 to 1974, was very helpful in all aspects of the planning of the conference. The programme itself and the list of participants reflects the efforts of the other members of the programme committee who worked closely with me: A. B. Atkinson, F. Forte, E. Gromov, S. Kolm and J. Paelinck. Robert Inman's excellent summary of the discussion appears at the end of this volume.

Finally, I am grateful to my secretary, Jeannette Taylor, who managed the voluminous correspondence and distribution of manuscripts, and to Dr Ruth Waxman, who edited a sometimes difficult and irregular manuscript.

M.S.F.

List of Participants

Aaron, H., The Brookings Institution, USA.
Atkinson, A., University of Essex, UK.
Bernard, A., Commissariat Général du Plan, France.
Bessière, F., CEPREMAP, France.
Bradford, D., Princeton University, USA.
Breton, A., University of Toronto, Canada.
Bruno, M., Hebrew University of Jerusalem, Israel.
Bruno, S., University of Rome, Italy.
Fauvel, L., University of Paris, France.
Feldstein, M., Harvard University, USA.
Forte, F., University of Turin, Italy.
Frey, B., University of Konstanz, Germany.
Giardina, E., University of Catania, Italy.
Gromov, E., Institute of World Economy and World Relations, USSR.
Guesnerie, R., CEPREMAP, France.
Hochman, H., The Urban Institute, USA.
Inman, R., University of Pennsylvania, USA.
Jeanjean, P., Ministère de la Santé Publique et de la Sécurité Sociale, France.
Khachaturov, T., Academy of Sciences of the USSR.
Klaassen, L., Netherlands School of Economics, the Netherlands.
Klevorick, A., Yale University, USA.
Kolm, S.-C., CEPREMAP, France.
Layard, R., London School of Economics, UK.
Lengyel, L., Ministry of Finance, Hungary.
Machlup, F., Princeton University, USA.
Martsinkevich, V., Institute of World Economy and International Relations, Academy of Sciences, USSR.
Milleron, J.-C., Ecole Nationale de la Statistique et de l'Administration Economique, France.
Paelinck, J., Netherlands School of Economics, the Netherlands.
Pauly, M., Northwestern University, USA.
Pedone, A., University of Rome, Italy.
Reviglio, F., University of Turin, Italy.

Rey, M., Ivrea, Italy.
Sandmo, A., Norwegian School of Economics and Business Administration, Norway.
Sheshinski, E., Hebrew University of Jerusalem, Israel.
Stern, N., Oxford University, UK.
Stiglitz, J., Stanford University, USA.
Thédié, J., Ministère de l'Equipement, France.
Tulkens, H., CORE, University of Louvain, Belgium.
Vickrey, W., Columbia University, USA.
Weizsäcker, C. von, University of Bonn, Germany.

Introduction: The Economics of Public Services

Martin S. Feldstein

Economics has traditionally and primarily been the study of the private economy. Although there have been occasional theoretical and practical studies in the field of public economics, the public sector has generally been the neglected stepchild of economic analysis. The classic studies of Wicksell and Samuelson showed how the logic of competitive equilibrium and welfare economics could be expanded to include public goods, but they also posed apparently insuperable problems that temporarily inhibited more practical developments. Even the specialised literature in public finance has focused on problems of taxation and has largely ignored issues of public expenditure.

All of this is now changing rapidly. During the past 30 years, the public sector has grown rapidly and spread into a wide range of previously private activities. Economic analysis has responded to this increased importance of public-sector problems. At first, the new economic interest was focused on developing general rules for the optimal behaviour of public enterprises. In France and England, economists developed optimal pricing rules for nationalised industries. In the United States, cost–benefit algorithms were designed to evaluate government investment options.

More recently, economic analysis has gone beyond theoretical foundations and general rules to the study of particular types of public programmes. This work has combined theoretical analysis with econometric estimation. Much of this research has been positive economics: analyses of the behaviour of the individual public sectors and studies of how the public programme affects that sector and the economy as a whole. Other research has built on this analysis to develop optimal policies for these public services.

The current conference exemplifies these recent developments in public economics. While the previous International Economic Association conference on public economics (held at Biarritz in 1967) focused on the general theoretical foundations of public expenditure analysis, the Turin conference was designed to explore the specific contributions that economic analysis can make to the study of particular types of public programmes.

Although the focus of most of the studies was on individual public services, several common themes were present in many of the papers. Perhaps most common was the emphasis that considerations of *distributional equity,* as well as the traditional notion of economic efficiency, were important in the design and evaluation of public services. Aaron and Layard were primarily interested in the measurement of distributional effects in the framework of a life-cycle model. Aaron used econometric estimates of life-cycle earnings profiles and mortality patterns to study the net redistributional effects of the United States social security system, and concluded that, despite the progressivity of the benefit schedule, the programme as a whole is mildly regressive. Layard analysed the distributional aspects of the British educational system, emphasising the issues in measuring redistribution in a life-cycle model with intergenerational links. Other studies showed how considerations of distributional equity could be quantified and explicitly balanced against losses of economic efficiency. Atkinson developed a general analysis of optimal housing subsidies in a framework suggested by the theory of optimal taxation. He related this analysis to experience in the United States and Britain, with special attention to the problems raised by imperfections in the housing market. Atkinson's concern with balancing equity and efficiency considerations was paralleled in Michael Bruno's treatment of public education expenditures.

Another common theme was the role of *decentralisation.* Instead of examining the optimal behaviour of a single omniscient government unit, several papers discussed the role of local governments and of decentralised public enterprises, and the desirability of mixing public and private decision-making. Breton, in his analysis of the assignment of functions in a multilevel federal government, focused most directly on the optimal degree of decentralisation. Sheshinski also dealt with a two-level structure of government. He investigated the behaviour of local governments in a model in which the central government provides grants financed by income tax while the local government uses a property tax. Within this framework, the supply of the local public good is determined by an explicit voting model in which the preference of the median voter is decisive. In contrast, Stiglitz ignored the role of the central government and emphasised the mobility of individuals among local communities as well as their voting behaviour. In this extension of the Tiebout model, Stiglitz examined the optimality characteristics of potential equilibria and showed how particular policies could improve the equilibrium. Vickrey also developed a model of competing cities, but focused on the role of external economies of scale in production as the source of city size and, thus, of land rents. In this framework, he showed that land rents should be used to subsidise the decreasing cost industries and that these rents are just sufficient to provide the optimal subsidy.

The third general theme was the importance of *general equilibrium effects.* Several authors emphasised that public programmes are often large in relation to the corresponding private sector of the economy (as in housing, for example) or even large in relation to the economy as a whole (as in social insurance). Forte's discussion of Italian housing policies stressed their impact on all housing development and land use. The study by Carr-Hill and Stern, which presented an econometric model of the criminal justice system in England, was not only interesting in its own right but also a valuable example of the power of economic theory and econometric methods in the analysis of nonmarket systems. Because this service is presented at the local government level, their model required a general equilibrium analysis of the reciprocal relation between criminal activities, police services, and conviction rates. Feldstein presented econometric evidence based on a cross-section of countries to show that social security increased retirement and reduced private savings. He then discussed the substantial impact on the distribution of income and wealth that is implied by this change in capital accumulation. In contrast to this emphasis on the long-run effect, Jeanjean used a short-term econometric model of the French economy to study in a general equilibrium framework the effect of the social security system on stabilisation policy.

The development of general methods of public expenditure planning was not neglected. Bernard extended earlier work on optimal taxation and public pricing, emphasising the problems associated with sectoral budget constraints and production efficiency in the case of profit taxation. In contrast to this global constrained optimisation approach. Thédié developed a partial-equilibrium analysis that would be appropriate for individual project evaluation.

Although the primary emphasis of the conference was on micro-economic problems, macro-economic aspects appeared a number of times. Klaasen and Eizenga stressed that some public services that are generally considered to be consumption expenditures should be treated as factors of production in aggregate growth analysis. Frey extended a short-term macro-econometric model by making government behaviour endogenous and assuming that governments act on the basis of their party ideology and their desire to remain in power while voters respond to the economy's short-run performance.

As this brief and partial description indicates, the conference dealt with a wide variety of stimulating issues. There was a general feeling that economic analysis and econometric research could make useful contributions to the understanding and improvement of public services. There was also agreement that this work had just begun and that much remains for the future.

It is perhaps a chairman's prerogative to look beyond the conference and to try to identify some of the types of research in this area that are likely to be important in the next decade. First, it is clear that we are just beginning to see the development of analytic and econometric models of such mixed-market and nonmarket sectors as health, education and criminal justice. Realistic models with estimated parameters are a prerequisite for policy analysis. A comparison of such models across countries should yield insights into the effects of institutional differences.

Second, the analysis of institutional behaviour must be extended beyond the traditional model of the competitive firm. Nonprofit institutions and decentralised bureaucracies are the primary organisations in the public sector. Recent studies of the behaviour of hospitals, universities and local governments show that useful models can be developed for such institutions but that much more remains to be done. The private firms that operate in conjunction with public services are often in concentrated industries or are the owners of unique patented information. Recent studies of the behaviour of regulated firms and of the process of government contracting indicate some directions for further work.

A third and more difficult task is to improve the analysis of the political behaviour that influences public services. Two types of research are needed. First, the simple median-voter models should be extended by relaxing the assumption that each expenditure category is voted separately, and by incorporating such things as 'logrolling' and political systems with more than two parties. Second, the legislative and political process should be recognised as imposing further constraints on the set of economically feasible options. While there is great value in describing the policies that would be optimal in the absence of such constraints, the politically constrained optimum may be qualitatively different. The nature of these political constraints – for example, not reducing pre-existing benefit levels or not increasing taxes beyond a certain level – requires careful investigation.

Finally, the analysis of optimal policies should be extended to reflect our uncertainty about economic parameters. To do this properly requires more than the application of static rules of expected utility maximisation. Public-service programmes provide opportunities for experimentation and learning. A programme can evolve slowly but certain changes may be irreversible. The general theory of the optimal design of public services should explore this problem of dynamic adjustment in an uncertain economic structure.

These suggestions for the future should not detract from what has already been achieved. The Turin conference successfully showed that economists from several countries can use a common framework to discuss the economics of a wide range of public services. The papers and the discussion indicate the useful contribution that economic analysis and econometric research can make to the understanding and improvement of public services.

Part I
Economics of Housing Programmes

1 Housing Allowances, Income Maintenance and Income Taxation

A. B. Atkinson[1]
UNIVERSITY OF ESSEX

This paper is concerned with the relationship between income maintenance and housing subsidies. After reviewing some of the policy issues which have arisen in Britain and the United States, it examines the theoretical considerations underlying the design of housing subsidies in relation to household incomes.

I. INTRODUCTION

Housing policy is a complex and controversial subject. The purpose of this paper is to concentrate on one particular aspect of this problem: the provision of individual housing allowances and their relationship to income maintenance and income taxation. Housing assistance in this form has become increasingly popular in recent years. In Britain, around 3 million (20 per cent of total) households are estimated to be eligible for rent rebates under the 1972 Housing Finance Act; in the United States, a Housing Assistance Plan is seen by many commentators to be a major component in a reform of the welfare system. In the Netherlands, a housing allowance programme was introduced in 1970; in West Germany, 5 per cent of households have been receiving allowances covering all forms of tenure ever since 1965; and, in Denmark, a rental allowance covers 25 per cent of all rental units (10 per cent of households).[2]

Section II of this paper describes the main issues to be examined, and discusses their relationship to recent housing policy in Britain and the United States. Although the motivation for the paper stems from a concern with important policy issues, it should be stressed at the outset that the analysis is based on a number of strong assumptions (described in section III) and that the results derived in sections IV–VI are largely theoretical in nature. The main emphasis of the paper is on isolating the essential issues, rather than with making policy recommendations, and the concluding section (section VII) describes some of the further research necessary in this area.

[1] The author is most grateful to participants in the conference for their helpful comments. These have led to definite improvements in the presentation of this paper.

[2] See Welfeld (1972)

II. HOUSING ALLOWANCES: SOME OF THE ISSUES IN BRITAIN AND THE UNITED STATES

Housing policy in Britain and the United States in the post-war period has been concerned with both the supply and the demand sides of the housing markets. Here attention is focused on the latter, and in particular on the relationship between housing subsidies and income maintenance/income taxation. The overlap between these policies has long been recognised in the case of the income-tax treatment of housing outlays; the overlap between housing assistance programmes and income taxation is a more recent problem and one that has not received sufficient attention.

TAX TREATMENT OF HOUSING OUTLAYS

In both countries home-owners enjoy, under the income tax, substantial concessions, which in effect allow the deduction of housing costs from taxable income.[3] It has been argued that these concessions give rise to horizontal inequities[4] and many proposals have been put forward for their abolition. These proposals involve, ideally, the taxation of imputed rent accruing to owner-occupiers (as was the case in Britain until the abolition of Schedule A in 1963–4), but, in the event of this being administratively infeasible, it has been suggested that one could correct the horizontal inequities between owners and renters by permitting the deduction of rent for income-tax purposes.[5]

HOUSING SUBSIDIES AND INCOME REDISTRIBUTION

The choice between the two policies just outlined may be seen in terms of the relative treatment of housing and other expenditure. A general subsidy to housing may also be given directly by reducing the cost of housing, and it has been argued that – given a low income elasticity of demand – a general subsidy of this kind would supplement the redistributive impact of income taxation. In section IV, we examine whether a case can be made for a general housing subsidy as a purely income-redistributive measure. Such a general subsidy would involve an equal reduction in the price of housing to all households. This may be contrasted with tax deductibility, where the price of housing depends on the household's marginal tax rate, so that, if the marginal tax rate rises with income, the rich derive greater benefit. It may also be contrasted with the housing assistance schemes, in which the subsidy is *reduced* as income rises, and to which we now turn.

[3] Strictly speaking, taxable income excludes net rent plus interest payments plus (in the United States) property taxes. See Aaron (1972) for the United States.

[4] It is, of course, necessary to examine the incidence of these concessions in a general equilibrium framework.

[5] This has been suggested, for example, in Britain (by Anthony Crosland) and in Canada (see Bossons, 1970); in the United States it was permitted under the Civil War income tax (see Simons, 1938, p. 115).

HOUSING ASSISTANCE SCHEMES

The growth of interest in these schemes stems, in large part, from a desire to link housing subsidies to individual income and circumstances. In the 1960s, critics of British housing policy pointed to the fact that 'the assistance which a family obtains depends, to a large extent, on the housing sector in which it finds itself, and total housing costs often depend more on history than current ability to pay' (Cullingworth, p. 109). In the United States, Tobin argued similarly that housing 'subsidies are available only for an accidentally or arbitrarily selected few. The result is that some low income taxpayers are subsidising the rents of families with equal or higher incomes' (Tobin, 1970, p. 275).

In Britain, these considerations led to the Conservative Government's Housing Finance Act of 1972, which was aimed at securing 'fairness between one citizen and another in giving and receiving help towards housing costs'. The mechanism by which help is to be channelled to 'those most in need' is the rent rebate (or allowance) scheme, which covers all tenants.[6] There is a national scale of allowances,[7] and, making a few simplifying assumptions, the formula for the rebate paid can be written as

$$S = \max\ [0, \beta hX - \gamma Y] \tag{1.1}$$

where Y denotes income, X quantity of housing assumed, h cost of housing (so hX = rent), and β and γ are constants.[8] It should be noted that hX is actual housing outlay, but in certain circumstances (for instance, where the authority thinks that the house is larger than needed) the administrator may substitute a specified X^*.

In the United States, rent supplements have, in the past, been linked to public housing or to housing partially funded under government programmes, and it is only very recently that proposals have been made for general housing assistance to all tenants. These proposals have not yet reached such a definite state as in Britain, but in most cases the subsidy formula follows (1.1) in broad outline. The foreword to Aaron (1972), for example, suggested that the government 'should distribute the benefits of housing subsidies to low and moderate income families through allowances determined by personal income, net worth and local housing costs'. Under the 1970 proposals by the Nixon administration, tenants would have been required to pay a certain proportion of their income in rent (between 20 and 25 per cent) and the government would have paid the rest of a fair market rent up to a specified maximum.

The widespread introduction of housing assistance may eliminate some of

[6] Since 1930, local authorities have been able to apply differential rents for council (public housing) tenants. The number of schemes grew substantially after the mid-1950s, and by 1963–4 they were employed by 40 per cent of the local authorities. Although the central government issued guidance, in the form of a model scheme, the central direction of rent rebates came only with the 1972 Act.

[7] There is some minor scope for local discretion.

[8] In broad terms, β = 60 per cent, and γ = 17 or 25 per cent.

the inequities of previous housing subsidies, which themselves have been the subject of criticism. The first line of criticism concerns the relationship with the income-tax system. In the American discussion of welfare reform, attention has been drawn to the high marginal rates of taxation resulting from the combined effects of unco-ordinated schemes (see Aaron, 1973). In Britain, the rent rebate system means, for example, that a household on average earnings may face a marginal tax rate of 52 per cent,[9] which is not reached on the positive income-tax scale until well into the top 1 per cent. The design of housing assistance has to be considered, therefore, in relation to income taxation; the optimal value of γ has to be chosen in the light of the income-tax structure.

A second important criticism of housing assistance schemes concerns the problem of administration and its effectiveness in reaching eligible families. Experience in Britain with similar rebates for rates (local property taxes) suggests that benefits reach only half of those entitled to them.[10] In the United States, this problem of 'take-up' has received less attention, but evidence for the food-stamp programme suggests that it may be important. Steiner has referred to 'consistent evidence of client nonparticipation' (1971, p. 197). The reasons for this failure are not fully known, but they result, in part, from an administrative structure in which the benefit paid depends on both the income and the housing expenditure of the family. The fact that both items are required to compute the benefit that is due means that the allowance can neither be paid automatically through the income-tax (negative income-tax) machinery, nor can it be provided via the landlord (in the case of rented accommodation). This raises the important issue of how far a unified rent-allowance/income-maintenance policy is required. Under what conditions can the administration be decentralised into separate – if co-ordinated – programmes for housing subsidies and income maintenance? These questions are discussed in a preliminary way in section VI.

III. THE FRAMEWORK FOR THE ANALYSIS

Household behaviour. Households are assumed to have identical utility functions[11] $U(C, X, L)$, where C denotes other consumption and L labour supplied (as a fraction of the total hours), but to differ in their wage per hour (w). C is taken as the *numéraire.* Households have no income apart from labour income ($Y = wL$).

Housing supply. As was indicated earlier, the model makes a number of strong assumptions, particularly in the case of the supply side of the housing market. It is assumed that the cost of housing (h) is determined exogenously, although

[9] Income tax of 30 per cent, social security contribution of $4\frac{3}{4}$ per cent, withdrawal of rent rebate of 17 per cent.

[10] See, for example, Townsend (1973) and Meacher.

[11] U is assumed to be continuously differentiable and strictly concave. It is assumed that U_C, $U_X > 0$, and $U_L < 0$.

it may vary among individuals. This assumption is made not on the basis of reaslism, but because it allows us to focus on the elements of the demand side that are of importance.

Policy instruments. The policy instruments examined in this paper may be written in the general form $H(h, hX, Y)$ where the household budget constraint becomes

$$C + hX = Y - H(h, hX, Y) \tag{1.2}$$

If the joint distribution of w and h across households is given by $f(w, h)$ then the government budget constraint is given by

$$\int_0^\infty \int_0^\infty H(h, hX, Y)\, dw\, dh = 0 \tag{1.3}$$

(assuming that no net revenue is required). This general formulation contains a number of special cases, including:

(a) $H = H(Y - hX)$ which is the case where housing outlays are tax-deductible;
(b) $H = H_1\,(Y) - H_2(hX)$, which is the case where housing outlay is subsidised independently of the income of the recipient; and
(c) $H = H_1(Y) - H_2(h)X$, which is the case where the unit cost of housing is subsidised.

Policy objectives. It is assumed that the government's objectives are represented by a social welfare function of the form

$$W = \int_0^\infty \int_0^\infty G\{U(C, X, L)\} f(w, h)\, dw\, dh \tag{1.4}$$

where G is a concave function. It may be noted that this formulation allows for a range of concern from the strict utilitarian case ($G = U$) to the Rawlsian case ($G = \min U$), but that it excludes specific egalitarianism as defined by Tobin (1970), and that we have ruled out interdependencies between individual utility functions.

In approaching questions of housing policy, it is clear that recommendations often diverge because of differing views of the sources of inequality in the housing market. Most importantly, one must distinguish between situations where, in the long run, everyone faces the same housing cost per unit (h is equal for all households) and situations where there are long-run inequalities in access to housing. In the latter case, one is saying, in effect, that housing is different in this respect from most other commodities. In sections IV and

V, the former case (equal h) is considered; section VI deals with the case where housing is 'different'.

IV. A GENERAL SUBSIDY FOR HOUSING?

The view that there are no long-run inequalities in access to housing, and that it is only inequalities in incomes that are of concern, is held by a wide variety of authors.[12] As we have seen, however, this does not mean that there is no role to be played by housing assistance. In particular, where the scope for direct taxation is restricted,[13] it has been argued that housing subsidies, given a low income elasticity of demand, can supplement the redistributive impact of income taxation.

In order to examine this argument, let us consider first the case where the government subsidises housing outlay at rate β, in addition to imposing a linear income tax (with a negative tax component). The household budget constraint becomes

$$C + h(1 - \beta)X = w(1 - t)L + \alpha \tag{1.5}$$

and the government revenue constraint[14]

$$\alpha = \int_0^\infty [twL - h\beta X] f(w) dw \tag{1.6}$$

The government chooses α, β and t to maximise

$$W = \int_0^\infty G[U(C, X, L)] f(w) dw \tag{1.7}$$

subject to (1.6). We may form the Lagrangian

$$\mathcal{L} = W - \lambda \left[\alpha - \int_0^\infty [twL - h\beta X] f\, dw\right] \tag{1.8}$$

[12] For example: 'Public housing is proposed not on the ground of neighborhood effects but as a means of helping low-income people. If this is the case, why subsidise housing in particular?' (M. Friedman); 'The rent agreement is quite an ordinary commodity transaction which is . . . of no greater and no lesser interest to the worker than any other commodity transaction, with the exception of that which concerns the buying and selling of labour power' (F. Engels).

[13] It will be assumed throughout that lump-sum taxation, $T(w)$, is not possible and that the government is restricted to income taxation. Wage taxes are also assumed to be ruled out.

[14] The distribution is normalised so that $\int\int f\, dw\, dh = 1$, or, in the present case of constant h, $\int f\, dw = 1$.

and obtain[15]

$$\frac{\partial \mathcal{L}}{\partial \alpha} = \int_0^\infty \left[G'U_C - \lambda + \lambda \left[tw \frac{\partial L}{\partial \alpha} - h\beta \frac{\partial X}{\partial \alpha} \right] \right] f \, dw = 0 \tag{1.9}$$

$$\frac{\partial \mathcal{L}}{\partial \beta} = \int_0^\infty \left[G'U_C hX - \lambda hX + \lambda \left[tw \frac{\partial L}{\partial \beta} - h\beta \frac{\partial X}{\partial \beta} \right] \right] f \, dw = 0 \tag{1.10}$$

$$\frac{\partial \mathcal{L}}{\partial t} = \int_0^\infty \left[- G'U_C wL + \lambda wL + \lambda \left[tw \frac{\partial L}{\partial t} - h\beta \frac{\partial X}{\partial t} \right] \right] f \, dw = 0 \tag{1.11}$$

If we define (where $\lambda > 0$)

$$\Omega(w) = \frac{G'U_C}{\lambda} + \left[tw \frac{\partial L}{\partial \alpha} - h\beta \frac{\partial X}{\partial \alpha} - 1 \right] \tag{1.12}$$

the first-order conditions (1.9)–(1.11) may be re-written as

$$\frac{1}{\lambda} \frac{\partial \mathcal{L}}{\partial \alpha} = \int \Omega(w) \, f(w) \, dw = 0 \tag{1.13}$$

$$\frac{1}{\lambda} \frac{\partial \mathcal{L}}{\partial \beta} = \int \Omega(w) \, X f(w) \, dw + \int \left[tw \, S_{LX} + h\beta \, S_{XX} \right] f \, dw = 0 \tag{1.14}$$

$$\frac{1}{\lambda} \frac{\partial \mathcal{L}}{\partial t} = \int \Omega(w) \, (- wL) \, f(w) \, dw + \int w \left[tw \; S_{LL} + h\beta \, S_{XL} \right] f \, dw = 0 \tag{1.15}$$

where S_{ij} denotes the Slutsky terms (and L is measured negatively for this purpose).

The expression $\Omega(w)$ is of central importance. It can be seen that the first term is a declining function of w (given the assumptions about G and U); the last term is more problematical, since it depends on how the marginal propensities to consume change with w (and on the signs of t and β). If we define $R(w) = twL - h\beta X - \alpha$, then a sufficient condition for Ω to be a declining function of w is that $\partial R / \partial \alpha$ (the marginal tax paid as lump-sum income increases) be a nonincreasing function of w.[16] Let us also assume that all goods

[15] Using the fact that $\partial U / \partial \beta = U_C hX$, $\partial U / \partial t = - U_C wL$.

[16] This does not seem unreasonable; it is ensured, for example, in the Stone–Geary case. It may be noted that the same problem arises in trying to determine whether R rises or falls with w. It can be shown that the first-order conditions imply that

$$\int \Omega(w) \, R(w) f \, dw \leqslant 0$$

but this does not imply that $R' \geqslant 0$.

are normal and are Hicksian substitutes ($S_{ij} > 0$ for $i \neq j$). These assumptions, which do not seem unreasonable for the broad commodity groups considered here, imply that X is an increasing function of w and, hence, that the first term in (1.14) is non-positive. From this it may be deduced that $\beta < t$. Suppose $\beta \geqslant t$, then

$$\left(\frac{1-t}{t}\right)\left[tw\, S_{LX} + h\beta\, S_{XX}\right] = \left[w(1-t)S_{LX} + h(1-\beta)S_{XX}\right] + \frac{(\beta - t)}{t}\, hS_{XX}$$

$$= - S_{CX} + (1-t)\,\frac{(\beta - t)}{t}\, hS_{XX}$$

(using the properties of the Slutsky terms). This expression is strictly negative, and it follows that $\partial \mathcal{L}/\partial\beta < 0$.[17] We thus have:

> *Proposition 1.* If Ω is a nonincreasing function of w, and all goods are normal and Hicksian substitutes, the optimal rate of subsidy on housing is strictly less than the rate of income taxation.

It is an immediate corollary of proposition 1 that, where those conditions are satisfied, the tax deduction of housing outlay is not optimal, since it would involve

$$C + hX = \alpha + wL - t[wL - hX]$$

or $\beta = t$. The optimal policy could be achieved only if the deduction were limited to a certain proportion of housing outlays. We can also see that, if the income tax were to be replaced by a value-added tax, with a rate τ' on housing and a rate τ on other consumption, so that the budget constraint became

$$C(1+\tau) + hX(1+\tau') = wL + \alpha$$

then, where the conditions for proposition 1 are satisfied, the optimal tax on housing is positive ($\tau' > 0$). In other words, there may be a case for a reduced rate of value-added tax on housing, but there would not be a case for complete exemption.[18]

The case for subsidising housing ($\beta > 0$) depends on the nature of the demand for it. As noted earlier, it is commonly felt that the relevant factor is that housing is a necessity, in the sense that the income elasticity is less than unity. The empirical evidence does not, in fact, provide strong support for this,[19] but even if it were true, it would not necessarily provide a case for subsidies where other instruments for redistribution are available. This may be

[17] This requires $t < 1$, but the assumptions on the utility function ensure that $\partial\mathcal{L}/\partial t < 0$ for $t \geqslant 1$.

[18] There may, of course, be a case for total exemption where both value-added tax and an income tax are in effect.

[19] For the United States, see, for example, Aaron (1972), appendix C.

seen from (1.14). Suppose that we evalute $\partial\mathscr{L}/\partial\beta$ at $\beta = 0$. This will be positive where

$$\int \Omega(w)\, Xfdw + \int twS_{LX}fdw > 0$$

The first of these terms incorporates the distributional considerations. We have already seen, however, that, where α is chosen to satisfy (1.13), together with the not unreasonable conditions that X is a nondecreasing, and Ω is a non-increasing function of w, then the first term is nonpositive. In this situation, the case for a subsidy depends on the second (efficiency) term, which is positive where the goods are Hicksian substitutes.[20] Under quite reasonable conditions, therefore, there will be no 'equity' case for housing subsidies. The reason here is quite simple: where housing is a normal good, a housing subsidy is less progressive than a uniform per capita payment (α).

This point may be illustrated by reference to the Stone–Geary utility function commonly assumed in empirical demand studies:

$$U = b_C \log(C - C_0) + b_X \log(X - X_0) + b_L \log(1 - L)$$

where $b_C + b_X + b_L = 1$. The resulting demand relationships (where $L \geqslant 0$) may be written

$$C - C_0 = b_C M \tag{1.16}$$

$$h(1-\beta)(X - X_0) = b_X M \tag{1.17}$$

$$w(1-t)L = w(1-t) - b_L M \tag{1.18}$$

where

$$M = w(1-t) + \alpha - C_0 - h(1-\beta)X_0 \tag{1.19}$$

denotes 'full income'. From (1.13)–(1.15), we obtain

$$\frac{\partial\mathcal{L}}{\partial\beta} \sim \int \left[\Omega(w)b_X + \frac{t}{1-t}\, b_L b_X - \frac{\beta}{1-\beta}\, b_X(1-b_X)\right] M f\, dw$$

$$\frac{\partial\mathcal{L}}{\partial t} \sim \int \left[\Omega(w)(b_L - 1) + (b_L - 1)\frac{t}{1-t}\, b_L + \frac{\beta}{1-\beta}\, b_X b_L\right] M f\, dw$$

so that $\partial\mathcal{L}/\partial\beta$, $\partial\mathcal{L}/\partial t = 0$ implies $\beta = 0$. In this case, a subsidy on housing is not desirable, even though housing may have an income or expenditure elasticity of less than unity.[21]

[20] The relationship to the second-best results (for example, Green, 1961) will be clear. Where $\beta > 0$, there is a further, negative term.

[21] The expenditure on X relative to C rises or falls with M as

$$\frac{b_X}{h(1-\beta)X_0} \gtrless \frac{b_C}{C_0}$$

V. TAX DEDUCTIBILITY AND NON-LINEAR TAX SCHEDULES

In the previous section it was demonstrated that the need for housing subsidies depends on the other possible means of redistribution. Where the uniform subsidy α is chosen optimally, there is no equity argument for housing subsidies. In this section we examine further the relationship between subsidies and the scope for income taxation, examining the desirability of subsidies and tax deductions where the tax schedule may be freely varied (i.e. is not constrained to be linear, as it was in the previous section).

This question may be posed in general terms, allowing for nonlinearity of both the income-tax and housing-subsidy schedules:

$$C + H(hX) = Y - T(Y) \qquad (1.20)$$

This problem may be solved using the same approach as that of Mirrlees (1971).[22] The household maximisation is equivalent to maximising $U(C, X, Y/w)$ subject to (1.20) and gives the first-order conditions

$$U_X = hH' \cdot U_C, \quad (-U_Y) = (1 - T')U_C \qquad (1.21)$$

The government maximises (1.7) subject to the overall constraint

$$\int_0^\infty (C + hX - Y) f(w)\, dw = 0 \qquad (1.22)$$

Heuristically, this can be solved by introducing a multiplier δ associated with (1.22) and a multiplier $\mu(w)$ associated with the differential equation

$$U \frac{du}{dw} = U_w = -\frac{U_Y}{w} \qquad (1.23)$$

U is a state variable; X and Y are control variables; and C is determined from (1.21). The Hamiltonian may be written

$$H = \{G(U) - \delta\ [C + hX - Y]\}f + \mu U_w \qquad (1.24)$$

and the following necessary condition obtained:

$$\frac{\partial H}{\partial X} = -\delta f\left[h + \frac{\partial C}{\partial X}\bigg|_U\right] + \mu\left[U_{wX} + U_{wC}\frac{\partial C}{\partial X}\bigg|_U\right] = 0 \qquad (1.25)$$

$$\delta fh[1 - H'] = \frac{u}{w}\,[U_{YC}\, hH' - U_{YX}] \qquad (1.26)$$

From this it is clear that $U_{YC} = U_{YX} = 0$ implies that $H' = 1$ (since the right hand side is zero and $\delta > 0$); in other words, we have:

[22] The argument given here is only heuristic; for a fuller treatment, see Atkinson and Stiglitz.

Proposition 2. Where the utility function is additively separable in X and C, taken together, and L, then the optimal policy does not involve a subsidy on housing.

It should be emphasised that this result requires separability only between labour and all goods taken together; it does not require separability between housing and other goods.[23] Since the tax deductibility of a fraction θ of housing outlay would modify the household maximisation conditions to

$$U_X = h(1 - T'\theta)U_C$$

so that the left-hand side of (1.26) became $\delta f h T'\theta$, we have the corollary that, where the utility function is additively separable (as above), the deduction of part or all of housing outlay from taxable income is not optimal.

Where the only intrinsic differences between individuals are those related to earnings, and where the government can levy any desired nonlinear income tax, then separability of the utility function between labour and other goods implies:

(a) that housing outlays should not be tax-deductible;
(b) that housing outlays should not be subsidised.

More generally, we have seen in this and in the previous section that the case for a general subsidy on housing for income-redistributive reasons is likely to be limited to situations where the government's income-tax possibilities are restricted. This conclusion may, however, critically depend on the assumption that there are no intrinsic inequalities in access to housing, and we now examine this question.

VI. UNEQUAL ACCESS TO HOUSING

In this section, we consider the case where the price of housing varies across individuals, so that they are distinguished both by earnings possibilties (w) and by housing costs per unit (h).

The analysis of the optimal design of a general tax and housing allowance schedule raises a number of problems of considerable technical difficulty. In order, therefore, to make some limited progress with the question, I have made the following simplifying assumptions:

(a) that the income tax system is of the linear form examined in section IV; and

[23] This kind of 'second-best' result has an intuitive appeal. The reason why a first-best optimum cannot be attained is because of variations in w (and limited tax instruments); if the utility function is separable in w and other elements, then one should not introduce a distortion between choices in the separable sector.

(b) that the housing allowance is paid on the basis of housing costs per unit (h) rather than on the basis of housing expenditure (hX).

The first of these assumptions clearly rules out the aspects discussed in section V, but, in fact, a linear tax schedule closely approximate that in force in a number of countries.[24] The second of the assumptions limits attention to one of the two types of housing allowance scheme outlined in section III, but, given the power of the authorities to substitute a 'reasonable' rent for actual housing expenditure, it may be the closer approximation at least to the British system.

The housing allowance schedule examined here is of the form[25]

$$C + hX = \alpha(h) + \{1 - t(h)\}wL + \beta(h)hX \tag{1.27}$$

In other words, the housing subsidy consists of a payment $\alpha(h)$ related to rent per unit, plus a payment related to actual housing outlay (βhX), minus an adjustment related to income (part of $t(h)$).

The government aims to maximise

$$\int\int G\{U(C, X, L)\}\, f(w, h)dwdh \tag{1.28}$$

subject to the revenue constraint

$$\int\int [\alpha - twL + \beta hX]\, f(w, h)dwdh = 0 \tag{1.29}$$

with which is associated a multiplier λ. For any given $\hat{h}$ we obtain the first-order conditions (for $\lambda > 0$)

$$\int \left[\frac{G'U_C}{\lambda} - 1 + tw\frac{\partial L}{\partial \alpha} - \beta h\frac{\partial X}{\partial \alpha} \right] f(w, \hat{h})dw = 0$$

or

$$\int \Omega(w, \hat{h}) f(w, \hat{h})dw = 0 \tag{1.30}$$

$$\int \left[\left(\frac{G'U_C}{\lambda} - 1 \right) \hat{h}X + tw\frac{\partial L}{\partial \beta} - \beta\hat{h}\frac{\partial X}{\partial \beta} \right] f(w, \hat{h})dw = 0$$

$$\int \left[\left(\frac{G'U_C}{\lambda} - 1 \right) wL - tw\frac{\partial L}{\partial t} + \hat{h}\beta\frac{\partial X}{\partial t} \right] f(w, \hat{h})dw = 0$$

[24] The British income tax system involves a marginal tax rate of 30 per cent for all but the top few per cent of taxpayers. Under the tax credit proposals it would be extended to a negative income tax with the same marginal rate.

[25] This form differs from the British scheme in that the latter embodies a nonlinear tax on income, the marginal tax rate falling from 25 per cent, to 17 per cent, to zero.

For the case of the Stone–Geary utility function considered earlier, the last two equations reduce to:

$$\int\left[\Omega(w) + \frac{t}{1-t}\,b_L - \frac{\beta}{1-\beta}(1-b_X)\right]Mf(w,\hat{h})dw = 0 \qquad (1.31)$$

$$\int\left[\Omega(w) + \frac{t}{1-t}\,b_L - \frac{\beta}{1-\beta}\frac{b_X b_L}{1-b_L}\right]Mf(w,\hat{h})dw = 0 \qquad (1.32)$$

where $M = \alpha + w(1-t) - C_0 - h(1-\beta)X_0$ as before.

By the same argument as in section III, $\beta(h) = 0$ for all h. We are interested in how α, t vary with h. In order to consider this, let us assume that $G' = 1$ and that the distribution is of the form $f(w)g(h)$. It then follows that Ω is independent of h, and hence M. To ensure this, α is determined so that $\alpha(h) - hX_0 =$ constant (i.e. the lump-sum subsidy should fully compensate for variations in housing costs at the level of the 'committed expenditure' X_0) and $t(h)$ is the same for all h.[26] We have, therefore:

> *Proposition 3.* If the distributions of h and w are independent, and the utility function is Stone–Geary in form, then the optimal policy is to compensate for variations in housing costs at the 'committed' level of expenditure and for a uniform tax rate to be applied.

While based on very special assumptions, this result is of interest,[27] since it comes close to the policies put forward as alternatives to the British Housing Finance Act. In particular, the rate of income tax would be independent of housing costs. The income tax would be operated independently of the housing situation, and the housing subsidy would not depend on income. In this way, the administration of the two schemes could be separated, thus contributing to the elimination of the problem of a low rate of 'take-up'. The housing subsidy would be set at a level that levelled out differences in housing costs at a minimum standard of housing (X_0), which does seem to accord with views often expressed.

VII. CONCLUDING COMMENTS

It will be clear that this paper only scratches the surface of an important range of problems, and that only very limited guidance can be given to policy-makers on the basis of this analysis. Two areas in particular may be mentioned. First,

[26] The constancy of t can be seen from (1.31) and (1.32) to follow from the independence of M and Ω from h.

[27] In the case of the assumption about the distribution, it is not clear whether h would be positively or negatively correlated with w; there are arguments in both directions.

the importance of the case for housing subsidies depends very much on unequal access to housing, and the argument of section VI needs to be extended to allow more definite conclusions to be drawn. Second, the whole question of administrative costs, borne both by tax authorities and by individuals, needs much more careful attention. Especial reference should be made to the problem of low 'take-up'; this was referred to at the beginning of the paper and in the previous section, but, clearly, needs to be incorporated more explicitly into the analysis.

REFERENCES

Aaron, H. J., *Shelter and Subsidies* (Washington, DC: The Brookings Institution, 1972).
Aaron, H. J., *Why is Welfare So Hard to Reform?* (Washington, DC: The Brookings Institution, 1973).
Atkinson, A. B., and Stiglitz, J. E., *Lectures on Public Economics* (in preparation).
Bossons, J., 'Value of Comprehensive Tax Base', *Journal of Law and Economics,* 1970.
Cullingworth, J. B., *English Housing Trends* (London: Allen & Unwin, 1976).
Engels, F., *The Housing Question* (Martin Laurence, no date).
Green, H. A. J., 'The Social Optimum in the Presence of Monopoly and Taxation', *Review of Economic Studies,* Oct 1961.
Meacher, M., *Rate Rebates* (London: Child Poverty Action Group, 1972).
Mirrlees, J. A., 'An Exploration on the Theory of Optimum Income Taxation', *Review of Economic Studies,* Apr 1971.
Simons, H., *Personal Income Taxation* (Chicago: University of Chicago Press, 1938).
Steiner, G., *The State of Welfare* (Washington, DC: The Brookings Institution, 1973).
Tobin, J., 'On Limiting the Domain in Inequality', *Journal of Law and Economics,* 1970.
Townsend, P. B., 'Everyone His Own Home', *Royal Institute of British Architects Journal,* Jan 1973.
Welfeld, I. H., *European Housing Subsidy Systems* (Washington, DC: US Department of Housing and Urban Development, 1972).

2 Public Expenditure for Housing: The Italian Case

Francesco Forte
UNIVERSITY OF TURIN

Publicly financed positive action for housing may be justified on several grounds. One would hardly, however, consider as a good reason the pressure of the middle class to improve their living standards. In Italy, that pressure brought about a 25-year exemption from income tax on buildings for any nonluxury new housing, thus heavily damaging the source of revenue for local financing, particularly in expanding areas. The effectiveness of the low-cost housing programme financed through a 1 per cent tax on payrolls and additional State contributions, has been reduced by the fact that local authorities, who have to provide the land and the infrastructures, are increasingly indebted and finding it difficult to finance them, and by the complicated procedures for land condemnation and for the construction of these houses. The new law of 1971, which broadens the scope of the low-cost housing policy, has been impaired by similar factors and by additional bureaucratic complications, so that papers, rather than houses, have been produced. A much simpler solution, in which, at each regional level, global conventions – including land procurement, infrastructures, housing construction and/or urban renewal – are arranged with large contractors, is suggested.

Direct demand subsidies to low-income families do not seem to be adequate for solving the problems, because of the bottlenecks on the supply side and the very different local situations.

Publicly financed positive action for housing is carried on in various forms in most industrialised countries. There are several 'theoretical' reasons to support these interventions, which relate to peculiarities of this goal on the demand or on the supply side: a specific form of income redistribution in favour of the lower-income classes (the community may be willing to promote redistribution only if it concerns a given allocation of resources); development of a certain kind of savings and small property in specific forms in the working class; a lessening of the effects of monopolistic collusion and of inefficiencies and exploitation due to the effects of the urban land market on the supply of housing; a correction of inefficiencies in the behaviour of house-owners caused by the existence of reciprocal externalities; the removal of the negative externalities of bad housing and/or of urban decay that affect the community at large; and anti-cyclical action and relief from unemployment programmes.

There is, however, another reason, which is difficult to justify on the ground of equity or efficiency: that is, the pressure of the middle classes to improve their living standards and their wealth, and the interest in a market for middle-class housing – aided by the government – on the part of land developers, constructors and credit institutions.

This 'practical reason' explains a large share of Italian positive fiscal action in the housing area and, in particular, the exemption from income tax on buildings, that was granted in 1928, for a period of 25 years, to any kind of new construction that was not openly of a luxury type at the moment of its completion.[1] This exemption was renewed in 1949.[2] In the Italian tax system that was in force until the recent tax reform, this was the normal form of taxation on this kind of income; as a matter of fact, the progressive income tax was only a supplement to the sum of any kind of income of the taxpayers.

Without the exemptions, this tax should also have been one of the main sources of revenue for local finances: the municipal and provincial rate contributed the largest part of its global rate – 22–24 per cent. Since the assessment on buildings exempted from this tax was belated and imperfectly carried on, the exemption also damaged the taxable basis of the 'complementary' tax. The exemption has been carried on in the new lower-rate local tax that, since the tax reform, accompanies the State personal income tax.

Rooms built from 1949 to 1971 (including bathrooms, kitchens and other service areas) total 38,642 million. Practically all of them were granted the tax exemption. At an average rental value of 100,000 lire per year per room, the post-war tax-free gross income from buildings thus amounts to 3800 billion lire, with an expense deduction of 25 per cent to 2,850 billion. At the tax rate on buildings after the reform (around 13 per cent), the loss of yearly yield (entirely sustained by local authorities) is about 370 billions; at the tax rate before the reform (20–25 per cent), the loss of yearly yield (mostly sustained by local authorities) would currently be more than 600 million. In earlier years, when the stock of postwar buildings was smaller and rental values lower, the loss was proportionally less, but still large in constant-value terms. Public expenditure for housing has never been more than 250 billion lire per year and has usually been between 100 and 200 billion.

This tax exemption has heavily damaged the finances of large, growing cities, hindering their capacity to expand the supply of land provided with public utilities for new urban developments and for urban renewal. It also frustrates low-cost housing programmes, which presuppose that land is made available by the local authorities.[3]

In spite of this important exemption, however, the construction of flats in

[1] Changes in buildings soon after the exemption is granted are not taken into account.

[2] See *LRS*, 18 Jan 1949, no. 2, article 9.

[3] Post-war housing stock in large cities is about 60 per cent of the total stock. The exemption from tax on buildings subtracts more than 60 per cent of the tax yield.

Italy has been sizable, though not spectacular. As a rate per thousand inhabitants, it ranges from 5 to 7, far below the rate in Germany and, in most years, lower than the rate in France. As a percentage on national income, it ranges between 6 and 7·5 in current values and is slightly less in constant (1963) values. The first percentage is normally lower than the German and the French ones; the second is lower than the French and higher (after 1956) than the German one.

The number of persons per room is, on the average, 0·84 in the Centre–North and 1·20 in the South: but, allowing for vacant houses ('second' houses, buildings to be repaired, rural houses abandoned by emigrants, and so on) and for underoccupied houses, the index rises to 1·16 in the Centre–North and 1·54 in the South. To reach an index of 1, about 2 million rooms should be built, without taking into consideration the restorations, improvements and substitutions that are necessary to improve the conditions of unsuitable unhygienic housing.

The regional and local distribution of the rooms, is, however, very irregular. Southern low-income regions have very high indexes. A ranking of the regions with an income per capita of less than 90 per cent of the Italian average, and a ranking of the regions with an index per person per room of above the Italian average reveals a strong correlation, with the sole exception of Lazio, which includes Rome, where the income is above the average and where there is also an impressive metropolitan development that is fed by the immigrants coming from the South. At the other end, there is no correlation between the ranking of the 'wealthy' regions, i.e. those with an income per capita above the average, and the ranking of the regions with lower indexes of persons per room. This is because in the most industrialised regions there has been a large inflow of immigrants, which has aggravated the need for housing by the lower and the lower-middle classes.

Under the impulse of fiscal exemption (in addition to those previously mentioned, there are other exemptions from taxation on bond mortgages, on real estate and from the 'registry' tax), house-ownership in Italy has greatly increased, and it is now substantially greater than it is in West Germany and in France. More than 50 per cent of Italian families live in their own houses, and the number of upper- and middle-class owners of a second house (mostly enjoying fiscal exemption) is very large. In part, this high percentage is due to the large proportion of the population still living in rural areas, but the increase from 40 per cent in 1951 to 53 per cent in 1969 is almost entirely due to the development of house-ownership in urban and suburban areas. In large cities, families living in their own houses average 32 per cent. It is worth noting that, in Rome and in some cities of the Centre–South, the percentages are still higher. A large number of rented apartment houses belong to 'condominiums', i.e. to relatively small investors who have bought apartments here and there.[4]

[4] 'Condominiums' in the fifteen largest towns represent 52 per cent of the houses; assuming that all of the houses occupied by their owners are condominiums (certainly an

The amount of funds devoted by the public sector to subsidising programmes has decreased, over a period of time, both as a percentage of total investment in housing and as an absolute amount in constant values. The percentage of rooms built by the public sector decreased from 15–24 per cent in the years 1953–61, to 4–10 per cent in the next decade. The absolute amount also decreased substantially. This amount, however, is not entirely related to low-cost housing; a share of it (variable in time) refers to programmes of subsidised loans for house-purchasing in favour of employees or of families with a taxable income not higher than 4 million lire (which, due to the large underassessment of the personal tax before the recent tax reform, is quite a high amount). The regional distribution of funds clearly favours the more prosperous regions, where requests for loans are larger.

What is perhaps more impressive is the decrease of the percentage and of the absolute number of rooms built under the programme of the Agency of Housing for the Workers (Gescal), a genuine low-cost housing programme financed through a 1 per cent tax on payrolls and by additional State contributions. Its percentage for total housing construction, from 1962 to 1972, has never been more than 5 per cent and, in most years, has fallen to 3 per cent or less. This failure cannot be systematically attributed to a lack of funds. In fact, in 1971, Gescal had 500 billion lire of liquid funds to spend, against an aggregate expenditure of 817 billion from 1962 to 1972, plus 238 billion earmarked to pay for buildings under construction or just contracted. 1971 was a depression year and one would have expected that Gescal would have been able to act as an anti-cyclical fiscal weapon; but it was not possible to build more than 40,000 rooms, the lowest figure since 1965, which was also a year of depression, when the rooms built by Gescal numbered only 31,000.

Obviously, one might argue that, even if it were doubled, the yearly amount of funds spent by Gescal would not have been very much, since it would have increased the percentage of this programme in the decade to less than 5 per cent. But it may also be argued that, with the large social demand for housing in Italy, the pressure of the unions and the need to stimulate aggregate demand through fiscal actions in several of these years, Gescal could have obtained important additional amounts if it had been effective in spending its funds.

What are the reasons for the failure? Basically, they are the following.

(1) Very often municipalities had no land available to realise these programmes. Among the reasons for this were that they had not singled it out for expropriation, and/or did not have the funds, obtainable through loans, to carry on the expropriation, or were still going through the lengthy procedures preliminary to it.[5]

(2) Very often, because of the lack of funds to be obtained through loans,

excessive estimate), condominium houses rented are 20 per cent, as against 33 per cent rented by single private owners.

[5] In order to do so, they must carry on urban planning procedures.

municipalities had not endowed the land with the infrastructures that were necessary if it were to be built on.

(3) Prices set by Gescal for constructions were not considered interesting and offers were often not made by any contractor (this happened frequently in periods of rapidly increasing prices), so that the formal procedures, which must be carried on through the Local Agencies for Popular Buildings (IACPs) had to be repeated from the beginning.

(4) Sometimes the IACPs are inefficient bodies. This is not the case in most cities of Northern Italy but it is rather frequent in the South. Things are made even more difficult by the political resistance to expropriation and by the legal disputes related to it.

In October 1971[6] a law was passed to reinforce and broaden the public programme for housing by establishing better rules for expropriation, providing additional funds, devising new forms of intervention and concentrating all public operations in a three-stage system: the New Central Committee for Residental Buildings (CER) by the Ministry of Public Works; the regional administrations; and the IACPs, reorganised at a provincial level.

It was expected that it would be possible to devote 2500 billion lire to construction of low-cost housing and 450 billion to acquiring the land and providing it with public utilities in a three-year period (1971–4). The fact that this did not happen led to a very pessimistic attitude about the feasibility of public programmes in this area. Why is it that the law of 1971 has so far produced so much 'paper' (witnessing to bureaucratic activity) but so few houses? First of all, it should be said that it was absurd (or demagogic) to assume that a law of 22 October 1971 could produce any effect in that same year. But neither, because of procedural reasons related to the too-rigorous system set out by the law, could it be fruitful in the following years. In addition, many of the bodies involved in the planning failed to respect the time prescribed for their decisions, so that by 1973 the 'new' share of the programme was not yet operating. Regions, it should be remembered, are a newly created institution.

It must be added, however, that the 'old' share of the programme relating to Gescal funds experienced an acceleration in its initial stages; in 1972–3, Gescal contracted constructions for 600 billion lire. But most of the other funds were not mobilised. As for the ones for land procurement and development, the reason is very simple: these funds are available to municipalities not as *grants* but as *loans* at a reduced interest rate.[7]

Most municipalities have, by now, a very limited capacity of indebtment. Furthermore, procedures to get loans from the central institution entitled to grant them are slow. This is also due to the policy of the Central Bank, which aims to keep down the deficit of the public sector, sometimes in conflict with

[6] Law no. 865 of 22 Oct 1971, completed by Law no. 13 of 25 Feb 1972.

[7] To the contributions granted by the State to reduce the interest rate, there are sometimes added grants by the State, measured on the cost of the works. They differ for different kind of investments (schools, markets, social centres, and so on) and involve a complex procedure.

fiscal policy choices. But there is a bottleneck at the very beginning of the pattern of realisation of the programme.

A second failure lies in the fact that the 'new' funds given by the government to finance housing construction (except those allocated to Gescal) were conceived of as contributions on the interest rate, ranging from 4 per cent for projects by co-operatives with individual property, and 5 per cent for co-operatives with common property, to 5 per cent and 8 per cent for programmes by the IACPs and 6·89 per cent for programmes by the Ministry of Public Works to replace unhygienic houses and to build houses in places damaged by floods and earthquakes.[8]

In theory, the new programme should mobilise about 750 billion lire for construction, with a yearly grant of 50 billion on the interest rate. But in practice this requires that the Cassa Depositi e Prestiti (the Public Credit Agency, which finances local expenditures) should make the funds available (a choice that largely depends on the Central Bank) and that other credit institutions should be willing to supplement them with their share. Here there is clearly another bottleneck. Further, the green light to a public-finance and fiscal-policy action is, in this case, left to the decisions of monetary authorities and to credit-institution policies.

A third problem is created by the rules on the execution of construction by contracts. Severe and complex public-law rules have been conceived to prevent fraud, collusion among potential contractors, and excessive prices. The result, however, is often just the opposite of what was intended. Because of the delays and because of the fractioning of projects, construction costs eventually become greater and quality is often below desired levels.

To overcome these difficulties, a different system, based on 'conventions' of a global character, has been conceived. In the 1971 law, however, it has only a marginal place. As for construction under the programmes normally given to the IACPs, this can take place only where the latter fail to undertake them, and, then, only by public enterprises.

There is, in addition, a limited programme, with a contribution by the State of 4 billion lire, for constructions (which may subsequently be purchased by anybody) on municipal land, which is conceded for a maximum period of twenty-nine years to private or public entities. The contribution is such that, for loans of a maximum period of 25 years, the interest rate, inclusive of issuance costs and taxes, should not exceed 3 per cent plus amortisation charges. charges. Loans entitled to the contribution may cover up to 75 per cent of the total cost, which, however, also includes improvement costs.

The business enterprises that are granted the State contribution can perform any operation (from the land operation on), with their own planning and without being obliged to follow public-law rules. A great flexibility is thus reached.

[8] To these programmes one should add 300 billion lire made available, under the 1965 law, for State contributions to housing purchase loans to families with an income of a certain level. The above considerations apply also to this programme.

But this is still a marginal programme. It has been assessed that the 4 billion contribution may mobilise 50 billion lire in construction, entitled to the 3 per cent interest rate. Land, as such, is cost free, but urbanisation costs must be borne by the builders.

Because of the difficulties of public intervention in housing construction, the thesis has also been developed in Italy that the State should aid solution of the problem of housing through subsidies that pay the difference between an equitable rent that low-income families can afford and the actual rent as determined on the market. I do not question that, in given conditions, demand subsidies may be the best means to face the problem; but in my opinion they would at present be the wrong answer in Italy.

From the above picture one can clearly see that the scarcity of land suitable for building and the lack of public facilities necessary for adequate housing have been the main barriers to the realisation of construction programmes financed by public operators, when these programmes were given sizable funds. This, however, has not been a frequent case. State contributions were related to credit facilities that were difficult to raise. They did not take the form of straight capital grants.

If demand subsidies were given in a condition of limited supply of adequate housing, they would result in increased rents, and this, in our case, would not be a short-run phenomenon. This is due to the above-mentioned bottlenecks, which influence any kind of building.

It should be stressed that demand subsidies may to a large extent, be absorbed, by the supplies in a market where the supply is limited either by objective conditions, or by monopolistic practices, or by a combination of both. According to recent empirical findings, there is at present in Italy an increasing difference between the cost and the price of housing, as one moves from low-cost to medium, or to high-quality, supply.

For low-cost housing, construction costs are about 100–110 thousand lire per square metre, and sale prices are about 100–150. For medium housing, costs range between 115 and 120 thousand lire, and sale prices between 210 and 300 thousand lire, per square metre. For luxury housing, the corresponding figures are 145–160 thousand lire (costs) and 330–500 thousand lire (sale prices).[9] It can therefore be argued that the rate of exploitation increases in so far as purchasers or tenants increase. If this is true, then a demand subsidy would be mostly a transfer in favour of the supply, without much benefit to the poorer class of consumers.

As we have often seen, housing programmes have been halted by a monetary policy restricting the availability of funds. If this has been the case for investment expenditures in housing, why should the answer be different for the subsidies on housing rents? The only explanation of a different behaviour would be that in this second case the fiscal authority could have a better control of the choice, because it could allocate the funds in its general budget, the

[9] See CENSIS, *Quindicinale di note e commenti,* no. 191 (Sept 1973), p. 642.

deficit of which has to be globally financed. If fiscal policy really wants to give priority to housing, it may simply adopt a different financial arrangement from the very beginning, rather than artificially changing the type of intervention to obtain it.

The need for housing differs greatly in the various regions and areas; consequently, an undifferentiated subsidy would not be adequate. One would require that it be different for different places; but, then, direct action on the supply side appears a more efficient solution. It should be stressed that 'direct action', in this reasoning, does not at all imply direct construction by the government. On the contrary, not only construction, but also a considerable amount of other 'service' activity should be carried out by private firms – subcontracting, on private terms, to others, if they find it more workable.

Much unhygienic housing is in this condition because of inadequate sewerage, a poor water supply, and a scarcity of other public utilities. The stock of housing could be substantially improved if the necessary utilities were made available. To effect this, funds should be supplied for this purpose, not to supplement the rents of poor families living in these houses.

Furthermore, these subsidies will not help in urban renewal. Even if the programmes of housing financed by the government have systematically overlooked this aspect of the housing stock, concentrating, as they do, almost exclusively on other kinds of interventions, there is no inherent reason why this choice should not be changed.

Finally, housing costs are increased by the fractioned ways generally followed in building. By means of 'conventions' allowing large-scale enterprises to operate on large areas of land, from their preparation to actual construction, costs may be reduced and substantial innovations introduced with beneficial effects for the entire building sector.

A considerable amount of land is available for expropriation under the low-cost housing laws. In December 1971 it was 27,065 hectares, i.e. enough for the construction of 4·5 million rooms (including bathrooms and kitchens) and the public utilities relating to them, under average urban standards. By now, the availability has increased by at least 10 per cent. However, the distribution of this land among the various regions contrasts with the distribution of new constructions relative to indexes of need (taking into account the number of persons per room and the share of unhygienic dwellings). Here there is, among other things, an open disequilibrium between the North and the South plus the Rome area. But one could hardly increase the land available for low-cost housing development and renewal in these areas through subsidies on rents. Greater expenditures on local public facilities and on transportation services are probably the only effective answer here.

To some extent, the housing problem (at least in Italy) is a problem of funds for local finances. More land must be provided and endowed with public utilities and better communication systems.

REFERENCES

Aaron, Henry J., *Federal Housing Subsidies: History, Problems and Alternatives,* (Washington, DC: The Brookings Institution, 1973).

Aaron, Henry J., *Shelter and Subsidies: Who Benefits from Federal Housing Policies?* (Washington, DC: The Brookings Institution, 1972).

CENSIS, *Quindicinale di note e commenti* (several issues).

Ministero LL.PP, 'Relazione per il CIPE, attuazione del programma di edilizia residenziale' (29 Oct 1973) unpublished manuscript.

Villani, Andrea, *La politica dell'abitazione: analisis dell alternative di intervento publico – Il caso italiano,* (Milan: Franco Angeli, 1970).

Part II
Distributional Issues in Education

3 Efficiency and Equity in Public Education Expenditures

Michael Bruno [1]
THE MAURICE FALK INSTITUTE FOR ECONOMIC RESEARCH IN ISRAEL, JERUSALEM

The equilibrium distribution of schooling is studied when individuals differing in their natural endowments (n) decide on their schooling (S) on the basis of lifetime net earnings (I). The government affects the latter through the price of tuition and a given tax on earnings. The existence of positive interaction between S and n in earnings and a negative interaction on the resource-cost side makes for a strong positive correlation between the distributions of n and S, and a regressive tuition fee under pure efficiency. Social welfare objectives will modify this relationship in the direction of a more egalitarian S and I distribution, and the trade-off is quantifiable. A tentative numerical example based on Israeli data is given at the end.

I. INTRODUCTION

Recent literature on investment in education abounds in debates on policy issues concerned with the equity–efficiency quandary.[2] In going over it, one is struck by the contrast between the richness of interesting empirical findings and the relative sparseness of systematic analytical statement of the policy problems in a form that would be both sufficiently general and, at the same time, lend itself to quantitative application. Arrow (1971) has provided a good starting point in the direction of a theoretical framework for the analysis of equality in public expenditure. The present paper is an attempt to suggest a more detailed framework for the specific area of education and in a form that could be applied empirically.

A major element in an analysis of optimum educational expenditures is the behaviour attributed to the individual. For our purposes we adopt some version of a lifetime earnings approach (cf. Ben-Porath, 1967, and Atkinson, 1973) whereby an individual chooses the amount of education that he undertakes (beyond compulsory education) in a lifetime cost–benefit calculation. Costs

[1] I am indebted to A. Atkinson, Y. Ben-Porath, S. Colm, R. Gronau, R. Klinov-Malul, U. Litvin and the conference participants for helpful comments on an earlier draft.

[2] For a recent collection of articles on this issue see Schultz (1972).

include tuition fees and earnings that are forgone, and benefits include enhanced future net after-tax earnings (with, or without, additional consumption benefits). Individuals vary in their natural endowments, which may affect both their potential earnings (for given educational and other characteristics) and the production costs of providing them with formal education. The public sector can affect the individual's choice of education through the determination of (differential) tuition fees as well as through the tax system on future earnings. Optimality is here defined as maximisation of an individualistic social welfare function where equity considerations are applied across given cohorts.

Section II describes individual behaviour. Section III characterises the optimum choice of educational distribution and tuition fees under pure efficiency. This is compared, in section IV, with the solution that is obtained once equity considerations are introduced. Section V gives a numerical illustration for the distribution of human capital and educational expenditures among social groups in Israel.

II. THE MODEL – INDIVIDUAL BEHAVIOUR

We start with the following set of assumptions.

1. Individual earnings (y) depend on years of education completed (S) and on an index of natural endowments (n),[3]

$$y = b(S, n) \tag{3.1}$$

where $b_s > 0$ and $b_n > 0$. (Additional assumptions on the derivatives will be given below.) The population density function $f(n)$ is assumed given.

2. During the years of education (t; $0 < t < S$) the individual pays a tuition fee of $a(t, n)$ per period, where a is a government policy instrument that can vary with n and could, in principle, also take on negative values (net subsidy).

3. Individual earnings are taxed through a given progressive income-tax function

$$h = h(y) \tag{3.2}$$

where $0 < h_y < 1$ and $h_{yy} \geqslant 0$.

4. The individual maximises his lifetime (T) net wealth (I) with respect to S (for given a and h policies).

Denoting total lifetime gross income or wealth (discounted at rate r) by Y, total tax payments by H and total tuition fees by A, the individual thus maximises

[3] The latter here encompasses all of the unexplained regression residuals (from y on S) that are the result of endowments like home environment, as well as natural 'ability', and so on. Changes in y are defined net of other measurable changing characteristics, such as age and experience.

$$I = Y - H - A = \int_S^T b(S, n)e^{-rt}dt - \int_S^T h[b(S, n)]\, e^{-rt}dt - \int_0^S a(n, t)e^{-rt}dt$$

$$= (b - h)\frac{e^{-rS} - e^{-rT}}{r} - \int_0^S ae^{-rt}dt \tag{3.3}$$

Differentiating (3.3) by S and multiplying by e^{rS}, the first-order necessary condition for an interior maximum gives

$$g(S, n) = -(b - h) + Db_s(1 - h_y) = a(S, n) \tag{3.4}$$

where $D = 1 - e^{-r(T-S)}/r > 0$.[4] b, h, etc., are all evaluated at S. $g(S, n)$ is the undiscounted net private benefit from an additional year of schooling (at S), the first, negative term being net earnings forgone at S,[5] and the second, positive term being net additional earnings during the subsequent lifetime ($S < t \leqslant T$). $a(S, n)$ is the given tuition cost (or receipt) at year S.

Equation (3.4) can also form the basis of private rate-of-return calculations – or given observed a and S one calculates r as the rate that equates g to a in (3.4).[6] Note that g could, in principle, be negative. In particular this could be the case if we were to introduce uncertainty into future b_s levels, or if interest rates r that face the individual borrower are above social rates (say, involving a high-risk premium).

Consider now the second-order condition for a maximum: $I_{ss} < 0$. A necessary and sufficient condition is that the marginal tuition fees (a_s) be greater than the marginal schooling benefit (g_s). In particular, this will happen if $a_s > 0$ while $g_s < 0$, giving us

$$e^{rS}I_{ss} = g_s - a_s = (1 - h_y)[D_s b_s + (Db_{ss} - b_s)] - Db_s^2 h_{yy} - a_s \tag{3.5}$$

Since $D_s = rD - 1 \leqslant 0$ and $h_{yy} \geqslant 0$, we shall always have $g_s < 0$, providing the following assumption is made.

5. $b_{ss}/b_s < 1/D$ ($\leqslant r$), i.e. incremental income from education rises at a rate *less* than the discount factor $1/D$. To this we shall also add the next assumption.

[4] For most realistic situations, $e^{-r(T-S)}$ is very small and, thus, D is very close to $1/r$. It is also worth noting that, instead of assuming T to be fixed, one could (as in Atkinson, 1973) assume the working life ($T - S$) to be constant. There is even some empirical evidence supporting such an assumption (see Mincer, 1974). In any case, the theoretical results turn out extremely similar.

[5] Note that in the way (3.3) is formulated there are no earnings during studies. This could be modified. If, for example, in the year $t(t \leqslant S)$, an individual can earn $\delta b(t)$, where $0 < \delta < 1$, we must add an integral $\int_0^S \delta b(t)e^{-rt}dt$ in (3.3), and in (3.4) we must write $(1 - \delta)b$ instead of b. This will be used in the empirical illustration (section V).

[6] For example, if a or $(a - \delta b) \sim 0$ and $D \sim 1/r$ one gets simple $b_S(1 - h_y)/(b - h) \sim r$, i.e. the rate of change of net income equals the interest rate (see also Mincer, 1974).

6. $b_s/b > r\ (\geqslant 1/D)$, i.e. income rises with S at a rate that is *higher* than r.

Assumptions 5 and 6 together ensure a positive and diminishing gross marginal product of S ($Y_s > 0$, $Y_{ss} < 0$), since we have

$$e^{rs}Y_s = Db_s - b$$

and

$$e^{rs}Y_{ss} = (Db_{ss} - b_s) - (b_s - rb)$$

As long as the policy for $a(S)$ ensures that $\partial a/\partial S > \partial g/\partial S$ (this is usually ensured automatically by having $a_s \geqslant 0$), the solution for S (denoted by $\bar{S}$) is unique.

Next, look at the sensitivity of schooling benefits to differential endowments (n).[7] We have

$$g_n = (1 - h_y)(Db_{sn} - b_n) - Db_s b_n h_{yy} \tag{3.7}$$

Thus,
$$g_n \gtreqless 0 \; IFF \; \frac{Db_{sn} - b_n}{Db_s b_n} \gtreqless \frac{h_{yy}}{1 - h_y}$$

The following assumption on positive interaction between S and n seems to make empirical sense.[8]

7. $Y_{sn} = Db_{sn} - b_n > 0$.

Thus, if marginal tax progressivity (h_{yy}) is sufficiently small, we shall find that $g_n > 0$, but this, of course, is not automatically ensured. However, there is an additional point to be noted. Suppose that the discount rate r varies across individuals either because of capital market imperfections or because of differential attitudes to risk. If, as is sometimes claimed, r is negatively correlated with n, we could make D a positive function of n ($D_n > 0$) and in (3.7) we have to add another positive term, $D_n b_s(1 - h_b)$. This would strengthen the case for $g_n > 0$.

The importance of the signs of these derivatives derives from the resulting distribution of individual equilibrium schooling levels $[\bar{S}(n)]$ across the population distribution of n. We have

$$\frac{d\bar{S}(n)}{dn} = \frac{g_n - a_n}{a_s - g_s} \tag{3.8}$$

The denominator in (3.8) is positive by the previous second-order condition for a maximum. Thus, the better endowed will demand and get more schooling

[7] The implied assumption of continuity and differentiability with respect to n is only a matter of analytical convenience. One could prove analogous results for discrete changes in n.

[8] For empirical evidence of positive interaction between S and n ($b_{sn} > 0$), see Hause (1972) and de Wolff and Van Slijpe (1973). Also note that, in Becker's (1964) theoretical analysis, $y = b(n, s)$ takes the simple multiplicative form $y = n\beta(S)$, in which case assumption 7 becomes synonymous with assumption 6.

$(d\bar{S}(n)/dn > 0)$[9] if, and only if, $g_n > a_n$. In the special case in which tuition fees are the same for all $(a_n = 0)$, this condition is simply $g_n > 0$. It will *a fortiori* be the result if, also, $a_n < 0$. *Figure 3.1* gives a geometric representation

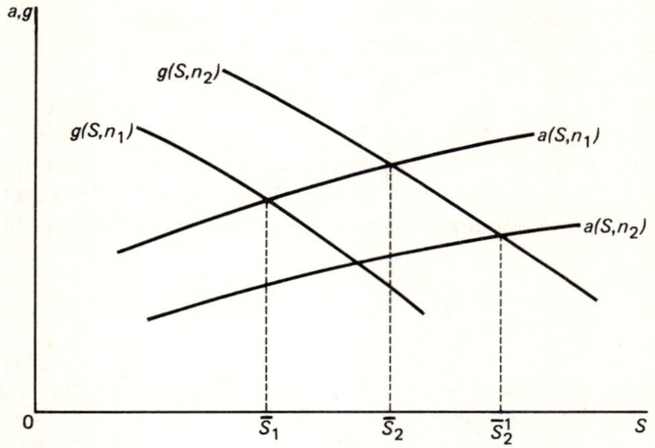

Fig. 3.1

for the case $a_s > 0, g_s < 0, g_n > 0$, where $a_n = 0$ $(\bar{S}_2)$ or $a_n < 0$ $(\bar{S}_2^1)$. We have $\bar{S}_2^1 > \bar{S}_2 > \bar{S}_1$ (for the discrete comparison $n_2 > n_1$).

III. REAL PRODUCTION COSTS AND SOCIAL EFFICIENCY

So far, we have not introduced real resource costs for the educational system itself. These may, or may not, find expression in the level of individual tuition fees $A(S, n)$, depending on institutional and government policy arrangements. Let us now start off from a productive efficiency standpoint and examine the optimum quantity and distribution of human capital under pure efficiency, i.e. marginal cost pricing. We first introduce assumptions on the cost function $C(S, n)$.

8. Cumulative input costs of the educational system $C(S, n)$ for each individual n and schooling level S have the following properties:

(i) there are positive and increasing (or constant) marginal costs with increasing S, i.e. $C_s > 0$, $C_{ss} \geqslant 0$ (for all n);
(ii) for greater individual endowment, both costs and marginal costs are smaller (or, at most, the same), i.e. $C_n \leqslant 0$ and $C_{ns} \leqslant 0$.

Assumption 8(ii), for which there is empirical evidence, can be interpreted as saying that an individual of higher n obtains a larger amount of costless

[9] This seems to be the case for all empirically recorded economies.

complementary education at home (books, mother's education, and so on) and, thus, requires less, in terms of the cost of formal schooling, in order to achieve what is required for a given S.

Let us leave aside questions of externalities and assume that aggregate demand for educated manpower is infinitely elastic at given $b(S, n)$ levels. For a stationary population and distribution $f(n)$, maximisation of net aggregate social wealth $\int [Y(S, n) - C(S, n)] f(n) dn$ implies that[10]

$$C_s = Y_s \tag{3.9}$$

Denote the solution of (3.9) by $S^*(n)$. By assumptions 6 and 8, this must be positive if $C(S, n) = 0$ at $S = 0$. Assumptions 5, 6 and 8 also ensure uniqueness of $S^*(n)$ as a maximum point ($C_{ss} - Y_{ss} > 0$). Next we have (by assumptions 5–8):

$$\frac{dS^*(n)}{dn} = \frac{Y_{sn} - C_{sn}}{C_{ss} - Y_{ss}} > 0 \tag{3.10}$$

Thus, from a pure efficiency standpoint, it would pay to let the better endowned obtain more schooling.

At this point, we can tie up the present analysis with that of the previous section and ask what would be the kind of policy that would induce individuals to choose $\bar{S} = S^*$. The answer, of course, is a version of marginal cost pricing for tuition. At the required level of S we must have both $C_s = Y_s$ and $I_s = Y_s - H_s - A_s = 0$. Thus, the policy rule must be $A_s = a(S, n)e^{-rS} = C_s - H_s$ at $S = S^*(n)$, or

$$a(S, n) = e^{rS} C_s - (Db_s h_y - h) \tag{3.11}$$

Note that equation (3.11) determines the tuition fee only in the marginal year. As long as there are no individual budgetary restrictions on tuition pricing policy, any $a(t, n)$ that has the 'right' signed slopes (see section II), i.e. $a_t > 0$ and $a_n < g_n$, and satisfies the boundary condition (3.11), can bring about the 'efficient' solution.

It is implicitly assumed here that the government, directly or indirectly, takes care of deficits or surpluses in the educational cost accounts of each individual through lump-sum taxes or transfers. If not, then additional restrictions on total $A(n, s)$ levels have to be introduced. However, consider a self-financing system where (3.11) is used as a basis for determining $a(t, n)$ for *all* t and n (including intra-marginal years). We then find that $A(S, n) = C(S, n) - H(S, n) + R(n)$, where $R(n)$ is a constant of integration depending only on n.[11] For annual tuition fees we have, differentiating (3.11)

[10] For a stationary population and fixed $f(n)$, each cohort must be distributed according to the same density function $f(n)$, so that one can think of this social optimum as calculated for each cohort at time $t = 0$.

[11] In fact, if $A(0, n) = C(0, n) = 0$ we have $R(n) = H(0, n)$.

$$a_n = e^{rS}C_{sn} - [h_y\ (Db_{sn} - b_n) + Db_s b_n h_{yy}] < 0 \tag{3.12}$$

(by assumptions 7 and 8); i.e., 'efficient' tuition policy, as expected, should be *regressive* with respect to n. Next,

$$a_s = e^{rS}(C_{ss} + rC_s) + h_y(b_s - Db_{ss}) + (1 - rD)b_s h_y - Db_s^2 h_{yy} > 0 \tag{3.13}$$

if the last (and the only negative) term, involving h_{yy}, is sufficiently small.

IV. EQUITY CONSIDERATIONS

We now introduce more general social welfare considerations in the choice of a distribution of human capital. A comprehensive approach to redistribution would require the simultaneous optimisation of the whole tax-transfer and government expenditure system. Instead, we choose to suboptimise in a more limited second-best case in which the tax-transfer system and the noneducational expenditures are given, and in which the only additional redistribution possible is through the reallocation of the educational budget among a given cohort. The following assumptions are now added.

9. The government budget constraint extends over the lifetime of a *cohort*, given fixed noneducational expenditures G. Thus

$$\int H\, f(n)dn + \int A\, f(n)dn = \int C f(n)\, dn + G \tag{3.14}$$

This implies that, given G, interpersonal transfers are possible only through the tax function H and the educational expenditures and receipts (C and A).[12] This formulation implies that intertemporal government borrowing and lending within the lifetime of the cohort are possible (implying borrowing from other cohorts or from abroad).

10. Society maximises a social welfare function of the form

$$\text{Max} \int U(I)\, f(n)dn \tag{3.15}$$

where $U' > 0$, $U'' \leqslant 0$.

We now continue to assume individual net wealth as maximising behaviour, subject to tuition-fee policy, while the latter is determined as part of social welfare maximisation (3.15). When written out in a general form, the result is a rather messy calculus-of-variations problem.[13] However, one can greatly simplify the analysis if one confines A and a to a single parameter family, in which case we are dealing with simple maximisation. An example that will

[12] The tax function is assumed given, but, in principle, one could generalise – introduce parameters in h and optimise.

[13] Note that from individual maximising behaviour we find $\bar{S}$ as a function of A_S. One thus obtains a function, involving both A and A_S, the solution of which cannot be easily characterised unless one chooses particular specifications of the functions involved.

also be used in the empirical illustration in the next section is to assume that $a(t, n)$ is a geometric series with the first element a variable policy parameter:

$$a(t, n) = a_0(n)e^{mt} \ (0 \leqslant t \leqslant S) \tag{3.16}$$

where m is a given positive parameter,[14] so that

$$A(S, n) = a_0 \frac{1 - e^{-(r-m)S}}{r - m} \quad \text{if } m \neq r$$
$$= a_0 S \qquad\qquad \text{if } m = r \tag{3.17}$$

In writing down first-order conditions for a maximum, we can now choose to maximise with respect to the amount of education (S) of each individual, assuming that tuition fees have been adjusted accordingly.

Denoting the Lagrangian multiplier for the budget constraint (3.14) by λ, and noting that $H + A = Y - I$, we have

$$U_I I_{\bar{s}} + \lambda\,(Y_s - I_{\bar{s}} - C_s) = 0$$
$$\frac{1}{\lambda} U_I = 1 + \frac{C_s - Y_s}{I_{\bar{s}}} \tag{3.18}$$

for all n. The solution of (3.18) will be denoted by $\hat{S}(n)$.

$I_{\bar{s}}$ denotes the derivative of I with respect to S after substituting for the a function from (3.5) into (3.3). For instance, if one takes the example of (3.16) and (3.17), one obtains, for the case $r \neq m$,

$$I_{\bar{s}} = \frac{\partial I}{\partial a_0} \frac{\partial(ge^{-mS})}{\partial S} = \frac{e^{-mS} - e^{-rS}}{r - m}\left(mg - \frac{\partial g}{\partial S} \ 0 >\right) \tag{3.19}$$

The optimality condition (3.18) can be given a rather straightforward interpretation. By aggregating it over n one can represent λ as a weighted population average of U_I.

Now, denote by $\tilde{I}$ the level of net wealth for which $U_I(\tilde{I}) = \lambda$. Equation (3.18) then tells us that for all $I < \tilde{I}(U_I > \lambda)$, $C_s > Y_s$ and, therefore, $\hat{S}(n) > S^*(n)$ (because $C_s - Y_s$ is an increasing function of S, and S^* is the level that makes $C_s = Y_s$). Likewise, for all $I > \tilde{I}(U_I < \lambda)$, $C_s < Y_s$ and $\hat{S}(n) < S^*(n)$. If we also have $\partial I_{\hat{s}}/\partial S < 0$, the above property becomes monotonic in both directions, i.e. the (absolute) distance $|\hat{S}(n) - S^*(n)|$ increases with $|\tilde{I}(n) - I(n)|$. The result of introducing the maximand (3.15) instead of $U(I) = I$ (which is the 'efficient' solution) obviously contracts the distribution of human capital in a direction of greater equality (see Figure 3.2).

As for the policy concerning tuition fees, given $\hat{S}$ we determine $a(S, n)$ on the basis of (3.4), and with suitable assumptions this may now be rising with

[14] One could, in principle, also optimise on m, but this is not done here. However, in the next section we give numerical illustrations with alternative values of m.

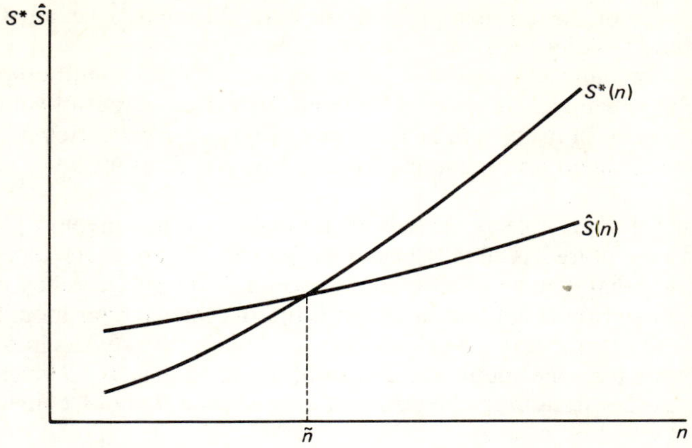

Fig. 3.2

n, for given $\bar{S}$, rather than falling, as under pure efficiency. It is hard to make any more precise statements unless the various functions are specified in greater detail. However, using empirical estimates of C_S, Y_S and $I_{\bar{S}}$ for various S and n levels, we can look at alternative 'optimum' distributions $\hat{S}(n)$ for alternative specifications of social welfare. Thus, supposing that we assume 'constant relative inequality aversion' (with parameter ρ), i.e. $U(I) = I^{1-\rho}/(1-\rho)$, we obtain from (3.18) the following expression:

$$\frac{I_1^{-\rho}}{I_2} = \frac{1+(C_{S_1}-Y_{S_1})/I_{\bar{S}_1}}{1+(C_{S_2}-Y_{S_2})/I_{\bar{S}_2}} \tag{3.20}$$

For any pair n_1, n_2 (and resulting $\hat{S}_1, \hat{S}_2$), (3.20) is an equilibrium condition involving only $\hat{S}_1, \hat{S}_2, n_1, n_2$ and ρ (see the next section).

One could use different specifications for the welfare function. For example, a case could be made for explicitly introducing S into U (in addition to the indirect utility through I). This might reflect direct individual consumption benefits from education, or it could also represent the social benefits from educational equality *per se.* In that case, we write $U(I, S)$, and in equations (3.15) and (3.18) we must everywhere write $U_I + U_S/I_{\bar{S}}$ instead of U_I (where U_I, U_S and $I_{\bar{S}}$ are positive). The trade-off between equity and efficiency can be calculated by working out the difference in net output arising from the $S^*(n)$ and $\hat{S}(n)$ solutions. A word of warning might be in place here. Our model takes the distribution of n as given and considered redistribution of S across given cohorts. There is no doubt that a more egalitarian distribution of S in one generation would change that part of the distribution of n that is due to home endowments. When looked upon from an intergenerational point of view, the long-run trade-off would then probably be quite different,[15] i.e. an egalitarian policy would look less 'costly'.

To this one must add a reservation on account of the assumption of infinitely elastic demand for education labour. Increased output of education manpower tends in itself to reduce the rate of return to education as well as the income differentials originating from an unequal distribution of human capital.

Among other possible extensions of the analysis, simultaneous optimisation for the tax structure has already been mentioned.[16] There is one aspect of the tax structure that may be of particular importance for public policy in the present human capital context, and that is international labour mobility (for instance, the brain drain). The ability to spend one's first S years in the educational system of one country and most of the remaining $T-S$ years in another puts constraints on the trade-off between the H and A policies of any one country.

Finally, the model might gain considerably in realism if the assumption of full certainty in individual behaviour were relaxed. The probability of drop-out and the uncertainty of future income streams should be explicitly accounted for. But this is a convenient point to 'drop out' of the analytical discussion.

V. A NUMERICAL ILLUSTRATION

We shall use Israeli data to illustrate possible empirical applications of the preceding analysis. However, the reader should be warned that some of the estimates are very crude and that the example should be considered as only a tentative suggestion for further work.

In Tables 3.1–3.3 are preserved some backround data on the education (Table 3.1), achievements (Table 3.2) and continuation rates (Table 3.3) of Jewish students, grouped according to the countries of origin of either the students or of their parents. It is quite apparent that the population can be divided into two major groups of almost equal size, the one comprising Jews of European or American descent (henceforth 'EURAM'),[17] and the other comprising Jews of Asian or North African descent ('ASAF'). The ASAF group have an average income level equal to about one half of that of the EURAM group, and this also more or less, corresponds to the relative investment in human capital embodied in the two groups.

Table 3.1 shows that there has been a considerable upgrading of education

[15] There is a related identification problem even within a given cohort. There must be some trade-off also between C_n and b_n. The more that is invested in the education of a specific low n group, the less will be the subsequent income differentials at any given S.

[16] In fact, Atkinson's use of such a model (see Atkinson, 1973) involves only tax optimisation.

[17] Unless otherwise specified, this will also include Israelis born to Israeli parents.

TABLE 3.1

JEWISH POPULATION AGED 14 AND ABOVE BY NUMBER OF YEARS OF SCHOOLING AND CONTINENT OF BIRTH, 1961–72 (PER CENT)

	Years of schooling								Number in population
	Total	*0*	*1–4*	*5–8*	*9–12*	*13–15*		*16+*	*1961–71 (thousand)*
Born in Asia–Africa (AA)									
1961	100·0	31·3	10·0	35·9	19·0		3·0		436
1965	100·0	26·2	10·0	38·0	22·2		3·5		
1970	100·0	23·6	8·4	38·3	25·0	3·4		1·3	
1972	100·0	22·7	7·9	36·9	27·5	3·5		1·5	635
Born in Europe–America (EA)									
1961	100·0	3·2	7·5	37·5	38·3		12·6		636
1965	100·0	2·8	8·9	35·1	39·9		13·3		
1970	100·0	2·6	8·2	33·3	38·7	7·9		9·3	
1972	100·0	2·4	8·4	30·6	39·3	10·5		8·8	691
Born in Israel (IS)									
1961	100·0	2·1	1·9	26·1	53·8		15·1		220
1965	100·0	1·4	1·1	24·0	57·3		16·2		
1970	100·0	1·1	1·2	21·6	58·4	12·1		5·6	
1972	100·0	1·1	1·0	19·3	60·1	12·3		6·2	568
Of whom, father AA	100·0	1·3	1·3	33·1	59·3	4·2		0·8	201
EA	100·0	0·4	0·3	8·6	61·7	18·7		10·3	279
IS	100·0	2·6	2·6	19·0	57·4	11·8		6·6	88

Sources: For 1961: CBS, Population and Housing Census.
For 1965–72: CBS, Labour Force Surveys.

TABLE 3.2

PERCENTAGE OF JEWISH CHILDREN WHO RECEIVED GRADES ABOVE 70 IN THE SEKER,[a] BY SIZE OF FAMILY AND FATHER'S COUNTRY OF ORIGIN

Father's country of origin	*Total*	*Number of children in family* 1–3	4	5	6	7	8	9+	*Percentage of children from families of five children or more*
Total	53·5	71·4	54·8	42·7	36·1	32·7	30·4	27·2	42·7
Israel	74·9	82·2	68·2	57·5	49·4	52·3	39·3	50·6	16·7
Europe	74·0	77·1	68·3	56·6	49·8	46·7	46·0	45·9	8·2
America	61·3	63·5	57·5	45·1	50·0	49·9	(25·0)	62·5	11·3
Australia	78·5	83·4	83·2	—	—	—	—	—	—
Turkey	44·7	46·9	50·5	33·9	47·5	27·5	37·5	24·5	22·0
Iran	36·2	50·6	41·3	34·0	34·6	30·4	28·3	29·6	68·7
Iraq	42·6	62·3	49·2	41·9	37·3	33·0	30·2	23·6	59·0
Yemen	38·2	53·2	53·4	41·1	35·5	35·4	30·6	28·2	79·0
Others countries in Asia	48·3	64·4	52·4	41·2	32·4	37·6	36·7	31·0	48·9
North Africa	33·7	51·9	39·4	36·4	31·4	29·0	28·1	25·3	73·4

[a]The *Seker* is a general examination given to all eighth-grade pupils in the country.
Source: Ministry of Education and Culture.

TABLE 3.3

CONTINUATION RATES OF JEWISH STUDENTS BY ORIGIN, 1969–70

Origin	*Entrants to first grade*	*Reached eighth grade*	*Reached ninth grade*		*Reached twelfth grade*		*Passed matriculation examination*
			Academic	*Other*	*Academic*	*Other*	
Asia–Africa	100·0	90·5	24	48	11	12	6
Europe–America–Israel	100·0	95·0	55	40	42	21	35

Source: Ministry of Education and Culture.

in all groups over the last decade, but that there have been only slight improvements in the *relative* distribution. The same finding could also be summarised in terms of human capital formation measured at cost (figures are not given here). As Tables 3.2 and 3.3 indicate, there is a serious ASAF drop-out problem at the secondary-school stage, and this is only gradually being overcome. An indication of the improvements can be seen by looking at school participation rates at ages 14–17: these have risen from 27 per cent (1963) to 48 per cent (1972) for ASAF, compared to 61 and 78 per cent, respectively, for EURAM. The rates for higher education have risen over roughly the same period from 1·6 to 2·5 per thousand for ASAF, the figures for EURAM being 10·7 and 13·4, respectively. However, the remaining gap at the university level is still considerable. By 1972 there were still only 5600 ASAF students, as compared with 32,300 EURAM.

This differential participation rate, as well as the considerable increase in public expenditure on higher education, explains the overall regressivity of public education expenditure. The government has, however, exerted itself on this matter and has introduced special programmes of supplementary education specifically designed to increase the participation rate of ASAF students at the various stages of the educational process. At the higher education level, for example, many ASAF students now obtain an extra study period of six to nine months between the termination of their army service and the formal beginning of their first academic year. There are other experiments and special institutional arrangements and programmes, reaching back to the kindergarten stage.

With this background in mind, we proceed tentatively to apply some elements of our model to a two-group subdivision of the population. A is used to denote the ASAF group, and E the EURAM group.

A recent detailed study of the earnings function for Israeli males (Amir, 1974) suggests a net income difference between the two groups – after taking into account individual education, age, and number of years in the country –

of 12–16 per cent.[18] One has to be very careful in interpreting such a difference. Since there is certainly no overt discrimination, it may be the result of differences in educational quality[19] as well as differences in home endowment. For our purpose, let us identify it as our variable n. We take it that $n_E = 1$ and $n_A = 0{\cdot}85$, and assume the multiplicative form $b(S, n) = n\beta(S)$. Likewise, on general considerations such as those mentioned above, we simply assume $C_s(A) = 1{\cdot}25C_s(E)$.[20]

Table 3.4 shows the basic cost and income data by stage of education for the the case $n = 1$.

TABLE 3.4

COSTS OF EDUCATION AND EARNINGS BY STAGE OF EDUCATION
(thousands of 1970–1 Israeli pounds)

Stage of education	*Years of education* (S)	*Average production costs per student per annum*[a] ($e^{rS}C_s$)	*Expected earnings at end of stage*[b] [$b(S)$]
Primary	1–8	1·2	9·2
Secondary	9–12	2·2	11·0
Higher	13–15	5·4	13·1
Postgraduate	16–18		15·6

[a]Costs relate to humanities (or social science) studies. Technical–scientific schooling involves a cost of 3500 Israeli pounds per annum at the secondary level and up to 14,00 per annum for higher education. Data are based on an ongoing Falk Institute study by Z. Herkovitz.

[b]Based on the regression study by Amir (1974).

We apply our model to the choice of supplying an 'average' extra year of higher education to two individuals, A and E, belonging to the same cohort. Assume $r = 5$ per cent,[21] $\delta_E = 0{\cdot}4$, $\delta_A = 0{\cdot}27$ (proportion of time worked during study)[22] and $S = 14$. Since e^{-rT} is negligibly small, we can write (3.6) in the form $e^{rS}Y_s = [(b_s/r) - (1 - \delta)b]$. We thus get (using $b_s = n2100/3 = n700$):

[18] Depending on whether or not one takes into account occupational subdivision. The study is based on 1968–9 data and is being carried out at the Falk Institute.

[19] In large part, the population has been educated in different countries with different educational systems. The more homogenous subsample of the locally educated is too small to offer any detailed systematic analysis.

[20] A combination of the 1·25 coefficient for costs and 0·85 for differential income may be too pessimistic.

[21] At this rate, investment in E is profitable (on an efficiency basis) and investment in A is not (see below).

[22] See footnote 5 above. Figures based on a 1970–1 student survey prepared for the Ministry of Education.

$$e^{rS}(Y_s - C_s)_A = -2240$$
$$e^{rS}(Y_s - C_s)_E = 1400$$

The rates of interest at which $Y_s = C_s$ are $r_A = 4{\cdot}2$ per cent, and $r_E = 5{\cdot}6$ per cent. In a similar fashion, we can use equation (3.4) to work out the level of tuition fee (a) at which such choice would be just profitable from the point of view of the private individuals concerned. This is $a_A = 90$, $a_E = 895$.[23] It is interesting to note that the actual average net tuition fees in 1970–71 were 85 and 530, respectively, for the two groups.[24]

We now apply the analysis of equation (3.20), using the constant elasticity utility function $U = I^{1-\rho}/(1-\rho)$, where ρ is the elasticity of the marginal utility schedule, or, in the terminology of Atkinson (1970), the 'parameter of inequality aversion'. The ratio of marginal utilities for equation (3.20) in the present case takes the form $(I_A/I_E)^{\rho}$.

Let us now estimate the level of ρ that would make society just indifferent at the margin between giving the above level of higher education to the two individuals. Using equations (3.19), (3.20) and (3.3) with suitable data, we obtain the results shown in Table 3.5 for alternative assumptions about m (0·05, 0·10, 0·25) and b_{ss})·40).[25]

The resulting estimate of ρ (ranging from 17 to 4) turns out to be quite sensitive to the second derivative of the income function (b_{ss}): the lower b_{ss}

TABLE 3.5

ESTIMATES OF NET WEALTH (AND INCREMENTS $I_{\bar{S}}$) UNDER ALTERNATIVE SPECIFICATIONS OF m, ρ AND b_{SS} (FOR $S = 14$)[a]

		$m = 0{\cdot}05$		$m = 0{\cdot}10$		$m = 0{\cdot}25$	
$e^{rS}I_{\bar{S}}$	A	9·5	(3·4)	6·8	(2·4)	3·3	(1·2)
	E	12·1	(5·4)	8·7	(3·9)	4·6	(2·4)
$e^{rS}I$	A	177·5		177·9		178·4	
	E	191·4		195·0		199·8	
ρ		4·4	(10·7)	4·9	(11·7)	7·8	(16·9)

[a] $b_{SS} = 0$; figures in parentheses are for the case $b_{SS} = 40$.

[23] $h(7400) = 50$, $h_y(10{,}200) = 0{\cdot}375$; $h(7200) = 45$, $h_y(12{,}00) = 0{\cdot}425$ (based on official tax tables). Thus, $a_A = -(7400 - 50) + (595)(0{\cdot}625)/0{\cdot}05 = 90$; $a_E = -(7200 - 45) + (700)(0{\cdot}575)/0{\cdot}05 = 895$.

[24] These data are based on the student expenditure and income survey mentioned in footnote 22. Average direct tuition fees (including books and so on) were 1100, and average grants per student were 1025 (ASAF) and 580 (EURAM), respectively.

[25] The case $b_{SS} = 0$ corresponds to an interpretation of the data by which years of education add constant *absolute* changes in income, while $b_{SS} = 40$ corresponds to constant *proportional* changes.

(change in future earnings additions) is, the greater is the reduction required in tuition fees to affect a choice of an additional year. ρ is less sensitive to the assumed rate of change of tuition fees (m). The lower m is, the higher is the share of tuition costs that is borne institutionally by the EURAM group, and the less 'educational inequality aversion' is required in order to obtain the required indifference.

Finally, we can ask what the net output loss in the present educational equality solution is when compared with a pure efficiency case ($Y_s = C_s$). The answer depends on what we assume to be the S_A, S_E levels for the latter. The data on the cost side (for higher education, in particular) are not sufficiently refined for C_s to be estimated separately, year by year. If the latter were constant up to $S = 18$ (which is quite unlikely), a shift of education from $S_E = 18$ and $S_A = 8$ (end of primary education only, at which it is just efficient) to $S_A = S_E = 14$ (previous point) might involve a net output[26] loss of 12 per cent, of which each individual contributes about one half.[27] But, for the various reasons mentioned here and in the previous section, this most probably gives a highly exaggerated picture of the cost to society of obtaining equity at the expense of efficiency.

REFERENCES

Amir, Shmuel, 'Earned Income of Male Employees in Israel, 1968/69' (Jerusalem, 1974). Draft in Hebrew.

Arrow, Kenneth J., 'A Utilitarian Approach to the Concept of Equality in Public Expenditures', *Quarterly Journal of Economics,* LXXXV (Aug 1971), pp. 409–15.

Atkinson, Anthony B., 'On the Measurement of Inequality', *Journal of Economic Theory,* II (Sep 1970), pp. 244–63.

Atkinson, Anthony B., 'How Progressive Should Income Tax Be?', in *Essays on Modern Economics,* ed. J. M. Parkin (London: Longman, 1973), pp. 90–109.

Becker, Gary S., *Human Capital: A Theoretical and Empirical Analysis, with Special Reference to Education,* National Bureau of Economic Research: General Series no. 80 (New York and London: Columbia University Press, 1964).

Ben-Porath, Yoram, 'The Production of Human Capital and the Life Cycle of Earnings', *Journal of Political Economy,* LXXV (Aug 1967), pp. 352–65.

De Wolff, P., and Van Slijpe, A. R. D., 'Relation between Income, Intelligence, Education and Social Background', *European Economic Review,* no. 4, 1973.

Hause, John C., 'Earnings Profile: Ability and Schooling', in *Investment in Education: The Equity–Efficiency Quandary,* ed. Theodore W. Schultz (Chicago: Chicago University Press, 1972). Also appeared in *Journal of Political Economy,* LXXX, no. 3, part II (May–June 1972), pp. S109–38.

Mincer, Jacob, *Schooling, Experience, and Earnings,* National Bureau of Economic Research: 'Human Behavior and Social Institution', no. 2. (New York and London: Columbia University Press, 1974).

Schultz, Theodore W. (ed.): (see reference under Hause, John C.

[26] This is calculated by taking into account production costs, output forgone, and changes in future output streams.

[27] Thus, moving a member of ASAF up to $S = 14$, for each member of EURAM already there, costs approximately 6 per cent of their joint output.

4 On Measuring the Redistribution of Lifetime Income[1]

Richard Layard
LONDON SCHOOL OF ECONOMICS

Much so-called redistribution is between similar people at different stages of life or fortune. The proper approach, therefore, is to look at redistribution between lifetime incomes. But this raises problems of choosing the discount rate and of specifying the assumptions about alternative policies. After discussion of these, attention is focused on specific problems that arise in relation to education, especially the distinction between incidence on parents and on children. Finally, the lifetime approach is applied to various educational policy options in Britain. Here only the effects on children are examined, using a new British earnings function. For any policy, this generates a distribution of incomes (present values). Each distribution is measured for equality, using the Atkinson index, so that a policy is desirable if it raises equality proportionately more than it reduces average income.

I. INTRODUCTION

How far, if at all, does the State reduce inequality? Or, how far does a particular policy affect it? To answer these questions one has to compare the *actual* distribution of income after taxes and benefits (a vector $\underline{V}^A$) with some *hypothetical* alternative distribution ($\underline{V}^H$).[2] The measure of income normally used in such analyses is current annual income, regardless of the past or future income of those concerned (Nicholson, 1964; CSO, 1972; Musgrave, 1964). But this is unsatisfactory, partly because a person's current income is a bad measure of his underlying real income, and especially because much government activity redistributes a person's lifetime income over his lifetime more than it alters its total. The 'annual-income approach' thus gives the wrong impression in two

[1] This paper arises from work done jointly with Mark Stewart, who did the computing with superb efficiency. The author is also most grateful to M. J. Bowman, P. Dasgupta, A. Flowerdew, R. Jackman, A. R. Prest, G. Psacharopoulos, A. K. Sen. C. Von Weizsäcker and B. A. Weisbrod for comments and helpful discussions on various points and to the Social Science Research Council for financial support.

[2] These correspond respectively to the United Kingdom Central Statistical Office's 'final' and 'original' distributions (CSO, 1972).

ways: first, it exaggerates the basic inequality of incomes and then it exaggerates the amount of redistribution.

It is particularly important to take the life-cycle perspective when considering social service expenditures, since, unlike such programmes as roads and defence, the social services typically involve payments by workers to support nonworkers such as children, pensioners, the sick or the unemployed. Since individuals do not remain in these dependent categories throughout their lives, current beneficiaries will, at other times, be supporting people who are similar to themselves but at a different stage of their life-cycle or of their fortunes. One may speculate on why such transfers are actually made or may be desirable. In terms of welfare economics many of them may be defended on grounds of the failure of capital and insurance markets or as merit wants, rather than on grounds of equity, and Arrow (1963) has argued that

> a good part of the preference for redistribution expressed in government taxation and expenditure policies and private charity can be reinterpreted as desire for insurance. It is noteworthy that virtually nowhere is there a system of subsidies that has as its aim simply an equalization of income.

This paper, however, is not concerned with how to explain or justify State action, but with how to measure its effects on the inequality of *ex post* lifetime incomes.

Section II justifies the use of lifetime rather than annual income to measure $\underline{V}^A$ and considers the problems of measuring it when capital markets are imperfect and some people live longer than others. Section III discusses how to measure $\underline{V}^H$ using relevant alternative policy assumptions with clearly defined non-steady-state time dimensions; it also considers the distinction between the effects of policy on *ex ante* and *ex post* income. Section IV deals briefly with the parametric representation of redistribution and adopts a framework within which the distributional and efficiency effects of policies can be computed in a commensurable way. It also rehearses some handy rules of thumb for measuring distributional effects, subject to one caution, which is often overlooked. Section V applies these ideas to education. First it contrasts approaches that look at effects on parents with those that look at effects on children, and supports Jencks's argument that education may not be a very suitable means towards income equalisation. It then proceeds to compute the equity and efficiency effects of various possible policies in Britain, using a newly estimated earnings function. It tentatively concludes that new cash subsidies to upper secondary education might be efficient and not too inequitable, but that a reduction in higher education subsidies might be efficient and equitable.

II. LIFETIME INCOME AS THE MEASURE OF INDIVIDUAL WELFARE

WHY LIFETIME INCOME?

There are well-known objections to using income within a limited time period as an indicator of economic welfare. First, it includes transitory income, which, according to Friedman (1957, p. 189) accounts for between 15 per cent and 30 per cent of the cross-sectional variance in the annual incomes of urban families. Then, there are the earnings variations that reflect differential investments in human capital; if we include in this category the effects of schooling and on-the-job training, these compensating differentials account for at least 30 per cent of the cross-sectional variance of the log of earnings in the work force (Mincer, 1972). However, there is no obvious reason why earnings distribution should exclude those who have zero earnings because they are still at school, and, if all aged over, say, sixteen were included, differential human capital investment would explain an even greater share of earnings inequality. Then there is the problem of retirement, which means that the economic welfare of a man with a given income at 60 is quite different from that of a man with the same income but with 20 more years of work ahead of him. Finally, there is the effect on welfare of the ownership of wealth, as opposed to the receipt of income from it.

However, various ways around these problems have been suggested that focus on annual consumption rather than on income as a measure of welfare. One is to compute for each individual the annuity that he could take out on the strength of his current wealth and expected earnings (Weisbrod and Hansen 1968).[3] This is the standard of consumption that the person could maintain for the rest of his life if he planned no bequest. An alternative is to take a person's actual current consumption as the measure of his welfare (Kaldor, 1955), though this is less good since it ignores any satisfaction he may be getting from accumulation for purposes of bequest.

These ideas are certainly more consistent with standard theory than is the notion that individual welfare depends on current income. However, in measuring inequalities in welfare one must have some social welfare function in mind, in which both justice and efficiency play a part. The measures of welfare proposed in the last paragraph imply that the justice of the current-period distribution of consumption can be assessed independently of the past consumption of each of those currently consuming.[4] If one accepts the continuity of the personality, this would seem impossible. Additive utilitarians would, of course, argue that social welfare in one period depends only on the sum of happinesses, regardless of their distribution among persons. If this were so, social welfare over many periods should also be independent of the grouping of sequential states of mind within individuals. But additive utilitarianism is morally unattractive (Sen, 1973a). Thus, if social welfare in one period depends not only on the sum of happiness, but also on its inequality, intertemporal social welfare must take into account the grouping of 'happinesses' in different periods as between individuals. So we may say, fairly generally, that

[3] Weisbrod and Hansen were able to allow only for wealth and current earnings.

[4] Of course, in the full life-cycle model with perfect capital markets and perfect foresight, present consumption and potential future consumption will be related to past consumption. But the assumptions are rather stringent.

$$W = W[U_1(C_{11}, \ldots, C_{1T_1}), \ldots, U_n(C_{n1}, \ldots, C_{nT_n})]$$

where C_{ij} is the consumption (including gifts to others) of the ith person in the jth year of his life, T_i is his age when he dies and U_i is a cardinal measure of his lifetime welfare. W measures social welfare and is a symmetric and concave function of the Us. In practice, of course, there is no general way of taking into account the different utility functions of different members of society. So we assume a common utility function for all men. Ignoring, for the moment, the problem of varying lengths of life, we might write this utility function, for an individual living T periods, as

$$U = U[V(C_1, \ldots, C_T)]$$

where V is a linear homogeneous function, and U increases with V but at a declining rate.

THE DISCOUNT-RATE PROBLEM

The first practical problem, then, would then be to find an index that approximately measures V for each individual. In a perfect capital market we could take the present value of his consumption plus gifts to others, which would necessarily be equal to the present value of his after-tax earnings plus gifts from others.[5] But if capital markets are imperfect, two people with consumption streams having the same present value at some discount rate may differ both in utility and in the present value of their discounted incomes. If we knew the individual consumption streams this would pose no problem: we could simply assume some reasonable functional form for V. But we generally know only people's income streams. If, in addition, we knew their capital-market positions, we should again have no problem: we could either infer their maximal V or compute the consumption annuity that would give the same satisfaction.

But we normally know nothing about people's capital-market positions. Assuming, therefore, that we use a common discount rate, how should it be selected? There is probably greater variation among people in borrowing rates than in lending rates. Suppose, for a moment, two borrowers of equal ability and owning no nonhuman capital. Would we get better measures of their real income differences by using high or low discount rates? The individual with the lower borrowing rate will invest more in human capital and will, therefore, have a higher ratio of earnings in later life to earnings in earlier life.[6] If we

[5] (a) V should be computed at the interest rate net of tax.

(b) It is sometimes considered double-counting if bequests are treated as giving utility to donor and recipient. However, they clearly do just that.

(c) Some people consider inequalities of inherited wealth more or less inequitable than inequalities in earnings. Such judgements are not easily handled in the present framework, but could be handled in a wider one where psychic (nonmonetary) sources of satisfaction, especially leisure, were allowed for.

[6] For a good discussion of the relation of discount rates to annual, rather than lifetime, earnings, see Becker (1967). See also Brainard (1974).

evaluate their incomes using high discount rates we shall overlook this advantage. This is illustrated in Figure 4.1 for the traditional two-period case. Individual I has a lower borrowing rate than has individual II. They have the same original endowment and investment opportunities. I is better off than II. Yet, at a rate of interest equal to II's borrowing rate, II has a higher present value of income than I has, and, at a rate of interest equal to I's borrowing rate, the discounted incomes stand in a ratio that understates V^{I}/V^{II}.[7]

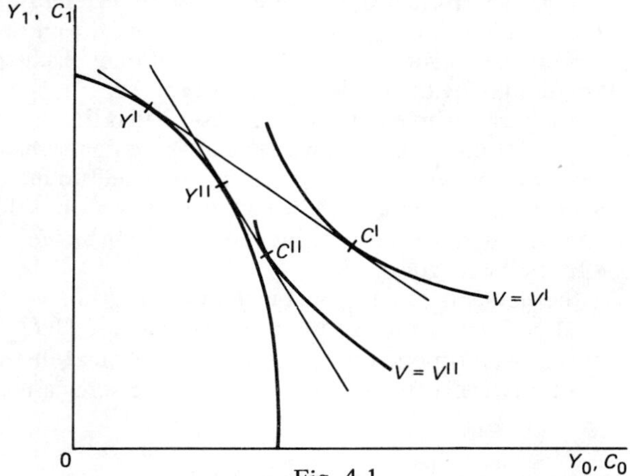

Fig. 4.1

Only at a rate less than the lower of the two rates, do we get a ratio of present values that correctly measures V^{I}/V^{II}. This argument suggests that, so long as interest rates and ability are independent, we should use low discount rates for borrowers. In fact, of course, people of higher-than-average ability tend to come from relatively well favoured families and therefore will be using lower discount rates. But higher ability, defined as a higher marginal rate of return on a given amount of human capital (Becker, 1967) will, other things being equal, lead a man to choose a higher ratio of later to earlier earnings; this provides a second reason for using low discount rates to make real income comparisons. The rates should perhaps be similar to those used for lenders, who have unearned incomes, so far ignored. In the empirical work in this paper, I concentrate on the estimates using a 5 per cent real rate.[8]

THE LENGTH-OF-LIFE PROBLEM

The next inescapable problem is the variation in length of life. Suppose that the length of individual lives was the same under all hypothetical distributions

[7] This can be seen geometrically by drawing a line through Y^{II}, parallel to $Y^{I}C^{I}$. The ratio of the horizontal intercepts of these two parallel lines measures the ratio of discounted incomes.

[8] As predicted above, inequality is higher when $i = \cdot 02$ and still higher when $i = 0$ (see Table 4.1 below).

of income. Now, compare two people with the same present value of income, one of whom lives to 80 and the other to 60. Which is better off? All of our normal judgements about inequality imply that the one who lives to be 80 is worse off, as he will have had a lower standard of living for most of his life. The most natural solution might be to measure a person's income by the annuity that, taken over his actual lifespan, has the same present value as his actual income stream, both being evaluated at some uniform rate of discount.[9] This is still not altogether satisfactory, since people have different needs at different ages. If these are known, or can be inferred from the chosen time paths of consumption, we might first deflate consumption at each age by some relevant weight before taking the equivalent annuity.

Some will object to this whole argument and assert that life, as such, is good (Meade, 1956). In this case, those who live long are richer than we have allowed. Likewise, State activity that lengthens life may add to income, even though each person's annual standard of living falls. I do not find this plausible. Those who do so might wish to compute individual welfare as the annuity already described times the length of life.

We now have the elements of our actual income distribution vector $\underline{V}^A$. The other practical problem is to measure its level of welfare $[W(\underline{V}^A)]$ and its inequality. However, we postpone this until we have looked at the problems of constructing the alternative vector $\underline{V}^H$, corresponding to some alternative set of policies.

III. THE EFFECTS OF GOVERNMENT POLICY

What alternatives are we to hypothesise and how do we compute their effects? The lifetime approach immediately raises problems that are concealed in the cross-section.[10] The chief new problems are, first, to identify a 'policy' and, second, to define the time period and historical context over which we consider substituting one policy for another.

[9] If they had no pure time preference, and given a positive interest rate, individuals would, choose a rising path of consumption. One might, therefore, prefer to compute for each individual a value A where the stream $A\ (1 + g)^t\ (t = 1, \ldots, T)$ has the same present value as the actual income stream, g could be based on observed rates of growth or on the outcome of maximising some suitable utility function subject to a given perfect capital-market constraint. However, comparisons of A so computed might tend to understate the real incomes of those who live long.

[10] For discussions of the problem in the single-year case see Musgrave (1964), Prest (1968), and Peacock and Shannon (1968). Prest (1968) is doubtful whether calculations so far made of the total effect of State expenditure and taxes are useful, while Musgrave (1964) thinks they are. There has also been considerable debate about how questions about these effects should be formulated. Peacock and Shannon (1968) suggest that the comparison should be put forward as one between a condition where government expenditure and taxes are as at present and one where government expenditure remained unchanged but everyone paid for his benefits. A more relevant alternative would seem to be one in which both the government expenditure and the corresponding taxes are abolished. The general equilibrium effect of such a change might well be less than that of the Peacock and Shannon alternative, and the question is more interesting.

IDENTIFYING POLICIES

If we follow the 'annual income' approach, we need only note that in the current year the government is paying out £*x* per pensioner, educating *y* students at a subsidy of £*z* per student, and so on. But if we want to know the future pensions that current policy implies for today's workers, or how much education today's students will have to supply to the next generation, we need to know the underlying principles governing today's policies. This raises questions such as: Do present pensions reflect a decision on the relative incomes of pensioners or on the tax rate out of which pensions are to be paid? The problems of defining a pension policy have been discussed by Asimokopoulos and Weldon (1968), though in fact, in Britain at any rate, government pension policies are spelt out in more explicit time streams than are most other policies (Atkinson, 1970a; Prest, 1970). As regards education, we are rarely given any explicit commitment. For example, ten years ago British students thought their maintenance grants had been fixed relative to the wage level, five years ago they thought they had been fixed relative to the price level, and now they appear to have been fixed relative to the nominal pound. This makes it peculiarly difficult to define present educational policies, and to examine their distributional effect, assuming them to be continued. One can, however, attempt to examine the impact of specified changes in policy, as is done in section V.

THE TIME PATH AND CONTEXT OF ALTERNATIVE POLICIES

When alternative policies are being considered, there is also the question of the timing of their substitution. This must depend on the question being asked. For example, economic historians might ask how State activity in education has affected the distribution of lifetime incomes. To answer this, they might attempt to compare the effect of the whole set of policies in force up to now (and those expected from now on) with the effects of zero State activity. This is illustrated in Figure 4.2(a), which indicates that, since State activity began (in year 0) and up to now (year *T*), varying policies (*A* to *D*) have been in force, and now we have policy *E*. This set of policies is to be compared with no policy (policy 0). For this purpose, the inner rationale of past policies need not be discovered, and we need only ask what happened from year to year.

If, however, we are interested in evaluating policy options, we can be interested only in policies that are real options now or in the future. The most natural way to evaluate an additional expenditure option *X* would be to imagine introducing it now in addition to the policies *E* that already appear to be in force. We thus compare $(X + E)$ with *E* as in Fig. 4.2(b), taking into account the whole population that will be affected by the introduction of *X*. The change will have these main types of effect:

(a) intra-cohort redistribution within each cohort;

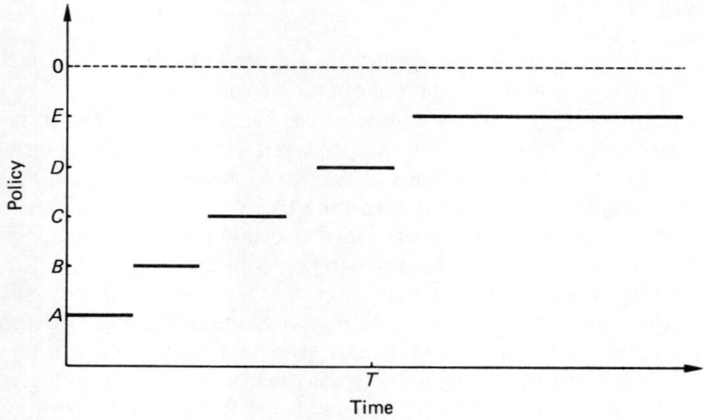

Fig. 4.2(a)

(b) inter-cohort redistribution between each pair of future cohorts whose education is not complete; and
(c) inter-cohort redistribution due to the impact effect on current earners (assuming, as I do throughout, that the expenditure is tax-financed).

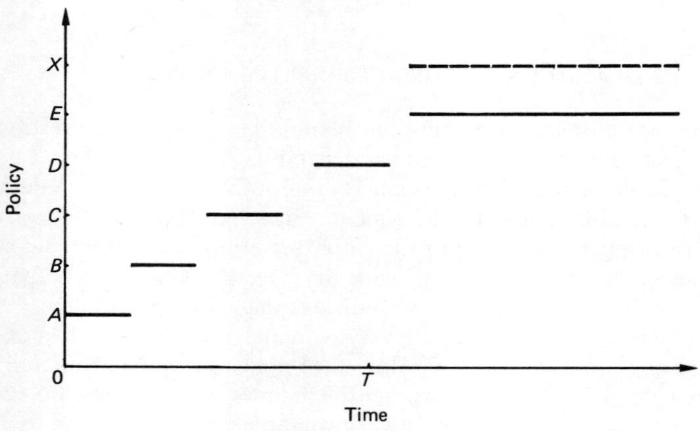

Fig. 4.2(b)

Effect (c) can be wished away either by pretending that the expenditure is financed by borrowing that is to be repaid by the benefiting cohort, or by pretending to compare policies $(X + E)$ and E as if they were in force for ever (see Fig. 4.2c).

Effect (b) can be simplified by further assuming, as the context of the comparison, either steady-state growth or, in the case of pure consumption transfers between generations, exogenously-given constant rates of growth of income and population. In these cases, many policies, constantly maintained,

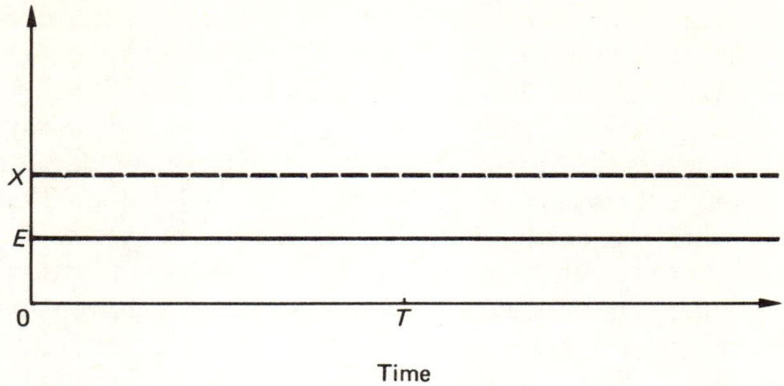

Fig. 4.2(c)

will affect all generations in the same way.[11] However, as regards steady-state growth, the historical record shows that the increase of measured inputs gives a good explanation of growth in output in the United States (Jorgesen and Griliches, 1967). Thus, little is gained by resorting to the steady-state fiction when attempting quantitative measures of redistribution. As regards exogenous growth, it does not seem credible, for example, that a tax-financed increase in pensions would not alter the rate of saving. Moreover, as soon as we return to historical time and introduce policy X at time T, we find that a tax-financed increase in educational outlays is bound to hurt present adults and a decrease in pensions is bound to hurt present pensioners. It is worth noting how many cohorts would actually be subject to these impact effects. A policy involving increased educational expenditure would, perhaps, have a harmful impact effect on 50-year cohorts of existing adults, whose education is finished and who could never gain from educational expansion; the impact would continue, in the case of the youngest cohort, for 50 years.

However, even though a historical context seems preferable for applied work on redistribution, some simplifying assumptions have to be made. In section V, I estimate the effects of various possible educational changes on the lifetime incomes of only one cohort of currently young people. I ignore the one-for-all effect of the additional taxes on existing adults. I also ignore, for lack of data, the impact of the changes on the incomes of the parents of the currently young cohort. Finally, I make a simplifying assumption about the extra taxes that the current cohort will need to pay in order to finance the extra expenditure on succeeding generations. As regards the tax adjustment, there are two problems. First, there is the new problem, introduced by the life-cycle approach, of determining the future numbers who will benefit from the policy, and the

[11] On exogenous growth, the chief proposition is that, if the rate of growth exceeds the interest rate, an additional pension proportional to the wage will make each generation better off (Samuelson, 1958; Cass and Yaari, 1961; and Aaron, 1966). By the same token, a youth endowment proportional to the wage will make everyone worse off. On steady-state growth with variable savings rates, Diamond (1965) has shown that, if the growth rate exceeds the rate of interest, an increase in the savings rate benefits all generations.

size of the tax bases from which these benefits could be financed. Second, there is the old problem of the tax instruments that would actually be chosen to finance the policy. Some, like Hansen and Weisbrod (1971), argue that it is impossible to answer this latter question – which is the same as saying that it is impossible to assess the distributional impact of a policy. Others (Pechman, 1970) have assumed (reasonably, in my view) that, unless there is good ground for assuming otherwise, expenditure changes will be financed by a mix of taxes equal to the average currently prevailing. Since, in Britain, taxation (including National Insurance) on families of a given size is roughly proportional (CSO, 1972), I assume that all tax changes affect the present values of all incomes equiproportionately. Since the inequality measure used is invariant with respect to scalar multiplication of all incomes, it is not necessary to compute the amount of the tax change; and, thus, the first problem (of projecting future expenditures and tax bases) can be avoided.

EX ANTE AND EX POST REDISTRIBUTION

Before coming to education, I shall make a brief digression to consider the effects of other social services and, in particular, the issue of *ex ante* versus *ex post* redistribution. Clearly, many social services have an insurance aspect – health care and sickness benefit (against disease), pensions (against longevity), family support (against unwanted children?). Any insurance scheme redistributes *ex post* income, from the lucky to the unlucky. In a cross-section or lifetime analysis that measures actual individual income, it would thus appear as equalising when compared with the absence of insurance.[12] However, if there were no State insurance, there would be private insurance. State insurance can, therefore, be redistributive *ex post*, as compared with no State insurance, for either of two reasons. First, it could simply have a wider coverage than the private scheme it displaces, even though each is equally redistributive *ex ante*. Second, it could be more redistributive *ex ante*. A private insurance company will, of course, redistribute towards people who have defects it does not know about. But it cannot redistribute to people who have defects that are known in advance; otherwise, it will be bankrupted by 'adverse selection'. For example, a scheme that included benefits in excess of premiums to people with multiple sclerosis would soon have no takers other than sufferers from that affliction.

To illustrate the distinction between these two possible effects of State insurance, we may suppose that, at birth, the income that we should predict

[12] Nicholson (1964) does not take this *ex post* approach. He measures the National Health Service benefits to an individual not as the value of services rendered, but as their expected value. However, the benefits from the old-age pension are recorded at their actual current value, although the pension scheme is also an insurance scheme providing a given expected value of benefits at each age (whether one is alive or dead), which is of course less than the actual old-age pension. This is less inconsistent than it might appear, since, for distributional purposes, the value of a given cover needs to be adjusted for the *ex post* length of life, as we have seen.

for the ith individual from our knowledge of his and his family's characteristics (a vector X_i), together with some general knowledge of the world as it will be during his life, is $f^A(X_i)$. Multiplied with this is a random term, U_i^A, with mean unity, which we may suppose independent of the person's characteristics. So

$$Y_i^A = f^A(X_i)\, U_i^A$$

and the inequality of income, as measured by the variance of log income, is, if log X and log U^A are independent,

$$\text{var}\,[\log Y^A] = \text{var}\,[\log f^A(X)] + \text{var}\,[\log (U^A)]$$

The left-hand expression measures inequality *ex post,* and the expression in the middle measures it *ex ante.* If we now construct the hypothetical alternative distribution, we have

$$\text{var}\,[\log Y^H] = \text{var}\,[\log f^H(X)] + \text{var}\,[\log U^H]$$

Ex post inequality reduction consists of *ex ante* redistribution (var $[\log f^A(X)]$ – var $[\log f^H(X)]$) plus the effects of extended insurance (var $[(\log U^A]$ – var $[\log U^H]$).

Should the analysis of redistribution be confined to *ex ante* income? Surely not.[13] The misfortunes of life are in no way either more or less serious than the misfortunes of birth. Arrow (1963) implies that governments tend, in fact, to be more concerned with the former. It would certainly be interesting to partition the effects of government activity into the two components above. But casual inspection suggests that most governments run many programmes that are *ex ante* equalising. Most government health-care and sickness-benefit schemes are not financed in a way related to a person's health risk but, rather, in relation to income, which is inversely related to health risk. Programmes of poor relief are the same. Likewise child-aid programmes such as family allowances, child tax credits, and universal education must equalise *ex ante* income, for they raise the standard of living of children in larger familes, where the standard of living is, on average, lower than in smaller families.[14] (They also,

[13] Gambling, of course, causes a problem here. If two gamblers start with the same incomes and voluntarily gamble so that they end up with different ones, we ought not necessarily to say that inequality has increased. However, if we used the Atkinson (1970b) approach (see section IV below), we should not necessarily say that it had. For the rationale of that approach is that the social welfare function is concave in individual utilities. If, in addition, utility is concave in income, the social welfare function is concave in individual incomes, as is generally assumed. But if we allowed increasing marginal utility of income, we might say that social welfare and 'equality' had increased *ex post* by permitting the gamble. So the *ex post* approach would still be preferable. The practical problem, however, is that we have to assume uniform tastes, and, therefore, assume diminishing marginal utility.

[14] It is true that larger families often have higher incomes and pay higher taxes, but it would be most unusual for the average tax payments of families with X children to exceed, by a multiple X, those of families with one child. In addition, there is a transfer to families with children from families with none.

of course, raise the standard of living of the parents, but parents who choose larger families cannot necessarily be considered worse off than those parents of the same income who have smaller families.)

IV. THE PARAMETRIC REPRESENTATION OF REDISTRIBUTION

Suppose we have now constructed out two income vectors $\underline{V}^A$ and $\underline{V}^H$. What is an appropriate way to compare them? We could of course compare them for social welfare, using some explicit concave social welfare function. In this case, we prefer $\underline{V}^H$ to $\underline{V}^A$ if $W(\underline{V}^H)$ exceeds $W(\underline{V}^A)$. However, suppose, as is often the case, that we want to look separately at the equity and efficiency aspects of the policy. The efficiency effects can be measured by the ratio of the average present values $\bar{V}^A/\bar{V}^H$. The equity effects could be measured by any of a number of inequality measures (Sen, 1973a). However, it would be desirable if the inequality measure implied some specific trade-off between equality and efficiency so that, if we knew both equality and efficiency effects, we could say whether social welfare had improved. This is the virtue of the Atkinson (1970b) inequality measure, as opposed to, for example, the coefficient of variation of income or the standard deviation of the logs.[15] The trade-off is as follows. Social welfare (W) is a concave function of $\underline{V}$. Equally-distributed equivalent income (V_{EDE}) is defined as that income which, if everybody had it, would produce the same social welfare as the actual income distribution vector $\underline{V}$. So

$$W(V_{EDE}, \ldots, V_{EDE}) = W(V_1, \ldots, V_n)$$

Because the welfare function is concave,

$$V_{EDE} < V$$

The Atkinson inequality measure is then

$$I = 1 - \frac{V_{EDE}}{\bar{V}} \qquad 0 \leqslant I \leqslant 1$$

To get the trade-off we note that

$$V_{EDE} = (1 - I)\bar{V}$$

If social welfare increases under the hypothetical alternative policy, then

[15] As Sen (1973b) implies, the Gini coefficient implies the same trade-off, since, in the Atkinson terminology (see below),

$$V_{EDE} = \bar{V}(1 - G)$$

where G is the Gini coefficient. But the welfare function corresponding to the Gini coefficient is less appealing than that used by Atkinson.

$$V_{EDE}^{H} > V_{EDE}^{A}$$

Therefore,

$$\frac{1-I^H}{1-I^A} > \frac{\bar{V}^A}{\bar{V}^H}$$

or, for small changes, $\Delta\, \ell n\, (1-I) > -\Delta\, \ell n\, \bar{V}$

The proportional increase in 'equality' must exceed the proportional fall in total output.

In Section V, I compute measures of both of these for each policy change, using for the inequality measure the Atkinson welfare function

$$W = \frac{1}{\alpha} \sum V_i^{\alpha} \quad \alpha < 1$$

taking $\alpha = -1$. The combined effect of any two policies can be roughly inferred by adding their separate effects, provided that the effects of both policies on a given individual are small and additive.

RULES OF THUMB

However, in speculating about the effects of policy it is also helpful to have some principles that enable one to infer, where possible, without doing detailed calculations, whether a policy is equalising or not. It often happens that policies are of a form that enables one to make such inferences. One such case is when a policy clearly shifts the Lorenz curve either in or out along its whole length, so that inequality rises or falls using any concave W. An example is where a policy confers benefits (B) and imposes costs (C) in a way uniquely related to income (V), so that

$$B(V_{\min}) - C(V_{\min}) > 0 \qquad (4.1)$$

$$-1 < \frac{dB}{dV} - \frac{dC}{dV} < 0 \qquad \text{(all } V\text{)} \qquad (4.2)$$

$$\Sigma\, B(V_i) - \Sigma\, C(V_i) = 0 \qquad (4.3)$$

In this case the Lorenz curve after the policy lies wholly along or above the previous Lorenz curve, for the policy can be achieved entirely by transfers from richer to poorer.[16]

[16] For a proof that this implies nonintersecting Lorenz curves, see Sen (1973a). If we drop the assumption of zero efficiency effects and allow for some losses, such that $\Sigma B(V_i) - \Sigma C(V_i) < 0$, then no strict statement is possible, since total income changes. For people with incomes low enough to experience positive net benefits, the Lorenz curve rises, since they all gain and total income falls; so their relative income share rises. But the share of the richest man may rise if his proportional loss is less than the proportional loss in the economy as a whole. However if there is some income V^* such that for

For practical purposes it is often easier to analyse redistribution by looking not at the absolute change of B and C per unit change in income, but at the proportional change. Supposing that within the relevant range $B = a\ V^{\alpha}$ and $C = b\ V^{\beta}$, and that conditions (4.1)–(4.3) hold within that range, then we can say that a policy raises the Lorenz curve throughout if $\alpha < \beta$.[17] This is an extremely useful approach.[18] It says, for example, that, if a programme is financed by a proportional tax, it equalises if benefits rise more slowly than income does.

A PROPOSITION ABOUT GROUP BENEFITS

However, when we turn to real world policies, there is one caveat. Most policies produce benefits that are not uniquely related to income. Suppose, instead, that a policy confers a given small benefit (α) on all members of a group (group 1) financed by a proportional tax on the whole population (groups 1 and 2). One might suppose that, if the average income of group 1 were above the average income of group 2, the policy would necessarily be disequalising, since group 1 has net gains and group 2 (with lower average income) loses. But this does not follow if the income distributions of the two groups overlap sufficiently. Intuitively, one can see this by supposing initially that the two groups have the same distribution. Then, a given small benefit to either group

---

all incomes greater than V^* the proportional loss exceeds that for the economy as a whole, then the Lorenz curve will rise for all incomes above V^*. And, if the proportional loss in the whole economy is not great, then V^* will lie close to the income for which net benefits are zero, and the Lorenz curve is likely to lie above its old level throughout its range.

[17] Again, if condition (4.3) does not hold, this does not strictly follow.

[18] It is perhaps a more convenient one than the traditional two-person classroom illustration that is sometimes used. In this, person 1 is richer than person 2 and therefore bears more costs. We then show that redistribution occurs if the project is efficient and $B_1/B_2 < C_1/C_2$. The proof is:

$$B_1 - C_1 = C_2 - B_2 \qquad \text{(the efficiency condition)}$$

Therefore $$C_1\left(\frac{B_1}{C_1} - 1\right) = C_2\left(1 - \frac{B_2}{C_2}\right)$$

Therefore $$\left(1 - \frac{B_2}{C_2}\right)\left(\frac{B_1}{C_1} - 1\right) = \frac{C_1}{C_2} > 1$$

Therefore $$2 > \frac{B_1}{C_1} + \frac{B_2}{C_2}$$

But $$\frac{B_1}{C_1} < \frac{B_2}{C_2}$$

Therefore $$\frac{B_1}{C_1} < 1$$

One can also show that an inefficient project hurts person 1 proportionately more than person 2 if $C_1/V_1 > C_2/V_2$.

is definitely equalising (and the tax that finances it leaves inequality unchanged). Now move one rich man from group 2 to group 1. Provided that both groups are large, the policy is still equalising, although group 1 is, on average, richer than group 2. In fact, the policy may be equalising for many more different compositions of the groups. Suppose that there are only two income classes in the population, the poor (with uniform incomes Y_P) and the rich (with uniform incomes Y_R), and that group 1 comprises a proportion p_1 of the poor and a proportion r_1 of the rich ($p_1 < r_1$). The policy is equalising if the proportional increase in the average income of the poor (in groups 1 and 2) exceeds that of the rich (in groups 1 and 2), i.e. if

$$\frac{\alpha p_1}{Y_P} > \frac{\alpha r_1}{Y_R} \text{ or } \frac{p_1}{r_1} > \frac{Y_P}{Y_R}$$

The groups must be not too dissimilar (p_1/r_1 too low), but can be more dissimilar the greater the relative poverty of the poor. For, the poorer the poor, the greater the proportional improvement in their income resulting from the gift of α to the few of them in the privileged group 1.

To complete the story, a gift of α to the members of group 2 is necessarily equalising, since

$$\frac{p_2}{r_2} > 1 > \frac{Y_P}{Y_R}$$

Thus, it is perfectly possible that, if the population concists of two (or more) mutually exclusive groups, it is equalising to provide each of them in turn with a given benefit financed by a proportional tax.[19] However, this requires that the groups be not too dissimilar. With the caveat of the preceding paragraph in mind, we can turn to the specific analysis of public support for education.

V. EDUCATION AND REDISTRIBUTION

ANALYSIS BY PARENTS' INCOME

The traditional approach has been to allocate the estimated benefits of this between individuals according to the income class of their parents. Individual benefits have been estimated as the cost of the subsidy, as would be appropriate if the subsidy had no effect on private choice. Examples of this approach applied to higher education may be found in Glennerster (1972) for Great Britain, and Pechman (1970) for California. The Glennerster analysis showed that, as one goes up the occupational scale and, presumably, the (average) income scale, the probability of having a child at university, and receiving a

[19] An example occurs in Table 4.1 (i = ·05), where a given benefit to early leavers raises equality by ·050 per cent, and extending the benefit to all raises equality by a further ·005 per cent.

(uniform) benefit thereby, rises faster than the level of taxes paid per family. If we suppose that this process can be represented by

$$P(B) = aV^{\alpha}; C = bV^{\beta}$$

it is likely to be disequalising, since $\alpha > \beta$.

In the case of California, the position is more complicated, partly because there exist different levels of benefits, but mainly because the probability of receiving a benefit is not a monotonic function of income. This has led to a somewhat confused debate. Hansen and Weisbrod (1969 and 1971) groups the population according to their level of benefits and then showed that those who received higher levels of benefit had higher average incomes and paid, on average, (total) taxes less than the benefits they received. By contrast, Pechman (1970) grouped the population by income level and showed that the higher education benefits received by the richest income groups were, on average, less than the taxes they paid that could be attributed to higher education.[20] Finally, Hartman (1970) explained how these apparently contradictory findings could be consistent with a given set of data. However, he did not offer a criterion for deciding whether the system was equalising or not and concluded that it was both '(a) regressive and (b) progressive'. This paradox could easily be settled, of course, by the simple device of measuring the inequality of $\underline{V}^A$ and $\underline{V}^H$.

ANALYSIS BY CHILD'S INCOME

It is, in any case, unsatisfactory to suppose that the incidence of educational expenditures is wholly on parents, so, running to the opposite extreme, Jencks (1972) proceeds on the assumption that the relevant impact is on children. His argument is by now so notorious that, were it not still misunderstood, it could be taken as read. Jencks starts from the low correlation (·35) between income and years of schooling for native, white, nonfarm males in the United States.[21] According to some economist critics, this is the wrong place to start, the right place being the estimated effect of education on income (the regression coefficient) and not the power of education to explain income. However, for distributional purposes, the correlation coefficient *is* the right place to start. For, whatever education can do to income, a low correlation indicates that many people with low education have high incomes, and *vice versa.* So, steps to augment the incomes of people with little education will involve many transfers from richer to poorer people. They would, of course, be equalising, but only mildly so.

[20] Even taking into account the parents' income only, it is important to allow for lifetime income. The richest taxpayers in a given year may often be too old to have college-age children and the poorest taxpayers to young.

[21] The correlation is the average of the correlation for different age groups. It is not, of course, a correlation of schooling and lifetime income, which would need to take into account the shorter working lives of those more schooled.

To clarify the issue, let us review a few possible policies. First, imagine giving each child a better-quality elementary education (of the same value for each child). Suppose that this were financed by a tax rising with income. Then, the net benefit of the policy would fall with income ($dB/dV - dC/dV < 0$) and the policy, if efficient, would be redistributive. But the redistribution comes from the fact that taxes rise with income. Now, imagine a compensatory educational policy where more education was given only to those who had least of it, again financed by a tax rising with income. This might, or might not, be more equalising, depending on how many of the poor had more than the minimum of education. But, since there will certainly be some in this category, such a policy will involve many transfers from poorer to richer, even though these are outweighed by transfers from richer to poorer. Though equalising, the policy will reduce inequality relatively little, compared with the use of the same tax receipts as income transfers. By the same token, expenditure on higher education would involve many transfers from richer to poorer and might not be as disequalising as one might suppose.

There is, however, one point that Jencks overlooks with regard to the incidence of educational expenditure on children. He assumes that social mobility (i.e. the correlation of fathers' and sons' incomes) is not directly relevant to the problem of income distribution. However, this is not the case if we are interested in lifetime income. For a child's standard of living in youth is determined by his father's income and in adulthood by his own. The inequality of lifetime income may thus be substantially reduced by reducing this correlation.[22]

INCIDENCE ON PARENTS AND CHILDREN

However, viewed more widely, educational spending must be seen as affecting both parents and children (Stiglitz, 1973). According to Bowles (1972), the correlation between father's income and son's schooling is mugh higher (·60) than the correlation between son's income and schooling (·36).[23] This means that, in so far as educational expenditure affects income distribution, it may do so at least as much through its effects on parents' incomes as on children's. In discussing the incidence of possible policy changes in Great Britain, we shall consider both types of effect. For numerical purposes, however, we unfortunately have to ignore the effects on parents, since no data are available on the

[22] If lifetime income consists of a fraction of father's income and a fraction of own income so that $V = a\ V_F + b\ V_O$, then

$$\text{var}(V) = a^2\ \text{var}(V_F) + b^2\ \text{var}(V_O) + 2\,ab\ \text{cov}(V_F, V_O)$$

According to Bowles (1972, p.S247), the correlation of father's and son's incomes is 0·30.

[23] Jencks (1972), using data on father's occupation, gets the reverse ranking. He finds that

r (father's occupation, son's schooling) = ·49
r (son's occupation, son's schooling) = ·69
and r (father's occupation, son's occupation) = ·44

income of the parents of children with different completed years of schooling. Since children's schooling, parents' income and children's income are all positively correlated, a policy that has similar effects on a child and on his parents is likely to (dis)equalise through its effects on both sets of incomes. But this is not necessarily the case. For example, a subsidy to the brillaint child of poor parents could disequalise through its effect on the child's income but equalise through its effects on that of the parents. A policy that has opposite effects on a child and his parents (like a reduction in the minimum compulsory school leaving age – see below) could also have this same set of results.

COMPUTING LIFETIME INCOME IN THE UNITED KINGDOM ($\underline{V}^A$)

The numerical analysis is for the cohort of working males aged 25–29 in 1971 and relies on cross-sectional data from the 1971 General Household Survey.[24] First, we compute their $\underline{V}^A$, and then their $\underline{V}^H$ under different policy assumptions. Getting $\underline{V}^A$ involves two steps. First we run an earnings function for all working males aged 15–65. This (the first earnings function for Britain that includes education)[25] comes out as follows (*SE*s are shown in brackets; R^2 = ·496, and *SE* = ·344):

$$
\begin{aligned}
\ln Y = \; & 2{\cdot}777 + {\cdot}948 \underset{(\cdot 028)}{\ln W} + \underset{(\cdot 041)}{\cdot 092C} + \underset{(\cdot 024)}{\cdot 110T} \\
& + \underset{(\cdot 044)}{\cdot 114F_1} + \underset{(\cdot 044)}{\cdot 053F_2} + \underset{(\cdot 052)}{\cdot 163F_3} + \underset{(\cdot 046)}{\cdot 184F_4} + \underset{(\cdot 050)}{\cdot 139F_5} \\
& + \underset{(\cdot 024)}{\cdot 093S_{15}} + \underset{(\cdot 033)}{\cdot 140S_{16}} + \underset{(\cdot 047)}{\cdot 214S_{17}} + \underset{(\cdot 052)}{\cdot 300S_{18}} + \underset{(\cdot 043)}{\cdot 507S_{19+}} \\
& + \underset{(\cdot 003)}{\cdot 030(A-S)} - \underset{(\cdot 00005)}{\cdot 00052(A-S)^2} + e
\end{aligned}
\qquad (4.4)
$$

where the variables are

Y after-tax earnings in previous 12 months (using tax rates for married men with no children)
W weeks worked in previous 12 months
C country of birth (1 = British Isles, 0 = other)
T type of secondary school (1 = selective entry, 0 = other)
F father's socio-economic group
F_1 1 = semi-skilled manual, 0 = other
F_2 1 = skilled manual and self-employed non-professional, 0 = other

[24] The General Household Survey is an annual national survey begun in 1971 (OPCAS, 1971). Different households are interviewed each year. The present preliminary analysis is confined to members of the labour force who when interviewed had worked at least one week in the last year, and who were interviewed in the last quarter of the year. There were 1868 such men aged 15–65. I am most grateful to the OPCAS for providing the survey tapes, and to Mrs Anne Thomas for help in understanding them.

[25] See also Hill (1959).

F_3 1 = intermediate and junior non-manual, 0 = other
F_4 1 = employers and managers, 0 = other
F_5 1 = professionals, 0 = other
(omitted group is unskilled manual)

S age on completing full-time education
S_{15}, S_{16}, S_{17}, S_{18}, S_{19+} indicate age shown by subscript
(omitted group is those who completed at 14 and under)

A age last birthday

This function is broadly similar to that used by Mincer (1972), but differs in three important respects. First, the dependent variable is after-tax earnings, which would be quite appropriate in a supply-side model such as Mincer's, and is the concept relevant to distribution. Second, schooling is treated as a dummy variable to avoid imposing equal private rates of return to each level of schooling.[26] Third, we include a dummy variable for type of secondary school (selective or nonselective); this is intended to catch at least some small part of the important effect of ability on income.

Once the earnings function is obtained, we confine ourselves to those members of the sample aged 25–29 in 1971. For each individual we then estimate his income at each age (A) from (S + 1) to 65, using equation (4.4) but replacing $\ell n\ W$ by ℓn 52, and multiplying the resulting estimate by $(1{\cdot}02)^{A-27}$, 2 per cent being the assumed rate of growth of real age–education-specific earnings. We thus assume that the individual's error (e) computed from the regression equation stays with him for life, but attempt to eliminate transitory components of annual income in 1971 by replacing $\ell n\ W$ by ℓn 52.[27] The present value of the individual's earnings (V^A) is got by discounting this stream back to age 15 and then adding to it the present value of any maintenance grants paid. (No tuition fees are paid by British students in Britain, except in private schools.) Unfortunately, no data are available on inherited wealth; otherwise, the discounted stream of bequests ought to be added in. The expected value of pensions should also be added in, but would involve many assumptions. If it is proportional to the included items, the exclusion of pensions does not affect the measurement of inequality. In addition, since we know little about how long the different individuals will live, no adjustment is made for length of life. The computed inequality of lifetime income at a 5 per cent discount rate is ·0707.[28]

[26] Of course, in Mincer's model, if the (common) rate of return to education equals the private discount rate, all inequality of annual incomes due to educational differences disappears when discounted lifetime income is considered.

[27] The sample included 213 individuals aged 25–29. Of these, six had error terms such that $|e| > 1$. These six were eliminated from the present preliminary analysis.

[28] This figure, like all that follow, is based on a sample of 207 (see the previous footnote). For the full 213, lifetime inequality is ·116, compared with inequality of 1971 incomes of ·157 (or ·119 if variations in weeks worked are excluded). In the whole sample aged 15–65, cross-sectional inequality is ·264.

THE IMPACT OF EDUCATIONAL POLICY CHANGE (COMPUTING $\underline{V}^H$)

We now construct various hypothetical vectors $\underline{V}^H$ by examining various possible educational policy changes.[29] As already explained, in all cases we assume that the additional taxes paid by the cohort to finance the same educational changes for succeeding generations are in the form of taxes proportional to consumption. So these are ignored altogether in obtaining our measures of inequality change $\Delta \ln (1 - I)$ shown in Table 4.1. Adjacent to these measures is shown the fall in total output $(- \Delta \ln \bar{V})$. This needs some explaining. The policy changes experienced by the current cohort also affect the elder generation, who partially pay for them. Though we cannot allocate this burden among people, its total must be taken into account in evaluating the efficiency effects of the project. $\bar{V}^H$ is therefore computed as follows. First, we compute the social present value (S) of the policy per person whose quantity of education was affected by it. The constituent elements in this calculation are shown in Table 4.2. If the project affected the quantity of education of a proportion p of the cohort, we then compute[30]

$$\bar{V}^H = \bar{V}^A + pS$$

Finally, Table 4.1 shows, on the right-hand side, the relative total cost of the policy to public funds. This includes only the outlays by taxpayers and not any additional tax receipts resulting from higher incomes generated by the project. It may not be a very important magnitude but is often looked at closely by governments. We can now examine the policies to be evaluated in this way.

(a) *Qualitative improvements in universal education*

These affect children and not parents. We examine the effects of an investment of £20 extra per annum on each child's education throughout his compulsory school life. Unfortunately, we have no idea what the rate of return to this would be. Jencks, Coleman and others imply that in terms of measurable outcomes it is small, though Jencks stresses that children may enjoy qualitatively better schools more. Suppose, for illustration, that the social rate of return is 3 per cent and takes the form of a constant income stream from the year of the investment until retirement. (While the individual is still being educated, the benefit will be in the form of improved ability to learn plus psychic benefits.)[31] Then each individual's present value at 15 would rise by a constant depending on the discount rate. This appears as equalising, since a given ab-

[29] For the detailed calculations, see a note available, on request, from the author.

[30] It is right to relate the total effects of the project to the present value of one cohort so long as one is only measuring inequality in one cohort. A more desirable approach would be to include all relevant cohorts, in which case the effects for each cohort would be measured in terms of present values when the members of that cohort were aged 15, and not when members of the cohort aged 25–29 in 1971 were aged 15.

[31] For simplicity, I assume that this is taxable.

TABLE 4.1

INEQUALITY AND EFFICIENCY EFFECTS OF DIFFERENT EDUCATIONAL POLICIES

Policy	$i = 0$			$i = \cdot 02$			$i = \cdot 05$			Cost to public funds Policy (a) = 1		
	I	$\frac{\Delta \ell n}{(1-I)}$ %	$-\frac{\Delta \ell n}{\bar{V}}$ %	I	$\frac{\Delta \ell n}{(1-I)}$ %	$-\frac{\Delta \ell n}{\bar{V}}$ %	I	$\frac{\Delta \ell n}{(1-I)}$ %	$-\frac{\Delta \ell n}{\bar{V}}$ %	$i = 0$	$i = \cdot 02$	$i = \cdot 05$
Present policy (I^A)	·079101	–	–	·075676	–	–	·070574	–	–	–	–	–
(a) Qualitative improvement in universal schooling	·078760	+·037	−·130	·075282	+·043	−·008	·070068	+·377	+·377	1·00	1·00	1·00
(b) Qualitative improvement for early leavers	·078723	+·041	−·083	·075262	+·045	−·005	·070113	+·050	+·242	·64	·64	·64
(c) Raising minimum school leaving age	·075839	+·354	−8·152	·073543	+·231	−6·195	·070022	+·059	−2·010	·93	·84	·71
(d) Maintenance grants in 16th year $\eta = 0$	·079152	−·005	0	·075722	−·005	0	·070490	+·009	0	·54	·47	·39
$\eta = 1$(I)	·079127	−·003	−·175	·075686	−·001	−·116	·070440	+·014	+·015	·78	·70	·59
(II)	·078637	+·050	−·778	·075303	+·040	−·727	·070266	+·033	−·617	·78	·70	·59
(e) Maintenance grants in 17th year $\eta = 0$	·079202	−·011	0	·075807	−·014	0	·070656	−·009	0	·31	·27	·21
$\eta = 1$(I)	·079191	−·010	−·160	·075788	−·012	−·120	·070618	−·005	−·034	·45	·39	·32
(II)	·079037	+·007	−·662	·075630	+·005	−·619	·070453	+·013	−·529	·45	·39	·32
(f) Maintenance grants in 18th year $\eta = 0$	·079216	−·012	0	·075833	−·017	0	·070725	−·016	0	·23	·20	·15
$\eta = 1$(I)	·079210	−·012	−·116	·075819	−·015	−·091	·070686	−·012	−·038	·31	·27	·21
(II)	·079126	−·003	−·462	·075670	+·001	−·426	·070415	+·017	−·355	·31	·27	·21
(g) Fees in higher education $\eta = 0$	·078909	+·021	0	·075464	+·023	0	·070562	+·001	0	−·15	−·13	−·10
$\eta = 1$(I)	·078900	+·022	+·082	·075435	+·026	+·027	·070465	+·012	−·078	−·11	−·09	−·07
(II)	·079271	−·104	+·480	·076878	−·130	+·421	·072419	−1·198	+·312	−·11	−·09	−·07

Note: On computation of parameters, see text.

TABLE 4.2

NET SOCIAL BENEFITS PER PERSON RECEIVING ADDITIONAL EDUCATION (PRESENT VALUES AT AGE 15, POUNDS STERLING, 1971 PRICES)

			$i = 0$	$i = \cdot 02$	$i = \cdot 05$
(a) Qualitative improvement in universal schooling + (b)					
		Change in after-tax earnings	233	157	100
		Change in taxes generated	100	67	43
		– New institutional subsidy	–200	–219	–251
(c) Raising minimum school leaving age					
		Change in after-tax earnings	3619	2014	959
		Change in taxes generated	1551	863	411
		– Existing institutional subsidy	–291	–285	–277
(d) Maintenance grants in 16th year					
$\eta = 1$	(I)	$\bar{B}$	131	128	125
		+ Change in taxes generated	1551	863	411
		– Existing institutional subsidy	–291	–285	–277
		– New cash subsidy	–300	–294	–285
	(II)	Change in after-tax earnings	3619	2014	959
		+ Change in taxes generated	1551	863	411
		– Existing institutional subsidy	–291	–285	–277
(e) Maintenance grants in 17th year					
$\eta = 1$	(I)	$\bar{B}$	132	127	120
		+ Change in taxes generated	2347	1295	607
		– Existing institutional subsidy	–386	–371	–350
		– New cash subsidy	–300	–288	–272
	(II)	Change in after-tax earnings	5477	3023	1417
		+ Change in taxes generated	2347	1295	607
		–Existing institutional subsidy	–386	–371	–350
(f) Maintenance grants in 18th year					
$\eta = 1$	(I)	$\bar{B}$	133	126	115
		+ Change in taxes generated	2798	1515	682
		– Existing institutional subsidy	–386	–363	–333
		– New cash subsidy	–300	–282	–259
	(II)	Change in after-tax earnings	6528	3534	1592
		+ Change in taxes generated	2798	1515	682
		– Existing institutional subsidy	–386	–363	–333
(g) Fees in higher education[a]					
$\eta = 1$	(I)	$\bar{B}$	–405	–367	–317
		+ Change in taxes generated	–5715	–3113	–1442
		+ Existing institutional subsidy	2172	1967	1703
		+ Existing cash subsidy	1068	967	837
	(II)	Change in after-tax earnings	–13335	–7264	–3366
		+ Change in taxes generated	–5715	–3113	–1442
		+ Existing institutional subsidy	2172	1967	1703

[a] In case (g) we show the social benefit that would result had each person who previously received higher education had not received it.

Note: For policies (d)–(g) a uniform value for income changes was calculated for all persons affected, using mean values for all background variables (averaged over the whole sample). For policy (c) individual earnings estimates were used. However, to avoid confusion, the same 'uniform' values have been shown in this table under (c) as under (d).

solute amount has been given to each person and a given proportional amount removed (in the language of section IV, $\beta = 1, \alpha < 1$). At a 2 per cent interest rate, the increase in equality is ·04 per cent and there is no loss in total output. The policy is therefore desirable. On the other hand, at a 5 per cent rate of interest, the increase in equality is outweighed by the loss of output and the policy should not be pursued. This conflict of findings highlights the problem that arises when one wishes to use one (low) rate of interest to measure existing lifetime income in a way that correctly reflects inequality, and another (higher) rate of interest (or set of rates) to measure changes in income as experienced by those concerned. This problem really cannot be overcome until data on consumption streams become available.

(b) *Qualitative improvements of early leavers only*

If the qualitative improvements could be restricted to less able children, they would of course be more equalising. Suppose, for example, that it were administratively possible to identify children who were going to leave at the minimum school-leaving age of 15 (for this cohort) and £20 per annum were then spent on each of these children. The rate of return is again uncertain; suppose it is 3 per cent. Then, at a 2 per cent rate of interest, this 'selective' policy appears as more equalising than the same policy applied to all children. At a 5 per cent rate of interest, there is already so much overlap in lifetime income among those who leave later that the selective policy is actually less equalising than the universal one.

(c) *Raising the compulsory minimum school-leaving age*

Another policy that may benefit early leavers is the raising of the minimum compulsory school-leaving age, which was 15 for our cohort but was raised to 16 in 1972–3. Since the option of staying on was available without compulsion to do so, staying on was clearly judged undesirable by the family decision-makers, whoever they were. This may be because the costs of an extra year of schooling for a child may normally be borne mainly by the parents. A 16-year-old British male worker normally lives with his parents and pays them for board and lodging; a 16-year-old schoolboy pays them nothing. Unless his alternative wages were much higher than his board and lodging, he may lose little by staying on a year. If he bears none of the earnings forgone, he gains the present value of his increased earnings from 16 onwards. But this probably overstates the gain, as the individual may hate school. We therefore attribute the full cost of earnings forgone to the child, so that he is assessed as gaining only if the private present value of the differences in after-tax earnings is positive. In our calculations we should, of course, allow for the effects that more staying on will have upon the wages of stayers-on. But, thoughout this analysis, we assume, instead, perfect substitution among different types of labour.[32] As

[32] For evidence on elasticities of substitution see Dougherty (1972) and Fallon and Layard (1973).

a result, equality rises and, at interest rates of 5 per cent or below, so does output.

(d)–(g) *Changing cash support for students in post-compulsory education*

An alternative policy for widening education opportunity is higher financial subsidies, such as cash maintenance grants to those who stay on at school. Extremely little is known about the effects of variation in the price of education upon quantity demanded. Suppose, first, that there is no effect ($\eta = 0$). Then, those affected gain the full value of the extra subsidy. Probably the main people affected are the parents, who would otherwise have been bearing that part of the cost of the child's education. The child may also experience some increase in his living standard. Lacking data on parents, we attribute the whole gain to the children.[33] The expenditure is pure transfer and has no efficiency implications.

Suppose now that the subsidy did induce an increase in staying on. Handa and Skolnik (1972) provide tenuous evidence that the demand elasticity may be unitary, and we shall assume this. In this case,

$$q_1 = q_0 \frac{p_0}{p_1}$$

where q_0 and p_0 are the present numbers staying-on and present private costs, and q_1 and p_1 are the values after the policy change. We assume that the $(q_1 - q_0)$ new stayers-on are selected randomly from those who previously took the next-lower level of education.

For those who already stay on, the benefits are, as before, $(p_0 - p_1)$. But what are they for the new stayers-on? The normal approach (approach I) would be to estimate their gain in consumer surplus. In this case, the average gain is measured by the average value of $p(q) - p_1$, over the range q_0 to q_1, in Figure 4.3, where $p(q)$ is the demand price. This, before discounting, is[34]

$$\bar{B} = p_0\, p_1 \frac{\log p_0 - \log p_1}{p_0 - p_1} - p_1$$

[33] This, and what follows, may not be entirely consistent with out treatment of the raising of the minimum school-leaving age, where the net gain of the family may be negative and yet we show gains.

[34] If $p(q) = kq^{-1}$, $\int_{q_0}^{q_1} kq^{-1}\, dq = k\,(\log p_0 - \log p_1)$.

Therefore, average surplus $= \dfrac{k\,(\log p_0 - \log p_1)}{k/p_1 - k/p_0} - p_1$.

If p rises, $\bar{B} = -\,p_0\, p_1 \dfrac{\log p_1 - \log p_0}{p_1 - p_0} + p_0$.

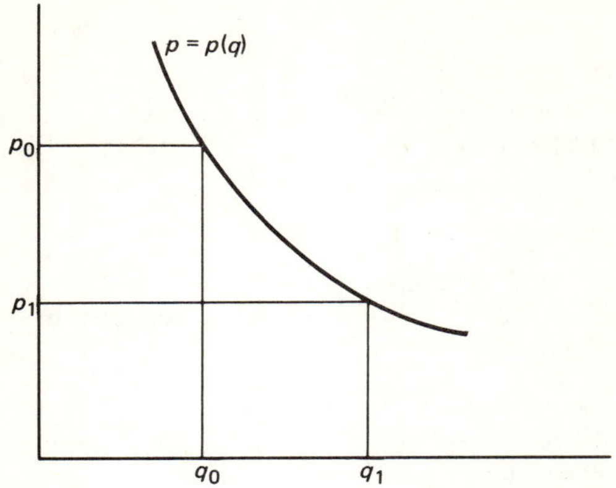

Fig. 4.3

Welfare Effects of an Educational Subsidy

This assumes, of course, that education is available at each age for those who demand it at the going price; this is broadly true in Britain, though demanders may not be able to get the exact kind of education that they want. The gain so measured may be divided between parents and children, and may even include losses for parents. However, we again impute all of the effects to children. The resulting calculations for equality and output change are shown in Table 4.1 on the rows marked $\eta = 1$ (I).

However, this approach assumes that the marginal individual in each situation is not only indifferent about staying on or leaving, but that he would *ex post* get zero benefit from staying on. In other words, it assumes on his part a perfect knowledge of monetary income streams. If we adopt the alternative 'human capital' approach (II), we measure the benefits for him. In this approach, psychic benefits are omitted, since there is no way of inferring them. We now measure private benefits as the change in the present value of after-tax earnings plus the present value of any maintenance grant gained. This approach is adopted in the rows marked $\eta = 1$ (II).

Finally we should review the calculation of the social present value of the effect of educating one extra person (S), the elements of the calculations being shown in Table 4.2.[35] This is the sum of the present value of the items listed:[36]

[35] We are, of course, omitting all external effects (other than taxes), including externalities connected with the so-called screening hypothesis. For evidence that this hypothesis may not be quantitatively important, see Layard and Psacharopoulos (1974).

[36] The scheme is different when one less person is educated; see Table 4.2. In Britain, and except for students of 19 and over, existing cash subsidies are approximately zero.

Assumption I	*Beneficiary*
$\bar{B}$	Educated person
+ Change in taxes generated – Existing institutional subsidy – Existing cash subsidy – New cash subsidy	Taxpayers

Assumption II	
Change in after-tax earnings + Existing cash subsidy + New cash subsidy	Educated person
+ Change in taxes generated – Existing institutional subsidy – Existing cash subsidy – New cash subsidy	Taxpayers

There are no a priori remarks that one can make about the sum of these items (i.e. S). Under assumption I, we know that $\bar{B} <$ new cash subsidy, so that $S > 0$ only if additional taxes exceed the existing subsidies. Under assumption II, if capital markets were perfect and knowledge likewise, net private benefits without the new cash subsidy would be zero, so the same condition for social gain applies. However, in practice, net private benefits so computed are not zero.

Using this framework we now evaluate the following policies:[37]

(d) maintenance grant for all children at school in the 16th year raised from zero to £300;
(e) maintenance grant for all children at school in their 17th year raised from zero to £300;
(f) maintenance grant for all children at school in their 18th year raised from zero to £300; and
(g) higher-education fees raised from zero to £300.

The conclusions to be drawn differ with the assumptions made. This may be due in part to the small sample numbers used in this preliminary exercise.[38] It may also be due to the high degree of overlap in the income distributions of the different groups;[39] as suggested in section IV, this makes the inequality

[37] At a later stage, further policies will be considered (for instance, differential grants related to father's occupation).

[38] The work reported here is the first item in a collaborative programme of work on income distribution using the *General Household Survey* data. This will cover, *inter alia*, the supply of working hours, labour force participation, and the determinants of unemployment – all of which are ignored in the present paper.

[39] At $i = \cdot05$, $\bar{V}$ for those who completed full-time education at different ages (using the full sample of 213 rather than the 207 used in Table 4.1) is: 14, £30,421; 15, £28,114; 16, £27,057; 17, £26,649; 18, £35,602; 19+, £32,169; all groups, £28,752.

effects of different policies very sensitive to specific assumptions. I shall concentrate on the case of $i = \cdot 05$, $\eta = 1$ (I). In this case, grants to 16-year-olds in school would have been equalising, but would have induced some loss of output, making the policy of marginal social value at the chosen level of inequality aversion. Grants to 17- and 18-year-olds, though disequalising, may be justified by the induced gain in output, while fees in higher education may be equalising and efficient. These findings, though tentative, make quite good sense, bearing in mind the massive current subsidies to higher education and the strange form of the educational pyramid, whereby most people either end their education at 19 or over or at below 17.

I do not claim to have solved the discount rate problem which lies at the heart of all analyses of lifetime welfare, but I hope to have clarified some of the issues, and to have adopted a useful framework within which distributional and efficiency effects of policies can be simultaneously viewed.

REFERENCES

Aaron, H. J., 'The Social Insurance Paradox', *Canadian Journal of Economic and Political Science,* Aug 1966.

Arrow, K. J., 'Uncertainty and the Welfare Economics of Medical Care', *American Economic Review,* Dec 1963.

Asimokopoulos, A., and Weldon, J. C., 'On the Theory of Government Pension Plans', *Canadian Journal of Economics,* 1968.

Atkinson, A. B., 'National Superannuation: Redistribution and Values for Money', *Bulletin of the Oxford University Institute of Economics and Statistics,* Aug 1970.

Atkinson, A. B., 'On the Measurement of Inequality', *Journal of Economic Theory,* Aug 1970.

Becker, G. S., *Human Capital and the Personal Distribution of Income,* The Woytinsky Lecture (University of Michigan Press, 1967).

Bowles, S., 'Schooling and Inequality from Generation to Generation', *Journal of Political Economy,* May/June 1972, part II.

Brainard, W., in *Efficiency in Universities: The La Paz Papers,* ed. K. G. Lumsden (Elsevier, 1974).

Cass, D., and Yaari, M. E., 'A Re-examination of the Pure Consumption Loan Model', *Journal of Political Economy,* Aug 1966.

Diamond, P. A., 'National Debt in a Neo-Classical Growth Model', *American Economic Review,* Dec 1965.

Dougherty, C. R. S., 'Estimates of Labour Aggregation Functions', *Journal of Political Economy,* Nov 1972.

Fallon, P., and Layard, R., 'Capital–Skill Complementarity, Income Distribution and Output Accounting' (Higher Education Research Unit, London School of Economics, 1973), mimeo.

Friedman, M., *A Theory of the Consumption Function* (Princeton University Press, 1957).

Glennerster, H., 'Education and Inequality', in *Labour and Inequality,* ed. P. Townsend and N. Bosanquet (Fabian Society, 1972).

Handa, M. L., and Skolnik, M. L., 'Empirical Analysis of the Demand for Education in Canada', in *Canadian Higher Education in the Seventies,* ed. S. Ostry (Economic Council of Canada, May 1972).

Hansen, W. L., and Weisbrod, B. A., 'The Distribution of Costs and Benefits of Higher Education: the Case of California', *Journal of Human Resources,* Spring 1969.

Hansen, W. L., and Weisbrod, B. A., 'On the Distribution of Costs and Benefits of Public Higher Education: Reply', *Journal of Human Resources,* Summer 1971.

Hartman, R., 'A Comment on the Pechman–Hansen–Weisbrod Controversy', *Journal of Human Resources*, Fall 1970.

Hill, T. P., 'An Analysis of the Distribution of Wages and Salaries in Great Britain', *Econometrica,* July 1959.

Jorgensen, D. W., and Griliches, Z., 'The Explanation of Productivity Change', *Review of Economic Studies,* 1967.

Jencks, C., et al., *Inequality* (New York: Basic Books, 1972).

Kaldor, N., 'An Expenditure Tax' (1955), in R. Bird and O. Oldman, *Readings on Taxation in Developing Countries* (Johns Hopkins Press, 1964).

Layard, R., and Psacharopoulos, G., 'The Screening Hypothesis and the Social Returns to Education', *Journal of Political Economy*, Sep 1974.

Meade, J. E., *The Theory of International and Economic Policy:* Vol. II, *Trade and Welfare* (Oxford University Press, 1956).

Mincer, J., *Schooling, Experience and Earnings,* National Bureau of Economic Research: 'Human Behavior and Social Institutions', no. 2 (New York and London: Columbia University Press, 1974).

Musgrave, R. A., 'Estimating the Distribution of the Tax Burden', in *Income Redistribution and the Statistical Foundations of Economic Policy,* ed. C. Clark and G. Stuvel (London: Bowes and Bowes, 1964).

Nicholson, J. L., 'Redistribution of Income in the UK in 1959, 1957 and 1953', ibid. (1964).

Office of Population Censuses and Surveys (OPCAS), Social Survey Division, *The General Household Survey, Introductory Report* (London: HMSO, 1973).

Peacock, A., and Shannon, R., 'The Welfare State and the Redistribution of Income', *Westminster Bank Review,* Aug 1968.

Pechman, J., 'The Distribution Effects of Public Higher Education in California', *Journal of Human Resources,* Summer 1970.

Prest, A. R., 'The Budget and Interpersonal Distribution', *Public Finance,* nos. 1–2 (1968).

Prest, A. R., 'Some Redistributional Aspects of the National Superannuation Fund', *Three Banks Review,* June 1970.

Samuelson, P. A., 'An Exact Consumption–Loan Model of Interest with and without the Social Contrivance of Money', *Journal of Political Economy,* Dec 1958.

Sen, A. K., *On Economic Inequality* (Oxford University Press, 1973).

Sen, A. K., 'Aggregation and Income Distribution' (paper presented to the International Seminar on Public Economics, Siena, Sep 1973).

Stiglitz, J., 'Education and Inequality', *Annals of the American Academy of Political and Social Science,* CDIX, Sep 1973.

Verry, D., and Layard, R., 'Cost Functions for University Teaching and Research', (Higher Education Research Unit, London School of Economics, 1973), mimeo.

Weisbrod, B. A. and Hansen, W. L., 'An Income–Net–Worth Approach to Measuring Economic Welfare', *American Economic Review,* Dec 1969.

Part III
The Criminal Justice System

5 Jury Size and Composition: An Economic Approach

Alvin K. Klevorick
YALE UNIVERSITY

The facilities and processes that governments provide for resolving legal disputes constitute an important public service. For the resolution of some of these disputes, society turns to a body of laymen – a jury. In considering the jury as a conflict-resolving instrument, several interrelated questions arise concerning the jury's size, the way its members are selected, and the voting rule that it uses in reaching its decision. This paper presents a theoretical structure to help address these questions. The model, which uses a statistical decision-theoretic framework, is then used to examine the specific issue of how 'representative' a jury should be.

I. INTRODUCTION

It is difficult to think of a society of heterogeneous individuals in which disputes would not arise. One set of public services that governments usually provide consists of the facilities and processes for the resolution of such disputes. The resources expended for these public services, which have received relatively little attention from economists, include the use of courthouses and administrative agency buildings, and the time of judges, prosecutors, public defenders, courthouse personnel, members of administrative agencies, and the staffs and assistants of these individuals.

Of course, not all disputes reach the stage where government facilities and services are called upon for assistance. In fact, the nature and structure of the particular set of services provided by the government help to determine which conflicts will be resolved inside, and which outside, the framework of govern-

[1] This is a revised version of a paper prepared for the International Economic Association Conference on the Economics of Public Services held on 1–6 April, 1974 at Turin, Italy. Without implying any responsibility on their part, the author wishes to thank B. Ackerman, G. Calabresi, G. Hazard Jr, A. Leff, B. Margolin, K. Peck, S. Rose-Ackerman, and J. Tobin for their helpful discussions. In revising the paper, I benefited greatly from the discussion of the paper at the conference and, in particular, from the extremely helpful comments of the discussant, C. von Weizsäcker. The research described in this paper was supported by grants from the National Science Foundation and from the Ford Foundation.

ment institutions. For example, the structure of liability rules, the court-established precedents for similar cases, and the current extent of court delay – all characteristics of the government's dispute-resolution service – will be among the factors that a potential plaintiff in an accident case will weigh in deciding whether to go to court. Moreover, not all disputants will employ the same set of government institutions. Different processes and facilities will be used in settling different conflicts.

In resolving some legal disputes, society turns to a selected body of laymen – a jury–for the decision. This particular 'government service' – the jury – is the focus of the present paper. In considering the use of the jury as a conflict-resolving instrument, several interrelated questions arise. How large should the jury be? What should the composition of this jury be; alternatively, how should its members be selected? What voting rule should the jury use to reach its decision in resolving the dispute at hand?

As the result of several relatively recent US Supreme Court decisions,[2] there has been a revival of interest in these questions in the United States. The decisions upheld, under particular circumstances, the constitutionality of juries comprised of fewer than 12 persons and of decisions reached by nonunanimous 12-person juries. The aim of this paper is to provide a theoretical structure to help address these questions of jury size, composition, and voting rule. It is not intended to serve as a comprehensive study of the jury. Instead, I shall present a model, shaped in the statistical decision-theoretic mould, that I hope will be helpful in organising and clarifying thought about the relevant current questions concerning the jury.

The model will not be able to specify how juries should be structured, but it will be useful in pinpointing the empirical information (or empirical guesses) needed to reach such decisions. It will suggest what data are relevant for making such choices and how different values for the critical quantities affect the choices made. Although one would like to have 'hard numbers' to demonstrate the effects of these critical choices, it seems that, at least for the present, there still remains considerable scope for the kind of insights that a theoretical model might provide.

For example, the empirical research, to date, on the issue of jury size seems a very slender reed upon which to base any decision concerning whether six-member juries behave differently from ('better' than?) 12-member juries. Much of the empirical research on this question is largely descriptive and anecdotal.[3] In the less anecdotal pieces, one approach compares actual jury decisions in two sets of civil cases tried in the same jurisdiction at different times – one set when jury size was fixed at 12, the other when it was reduced to six.[4] In these

[2] *Williams v. Florida,* 399 US 78 (1970); *Johnson v. Louisiana,* 406 US 356 (1972); *Apodaca v. Oregon,* 406 US 404 (1972); *Colgrove v. Battin,* 413 US 149 (1973).

[3] See Zeisel's criticism of the empirical evidence cited by the Supreme Court in the *Williams* case (Zeisel, 1971, pp. 713–15).

[4] Examples of this approach are Beiser (1973), Mills (1973).

studies, there is little stratification by type of case. When the cases are stratified sufficiently to lend credence to the comparability of the cases within a group, the numbers in each class are so small that meaningful statistical analysis of differences in the performances of the two sizes of jury for a particular type of case becomes almost impossible. Furthermore, some of the differences in performance that are considered in these papers seem of questionable relevance.[5] The other major empirical approach to the jury-size issue compares the decisions of mock juries of different sizes when each mock jury views the same case via videotape. In addition to difficulties specific to particular studies of this type, the general approach suffers, of course, from all of the problems associated with trying to draw inferences about actual decision-making situations from experimental ones.[6]

Given the state of empirical research on the jury questions mentioned earlier,[7] it seems reasonable to pursue the theoretical route a bit further. While the present model abstracts drastically from the richness of the jury as an institution, it is more attentive to two aspects that previous probabilistic models have suppressed: differences among jurors and the nonindependence of juror decision-making. Some previous probabilistic models essentially assume that jurors are identical or, at least, that they can be considered independent drawings from the same distribution.[8] Those models that do recognise differences among jurors still regard the jury as a collection of individual decision-makers whose decisions are independent of each other.[9] By contrast, the model in the present paper will focus on the importance of differences among jurors and the dependent elements in their decision-making processes.

After delineating the basic theoretical structure, we shall use the model to examine how representative a jury should be. The representativeness issue was highlighted by the Supreme Court's opinion in *Williams v. Florida.* The court saw little problem with reducing jury size from 12 to six so long as the jury

[5] Such studies may yield some insight into the difference in the time required when a six-person rather than a 12-person jury is used. Even here, though, inadequate stratification of cases limits the contribution that these studies can make. But we surely do not learn much when they compare the percentage of cases won by the plaintiff with the percentage of cases won by the defendant, or when they examine differences in the amount awarded, measured either absolutely or as a percentage of the amount requested in the complaint. (Results on the amount awarded as a percentage of the amount requested in the complaint convey especially little information in cases where the jury does not know the latter amount.)

[6] Some of these problems are discussed briefly in Kessler (1973), in which, only one case was used. Each of the 16 mock juries that Kessler used found for the defendant or reached no verdict, the latter being the result for two of the eight six-person juries and for one of the eight 12-person juries. The experiment does provide some useful insights into the degree of participation in juries of different sizes, but even here the value of the study's implications is diminished by the fact that only one case was examined.

[7] Erlanger (1970) provides a fairly complete bibliographic survey of social science writings on the jury during the period 1925–70.

[8] Gelfand and Solomon (1973).

[9] Gelfand and Solomon (1973), Walbert (1971), and Zeisel (1971).

continued to be a cross-section representative of the community. In the court's view, if the six members were representative of the community, the reduction in size would not substantially reduce the protection afforded the defendant. Of course, as Zeisel has demonstrated in the context of a simple two-class society, reducing the size of the jury reduces the possibility of obtaining a representative jury.[10]

The issue that we raise here is a different one. There is, to be sure, a spectrum of reasons that one could offer for having representative juries. I shall present a model of the most instrumental function of the jury. Then, drawing upon the economist's model of portfolio selection and using that model as a metaphor in viewing the question of jury composition, I shall examine the degree to which, and the conditions under which, jury representatives serves this most instrumental function. I shall also try, at the end, to suggest an alternative reason for representativeness of the jury which I have not seen articulated in this way elsewhere.[11] This reason, which lies at the least instrumental end of the spectrum, focuses on jury representativeness as a political symbol, as a value in its own right.

II. THE BASIC APPROACH AND THE UNIT OF ANALYSIS

The approach taken here begins by specifying a social loss function encompassing the variety of 'costs' associated with running a jury system. These 'costs' include both readily monetisable economic costs and less quantifiable non-economic costs engendered by the jury.[12] The jury's sole function is taken to be the most instrumental one ascribed to it – fact-finding. The social loss function thus will summarise the social 'costs' resulting from the jury's fact-finding function. Society's goal is to minimise this social loss function, and the optimal jury system is the one that achieves this minimum.

The analysis focuses on the criminal jury, and it takes a partial, analytic view of it. I abstract from the reverberations that institutional changes in the jury may have on the number of jury trials itself. For example, while I assume that an erroneous conviction affects the total incidence of crime, I do not consider how this increase in criminal activity affects the number of criminal trials and, hence the total cost that society is trying to minimise in designing a jury system. I also do not explore how changing the efficiency of the jury would affect the extent and nature of plea bargaining. Especially since such a

[10] Zeisel (1971), pp. 715–16.

[11] For a discussion of the variety of functions attributed to the jury, see, for example, Broeder (1954).

[12] Our approach is similar to the one that Posner (1973) uses in his economic analysis of legal procedure and judicial administration. His 'direct costs' correspond to our economic costs, and his 'error costs' to our noneconomic costs. The basic framework used here also seems closer to the mathematical model of legal rulemaking that Tribe finds more enlightening (though still far from satisfactory) than it is to the simpler model, which he finds more misleading than helpful (Tribe, 1971b, pp. 1378–93).

small fraction of criminal cases is resolved by means of jury trial, these questions are very important. Nevertheless, I shall not discuss them in this paper.

The object of the analysis will be a single case in which the individual has been charged with a particular crime. I shall assume that the jury that is chosen to hear the case has only three alternatives. It can find the defendant guilty of the crime, it can declare him innocent, or it can reach no decision (it can 'hang'). In particular, the possibility that the jury might find the defendant guilty of a lesser charge is excluded from consideration.[13] Our analysis takes the defendant and the charge against him as given, and discusses the situation in which the jury, faced with these three alternatives, must be chosen before the in-court proceedings have begun. A simpler and narrower analysis would ask how to select the 'optimal' jury after the in-court proceedings have already been completed. Finally, while remaining within our partial-analytic framework, the most general analysis would ask what kind of jury panel we would want, *given only* the number of cases and the composition of charges to be evaluated.[14] This last decision involves optimally choosing the panel from which juries for particular cases will be drawn.

The conclusions that one reaches about optimal jury composition will depend on the level of analysis that one chooses. It may, for example, turn out that a fully representative jury is optimal when one defendant is to be tried on a particular charge but not when another defendant is to be tried for a different crime. The degree of representativeness that is optimal for the juror panel as a whole may differ from the one that is optimal for the jury for any particular case.

III. THE ECONOMIC COSTS OF THE JURY

We must begin with a concrete discussion of the costs of the jury system. The monetisable economic costs represent the value of all of the resources that society devotes to the jury system, including the value of judges' time, the value of lawyers' time, the value of the time of courthouse personnel, the value of courthouse space, the subsistence expenses and travel expenses of jurors, and the value of jurors' time. Since these costs are described in some detail elsewhere,[15] I shall restrict myself to some observations about them.

First, it should be clear that, in measuring the economic costs of the jury, one is concerned only with the incremental costs of using a jury. It would, for example, be incorrect, to count as a cost of the jury system the value of the

[13] Of course, this excludes a number of interesting aspects of jury deliberation, for example, jurors' *de minimis* sentiments about the law and jurors' views about unpopular laws. For a fascinating discussion of these and other aspects of jury decisions, see Kalven and Zeisel (1966).

[14] The Jury Selection and Service Act of 1968, 28 USC § §1861–9 (1970), sets forth the procedures to be used by Federal district courts in the United States in selecting jury panels.

[15] See, for example, Martin (1972) and Powell (1971, pp. 94–9).

entire time that judges spend in cases tried to a jury. Given the assumptions we have made, eliminating any jury trial currently taking place would mean replacing it by a bench trial. Hence, it is only the extra time that the judge must spend for a jury trial, as opposed to a bench one, that should be assessed as a cost of the jury system. Since time differences have many potential sources, evaluating this difference in time consumed will be a fairly complicated task.

Second, in considering the additional economic costs that society incurs because it uses juries, it is useful to distinguish between the fixed costs and the variable costs of having a jury trial.[16] The fixed costs are incurred as soon as it is decided to try a case to a jury rather than to a judge. In particular, these costs do not vary with the size or composition of the jury. For example, having juries decide cases requires an administrative structure to poll the community, to determine who is eligible for jury duty, and to maintain up-to-date lists of such people. Some of the costs incurred in establishing and operating this structure are independent of the number of people on each jury and the characteristics of those people, and, hence, they constitute a fixed cost of the jury system.

The variable costs of the system are those resource costs associated with running a jury which depend on the kind of jury one uses. The model developed here focuses on two particularly important sources of variation. First, the cost of running a jury varies with the number of jurors. For example, the daily incremental subsistence expenses of the jury can be expected to vary directly with jury size. In addition, if the total time required for a jury trial varies with the number of jurors, then jury size will also affect this determinant of the total incremental subsistence costs of the jury.[17]

Another resource cost that varies with the number of jurors used is the opportunity cost of jurors' time – the sum of the social marginal products of the jurors for the period for which they serve.[18] The opportunity cost of

[16] Indeed, one issue in the debate about whether to use six- or 12-member juries concerns whether or not some jury costs are fixed – at least, for juries in this size range.

[17] Advocates of the six-member jury argue that the smaller jury will save the government money because fewer jurors will receive juror fees, and because the trial that uses the smaller jury will require less time from its beginning to the jury's verdict. But empirical evidence concerning the difference in time required is, on the whole, inconclusive and particularly uninformative, because of the researchers' inability to stratify cases appropriately. See Beiser (1973) and Mills (1973). Beiser's figures show that the average length of trials by six-person civil juries is less than the average length of trials by 12-member civil juries, with the largest source of difference being jury deliberation time. But his data are skewed, and the median trial length is the same for both types of jury (Beiser, 1973, table X).

[18] This assumes that we can ignore interactions among jurors in producing goods and services. This measure of the resource cost of jurors' time also ignores the nonpecuniary benefits and costs associated with jury duty. If, for example, an individual derives nonpecuniary income from jury duty (because, perhaps, he views it as having an educational function for him), his social marginal product overstates the social loss resulting from his jury service. In using this measure, we are also implicitly assuming that the economy is operating at full employment.

jurors' time also provides an example of the second way in which the cost of a jury trial can vary. It will change as the composition of the jury changes. If, for example, the time required for a jury trial depends only on the number of jurors, then holding fixed the number of people on the jury, but replacing one individual with another whose social marginal product is higher or lower will change the jury's demand on society's resources.[19]

My last observation concerns the relative magnitudes of the economic costs of the jury. It is difficult to obtain precise estimates of the incremental costs of judges' and lawyers' time resulting from the use of jury trials rather than of bench trials. In fact, I have seen no such estimates. I should hazard a guess, however, that the largest economic costs of the jury are those associated with the jurors themselves, and that the greatest single resource cost of the jury consists of the goods and services that the jurors would have produced had they not been empanelled.[20]

The model developed in this paper will focus on the economic cost attributable to the use of jurors' time and, particularly, on the way that cost changes as the composition of the jury changes. Essentially, I shall treat all other costs of the jury system – judges' time, lawyers' time, use of courthouse space, and so on – as fixed and invarient with the size and composition of the jury. This simplifying assumption will help to highlight some ideas about jury size and composition.

IV. THE NON-ECONOMIC COSTS OF THE JURY

Let us turn now to the noneconomic costs of the jury system and focus on an individual trial where the defendant has been charged with a particular crime. It will be assumed that there is a true state of nature: the defendant either did commit the crime with which he is charged or he did not. The principal noneconomic social costs are those of making mistakes in deciding what the true state of affairs is; that is, in deciding whether the defendant is guilty in fact (which we shall denote G) or innocent in fact (denoted I). Hence, we are measuring the noneconomic social costs of the jury relative to the social costs that a perfectly accurate fact-finder would engender. When the jury reaches the same verdict as the perfect fact-finder would reach, no noneconomic social

[19] There are also less important ways in which the jury's composition affects it economic cost. For example, changing the jury's geographical composition will probably alter the incremental travel expenses that society incurs because of the trial.

[20] Martin estimates that the opportunity costs of jurors' time in Federal and non-Federal courts in the United States in 1962 totalled \$ 233 million (in 1958 dollars). The estimated aggregate juror fees spent in the United States in the same year were \$89 million (also in 1958 dollars). Martin's comparison of the opportunity costs of two different juror-selection systems – a random selection system and a 'keyman' jury-selection method – illustrates how these costs vary with changes in the composition of the juries (Martin, 1972, pp. 683–6).

costs are incurred; when the two verdicts diverge, the jury has generated non-economic social costs.[21]

The jury can declare the defendant legally guilty, which I shall refer to as a conviction (denoted *C*); or it can declare him legally innocent, which I shall call an acquittal (denoted *A*); or it can reach no verdict (leave it hanging, denoted *H*). Social noneconomic costs are associated with convicting an individual who is innocent (deciding *C* when *I* is the true state) and with acquitting a defendant who is guilty (deciding *A* when *G* is the true state). If one regards the null hypothesis as the statement 'The defendant is innocent', then these two possible mistakes are, respectively, the type I error and the type II error of classical statistical hypothesis testing. In declaring *C* when *I* is the true state, the jury is rejecting the null hypothesis when it should accept it; while, in declaring *A* when *G* is the true state, the jury is accepting the null hypothesis when it should be rejected.

The corresponding social costs are the costs of committing type I and type II errors. In the former case, the costs include the goods and services that society forgoes if the punishment involves imprisonment (taking into account both the forgone social marginal product of the individual and the resource cost of his imprisonment); the loss that the innocent individual suffers as the result of being labelled a criminal; the effects on the total incidence of crime that ensue because the system convicts innocent individuals; and the effects on the social state of mind of having such a system.[22] The social costs associated with a type II error include the cost of having an individual who has committed a crime free to commit another one, and the effects on the total level of crime and on the social state of mind of having a system that acquits defendants who are in fact guilty. Of course, in computing the social cost of a type II error, one must take account of the benefits that society obtains from the error: the marginal social product of the truly guilty individual when he is free and the resource costs of his imprisonment that are saved.

There remains for consideration the set of cases in which the jury neither acquits nor convicts the defendant. Such a decision, or, rather, such a non-decision, could be considered a 'mistake'. Either *I* or *G* is the true state, and the jury does not declare which one actually obtains. To be sure, the resource cost of running a jury trial in which the jury does not reach a decision is real and will be counted among the economic costs discussed earlier. The question is what additional social costs result from such an outcome. The answer depends on what happens if the jury remains undecided and on the true state of nature.

[21] It should be noted that, in examining the jury's most instrumental function, I do not number among the costs or benefits of using a jury the fact that a body of laymen is making an important decision of this type.

[22] The conviction of innocent individuals will affect the total incidence of crime, in part because such convictions alter the expected marginal cost to a potential offender (see Stigler, 1970). See Posner (1973, pp. 410–15) for a more complete discussion of how convicting the innocent affects the total level of criminal activity.

Suppose that there is no retrial and that the jury's verdict is allowed to stand as a nondecision. If G is the true state, the outcome H has the same social costs as an acquittal, except that society need not face the *de jure* acquittal of a guilty individual, but only his *de facto* acquittal. If, instead, I is the true state, the social costs do not involve any forgone goods and services due to imprisonment as they do when a type I error is committeed. They do, however, include costs similar to, but not the same as, all the other costs resulting from the conviction of an innocent individual. The two sets of costs differ because the stigma attached to an individual whose true innocence has not been affirmatively declared differs from that attached to an innocent person who has been declared guilty. Hence, the effects of the two situations are different for the individual and for the society that must recognise that it imposes this cost on individuals.

All of this assumes that the case is not retried; but, suppose, to the contrary, that it is. If G is the true state, then the additional social costs resulting from this particular 'hung' (undecided) jury are those associated with having a guilty individual free for the interval between the two trials. If, on the other hand, the defendant is, in fact, innocent, the added social costs are those associated with having a truly innocent individual not acquitted and, therefore, branded during the interval as a potential criminal.

Note that viewing the trial process from a statistical decision-theoretic perspective raises interesting questions about how a hung-jury verdict should be regarded if the case is retried. Specifically, how should the information from the hung jury's deliberation be treated? Should the new jury deliberate without access to information about which issues the original jurors agreed on and which ones caused them to split? If the *sequence* of trials is viewed as an attempt to find the facts leading to a determination of guilt or innocence, then this information should be passed on from one fact-finding body to the next. The jury in the retrial could attach to its predecessor's deliberations whatever weight it saw fit to attach to them, but to disregard totally that prior jury's view of the settled and unsettled issues is to discard potentially useful information. To be sure, there may be very good reasons – resting on grounds other than the fact-finding function of juries – for requiring a retrial not to be treated differently from the original trial, and for requiring that all issues be aired again *ab novo.* But using a statistical decision theory approach in analysing the jury's fact-finding function raises some question about this treatment of re-trials.

Returning to the measurement of the social noneconomic costs of a hung jury, we should recognise that the appropriate evaluation of these costs must be resolved, in the end, by the empirical examination of the sequels to hung-jury trials. For example, with what frequency are such cases retried? In examining a single case and asking about the optimal size and composition of the jury to decide that case, it is possible, though, to treat a hung-jury outcome in either of the ways discussed.[23] In what follows, hung juries will be treated as

[23] Note, though, that, if one were to assume that hung juries always lead to retrials – so that all cases are pursued until a conviction or an acquittal is obtained – then, in

final decisions. But we shall distinguish between those instances in which the jury reaches no verdict when I is the true state and those cases in which it does so when G is the true state. The former will be called a hung-jury error of type I, the latter a hung-jury error of type II.

V. THE SOCIAL LOSS FUNCTION

It is now necessary to specify how the social loss function aggregates the several kinds of social costs that a criminal jury system entails. First, some notation will be helpful. Define the following quantities:

$p = P(C \mid I) =$ the probability of convicting an innocent individual, i.e. the probability of a type I error;
$s = P(A \mid G) =$ the probability of acquitting a guilty individual, i.e. the probability of a type II error;
$p' = P(H \mid I) =$ the probability of the jury reaching no verdict when the defendant is innocent, i.e. the probability of a hung-jury error of type I;
$s' = P(H \mid G) =$ the probability of the jury reaching no verdict when the defendant is guilty, i.e. the probability of a hung-jury error of type II;
$k_{\mathrm{I}} =$ the social cost associated with a type I error;
$k_{\mathrm{II}} =$ the social cost associated with a type II error;
$k_{\mathrm{I}}' =$ the social cost associated with a hung-jury error of type I;
$k_{\mathrm{II}}' =$ the social cost associated with a hung-jury error of type II; and
$W =$ the economic cost of the jury.

In its most general form, the social loss function for the single trial under consideration, involving a particular defendant charged with a specific crime, can be written as

$$L = L(p, s, p', s', k_{\mathrm{I}}, k_{\mathrm{II}}, k_{\mathrm{I}}', k_{\mathrm{II}}', W) \tag{5.1}$$

Each of the first partial derivatives of this function is positive, since a *ceteris paribus* increase in any of the determinants of social cost makes society worse off. We might also assume that the second own partial derivatives are non-negative. This implies that the marginal social loss due to a *ceteris paribus* increment in any factor determining social cost remains constant, or increases as the level of that factor rises.

Once the given trial is specified, the social costs associated with making different errors – k_{I}, k_{II}, k_{I}'' k_{II}' – are determined. The probabilities of making these errors may also be affected by the specific trial being considered. For example, the probability that a decision-maker will err in deciding a murder case may differ from the probability that he will err in deciding a shoplifting

deciding on the optimal jury for the first trial, it would be necessary to take into account the expected cost of the string of future trials that might be required.

case. But, while knowledge of the defendant and of the crime with which he is charged suffices to determine the several k values, it is not sufficient for calculation of the error probabilities. On the contrary, the error probabilities and the economic costs W of deciding the case depend on the size and composition of the jury selected to try it.

For the trial being considered, a jury of a particular size and a particular composition will generate a set of values for the vector of factors on which L depends, and the 'optimal jury' for this case would be the one with the lowest resulting social loss figure. Without further assumptions about the nature of society's loss function,[24] it is impossible to say very much about the nature of the optimal jury. To go further, I shall make assumptions that restrict the form that the loss function can take and thereby confine the nature of the juror selection process. Nevertheless, these assumptions leave a fairly wide scope for the kinds of social trade-off that interest us. Moreover, they yield a model that serves as a useful heuristic device for illuminating the process of optimal jury selection.

It should be emphasised that, up to this point, I have been intentionally vague about how one might measure the social noneconomic costs of the jury – k_{I}, k_{II}, k'_{I}, and k'_{II}. I now want to assume that, while these noneconomic social costs may not be monetisable, they are comparable with one another and can be measured on a scale that is unique up to a positive linear transformation. Denote the level of noneconomic social costs measured on this scale by K. *Ex post,* the variable K will then take on one of five values, 0, k_{I}, k_{II}, k'_{I} or k'_{II}, depending on which error, if any, is made. Of course, the only cases in which the value of k will be zero, will be those where no error is made – that is, where an innocent defendant is acquitted or a guilty one convicted.

Assume, further, that the social decision-maker can compare different combinations of noneconomic social costs and economic social costs. Given any two (K, W) pairs, he can indicate which combination he prefers or whether he has no preference. Finally, assume that in choosing among combinations of noneconomic and economic social costs our decision-maker satisfies the von Neumann–Morgenstern axioms.[25] Hence, the disutility function $D(K, W)$, which represents his preferences in the choice between noneconomic and economic costs, is a von Neumann–Morgenstern (dis)utility function. It is unique up to a positive linear transformation and is a utility function in the probabilistic sense. Faced with a choice between lotteries of (K, W) combinations, the social decision-maker will choose the one with the highest expected utility (lowest expected disutility).

[24] The decision-making unit choosing the jury on society's behalf is assumed to follow the dictates of the social preference ordering (which we assume exists). The decision-maker is an objective jury selector who is not directly involved in the specific trial for which he is selecting the jury. In particular, I am not arguing that the common current procedure – which employs the judge, the prosecutor, and the defence attorneys – fits this description.

[25] Von Neumann and Morgenstern (1947), chapter 1, section 3 and appendix.

What choice situation does society face in selecting a jury? We shall assume that using a jury of a specific size and composition will engender the same social economic cost no matter what may be the true state of nature – innocence or guilt of the defendant. By contrast, the social nonecomic cost of using that jury depends upon the true state of nature. Hence, the disutility of using a particular jury, call it J^0, is conditional on the defendant's true state.

Consider, first, the disutility if the defendant is innocent. Since the jury's decision will be stochastic, all that the social decision-maker can compute is the expected social disutility of this jury conditional on I being the true state of nature. Denote this expected disutility of $ED(K, W|I, J^0)$. Using the notation introduced earlier, and recalling that p, p', and W depend on the particular jury J^0, we have

$$ED(K, W|I, J^0) = D(k_{\text{I}}, W)p + D(k'_{\text{I}}, W)p' + D(0, W)(1 - p - p') \quad (5.2)$$

Note that, by definition, the jury will acquit the innocent defendant with probability $1 - p - p'$, and that in this case there are no social noneconomic costs. This is the event captured by the last term in the sum in (5.2).

Similarly, the expected social disutility of this jury conditional on the defendant's being guilty, denoted $ED(K, W/G, J^0)$, can be written as

$$ED(K, W|G, J^0) = D(k_{\text{II}}, W)s + D(k'_{\text{II}}, W)s' + D(0, W)(1 - s - s') \quad (5.3)$$

where s, s', and W all depend on the particular jury J^0. Note that no social noneconomic cost is incurred when the jury convicts the guilty defendant, and this will occur with probability $1 - s - s'$.

If the decision-maker's preferences with regard to outcomes are transitive and if he accepts the principle of substitutability for strategies[26] – both of which are compelling principles of consistent behavior – his indifference curves in the space of conditional expected disutilities are negatively sloped, parallel straight lines. The set of $ED(K, W|I)$ and $ED(K, W|G)$ pairs yielding any given level of disutility lie along a negatively sloped straight line. This is illustrated in Figure 5.1, where $\mathcal{L}_1$, $\mathcal{L}_2$, and $\mathcal{L}_3$ are three such indifference curves. The social decision-maker's disutility increases as we move northeast, so that any point on $\mathcal{L}_1$ is preferred to any point on $\mathcal{L}_2$, and any point on $\mathcal{L}_2$ is, in turn, preferred to any point on $\mathcal{L}_3$.

The particular jury, J^0, will generate a point in the space of conditional expected disutilities, say the point marked J^0 in Fig. 5.1. Specifying different jury sizes or compositions will generate different combinations of conditional expected disutilities, as indicated, for example, by the points J' and J'' in the figure. The social decision-maker's objective is to reach the lowest indifference curve that he can, to select that jury which maps into a point that is as far south-west in the figure as possible.

[26] Raiffa (1968), pp. 145–8.

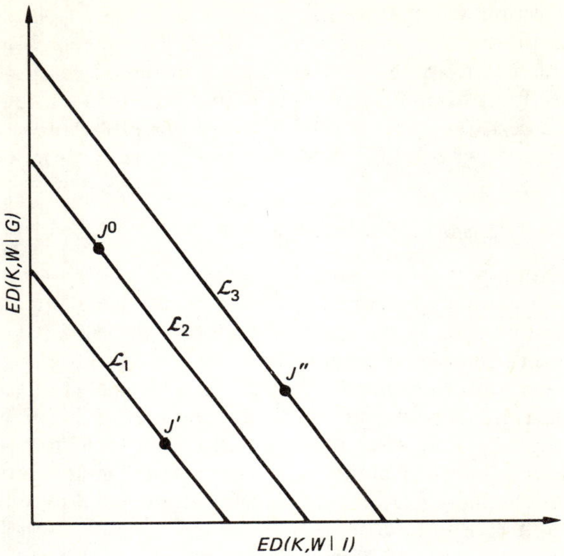

Fig. 5.1

This can be stated more precisely. Any one indifference curve can be written as

$$ED(K,\ W|G) = aED(K,\ W|I) + b$$

where $a < 0$ is the slope of the curve and b is its intercept on the $ED(K,\ W|G)$ axis. Obviously, this can be rewritten as

$$\alpha ED(K,\ W|G) + (1-\alpha)ED(K,\ W|I) = \beta$$

where $\alpha = 1/1 - a$, with $0 \leqslant \alpha \leqslant 1$, and $\beta = b/1 - a$. The decision-maker's problem is to find the jury yielding the minimum value for b or, equivalently, since a is a fixed negative parameter that depends only on the decision-maker's preferences and does not change with the jury, to find the jury with the minimum β. Hence, the social decision-maker's problem is to choose the jury J whose size and composition solve the problem in (5.4):

$$\min_J L(J) = \alpha ED(K,\ W|G,J) + (1-\alpha)ED(K,\ W|I,J) \tag{5.4}$$

where the conditional expected disutilities are as defined in (5.2) and (5.3).

The direction numbers α and $1-\alpha$ depend solely on the social decision-maker's preferences in the choice between the two types of conditional expected losses. It follows from their definition that the weights in the objective function in (5.4) are non-negative and sum to 1. Hence, it is, as Raiffa puts it, 'a semantic question' whether we call them 'probabilities.[27] Nevertheless, most Bayesian decision theorists would argue that α and $1 - \alpha$ represent the decision-maker's prior subjective probability assessment of the true states of nature. That is, in specifying his indifference curves between the conditional expected disutilities, the decision-maker implicitly reveals his probability assessment, *prior* to the trial, of whether the defendant is guilty (α) or is innocent ($1 - \alpha$).

VI. A NOTE ON THE 'PRESUMPTION OF INNOCENCE'

This interpretation of α raises a natural question about the formulation in (5.4). Specifically, can one reconcile with the traditional affirmation of the 'presumption of innocence' the idea that the social decision-maker selecting the jury's size and composition is predisposed to see guilt as more probable? There are several ways to respond. First, the decision-maker selecting the jury – choosing its size and its composition – is not the trier of fact. The latter role is played by the jury itself. Hence, to say that the jury selection mechanism has implicit in it a prior probability of the defendant's guilt is not to say that when the case is actually tried the defendant is confronted by something less than a presumption of innocence.

Second, *if* one wanted to interpret the 'presumption of innocence' as meaning that the prior probability of the defendant's guilt is zero, then this assumption could be built into the jury selection rule in (5.4). Specifically, one would simply set $\alpha = 0$ and, hence, $1 - \alpha = 1$. While the jury selector can take $\alpha = 0$, I would argue that this is a wholly inappropriate translation of the presumption of innocence for the trier of fact to employ. The reason is quite simple. If the trier of fact were to take a Bayesian stance, he would formulate a prior probability of guilt and use the in-court proceedings to modify it, thereby generating a posterior density function over the states of nature – I and G. Taking the prior probability of guilt to be zero would imply that in each and every case the posterior probability of guilt would be zero. Under any standard of reasonable doubt, every defendant would be acquitted! Of course, the issue here goes to the more basic question of whether it is wise to have the trier of fact use Bayesian methods at all. But one of the major problems with using such methods in trials themselves is formulating the presumption of innocence in terms of a prior probability distribution.[28] Since the decision-maker selecting the jury never uses the prior probabilities α and $1 - \alpha$ to derive posterior probabilities of guilt and innocence, one might object less strenuously to setting those prior probabilities equal to 0 and 1 respectively. These values would simply constitute one possible set of social preferences with respect to the conditional expected disutility of acquitting (or not convicting) guilty individuals relative to

[27] Raiffa (1968), p. 146.

[28] Compare Tribe's discussion of the problems associated with setting the prior probability of guilt at some artificially low level on the pretence that the defendant's indictment was equivalent to random selection (Tribe, 1971b, footnote 132).

the conditional expected disutility of convicting (or not acquitting) innocent individuals.

A last possible way of reconciling the presumption of innocence with the jury selector's implicit use of a prior probability of guilt invokes the distinction that Tribe emphasises between that presumption as a normative judgement and as a factual judgement.[29] Specifically, we can regard as a normative judgement the presumption 'that society *ought* to *speak* of accused men as innocent, and *treat* them as innocent, until they have been properly convicted after all they have to offer in their defense has been carefully weighed'.[30] At the same time, society can realistically face the factual judgement that some (a substantial?) percentage of those tried for crimes are, in fact, guilty of the crime with which they are charged. We can retain and draw upon the 'presumption of innocence' as a normative guide for the trier of fact in approaching a given defendant in the course of his trial. Nevertheless, the social decision-maker choosing the kind of jury to use need not cringe at the implicit introduction of a factual judgement concerning the defendant's probable guilt.[31]

VII. THE PORTFOLIO SELECTION ANALOGY

We shall assume, then, that the social decision-maker's task is to determine the characteristics of the jury that solves the problem in (5.4). The formulation in (5.4) suggests the broad outlines of the analogy with portfolio selection. The acquisition of any portfolio of assets entails a specific expenditure of funds by the investor. As a result of his initial outlay and of his choice of portfolio, the investor will obtain a return, and this return will depend on which state of nature is the true one. If the investor satisfies the von Neumann–Morgenstern axioms and the substitutability principle in strategy space, he will use his subjective distribution over the possible states of nature and maximise his expected utility.[32]

The problem that society confronts in trying to decide what kind of jury to use, namely (5.4), fits quite well with this description of the investor's problem. While one might expect the typical investor to consider a fairly large number of states of nature, there are only two alternative true states in the jury problem – guilt and innocence. The economic costs of using a particular jury (W) are incurred no matter what the true state is, and they correspond to the

[29] Tribe (1971b), pp. 1370–1.

[30] Tribe (1971b), p. 1371; emphasis in original.

[31] 'The suspicion that many [accused individuals] are *in fact* guilty need not undermine either [the] normative conclusion or its symbolic expression through trial procedure, so long as jurors are not compelled to articulate their prior suspicions of guilt in an explicit and precise way' (Tribe 1971b, p. 1371; emphasis in original).

[32] Even if the investor uses objective historical data to derive a prior distribution, the adoption of that objective distribution as a prediction of the future constitutes a personal probability judgement. Hence, the distribution that he uses should be viewed as subjective even in that case.

investor's outlay on his portfolio. His initial outlay is also the same whether or not his assets perform well. The noneconomic costs of the jury (K) depend on the true state of nature, just as the investor's returns do. Of course, since the returns to the investor are commensurate with the outlay on the portfolio, his utility function has only one argument. By contrast, the jury selector's expected disutility function – which evaluates the outcome in each state of nature – is a function of two arguments, since the noneconomic costs may not be monetisable. And, just as the investor chooses the portfolio that maximises the expected value of his conditional utilities – with the weights equal to his subjective probabilities for alternative states – so the jury selector chooses the jury that minimises the expected value of his conditional expected disutilities – with the weights being his prior probabilities for the two alternative states.

Perhaps the most important similarity is that, in both the jury problem and the investment problem, the outcome depends not only on the total resources expended, – the economic costs W, in the one case, and the size of the portfolio, in the other – but also on the way in which those resources are expended. What securities are purchased by the portfolio investor? How many different kinds of securities are bought, and how much is invested in each type of asset? In the jury case, how many jurors are used to try the case and how is the jury composed? How many different 'types' of jurors are employed and how many jurors of each type hear the case? To pursue this part of the metaphor, viewing jurors as assets to be optimally combined in the portfolio of the jury box, we need a more precise model of the individual juror and of interactions among jurors.

VIII. THE INDIVIDUAL JUROR

Our model of the individual juror's decision-making process is quite simple. For any given trial, we assume that, after the juror has viewed the in-court proceedings (which I shall loosely call the 'evidence'), he first takes all that he has seen and heard in court, sifts through it, reflects on it, and arrives at a probability of guilt for the defendant. Second, he attempts to evaluate the degree of certainty that he would require in making decisions in his own life where the risks to him were as substantial as those faced by the defendant in the case he has viewed.[33] This yields his standard of reasonable doubt for the case. Finally, he compares his evaluation of the probability of guilt with his standard of reasonable doubt for the case. If the probability of guilt that he calculates exceeds the probability required by his standard of reasonable doubt, he votes to convict the defendant. Otherwise, he votes to acquit the accused.

I am not asserting that any juror does, in fact, go through exactly this thought process; nor am I suggesting that any juror necessarily should. In par-

[33] This is the interpretation of reasonable doubt that at least some legal scholars would have the juror use in a criminal case. See, for example, Winter (1971), p. 342.

ticular, I am not prepared to argue here the case for the use of Bayesian methods by the trier of fact.[34] The model used here simply decomposes the juror's decision-making process into the three steps described for analytical purposes. It places a particular analytical grid on the 'true' historical description of what the juror does. If you will, we are saying that no matter how *gestalt* the juror's decision process may actually be, we shall view him as acting 'as if' he proceeded according to the steps that we have described.

I shall assume that the juror's decision-making process has stochastic elements in it; it is not perfectly deterministic and predictable. An outside observer who knew all there was to know about the juror prior to the trial and who was omniscient with respect to the trial, observing *every* element of the in-court proceedings, could not predict with certainty how the particular juror would vote after the trial and *before* any jury deliberation. There are two sources of randomness which seem important.

First, there is the stochastic element in going from the in-court proceedings to the juror's evaluation of the probability that the defendant is guilty. There are random factors in the juror's observation and evaluation of the evidence. Even given the identical set of in-court proceedings (as perceived by our omniscient objective observer), on different occasions our juror could arrive at different values for the probability that the defendant is guilty. Second, randomness arises in the juror's standard of reasonable doubt. If we could confront the juror with the same trial on two distinct, but hypothetically identical, occasions, he might employ a different standard in each of the two cases. I think that the standard of reasonable doubt is sufficiently vague for us not to be able to expect a juror to be perfectly consistent in applying it.

To express this view of the juror's decision process more precisely, denote the in-court proceedings as perceived by our objective omniscient observer by Z.[35] The juror's view of the defendant's guilt is assumed to be based solely on Z, and there exists a mapping that carries the evidence Z into a probability of guilt. This mapping, denoted f, is assumed to be stochastic and the random variable is denoted X_1.[36]

[34] For a discussion of this issue, see Finkelstein and Fairley (1970 and 1971) and Tribe (1971a and b).

[35] If one could enumerate all the characteristics of the in-court proceedings (or evidence) and measure the level of each characteristic in a given trial on a cardinal scale, Z could be represented as a vector. It suffices, however, to think of Z as representing the particular configuration of in-court proceedings that has been observed, without considering more explicitly how one might express Z (other than by giving the objective omniscient observer's historical description of what occurred).

[36] The in-court proceedings include the fact that the defendant has been apprehended, arraigned, indicted, and brought to trial. If the juror follows the directive that he is given, and at the start of the trial presumes the defendant to be innocent, these aspects of the evidence will not affect his determination of the probability of guilt at the trial's close. But if the juror under consideration does not follow this instruction and, instead, views this set of events as bearing on the defendant's guilt, his use of some prior probability of guilt is subsumed in his f mapping.

Hence, having viewed the same trial as the objective omniscient observer, the individual juror reaches the conclusion that the probability that the defendant is guilty as $f(Z, X_1)$. He then compares this number with his standard of reasonable doubt to decide whether or not to convict. Denote the deterministic part of that standard by R and the stochastic component by X_2 (a random variable with mean zero), so that the number with which the juror compares $f(Z, X_1)$ is $R + X_2$. The juror's decision rule is thus

$$\left.\begin{array}{ll} C & \text{if } f(Z, x_1) > R + x_2 \\ A & \text{if } f(Z, x_1) \leqslant R + x_2 \end{array}\right\} \quad (5.5)$$

where x_1 is a particular realisation of the random variable X_1, and x_2 is a particular realisation of the random variable X_2.

In what follows I shall focus only on the fact that the juror's decision-making process is stochastic, and I shall not differentiate between the sources of uncertainty. Hence, it will be notationally simpler to summarise all of the uncertainty by a single random variable X. Denote the density function of X by $g(X)$, and assume that the mean of X is zero. Introducing the new mapping $F(Z, X)$, we can write the juror's decision rule as

$$\left.\begin{array}{ll} C & \text{if } F(Z, x) > R \\ A & \text{if } F(Z, x) \leqslant R \end{array}\right\} \quad (5.6)$$

where x is the particular realisation of the random variable X.

Before the particular juror actually reaches his decision in the case, all we can calculate is the probability that he will vote to convict and the probability that he will vote to acquit because the value that the random X will assume is still unknown. Using the information available after the in-court proceedings are complete, we can calculate the following probabilities for the individual juror being considered:

$$\left.\begin{array}{ll} & P(C|Z) = {}_T\int g(X)dX \\ & P(A|Z) = {}_{\overline{T}}\int g(X)dX = 1 - Pr(C/Z) \\ \text{where} & T = \{x|F(Z, x) - R > 0\} \\ \text{and} & \overline{T} = \{x|F(Z, x) - R \leqslant 0\} \end{array}\right\} \quad (5.7)$$

The set T is simply the set of values of the random variable X such that, given the in-court proceedings Z, this juror will vote to convict the defendant, and $\overline{T}$ is the complement of that set.

The juror's decision may be in error – he may vote to convict an innocent individual or he may vote to acquit a guilty defendant. If the particular configuration of evidence Z could have been generated only by an innocent defendant, we should immediately have our juror's probability of making a type I error, namely $P(C \mid Z)$ in (5.7), and we should know that he could not make a type II error in this trial. On the other hand, if only a guilty defendant could have led to Z occurring, then the probability of a type I error would obviously be zero and the probability of a type II error would be equal to $P(A|Z)$ in (5.7).

Unfortunately, matters are not quite so simple. The same configuration of evidence and in-court proceedings could probably be generated by a guilty defendant or by an innocent defendant, and jury trials are most likely to occur when there is substantial uncertainty about which of these is, in fact, the case. It simply is not possible to partition the evidence space into two sets so that Z is in one set if, and only if, I is true, and, in the other set if, and only if, G is the true state of nature.

If the juror's standard of reasonable doubt depends only on the penalty that the defendant will face if convicted, then the juror must reach the same conclusion when the same Z is generated, whether the defendant is truly innocent or is truly guilty. Hence, if Z can be generated whether I or G is the true state, the juror necessarily has a positive probability of making at least a type I error or a type II error. If both probabilities in (5.7) are positive, then there is a positive probability that the juror will make each type of error. Denote by $P(Z|I)$ the probability that an innocent defendant would generate the particular set of in-court proceedings observed, and by $P(Z|G)$ the corresponding probability for a truly guilty person. Then, we have the probabilities of a type I and a type II error for the individual juror for this case:

$$\left.\begin{aligned} P(C\,|\,I, Z) &= P(Z\,|\,I)\int_T g(X)dX \\ P(A|G, Z) &= P(Z|G)\int_{\overline{T}} g(X)dX \end{aligned}\right\} \qquad (5.8)$$

This discussion of the juror's decision process assumes that the in-court proceedings are over and that the juror is deciding how to vote on the verdict. The social decision-maker's selection of the optimal jury to try the given case must, however, be made before the in-court proceedings begin. He must solve the problem in (5.4) before, not after, Z is revealed. Hence, in considering the probability that a particular individual will make errors in deciding the case, the social decision-maker is not interested solely in the probabilities in (5.8).

What he must consider is the set of all of the possible configurations of in-court proceedings for the case at hand. Suppose that there are m such possible configurations, Z_i, $i = 1, \ldots, m$. For each Z_i, there is a set of values of the random variable X for which the potential juror would convict the defendant on the charge presented; that is, a set of x values such that $F(Z_i, x) - R > 0$. We shall denote this set $T(Z_i)$. The definition of $T(Z_i)$ is analogous. It is the set of x values for which the potential juror would acquit *when* the in-court proceedings are Z_i. Hence, the probability that the juror will convict, given Z_i, is simply $P(C|Z_i) = \int_{T(Z_i)} g(X)dX$, and the probability that he will acquit is

$\int_{\overline{T}(Z_i)} g(X)dX$. The probability that this juror will make a type I error and the probability that he will make a type II error when Z_i describes the in-court proceedings are given by (5.8) with the appropriate substitution of Z_i for Z, $T(Z_i)$ for T and $\overline{T}(Z_i)$ for $\overline{T}$.

These error probabilities are conditional on the fact that incourt proceedings of type Z_i characterise the case. The jury selector, however, is concerned with the unconditional probabilities of error. To obtain these he must have a subjective probability distribution over the possible configurations of evidence that might arise, given the particular defendant charged with the particular crime. Denote by $h(Z_i)$ the decision-maker's probability estimate that the ith type of evidence situation will occur. Then, the unconditional probabilities that the individual juror considered will make type I and type II errors are, respectively,

$$\left.\begin{aligned} P(C|I) &= \sum_{i=1}^{m} h(Z_i)P(Z_i|I) \int_{T(Z_i)} g(X)dX \\ \textit{and} \qquad P(A|G) &= \sum_{i=1}^{m} h(Z_i)P(Z_i|G) \int_{\overline{T}(Z_i)} g(X)dX \end{aligned}\right\} \tag{5.9}$$

These are the error probabilities on which the social decision-maker will focus when he considers whether or not to select the particular juror whom we have been considering.

IX. DIFFERENCES AMONG JURORS

This model of juror decision-making could be used to calculate the error probabilities for each potential juror. For each one, we would conclude with probabilities of the type shown in (5.9). We should expect these error probabilities to differ among jurors, since we expect people to differ in the way they process the same in-court proceedings and in their standards of reasonable doubt. They differ in their ability to understand arguments and to understand and interpret the testimony of expert witnesses. Alternative potential jurors might put the same set of in-court proceedings together in different ways. They might differ in their capacities to judge the credibility of witnesses and to sift what some might view as the courtroom 'drama' from the 'hard facts'. Of course, different people will have different biases – be they racial, ethnic, class, or other – and they will also bring these biases to bear on their perception of the trial.

Clearly, one could go on to enumerate many other ways in which potential jurors might differ. The last one I shall point out here, and a very important one, is that they will differ in their life experiences and in the ways in which they have internalised these divergent experiences. To the extent that each juror draws upon his own experience to determine his standard of reasonable doubt for the case, this difference among potential triers of fact will lead each of them to use a different standard in judging whether the probability of guilt that he derives from the in-court proceedings is high enough to justify a conviction.

Differences among jurors are, of course, at the heart of the justification for the jury system. Use of the jury as a fact-finding unit is premised upon the view that different people see things differently, that 'Twelve jurors have seen a larger slice of life than a single judge.'[37] Unfortunately, however, there has been very little empirical research on how differences in jurors' backgrounds influence their verdicts.[38]

In terms of our formal model, jurors' verdicts might differ because the F function, which maps the in-court proceedings into a probability of guilt, may differ from one juror to the next; because the R value for the standard of reasonable doubt may vary with the juror; and because the values of the random variables affecting the jurors' decisions may not be the same. Using the superscript j to denote the jth juror, the decision rule for this juror is

$$\left.\begin{array}{ll} C & \text{if } F^j(Z, x^j) > R^j \\ A & \text{if } F^j(Z, x^j) \leqslant R^j \end{array}\right\} \qquad (5.10)$$

Faced with a given set of in-court proceedings, one potential juror trying the case alone may decide to convict, while another may acquit the particular defendant of the specific crime with which he is charged.

Jurors may also differ in the density functions for the random factors in their decision processes. That is, the density function of X^j, denoted $g^j(X^j)$, may not be the same as that of $x^{j'}$, denoted $g^{j'}(X^{j'})$. Hence, the *probabilites* that two jurors faced with the same configuration of evidence, Z_i, will vote for

[37] See, for example, Broeder (1954), p. 388; Winter (1971), footnote 7; and Zeisel (1971), p. 715.

[38] For example, one reviewer of Kalven and Zeisel's leading study, *The American Jury,* specifically noted the absence of any examination of how differences in jurors' experiences might lead them to vote differently (Goldstein, 1967, p. 151). The British counterpart of the Chicago Jury Project – the London School of Economics (LSE) Jury Project – provides some limited evidence on the importance of differences in juror backgrounds. In a report on part of the LSE study, Sealy and Cornish (1973) find that age is the only major socio-demographic characteristic having a consistent effect on juror verdicts, with younger people generally being more lenient. Mock juries were used to view two different trials involving a total of three different defendants, and the unit of observation was the juror's verdict *after* the jury deliberation was completed. Hence, the results do not significantly increase our understanding of how variations in jurors' experiences might cause their individual predeliberation votes to differ.

conviction may differ because their F^j functions, R^j values, *or* density functions $g^j(X^j)$ differ.

For the *j*th juror, the set $T^j(Z_i) = \{x^j | F^j(Z_i, x^j) > R^j\}$ and the set $\overline{T}^j(Z_i) = \{x^j | F^j(Z_i, x^j) \leqslant R^j\}$, with the result that the *j*th juror's error probabilities for the trial of a particular defendant charged with a specific crime are

$$\left.\begin{aligned} P(C|I, j) &= \sum_{i=1}^{m} h(Z_i)P(Z_i|I) \int_{T^j(Z_i)} g^j(X^j)dX^j \\ P(A|G, j) &= \sum_{i=1}^{m} h(Z_i)P(Z_i|G) \int_{\overline{T}^j(Z_i)} g^j(X^j)dX^j \end{aligned}\right\} \qquad (5.11)$$

As is clear from (5.11), the error probabilities for different potential jurors have some common determinants. They all depend on the social decision-maker's judgements concerning the probability that a guilty (an innocent) defendant would generate a particular set of in-court proceedings and the probabilities with which different evidence configurations can be expected to arise. But each potential juror's error probabilities also depend on that individual's specific characteristics via the density function $g^j(X^j)$ and the sets $T^j(Z_i)$ and $\overline{T}^j(Z_i)$. For notational convenience, let us denote $P(C|I, j)$, the probability that the *j*th juror acting alone would make a type I error, by p_j, and $P(A|G, j)$, the probability that acting alone he would make a type II error, by s_j.

Using the *j*th potential juror to try the case will engender a particular social economic cost. This will equal the incremental subsistence and incremental travel expenses of the juror, *plus* the social opportunity cost of his time for the duration of the trial. In what follows, I shall take the length of the trial under consideration to be fixed and independent of the size and composition of the jury, the true state of nature, and the verdict.[39] Given this assumption, we can precisely measure the social economic cost of using juror *j* to try the case, and I shall denote this quantity w_j.

Our description of the individual juror as a risky asset to be considered by the jury selector is now complete. It costs w_j dollars to invest in the *j*th potential juror. If he were to decide the case alone, he would return expected non-economic social costs of $p_j k_{\mathrm{I}}$ if the true state of nature were *I*, and of $s_j k_{\mathrm{II}}$ if the true state were *G*. With this information, the social decision-maker could now decide which potential juror to use if only one juror were to try the case. But if juries of a size larger than one are to be considered, this description of each risky asset will not suffice.

[39] In the light of the inconclusive nature of the empirical results on the time required for trials by juries of different sizes (see Beiser, 1973; Mills, 1973), the weakest part of this assumption would appear to be the fact that one might expect trials resulting in hung juries to take longer than do other trials.

In considering the use of more than one juror, the social decision-maker is essentially choosing a portfolio of risky assets. And one of the main lessons of the portfolio theory developed in the last twenty years is that optimal portfolio selection requires consideration of more than the individual characteristics of a given security (for example, its mean and variance). It requires that careful attention be paid to the stochastic relationship between the returns to one asset and the returns to another. Analogously, in selecting the optimal portfolio of jurors, one must consider not only how 'good' an asset each one is when considered by himself (measured in terms of the loss function in equation 5.4), but also how he interacts with other jurors. The value of a portfolio of jurors cannot be determined from the characteristics of each juror acting alone.

X. THE JURY DELIBERATIONS

Jury deliberations constitute a fascinating type of small-group decision process, and various kinds of information have been collected about them.[40] Most of the available evidence comes from post-trial interviews with jurors in actual cases and from records of the actual deliberations of mock juries. In analysing jury behaviour, these data can be supplemented by the results of social psychologists who have studied small-group behaviour in different experimental decision-making situations.[41] But, while much data exists on jury deliberations, there is no single widely accepted theory of how juries reach their final decisions.

One of the major hypotheses on the subject was put forth by Kalven and Zeisel near the end of *The American Jury.* Using data from a pilot study of the Chicago Jury Project, they examined the relationship between the jury's vote on the first ballot *before* any discussion has taken place and the final vote *after* deliberation has been concluded. The data show that when there is a first-ballot majority for conviction or for acquittal, somewhat more than 90 per cent of the final ballots yield a verdict in the same direction as the initial majority. In most of the cases where the first-ballot majority position is not followed, the jury does not reach a verdict.[42] Kalven and Zeisel go on to articulate their interpretation of the data as follows: 'this is only to say that *with very few exceptions the first ballot decides the outcome of the verdict.* And if this is true, then *the real decision is often made before the deliberation begins.*[43] They conclude with 'a radical hunch about the function of the deliberation

[40] See, for example, the research summarised by Erlanger (1970), Kalven and Zeisel (1966), and Kessler (1973).

[41] See, for example, the studies by Bales and Borgatta, Hare, Miller, Thomas and Fink, and others cited by Powell (1971, pp. 99–106); and the studies by Asch, Cartwright and Zander, Flament, Gerard, and others cited by Walbert (1971, pp. 542–5).

[42] 'Only with extreme infrequency does the minority succeed in persuading the majority to change its mind during the deliberation' (Kalven and Zeisel, 1966, p. 488).

[43] Kalven and Zeisel (1966), p. 488; emphasis in original. It should also be noted that the sample included ten cases in which the jury divided six–six on the initial ballot. The final ballots in those cases yielded five 'guilty' verdicts and five 'not guilty' verdicts.

process. Perhaps it does not so much decide the case as bring about the consensus, the outcome of which has been made highly likely by the distribution of first ballot votes.[44]

The Kalven–Zeisel 'majority persuasion' hypothesis could be used in our model as follows. The result that each juror would reach if the case were tried to him alone could be interpreted as his vote on the first ballot. Then, regarding the process of jury deliberation as carrying these initial votes to the final verdict, we would assume that a first-ballot majority for conviction results in a verdict of guilty, while a first-ballot majority for acquittal results in a verdict of not guilty.[45] This is the approach that Walbert uses in his note on *Williams* v. *Florida,* where he also marshals additional evidence from psychology experiments to support the 'majority persuasion' hypothesis.[46] Nevertheless, that hypothesis remains simply a 'hunch' and, as Walbert recognises explicitly, the results from other experimental settings are of questionable relevance for jury deliberations. The same 'majority persuasion' approach could be used here, with results, concerning the representativeness of the optimal jury, similar to those that we shall obtain.

Our introduction of stochastic elements into the individual juror's decision-making process and our incorporation of differences among jurors enable us to approach jury deliberations in a different way. We can follow an analytically simpler route that leads to similar results for our major question of jury representativeness. Specifically, I shall assume that the individual juror verdicts and the juror votes that we have been discussing are final-ballot votes. I shall also broaden the interpretation of the random variables X^j to include the results of jury deliberation. That is, X^j will be interpreted as reflecting not only stochastic aspects of the individual juror's mapping from in-court proceedings to probability of guilt, and stochastic aspects of his standard of reasonable doubt, but also the effects of discussion in the jury room. It should be emphasised that modelling the deliberation process in this way does not imply that the discussion is totally haphazard. On the contrary, depending on the assumptions made concerning the X^j random variables, that discussion can be portrayed as being quite structured indeed. Moreover, differences in the relationships among the X^j variables are at the heart of our message about the instrumental case for representative juries.

XI. THE JURY AS A PORTFOLIO OF JURORS

To simplify the analysis of jury composition, I shall assume that only three people serve on the jury. We could consider larger juries, but the presentation

[44] Kalven and Zeisel (1966), p. 489.

[45] If there were an even number of jurors, there would be the troublesome possibility of an evenly split initial ballot. This difficulty could be resolved by assuming that, as in Kalven and Zeisel's limited sample, 50 per cent of such cases resulted in convictions and 50 per cent in acquittals.

[46] Walbert (1971), p. 545.

would become notationally more cumbersome, without additional analytical insights being gained. The issues involved in selecting the optimal jury and, specifically, the optimal degree of representatives of the jury can be illustrated just as well with three-person juries. In particular, since the individual juror verdicts discussed earlier are taken to be juror votes on the final ballot, and since the unanimity rule prevails, very little generality is lost by having an odd number of jurors. For example, all three types of outcome – conviction, acquittal, and hung jury – are still possible.[47]

Since we have assumed that the social costs of different errors are known, once the defendant and the charge against him are given, all that we must determine for each potential jury is (a) the probability that it will make each type of error and (b) the economic cost incurred in using it. The latter, the jury's resource cost, is easily determined. Certain costs entailed in using a jury to try the case have been assumed to be fixed; these costs will be denoted B. The variable cost of using a particular jury is the sum of the jurors' incremental travel and incremental subsistence expenses plus the sum of the social opportunity costs of their time. It is the sum of the w_j values for the members of the jury.[48] Hence, the economic cost of using jury J, denoted $W(J)$, is

$$W(J) = B + \sum_{j \in J} w_j \tag{5.12}$$

While the social economic cost of jury J can thus be expressed succinctly in terms of the social economic costs of using its individual members, it is much more difficult to express the jury's error probabilities in terms of the probability distributions characterising its members' votes. To illustrate the problem, consider a calculation that is simpler than, but basic to, the ones we must actually perform. Suppose that jurors 1, 2, and 3 have just heard the case involving the defendant facing the given charge, and suppose that the evidence was the configuration Z_1. What is the probability that this jury will commit a type II error? It is clearly the probability that a truly guilty defendant would have generated the evidence Z_1 *times* the probability that all three jurors will vote to acquit given the evidence Z_1.

The latter is the probability in the tail of a joint distribution of three random variables, with one random variable for each juror. Specifically, denote by $V^j(Z)$ the random variable $F(Z, X^j) - R^j$ so that $V^j(Z)$ measures the difference between the jth juror's estimate of the probability of guilt given the in-court proceedings Z and his standard of reasonable doubt. This difference is a random variable because it is a function of the random variable X^j, and it depends

[47] If we were to use the 'majority persuasion' hypothesis and treat jurors' votes as their positions on the first ballot, then using an odd number of jurors would obviously eliminate the possibility of a hung jury.

[48] Recall that we are ignoring interactions among jurors in producing goods and services and that we are assuming that the length of the trial under consideration is fixed and independent of the composition of the jury, the true state of nature, and the verdict.

on the in-court proceedings because the juror's view of the probability of guilt is based on that evidence. Since both $F(Z, X^j)$ and R^j are probabilities, $V^j(Z)$ must lie in the closed interval $[-1, 1]$. If $V^j(Z) > 0$, the jth juror votes to convict; if $V^j(Z) \leqslant 0$, he votes to acquit. For each Z configuration, there will exist a joint distribution function of the V^j random variables for our three jurors; denote it $\theta(V^1, V^2, V^3 | Z)$. Then the probability that all three jurors will vote to acquit, given the evidence Z_1, is the probability that $V^1(Z_1) \leqslant 0$, $V^2(Z_1) \leqslant 0$, *and* $V^3(Z_1) \leqslant 0$ or $\Phi\,(0, 0, 0|Z_1)$. Hence, the probability that a jury comprised of jurors 1, 2 and 3 would acquit, given the evidence Z_1, is a tail probability – more precisely, the nonpositive orthant probability – of the multivariate distribution $\Phi(V_1, V_2, V_3 | Z_1)$.

We would like to express this tail probability in an analytically tractable form in terms of the parameters of the distributions for the individual jurors' decisions and the interactions among jurors. Using such an expression, we could examine how the type II error would change as we held the evidence fixed and varied the characteristics of the jurors (that is, the composition of the jury). Unfortunately, such analytically tractable representations do not exist for distributions that might be considered reasonable in this context – for example, the truncated multivariate normal distribution – except for special parameterisations that would impose overly strong restrictions on the relationship between the parameters of different jurors' distributions and on the type of interdependence among jurors.[49]

This means that the probability that the jury comprised of individuals 1, 2, and 3 will commit a type II error after observing Z_1 cannot be conveniently expressed in terms of the basic parameters of the jury decision process – the parameters of each juror's marginal distribution and the interactions among jurors. *A fortiori,* the type II error probability that the social decision-maker calculates for this jury and uses in selecting the optimal jury, knowing only the defendant and the charge against him – namely, $\sum_{i=1}^{m} h(Z_i)P(Z_i|G)\Phi\,(0, 0, 0|Z_i)$ – cannot be written compactly in terms of these basic parameters. The same difficulty arises in attempting to express the type I error probability and the hung-jury error probabilities for the given jury in terms of the characteristics of the individual jurors and their interactions with one another, since each of these error probabilities also involves computation of orthant probabilities.

Because of these difficulties, we shall pursue a different route. The alternative approach takes place at a less fundamental level of analysis, but it still serves well our investigation of the instrumental case for representative juries.

[49] For an idea of the types of restrictions one would need to impose, see Johnson and Kotz (1972, pp. 43–53) on the specifications needed to evaluate tail probabilities for the (untruncated) multivariate normal distribution.

We shall consider a fictional society in which there are $3N$ individuals divided into three groups (indexed 1, 2, 3) of equal size. Individuals are assumed to be grouped according to relevant socio-economic and demographic characteristics. We shall think of the groups as income classes, with income a nonincreasing function of group index number.

The random variable $V^j(Z)$ will be assumed to be identical for all members of a group, so that we need discuss only $V^1(Z)$, $V^2(Z)$, and $V^3(Z)$. To illustrate the implications of this assumption, suppose we were to choose a member of group 2 to view the case and reach a verdict independently. Then, viewed *before* the trial begins, the difference between the probability of guilt that this juror would calculate and his standard of reasonable doubt is distributed as the random variable $\sum_{i=1}^{m} V^2(Z_i)h(Z_i)$; and this is true no matter which member of group 2 we choose. As a result, the pretrial marginal distribution of the verdict that would be reached is the same for all members of the group. Naturally, the distribution of the $V^j(Z)$ random variables may differ for different values of j, and, hence, the pretrial marginal distributions of the verdicts of jurors from different groups may differ.

We shall also assume that the stochastic interaction among members of a group is the same no matter which particular members are involved. Furthermore, the stochastic interaction between any member of one group, say j, and any member (or members) of another group, say j', will be taken to be the same, regardless of which member of j and which member(s) of j' are interacting. Our general analysis imposes no further restrictions on juror interactions.

Of course, defining the relevant groups in any real society will be difficult and somewhat arbitrary, as it will depend on the stratifier's perception of the society and its goals. In discussions of the representativeness of juries and jury panels in the United States, one usually has in mind groups defined by socio-economic and demographic characteristics – age, race, sex, income class, and educational background.[50] Exactly how many groups one would want to delineate is an open question, and, clearly, the marginal verdict distributions of individuals in these real-world groups would not necessarily be identical. But I would argue that it is likely that jurors whose backgrounds and experiences are similar will view a given trial from similar perspectives and process the in-court proceedings in comparable ways. Moreover, to the extent that a juror's standard of reasonable doubt is based on his own experience, such jurors are likely to apply standards that are close to one another. The assumption that the random variable $V^j(Z)$ is the same for all members of group j expresses this looser, more tenuous, relationship in an extreme, though simpler, form.

It is also easier to discuss representativeness of three-person juries in this

[50] See, for example, Beiser (1973), section I; Finkelstein (1966); and Himelrick (1973).

fictional society than it is to discuss representativeness of juries or jury panels in any actual community. In this equally proportioned three-class society, a fully representative three-member panel would have one member from each group. A jury with two members from one group and one from another would be less representative, and all such juries – regardless of which group had two people on the panel and which had one – would be considered equally representative. Finally, the least representative type of panel would have members from only one group on it, and any such homogeneous jury would be as representative (or unrepresentative) as any other. If the groups in a real community were well defined, the analogous approach would be to measure the representativeness of a jury by the degree to which the distribution of groups on it approximated the distribution of these groups in the population as a whole. But there is no unambiguously superior method for gauging the similarity of these two distributions, and different approaches can yield different conclusions.[51]

The error probabilities for a jury drawn from our fictional community can be expressed in a way that emphasises the role of stochastic interactions among jurors. Denote by y_j the number of jurors from group j on the jury. Each y_j, $j = 1, 2, 3$, must be a non-negative integrer, and, since we are considering three-person juries, the sum of the y_j variables must equal three: $\sum_{j=1}^{3} y_j = 3$. It follows from our assumptions about the individuals in this fictional society and about the interactions among them that any jury is fully described by the vector $Y = (y_1, y_2, y_3)$ indicating how many members of each group are on the jury.

Consider the probability that the jury described by the vector Y – which we shall refer to as the jury Y – would vote to convict the defendant when he is, in fact, innocent; that is, consider $p(Y) = p(y_1, y_2, y_3)$. The probability that a member of the jth group deciding the case alone would make this type I error is p_j. Hence, if all individuals in the society behave independently of one another, no matter what group they belong to, then $p(Y)$ equals $p_1^{y_1} p_2^{y_2} p_3^{y_3}$. This is the case where no stochastic interaction occurs among jurors in the same group or between members of different groups.

To capture the stochastic interactions within the groups and between them, we need some further notation. Define the following quantites:

[51] Real communities would present a number of specific difficulties that do not arise in the case of three-person juries in our fictional society. For instance, if the number of relevant groups were to exceed the number of jurors (or the number of people on the panel from which jurors are selected), some groups would necessarilly be excluded from the jury (or the panel). For an example of how statistical techniques can be used to evaluate arguments concerning discrimination in jury empanelling procedures, see Finkelstein (1966).

p_{jjj} = the probability that a jury composed of only group j members will commit a type I error;

p_{jjl} = the probability that a jury composed of two members of group j and one member of group l will commit a type I error;

p_{123} = the probability that a jury with one member from each group will commit a type I error;

$\hat{p}_{jjj} = p_{jjj} - p_j^3$;

$\hat{p}_{jjl} = p_{jjl} - p_j^2 p_l$;

$\hat{p}_{123} = p_{123} - p_1 p_2 p_3$.

The quantities denoted with carets indicate the increases or decreases in jury type I error probabilities that result from stochastic interactions among jury members' decisions. For example, $\hat{p}_{jjj}$ equals the contribution that stochastic interactions among members of group j make to the probability that a jury composed solely of individuals from that group will commit a type I error. If the individuals in the group are stochastically independent – if neither the random components of their perception and processing of the evidence nor the random elements in their standards of reasonable doubt are related to one another – then $\hat{p}_{jjj} = 0$. The higher the correlation of the stochastic elements of their decisions, the higher the value of $\hat{p}_{jjj}$. In the extreme case where the decisions of members of group j are perfectly dependent, $\hat{p}_{jjj} = p_j - p_j^3$.

The careted quantities – the probability differences – correspond to the convariance terms in a mean-variance portfolio analysis. Just as it is possible to have securities the returns of which are negatively correlated, so it is also possible that the stochastic elements of juror decisions could be negatively related. Suppose, for example, that high values of X^1 (the random component of a group 1 juror's decision) occur when low values of X^3 (the random component of a group 3 juror's decision) are realised and *vice versa;* when a group 1 is more likely to convict, a group 3 juror is more likely to acquit, and *vice versa.* For this illustration, assume also that the decisions of members of the same group are stochastically independent. Then, p_{113} would be smaller than $p_1^2 p_3$, so that $\hat{p}_{113}$ would be negative. Similarly, $\hat{p}_{133}$ would be negative because p_{133} would be smaller than $p_1 p_3^2$. Of course, this reduction of the type I error would come at the cost of an increased probability of a hung-jury error of type I, since the negative correlation between the group 1 and group 3 jurors' decisions would increase the probability that they would not reach a unanimous verdict.

With the introduction of one other function, we can express the probability that jury Y will make a type I error in terms of the individual p_js and the probability differences (the $\hat{p}$s). Specifically, define the indicator function θ as follows:

$$\theta(u) = \begin{cases} 1 \text{ if } u > 0 \\ 0 \text{ if } u \leqslant 0 \end{cases} \tag{5.13}$$

Then,

$$p(Y) = p_1^{y_1} p_2^{y_2} p_3^{y_3} + \sum_j \sum_{l \neq j} \theta(y_j - 1)\theta(y_l)\hat{p}_{jjl}$$

$$+ \sum_j \theta(y_j - 2)\hat{p}_{jjj} + \theta(y_1)\theta(y_2)\theta(y_3)\hat{p}_{123} \qquad (5.14)$$

Equation (5.14) is basically a notational device to help focus attention on the role that stochastic interactions among jurors play in determining the probability that a jury of a particular composition will convict the defendant if he is truly innocent. The reader can easily verify that (5.14) provides the correct probability of a type I error for each possible kind of jury.[52]

Now, consider the probability $p'(Y)$ that jury Y will commit a hung-jury error of type I by reaching no decision when the defendant is innocent. It is most convenient to express $p'(Y)$ as the probability that jury Y will neither convict nor acquit the defendant when I is the true state. To this end, denote by $\pi(Y)$ the probability that jury Y acquits when the defendant is innocent: $\pi(Y) = P(A|I, Y)$. In terms of the notation used earlier in formulating the social loss function, $\pi = 1 - p - p'$.[53] If we now define π_j as the probability that a member of the jth group deciding the case alone would acquit the defendant given that he is truly innocent, so that $\pi_j = 1 - p_j$, and introduce notation analogous to that introduced for p, we can write

$$\pi(Y) = \pi_1^{y_1} \pi_2^{y_2} \pi_3^{y_3} + \sum_j \sum_{l \neq j} \theta(y_j - 1)\theta(y_l)\hat{\pi}_{jjl}$$

$$+ \sum_j \theta(y_j - 2)\hat{\pi}_{jjj} + \theta(y_1)\theta(y_2)\theta(y_3)\hat{\pi}_{123} \qquad (5.15)$$

This is essentially a notational device that emphasises how stochastic interactions among jurors influence the probability that a particular jury will acquit

[52] For example, consider a jury with one member of group 1 and two members of group 2: $Y = (1, 2, 0)$. The first term on the right-hand side of (5.14) contributes $p_1 p_2^2$. The terms in the second sum are all zero except for the term for $j = 2, l = 1$, which contributes $\hat{p}_{221}$. To see this, note that $\theta(y_1 - 1) = \theta(0) = 0$ and $\theta(y_2 - 1) = \theta(-1) = 0$; so the only terms in the sum that could be positive are the ones with $j = 2$. Since $\theta(y_3) = \theta(0) = 0$ while $\theta(y_1) = \theta(1) = 1$, the only positive term is the one for $j = 2, l = 1$, as asserted. All three terms in the third sum are zero, because the largest y_j is y_2, and, hence, the largest value of $\theta(y_j - 2)$ is $\theta(y_2 - 2) = \theta(0) = 0$. The final term on the right-hand side is zero because $\theta(y_3) = \theta(0) = 0$. Hence, (5.14) indicates that $p(Y) = p_1 p_2^2 + \hat{p}_{221} = p_{221}$, which is correct.

[53] In that discussion it was most natural to express $P(A|I)$ as the residual probability in terms of $P(C|I)$ and $P(H|I)$, but now it is more convenient to express $p' = P(H|I)$ in terms of $p = P(C|I)$ and $\pi = P(A|I)$.

the defendant if he is actually innocent. Using (5.14) and (5.15), the probability that jury Y will remain undecided when I is the true state can be expressed in terms of the y_j variables, since

$$p'(Y) = 1 - p(Y) - \pi(Y) \tag{5.16}$$

An analogous notational structure can be used to express the error probabilities in terms of the y_j variables when the true state of nature is G. In particular, we would express the probability of a hung-jury error of type II, $s'(Y)$, as the probability that jury Y will neither convict nor acquit the defendant when G is the true state. Denoting by $\sigma(Y)$ the probability that jury Y convicts when the defendant is guilty, we would then write

$$s'(Y) = 1 - s(Y) - \sigma(Y) \tag{5.16$'$}$$

If we consider the groups as income classes, if factor markets are competitive, if there is no difference between private and social marginal products, and if members of a group have the same work–leisure preferences, then the social opportunity cost of a juror's time will be the same for all members of a group. In addition, we shall assume that the incremental travel and subsistence expenses are the same for all jurors. Hence, the economic cost of a juror depends only on the group to which he belongs. Denoting by w_j, the social economic cost of using a member of group j as a juror, our earlier assumption that income is a nonincreasing function of group index number becomes $w_1 \geqslant w_2 \geqslant w_3$, and the expression in (5.12) specialises to

$$W(Y) = B + \sum_{j=1}^{3} w_j y_j \tag{5.17}$$

where $W(Y)$ is the resource cost of using jury Y.

This expression for jury Y's economic cost and the expressions for its error probabilities – (5.14), (5.15) and (5.16), and their analogues for the case in which G is the true state – all in terms of the y_js, can be used to state as a nonlinear integer programming problem the problem facing this community's jury composer. His problem resembles a capital-budgeting problem where different classes of large-scale investments are being considered, and where the projects, the stochastic returns of which are characterised by a specific dependence structure, can be undertaken only in integral units. Of course, for a problem as small as the one considered here, it is easy enough to use an exhaustive enumeration of possibilities to find the optimal jury. For larger jury panels, the problem would probably be solved by using some clever enumeration technique – for example, an efficient branch-and-bound method.

My interest now is not, however, in solving the decision-maker's problem formally for particular configurations of parameter values. Rather, I am concerned with how the character of the solution changes as the structure of the community changes, and, in particular, with whether one can make an *a priori* case for a representative jury – for a well-diversified portfolio of jurors. For this purpose, it is important to recognise the formal nature of the decision problem and its strong correspondence with portfolio selection problems. Nevertheless, the basic message can be conveyed by considering a set of examples in somewhat less formal terms, and this is what I shall do. We shall see that the critical elements determining whether or not to have a broadly representative jury are: the structure of the marginal probabilities of error (that is, the probabilities that individual members of different groups would err if they were to decide the case alone); the nature of the stochastic interactions within and across the three groups; the structure of the social opportunity costs in the society; the relative disutility that the society attaches to different kinds of errors; and the prior probability of guilt used by the jury selector. That a firm *a priori* case cannot be made for a representative jury will be seen when we focus on that institution's most instrumental function – fact-finding.

XII. THE INCONCLUSIVE A PRIORI INSTRUMENTAL CASE FOR REPRESENTATIVE JURIES

For the purpose of this discussion, I shall assume that the disutility function $D(K, W)$ is additively separable in K and W:

$$D(K, W) = D^1(K) + D^2(W) \tag{5.18}$$

where both $D^1(K)$ and $D^2(W)$ are von Neumann–Morgenstern disutility functions. The marginal disutility of noneconomic costs is independent of the level of economic costs, and the marginal disutility of economic costs is invariant with *ceteris paribus* changes in the level of noneconomic costs. With (5.18) as the disutility function, the social loss function in (5.4) becomes

$$L(Y) = \alpha[ED^1(K|G, Y) + ED^2(W|G, Y)] + (1-\alpha)[ED^1(K|I, Y) + ED^2(W|I, Y)]$$

Since the social economic costs of using jury Y are assumed to be independent of the jury's verdict and the true state of nature,

$$ED^2(W|G, Y) = ED^2(W|I, Y) = D^2(W|Y)$$

Hence, using the expression for the resource cost of jury Y given by (5.17), the social loss function $L(Y)$ simplifies to

$$L(Y) = \alpha ED^1(K|G, Y) + (1-\alpha)ED^1(K|I, Y) + D^2(B + \sum_{j=1}^{3} w_j y_j) \tag{5.19}$$

The expected disutility of noneconomic costs conditional on the defendant's being guilty has several components:

$$ED^1(K|G, Y) = s(Y)D^1(k_{\text{II}}) + s'(Y)D^1(k'_{\text{II}}) + \sigma(Y)D^1(0) \tag{5.20}$$

where $D^1(k_{II}) > D^1(k'_{II}) > D^1(0)$. Similarly, the expected disutility of noneconomic costs conditional on I being the true state also has several components:

$$ED^1(K|I,\ Y) = p(Y)D^1(k_I) + p'(Y)D^1(k'_I) + \pi(Y)D^1(0) \qquad (5.20')$$

with $D^1(k_I) > D^1(k'_I) > D^1(0)$. Since $D^1(K)$ is a von Neumann–Morgenstern disutility function, unique up to a positive linear transformation, we can without loss of generality, set its origin at $K = 0$ so that $D^1(0) = 0$: the disutility of the (zero) noneconomic costs of a correct decision is zero. Using this simplification and the equations for $p'(Y)$ and $s'(Y)$ in (5.16) and (5.16′), respectively, in the expressions for the conditional expected disutilities, the social loss function can be written as

$$\begin{aligned} L(Y) = {} & \alpha\{[D^1(k_{II}) - D^1(k'_{II})]\,s(Y) - D^1(k'_{II})\sigma(Y) + D^1(k'_{II})\} \\ & + (1-\alpha)\{[D^1(k_I) - D^1(k'_I)]\,p(Y) - D^1(k'_I)\pi(Y) + D^1(k'_I)\} \\ & + D^2(B + \sum_{j=1}^{3} w_j y_j) \end{aligned} \qquad (5.21)$$

It should be clear that, if the social decision-maker changed the prior probability of guilt that he was (implicitly) using, the optimal jury might well change. For example, suppose that two differently composed juries drawn from our fictional society – call them Y' and Y'' – engender the same social economic cost, but that the expected disutility of noneconomic costs conditional on the defendant's being guilty is much higher for jury Y' than for Y'' and that the opposite is true for the expected disutility of noneconomic costs conditional on I being the true state:

$$ED^1(K|G,\ Y) \gg ED^1(K|G,\ Y'')$$

and

$$ED^1(K|I,\ Y'') \gg ED^1(K|I,\ Y')$$

Then, clearly, for very low values of α, the social decision-maker would prefer jury Y' to jury Y''. As the implicit prior probability of guilt increases from 0 to 1, however, there would be a point, say $\hat{\alpha}$, at which the decision-maker would have no preference one way or the other. For all values of α in the interval $(\hat{\alpha}, 1)$, the decision-maker would choose jury Y'' rather than Y'.

In a forthcoming paper I shall use numerical calculations to explore in detail how the optimal jury varies with the value of α as well as with the social disutilities of different kinds of errors and the structure of the community. The expositional limitations imposed by analytical examples are, however, rather severe. If we set α at some arbitrary level between 0 and 1, we have to consider four independent parameters – the coefficients of $s(Y)$, $\alpha(Y)$, $p(Y)$, and $\pi(Y)$ in (5.21) – as well as the structure of marginal probabilities of error of potential jurors, the structure of stochastic interactions among individuals in the society, and the structure of social opportunity costs in the community. A number of simplifications could be used to reduce the dimension of the parameter space to expositionally manageable proportions. For example, by setting the social noneconomic cost of the two hung-jury errors equal to zero, we could reduce the parameter space to two dimensions.

I have chosen an alternative simplification which also yields a two-dimensional parameter space and which leaves the social decision-maker with important social trade-offs. Specifically, I shall consider the special case in which the social decision-maker implicitly sets the prior probability of the defendant's guilt at zero. Hence, he uses weights of $\alpha = 0$ and $1 - \alpha = 1$ in the loss function in (5.21). Even with this extreme resolution of the question of the prior probability of guilt, the jury selector must still balance the cost of convicting an innocent individual, the cost of reaching no decision when the defendant is innocent, and the economic cost of the jury. In addition, we shall assume throughout that $0 < p_j < 1$ for each j. No member of the society will always commit a type I error if he decides the case alone, but there is some positive probability that each individual will make such a mistake if he arrives at a verdict on his own. Hence, the 'obvious' solution for the $\alpha = 0$ case, of choosing jurors who would always vote to acquit, is not feasible. Moreover, because there are several costs to be balanced, the closest approximation to the 'obvious' solution – selecting jurors with the highest probability of acquitting – is not necessarily optimal. Since the conclusion we reach is that diversification of the portfolio of jurors is sometimes, but not always optimal, and since that result can be demonstrated using a social loss function with $\alpha = 0$, this simplification does not really impede our analysis.

For this specialisation, in which $\alpha = 0$, the social loss function is

$$L(Y) = [d_C - d_H]p(Y) - d_H\pi(Y) + d_H + D^2(B + \sum_{j=1}^{3} w_j y_j) \quad (5.22)$$

where, for notational simplicity, $D^1(k_\text{I})$ is denoted as d_C (C being mnemonic for 'conviction'), and $D^1(k_\text{I}')$ as d_H (H being mnemonic for 'hung jury'). From our earlier assumptions, we have $d_C - d_H > 0$ and $d_H > 0$. If the expressions in (5.14) and (5.15) are substituted for $p(Y)$ and $\pi(Y)$, respectively, this loss function can be written explicitly in terms of the y_js – the number of members of each group serving on the jury – which are the choice variables in the problem.

The function in (5.22) is the one that the social decision-maker in our fictional society wants to minimise. Let us now consider what kind of jury he would choose under alternative assumptions about the structure of the community. In particular, how representative is the optimal jury in each case?

First, consider the case in which *all* jurors act independently of one another. Knowing the way one juror will vote would not alter our probability distribution for any other juror's vote, regardless of whether the second juror is in the same group as the first one or in a different class. In this case, all the probability differences discussed in section II are zero: all the $\hat{p}$s and all the $\hat{\pi}$s are zero. Hence, $p(Y) = p_1^{y_1} p_2^{y_2} p_3^{y_3}$ and $\pi(Y) = \pi_1^{y_1} \pi_2^{y_2} \pi_3^{y_3}$, or, since $\pi_j = 1 - p_j$, we have $\pi(Y) = (1 - p_1)^{y_1}(1 - p_2)^{y_2}(1 - p_3)^{y_3}$. The social loss function becomes

$$L(Y) = (d_C - d_H)p_1^{y_1} p_2^{y_2} p_3^{y_3} - d_H(1 - p_1)^{y_1}(1 - p_2)^{y_2}(1 - p_3)^{y_3} + d_H + D^2(B + \sum_{j=1}^{3} w_j y_j) \quad (5.23)$$

Suppose that the probability of convicting a truly innocent defendant were the same for all potential jurors: $p_1 = p_2 = p_3$. Then, regardless of the structure of economic opportunity costs for the several groups, there would be no reason for diversifying the portfolio of jurors. Either members of different groups would have the same economic costs or they would not. In the former case, with $w_1 = w_2 = w_3$, it would make no difference, in terms of economic or noneconomic costs, which groups served on the panel. On the other hand, if the w_js were unequal, then the jury selector would choose the entire jury from the group with the lowest economic opportunity cost.

Similarly, when there are no stochastic interactions among jurors, differences in the error probabilities of different groups do not suffice to ensure the optimality of a representative jury. For example, suppose that group 1 has the lowest probability of commiting a type I error, that groups 2's probability of making such a mistake is higher, and that group 3 is most likely to convict the defendant if he is truly innocent: $p_1 < p_2 < p_3$. Then, if all the w_js are equal, the decision-maker minimising (5.23) will set $y_1 = 3$, $y_2 = y_3 = 0$. The optimal jury would be the least representative kind, comprised of members of group 1 only.

If, however, the error probabilities *and* the economic opportunity costs differ across the groups, a nonhomogeneous jury may be optimal. Whether or not it will be so depends, in part, on how large the differences in the p_js and the w_js are. The optimality of a heterogeneous jury in this case also depends on how the disutility of an incorrect conviction (d_C) compares with the disutility of a nondecision when the individual is truly innocent (d_H), and on how these disutilities and the difference between them stand in relation to the disutility of social economic opportunity costs. If the group with the lowest probability of error (p_j) has the highest economic opportunity cost (w_j), one can easily generate disutility functions for which a mixed jury is optimal. In this case, the asset with the highest probability of paying off – the class of jurors with the lowest probability of erring – is so expensive that society cannot afford to hold a three-juror portfolio consisting only of jurors of that class.

But the most representative type of jury – with one member from each group – may still not be optimal. The jury selector might choose to diversify, but only to the extent of holding two types of assets and not to including all three in the jury portfolio. Note also that, if the most competent group of potential jurors – the group with the lowest p_j has a sufficiently high opportunity cost, and if the disutility of economic costs is significant relative to non-economic costs, the jury that minimises the social loss function in (5.23) may not contain any members of this most accurate group.

In sum, when all potential jurors behave independently of one another, regardless of the group to which they belong, there are circumstances under which a fully representative jury is optimal. But there are also configurations of error probabilities, opportunity costs and disutility levels for which a homogeneous jury minimises the social loss function, and situations in which a jury composed of members of only two groups is best. Essential to the case for broadening representation on the jury are differences in the probabilities with which members of different groups will vote to convict when the defendant is innocent, and variations in the opportunity costs of their time. When stochastic interactions are absent, the argument for a fully representative jury in our fictional community will be strongest when the ranking of error probabilities across groups is exactly the opposite of the ranking of economic opportunity costs: if $p_1 < p_2 < p_3$ while $w_1 > w_2 > w_3$.

The second community that we shall consider is structured very differently from the first one. In this society, the votes of individuals in the same group are perfectly correlated, while the random variables representing the verdicts of jurors in different groups are independent of one another. Once we know the way one juror from group j would decide the case if he were acting alone, we know exactly how any other juror from that class would vote, but we know nothing more about what verdict an individual from either of the other two classes would reach. For this society, the probability differences for a fully representative jury, $\hat{p}_{123}$ and $\hat{\pi}_{123}$, are both zero. But all the other probability increments are positive: $\hat{p}_{jjl} = p_j p_l - p_j^2 p_l$, $\hat{p}_{jjj} = p_j - p_j^3$, $\hat{\pi}_{jjl} = \pi_j \pi_l - \pi_j^2 \pi_l$, and $\hat{\pi}_{jjj} = \pi_j - \pi_j^3$. The social loss function for this community can be written as

$$
\begin{aligned}
L(Y) = {} & (d_C - d_H) p_1^{\theta(y_1)} p_2^{\theta(y_2)} p_3^{\theta(y_3)} \\
& - d_H (1 - p_1)^{\theta(y_1)} (1 - p_2)^{\theta(y_2)} (1 - p_3)^{\theta(y_3)} \\
& + d_H + D^2 \left(B + \sum_{j=1}^{3} w_j y_j \right)
\end{aligned}
\tag{5.24}
$$

where $\theta(\cdot)$ is the indicator function introduced earlier.

The critical feature of a jury in this society is that, if one member of group j is on it, adding a second member of that group to the panel will not change the probability that the jury will convict (or that it will acquit) the truly innocent defendant. In sharp contrast, increasing the number of groups represented on the jury decreases the probability of a type I error, $p(Y)$, and it also decreases the probability of acquitting the defendant if he is actually innocent, $\pi(Y)$. Since society would like $p(Y)$ to be as small as possible and $\pi(Y)$ to be as large as possible, a trade-off must be confronted in deciding whether to diversify the portfolio of jurors, even in the absence of differences in the opportunity costs of members of different groups. As the jury becomes more representative, it becomes less likely that the panel will engender the disutility of convicting a truly innocent man. But, at the same time, it becomes more likely that the jury will not reach a unanimous verdict when I is the true state of nature, and, thus, the probability increases that society will incur the associated hung-jury costs. Even if the economic opportunity cost of an individual's time is the same for all individuals, regardless of group affiliation, variations in the optimal degree of representativeness will result from differences in the relationship between d_C and d_H and differences in the structure of the p_js.

Suppose, then, that $w_1 = w_2 = w_3$, so that $D^2\left(B + \sum_{j=1}^{3} w_j y_j\right)$ is the same no matter how the jury is composed. Then, if $d_C - d_H$ is sufficiently larger than d_H, the social decision-maker minimising $L(Y)$ is essentially concerned only with minimising $p(Y) = p_1^{\theta(y_1)} p_2^{\theta(y_2)} p_3^{\theta(y_3)}$. In this case, the optimal jury would be fully representative with one member from each group serving on the panel. Note that the optimal solution would have $y_1 = y_2 = y_3 = 1$, regardless of the differences in the p_js; that is, no matter how much variation there is among classes in the probability of making a type I error when reaching a verdict alone.

This case provides an interesting illustration of the usefulness of the portfolio metaphor with its focus on interactions among jurors. One might casually think, 'If you want good fact-finders, you do not want representative juries.' But here we have a case in which members of one group could significantly dominate members of the other two in performing the fact-finding function alone – say, if p_1 were much smaller than p_2 and p_3 – and yet the optimal jury would contain only one member of that group. The social decision-maker would choose a fully representative jury despite the apparently superior fact-finding skills of group 1 individuals. The explanation rests with the stochastic interactions among jurors – in particular, in this example, with the perfect correlation of the verdicts of jurors belonging to the same group in society. This example illustrates the point that the value of a particular juror as a fact-finder depends not only on how well he makes decisions in isolation, but also on the characteristics of the other jurors with whom he will serve.

Retaining the assumption that all w_js are equal, consider the other extreme case where d_C is insignificantly larger than d_H. This is the somewhat implausible circumstance in which having the jury reach no decision when the defendant is truly innocent is almost as costly (in noneconomic terms) as having it err by convicting him. In this instance, minimising $L(Y)$ in (5.24) is almost equivalent to maximising $\pi(Y) = (1 - p_1)^{\theta(y_1)}(1 - p_2)^{\theta(y_2)}(1 - p_3)^{\theta(y_3)}$. The optimal jury will be homogeneous, comprised only of members of the group with the lowest p_j.

Clearly, by varying the ratio of d_H to d_C between the two extremes that we have examined (zero and unity), and by varying the structure of the p_js, we can generate other cases in which a fully representative jury would be optimal and yet others in which a homogenous jury would be optimal. Examples could also be constructed in which the jury minimising the social loss function would be composed of two members from one group and one from another. Differences in the economic cost of using members of different groups will affect the strength of the argument for a representative jury in this society just as they did in the first community that we considered. The higher are the economic costs of those individuals with the lower error probabilities, the stronger is the case for diversifying the portfolio of jurors. On the other hand, to the extent that the ranking of the p_js matches that of the w_js, the case for broad representation is weakened. But, as we have seen, unlike the community in which all individuals' verdicts are reached independently, representative juries may be desirable in our second society even if all individuals' economic opportunity costs are the same.

We could go on to consider more complicated, less extreme structures for the stochastic interactions among individuals in the community. For example, the next logical step might be to retain the assumption of stochastic independence of the verdicts of jurors in different groups but to assume that the votes of individuals in the same group are (highly) positively correlated rather than perfectly correlated. Obviously, the strong argument that could be made for a fully representative jury in the case of the second community that we considered would weaken as the degree of correlation between jurors in the same group decreased. We could then go on to allow for positive or negative correlation between the verdicts of jurors in different classes, requiring only that the correlations between jurors in the same group be positive and higher than those between jurors in different groups.

In such societies, with richer structures of interrelationships, the conclusion would be the same as the one reached in the two very simply structured communities that we have considered: diversification of the portfolio of jurors is sometimes, but not always, optimal. For some sets of parameter values, a fully representative jury is optimal, for others a homogeneous jury is best, and, for yet other configurations of parameters, a somewhat (but not fully) diversified jury minimises the social loss function. We have indicated the kinds of parameter structures that would tend to make more or less diversification optimal. But the *a priori* instrumental case for representative juries is inconclusive. Without empirical information – either actual data or empirical guesses – concerning the particular community, one cannot state how representative the best fact-finding jury would be.

XIII. JURY REPRESENTATIVENESS AS A POLITICAL SYMBOL: A CONCLUDING NOTE

Although representativeness of the jury does not necessarily serve the instrumental function of fact-finding, I would argue that it does serve a very important but much less instrumental function. It constitutes an important symbolic expression of our societal belief in, and commitment to, democracy. In this sense, representativeness of the jury is a value in its own right. One need not (perhaps, should not try to) derive its usefulness by positing some other goal and demonstrating the role that representativeness plays in achieving that other goal.[54]

The importance of jury representativeness as a political symbol can be suggested by considering the potential for such symbolic expression in each of the branches of government: the executive, the legislature, and the judiciary. While all citizens are meant to have an equal voice (one man, one vote) in choosing the executive, we do not expect the executive to be representatively responsive in each decision he makes. Similarly, while members of the legislature are elected democratically, they are not expected to take the proportional pulse of their constituents when voting on each and every legislative issue. Finally, we do not expect judges, be they elected or appointed, to decide cases on the basis of a proportional weighing of the opinions of individuals in the community. Judicial decisions may reflect the sense of the community or its conventional morality',[55] but individual judicial decisions are not to be rendered in a democratically representative way.

The jury, however, can be representative. It can provide symbolic reinforcement of the democratic myth (where 'myth' is used in a positive and not a pejorative sense) by being an institution that makes individual decisions on a representative basis. The communication of the symbolic value of representative juries is probably quite effective. While few people actually serve on juries, surveys have shown that many more people know someone who has served.[56] At least some trials receive a substantial amount of publicity. People may not know about many jury trials, but they are at least aware of, and informed about, several major ones each year. To the extent that publicity is given to the courtroom juror selection process – the *voir dire* – in reporting these cases, the representativeness of the jury and the importance of having decisions made by representative bodies is brought into even sharper focus. Finally, the symbolic value of the representativeness of the jury is heightened because that body is making a decision that everyone will recognise as being of major importance for one or more named individuals. The ordinary citizen can easily grasp the importance of the decision, as contrasted, for example, with some legislative issue the ramifications of which he may find quite difficult to trace. Requiring that this jury decision be made by a representative group of individuals can provide a powerful restatement of our commitment to a particular political structure – democracy.

[54] In a forthcoming paper, I shall present my argument for this view in greater detail. I shall sketch only its broad outlines here. Compare Tribe (1971b), pp. 1391–2, where other aspects of the trial procedure are seen as 'ritual' that is meant to be expressive of certain moral relationships and principles.

[55] See Wellington (1973) for a development of this idea.

[56] Erlanger (1970), p. 354.

But we must still end with a question. If we accept that a major – perhaps the principal – justification of jury representativeness is its value as a political symbol, how representative does the jury have to be to give effective expression to the democratic principle? And, do the recent decisions upholding reductions in jury size and nonunanimous verdicts substantially reduce the politically symbolic power of the representative jury?

REFERENCES

Beiser, E. N., 'The Trial Jury: Empirical and Normative Considerations' (paper delivered at the 1973 Annual Meeting of the American Political Science Association, New Orleans, Louisiana, 4–8 Sep 1973).

Broeder, D. W., 'The Functions of the Jury: Facts or Fictions?', *University of Chicago Law Review,* XXI (1954), p. 386.

Erlanger, H. S., 'Jury Research in America; Its Past and Future', *Law and Society Review,* IV (1970), p. 345.

Finkelstein, M. O., 'The Application of Statistical Decision Theory to the Jury Discrimination Cases', *Harvard Law Review,* LXXX (1966), p. 338.

Finkelstein, M. O., and Fairley, W. B., 'A Bayesian Approach to Identification Evidence', *Harvard Law Review,* LXXXIII (1970), p. 489.

Finkelstein, M. O., and Fairley, W. B., 'A Comment on "Trial by Mathematics" ', *Harvard Law Review,* LXXXIV (1971), p. 1801.

Gelfand, A. E., and Solomon, H., 'A Study of Poisson's Models for Jury Verdicts in Criminal and Civil Trials', *Journal of the American Statistical Association,* LXVIII (1973), p. 271.

Goldstein, A. S., Book Review, *Law and Society Review,* I (1967), p. 148.

Himelrick, R. G., 'Federal Courts – Juror Selection – Under-Representation of Young Adults on Juror Source Lists', *Wayne Law Review,* XIX (1973), p. 1287.

Johnson, N., and Kotz, S., *Distributions in Statistics: Continuous Multivariate Distributions* (New York: John Wiley and Sons, 1972).

Kalven, H., and Zeisel, H., *The American Jury* (Boston, Mass.: Little, Brown and Co., 1966).

Kessler, J. B., 'An Empirical Study of Six- and Twelve-Member Jury Decision-Making Processes', *University of Michigan Journal of Law Reform,* VI (1973), p. 712.

Martin, D. L., 'The Economics of Jury Conscription', *Journal of Political Economy,* LXXX (1972), p. 680.

Mills, L. R., 'Six-Member and Twelve-Member Juries: An Empirical Study of Trial Results', *University of Michigan Journal of Law Reform,* VI (1973), p. 671.

Posner, R. A., 'An Economic Approach to Legal Procedure and Judicial Administration', *Journal of Legal Studies,* II (1973), p. 399.

Powell, D. M., 'Reducing the Size of Juries', *University of Michigan Journal of Law Reform,* V (1971), p. 87.

Raiffa, H., *Decision Analysis. Introductory Lectures on Choices under Uncertainty* (Reading, Mass.: Addison–Wesley, 1968).

Schulman, J., Shaver, P., Colman, R., Emrich, B., and Christie, R., 'Recipe for a Jury', *Psychology Today,* VI (1973), p. 37.

Sealy, A. P., and Cornish, W. R., 'Jurors and their Verdicts', *Modern Law Review,* XXXVI (1973), p. 496.

Stigler, G. J., 'Optimum Enforcement of Laws', *Journal of Political Economy,* LXXVIII (1970), p. 526.

Tribe, L. H., 'A Further Critique of Mathematical Proof', *Harvard Law Review,* LXXXIV (1971), p. 1810.

Tribe, L. H., 'Trial by Mathematics: Precision and Ritual in the Legal Process', *Harvard Law Review,* LXXXIV (1971), p. 1329.

Von Neumann, J., and Morgenstern, O., *Theory of Games and Economic Behavior* (Princeton: Princeton University Press, 1947).

Walbert, D. F., 'The Effect of Jury Size on the Probability of Conviction: An Evaluation of *Williams v. Florida', Case-Western Reserve Law Review,* XXII (1971). p. 529.

Wellington, H. H., 'Common Law Rules and Constitutional Double Standards: Some Notes on Adjudication', *Yale Law Journal,* LXXXIII (1973), p. 221.

Winter, R. K., Jr. 'The Jury and the Risk of Nonpersuasion', *Law and Society Review,* V (1971), p. 335.

Zeisel, H., '. . . And Then There Were None: The Diminution of the Federal Jury', *University of Chicago Law Review,* XXXVIII (1971), p. 710.

Zeisel, H., *Six-Man Juries, Majority Verdicts – What Difference Do They Make?,* Occasional Papers from the Law School, University of Chicago (1972).

Zeisel, H., 'The Waning of the American Jury', *American Bar Association Journal,* LVIII (1972), p. 367.

CASES

Apodaca v. Oregon, 406 US 404 (1972).
Colgrove v. Battin, 413 US 149 (1973).
Johnson v. Louisiana, 406 US 356 (1972).
Williams v. Florida, 399 US 78 (1970).

6 Theory and Estimation in Models of Crime and its Social Control and their Relations to Concepts of Social Output[1]

R. A. Carr-Hill* and N. H. Stern†

* UNIVERSITY OF SUSSEX
† ST CATHERINE'S COLLEGE, OXFORD

Following a short introduction, consideration is given (section II) to a model, developed by Becker (1968), that attempts to describe the generation of, and optimum punishment for, illegal activity. It is shown that this model has no optimum finite solution for the case where punishment is costless (fines, according to Becker). Possible modifications are then discussed and it is suggested that the notion of retribution is required in order to explain observed penalties.

Section III continues the econometric work of Carr-Hill and Stern (1973) on criminal statistics, using 1971 data for England and Wales. Results analogous to those for 1961 and 1966 are obtained, in that police practices seem important.

Section IV considers the policy implications of the previous sections.

I. INTRODUCTION

It is natural for an economist, when faced with a policy problem, to attempt to write down a model of the processes involved, together with a statement of objectives, perhaps involving a function to be maximised or minimised, and summarising the values of the policy-maker. This procedure is not easy at the best of times, but the problems involved in applying it to crime are particularly severe. For example, the appropriate area of policy concern is itself unclear;

[1] The econometric work of section III is a continuation of the work described in Carr-Hill and Stern (1973), and the acknowledgements that were contained in the first footnote of that paper apply here. In addition, the authors would like to thank David Deans and Jay Kynch for computing and research assistance. They are also grateful for the helpful comments of P. A. Diamond, Julian Le Grand, J. E. Stiglitz, and an Economic Theory Workshop at Oxford.

the distinct issues of assuring personal safety and the control of crime are often treated synonymously.

Section II of this paper presents some criticisms and extensions of Becker's economic theory of crime generation and policy towards its control.[2] It is argued that some of Becker's main conclusions are invalid or heavily circumscribed. Further, it will often be the case that society's choice problems as posed by Becker, will have no solution. This leads us to a discussion of alternative specifications of the problem.

Section III reports on an attempt to estimate a model suggested, in part, by the theory of the first section. This is a simultaneous-equations model based on data for a cross-section of United Kingdom police districts in 1971. This extends our earlier work on similar data for 1961 and 1966.[3]

Section IV discusses the specification of aims and policy areas and how, if at all, criminal statistics should be used as measures of the output of the public services designed to deal with crime, in the light of the theory of the second section and the experience with estimation described in the third.

II. THEORY

Becker was concerned with the optimum choice of the policy variables severity of punishment (f) and probability of conviction (p). He reached two main conclusions: (1) that at the optimum, the responsiveness of the level of offences to p should be greater than that to f;[4] and (2) that fines are, in general, preferable to other forms of punishment, and that the appropriate level of fines is given by the harm inflicted by the offender. We shall argue that the first of these conclusions is heavily circumscribed and that the result concerning the optimum level of fines is, in general, invalid.

We begin with a brief description of the model discussed by Becker. He supposes that, for a given level of p and f, there will be some level of offences O.[5] In order to achieve a probability of conviction p for a level of offences O, the public expenditure on the system of social control of crime[6] must be C. We thus have the two main functional relationships of the model, $O(p, f)$ and $C(O, p)$.

The objective is to minimise a social loss function

$$L(p, f) = D(O) + C(O, p) + bpfO \tag{6.1}$$

$D(O)$ is the level of damages deemed to flow from a level of offences O and is obtained by subtracting the gain to the offenders, $G(O)$, from the harm done

[2] See Becker (1968).

[3] See Carr-Hill and Stern (1973)

[4] This result was used, through an appeal to an expected utility model of criminal behaviour, to suggest that criminals would be risk preferrers, so that 'illegal activities "would not pay" (at the margin)'. (Becker, 1968, p. 207.)

[5] We follow Becker's notation here.

[6] Including the police, the criminal justice system, and various security measures.

to others, $H(O)$. The final term in the loss function is intended to measure the cost of punishment: pO is the total number of punishments, pfO the total 'amount' of punishment, and b is a factor translating amount into social loss (it is assumed that the translation can be taken as linear). Most of Becker's discussion is then concerned with the analysis and interpretation of the first-order conditions for this minimisation.

'OPTIMALITY' WHEN $b = 0$

Becker concentrates much of his attention on the case where the method of punishment is fines, for which, he argues, $b = 0$. The reason offered is that a fine is merely a transfer payment from the finee to the public authorities. We shall return to this argument shortly, but, meanwhile, we discuss the following optimisation problem.

I. Minimise $L(p, f)$ $\qquad 0 \leqslant f \leqslant \infty, 0 \leqslant p \leqslant 1$

where $\quad L(p, f) = D(O) + C(O, p)$

Becker[7] adopts the assumption $p = 1$ for his discussion of the optimum level of f. With this assumption, we have

$$D'(\hat{O}) + C_o(\hat{O}, 1) = 0 \tag{6.2}$$

where C_o is the partial derivative of C with respect to O. If we suppose that offenders maximise net money gains, they push offences to the point where marginal money gains equal marginal money losses, so that $f = G'$. Using $D \equiv H - G$, we have[8]

$$\hat{f} = H'(O) + C_o(O, 1) \tag{6.3}$$

This is the condition on which Becker bases his case that fines should be equal to the costs (direct, H', and indirect in apprehending and punishing, C_o) inflicted by the offender and not on the special circumstances of the offender. The similarity with the economic theory of externalities is clear and we return to it later. If p were fixed at $\hat{p}$, rather than at unity, and we supposed that offenders maximised expected money gain, we should have, instead of (6.3),

$$\hat{p}\hat{f} = H'(\hat{O}) + C_o(\hat{O}, 1) \tag{6.3$'$}$$

The problem with Becker's approach is that inadequate attention is paid to the corners of the constraint set for problem I. Taking these into account, we have the following necessary conditions for an optimum

[7] See Becker (1968), p. 193, equations (28) and (29).

[8] The constraints are sufficiently well behaved for constraint qualifications to apply (see, for example, Abadie, 1967).

$$\left.\begin{aligned} f &\geqslant 0 \\ L_f = O_f(D' + C_o) &\geqslant 0 \end{aligned}\right\} \text{comp.} \tag{6.4a}$$

and either $$0 < p < 1, L_p = 0 \tag{6.4b}$$

or $$p = 0, L_p \geqslant 0 \tag{6.4c}$$

or $$p = 1, L_p \leqslant 0 \tag{6.4d}$$

where } comp. denotes complementary slackness

$$L_p = O_p(D' + C_o) + C_p$$

and where O_p, O_f are the partial derivatives of O with respect to p and f, and C_p is the partial derivative of $C(O, p)$ with respect to p. We suppose that O_f is strictly negative for $p > 0, f > 0$ and $C_p > 0$ for $O > 0, p \geqslant 0$.

We shall examine possible values of p and f satisfying the alternative necessary conditions to see if they could be optimum. We shall show that, in general, such values will not be optimal and, hence, that no optimum exists.

Suppose, now, that some pair (p, f) with $p > 0$ and $f > 0$ satisfied the necessary conditions. (6.4a) implies that $(D' + C_o) = 0$ (since $O_f < 0$). This, together with $C_p > 0$, implies that $L_p > 0$. By (6.4b) and (6.4d) this is a contradiction to $p > 0$. The economics of the argument are that, if f is chosen so that the net costs from the marginal offence $(D' + C_o)$ are zero, we save on apprehension costs by reducing p (since $C_p > 0$) while incurring no offsetting loss. Thus, no pair (p, f) with $p > 0, f > 0$.

The remaining possibilities are that $p = 0$, or $f = 0$ gives an optimum, or that no optimum exists. If we suppose that $O_f(0, f) = 0$ and $O_p(p, 0) = 0$, as seems natural,[9] $p = f = 0$ will give a minimum of L in the set of (p, f) where one or the other is zero. We have the situation, then, that either $p = f = 0$ is an optimum or that no optimum exists. Presumbly, it will usually be the case that there exist levels of p, f giving a smaller loss L in problem I than $p = f = 0$ – for example, those involving positive p and large values of f. We can conclude then, that problem I usually will have no solution.

We must conclude, therefore, that Becker's analysis of the first-order conditions that would have prevailed for an interior solution with $f > 0$, had it been the case that an optimum existed, is irrelevant. The analysis cannot, therefore, be used to justify his main conclusions that fines should be equal to damages from offences. The reason why no optimum exists is, loosely speak-

[9] The possible exceptions are that $O_p(p, 0)$ may be strictly negative if there is a perceived cost of appearing in court even when official penalties are zero, or $O_f(0, f)$ may be strictly negative if higher fines, in the absence of enforcement, restrain offenders by, for example, convincing them that the criminal acts are more reprehensible. In these cases it is easy to check from (6.4) that $p > 0, f = 0$ can never be optimum. In the case $O_f(0, f) < 0$, an optimum, if it exists, still requires that $p = 0$, but may require that $f > 0$. Such a policy would, in practice, be a dubious candidate for an optimum.

ing, that his problem leads to the conclusion that f should be indefinitely large.[10] In other words, if we imposed a large upper bound F on f (so that L would be minimised over a compact set and a solution would exist) the optimum would be at $f = F$ (since we have seen that the only alternatives are f or p zero). With $b = 0$, here are benefits from increasing f, but no costs. Naturally, with answers like these we have a misspecified problem. We return to this point later.[11]

Much of our discussion above applies to the general theory of externalities. Suppose that we were in a situation where everyone were made to pay a tax on a certain externality-producing good and that the tax were set at such a level that the total net social benefit from a marginal unit of the good were zero (the standard Pigovian rule). Now, suppose that a random sample of 99 per cent of the population be made to pay the tax. The change in social welfare from the adjustment of the level of the good is zero. If enforcement costs are reduced, then the change is beneficial.

THE SOCIAL COST OF FINES

Becker argued that $b = 0$ for fines since they are transfer payments. We have seen that this assumption can lead to a model without a solution. There are, however, direct objections to the argument. The assertion is based on an optimality condition from first-best welfare economics: the social marginal utility of income to each individual is equal and the common value is equal to the social marginal utility of public income.[12] In this case, a marginal transfer from an individual to the government does not increase or decrease social welfare. It is, of course, well known that the achievement of the first-best situation will usually require the levy of an appropriate set of lump-sum taxes that vary among individuals but that do not affect their behaviour on the margin. There are severe problems with the calculation and administration of such taxes. It is important, therefore, to examine policy in models where the assumption of the availability of lump-sum taxes is not made. There has recently been a good deal of work on the welfare economics of such models, i.e. on second-best welfare economics.[13] In such models, the transfer of income from an individual to the government, such as that involved in a fine, will usually have an impact on social welfare, even where the (limited) taxes are set optimally.

Our assessment of whether the transfer involved in a fine increases or de-

[10] Becker does seem to realise that there may be such a difficulty, at several points, but does not appreciate the full consequences of this for his discussion of the appropriate fine. See Becker (1968), pp. 183–4 (footnote 26), 189 ($b = 0$, and figure 4), and 193.

[11] Possible problems of nonexistence in a related model have been noted by Kolm (1973).

[12] These issues are discussed in Diamond and Mirrlees (1971)

[13] See, for example, Diamond and Mirrlees (1971), Baumol and Bradford (1970), and Stiglitz and Dasgupta (1971).

creases social welfare depends on whether we view a marginal unit of income to the finee as less, or as more, valuable than a unit to the government. In the former case $b < 0$ in Becker's model, and in the latter $b > 0$. It should be noted that we are abstracting from collection costs (as Becker does in his argument that $b = 0$), and that the deterrent benefit of fines is captured elsewhere in the loss function.

From this point of view, it seems that the decision-maker will often put a negative value on b. Some might view an offender as inherently less deserving than the alternative recipients of government income. Others might argue that the level of b should depend on the wealth of the offender. On the assumption of diminishing social marginal valuation of income, it could be argued that for rich offenders b is significantly negative, whereas for the poor offenders it might be closer to zero. On the other hand, many offenders are very poor, perhaps unable to obtain a job due to previous convictions, and in this case b may be positive.

We should be clear that, for punishments involving custodial treatment or supervision, b is much more likely to be positive, since the expenses involved in carrying out the punishment can be large.

We have been discussing the social cost or benefit of fines as a transfer. There may, of course, be other issues involved. Collection costs have already been mentioned. Social loss connected with the possibility of punishment of the wrong individual would increase as the level of punishment increased. We can thus view Harris's discussion[14] of this problem as an argument that b should be larger than it otherwise would be, although he preferred to include a separate term in the minimand.

OPTIMALITY WHEN b IS NON-ZERO

The case $b > 0$ has been extensively analysed by Becker. The problems of the possible nonexistence of a solution are less likely to arise, since the cost of punishment helps to keep down the level of f. We concentrate our discussion on two points: first, the existence problem when $b < 0$; second, assuming an optimum exists, the sensitivity of the optimum punishment to the level of b.

From the minimand (6.1) we have

$$L_f = O_f(D' + C_o) + bp\frac{\partial}{\partial f}(fO) \qquad (6.5)$$

At an optimum, if it exists, we must have $L_f \geqslant 0$. Where O_f and b are negative, and D' and C_o are positive, this can arise only if $(\partial/\partial f)(fO)$ is negative and sufficiently large in absolute magnitude to offset the first term of (6.5). As Becker noted,[15] this requires $\epsilon_f\ (= -\frac{f}{O} O_f)$ to be greater than one. The other

[14] See Harris (1970).

[15] See Becker (1968), p. 183, footnote 23.

way of achieving $L_f \geqslant 0$ would be $D' < 0$. It might be argued that, at very low levels of offences, an extra offence is beneficial because the gains to the offender outweigh the losses to the rest of the community. This kind of possibility is entertained by Becker in his discussion of fines. An alternative would be, following Durkheim,[16] that a small amount of illegal behaviour is needed to demonstrate the role of the legal norms to the majority of the community.[17] It seems, then, that existence of an optimum in the case $b < 0$ requires either that offences are so sensitive to f that higher fines will cause substantial loss of revenue, or so low that extra offences are seen as beneficial. If offences do not respond to f in this manner for any finite level of f, and offences are not viewed as beneficial at any level, then no optimum exists[18] for the case $b < 0$.

Relation of optimum fine to income of offenders

In our discussion of the social costs of fines, we indicated that b would be higher the poorer the finee, if we assume that the social marginal valuation of income decreases with income. There are two further considerations that we should take into account when discussing the relation of the optimum fine to the income of offenders: the deterrence value of a given fine will be higher[19] and the net social damage from an offence will be lower (for those offences involving transfers from victim to offender) if the offender is poorer.

To keep the argument simple we assume that $O = O(p, f)$, and, hence, is independent of the income of the offender. If offenders maximise expected utility, an assumption of constant absolute risk aversion would justify this specification of O (so that a rich man and a poor man would be equally likely to accept a given gamble). If we assume diminishing absolute risk aversion, so that the poor are less likely to commit offences, the following argument (that the poor should be subject to lower fines) is strengthened.[20]

The argument is now intuitively clear from the expression for the net social loss $L = D(O) + C(O, p) + bpfO$. For a poorer person D is lower and b is higher. Becker shows[21] that the optimum fine should be lower if $D(O)$ shifts downward

[16] See Durkheim (1954), chapter 3. The existence of a few acts of criminality contributes to a direct consciousness of the definition of criminal behaviour. This greater certainty makes individuals more able to act and, hence, better off.

[17] An alternative suggestion, made to us by Julian Le Grand, is that the government may regard some illegal activities as a lesser evil than alternative legal activities (for instance, propagandising against the government).

[18] Becker recognises this possibility in Becker (1968), p. 184, footnote 26.

[19] We assume diminishing absolute risk aversion (see, for example, Arrow, 1965).

[20] Similarly, it is weakened if the poor are more likely to commit offences. Constant relative risk aversion is often assumed and this would imply decreasing absolute risk aversion. There are other arguments that indicate that the poor may be more likely to commit offences, although these widen the scope of the model. For example, for the poor, alternative legal activities may be inferior, or concern with court appearances less severe.

[21] This is demonstrated in the appendix to Becker (1968).

or if b shifts upward. On both counts, therefore, poorer offenders should face lower fines.

Thus, in contrast to Becker, we have the result that, in the case where the model admits of a solution, the optimum fine should depend on the circumstances of the offender, and is not, therefore, simply equal to the damage done by the offence.

MODIFICATIONS TO THE BECKER MODEL

We have hitherto been discussing the structure and logical consistency of Becker's model and his results. We now briefly present two modifications of his model that are important in practice and affect the interpretation of the econometric results in Section III. They derive from two simple observations: first, that the punishment meted out by the sentencer is only a part of the perceived punishment, and, second, that many offences go unreported.

These statements are very plausible from the common-sense point of view and we offer two tables from previous researches to show that the effects appear to be quantitatively important.

A random sample of 808 young men aged between 15 and 22 were interviewed in 1963 in a survey arranged by Willcock and Stokes for the Government Social Survey.[22] The interviewees were questioned about the assumed consequences of appearing in court, and were specifically asked 'which things would worry them most about being found out by the police'. They were asked to rank the eight causes of concern that are shown, together with the results, in Table 6.1. Even offenders who had committed a wide variety of offences ranked the worries in roughly the order indicated in the table.

The National Opinion Research Centre (Chicago) has made estimates based on a survey that covered a random sample of 32,966 households and that inquired of each whether its members had been the victim of any offences. These results were compared with the officially reported offences, as shown in Table 6.2. Such surveys have been carried out in other countries, with similar results.

The reporting ratio implicit in Table 6.2 varies widely between offences and there is no large representative subclass of offences that has a reporting ratio close to unity. Vehicle theft is something of a 'special case' and the reporting ratio greater than unity is presumably due to false insurance claims and 'borrowings' initially thought to be thefts.

The fixed cost of conviction A

We introduce the two modifications separately. We suppose that the punishment from conviction can be separated into two parts: $\overline{f}$, which is a measure of the punishment meted out by the court and is subject to the court's

[22] See Willcock and Stokes (1968).

TABLE 6.1

YOUNG PERSONS' WORRIES ABOUT COURT APPEARANCES

Cause of concern	*Mean rank*	*Percentage placing item first*
1. What my family would think about it	2·38	49
2. The chances of losing my job	2·96	22
3. Publicity or shame of having to appear in court	3·88	12
4. The punishment I might get	4·40	10
5. What my girl friend would think	4·72	6
6. Whether I should get fair treatment in court	6·07	2
7. What my mates would think	6·08	1
8. What might happen to me between being found out and appearing in court	6·20	2

Source: Willcock and Stokes (1968).

TABLE 6.2

ESTIMATES OF RELATION BETWEEN REPORTED OFFENCES AND TOTAL OFFENCES

Offence	*NORC*	*UCR(B)*
Homicide	3·0	5·1
Forcible rape	42·5	11·6
Robbery	94·0	61·4
Aggravated assault	218·3	106·6
Burglary	949·1	296·6
Larceny (of more than $50 worth)	606·5	267·4
Vehicle theft	206·2	226·0
	2119·6	974·7

Note: The first column is the number of offences per 100,000 population found in the NORC survey and the second is the relevant number of officially reported crimes.

Source: Enniss (1967), p. 8.

control, and A, the punishment associated with conviction *per se.*[23] The total perceived punishment, if A is measured in terms of income to the offender, is $A + \bar{f}$.

We suppose that the social loss from punishment can be written $(gA + b\bar{f})$. In the case of fines, A involves no transfer from the offender to the public, whereas $\bar{f}$ does. We should, therefore, take $g = b + 1$ and interpret g as the social marginal utility of income to the offender (again abstracting from collection costs). In the case of imprisonment, we might suppose that b is considerably larger than g.

We now have a minimand

$$L(p, \bar{f}) = D(O) + C(O, p) + (gA + b\bar{f})pO$$

where we should remember that $O = O(p, A + \bar{f})$. We rewrite this as

$$L(p, \bar{f}) = D(O) + C(O, p) + b(A + \bar{f})pO + (g - b)ApO \qquad (6.6)$$

Examination of (6.6) shows us the effects of the introduction of A. Comparison of the first three terms of (6.6) with expression (6.1) shows that they represent the original problem with $A + \bar{f}$ substituted for f. If the fourth term in (6.6) were equal to zero and the problem embodied in (6.1) had a solution f^*, then the problem represented by (6.6) would have solution $\bar{f} = f^* - A$. From this point of view, the recognition that A should appear in the problem implies that the punishment should be correspondingly reduced.

The fourth term in (6.6) is decreasing or increasing in $\bar{f}$ as g is greater or less than b. Thus, the effect of the fourth term in (6.6) is in the direction of increasing optimum punishment if $g > b$, and of reducing it if $g < b$. A similar conclusion would follow if the term were interpreted as an addition to the C function. We can say, therefore, that, in the case of costly punishment, such as imprisonment, the recognition that loss from conviction *per se* should appear in the problem leads to lower recommendations for the appropriate punishment. There is a similar presumption in the case of fines, although here we cannot rule out the prospect that the effect of the last term in (6.6) might result in a net increase in punishment.

Similar conclusions emerge from a discussion of the effects of shifts in the parameter A on the first-order conditions describing the optimum $p, \bar{f}$.[24] It appears that one cannot rule out the case that, if g is high relative to b, the optimum punishment can increase with A.

A further consequence of the introduction of A is that one has to take care in the interpretation of empirical results concerning the magnitude of the elasticity of offences with respect to the level of punishment. Measured proportional variations in $\bar{f}$ are larger than the proportional variations in total punishment $A + \bar{f}$, and so we underestimate the elasticity with respect to *total*

[23] Since a very high proportion of those appearing in court are convicted, we do not separate the notions of conviction and court appearance.

[24] See the mathematical appendix to Becker (1968).

punishment. Thus, we cannot necessarily conclude from the emprical observation $\epsilon_p > \epsilon_{\bar{f}}$ that ϵ_p is larger than the elasticity with respect to total punishment and, hence, through risk-preference, that 'crime does not pay'.[25]

Under-reporting

We have to distinguish the recorded number of offences from the 'true' number. We denote the latter by O^* and retain O for the former. We write $O^* = kO$ where k is a measure of the degree of under-reporting. We also have to distinguish the recorded and 'true' clear-up rates p and p^*, where $p^* = p/k$, since $p^*O^* = pO$, the number of convictions. In the expression for L (see equation (6.1)), one would expect the damages from offences to depend on O^*, whereas the costs of apprehension would depend on O, p. It is unclear where O^* depends on p or on p^*, although there is little evidence in favour of the latter.[27]

The above modifications do not seriously alter the analysis and conclusions from the Becker model unless k depends on p (or p^*) or f directly, or through O (or O^*). Such a dependence is certainly possible if punishments are high, so that there might be a lack of willingness to report to the police.[28] Naturally, it is rather hard to know what, in general, are the main determinants of k.

The purpose of introducing k is to make the point that we must always be careful, when interpreting empirical work based on recorded O and p, to be aware of possible effects that are operating through the recording ratio k. We have discussed this problem at length in Carr-Hill and Stern (1973) and refer the reader there for details of identification problems that arise. We return to this point when we interpret some of our empirical results in Section III.

SOME CONCLUSIONS FROM THE THEORETICAL ANALYSIS

We began our discussion of Becker's model by pointing out that in one of the cases that he saw to be central, where the punishment is a fine, the optimisation problem, as posed, has no solution. The problem thus, is, misspecified, at least for this case. In our view, there are bound to be problems with any model that tries to explain current Western punishment systems in terms based essentially on weighing economic costs and benefits that are fairly narrowly defined. We elaborate this point below. Nevertheless, the economic calculus certainly plays a role in analyses of appropriate punishment and it is important that it be properly applied.

[25] See the beginning of section II of this paper and Becker (1968). Ehrlich (1973) has used risk-preference interpretations of his empirical work on United States data.

[26] This point is noted in Carr-Hill and Stern (1973). It has also been noted, at great length, by Brown and Reynolds (1973), who pointed out (effectively) that punishment generally includes confiscation of the proceeds of offences.

[27] See Willcock and Stokes (1968).

[28] Alternatively, k might depend negatively on p or p^*, because people want revenge or the return of stolen goods, and their enthusiasm to report depends on the likelihood of police 'success'.

We summarise first those arguments that accept the framework of the economic calculus but suggest that it has been misapplied. The points are limited to those cases where an optimum exists: the conditions where this is more likely were discussed in the third part of this section. The main complaint is that the analysis is based on first-best welfare economics, so that there is an implicit assumption of equal social marginal valuation of income. In the absence of lump-sum taxes, this assumption is unwarranted; and, if it is omitted, one of Becker's main conclusions – that fines should be independent of the circumstances of the individual – disappears. On the assumption of diminishing social marginal valuation of income, we were led to the conclusion that *ceteris paribus,* the poorer the offender the lower should be the fine.

There seems to be evidence that such a policy is often followed. For example, in Sweden many offences are punished by means of the day fine, which related the fine to the income of the offender.[29]

The second suggested modification to Becker's analysis was that the perceived loss from conviction *per se* be included. We saw, in general, that this would be a further argument for lower punishments.

Again, there are examples that indicate that such a sentencing policy is often followed. The general question is examined in Martin and Webster (1971).

We saw earlier that putting $b = 0$ in Becker's model led to the apparent conclusion that f should be indefinitely large. We turn now to the reasons why, in the real world, we do not choose the very high punishments that seem to follow from this approach when punishment is 'costless' (so that we concentrate attention on fines).

We shall argue that, although there are several 'economic' reasons for rejecting infinite punishments, these are not sufficiently strong to explain why small fines for relatively minor offences are not increased. It seems that we require the concept of retribution to understand current penal systems.

The first of the 'economic' reasons is the existence of a perceived cost of conviction, A. This will not, however, avert the solution $f = \infty$, because A is finite and $g > b = 0$ (see the previous subsection). Second, very large fines will force up the cost of punishment by increasing the finee's poverty and, therefore, his social marginal valuation of income. It seems doubtful that, in general, fines are pushed to the point where the resulting poverty of the finee is the overriding argument against further increases. Further, there are ways of increasing fines, whilst retaining differentials between offences, that would not increase the social cost of punishment very severely. For example, one might suggest that many fines, instead of being just one payment, be repeated for a few years after the event, thus increasing the fine without producing penury in any year. If, by the consequent deterrence, this decreases, the social loss L as modelled, it would be hard to produce an economic argument against it based on considerations that are embodied in the analysis up to this point.

A third argument for keeping down fines may be that, at very low levels of

[29] There may also be retributivist reasons for this: See Walker (1969), pp. 106–7.

offences, the net damage from the offences is negative. In other words, if penalties are high, offences are committed only by those whose personal benefit from committing the offence is very high and might outweigh, in the social calculus, the harm done to others. There are, doubtless, examples of beneficial offences: for example, one might argue that it is better that a speed limit be broken to take a severely injured person to hospital than that it be observed and the person die. It would be difficult to argue, however, that where fines are high enough the residual offences are, *on average,*[30] beneficial. One would have to be both a very strong believer in *homo economicus* and to argue that most personal 'gains' should enter the social welfare function. In other words, one would need to argue that individuals carried out acts where expected benefits exceeded expected costs, and that their expected benefits should be included in the social calculus. In the case of the expected benefit involved in, say, deciding to commit an assault, few would accept this. There may, however, be specific types of offences for which this type of argument is appropriate: for example, parking offences.

Fourth, one might argue that the social loss from fines is negative because government revenue is very valuable, and that they should not be pushed so far that this revenue begins to drop off severely. This is basically the motivation for the model of Kolm (1973) in his discussion of income tax evasion. We should guess that this argument would be unconvincing to many if it were put a little more openly, as follows: 'We should not raise fines from current levels because offences would drop off so sharply that we should lose fine revenue.' One could think of examples of revenue-raising opportunities that are not accepted.

The fifth argument concerns the effect on offences of the structure of relative penalties. If the fine for a certain offence is high, an offender might be more likely to commit other, and perhaps more serious, offences, either instead or in order to limit the probability of being apprehended. This argument would not be significant in the absence of upper limits to punishment, since differentials could be maintained while increasing all punishments. It assumes significance when there is an upper limit to penalties. It is difficult to judge the quantitative importance of this argument. We should suggest, however, that the effect on *other* offence levels of, say, doubling the fines for minor acts of vandalism might be small.

A sixth, and related, point is that the level of punishment might enter the C (cost of apprehension) function directly, in the sense that individuals have a greater incentive to take evasive action, and to hire better lawyers if caught, if penalties are high.[31] We should suggest that, for minor offences, the component (A) of punishment representing the perceived cost of court appearance may be

[30] We are averaging across *types* of offence that are being committed on the margin.

[31] Becker (1968), p. 184, refers to the possibility that punishment levels may enter C through juries being unwilling to convict if punishment levels are set very high. We dismiss this point in more detail in the second part of section IV.

sufficiently high for the effect of changes in the punishment meted out in court ($\bar{f}$) on evasive action to be small.

Our seventh consideration is an argument that we include here because some might describe it as economic, although we should prefer to call it retributive. This is any cost that is associated with punishing the innocent. On a utilitarian basis, one might argue that the only cost associated is that concerned with the transfer, and that this has already been included in the social loss function. We feel, therefore, that the argument should be classified as retributive, since it is based on the notion that we should punish *only* those who have done wrong. As an explanation of the feeling that there is a cost to punishing the innocent, one might invoke, irresponse, a principle of 'horizontal equity' that says that individuals of like situation should be treated similarly. Innocent individuals should therefore be treated alike and violations of this principle should impose costs. This seems very close to the retributive position, since one has to argue that the overriding sense in which people are alike is in whether they are innocent or guilty. Otherwise, one would not be able to argue against fining the *unique* (say), richest person in the economy for an offence that he did not commit. Further, one might argue that a principle of horizontal equity refers to *ex ante* rather than *ex post* positions, so that it has not been violated if each innocent person is equally likely of being found guilty of an offence.

Leaving aside, however, the question of whether to classify the argument as economic or retributive, it does not seem powerful enough to explain why fines for minor offences are not raised, since, at low levels of punishment, it is the fact of convicting the innocent that is found offensive, rather than precise punishment levels. This is not to deny its possible importance when discussing capital punishment, for example. The possibility of punishing the innocent is likely to affect jury behaviour too, and we return to this point in the second part of Section IV.

The possibility of punishing the innocent raises an issue relevant to the behavioural specification of the Becker model. Under an expected utility model, the decision whether to commit an offence would depend on the difference between the expected utility of being punished, if innocent, and the expected utility of being punished, if guilty. This raises some interesting questions – for example, the granting of extra powers to the police in certain situations may increase offences, unless the probability of punishing the guilty is increased sufficiently to compensate for the increased probability of punishing the innocent.[32]

The distinction between *ex ante* and *ex post* introduces the eighth argument. Up to now, our concentration has been on *ex post* phenomena (in the sense that our loss function evaluates what has happened in the society) rather than on the evaluation *ex ante* of various outcomes with different probabilities. It seems to us that a mixture of the two approaches is needed. The fear of being assaulted and the occurrence of an assault are both real losses to an

[32] See Harris (1970) for a discussion of other problems related to the increase of police powers.

individual. One can argue that, if individuals perceive probabilities correctly, the utilitarian sum *ex post* and expected utility *ex ante* are the same, so that a concern with either or both yields the same policy. However, if individuals do not perceive probabilities correctly, or if some fears or expectations are deemed to enter the social loss function while others are not, then a concern with *ex ante* as well as *ex post* welfare will require a modification to our social loss function. We briefly return to this point in the fourth part of Section IV. Its relevance here to the social loss from punishment is the *ex ante* cost associated with the fear of punishment from the point of view of either the offender or the innocent.[33] Given an estimate of the sentencers' and legislators' perception of an innocent individual's fear of being mistakenly punished, and a guess at their evaluation of the loss due to the generation of fear in offenders, we suppose again that this does not explain why, in fact, fines for minor offences are not raised substantially. We have seen that deterrence theories often fail to provide a reason for the level of the fine that is viewed as just. The remaining argument would appear to be that the punishment is deemed to be the appropriate level of retribution.

Although humanitarian principles could set a limit on the levels of punishment to be used they do not provide an argument why low fines should not be raised.

This is not the place for a lengthy discussion of the appropriate place of retribution in sentencing systems. We have merely come to the conclusion that it does play an important role in actual sentencing systems. The reader can doubtless think of situations, often viewed as just, which seem to require retributive arguments for explanation. One example would be the notion of equality of punishment for similar offences. If individuals committing the same offence have different preferences or inclinations, the advocate of the social calculus would have to argue for different treatment. To many people this would often appear unjust.[34]

The reader is referred, for further discussion of retributionism, utilitarianism and reductivism in punishment, to Hart (1968) and Walker (1969). Reductivism refers to a concern to reduce offences at as little cost as possible. This is advocated by Walker, although he distinguishes it from utilitarianism. It is clear, however, that the reductivist and utilitarian approaches (which include the Becker approach if utilitarianism is interpreted widely) are close.

It would be possible to incorporate retributive considerations in a policy model. If retribution is regarded as a reasonable social objective, we can include it in the term measuring the net social cost of punishment. For example, bf, the social cost for a punishment f, might be replaced by a function such as $S(f)$, which is illustrated in Figure 6.1. In the case where the punishment *per se* is seen to be costless, the minimum would occur at the f deemed to be the

[33] Julian le Grand has made this point to us.

[34] Not least the offender who received the heavier punishment. See the second part of Section IV.

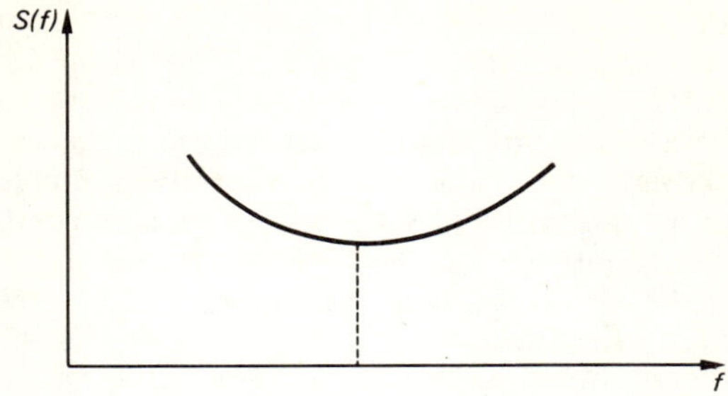

Fig. 6.1

appropriate retribution for the offence. If the punishment *per se* had a cost (positive or negative), this would have to be added to the $S(f)$ of Fig. 6.1.

Alternatively, one might argue that retribution is not an appropriate social objective, but that attitudes are such that it has to be acknowledged in constraints on policy. For example, juries may be unlikely to convict if they feel that the punishment is unjust. The perception of the injustice of punishment might so embitter those who are punished in this way that they become more likely to offend again.

The incorporation of such considerations into policy models is a subject for further research and we return to it briefly in Section IV. Many of the considerations have been discussed by penologists. A formal analysis of the possible solutions to systems incorporating different aims of a penal system would be a useful addition to these discussions. Meanwhile, however, we should be suspicious of attempts, such as Becker's, to explain existing systems purely in terms of a social cost–benefit calculus.

III. THE ESTIMATION OF A SIMULTANEOUS EQUATIONS MODEL OF THE SUPPLY AND CONTROL OF RECORDED OFFENCES IN ENGLAND AND WALES IN 1971

DATA, MODEL AND ESTIMATION TECHNIQUE

In this section we report on the continuation of the econometric work described in Carr-Hill and Stern (1973), and some of the arguments mentioned here are elaborated there. That work was on a cross-section of police districts for England and Wales in 1961 and 1966. As these were census and sample-census years, data were available on variables such as the age composition of the population. 1971 was another census year, so allowing us to repeat the exercise. The main way in which the data base for 1971 differed from that for the other two years was in the reduction, through amalgamation, in the number of police districts. Whereas we could use data on 110 districts in 1966, we had only 41 observations in 1971. Further, in 1961 and 1966 we could separate urban areas from rural areas and still retain enough observations on urban areas (66) for estimation purposes. We saw, for the 1961 and 1966 data, that urban and rural areas are better treated separately; so the inability to perform a similar split in 1971 is a second reason to expect our 'fits' on the 1971 data to be a little worse. Nevertheless, we did find that certain important features that occurred in our results for 1961 and 1966 reappeared in the 1971 analysis.

Our main data sources (see Table 6.3) were as follows: published 1971 census data (denoted 'Census' in Table 6.3), the Home Office publication *Supplementary Statistics Relating to Crime and Criminal Proceedings* for 1971 (*Supp. Stats.*) and the publication *Police Force Statistics* for 1971–2 (*PFS*) put out by the local-authority treasurers.

TABLE 6.3

INCLUDED EXOGENOUS VARIABLES IN MODEL FOR 1966 AND 1971, URBAN AND RURAL POOLED

	Variable	*Definition*	*Source*[a]
Equation 1	*F*	The proportion of convicted offenders[b] given custodial treatment	*Supp. Stats.*
	A	Proportion of young (15–24) males in population	Census
	S	Proportion of population that is working class (specifically, socio-economic groups 7, 10, 11, 15)[c]	Census
	% urban	Proportion of the area of the police district that is urbanised	*PFS*
	E	Total police expenditure per officer	*PFS*
Equation 2	*A*	See equation 1	
	S	See equation 1	
	N	Population	*PFS*
	E	See equation 1	
	V	Proportion of offences that are violent[b]	*Supp. Stats.*
	% urban	See equation 1	
Equation 3	*M*	Proportion of population that is middle class (specifically, socio-economic groups 5, 6, 8, 9, 12, 14)[c]	Census
	V	See equation 2	
	% urban	See equation 1	

[a] Sources are defined in the first part of section III.

[b] Custodial treatment and violent offences are defined in a data appendix available from the authors. We should have liked to incorporate in *F* data on the length of sentences, but the available data proved inadequate.

[c] At the time of writing (Jan 1974), the 1971 census data on socio-economic groups are unpublished. We have therefore used the data on 1966. The coefficient of the correlation between the variables log *S* for 1966 and for 1961 was 0·927, and that between the variables log *M* for 1966 and for 1961 was 0·869. The observations were for 110 local authority districts (covering – almost – the whole of England and Wales). It can therefore be concluded that the social class measures are fairly stable over time. The model will be re-estimated as soon as the 1971 social class data are published.

Notes

1. The Endogenous variables used were as follows.

Y All indictable offences per head of population (source: *Supp. Stats.*).

P Clear-up rate: proportion of crimes deemed to have been solved (defined in data appendix available from authors). This information is unpublished and was kindly made available by the Home Office.

C Number of policemen per capita (source: *PFS*).

2. The natural logarithms of the above variables were used in the estimation, and these logarithms are denoted by the corresponding lower-case letters (except % urban, which was logged for estimation but has not been allocated an upper-case letter).

3. The data cover all the police districts in England and Wales except for the Metropolitan Police District (MPD) and some adjacent authorities. The MPD and these authorities were omitted because the overlap with several local authorities made census data difficult to ascribe.

We shall now describe in brief the model we estimated. We hope that most readers will, *prima facie,* view as reasonable the variables included in the model. The economic and criminological justification for their inclusion is given in Carr-Hill and Stern (1970 and 1973) and is also motivated by the experience of the results for 1961 and 1966.

The first equation is intended to 'explain' recorded offences per capita and is an extension of the offence function described in section II above. The number of offences was the total of all indictable offences in the area.[35] We included variables intended to measure the probability of apprehension and the severity of punishment. The precise measures used and the notation adopted are given in Table 6.3. Further variables that might occur naturally to a deterrence theorist and that were included in the first equation are the number of policemen per capita and a measure of the equipment available to each officer. Since different groups are often asserted to be differentially prone to offending, we included, in addition, social indicators intended to capture in an appropriate manner the class and age structure of the population (see Table 6.3). The final variable in the first equation is the proportion of the area that is urbanised (there were 10 of the 41 observations for which this proportion was 100 per cent).

The second equation is intended to model the determination of the proportion of offences solved. Following section II, we include the number of policemen per capita, the number of offences, and the expenditure per officer. We also use a measure of crime-mix based on violent offences, since in these cases the offender is often easier to identify. The age and social-class indicators of the first equation were also included, since there may be differential immunity among groups. The population of the area was included as an attempt to capture scale effects, as was, finally, the proportion of the area urbanised.

The third equation models the determination of the number of policemen per capita. This process is influenced by central allocation, local pressures and

[35] Indictable offences are those deemed to be serious enough to warrant the possibility of trial by jury.

demands, and recruitment. The centre[36] looks at the number of offences per capita, clear-up rates, and the proportion of the area urbanised, and therefore these variables were included. The proportion of offences that are violent and the proportion of the population that is middle class were included as an attempt to capture local pressures for 'law and order'.[37]

We should emphasise that the model is one that deals with *recorded* offences. This naturally, is, all that published data can accommodate. We should always be aware that some of the variables in the first equation may be influencing the proportion of offences that enter the record book, as well as the 'actual' number of offences committed. The problems associated with this difficulty have been noted in section II above and are discussed at length in Carr-Hill and Stern (1973). We refer the reader to this earlier paper for details, and in discussing results will use interpretations involving the difference between recorded and actual offences.

The results from estimating the model that is described above and specified in Table 6.3 are presented in Table 6.4(a) under the heading '1971 Urban and Rural Pooled'. The estimation procedure was the full-information maximum likelihood option (FIML) on the SIMUL 7 programme developed at the LSE by Cliff Wymer and kindly made available by him.[38] We made the assumption that the errors were cross-sectionally independent (as between police districts) and multivariate normal across the three equations. Alternative interpretations of the FIML estimator are available if one wishes to drop the normality assumption.[39]

We began by estimating this 'large' model in order to make direct comparisons with the previous years. Just as in the models for 1961 and 1966, we went on to look for a model that produced more satisfactory results for the particular year. This was conducted by excluding insignificant variables from equations.

There was no rigid criterion, but our guidelines were the significance levels of the coefficients and the chi-square value of the log-likelihood ratio. This latter value is a measure of the amount by which the maximum likelihood increases when all the overidentifying restrictions are taken off.[40] By placing emphasis on this, we are therefore stressing a measure of how well the model is specified. The results of this search are reported in Table 6.4(b) under the heading '1971 Urban and Rural Pooled Restricted'.

The derived reduced form from the model of Table 6.4(b) is presented in Table 6.6. Results from 1966 are presented in Table 6.5 for comparative pur-

[36] This statement is based on discussions with the Home Office.

[37] All the variables described might also influence recruitment.

[38] The programme was run on the Oxford University 1906 computer. It was adapted for the 1906 by Jerry Hausman, and David Deans carried out the programming for our date. See footnote 1 above and the first footnote of Carr-Hill and Stern (1973).

[39] See Malinvaud (1970), chapter 16.

[40] That the distribution of the particular statistic is asymptotically chi-square is demonstrated in various textbooks on multivariate analysis.

TABLE 6.4(a)

1971 URBAN AND RURAL POOLED

Variable to be explained	*Explanatory variables*								
	p	*c*	*f*	*a*	*s*	*%urban*	*e*	*const.*	
y	–0·91	+0·71	–0·20	+0·12	+0·25	+0·07	+0·05	+5·85	
	(0·89)	(0·47)	(0·16)	(0·32)	(0·22)	(0·04)	(0·65)	(10·60)	
	1·02	1·52	1·27	0·38	1·08	1·61	0·07	0·55	
	y	*c*	*a*	*s*	*n*	*e*	*v*	*%urban*	*const.*
p	–0·56	+1·14	+0·03	–0·03	+0·01	+0·12	+0·39	–0·03	+7·74
	(0·52)	(1·49)	(0·20)	(0·18)	(0·04)	(0·76)	(0·42)	(0·05)	(4·52)
	1·07	0·76	0·15	0·16	0·16	0·16	0·92	0·51	1·71
	y	*p*	*m*	*v*	*%urban*	*const.*			
c	+0·56	+1·12	+0·07	–0·36	+0·02	9·91			
	(0·25)	(0·55)	(0·41)	(0·18)	(0·05)	(5·32)			
	2·26	2·04	0·18	2·04	0·37	1·86			

					Variance	
Covariance matrix of residuals	0·032			*y*	0·106	*Chi-square value of log-likelihood ratio:* 1·276 with 4 degrees of freedom
	0·019	0·020		*p*	0·017	
	–0·020	–0·020	0·020	*c*	0.032	

Notes

1. See Table 6.3 for definition of variables. The logarithmic form of all variables was used.
2. The number in brackets below a coefficient is the asymptotic standard error. Below this is the *T* value.
3. Chi-square values discussed in text.
4. Programme: FIML option on SIMUL 7 run on Oxford University ICL 1906A computer.
5. The constant terms are affected by the scaling of variables. The scalings for 6.4 (a) and (b) are identical.

poses. The models used are similar to those of Table 6.4, and the results are taken from Carr-Hill and Stern (1973).

THE RESULTS

We base our discussion on the model for 1971 of Table 6.4(b) and on the comparison of this with the model for 1966 of Table 6.5(b). We note that significance levels are lower in 1971 than in 1966. We presume that this is largely due to the lower number of observations (41 compared with 110). Thus, for 1971 we accept coefficients with asymptotic *T* values of above unity as being

TABLE 6.4(b)

1971 URBAN AND RURAL POOLED RESTRICTED

Variable to be explained	*Explanatory variables*						
	p	*c*	*f*	*a*	*s*	*%urban*	*const.*
y	−1·05	+0·64	−0·21	+0·12	+0·26	+0·07	+7·02
	(0·54)	(0·38)	(0·16)	(0·30)	(0·20)	(0·04)	(3·79)
	1·93	1·66	1·29	0·42	1·27	1·64	1·85
	y	*c*	*n*	*e*	*v*	*%urban*	*const.*
p	−0·51	+0·98	0·00	+0·10	+0·35	−0·02	+7·71
	(0·43)	(0·95)	(0·02)	(0·54)	(0·25)	(0·04)	(3·42)
	1·19	1·03	0·18	0·18	1·43	1·58	2·25
	y	*p*	*m*	*v*	*%urban*	*const.*	
c	+0·56	+1·23	+0·07	−0·38	+0·02	−10·70	
	(0·25)	(0·63)	(0·37)	(0·19)	(0·05)	(5·70)	
	2·22	1·95	0·20	2·02	0·44	1·88	

Covariance matrix of residuals					*Variance*	*Chi-square value of log-likelihood ratio:*
	0·034			*y*	0·106	
	0·018	0·017		*p*	0·017	
	−0·021	−0·019	0·022	*c*	0·032	2·314 with 7 d.o.f.

Notes: As for Table 6.4(a).

significantly different from zero and, therefore, qualifying for discussion.[41] For the 1966 results we adopt the more stringent requirement of asymptotic *T* values above 2. The chi-square values of the log-likelihood ratio, goodness-of-fit and variance–covariance matrix of residuals are discussed in the next subsection.

In the offence equation for 1971 we again find that variables stressed as important in deterrence theories – the probability of detection *p* and the severity of punishment *f* – appear as important with the coefficient appropriately signed. The responsiveness to the probability of being caught is again a good deal higher than that to the severity of punishment. We should emphasise, however, a point noted earlier (section II): that, to the extent that there is a fixed element in a punishment (for instance, the perceived cost of court appearance *per se*), we underestimate the responsiveness of offences to perceived severity of punishment. For 1971, the estimated elasticity of *O* with respect to *p* is much higher[42] than in previous years, and it seems unlikely that

[41] The confidence with which claims are made is therefore correspondingly reduced.

[42] The general perception of *p* may have improved, so reducing downward bias from 'errors in variables'.

TABLE 6.5(a)

1966 URBAN AND RURAL POOLED

Variable to be explained	*Explanatory variables*								
	p	*c*	*f*	*a*	*s*	*%urban*	*e*	*const.*	
y	–0·58	+0·76	–0·17	+0·62	+0·11	+0·45	+0·41	–1·60	
	(0·24)	(0·22)	(0·09)	(0·15)	(0·13)	(0·09)	(0·14)	(2·29)	
	2·45	3·46	1·87	4·27	0·87	4·95	2·84	0·70	
	y	*c*	*a*	*s*	*n*	*e*	*v*	*%urban*	*const.*
p	–0·26)	–1·28	+0·11	+0·15	–0·18	+0·08	–0·09	+0·50	–12·25
	(0·53)	(1·53)	(0·38)	(0·20)	(0·13)	(0·28)	(0·27)	(0·41)	(12·02)
	0·49	0·75	0·29	0·75	1·39	0·29	0·36	1·21	1·02
	y	*p*	*m*	*v*	*%urban*	*const.*			
c	–0·01	+1·24	–0·91	–0·45	+0·41	–3·76			
	(0·09)	(0·41)	(0·42)	(0·12)	(0·11)	(2·33)			
	0·12	3·03	2·11	3·83	3·80	1·61			

Covariance matrix of residuals					*Variance*	*Chi-square value of log-likelihood ratio:*
	0·039			*y*	0·175	15·661 with 4 d.o.f.
	0·010	0·049		*p*	0·028	
	–0·004	0·001	0·055	*c*	0·042	

Notes: See notes to Table 6.4(a). See also Carr-Hill and Stern (1973), tables 2 (i) and A (iv).

underestimation of the elasticity with respect to *f* could be sufficiently large to close the gap between the two elasticities.

For both 1971 and 1966, the first equation gives rise to the phenomenon that the more police there are the more offences there are, and the coefficients in the two years are of similar magnitude. We have suggested in our 1973 paper that such a positive relation has to be explained through more police recording more offences, since it seems unlikely that many more offences actually do occur. This is an illustration of the importance of seeing the model as one of behaviour of the population *together with* the interaction of this behaviour with the practices of the institutions of social control. We return to this point in section IV, in our discussion of the use of crime figures.

By 1971, the proportion of young males (aged 15–24) has ceased to be a significant determinant of the level of offences (after appearing as significant and positive in 1966 and insignificant in 1961). If young males do, *in fact,* commit more offences than average, then the absence of significance in the first equation implies that *fewer* than average of these offences are recorded. This may be due to the type or circumstance of the offence committed or to the differential recording practices of the police. If the proneness-to-offend

TABLE 6.5(b)

1966 URBAN AND RURAL POOLED RESTRICTED

Variable to be explained	*Explanatory variables*							
	p	*c*	*f*	*a*	*s*	*%urban*	*e*	*const.*
y	−0·59	+0·74	−0·17	+0·63	+0·11	+0·45	+0·40	−1·64
	(0·24)	(0·22)	(0·09)	(0·15)	(0·13)	(0·09)	(0·14)	(2·28)
	2·50	3·41	1·86	4·29	0·88	4·92	2·81	0·72
	c	*n*	*%urban*	*const.*				
p	−1·15	−0·16	+0·31	−8·82				
	(0·34)	(0·04)	(0·11)	(2·62)				
	3·39	4·31	2·76	3·37				
	p	*m*	*v*	*%urban*	*const.*			
c	+1·22	−0·86	−0·44	+0·40	−3·98			
	(0·41)	(0·39)	(0·11)	(0·08)	(2·18)			
	2·98	2·23	3·88	5·22	1·82			

Covariance matrix of residuals				*Variance*		*Chi-square value of log-likelihood ratio:*
	0·039			*y*	0·175	
	0·001	0·040		*p*	0·028	
	−0·005	−0·007	0·053	*c*	0·042	17·057 with 10 d.o.f.

Notes: As for Table 6.5(a).

was similar in 1971 to 1966, then the change in the estimated equation must have been due to recording phenomena. The result illustrates that we must be rather careful with the type of argument that, starting from an observation that young males appear prominently amongst convicted offenders, would proceed to the conclusion that areas with relatively many young males will have relatively high crime rates.

We do not wish to argue that the effect of the social class indicator has changed very much, since in our 1966 urban results the coefficient is fairly close to the 1971 figure (the 1966 urban figure being +0·31 with a *T* value of 1·97; see Table 2(i) in Carr-Hill and Stern (1973)). The proportion of the area urbanised is again significant, although the importance has declined. The reason may be that, as a result of the amalgamations, it now distinguishes less sharply between urban and rural areas: whereas in 1966 the urban proportion was 100 per cent for 66 out of 110 districts, in 1971 it was 100 per cent for 10 out of 41.

The coefficient of expenditure per policeman is now insignificant, as it was in 1961.[43]

[43] Between 1961 and 1966 there was an increased emphasis on efficiency within a well established geographical structure. Between 1966 and 1971 there was a major geographical reorganisation, which may have had its own dysfunctions.

The changes in the second equation, modelling the determination of the clear-up rate are more substantial. We now have, as in the Becker model, a positive relationship between the number of policemen per capita and the clear-up rate, and a negative relation between offences and the clear-up rate. The positive effect of c on p may be due, simply, to more minor offences being reported and cleared-up simultaneously. It does indicate, however, that the 'weeding-out' effect seems to have diminished in importance. We suggested, for 1966, when discussing the negative c coefficient, that more police in an area might result in a diversion to another area of offences that are easily cleared up, so diminishing the clear-up rate; i.e. these easily solved offences are weeded out. The larger police districts may have diminished the scope for such diversion.

The p equation does now seem to be a more direct model of the process of crime-solving than it was before. This may be due to increasing concern with analysis and allocation of police activities.

The positive effect of the number of violent offences reappears (after being significant in 1961 and disappearing in 1966). The proportion of the area urbanised now plays no role, perhaps for the reason described in the discussion of the first equation.

The behaviour of the size variable n is interesting. We noted diminishing returns to scale in crime-solving in both 1961 and 1966, but with the reorganisation of the police districts this phenomenon seems to have disappeared. There would seem to be several possible explanations. First, mapping p as a function of size of police district, holding other variables constant, might produce graphs as in Figure 6.2(a) and (b). If the sizes of police districts in 1966 were clustered round the points 1966 marked on the figures, and similarly for 1971, we should

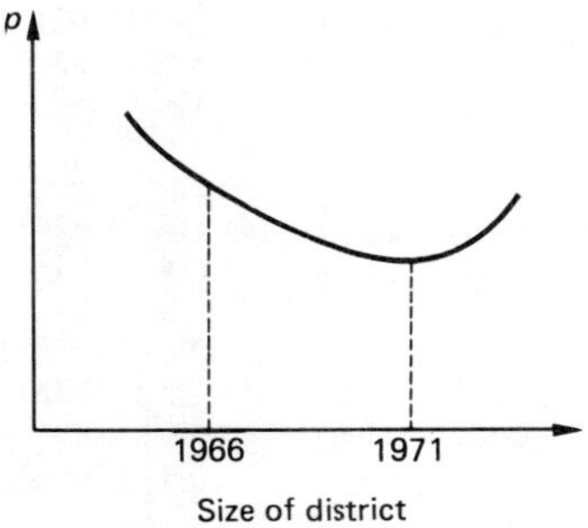

Fig. 6.2(a)

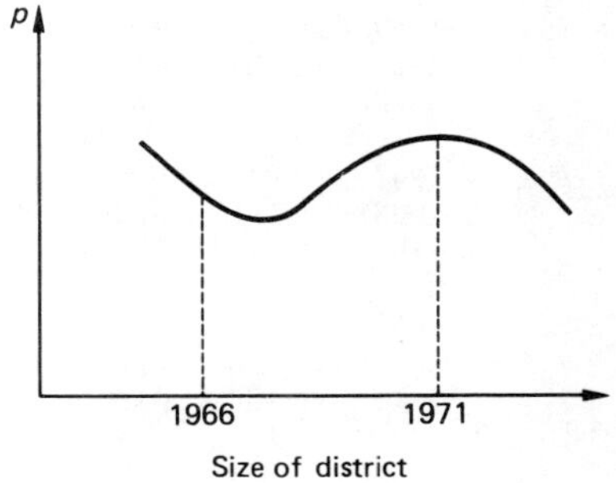

Fig. 6.2(b)

obtain estimates for the two years as quoted. The graph in Fig. 6.2(a) suggests that the new size of district may represent a local minimum for efficiency rather than a local maximum. Presumably the authorities feel confident that a graph as in Fig. 6.2(b) is more likely. Naturally, any shift of the curve between the years could be superimposed on a similar diagram.

An alternative explanation could be that the size of district was, in 1961 and 1966, capturing effects on clear-up rates due to the size of cities. It may be that larger cities, with, for example, greater anonymity, present more severe detection problems.[44] With less than a quarter of the districts fully urbanised in 1971, the population of the district would cease to play this role.

The third equation in 1971 may again represent an effect of increasing formality, and care in allocation, in police practices. The number of police now increases with the number of offences where such an effect was not observed in 1961 and 1966. Recruitment, however, may still be an important problem, as it appears to be the explanation of the positive effect of p and the negative effect of v on the number of offences. Both a high clear-up rate and a low level of violent offences in an area presumably make it more attractive to be a policeman.

VARIANCE–COVARIANCE MATRIX OF RESIDUALS AND TESTS OF MODEL SPECIFICATION

We focus our discussion of the residuals on the matrices of Table 6.4(b) and Table 6.6. We use as an indication of the goodness-of-fit of each equation the ratio of residual variance to total variance in the derived reduced form (Table

TABLE 6.6

1971 URBAN AND RURAL POOLED RESTRICTED: DERIVED REDUCED FORM

Endogenous variables	*Exogenous variables*								
	f	*a*	*s*	*%urban*	*n*	*v*	*m*	*e*	*const.*
y	–0·36	+0·21	0·44	0·15	0·01	–0·47	0·24	0·21	–5·69
	(0·25)	(0·48)	(0·30)	(0·04)	(0·02)	(0·18)	(0·55)	(6·44)	(6·93)
	1·45	0·44	1·44	3·81	0·44	2·54	0·43	0·49	0·82
p	0·07	–0·04	–0·09	–0·02	–0·02	0·21	–0·40	–0·52	14·62
	(0·08)	(0·11)	(0·10)	(0·02)	(0·03)	(0·09)	(0·40)	(0·24)	(3·89)
	0·89	0·41	0·90	1·10	0·89	2·28	1·00	2·16	3·76
c	–0·11	0·07	0·14	0·08	–0·02	–0·38	–0·28	–0·52	4·05
	(0·10)	(0·16)	(0·12)	(0·02)	(0·03)	(0·10)	(0·42)	(0·25)	(4·12)
	1·14	0·43	1·15	3·25	0·88	3·85	0·66	2·06	0·98

Covariance matrix of residuals					*Variance*
	0·041			*y*	0·106
	–0·004	0·007		*p*	0·017
	0·011	–0·003	0·010	*c*	0·032

Notes: See Table 6.5.

[44] There may also be different reporting effects on the number of offences.

6.6); for 1971 this was 39, 41 and 31 per cent for *y, p* and *c*, respectively, as compared with the 1966 urban results of 29, 61 and 80 per cent (see Carr-Hill and Stern, 1973, section 4.3). The increase in explained variance for *p* and *c* is striking and confirms our view, formed from an examination of the coefficients, that the rationalisation of police practices is manifesting itself in the statistics.

The variance–covariance matrix in the structure (Table 6.4 b) is of interest in understanding the behavioural and institutional relations underlying the model. We now have residual variance in the *p* equation exactly equal to the observed variance, whereas in 1966 the residual variance was the larger. The (technical) reason that the observed variance of *p* in 1971 is no larger than the 'noise' element is as follows. Consider the system effects of a positive disturbance in *p*. This works to decrease *y* through the negative first-equation coefficient of *p*, but to increase *y* through the correlation of the first- and second-equation disturbances. It works to increase *c* through the positive third-equation coefficient of *p*, but to decrease *c* through the negative correlation of the second- and third- equation disturbances. The effects on *y, c* through the coefficients in the first and third equations tend to amplify the original disturbances on *p* when fed back into the second equation. The effects through the cross-equation correlation of disturbances tend to dampen the original disturbance on *p*. These latter effects seem to dominate, since, *after* the variation produced by the exogenous variables is added to the effects already discussed, the observed variance is no greater than the estimated variance of the 'noise' element.

It is interesting to note that the change in sign of the *c* coefficient in the *p* equation between 1966 and 1971 has occurred together with the appearance, in 1971, of an important negative correlation between the residuals of the second and third equations (–0·88). Again, one explanation might lie in Chief Constable behaviour. A Chief Constable with fewer policemen than is normal will show fewer clear-ups through the direct effect of *c* in the *p* equation. He may therefore have an incentive to influence the measured clear-up rate so that it is higher than it would otherwise be.[45]

We now turn to the chi-square values of the log-likelihood ratio for the models of Tables 6.4(a) and (b). The chi-square value shown represents a test of the overidentifying restrictions in that it is a measure of the amount that the likelihood increases when the overidentifying restrictions are relaxed, so that, loosely, low values represent 'good' models. The null hypothesis that the overidentifying restrictions are correct is accepted at the 80 per cent level for the model of Table 6.4(a) – the 1971 'full' model – and at the 90 per cent level for the model of Table 6.4(b) – 1971 restricted. The test of the model of Table 6.4(b) against that of 6.4(a) gives a chi-square value of 2·314 – 1·276 =

[45] A similar argument explained the 1966 results reported in Carr-Hill and Stern (1973). There was a positive correlation between second- and third-equation errors in 1966 urban results (see Table 2 (i) in the paper cited). A larger number of policemen (positive disturbance in third equation) implied fewer clear-ups (negative *c* coefficient in *p* equation) and, hence, an incentive to influence clear-ups in a positive direction.

1·038 with three degrees of freedom; i.e. the null hypothesis that the extra restrictions – in Table 6.4(b) over Table 6.4(a) – are correct is accepted at the 70 per cent level.

The chi-square values of the test of the overidentifying restrictions lead to more comfortable acceptance of these restrictions than do comparable tests for 1961 and 1966 (see Carr-Hill and Stern, 1973).

IV. THE NOTION OF OUTPUT

INTRODUCTION

We want now to draw out some implications of these models for the measurement of output of social control policies. We shall make three main points: that the introduction of retribution as an apparently essential component in reasonable models of current penal policy implies a reconsideration of Becker's 'social loss function'; that the introduction of the differences between actual and formal punishment and between actual and recorded offences make it very difficult to make confident deductions about the effects of any social control policy; and that the correct concern of social policy in this area should be personal safety, both objectively and subjectively defined, rather than control of (legally defined) crime *per se.*

RETRIBUTION AND THE 'SOCIAL LOSS FUNCTION'

The argument in section II indicates that 'pure' economic cost–benefit arguments based on the standard type of social welfare function cannot account for our present penal policies. Nor can they account for our apparent sense of injustice at unequal treatment before the law. We must therefore discuss how retribution might be included in a model of social policy toward crime. It should be emphasised that such a discussion should be distinguished from an attempt to justify retribution as a social goal.

We have to distinguish several different ways[46] in which retributivist considerations might be important.

(a) *As a general justifying aim of punishment.* In unsophisticated form this means that the penal system is designed to ensure that offenders atone by suffering for their offence. Although a utilitarian can appeal to the beneficial consequences in terms of the reduction of crime attained through punishment, he cannot easily account for our predilection for punishing only the guilty.[47] This more limited form of retribution is called 'distributive retribution' and

[46] Most of these distinctions are derived from Hart (1968), as are the names.

[47] It is not enough to say that the indirect utility in maintaining respect for the law by not punishing the innocent is always greater than the utility to be derived from punishing the innocent: as a *principle* this is beyond utilitarian considerations, and empirically it may not always be true!

can be absorbed into our social loss function relatively simply by increasing the social cost of punishment, *b*, on the grounds that a higher number or severity of punishments implies a greater likelihood or cost of punishing the innocent.[48]

We argued towards the end of section II that an appeal to a 'principle of horizontal equity', in the attachment of a cost to punishing the innocent, would reduce to the notion of distributive retribution.

(b) *In our system of fixing penalties.* There are two common assumptions about the 'appropriate' penalties that should be imposed on an offender: consistency, i.e. that similar offences should be similarly penalised; and harm, i.e. that the severity of the sentence should be related to the harm done by the offence, whether or not the incidence of such offences is thereby reduced. The utilitarian approach would arrange the penalties with a view to reducing 'appropriately' the frequency of types of offences prohibited by the criminal law. This would entail, for some very frequent but minor offences, a severity of punishment that would be generally unacceptable.[49] The second of these considerations could be captured by adding to the social loss function a further term of the type shown in Fig. 6.1. The first would require the social loss function to contain an element that was an increasing function of a measure of the spread of punishments for a particular offence. Measures of inequality are discussed in Atkinson (1970).

(c) *Concern with those 'get away'.* Another facet of concern with equal treatment before the law is anger with those who 'get away' with an illegal act. This would imply that *p* be an argument of the social loss function as an 'output' in its own right, i.e. in addition to the effect through offences, costs of apprehension and punishment costs. This function might increase in *p* for very low levels of *p* (corresponding to a view that those few who were caught were unlucky) but would be a decreasing function thereafter. One might also wish to include the incomes of those who 'escape', since the anger is often the greater when there is a suspicion that the immunity has been bought in some way.

One might argue that some 'principle of horizontal equity' underlies the feeling discussed (i.e. all the guilty should be treated equally), but, again, this is confused by the doubt as to whether the principle applies *ex ante* or *ex post.* It might be enough to satisfy the principle if everyone had an equal chance of getting away.

(d) *Retribution elsewhere in the model.* One need not discuss retribution in the model solely in terms of the minimand. It may be important to recognise retributivist feelings in participants in the system. For example, juries may be reluctant to convict if they feel that prospect penalties are likely to be unjust. It is natural to suppose that the measure of reasonable doubt used by a jury is a function (however vague) of previous convictions of the innocent. Alterna-

[48] See Harris (1970).

[49] However measurable, we can see no justification (not until the oil crisis gets worse, anyway) for severely punishing an incorrigible bicycle borrower.

tively, an individual may be so embittered by treatment that he regards as unjust that he becomes more likely to offend than he would be were the punishment been less severe. The former consideration would imply that the cost of obtaining convictions might increase with f for high levels of f. The second would give offences increasing in f over a certain range.

MISMEASUREMENT OF OFFENCES AND PUNISHMENTS

Offences

The work described in section III shows that, in order to understand the recorded statistics of crime and social control, we must consider the processes, both formal and informal, that separate the recording of an offence (which, itself, is not a guarantee that the act referred to is illegal) from the commission of an act that, had it been reported, would probably have been recorded.[50] In particular, the positive coefficients obtained for C and O in the first and third equations, respectively, lead us to suggest that it is possible for an increased size of police force to produce more recorded crimes, which in turn leads to a greater allocation of police to that area. Therefore, when assessing the social output in the field of crime and social control,[51] one must be wary of using recorded offences to measure the level of crime.

This leads to a more general point: police statistics have been designed and developed for internal administrative purposes,[52] and not just because of a desire to measure a component of social welfare. As a result, administrative convenience has in part determined the classifications adopted and the care taken over the compilation of different tabulations.[53] In terms of their effect

[50] An incident is recorded as an offence only if the police are reasonable certain that a crime has been committed. This is obviously less open to scrutiny than an adjudication of guilt in a court of law.

[51] For some years now, most industrialised countries have been experiencing a 'crime wave', as reported by their police commissioners and the media. Whether or not this represents a real increase in criminal events is very difficult to judge. For example, Pope (no date) shows that, although the number of cases of mugging that were reported in a local paper covering a fixed geographical region were twice as many in 1972 as in 1962, all the incidents reported in 1962 occurred *inside* the region served by the paper, but one-third of the incidents reported in 1972 were 'foreign' incidents. The rise, even in offences reported in the paper, was actually only 33 per cent, not, as it seemed, 100 per cent. The police can come under similar, though less severe, influences in the frequency of recording and reporting offences.

[52] Even more generally, decisions on the type of police statistics that are collected have not changed significantly for several decades, partly because of a desire to maintain comparability, and partly because of a steady increase in bureaucracy. As Perks (1967) notes, there is a strong conservative tendency in the collection of criminal statistics.

[53] Examples are: the combination, under the category of 'larceny by a servant', of certain forms of embezzlement in business and of offences such as that of a domestic servent who helps himself to food in an employer's household; and the classification of an incident involving several different charges under the incident that goes furthest in terms of formal procedure.

on people's lives, dissimilar incidents may be grouped together and cognate incidents may be grouped separately. Except in very crude ways, neither the amount of harm nor the unexpectedness of the event are used to classify recorded offences.[54] We shall return to these and other similar points in our concluding remarks.

Punishment

We pointed out in the fourth part of section II that individuals perceive[55] a substantial cost (A) in court appearance *per se,* and we showed how this might be incorporated into the model and how it would affect the results. In this case, information about the size of A (and its distribution) is important for social policy. It is surprising that very little formal research has been conducted in this area, especially as the recommendations of the Willink Commission, which have been progressively implemented over the last decade in terms of more formalised police procedures, may have implied substantial increases in A.[56]

THE APPROPRIATE SOCIAL POLICY CONCERN: CONTROL OF CRIME OR PERSONAL SAFETY AND FEAR OF CRIME?

Finally, we return to the point that we made at the beginning of this paper: it is not obvious that the control of (legally defined) crime is a clearly definable social policy concern. The police include control of traffic and various forms of registration among their duties; and other agencies (the Inland Revenue, Factory Inspectorate, and so on.) monitor certain transgressions of the law. If control of crime is the aim, then we have to solve the problem of the 'dark number'; but one of the main reasons why the 'dark number' is so large is that not all legally defined crime *per se* is a source of anxiety (since not all crime – for instance, successful soliciting for prostitution – produces identifiable injuries).

A more coherent policy goal might be the control of avoidable and unexpected harm that people suffer at home, in the street, or at work; only a small proportion[57] of these events is as a result of a crime. Are there any good

[54] The criminal statistics do distinguish attempts from completed acts and indecent assault from unlawful sexual intercourse, but neither by level of injury, nor by situational context.

[55] Well documented in Martin and Webster (1971).

[56] Previously, the local policeman on the beat used to exercise a considerable amount of discretion in 'ticking off' minor miscreants in the neighbourhood; Willink (1962) urged them to institute formal procedures. Thus, the incidence of costs such as A has increased. With more information available, and more rapidly available, to the police, the size of A itself may also have increased.

[57] The World Health Organisation statistics for cause of death show that in all industrialised countries 'deaths from unnatural causes' are several times more numerous than murders.

reasons for distinguishing accidents from crimes for the purposes of such a social policy goal? First, the physical injury does not change according to the intent; and, second, the boundary dividing criminal negligence from accidental is, to a large extent, arbitrary. In the United Kingdom, a shopkeeper who sells adulterated food may be convicted under the Food and Drug Acts even if he had no means of knowing whether it was adulterated (say, because it was tinned).

It may be true that people are usually much more worried about the likelihood of a criminal unexpected event than an accidental incident, and that this probably affects their life style.[58] But this fear of harm should be treated in addition to, and separately from, the counting of actual instances of harm.[59] The appropriate treatment of this fear of harm raises two interesting questions. The first concerns the determinants of individuals' perceptions of the probability of harm. We know of very little research on this topic and further empirical work could be of great interest.[60]

The second question concerns the policy issue of the appropriate relation between the perceived probability of harm (say, q) and the actual probability of harm (q^*). If one takes a group of identical individuals, then the *ex ante* individual expected utility *using* q^* equals the *ex post* utilitarian sum of utilities. The *ex post* utilitarian sum is, therefore, maximised over the range of q when $q = q^*$ so that individuals take actions to maximise the expected utility using q^*. The problem, however, is not necessarily this simple. We may not be interested in maximising the *ex post* utilitarian sum. We have the problem of *ex post* versus *ex ante*: if $q < q^*$, *ex ante* utility will be higher than for $q = q^*$, but the *ex post* utilitarian sum will be lower. We have the further problem of the appropriate combination of individual utilities into social welfare. In addition, individuals may be particularly bad judges of their own best interests in such situations. Finally, we repeat the former question of just how one goes about influencing q.

REFERENCES

Abadie, J. (ed.), *Non-Linear Programming* (Amsterdam: North Holland, 1967.)

Arrow, K. J., *Aspects of the Theory of Risk-Bearing* (Helsinki: Yrjö Jahnssonin Säätiö, 1965.)

[58] See the results of victimisation surveys conducted mainly in the United States; for example, the National Crime Panel carried out by the Statistics Division of the National Institute for Law Enforcement and Criminal Justice.

[59] If we counted the actual instances of harm that would have taken place in the absence of various precautions and changes in life-style we should overestimate the harm. This is similar to the standard economic argument that a measure of utility loss using quantity bought just before a price change will overestimate the loss, and using quantity after the price change will underestimate the loss.

[60] We noted in footnote 51 that the information the public receives concerning the probability of harm can be very misleading.

Atkinson, A. B., 'On the Measurement of Inequality', *Journal of Economic Theory,* Sep 1970.

Baumol, W. J., and Bradford, D. F., 'Optimal Departures from Marginal Cost Pricing', *American Economic Review,* June 1970.

Becker, G. S., 'Crime and Punishment: An Economic Approach', *Journal of Political Economy,* Mar 1968.

Brown, W. W., and Reynolds, M. O., 'Crime and "Punishment": Risk Implications', *Journal of Economic Theory,* Oct 1973.

Carr-Hill, R. A., and Stern, N. H., 'An Econometric Model of the Supply and Control of Offences in England and Wales', *Journal of Public Economics,* Nov 1973.

Carr-Hill, R. A., and Stern, N. H., 'Criminological Theories and Variations in Recorded Statistics of Police Work, Offender Behaviour and Judicial Activity in England and Wales in the early 1960's' (Dec 1970), mimeo.

Diamond, P. A., and Mirrlees, J. A., 'Optimum Taxation and Public Production', parts I and II', *American Economic Review* Mar and June 1971.

Durkheim, E., *Rules of Sociological Method* (New York: The Free Press, 1964).

Ehrlich, I., 'Participation in Illegitimate Activities: A Theoretical and Empirical Investigation', *Journal of Political Economy,* May/June 1973.

Enniss, P. H., 'Criminal Victimisation in the U.S.' (National Opinion Research Centre, University of Chicago, May 1967).

Harris, J. R., 'On the Economics of Law and Order', *Journal of Political Economy,* Jan/Feb 1970.

Hart, H. L. A., *Punishment and Responsibility* (Oxford: The Clarendon Press, 1968).

Kolm, S. C., 'A Note on Optimum Tax Evasion', *Journal of Public Economics,* July 1973.

Malinvaud, E., *Statistical Methods of Econometrics,* 2nd edn (Amsterdam: North Holland, 1970).

Martin, J. P., and Webster, D., *Social Consequences of Convictions* (London: Heinemann, 1971).

Perks, W., *Report of the Departmental Committee on Criminal Statistics,* Cmnd 3448 (London: HMSO, 1967).

Pope, L., 'Press Representations and Alternative Interpretations' (unpublished dissertation for BA Social Sciences, Sussex University).

Stiglitz, J. E., and Dasgupta, P., 'Differential Taxation, Public Goods and Economic Efficiency', *Review of Economic Studies,* Apr 1971.

Walker, N., *Sentencing in a Rational Society* (London: Allen Lane, The Penguin Press, 1969).

Willcock, H. D., and Stokes, J., *Deterrents to Crime Among Youths aged 15 to 21,* Government Social Survey Report no. SS356, part II (London, 1968).

Willink, H. V., *Royal Commission on the Police,* Cmnd 1728 (London: HMSO, 1962).

Part IV
Economic Effects of Social Security

7 Demographic Effects on the Equity of Social Security Benefits

Henry J. Aaron[1]

BROOKINGS INSTITUTION AND UNIVERSITY OF MARYLAND

WITH THE ASSISTANCE OF PHILIP SPEVAK

This paper examines the impact on social security benefits and taxes of (a) differential mortality by race, income, education, sex, and marital status; (b) differing ages of entry into the labour force; and (c) different lifetime earnings profiles.

Although the United States retirement-benefit formula is progressive and taxes are proportional, it is shown that these three demographic effects cause the system to favour upper-income over lower-income households.

If the system is to have progressive effects on income distribution, as its advocates have long maintained, a progressive payroll tax is indicated.

I. THE ISSUE

The benefit structure of every social security system in the world is proportional or progressive with respect to earnings.[2] All benefit formulas fall into one of three categories. Ranging from most to least progressive, benefits are: (a) unrelated to past earnings levels; (b) progressively related to earnings – i.e. benefits rise with earnings, but less than proportionately; or (c) directly and proportionately related to earnings. All of these formulas may be adjusted for years of coverage under the system, and the second and third may be subject to maximums and minimums, a feature that adds to progressivity by establishing a floor under, or ceiling to, benefits, depending on how low or high

[1] The author is a member of the Economic Studies Program of the Brookings Institution and of the Economics Department at the University of Maryland. The views expressed are those of the author, and not necessarily those of the officers, trustees, or other staff members of the Brookings Institution or the University of Maryland.

The author wishes to thank Christine De Fontenay for extensive programming assistance.

[2] Throughout this paper I shall refer interchangeably to 'social security' and 'retirement system'. In fact, of course, the term 'social security' everywhere denotes far more than retirement benefits. The analysis, as noted is limited to retirement benefits.

average earnings are. In addition, some countries employ means tests for some or all benefits paid to the aged.[3]

Most countries finance benefits, at least in part, by taxes levied on employees, employers, or both. In those countries where benefits are related to earnings, taxes on employees are usually limited to that part of earnings used in computing benefits. Taxes on employers may or may not be so limited.

In combination, the tax and benefit formulas would seem to equalise incomes. This statement holds for both annual and lifetime incomes. Annual incomes are equalised at least up to the earnings level at which payroll taxes cease to apply, since such taxes are usually proportional, while benefits are paid to older persons whose current earnings typically are negligible or nonexistent. Lifetime income seems to be equalised whenever benefits are of the first two types, because a tax that is proportional is combined with a progressive benefit structure. The least-equalising systems are those that entail proportional earnings taxes and proportional benefit formulas. When benefits are set equal to taxes paid, plus compound interest at a market rate of interest, all elements of equalisation are removed.

Whatever nominal progressivity a country's legislators may incorporate in its retirement system, the actual effect of the system on income inequality is conditioned by the differential behaviour of various economic groups. It is conceivable that such behaviour may undo or reduce progressivity built into a tax-benefit formula or convert a nominally progressive system into a regressive one. For example, if mortality rates are higher among the poor than among the rich, fewer low-income than upper-income persons may survive to receive benefits. In addition, the social security system may redistribute income in unanticipated ways among groups classified by characteristics incidental to, or independent of, the operation of the social security system itself.

For example, Milton Friedman has speculated that, despite its nominally progressive character, the old-age and survivor insurance (OASI) system in the United States actually is far less progressive than its appearance suggests and may be regressive because:

(a) Persons in high income classes typically start working at a later age and so will tend to pay taxes for a shorter period.

(b) Persons in high income classes have a higher life expectancy, and so will tend to receive benefits for a longer period.

(c) The employer tax is excluded from the personal tax base, which is of much greater advantage to persons in high income classes.

(d) Even more important, the social security benefit is not subject to the personal income tax, which, again, is a greater advantage to persons in high income classes.

(e) The self-employed pay a lower tax rate, and while some are in low

[3] In Table 6A.1 (see Appendix A below) all countries with national retirement systems are classified among the three categories of benefit formulas.

income groups, many, particularly professionals, are in high income groups. (Cohen and Friedman, 1972, p. 35.)

The third and fourth of these factors are best thought of as attributes of the personal and corporate income tax system rather than of the retirement system.

A sixth source of reduced progressivity or regressivity is the exclusion, from the calculation of the average wage on which benefits are based, of years when earnings were low. Currently, retirees must average earnings over the number of years elapsed since 1950, less five. The privilege of dropping out years of low earnings is of greatest relative value to those whose earnings rise most over their life-cycle, an attribute of earnings profiles of white males and, especially, of the highly educated. It is likely that the number of years used in computing benefits will not be permitted to increase materially and may be reduced, particularly if significant rates of inflation persist. The consideration of earnings covering most of the working life when money wages are rising sharply will relate benefits to money wages that are meagre by current standards. For this reason, the number of years over which earnings are averaged in order to compute benefits may have an important effect on the relative size of benefits. (See Pechman et al., 1968, appendix A.)

The tendency of professional persons, usually with above average earnings, to continue working past 65 and to forgo retirement benefits may generate a contrary tendency. The operation of these factors could cause the ratio of benefits to taxes to vary by such characteristics as race, place of residence, or educational level, which themselves are not used in determining benefits or taxes, but, nonetheless, are highly relevant in assessing the distributional consequences of the social security system.

Although Professor Friedman's remarks are directed specifically to the United States social security system, they are generally relevant wherever any of the six factors just mentioned are relevant. In particular, variations in mortality rates by income class are likely to exist elsewhere, though perhaps less sharply in countries with national health insurance plans.

II. APPLICATION: THE UNITED STATES SYSTEM

Unfortunately, the data necessary for measuring the importance of the factors listed in Section I are not readily available. One attempt was made by Okonkwo (no date). He calculated the internal rate of return of social security to white and nonwhite couples and single workers who entered the labour force at various ages. He used historical data on taxes paid for workers who were 18 years old in 1937, when the United States social security system came into operation. Workers were assumed to continue working until 1984, at which time they would retire and receive benefits. At each point *after* retirement, benefits were reduced by the probability that the worker (and/or his spouse) had not survived to receive them. Okonkwo found that the internal rate of return is higher for couples than for single workers (because couples receive benefits 50 per cent larger than those of single retirees), higher for nonwhites than for whites (because the average earnings of nonwhites is lower than that of whites and the benefit formula is progressive), and higher for whites than for nonwhites with equal earnings (because the survival rate of nonwhites is lower than that of whites).

The present study examines the impact of ages of entry into the labour force, earning profiles, and mortality rates on the relative rates of return from old-age insurance in the United States. The results are consistent with Okonkwo's, though more detailed. Atkinson (1970) carried out a similar study, of a retirement system proposed, but not implemented, by the Labour Party in the United Kingdom. In this paper, Atkinson calculated, among other things, the impact on the internal rate of return of differential mortality rates by wealth category.

Workers are distinguished by the following characteristics.

Sex	(male, female) $i = 1, 2$.
Race	(white, nonwhite) $j = 1, 2$.
Education	(0–8, 9–11, 12, 13–15, 16, 17+) $k = 1, \ldots, 6$
Age	(14–19, 20–24, 25–34, 35–44, 45–54, 55–59, 60–64, 65–71, 72+) $m = 1, \ldots, 9$.
SMSA	(SMSA, non-SMSA) $n = 1, 2$.
Region	(North-east, North-central, West, South) $p = 1, \ldots, 4$
Union status	(union, non-union) $q = 1, 2$.
Marital status	(married, not married) $r = 1, 2$.

Following Hall, the logarithm of earnings was regressed on dummy variables for the preceding characteristics. Data were taken from the 1967 Survey of Economic Opportunity (SEO).[4] The equation used was as follows:

$$\log E^{ij}{}_{klmnpq} = \sum_{k} \sum_{m} a_{km} + \sum_{n} b_n + \sum_{p} c_p + \sum_{q} d_q + \sum_{r} e_r + h \quad (7.1)$$

where E is earnings, he is the earnings level for the one possible dummy variable that is omitted from each set to prevent singularity, and a, b, c, d and e are 1 when the worker has the indicated characteristics, and 0 otherwise. Separate regressions were run for white males, nonwhite males, white females, and nonwhite females, allowing complete interaction between race and sex, on the one

[4] Unlike Hall (1970), who was interested in earning capacity and, hence, used instrumental variables to estimate potential wages, I am interested in payroll taxes and social security benefits, both of which are based on actual earnings and, hence, use actual wages and salaries.

hand, and each of the variables, on the other. This procedure is capable of generating a maximum of 768 cross-sectional lifetime earnings profiles for various types of workers, classified by sex, race, education, place of residence, union status and marital status. In fact, the number generated is smaller, because some age–education cells are unrepresented in the sample. The estimated coefficients from equation (7.1) appear as in Table 7A.2.

The earnings profiles of certain groups are flatter, and peak earlier, than do those of others. In general, nonwhites, females, and those with meagre education not only earn less, but also experience less relative increase of, and an earlier decline in, earnings than do well-educated white males. The other characteristics – place of residence, union status, and marital status – are not allowed to interact with age, because of limitations within the regression programme used; hence, they affect the level of earnings and the absolute change, but not the rate of growth or decline, from one age bracket to another. The relationship between earnings, race, sex and education is one that has been commonly observed in previous research (see, for example, Hall, 1970; Morgan, 1962; and Weiss, 1970). It reflects the deferred returns to formal education, the access of white males to jobs in which learning-by-doing is important, and, possibly, the complementarity between investment in nonspecific human capital (formal education) and job-specific human capital (on-the-job training).

The next stage requires that each class of workers be 'exposed' to social security taxes and benefits. At this point, the fact that the social security system and the various earnings profiles are continuously evolving requires a number of *ad hoc* assumptions in order to convert into dynamic forms the cross-sectional snapshots generated by equation (7.1) and the social security system as it exists at a specific time.

The following assumptions are made concerning earnings.

(1) The profiles generated by equation (7.1) apply to the year 1966.
(2) Each year thereafter, earnings rise by g per cent (g will be allowed to vary in appraising the effects of the system). Consequently, the level of earnings profiles increases with time but the shape does not change. A worker who is, say, 20 in 1966 receives in that year the earnings for the cohort of 20–24 year olds with his education and other characteristics; and in 1976, for example, he receives the earnings for the cohort of 25–34 year olds with his characteristics, calculated for 1966 and multiplied by $(1 + g)^{10}$. Similar calculations will give his earnings for each year until he retires, at age 65.

The worker faces payroll taxes on all earnings up to a taxable maximum. The maximum is set at \$7800 for 1966 and is assumed to rise g per cent per year; thus, the taxable maximum in years after 1966 is \$7800 $(1 + g)^n$.[5] The worker is assumed to bear the payroll tax collected from employers on his

[5] The actual taxable ceiling reach S7800 only in 1968.

earnings, as well as his own tax.[6] This assumption is consistent with recent empirical work by Brittain (1972) and with a short-run model in which the supply elasticity of labour is zero. Within the framework of a one-sector growth model, however, Feldstein (1972) has shown that the value of the supply elasticity of labour is unimportant in appraising the long-term incidence of a wage tax. The incidence depends, rather, on the effect of the wage tax on capital accumulation and, hence, on labour's marginal productivity.

A similar procedure is used in computing retirement benefits. These are based on an average wage computed as the average *taxable* wages during a stipulated number of years, currently the number of years elapsed since 1950, less five. This formula is likely to be changed, for reasons stated earlier.[7] In any case, the number of years of earnings included in the computation of the average wage is treated as a variable over the range 5–35. The benefit formula used in the computations is shown in Table 7A.4 (appendix A below). It is progressive over four steps; each step is assumed to be broadened g per cent per year.

The final step is the computation of the present expected value of benefits and taxes for workers with various socio-economic characteristics. To compute these values, given the benefit and tax formulas, it is necessary to know only a discount rate and the survival probabilities for various classes of workers. The discount rate, d, employed is $(g + \cdot 02)$. This number is approximately the sum of the rate of growth in money wages (g) and the rate of growth in the labour force; this sum has been shown to be approximately equal to the rate of return that workers will receive under a mature pay-as-you-go pension system (see Aaron, 1966, and Pechman et al., 1968). While the United States system is not fully mature and deviates slightly from pay-as-you-go, this assumption does little violence to the facts.

The survival probabilities, based on data contained in Kitagawa and Hauser (1973) are computed from age-specific mortality rates differentiated by race (white, nonwhite), marital status (married, not married), sex (male, female), education (0–7 years, 8, 9–11, 12, 13+), and income (six levels). Because the income categories in Kitagawa and Hauser are defined for family income in 1959, while the earnings profiles computed from the SEO refer to individual wage and salaries, the rather unsatisfactory expedient of converting family earning categories into percentile classes was employed. The mortality-rate adjustments for these percentiles of family income in 1959 were applied to the corresponding SEO-based percentile classes of earnings. The computed mortality rates and more details on their derivation appear in Appendix B.

All workers in the computation were assumed to be 14 years old in 1966,

[6] The applicable rates are shown in Table 7A.3 (appendix A below).

[7] In fact, the social security system was 'overfinanced' during the 1960s, since taxes and benefits were calculated on the assumption that earnings would not rise. Increases in earnings generate more revenues than benefits, becauase of the progressive nature of the benefit formula. Thus, some liberalisation by allowing more years to be excluded in the computation of the average wage would be consistent with overall balance, given growth in earnings.

hence 22 in 1974. Contrary to fact, all 14 year olds are assumed to survive with certainty to age 21. They enter the labour force at an arbitrary age a, and pay taxes, the present value of which is reduced by the discount rate and the probability that they have died, until age 65, at which they commence to receive benefits. If they are single, the present expected value of benefits, like that of taxes, is the sum of actual benefits, reduced by the discount rate and the probability that they have died. The mortality rate at age 100 is assumed to be 1·00. If retirees are married, the computation of benefits is much more complex. Married workers are assumed, with certainty, to be married at age 65 and, hence, to be eligible in that year for couples' benefits equal to 1·5 times the benefits payable to single retirees. At age 66 such households will receive couples' benefits if both husband and wife survive. If one spouse dies, the other receives the benefits payable to single retirees.[8] If both die, benefits cease. I ignore lump-sum death benefits entirely.

III. RESULTS

The simulations indicate that differential mortality rates fully offset the progressivity of the retirement benefit formula. Variations in age of entry into the labour force, associated with differences in educational attainment, reinforce these effects. Together these factors make the social security benefit–cost ratio rise with educational attainment, rather than fall, as suggested by the benefit formula. In short, retirement benefits are regressive, not progressive, as the proportional tax and, apparently, progressive benefit structure suggest. Variation in the shape of earnings profiles further reinforces these results.

The results shown in Table 7.1 display relative benefit–cost ratios of retirement benefits where education, race, and marital status are allowed to vary.[9]

[8] This assumption reflects legislation enacted in 1972, but is contrary to the law as it stood in 1966, when widows (or widowers, if their benefits were based on the wife's earnings) received 82½ per cent of the benefit payable to single retirees. Formally, the present value of benefits payable at age a, $BP(a)$, $(65 \leqslant a \leqslant 99)$ to a worker who will be married at age 65 is

$$BP(a) = B(1+d)^{-(a-14)}\left[1{\cdot}5 \times P^m(a) \times S(65) + (1 - P^m(a) - \frac{1-S(a)}{S(65)} \times \frac{1-\bar{S}(a)}{S(65)}\right]$$

where $S(a)$ and $\bar{S}(a)$ are the probabilities that a worker survives to age a and that the worker's spouse survives to age a, and where $P^m(a)$ is the probability that a married worker who has survived with spouse to age 65 is married at age a. $P^m(a)$ is defined as $[S(a)/S(65)] \times [\bar{S}(a)/S(65)]$. In this form, workers and spouses are assumed to be the same age.

[9] Relative benefit–cost ratios are defined as the ratio calculated for the relevant cell, divided by the ratio for white married men with 12 years of education, as described in the note to each table. This procedure is employed because the absolute benefit–cost ratios have no meaning outside actuarial calculations, which show whether the streams of taxes and benefits have the same present value at some discount rate. In addition, certain simplifications, described in the text below, undermine the significance of absolute values of the ratios, but probably do not seriously affect their relative values.

TABLE 7.1

RELATIVE BENEFIT–COST RATIOS BY RACE, EDUCATION AND MARITAL STATUS[a]

Educational attainment (years)	*Married couples*						*Single workers*			
	Male earner only		*Two earners* A		*Two earners* B		*Males*		*Females*	
	White	*Nonwhite*	*White*	*Nonwhite*	*White*	*Nonwhite*	*White*	*Nonwhite*	*White*	*Nonwhite*
0– 8	·95	1·41	·73	1·02	·57	·80	·44	·44	·75	·87
9–11	1·00	1·49	·76	1·08	·60	·84	·46	·48	·88	·97
12	1·00	1·29	·74	·95	·60	·73	·46	·43	·82	·79
13–15	1·13	1·45	·82	1·07	·68	·82	·47	·46	·90	·88
16	1·15	1·28	·80	·92	·69	·72	·47	·41	·89	·76
17+	1·15	1·20	·81	·85	·70	·68	·48	·40	·92	·76

A = where female's earnings are 0·3 as a fraction of male's.
B = where female's earnings are 1·0 as a fraction of male's.

[a]Earnings profiles refer to male union members, living in an SMSA in the North-east Census region, who enter the labour force at age 18. Money wages are assumed not to grow and benefits are based on earnings in the highest 40 years. Workers with more than 12 years of education may be regarded as working as well as going to school. Workers with less than 12 years of attainment are assumed not to have taxable earnings until age 18.

The benefit–cost ratio of a white, married, male union member with 12 years of education, living in an SMSA in the North-east Census region, assuming no earnings growth and a benefit computation period of 40 years, is normalised to 1·00.

Table 7.1 embodies two unrealistic assumptions: (a) that all workers enter the labour force at age 18; and (b) that money wages do not change. These assumptions will be relaxed in Tables 7.2 and 7.3. Associated with each cell in Table 7.1 is an estimated lifetime earnings profile.[10] For white married families, the inverse correlation between education and income, on the one hand, and mortality rates, on the other, causes the benefit–cost ratio to rise with education. The better survival probabilities of those with more education (and higher income) mean that a new labour force entrant has a greater chance of surviving to retirement; given that he is married at retirement, higher survival probabilities also assure a longer period during which the couple will receive the 50 per cent larger benefits paid to surviving couples and during which at least one member of the couple will survive. These effects more than offset the progressivity in the benefit formula that causes the ratio of benefits to average earnings to decline as earnings rise. The benefit–cost ratio is drastically reduced when both spouses are employed, because the second earner bears payroll taxes from the first dollar of earnings, but receives net benefits only when benefits based on that earnings history equal 50 per cent of the benefits to which the primary earner is entitled. In general, where the second earner receives 30, 65, 100 or 150 per cent of the earnings of the first worker, the respective benefit–cost ratios of married couples with two earners are approximately 25, 35, 40 and 42 per cent below those of married couples with one earner.

By contrast, benefit–cost ratios of married nonwhite families exhibit an irregular pattern and exceed those of whites. Since nonwhite men earn less than white men, they are exposed to greater progressivity in the benefit formula than whites are, a factor that more than offsets the higher mortality rates of nonwhite men. Then survival probabilities of nonwhite women are higher beyond, but lower before, age 65 than are those of white women.[11] Since the simulations assume, for simplicity, that the spouse of a man who survives to 65 also survives to 65, this procedure creates in the results a bias in favour of nonwhites that is not present in the system. The higher ratios of nonwhite married men occur despite the fact that their survival probabilities are lower than those of whites. Once again, the benefit–cost ratios of married couples with two earners are far below those of couples with one earner.

Unmarried male workers have lower survival probabilities and earn less than married workers. In combination, these factors reduce benefit–cost ratios and make them slightly regressive for whites and irregularly progressive for non-

[10] These earnings are not shown, but they can be calculated from values shown in Table 7A.2 (Appendix A below). Earnings of whites exceed those of nonwhites and rise montonically with education, except for whites with 17 or more years of education, who earn somewhat less than whites with 16 years of education, using simple undiscounted lifetime averages. Earnings of white (nonwhite) married men exceed those of single men by 68 (59) per cent.

[11] On balance, the mortality rates for nonwhite women are unrealistically low (5 per cent of nonwhite women survive to age 99), but this factor has little effect on the results. See Tables 7.4–7.6 below.

whites. Single women encounter much higher ratios than do single men, because of both lower earnings and higher survival probabilities. As with married couples, the pattern for whites is regressive; that of nonwhites is irregularly progressive.

The relative benefit–cost ratios of married workers with selected educational attainments and various ages of entry into the labour force are shown in Table 7.2. Workers with greater educational attainment are likely to enter the labour force at a later age than workers with less schooling. Consequently, Table 7.2 should be read diagonally from upper left to lower right for the most plausible cases. Italic type is used to indicate those combinations of education and labour-force entry that I judge to be most realistic. Given this perspective, it is apparent that the better educated (and higher income) are white workers. The effects of greater longevity and later entry into the labour force overwhelm the progressivity of the benefit formula. Among nonwhites no simple pattern is apparent.

TABLE 7.2

RELATIVE BENEFIT–COST RATIOS OF SELECTED MARRIED WORKERS WHO ENTER THE LABOUR FORCE AT VARIOUS AGES[a]

Race and educational attainment (in years)		*Age at entry into labour force* 14	18	21	24	27	30
White	0–8	*·94*	·95	·98	1·06	1·14	1·22
	12	·98	*1·00*	1·04	1·14	1·22	1·29
	16	1·11	1·15	*1·18*	1·24	1·30	1·38
	17+	1·12	1·15	1·19	*1·26*	1·32	1·40
Nonwhite	0–8	*1·40*	1·41	1·45	1·56	1·68	1·82
	12	1·25	*1·29*	1·35	1·48	1·59	1·69
	16	1·25	1·28	*1·32*	1·42	1·51	1·61
	17+	1·18	1·20	1·24	*1·35*	1·43	1·50

[a]Workers are married males who live in an SMSA in the North-east Census region and are union members. Earnings are assumed not to grow and benefits are based on earnings in the highest 40 years.

The benefit–cost ratio of a white, married, male union member with 12 years of education, living in an SMSA in the North-east Census region, assuming no earnings growth and a benefit computation period of 40 years, is normalised to 1·00.

The second unrealistic assumption embodied in the preceding tables is that money wages are stable. In fact, money wages rose roughly 4 per cent per year between 1950 and 1965; since then, the pace of growth has accelerated. When money wages are rising, retirement benefits are often not based on average nominal earnings over the entire life-cycle. Two alternative methods are commonly used. One is to convert wages each year into an index. For example, wages may be recorded as a multiple of the current minimum wage or median wage. At retirement, the worker's index values are averaged, and benefits are then based on his index and on the current minimum or average wage. This method is used in the Federal Republic of Germany. Alternatively, benefits may be based on average earnings in a smaller number of years (say, 20, 10 or five) than are contained in the typical working life. Since no move has been made toward indexing in the United States, I assume that problems created by rapid growth in money wages will be met by reducing the number of years of earnings included in benefit computation. The faster money wages grow, the shorter will be the benefit computation period.

Table 7.3 shows, for workers with various amounts of education, how the relative benefit–cost ratios are affected by variations in the growth of money

TABLE 7.3

RELATIVE BENEFIT–COST RATIOS OF SELECTED WORKERS WHEN GROWTH OF MONEY WAGES AND THE NUMBER OF YEARS OF EARNINGS USED IN COMPUTING BENEFITS VARY[a]

		Growth in wages (Computation period)		
Education		*3% (20 years)*	*6% (10 years)*	*10% (5 years)*
Whites	0–8	·78	·74	·73
	9–11	·81	·80	·80
	12	·81	·82	·86
	13–15	·92	·93	·97
	16	·93	·94	·98
	17+	·94	·95	·99
Nonwhites	0–8	1·25	1·21	1·20
	9–11	1·38	1·36	1·36
	12	1·15	1·16	1·15
	13–15	1·32	1·33	1·46
	16	1·21	1·24	1·29
	17+	1·02	1·03	1·08

[a]Benefit–cost ratios apply to married males, living in an SMSA in the North-east Census region, who are union members and enter the labour force at age 18.

The benefit–cost ratio of a white, married, male union member with 12 years of education, living in an SMSA in the North-east Census region, assuming no earnings growth and a benefit computation period of 40 years, is normalised to 1·00.

wages and in the benefit computation period. Because the earnings profiles of well educated workers tend to rise more and peak later than do those of less educated workers, shortening the benefit computation period should favour the relatively well educated. Table 7.3 reveals just such a pattern for whites. This table shows that, all other things being equal, the smaller the number of years of earnings included in computing benefits, the greater will be the relative advantage of well educated and upper-income workers under the social security system. For nonwhites, this pattern is less striking, because the variation in earnings of nonwhites over the life-cycle has been less pronounced than that of whites has.

Although the calculations presented thus far are rather complex, they embody a number of oversimplifications and ignore some highly important situations. Perhaps the most important is the failure to account for benefits paid to survivors of non-aged deceased persons. Tables 7.4, 7.5, and 7.6 remedy this omission. As is apparent, the benefit–cost ratios across educational classes

TABLE 7.4

RELATIVE BENEFIT–COST RATIOS BY RACE, EDUCATION AND MARITAL STATUS[a]

Educational attainment (years)	*Married males*		*Nonmarried-males*		*Nonmarried-females*	
	White	*Nonwhite*	*White*	*Nonwhite*	*White*	*Nonwhite*
0–8	1·11	1·69	·32	·31	·54	·72
9–11	1·07	1·58	·33	·35	·63	·77
12	1·00	1·00	·33	·31	·59	·63
13–15	1·12	1·39	·34	·33	·64	·68
16	1·13	1·22	·34	·29	·63	·59
17+	1·11	1·14	·35	·28	·66	·59

[a]Earnings profiles refer to male union members, living in an SMSA in the North-east Census region, who enter the labour force at age 18. Money wages are assumed not to grow, and benefits are based on earnings in the highest 40 years. Workers with more than 12 years of education may be regarded as working as well as going to school. Workers with less than 12 years of attainment are assumed not to have taxable earnings until age 18.

The benefit–cost ratio of a white, married, male union member with 12 years of education, living in an SMSA in the North-east Census region, assuming no earnings growth and a benefit computation period of 40 years, is normalised to 1·00. *Benefits include survivor benefits, and nonwhite women are given the mortality rates of white women.*

are virtually identical (Table 7.4), although differences related to race and marital status persist. Once again, the pattern for married nonwhites is clearly progressive. The fact that survivor benefits accrue differentially to households that do not survive to retirement undoes the regressivity in Table 7.1, but does not restore the progressivity contained in the benefit formula. In the same degree, the regressive patterns (for whites) shown in Tables 7.2 and 7.3 are softened, but not removed, in Tables 7.5 and 7.6. Other included oversimplifications that will not be removed are the assumptions that husbands and wives are the same age, that wives of married workers survive to age 65 if the worker does, and that workers abruptly enter the labour force at a certain age and leave it at age 65. The calculation of all benefits from age 65 is inaccurate in two ways. Workers may receive benefits between ages 62 and 65, but at an actuarially reduced amount, so that expected lifetime cost is the same.[12] Also,

[12] One corollary of this paper is that the actuarial reduction should vary by the socio-economic characteristics of the retiree.

TABLE 7.5

RELATIVE BENEFIT–COST RATIOS OF SELECTED MARRIED WORKERS WHO ENTER THE LABOUR FORCE AT VARIOUS AGES[a]

Race and educational attainment (in years)		*Age of entry into labour force* 14	18	21	24	27	30
White	0–8	1·08	1·11	1·15	1·24	1·33	1·43
	12	·98	1·00	1·04	1·14	1·22	1·29
	16	1·10	1·13	1·17	1·22	1·29	1·37
	17+	1·08	1·11	1·15	1·21	1·28	1·40
Nonwhite	0–8	1·65	1·69	1·74	1·86	1·97	2·11
	12	1·22	1·27	1·32	1·45	1·56	1·66
	16	1·18	1·21	1·27	1·36	1·45	1·55
	17+	1·12	1·14	1·18	1·28	1·36	1·44

[a]Workers are married males who live in an SMSA in the North-east Census region and are union members. Earnings are assumed not to grow, and benefits are based on earnings in the highest 40 years.

The benefit–cost ratio of a white, male union member with 12 years of education, living in an SMSA in the North-east Census region, assuming no earnings growth and a benefit computation period of 40 years, is normalised to 1·00. *Benefits include survivor benefits, and nonwhite women are given the mortality rates of white women.*

many workers forgo benefits at age 65 in order to continue working, although benefits are not actuarially increased. Since professional workers (i.e. those with relatively high education and lifetime income) are more likely to continue working past age 65, this behaviour may be viewed as imparting progressivity to the system. I have not included it because the decision to forgo benefits is voluntary, while the payment of taxes and eligibility for benefits are not. In addition, some elements of the relationships employed are implausible, an example being that nonwhite women have unrealistically high survival rates.[13] Furthermore, some important interactions in the earnings function have been ignored, such as the interaction of the contributions that sex, union status and educational level make to earnings. I shall not attempt to remedy these over-simplifications, because I do not think that doing so would alter the general thrust of the results reported here. It is my hope that actuaries, who are better able to perform such calculations with precision, will address in public the questions raised here.[14]

Unless such actuarial calculations overturn the results shown here, a major implication for public policy emerges. If United States legislators wish to

[13] In Tables 7.1–7.3. Tables 7.4–7.6 apply to nonwhite women the mortality rates of white women.

[14] It is difficult to believe that no study of the impact of differential mortality rates has been undertaken by social security actuaries, as this question is paramount in the setting of rates for private insurance. Aside from the study by Okonkwo, however, I have seen no empirical examination of this question.

TABLE 7.6

RELATIVE BENEFIT–COST RATIOS OF SELECTED WORKERS WHEN GROWTH OF MONEY WAGES AND THE NUMBER OF YEARS OF EARNINGS USED IN COMPUTING BENEFITS VARY[a]

		Growth in wages (Computation period)		
Education		*3% (20 years)*	*6% (10 years)*	*10% (5 years)*
Whites	0–8	·97	·98	·91
	9–11	·91	·92	·91
	12	·86	·88	·90
	13–15	·99	1·01	1·06
	16	1·06	1·06	1·14
	17+	1·03	1·03	1·11
Nonwhites	0–8	1·63	1·46	1·33
	9–11	1·56	1·43	1·33
	12	1·19	1·19	1·10
	13–15	1·33	1·31	1·31
	16	1·17	1·23	1·21
	17+	1·01	1·04	1·08

[a]Benefit–cost ratios apply to married males, living in an SMSA in the North-east Census region, who are union members and enter the labour force at age 18.

The benefit–cost ratio of a white, married, male union member with 12 years of education, living in an SMSA in the North-east Census region, assuming no earnings growth and a benefit computation period of 40 years, is normalised to 1·00. *Benefits include survivor benefits, and nonwhite women are given the mortality rates of white women.*

establish the progressivity within the social security system that has been the declared intent of its advocates for three decades, it is necessary to make one of two changes in the system to offset the differentially higher mortality, and the earlier labour force entry, of workers with little education and low income. Under one approach, the progressivity of the benefit formula could be increased. Alternatively, the proportional payroll tax rate could be replaced with a graduated tax. In principle, one could apply to different classes of workers different tax rates, based on their expected mortality, age of entry into the labour force, and, possibly, other characteristics. While variation in tax rates by race would probably be constitutionally impermissible, variation of tax rates by income class or, possibly, by educational attainment (since cessation of education usually marks the commencement of fulltime employment) would be permissible. As a practical matter, rough equity could be achieved by graduating the payroll tax with respect to income. Since the payroll tax has already been severely criticised in the United States for the burdens that it currently imposes on low-wage workers, this solution has considerable attractiveness. Until now, traditional supporters of social security have successfully opposed conversion of the payroll tax into a progressive tax on earnings, because, they have held, the introduction of progressivity would violate the insurance principles on which, they allege, the social security system rests.[15] The analysis presented in this paper indicates that a progressive payroll tax is not only consistent with, but implied by, insurance principles.

The results further support the widely recognised tendency for social security to treat families with two workers less generously than it treats one-earner families. It is unclear why this pattern of discrimination should be allowed to persist.[16]

All calculations in this paper have been based on United States data, but the lessons have general applicability. Differential mortality rates and the tendency of well-educated workers to enter the labour force later than poorly educated workers do are not uniquely American characteristics. Wherever payroll taxes are employed to finance all, or a large part, of the retirement benefits that are proportionally, or even progressively, related to past earnings, these forces will make a nominally proportional, and possibly even a progressive, system into an effectively regressive one. This fact cannot be apprehended from benefit and tax formulas alone, but requires explicit analysis based on the mortality rates and labour force experiences of various workers.

REFERENCES

Aaron, Henry J., 'The Social Insurance Paradox', *Canadian Journal of Economics and Political Science,* XXXII, no. 3 (Aug 1966), pp. 371–4.

Atkinson, A. B., 'National Superannuation: Redistribution and Value for Money', *Bulletin of the Oxford University Institute of Economics and Statistics,* XXXII, no. 3 (Aug 1970).

Brittain, John, *The Payroll Tax for Social Security*, (Washington, DC: The Brookings Institution, 1972).

Cohen, Wilbur, and Friedman, Milton, *Social Security Universal or Selective?* (American Enterprise Institute, 1972).

Feldstein, Martin, *Tax Incidence in a Growing Economy with Variable Factor Supply,* Harvard Institute of Economic Research, Discussion Paper no. 263 (Dec 1972).

Hall, Robert E., *Wages, Income and Hours of Work in the U.S. Labor Force,* MIT Department of Economics Working Paper no. 62 (Aug 1970).

Kitagawa, Evelyn M., and Hauser, Philip M., *Differential Mortality in the United States* (Cambridge, Mass: Harvard University Press, 1973).

Morgan, James, 'The Anatomy of Income Distribution', *Review of Economics and Statistics,* XLVI, no. 3 (Aug 1962), pp. 270–83.

Okonkwo, Ubadigbo, 'Individual Equity Under Social Security: Some Black–White Comparisons' (no date), mimeo.

Pechman, Joseph A., Aaron, Henry J., and Taussig, Michael K., *Social Security: Perspectives for Reform* (Washington, DC: The Brookings Institution, 1968).

Weiss, Randall, 'The Effect of Education on the Earnings of Blacks and Whites', *Review of Economics and Statistics,* LII, no. 2 (May 1970), pp. 150–9.

[15] For a demonstration that this latter contention is false, see Pechman et al (1968)

[16] For a recommended solution to this problem, see ibid.

APPENDIX A

TABLE 7A.1

CLASSIFICATION OF COUNTRIES BY TYPE OF BENEFIT FORMULA

Region	*Benefits not related to earnings*	*Benefits progressively related to earnings*	*Benefits proportional to earnings*
Europe and related	Denmark	Australia	Belgium
	Finland	Austria	Canada
	Ireland	GDR	France
	Netherlands	Israel	Federal Rep. Germany
	New Zealand	Luxembourg	Italy
	Norway	Switzerland	Portugal
	Sweden	United Kingdom	Spain
		USA	
Latin America		Bolivia	Argentina
		Costa Rica	Brazil
		Mexico	Chile
		Uruguay	Colombia
		Venezuela	Cuba
			Dominican Rep.
			Ecuador
			El Salvador
			Guatemala
			Guyana
			Haiti
			Jamaica
			Nicaragua
			Panama
			Paraguay
			Peru
Asia	Ceylon	Japan	Taiwan
		Philippines	China
			India
			Iran
			Iraq
			Lebanon
			Malaysia
			Saudi Arabia
			Singapore
			Syria
			Turkey
Africa	Burundi	Libya	Algeria
		Malagasay Rep.	Cameroon
		South Africa	Cent. African Rep.
			Congo
			Dahomey
			Gabon
			Ghana

Table 7A.1 *continued*

Region	*Benefits not related to earnings*	*Benefits progressively related to earnings*	*Benefits proportional to earnings*
			Guinea
			Ivory Coast
			Kenya
			Mali
			Mauretania
			Morocco
			Niger
			Nigeria
			Ruanda
			Tanzania
			Togo
			Uganda
			UAR
			Upper Volta
			Zaire
			Zambia
Socialist		Albania	Bulgaria
		Poland	Czechoslovakia
		Romania	Hungary
			North Viet Nam
			Yugoslavia
			USSR
Other	Cyprus	Greece	Barbados
	Iceland	Trinidad and Tobago	
	Mauritius		
	Nauru		

Source: Social Security Administration, US Department of Health, Education, and Welfare, *Social Security Programs Throughout the World, 1971,* Research Report no. 40 (Washington, DC: US Government Printing Office, 1971).

TABLE 7A.2

COEFFICIENTS OF REGRESSION OF THE LOGARITHM OF WAGES AND SALARIES ON DEMOGRAPHIC CHARACTERISTICS

Characteristic		*Coefficients*			
		White males	*White females*	*Nonwhite males*	*Nonwhite females*
Constant		5·7375	3·647	5·5592	4·3198
Education,	age:				
0–8,	14–19	–	–	–	–
0–8,	20–24	2·0217	2·593	2·2401	1·5487
0–8,	25–34	2·3539	3·039	2·3140	1·9489
0–8,	35–44	2·4784	3·112	2·2827	2·0117
0–8,	45–54	2·4589	3·216	2·2535	1·9701
0–8,	55–59	2·3820	3·153	2·2563	1·7204
0–8,	60–64	2·1394	2·867	1·7768	1·5362
0–8,	65–71	1·4661	2·514	1·2147	1·2675
0–8,	72+	1·1433	1·837	–·5202	·6693
9–11,	14–19	·0959	·638	·1768	·1743
9–11,	20–24	2·3133	2·799	2·0176	1·5022
9–11,	25–34	2·5911	2·994	2·2898	2·1109
9–11,	35–44	2·7776	3·219	2·3866	2·2391
9–11,	45–54	2·7372	3·436	2·5408	2·3236
9–11,	55–59	2·6987	3·427	2·2150	2·1845
9–11,	60–64	2·5275	3·227	2·2791	2·2312
9–11,	65–71	2·0838	2·644	1·6910	1·0021
9–11,	72+	1·3453	2·554	2·1519	·5202
12,	14–19	1·0385	2·116	·9610	1·2035
12,	20–24	2·4860	3·396	2·1405	2·1449
12,	25–34	2·8069	3·402	2·5105	2·5902
12,	35–44	2·8601	3·573	2·6048	2·5343
12,	45–54	2·8660	3·662	2·4552	2·5745
12,	55–59	2·8662	3·787	2·3428	2·6472
12,	60–64	2·8529	3·550	2·6058	2·3727
12,	65–71	1·9032	3·151	1·8696	2·0054
12,	72+	1·1342	2·660	1·8589	3·4051
13–15,	14–19	1·1650	1·984	1·1579	1·7091
13–15,	20–24	1·9662	3·160	2·1303	2·0232
13–15,	25–34	2·8666	3·269	2·5681	2·7606
13–15,	35–44	3·1079	3·567	2·9339	2·8620
13–15,	45–54	3·1084	3·692	2·7954	2·5948
13–15,	55–59	2·9739	3·506	2·7566	2·5370
13–15,	60–64	3·1646	3·741	1·5544	2·5236

Table 7A.2 continued

Characteristic		*Coefficients*			
		White males	*White females*	*Nonwhite males*	*Nonwhite females*
Education,	age:				
13–15,	65–71	2·1532	3·738	2·4295	2·2078
13–15,	72+	1·5780	3·486	2·6407	1·8411
16,	14–19	–	2·150	–	–
16,	20–24	1·8281	3·490	1·8360	2·6245
16,	25–34	3·0213	3·845	2·9581	3·4841
16,	35–44	3·2893	3·720	3·1650	3·5072
16,	45–54	3·3986	4·178	2·9757	3·4260
16,	55–59	3·3166	4·398	3·0536	2·9796
16,	60–64	3·2673	4·213	3·0129	2·2974
16,	65–71	2·3000	4·211	2·3086	2·3774
16,	72+	2·4616	3·137	2·7754	–
17+,	14–19	–	–	–	–
17+,	20–24	1·9343	3·838	1·2465	2·8949
17+,	25–34	2·9173	4·029	2·7389	3·3774
17+,	35–44	3·3314	4·181	3·0602	3·8212
17+,	45–54	3·4611	4·522	3·0188	3·9926
17+,	55–59	3·1627	4·602	2·8526	3·8553
17+,	60–64	3·1435	4·835	2·6910	3·2546
17+,	65–71	2·5933	3·845	3·0311	2·7480
17+,	72+	2·2372	2·201	–	–
SMSA					
Outside		–	–	–	–
Inside		·2165	·0204	·4040	·6505
Region					
North-east		·0490	·0213	·0196	·1627
North-central		·0399	·0115	·0329	·0532
West		–·0588	·0159	–·1936	–·2297
South		–	–	–	–
Union status					
Nonunion		–	–	–	–
Union		·02756	·0677	·4351	·4861
Marital status					
Married		–	–	–	–
Non married		–·5181	·0284	–·4642	·0792
$\bar{R}^2$		·6079	·3320	·5771	·4111

TABLE 7A.3

OASI PAYROLL TAX RATES IN 1966 AND SUCCEEDING YEARS

Year	*Employee (Combined tax on employee and employer)*	*Self-employed*[a]
1966	·0700	·0527
1967	·0710	·0537
1968	·0665	·0508
1969–70	·0745	·0559
1971–2	·0825	·0619
1973 on	·0905	·0634

[a]The self-employed OASI payroll tax rate is not shown separately. It is obtained by multiplying the self-employed OASDI rate by the ratio of the OASI rate to the OASDI rate for employees.

TABLE 7A.4

ANNUAL BENEFIT FORMULA

Benefit = 71·16 per cent of first \$1320 of earnings
25·88 per cent of next \$3480 of earnings
24·18 per cent of next \$1800 of earnings
28·43 per cent of next \$1200 of earnings

The size of the steps in the benefit formula in year n is increased by $(1 + g)^{n-1966}$

Minimum benefit in year n is \$55 $(1 + g)^{n-1966}$.

APPENDIX B: DESCRIPTION OF MORTALITY-RATE CALCULATIONS

Philip Spevak

The following is a description of the process used in the construction of mortality rates specific as to sex, race, marital status, age, education and income. It should permit any investigator to replicate the mortality tables used in this study. A limited number of copies of these tables are available on request.

The file containing the final mortality rates is a sex-dimensional array. The mortality rate variable, 'rate', is the subscripted rate (*ISEX, IRACE, MAR, IAGE, IED, INCM*). The subscripts are as follows:

ISEX = 1 (male)
2 (female)

IAGE = 1 (15–19 years)
2 (20–24 years)

IRACE = 1 (white)
2 (nonwhite)

MAR = 1 (married)
2 (not married)

IED = 1 (less than 8 years)
2 (8 years)
3 (9–11 years)
4 (12 years)
5 (13 and more years)

INCM = 1 (less than \$2000, or 13·1%)
2 (\$2000–3999, or 17·8%)
3 (\$4000–5999, or 23·3%)
4 (\$6000–7999, or 19·3%)
5 (\$8000–9999, or 11·5%)
6 (\$10,000 and over, or 15·1%)

3 (25–29 years)
4 (30–34 years)
5 (35–39 years)
6 (40–44 years)
7 (45–49 years)
8 (50–54 years)
9 (55–59 years)
10 (60–64 years)
11 (65–69 years)
12 (70–74 years)
13 (75–79 years)
14 (80–84 years)
15 (85 years and over)

CONDENSATION OF MARITAL STATUS

The mortality rates in table B.5 of Kitagawa and Hauser, *Differential Mortality in the United States,* were specific as to race, sex, marital status and age. There were four marital groups: single, married, widowed and divorced. All non-married groups were condensed into one category by weighting mortality rates by population within a particular race, sex and age cell. Population figures were obtained from the *United States Census of Population 1960, United States Summary* (table 176, pp. 425 ff.).

CORRECTION USING WHITE–NONWHITE DIFFERENTIALS

Using table 6.1 of Kitagawa and Hauser, each mortality rate was corrected for age reporting errors and for undercount errors. For example, for white males of ages 15–19, age reporting error was –3·6 per cent and undercount error was –3·8 per cent. The correction factor for this cell was 0·9274 = (1 – 0·036) x (1 – 0·038).

EDUCATION–INCOME ADJUSTMENT

Adjustment for education

Using table 2.8 of Kitagawa and Hauser, white mortality rates for ages 25 and over were made specific for educational background. Since table 2.8 actually consisted of mortality rates specific for sex, age and education, an index specific for sex, age and education was created by weighting each cell by population, using the *United States Census of Population 1960* (table 173). The average mortality for each age bracket was set equal to 1·00.

The index created included an income factor, since table 2.8 of Kitagawa and Hauser was not standardised for income. To remove the effect of income from the index, each value of the index was multiplied by the ratio representing the proportion of the index value attributable solely to education. This ratio was calculated using table 2.6 of Kitagawa and Hauser. For example, for white males of, 25–64 years old with 0–7 years of education, the ratio was 5 : 13.

Since ages over 65 were not made specific for income, the income effects of the education index for these ages were not removed.

Adjustment for income

Table 2.7 of Kitagawa and Hauser, showed mortality ratios by level of white family income standardised for age and education. Adjustment for income was made simply by multiplying by the relevant ratio.

Creation of education, income matrix

For each sex–age group for individuals of ages 25–64, an education–income matrix was created (5 x 6) by multiplying the education index by the income ratio for a particular sex–age bracket.

Ages 24 and under. Since no adjustment was made for education and income for ages 24 and under, all cells of the education – income matrix for these ages were 1·0.

Ages 65 and over. Since no adjustment was made for income for ages 65 and over, the education–income multipliers for all income columns of a particular education row were equal.

FINAL MORTALITY RATES FOR MALES

There were eight different race, sex, marital-status combinations. As male and female rates were calculated independently from this point, the following discussion of the calculation of male rates parallels the calculation of female rates, except that for the latter corresponding female rates and multipliers were used.

White married-male rates

For all ages, the race, sex, age and marital-status specific mortality rates calculated as described above were multiplied by the age-specific education–income matrix. This created 450 cells for white married males for ages 24 and under; the rates are not specific for education and income. For ages 65 and over, the rates are not specific for income.

White nonmarried rates

A marriage factor used to adjust white married rates was calculated by finding for each age bracket the cell that corresponded to the median level of education and income for white nonmarried individuals. The marriage factor was equal to white nonmarried mortality (not made specific for education and income) divided by white married mortality for the education–income cell corresponding to white nonmarried median education and income.

To determine white nonmarried rates, the marriage factor, specific for each age bracket, was multiplied by the white married rates, for all cells.

Nonwhite married rates

A race factor was calculated in the same manner as was the marital factor. The race factor for each age level was equal to nonwhite married mortality divided by the white married mortality rate in the cell corresponding to the median level of education and income for nonwhites.

Nonwhite married mortality was then determined by multiplying each age, education and, income specific cell for white married individuals by the race factor for each age bracket.

Nonwhite nonmarried rates

A nonwhite married factor for each age bracket was calculated equal to age-specific nonwhite nonmarried mortality divided by the age, education, and income specific nonwhite married rate cell corresponding to the median level of education and income for nonwhite nonmarried individuals of that age bracket.

The nonwhite nonmarried rate was determined by multiplying each age, education and income specific mortality rate for nonwhite married people by the age-specific nonwhite marriage factor.

8 Social Security and Private Savings: International Evidence in an Extended Life-Cycle Model[1]

Martin S. Feldstein
HARVARD UNIVERSITY

The extended life-cycle model shows that the impact of social security on private savings depends on two opposing effects: wealth replacement and induced retirement. The net impact can be determined only empirically. The current study uses data for a cross-sectional sample of developed countries so as to evaluate both effects. The evidence indicates that increases in the extent of social security coverage and in the relative level of benefits substantially depress the rate of private saving.

I. INTRODUCTION

Social insurance is becoming increasingly important everywhere in the Western world. In the United States, the recent expansion of such programmes has carried government spending for social insurance in 1973 to more than $85 billion, or 8·1 per cent of the national income. The basic social security cash benefits for the aged, for surviving dependants and for the disabled will, by themselves, exceed $55 billion. Total federal-government benefits for the aged and disabled will exceed $90 billion.

The vast magnitude of social insurance programmes suggests that they may have substantial unintended consequences. An unemployment insurance programme is intended to provide income to the unemployed and a sense of financial security to those who remain at work. It may also have important effects

[1] This research is part of a larger study of the effects of fiscal policies on capital formation and income distribution. The author is grateful to the National Science Foundation for financial support; to Larry Summers and Marie-Paul Donsimoni for assistance with the research; and to Franco Modigliani for discussions. Helpful comments on an earlier version of this paper were made by members of the Harvard Public Finance Seminar and by participants in the International Economic Association conference on the economics of public services, held in Turin, Italy.

[2] This includes health benefits to the aged, and cash benefits to aged veterans, to retired government employees, and to others not covered under social security.

on aggregate demand and on the functioning of the national labour market, reducing the cyclical variations in unemployment by automatically contributing to demand when unemployment is high, but increasing the general level of unemployment by distorting the incentives of employees and employers.[3] In an analogous way, health insurance programmes may protect individuals from the financial hardships of unexpected medical bills, but not without substantial, and often unanticipated, consequences in the entire health-care sector. Similar unintended effects can probably be identified by examining other types of social insurance. A better understanding of the full consequences of current social insurance programmes would permit them to evolve in the future in ways that strengthen their good aspects while reducing their harmful effects.

The present paper examines the effects of social security programmes on aggregate private saving. The extended life-cycle model presented in section II shows why the impact of social security cannot be determined *a priori*. It is clear that the introduction of public pensions for the aged permits working individuals to reduce their saving and still plan to enjoy the same level of consumption during retirement. However, the existence of social security benefits for the aged may increase the fraction of older persons who retired. This induced increase in retirement will, in itself, increase the volume of saving for retirement. The net impact of the 'wealth replacement effect' and the 'induced retirement effect' can be determined only empirically. This study uses data for a cross-sectional sample of developed countries in order to evaluate these two effects of the social security programme.

The evidence presented here indicates that the provision of public pensions for the aged substantially depresses the rate of private saving. If this is not offset by other government policies, the result is a decline in the rate of capital accumulation, with important long-run effects for the level and distribution of income.

The framework for the present analysis is an extension of the traditional life-cycle model. Section II presents this model of household saving and retirement in an economy with social security benefits. The second section develops the macro-economic implications in a way that is suitable for application to data for a cross-section of countries. The data sources and specific definitions of variables are discussed in section IV. The estimated savings function is presented in section V. Section VI discusses the estimated model of retirement behaviour. These results are used in section VII to assess the net impact of intercountry differences in social security programmes and of prospective changes in benefit levels. There is a brief concluding section.

II. THE MICRO-ECONOMICS OF HOUSEHOLD SAVING IN AN EXTENDED LIFE CYCLE MODEL

The familiar life cycle model emphasises the importance of saving during working years for consumption during retirement. The most obvious implication of

[3] This point is developed in section 5 of Feldstein (1973).

this familiar model is that social security, by providing income during retirement, reduces the amount of saving during working years. More specifically, if the combination of the social security tax and the benefits that it finances has no income effect, and if the pattern of work and retirement is fixed, the social security programme will reduce savings by just enough to leave consumption unchanged during retirement.

There is, however, a second effect of social security that would tend to increase personal saving. By providing non labour income to older persons, social security induces the aged to reduce their supply of labour. The formal analysis presented below shows that if younger workers correctly anticipate this subsequent reduction in labour supply, their saving may actually be increased.[4]

In many countries, social security benefits are paid to the aged only if they retire or if their earnings fall below a certain level. This 'retirement test' or 'earnings test' is, in effect, a high marginal rate of tax on the earnings of the aged. This increases the extent of retirement and, for any given level of earnings during old age, reduces the net income of the recipient of old-age benefits. It is clear that the earnings test is likely to increase the rate of saving during the earlier working years.

The net effect of social security on saving by the non-aged depends on the relative strength of the 'saving replacement effect' and the 'induced retirement effects'. This has important macro-economic implications for aggregate savings behaviour. When a new social security programme is introduced, it is likely to increase retirement rates as well as to substitute expected benefits for private saving. Eventually, however, the proportion of retirees reaches a limit and any increase in social security benefits reduces saving. More specifically, as the system matures, the 'induced retirement effect' will become increasingly small relative to the 'saving replacement effect'. These macro-economic implications are examined more fully below. First, however, it is useful to consider more explicitly the basic micro-economic saving behaviour.

The current analysis is a direct extension of the simple two-period 'life-cycle' model originally introduced by Irving Fisher (1930). The individual consumes C_i in period i ($i = 1, 2$) and enjoys leisure L_i in that period. For simplicity, I follow the common practice in specifying a multiperiod utility function and assume that the function is separable:

$$W = U(C_1, L_1) + V(C_2, L_2) \tag{8.1}$$

By an appropriate choice of units, the amount of labour supplied in each period may be written $1 - L_i$. The wage rate may also be normalised to 1, so that labour income in each period is $1 - L_i$.[5]

[4] This effect of anticipated retirement on personal saving could also explain the positive association between private pension and other savings that was found by Cagan (1965) and Katona (1965). See also Feldstein (1973c).

[5] $L_2 < 1$ implies that the individual does some work in period 2. $L_2 < L_2$ can include doing part-time work and full retirement at some time after the beginning of period 2.

Consider a social security programme that imposes a tax on all labour income at rate t. In the second period of an individual's life (i.e. after age 65), the programme provides benefits of B. These benefits may be subject to an 'earnings test': for every one dollar of labour income in period 2, the individual loses $\alpha < 1$ dollar of income. First-period consumption is thus

$$C_1 = (1 - t)(1 - L_1) - S \tag{8.2}$$

where S is savings. If a dollar saved at time 1 returns R dollars in period 2 (i.e. R is one plus the interest rate),[6] second-period consumption is

$$C_2 = RS + (1 - t)(1 - L_2) + B - \alpha(1 - L_2) \tag{8.3}$$

or

$$C_2 = RS + (1 - t - \alpha)(1 - L_2) + B$$

To contrast the extended life-cycle model in which retirement is endogenous with the traditional life-cycle model, I shall consider two different cases. In case I (the traditional life-cycle model), L_1 and L_2 are both fixed. In case II, the individual is free to vary his work during the second period; for simplicity, L_1 will be taken as fixed.

CASE I

With L_1 and L_2 fixed, S is the only variable that the individual can choose. The first-order condition is thus

$$\frac{dW}{dS} = - U_1 + V_1 R = 0 \tag{8.4}$$

Totally differentiating with respect to S, t, B and α yields

$$\begin{aligned}&[(1 - L_1)U_{11} - RV_{11}(1 - L_2)]\,dt + \\ &\quad (U_{11} + R^2 V_{11})dS - RV_{11}(1 - L_2)d\alpha + RV_{11}dB = 0\end{aligned} \tag{8.5}$$

The social security programme operates under a budget constraint[7]

$$B = Rt(1 - L_1) + (t + \alpha)(1 - L_2) \tag{8.6}$$

This implies that

$$dt = \frac{dB - (1 - L_2)d\alpha}{R(1 - L_1) + (1 - L_2)} \tag{8.7}$$

[6] Note that, since the individual's life is divided into only two periods, the 'interest rate' actually refers to the effect of compounding over many years. Even a 3 per cent annual rate would imply $R = 2$ if all first-period saving were taken to occur at age 45 and all second-period dissaving at age 70.

[7] This assumes that the social security taxes in period 1 earn the same rate of interest as the individual would have earned on private saving. If this is not true, there is an income effect; i.e. the lifetime budget constraint is altered.

Substituting this into equation (8.5) and collecting terms yields

$$(U_{11} + R^2 V_{11})dS = \frac{(U_{11} + R^2 V_{11})(1 - L_1)}{R(1 - L_1) + (1 - L_2)} \cdot [(1 - L_2)d\alpha - dB] \quad (8.8)$$

or

$$dS = \frac{(1 - L_1)(1 - L_2)}{R(1 - L_1) + (1 - L_2)}\, d\alpha - \frac{(1 - L_1)}{R(1 - L_1) + (1 - L_2)}\, dB \quad (8.9)$$

If, in the absence of this social security programme, the individual would have been fully retired in the second period (i.e. $L_2 = 1$), we obtain

$$\frac{dS}{d\alpha} = 0 \quad (8.10)$$

and

$$\frac{dS}{dB} = -\frac{1}{R} \quad (8.11)$$

The earnings test has no effect (equation 8.10), because there are no second-period earnings. Savings fall by $1/R$, just enough to offset the benefits B; i.e. $RdS + dB = 0$.

Alternatively, if the individual would have worked in the second period,

$$\frac{dS}{d\alpha} = \frac{(1 - L_1)(1 - L_2)}{R(1 - L_1) + (1 - L_2)} > 0 \quad (8.12)$$

and

$$\frac{dS}{dB} = \frac{-(1 - L_1)}{R(1 - L_1) + (1 - L_2)} < 0 \quad (8.13)$$

The earnings test increases savings (equation 8.12) because it reduces net earned income in the second period. The benefits reduce saving, but by less than the amount required to maintain the same level of consumption. The net effect of the social security programme is to reduce savings as long as the social security programme adds to second-period income: $dB - (1 - L_2)d\alpha > 0$.

CASE II

If the individual is free to vary his supply of labour in the second period (but L_1 is still fixed), there are two first-order conditions:

$$-U_1 + V_1 R = 0 \quad (8.14)$$

$$-V_1(1 - t_1 - \alpha) + V_2 = 0 \quad (8.15)$$

These may be totally differentiated to give two equations for dS and dL_2 as linear functions of $d\alpha$, dB and dt. The value of dt can again be eliminated by recognising the budget constraint of equation (8.6). The constraint now implies that

$$dt = \frac{dB - (1 - L_2)d\alpha + (t + \alpha)dL_2}{R(1 - L_1) + (1 - L_2)} \quad (8.16)$$

For the introduction of a new social security programme, these equations can be evaluated at $t = \alpha = B = 0$. The induced change in saving and second-period leisure are then given by the matrix equation

$$[A]\begin{bmatrix} dS \\ dL_2 \end{bmatrix} = \underline{a}\, d\alpha + \underline{b}\, dB \tag{8.17}$$

where

$$A = \begin{bmatrix} U_{11} + R^2 V_{11} & R(V_{12} - V_{11}) \\ R(V_{12} - V_{11}) & V_{11} + V_{22} - 2V_{12} \end{bmatrix}$$

$$\underline{a} = \begin{bmatrix} [R(1 - L_1) + 1 - L_2]^{-1}(1 - L_1)(1 - L_2)(U_{11} + R^2 V_{11}) \\ -[R(1 - L_1) + 1 - L_2]^{-1} R(1 - L_1)[V_1 + (V_{11} - V_{12})(1 - L_2)] \end{bmatrix}$$

and $$\underline{b} = -\begin{bmatrix} [R(1 - L_1) + 1 - L_2]^{-1}(1 - L_1)[U_{11} + R^2 V_{11}] \\ [R(1 - L_1) + 1 - L_2]^{-1}[V_1 - R(1 - L_1)(V_{11} - V_{12})] \end{bmatrix}$$

When equation (8.17) is solved, we obtain

$$|A| \cdot \frac{dS}{d\alpha} = [R(1 - L_1) + 1 - L_2]^{-1}(1 - L_1)[|A|(1 - L_2) - R^2(V_{11} - V_{12})V_1] \tag{8.18}$$

$$|A| \cdot \frac{dS}{dB} = -[R(1 - L_1) + 1 - L_2]^{-1}\, [|A|(1 - L_1) + R(V_{11} - V_{12})V_1] \tag{8.19}$$

$$|A| \cdot \frac{dL_2}{d\alpha} = -[R(1 - L_1) + 1 - L_2]^{-1} R(1 - L_1)(U_{11} + R^2 V_{11})V_1 \tag{8.20}$$

$$|A| \cdot \frac{dL_2}{dB} = -[R(1 - L_1) + 1 - L_2]^{-1}(U_{11} + R^2 V_{11})V_1 \tag{8.21}$$

The second-order conditions for the original equilibrium to be a maximum imply that the determinant $|A|$ is positive, so that $(U_{11} + R^2 V_{11}) < 0$. Equations (8.20) and (8.21) therefore unambiguously indicate that $dL_2/d\alpha > 0$ and $dL_2/dB > 0$, i.e. that both aspects of the social security programme induce an increase in second-period leisure. The effects on saving are less clear. If the reasonable assumption that $V_{11} - V_{12} < 0$ is made,[8] equation (8.18) implies that $dS/d\alpha > 0$. The earnings test, by reducing second-period net labour income, induces an increase in saving. Even with this assumption, the effect of B on savings is unclear. The net impact of social security on savings therefore is ambiguous.

The contrast between these two cases shows the significance of the induced retirement effect. In the empirical work developed below, it will be important

[8] In terms of a cardinal utility function, this would be true unless an increase in second-period leisure reduced the marginal utility of second-period consumption by more than it would be reduced by a unit increase in second-period consumption.

to separate the effects of wealth replacement with fixed retirement behaviour from the effects that operate through changes in retirement.

III. MACRO-ECONOMIC IMPLICATIONS AND THE AGGREGATE SAVING FUNCTION

In the traditional multiperiod life-cycle model, each individual works for a fixed period and then retires to consume the wealth that he has accumulated during his working years. This personal wealth is the only basis for consumption during retirement. The important implications of this model for aggregate saving were first derived by Harrod (1948) and Modigliani and Brumberg (1954), and later developed by Modigliani (1966 and 1970) and Tobin (1967). It follows from the life-cycle model than an economy without technical progress or population growth will have no net aggregate savings. In such a stationary economy, there will be an equilibrium aggregate ratio of wealth to income that depends on the time preference of individuals, the life-cycle timing of earnings and retirement, and the rate of interest.[9] With a constant ratio of wealth to aggregate income and no growth in aggregate income, there will be no net aggregate saving.

By contrast, a growing economy will require a continuing increase in wealth to maintain the equilibrium ratio of wealth to income. Economic growth is the well spring from which aggregate saving flows. In a growing economy, the workers who are saving at any time have a higher aggregate income out of which to save than the older retirees had when they were saving. The savings of each generation of workers therefore exceed the dissavings of the concurrent retirees. The result is positive net aggregate saving. More specifically, in an economy experiencing a steady-state growth, the ratio of private saving to national income will be approximately proportional to the rate of growth of national income, the factor of proportionality being the equilibrium ratio of wealth to income.[10]

In the extended life-cycle model of section II, the extent of retirement of older persons is endogenous and reflects the system of social insurance. The aggregate ratio of private wealth[11] to income depends, therefore, on the level of social security benefits (relative to individual income) and on the extent of labour-force participation by older individuals. Where social security old-age benefits are high relative to earnings, the desired ratio of wealth to income will be comparatively low for any given level of labour-force participation by

[9] The rate of interest will be determined simultaneously with the equilibrium ratio of wealth to income.

[10] A change in the rate of population growth changes the age structure of the population and therefore, alters the desired ratio of wealth to income. The proportional relation between the savings ratio and the growth rate is, therefore, only approximate.

[11] The term 'wealth' will always be used to denote 'private wealth', i.e. the accumulation of private saving. Wealth, therefore, specifically excludes the value of 'social security wealth', i.e. the discounted actuarial value of the public social security pensions to which individuals are entitled. See Feldstein (1973c).

older persons. But to the extent that social security increases the fraction of older persons who are retired, it will also increase the desired ratio of wealth to income.

In a stationary economy, the introduction of a social security programme would not alter the zero rate of saving that would otherwise prevail. Although workers would save less, the dissaving of retirees would fall by an equal amount. The level of consumption of the aged is maintained by transfer payments financed by a tax on workers. But, in a growing economy, the 'wealth replacement effect' of the social security programme lowers the aggregate rate of saving, while the 'induced retirement effect' increases the rate of saving.

This discussion implies that, if observations were available for a set of different steady-state growth situations, it would be appropriate to estimate a savings function of the form

$$\frac{S}{Y} = \left(\alpha_0 + \alpha_1 \frac{B}{Y} + \alpha_2\, LPAGED\right) \cdot G \tag{8.22}$$

where S is per capita private saving;
Y is per capita income;
B is social security benefits per aged person;
LPAGED is the labour-force participation of the aged; and
G is the rate of growth of national income.[12]

The composite term $\alpha_0 + \alpha_1 (B/Y) + \alpha_2\, LPAGED$ reflects the equilibrium ratio of wealth to national income. The coefficient α_1 measures the wealth replacement effect and is, therefore, negative. Since an increase in the equilibrium level of labour-force participation by the aged reduces their desired accumulation of wealth, the coefficient α_2 also is negative.

It is important to emphasise that this simple specification is appropriate for observations generated by economies experiencing steady-state growth. Any actual data will represent a situation of disequilibrium. The appropriate modification of equation (8.22) depends on the nature of the sample of available data. With observations for a single country over a period of only a few decades, the influence of changes in the long-run rate of growth (G) may be relatively small, while other disequilibrium factors may have substantial effects on the rate of savings. Cyclical variations in the level of income and changes in the ratio of wealth to income may be particularly important.[13]

[12] The analysis of section II also suggests a variable corresponding to the 'tax' on earnings (α). This would affect *LPAGED* but would also have a direct effect on S/Y when those who are not retired pay the 'tax', i.e. when it is not just a retirement test. Unfortunately, the data generally are not suitable for distinguishing these two aspects.

[13] Ando and Modigliani (1963) develop an application of the traditional life cycle model to aggregate time-series data for the United States. Feldstein (1974) applies the extended life-cycle model to the effects of social security in a study of United States saving for 1929 to 1971. Munnell's (1974) analysis explicitly includes the labour-force participation of the aged in such aggregate time-series savings equations.

These particular disequilibrium factors may be relatively unimportant when the data relates to a cross-section of countries for each of which savings and income have been averaged over a number of years so as to reduce the influence of cyclical variations. The important aspects of disequilibrium in such an international cross-section are more likely to relate to the departure of the population age structure from the stationary age structure implied by the rate of population growth. More specifically, the savings rate will be depressed by an increase in the dependency ratio (i.e. the ratio of minors to persons of working age) and in the ratio of aged persons to persons of working age.[14] A greater life expectancy may be expected, *ceteris paribus,* to postpone the average age at retirement. For any given age pattern of retirement, a greater life expectancy (evaluated near the beginning of the normal retirement period) will increase the number of expected years of retirement and, therefore, the desired ratio of wealth to income.

In extending the simple steady-state specification of equation (8.22) to reflect these disequilibrium factors, it is no longer clear how the nonlinear structure should be generalised. Since that multiplicative specification was itself an approximation,[15] the first step may be to avoid further arbitrary nonlinearities by using a simple linear equation:

$$\frac{S}{Y} = \beta_0 + \beta_1 G + \beta_2 \left(\frac{B}{Y}\right) + \beta_3 LPAGED + \beta_4 DEP + \beta_5 AGED + \beta_6\ LEAGED \tag{8.23}$$

where *DEP* is the ratio of dependants (minors) to non-aged adults;
AGED is the ration of aged persons to non-aged adults; and
LEAGED is the life expectancy at the beginning of the period denoted as 'aged'.

The impact of a social security programme on retirement behaviour and on saving may develop with a lag. This is particularly important for the impact on retirement behaviour. A social security programme may induce an individual to plan an earlier retirement and to save more to supplement his social security benefits, so that earlier retirement would be preferable to continued work. When a new social security programme is introduced, workers nearing the 'retirement' age do not have sufficient time to increase their personal wealth substantially and may therefore choose not to retire early. For any given level of labour-force participation by the aged, the effect of the age of the social security system is unclear. The retired, or those nearing retirement, might respond to the introduction of a new social security programme by a sharp reduction in saving or by an increase in dissaving. This would imply a short-

[14] See Mikessel and Zinser (1973), Leff (1969) and Modigliani (1970). Note that all increases in the aged population will lower savings, even if they are not retired; the working aged will save less than workers in the pre-retirement period, because they have fewer years of potential retirement.

[15] See footnote 9 above.

run effect greater than the long-run effect. But the interaction may be more complex: as the system matures, a larger fraction of the population plans to retire, and, therefore, the aggregate saving rate becomes more sensitive to changes in the ratio of benefits to income. This suggests that the entire history of the social security programme is relevant to the current rate of saving. Nevertheless, it may be useful to include a measure of the age of the social security programme, either linearly or as modifying the effect of B/Y in equation (8.23).

Finally, the homogeneity of savings with respect to income must be considered. In the traditional life-cycle model, it is customary to assume that the *share* of total lifetime income that the individual allocates to retirement consumption is independent of his absolute level of income. This implies that the aggregate ratio of wealth to income (and therefore, in steady-state growth, the aggregate ratio of savings to income), is independent of the level of per capita income. The extended life-cycle model suggests that actual behaviour may be more complex. It seems likely, although obviously not logically necessary, that a higher absolute level of income will induce more retirement and earlier retirement. When income is very low, retirement may be no more pleasant than is continued work, while higher incomes may permit a relatively more comfortable and appealing retirement. If higher income does induce more retirement,[16] it will also raise the desired ratio of wealth to income and, therefore, the aggregate ratio of saving to income. This may explain the positive effect of per capita income that has been observed in previous international studies (Houthakker, 1965, and Modigliani, 1970) in which no adjustment was made for intercountry differences in the labour force participation of the aged.[17] It suggests that, if the savings function contains a variable that measures the labour-force participation of the aged, the level of per capita income will cease to have a positive effect.

The importance of corporate saving as a component of private saving varies substantially among the countries of the sample. Whereas some governments have, by means of tax incentives, encouraged corporate saving,[18] in an attempt to increase aggregate saving, others have discouraged it, believing that the capital market would allocate resources more efficiently. Traditional Keynesian theory relating consumption to disposable income implies that a higher rate of corporate saving would increase total private saving. By contrast, the Fisherian theory relates consumption only to labour income and the capital stock, and thus makes total saving independent of the rate of corporate saving. However, as I have discussed elsewhere (Feldstein, 1973b; Feldstein and Fane, 1973), in advocating a model of consumption behaviour that I have called the 'capital

[16] Evidence that this is so is presented in section VI below.

[17] This effect of income on retirement may also explain why aggregate consumption functions estimated with long time-series for an individual country have a positive constant term, implying that the ratio of savings to income rises with per capita income.

[18] For evidence of the efficacy of these incentives in increasing corporate saving in the United States and the United Kingdom, see Brittain (1966) and Feldstein (1970).

income hypothesis', capital *income,* and not just the capital stock, influences the level of consumption. This implies that the level of corporate saving may, but need not, alter the aggregate saving level. Evidence for both the United States (Feldstein, 1973b) and the United Kingdom (Feldstein and Fane, 1973) indicates that a higher level of corporate saving does raise private saving, but by a relatively small amount. This is consistent with Modigliani's (1970) international cross-section evidence that a 1 per cent increase in the corporate saving ratio (i.e. the ratio of corporate saving to national income) raises the private saving ratio by between 0·20 per cent and 0·50 per cent, depending on the other variables in the model. Because of the large standard errors associated with these estimates, Modigliani concluded that the international evidence provided no clear-cut resolution of the question. The corporate saving ratio will be included in the extended life-cycle specification to see whether any sharper conclusions can be drawn when other important influences on private saving have been taken into account.

IV. DEFINITIONS AND DATA

The basic data required to estimate the effect of social security in the extended life-cycle model have been collected for a 15-country sample that includes all of the major developed nonsocialist nations.[19] Observations on savings and economic growth generally are averages for the period 1954–60. The more stable demographic variables are, typically, values for a single year, while the social security programme variables are averages for 1958–60. This section provides more precise definitions of the variables and discusses the sources of data.

For several of the variables, it is possible to use the data previously employed by Modigliani (1970) to estimate the aggregate saving function implied by a traditional life-cycle model. The data on the private saving rate (S/Y), real per capita income (Y), the rate of economic growth (G), the ratio of minor dependants to adults of working age (DEP) and the ratio of older individuals to adults of working age (AGE) are all the same in this study as in Modigliani's. The construction and sources of these variables are described by Modigliani and need be summarised here only very briefly.[20]

The private saving rate (S/Y) is the ratio of total private savings to private national income. The actual values are averages for several years (usually 1954–60) based on data in different volumes of the *United Nations Yearbook of National Account Statistics.* It is important to note that such private saving

[19] The countries in the sample are Australia, Austria, Belgium, Canada, Costa Rica, France, Italy, Japan, the Netherlands, Norway, Spain, Trinidad, the United Kingdom, the United States, and West Germany.

[20] Modigliani's sources and methods were based on earlier work by Houthakker (1961, 1965), thus permitting the current results to be compared with the earlier studies.

includes accumulation in private pensions and net corporate saving, but excludes accumulation of government social security reserves. There is substantial variation in this saving rate within the sample, from a low of 7·10 per cent to a high of 21·05 per cent.

The income variable (*Y*) for each country is national income divided by population and converted to real US dollars by deflating by the appropriate price index and converting at the official exchange rate. The actual value used in the estimates is, again, an average of annual observations for several years. Because the conversion to US dollars is clearly the weakest link in this calculation, it should be noted that the US dollar equivalents of local incomes are relevant only for testing the homogeneity hypothesis. For all other purposes, local income enters each variable as part of a ratio that makes the exchange rate irrelevant.

The rate of growth (*G*) is computed from the real aggregate private national incomes in the first and last year of each country's sample period. More specifically, *G* is the implicit constant annual percentage rate at which national income grew during the sample period. There is, again, substantial variation, from a low of 2·2 per cent to a high of 9·9 per cent. The use of a six-year interval is intended to avoid biasing the estimated long-term growth rate by short-run cyclical fluctuations. Since the relevant growth rate is the rate that has been sustained over the lifetime of the current adult population and is expected, by current workers, to continue during their working life, the use of only a six-year period clearly reflects a faith that the permanent intercountry variance is large relative to the transitive intracountry variance after a relatively short cycle has been removed by averaging. The validity of this assumption and the appropriateness of this estimate should surely be tested as more data develop in the future.

The *United Nations Demographic Yearbook* provides information on the age structure of the population. The dependency ratio (*DEP*) is defined as the ratio of the number of persons under 20 to the number of adults between 20 and 65. At the other end of the population structure, the variable *AGE* is the ratio of the number of persons 65 and over to the number between 20 and 65. Data on life expectancy at age 65 (*LE*65) also are presented in this source.

The extent of an individual's labour-force participation is, in principle, capable of infinite gradations. The older individual need not completely retire in order to increase his consumption of leisure. Shorter hours, longer vacations and less arduous work are among his possible alternatives. Unfortunately, there is no way to measure these subtle changes in labour-force participation. The only available data for our sample of countries are classified on the basis of a simple distinction between 'economically active' and 'economically inactive' persons (UN, *Demographic Circular no. 24,* 1958). Because of this, the labour force participation of older persons (*LPAGED*) is measured as the percentage of men aged 65 and older who are economically active. It is to be hoped that income losses associated with reducing effort while remaining economically active are small relative to the income loss of becoming economically inactive.

If so, the current measure is appropriate for our purpose.[21]

There are two separate dimensions involved in measuring the magnitude of social security benefits to the aged: the average benefits per aged recipient and the fraction of the population that is effectively covered by the programme of old-age insurance. Although the available data do not exactly correspond to these variables, we are fortunate in having separate quantitative information about both aspects. The International Labour Organisation's *Yearbook of Labor Statistics* provides the number of recipients of pensions for the aged, surviving dependants and the disabled. The same organisation's *Cost of Social Security* provides the total amount of the benefits received by these pensioners in each of the sample countries. Data were collected for the years 1958–60 and average values were computed after adjusting for local price changes. Although most of the survivors and many of the disabled will be above retirement age, some individuals in both groups will be younger. This broader statistical coverage may actually be an advantage. Individuals save not only for their own retirement, but also to support their survivors and to provide for themselves in case of illness, accident or other source of disability. More complete social insurance for these conditions will reduce private saving.[22]

The benefit level per old-age pensioner (B) is estimated as the ratio of the total amount of pensions received (by the aged, survivors and the disabled) to the total number of such pensions.[23] The variable used in the estimated saving function is the benefit level relative to average per capita income (B/Y); it therefore is unnecessary to convert local currencies to a common standard.[24]

It is more difficult to measure the fraction of the population that is effectively covered by the old-age insurance programme. The simplest measure is the ratio of the number of pension recipients to the number of persons over age 65; this will be denoted *SSPA* (for social security pension per aged person). There are three possible problems with this measure. First, the persons re-

[21] The *LPAGED* variable would be appropriate under more general conditions if the whole spectrum of reductions in labour supply tended to shift together; for example, if a country where labour-force participation among the aged was low were also a country where those who continued to work were employed for fewer hours. While many factors might lead to such an assumption, the social security 'retirement test' might have the opposite effect.

[22] Countries may, however, differ in the extent to which private provision for survivors or for invalidhood creates private saving. While ordinary life-insurance policies involve capital formation that is similar to retirement saving, term life insurance will do so to a lesser extent. Similarly, private group disability insurance would entail less capital formation than would individual saving to provide resources for such contingencies.

[23] When a married retired worker receives a social security pension, the statistics record one beneficiary, even though two persons are being supported. If the wife has previously worked and now collects a social security pension in her own right, the statistics record two pensioners. No attempt has been made to adjust the data for this.

[24] The ratio of benefits to per capita income is only an approximate measure of the ratio of benefits to the pensioner's alternative (or concurrent) earnings. In particular, international differences in labour-force participation rates and in the share of national income received by labour will cause the relative value of these two ratios to differ.

ceiving pensions include surviving dependants and invalids below the age of 65 and, in some countries, also retirees who are below the age of 65. Although the broader measure of beneficiaries is useful, relating it to the population over 65 may be misleading to the extent that the relevant age structure among countries.[25] Second, a retired couple may receive one or two pensions, depending on the wife's work history and on the relative sizes of the benefits available to the wife as a retired worker rather than as a dependant. Finally, in countries where old-age pensions are paid only to those who have retired, the ratio of pensions to aged population will reflect retirement decisions as well as the fraction of the population that is eligible for old-age pensions, and will therefore understate the eligibility rate. The best response to this problem is not clear. If the number of aged persons who collect pensions is relatively small because there is a strict retirement test and a low level of benefits, this may be a form of *de facto* low eligibility rate. With this interpretation, the variable *SSPA* should be used without further adjustment. Alternatively, the eligibility rate could be represented by using two variables: (1) a dummy variable that indicates the presence of a retirement test (*RT*);[26] and (2) the ratio of the number of pension recipients to the number of *persons* over age 65 (in countries with no retirement test) or to the number of *retired persons* over age 65 (in countries with a retirement test). This latter variable will be denoted *SSPARA* (for *SSPA* with retirement adjustment). Since retirement will be more common among those who are covered, *SSPARA* will overstate the fraction of the population that is effectively covered. Fortunately, in practice, the estimated saving function is quite insensitive to the choice between these two variables.

It is clear that these two aspects of the social security programme interact in influencing national saving. An increased level of benefits per pensioner will have a greater effect on the national saving rate if a larger fraction of the population is effectively covered. Similarly, an increase in the fraction of the population covered will have a greater effect if the benefit level is high. This suggests measuring the magnitude of the social security programme as the product of the relative-benefit-level variable and the eligibility variable. Using the eligibility variable without adjustment for retirement implies that the magnitude of the programme is measured as the benefits per person over 65 relative to mean per capita income. More formally, if *BPA* denotes benefits per aged person, the corresponding measure of social security is $(BPA/Y) = (B/Y)\,(SSPA)$. Alternatively, if the eligibility variable is adjusted for retirement, the programme is measured by benefits per *person* over 65 relative to mean per capita income if there is no retirement test, but by benefits per *retired person* over 65 where a retirement test is imposed: $BPARA/Y = (B/Y)\,(SSPARA)$. The relative merits of the alternative measures are clearly implied by the previous discussion of *SSPA* and *SSPARA*.

[25] The variables *DEP* and *AGE* will, however, partly offset such differences.

[26] The retirement-test variable is based on the description of retirement tests, earning tests and means tests in the Social Security Administration survey *Social Security Programs Throughout the World* (1971).

The product of the relative benefit level and the eligibility fraction is, of course, a restricted specification. A more general formulation would measure the social security programme by a constant elasticity function of the benefit level and the eligibility rate; for instance, Social Security = $(B/Y)^{\gamma}(SSPA)$. Although this nonlinear function could be included in the otherwise linear savings function, this has not been done in the current paper. The two-variable linear specification described above can be regarded as a linear approximation to the function

$$d(\text{Social Security}) = \gamma \frac{(\text{Social Security})}{B/Y} d(B/Y) + \frac{(\text{Social Security})}{SSPA} dSSPA \tag{8.24}$$

This decomposition of the change in social security must be borne in mind in evaluating the impact of differences in the benefit level and the eligibility rate.

One final characteristic of a nation's social security system that may influence the rate of saving is the age of the programme itself. In the early years of a social security old-age system, there will be a reduction in saving (or an increase in dissaving) among those who are already retired or near retired, but an increase in saving by those who are induced to plan for retirement. As the system matures, the possibility of dissaving is reduced and further benefit increases induce little extra retirement. It is difficult to imagine capturing these complex effects with the current small sample. Although various interactions between the age of the programme and the other variables might usefully be investigated, the current analysis will consider only a simple additive effect. More specifically, the variable *START*, the year in which the system started, is equivalent to including the age of the system in years.

The corporate saving ratio (*CSR*), i.e. the ratio of corporate saving to national income, is estimated with data on corporate saving (excluding the saving of public corporations) presented in the *United Nations Yearbook of National Accounts Statistics.* The ratio represents an average for the same years (generally 1954–60) as the private saving ratio.

Note that all ratio variables are expressed as *percentages,* to make the scales commensurate.

V. THE ESTIMATED SAVINGS FUNCTION

The estimates presented in this section provide strong support for the extended life-cycle model and show quite clearly that social security pensions substantially depress private saving. Although the number of observations is severely limited, the relative standard errors are reassuringly low. Moreover, the basic results are quite robust and generally change relatively little when additional, but insignificant, variables are added.

Despite the small size of the sample, the labour-force participation of the aged (*LPAGED*) is treated as endogenous, and the equation is estimated by two-stage least squares.[27] Although a case might obviously be made for regarding some of the other variables as endogenous, I think that the extent of simultaneity is much less, and, because of the small sample size, prefer to regard them as exogenous.[28] It clearly would be desirable to have a large enough sample to permit a thorough investigation of the simultaneity problem. Even the limited use of two-stage least squares in the current study must be interpreted with caution: because of the small size of the sample, consistency is a property of only limited interest. The actual coefficient values are quite similar to ordinary least-squares estimates that have been calculated but not presented here.

I have followed the procedure of Houthakker (1961, 1965) and Modigliani (1970) by weighting each observation to reflect the size of the country's population.[29] As a result, including Costa Rica and Trinidad in the sample has almost no effect on the estimates, since together they account for less than 1 per cent of the total sample weight. Moreover, restricting the sample to only 15 of Modigliani's 36 countries still retains 62 per cent of the original total sample weight and 97 per cent of the weight in his sample of 21 'fully developed' economies. The computer program adjusts the degrees of freedom, standard errors, and so on, for these weights. It is perhaps reassuring to note that re-estimating some of the basic equations without the weights did not alter any of the implications.

Table 8.1 presents the estimates of alternative specifications of the private savings function with social security eligibility measured by the number of pension recipients per aged individual. It should again be noted that the dependent variable is the ratio of private savings to national income and that social security benefits include only pensions for the aged, survivors and the disabled. The savings ratio has a mean of 12·7 per cent with a standard deviation of 4·1 per cent. The corrected R^2 values (i.e. $\bar{R}^2$) almost always exceed 0·90. Because the equations are estimated by two-stage least squares, I have instead presented the standard error of the estimate for each equation.

[27] Section VI discusses the specification of the retirement equation.

[28] Both the recent rate of growth and the level of per capita income are, to some extent, exogenous and dependent upon the national saving rate. Modigliani (1970) presents evidence and analysis to show that the simultaneity with the recent rate of growth is unlikely to be a serious problem. Similarly, the difference in saving rates is likely to be responsible for very little of the current international differences in income levels. Aaron (1967 and 1968) examined the hypothesis that the saving rate influences the percentage of national income spent on social insurance (including not only old-age pensions, but also health benefits, and so on) and concluded that the evidence does not support this hypothesis. Aaron's tests were not done in the framework of a consistently estimated simultaneous system, but it seems reasonable, from other evidence about the development of social insurance, to concur with his conclusion. These conjectures obviously deserve more careful investigation.

[29] There is also a correction for the number of years of data used in estimating each country's saving rate; for some countries the number of years used was one or two more or less than the standard seven years for 1954–60.

TABLE 8.1

PRIVATE SAVINGS FUNCTION WITH ENDOGENOUS RETIREMENT BEHAVIOUR

Equation	*G*	*AGE*	*DEP*	*LPAGED*	*BPA/Y*	*B/Y*	*SSPA*	100/*Y*	*LE65*	*RT*	*START*	*CSR*	*N*	*SE*
1.1	1·34 (0·17)	−1·09 (0·27)	−0·22 (0·07)	−0·25 (0·07)	−0·104 (0·022)				1·81 (0·78)				15	1·03
1.2	1·63 (0·41)	−0·98 (0·44)	−0·24 (0·10)	−0·24 (0·09)		−0·108 (0·047)	−0·083 (0·022)		2·03 1·01				15	1·22
1.3	1·02 (0·25)	−1·01 (0·28)	−0·16 (0·09)	−0·31 (0·08)	−0·090 (0·025)			8·31 (7·66)	1·60 (0·80)				15	1·01
1.4	0·84 (0·59)	−1·06 (0·39)	−0·16 (0·10)	−0·37 (0·11)		−0·067 (0·048)	−0·071 (0·020)	14·06 (8·24)	1·86 (0·90)				15	1·07
1.5	1·17 (0·19)	−1·11 (0·32)	−0·17 (0·08)	−0·26 (0·08)	−0·077 (0·022)								15	1·25
1.6	1·50 (0·47)	−0·86 (0·52)	−0·14 (0·09)	−0·23 (0·11)		−0·092 (0·055)	−0·056 (0·020)						15	1·44
1.7	1·48 (0·21)	−0·96 (0·30)	−0·22 (0·06)	−0·23 (0·07)	−0·095 (0·023)				2·20 (0·86)	1·03 (0·96)			15	1·02
1.8	1·64 (0·44)	−0·96 (0·50)	−0·23 (0·11)	−0·24 (0·10)		−0·104 (0·060)	−0·081 (0·029)		2·09 (1·17)	0·18 (1·45)			15	1·32
1.9	1·42 (0·20)	−1·04 (0·29)	−0·24 (0·07)	−0·25 (0·07)	−0·093 (0·027)				1·67 (0·83)		0·035 (0·047)		15	1·06
1.10	1·69 (0·45)	−0·91 (0·49)	−0·24 (0·10)	−0·24 (0·10)		−0·101 (0·053)	−0·074 (0·030)		1·84 (1·15)		0·029 (0·062)		15	1·30
1.11	1·31 (0·22)	−0·97 (0·32)	−0·14 (0·11)	−0·28 (0·08)	−0·092 (0·033)				0·78 (1·38)			0·099 (0·033)	13	1·11
1.12	0·98 (0·61)	−1·26 (0·43)	−0·15 (0·08)	−0·38 (0·08)		−0·026 (0·076)	−0·073 (0·024)		0·86 (1·07)			0·542 (0·441)	13	0·88

Note: The dependent variable is S/Y. All equations contain a constant term, which is not shown. Standard errors are shown in parentheses. Equations

Equation 1.1 contains the basic variables of the extended life-cycle model, with the effect of social security measured by the relative benefits per aged individual. Each of the coefficients has the anticipated sign, is of a reasonable order of magnitude, and is substantially larger than its standard error. A 1 per cent increase in the rate of growth of national income (*G*) raises the savings rate by 1·34 per cent (s.e. 0·17). An increase in the relative number of older persons (*AGE*) and of minor dependants (*DEP*) also decreases the saving rate in the expected way.[30] These findings confirm the basic implications of the traditional life-cycle model.

The coefficient of *LPAGED* (–0·25) shows the importance of taking the labour-force participation of the aged into account in analysing intercountry differences in saving behaviour. The fraction of men over 65 who are economically active has a sample mean of 41 per cent with a standard deviation of 9·7 per cent. A decrease in the labour-force participation rate from one standard deviation above the average to one standard deviation below the average would, therefore, increase the saving rate by an estimated 4·8 percentage points ((0·25)(19·4) = 4·8) or by about 38 per cent of the mean saving rate. A longer life expectancy should, *ceteris paribus,* increase the rate of saving. The coefficient of *LE*65 shows that a one-year increase in life expectancy at age 65 adds about 1·8 per cent to the saving rate. Note that this effect is evaluated with the retirement behaviour (*LPAGED*) held constant. The actual effect of greater life expectancy would probably be divided between a later retirement and a higher level of consumption; the net effect on saving would therefore be smaller.

The implied impact of the social security variable is very substantial. The level of social security benefits per aged individual as a percentage of per capita income (*BPA*/*Y*) has an average of 40 per cent in the current sample. The value for the United States is 35·6 per cent. The coefficient of –0·104 implies that the average level of relative benefits (40) reduces the private saving rate by 4·2 percentage points. The standard deviation of *BPA*/*Y* in the sample is 26, implying that an increase in the magnitude of the social security programme from one standard deviation below the sample average to one standard deviation above reduces the private saving rate by 5·4 percentage points, 43 per cent of the sample mean rate of saving.

This discussion of the impact of *BPA*/*Y* obscures the difference between changes in the benefit level and changes in the extent of coverage. In equation 1.2 the composite social security variable is replaced by its two components: the value of benefits per recipient relative to per capita income (*B*/*Y*), and the number of social security pension recipients as a percentage of the aged population (*SSPA*). None of the other coefficients is altered appreciably. The coefficient of the benefit-level variable (–0·108) is only slightly greater than the

[30] Recall that *AGE* is the number of persons over age 65 expressed as a percentage of those between 20 and 65. Similarly, *DEP* is the number of persons under 20 expressed as a percentage of those between 20 and 65.

coefficient of the coverage variable (–0·083); with such a small sample, the difference is not statistically significant. This difference in the magnitude of the coefficients is, however, consistent with the implications of the extended life-cycle model of section II. An increase in the fraction of the population covered (*SSPA*) will have two countervailing effects: a wealth replacement effect that reduces private saving, and an induced retirement effect that increases private saving. An increase in the benefit level (*B*/*Y*) will also have both effects, but the wealth replacement effect is likely to be relatively stronger.[31] If the observations represented steady-state situations in each country, the *LPAGED* variable would absorb the induced retirement effect, leaving the coefficients of the social security variables to measure only the wealth replacement effect. But the economies are not in a steady state and, in particular, the full long-run effects of the social security system on retirement behaviour have not generally been reached. When a new social security system is introduced or the coverage and relative benefits of an old system are increased, the short-run change in retirement behaviour is likely to be less than the long-run change. The model of section II implies that some younger workers will increase their saving in anticipation of future retirement. Until the retirement level has adjusted to its new equilibrium, this induced retirement effect on saving will not be fully adjusted for by including the *LPAGED* variable.

Equation 1.3 implies that the savings rate is not directly affected by the level of per capita income. More specifically, the inverse of mean income is used instead of the level, so that the variance of this variable will not be dominated by the highest-income countries. An alternative equation using the income level (not shown) leads to the same conclusions. The positive sign of the coefficient is the opposite of the usual assumption that savings may rise with income. It should be stressed, however, that the coefficient of the income variable measures only the direct effect of income with the retirement behaviour held constant. If a higher level of income decreases the labour-force participation of the aged, it will also increase the rate of saving. The next section presents evidence that this indirect life-cycle effect is quite important. Equation 1.4 shows a similar result for when the social security variable is divided into its components.

The sample range of the life-expectancy variable (*LE*65) is quite small (between 11·9 and 14·9 years). The coefficient therefore reflects intercountry differences that, because of the substantial intracountry variance, might not be perceived by local individuals. The observed coefficient, although large and statistically significant, may therefore be a spurious result. Further work on the general effects of life expectancy on retirement and savings is necessary in order to assess the appropriateness of this coefficient. Equations 1.5 and 1.6 show that omitting the *LE*65 variable does not appreciably alter any of the other conclusions.

[31] Evidence for this is presented in the next section, where intercountry differences in *LPAGED* are examined.

If a social security programme involves a retirement test as a condition of receiving benefits, the induced retirement effect is strengthened. This should be reflected in the actual labour-force participation of the aged and in the number of social security pensioners. The presence of a retirement test should not in itself increase the rate of saving. This is confirmed by the insignificant coefficient of the variable *RT* in equations 1.7 and 1.8.

Including the year in which the social security programme started (*START*) is equivalent to including the age of the programme. The insignificant coefficient (equations 1.9 and 1.10) probably should not be interpreted as signifying anything more than that the programme age does not have an additive linear effect on the rate of saving. Further work is required to develop an explicit model of the nonlinear way in which the effect of the social security programme changes as the system matures. The current sample is, unfortunately, too small to permit an analysis of these interactions. It is reassuring, however, that the other coefficients are not substantially affected by introducing the *START* variable.

The final pair of equations in Table 8.1 assess the effect of the corporate saving rate (*CSR*).[32] When the magnitude of the social security system is measured by the relative benefits per aged individual (equation 1.11), the point estimate of the coefficient of the *CSR* indicates that, if corporations save an additional 1 per cent of national income, the total private saving rate will increase by 0·10 percentage points. When the relative social security benefit level and the extent of coverage are separated (equation 1.12), the point estimate of the coefficient of *CSR* rises to 0·54. Although this second estimate is more than its standard error, both standard errors are too large to permit any precise conclusions from this evidence. The general impression that higher corporate saving has a positive effect on total private saving with a coefficient of approximately one-half is roughly consistent with the earlier time-series analysis (Feldstein, 1973; Feldstein and Fane, 1973) and with the estimates of Modigliani (1970) for an international cross-section.

In all of the estimates of Table 8.1, the extent of social security coverage is measured by the number of social security pension recipients per aged person. As was explained in section IV, this tends to understate the extent of coverage, the reason being that, in countries with a retirement test, some of the aged persons covered who are not yet receiving benefits are ineligible because they are still at work. An alternative variable measures eligibility by the number of pension recipients per aged *person* in countries without a retirement test, but by the number of pension recipients per aged *retiree* in countries with a retirement test. This variable, *SSPARA*, tends to overstate the extent of social security coverage. The same is true when *SSPARA* is combined with the relative benefit level to form (*BPARA*/*Y*), the product of (*B*/*Y*) and *SSPARA*. Table 8.2 shows that substituting *SSPARA* for *SSPA* and *SPARA* for *BPA* in the

[32] Note that, because of lack of data, it is now necessary to eliminate two countries (Italy and Norway).

TABLE 8.2

PRIVATE SAVINGS FUNCTION WITH ENDOGENOUS RETIREMENT BEHAVIOUR AND SOCIAL SECURITY ELIGIBILITY ADJUSTED FOR RETIREMENT TEST

Equation	*G*	*AGE*	*DEP*	*LPAGED*	*BPARA/Y*	*B/Y*	*SSPARA*	100/*Y*	*LE65*	*RT*	*START*	*CSR*	*N*	*SE*
2.1	0·96	–0·96	–0·18	–0·12	–0·065				0·81				15	1·34
	(0·23)	(0·36)	(0·08)	(0·08)	(0·021)				(0·91)					
2.2	1·28	–0·66	–0·16	–0·07		–0·114	–0·050		0·46				15	1·50
	(0·51)	(0·55)	(0·11)	(0·10)		(0·060)	(0·019)		(1·01)					
2.3	1·34	–0·80	–0·22	–0·13	–0·070				2·29	2·69			15	0·82
	(0·17)	(0·22)	(0·05)	(0·05)	(0·013)				(0·69)	(0·72)				
2.4	1·33	–0·80	–0·24	–0·13		–0·081	–0·057		2·23	3·00			15	0·86
	(0·29)	(0·30)	(0·06)	(0·05)		(0·034)	(0·011)		(0·75)	(0·79)				
2.5	1·16	–0·76	–0·18	–0·17	–0·064			4·89	2·17	2·58			15	0·79
	(0·28)	(0·22)	(0·07)	(0·07)	(0·015)			(6·25)	(0·69)	(0·71)				
2.6	1·03	–0·83	–0·20	–0·19		–0·061	–0·052		2·18	2·93			15	0·80
	(0·45)	(0·29)	(0·07)	(0·09)		(0·040)	(0·012)		(0·70)	(0·75)				
2.7	0·94	–0·93	–0·16	–0·11	–0·056								15	1·34
	(0·22)	(0·36)	(0·08)	(0·08)	(0·020)									
2.8	1·41	–0·48	–0·13	–0·04		–0·123	–0·045						15	1·49
	(0·52)	(0·56)	(0·10)	(0·10)		(0·059)	(0·018)							
2.9	1·16	–0·94	–0·23	–0·16	–0·055				0·72		0·068		15	1·25
	(0·27)	(0·33)	(0·09)	(0·07)	(0·021)				(0·84)		(0·051)			
2.10	1·45	–0·67	–0·21	–0·13		–0·096	–0·042		0·39		0·073		15	1·39
	(0·50)	(0·50)	(0·11)	(0·09)		(0·056)	(0·019)		(0·39)		(0·057)			
2·11	0·92	–0·97	–0·10	–0·20	–0·049				–0·28			0·35	13	1·41
	(0·25)	(0·44)	(0·15)	(0·09)	(0·030)				(1·56)			(0·38)		
2.12	0·20	–1·42	–0·10	–0·31		–0·050	–0·025		–0·63			0·95	13	1·42
	(0·85)	(0·85)	(0·15)	(0·15)		(0·126)	(0·027)		(1·46)			(0·70)		

Note: The dependent variable is *S/Y*. All equations contain a constant term, which is not shown. Standard errors are shown in parentheses. Equations are estimated by two-stage least squares with *LPAGED* endogenous. See text for definitions and data.

specification of Table 8.1 has little effect on the parameter estimates. The coefficients of *SSPARA* and *BPARA/Y* are somewhat smaller than the corresponding coefficients of *SSPA* and *BPA/Y*, but this reflects no more than the increase in the size of the new variables because of the smaller denominator. For all of the specifications, the equations of Table 8.2 have higher sums of squared residuals, indicating that the original specification is statistically preferable.

VI. SOCIAL SECURITY AND RETIREMENT BEHAVIOUR

In order to assess the extent to which social security programmes are responsible for international differences in saving rates, it is necessary to evaluate their indirect effect through induced retirement. The equations presented in the previous section show the effect on savings of the labour-force participation rate of men over 65 (*LPAGED*). In the present section is estimated the impact of social security programmes on this measure of retirement behaviour. The parameter estimates presented in these two sections (V and VI) will then be combined in section VII to assess the net effect of international differences in social security.

The extended life-cycle model of section II indicates the likely impact of social security on retirement behaviour. Equations (8.20) and (8.21) imply that a higher level of benefits and the existence of an earnings test or retirement test are both likely to decrease the labour-force participation rate of older persons.[33] The relative benefit level (*B/Y*) and the retirement-test dummy (*RT*) are therefore both included in the equation. The labour-force participation rate (*LPAGED*) also will reflect the extent of coverage of the social security programme. Using the number of beneficiaries per aged person (*SSPA*) to measure this would probably introduce a spurious negative correlation with *LPAGED*, because *SSPA* would be reduced in a country with a retirement test if, for any reason, the labour-force participation rate of covered older persons increased. By contrast, using the number of beneficiaries per aged person where there is no retirement test, and the number of beneficiaries per retiree where such a test does exist (i.e. *SSPARA*) would introduce a spurious positive correlation with *LPAGED*, because *SSPARA* would be increased in a country with a retirement test if, for any reason, the labour-force participation rate of uncovered older persons were increased.

International differences in life expectancy near the beginning of the normal retirement period (*LE*65) are likely to have some effect on retirement behaviour if they are correctly perceived by local individuals. An increase in life expectancy can be regarded as an increase in an individual's basic resource endowment. The likely effect of such an increased endowment is a greater demand for both goods and leisure; i.e. the period of retirement will increase, but by less

[33] This is true unless an increase in second-period leisure reduced the marginal utility of second-period consumption by more than it would be reduced by a unit increase in second-period consumption; see footnote 8 above.

than the increase in life expectancy. If the individual were merely to add the extra years of life to his retirement, he would have to reduce the average level of consumption during his working years and his original years of retirement. By contrast, if the individual were to postpone retirement by the increase in life expectancy, he would obtain a higher sustainable level of consumption with no increase in leisure. Of course, the response to greater life expectancy may be affected by international differences in the social security programmes. In particular, if the eligibility age or other provisions are adjusted to reflect the national mortality experience, the expected effects of life expectancy differences may be offset.

Although the effect of a higher wage level on the demand for leisure cannot be determined *a priori,* both the historical evidence and survey results indicate that the income effects generally dominate substitution effects. The same is likely to be true for the effect, on retirement, of an increase in the wage level. When wages are low, the individual is likely to allocate more of his total endowment of years to the production of income, and fewer to the leisure of retirement. As wages rise, the marginal value of consumption falls and the possibility of a comfortable retirement increases. For an increase in the level of per capita income, the importance of the income effect relative to the consumption effect is likely to be even greater. Aaron (1968) has shown the existence of such an inverse relation between per capita income and labour-force participation among older men.

The final variable that will be considered is the age of the social security programme. As has been noted a number of times in earlier sections, the extended life-cycle model suggests that the effects of a social security programme will not be the same in the short run and in the long run. It is most likely that the retirement rate will increase with the age of the system. Young workers will respond to the introduction of a social security programme by planning to retire and by saving more during their working life (including saving in private pensions), so as to supplement the social security pension. Older workers who had not planned to retire, and who have too little in private assets to make additional retirement preferable to continued work, may often choose to continue working. As the system matures, everyone has the opportunity to anticipate retirement and, therefore, to save accordingly. As usual, there is a countervailing effect: when the social security programme is introduced, there will be older workers who have been saving in order to retire at a later time; the introduction of the social security programme will raise their effective wealth and, thus, induce them to retire earlier. The effect of the programme's age is further complicated by the fact that, long after the programme has begun, there may be substantial changes in the coverage and relative benefits. All of these aspects require further analysis if we are fully to understand the impact of social security programmes. Here, I shall do no more than add a measure of the age of the social security programme (i.e. the variable *START*), so as to assess a net effect of this factor. As before, only a simple linear and additive form will be examined.

The proportion of men over age 65 who are still in the labour force (*LPAGED*) has a sample mean of 41 per cent with a standard deviation of 9·6 per cent, reflecting a range from 25 to 74 per cent. The results presented in this section show that most of this variation can be explained by the social security and income variables described above. However, the sensitivity of the parameter estimates to the particular form of the equation and to the measurement of the social security variables implies that the results should be regarded as preliminary and tentative. Moreover, the parameter estimates may be biased by the omission of a number of potentially important determinants of retirement behaviour, including the occupational structure of the economy (especially the role of agriculture), the extent of self-employment, the retirement provisions of private pensions, and the existence of compulsory retirement rules in employment.[34]

Equation 3.1 of Table 8.3 shows that higher levels of income and more substantial social security programmes both decrease the extent of labourforce participation of men over age 65 (*LPAGED*). More specifically, the coefficient of $100/Y$ implies that a higher per capita income reduces labour-force participation, but that this effect is much more important for low-income than for high-income countries. At a per capita income of \$600 (near the sample mean), an additional \$100 of income decreases the percentage of aged men in the labour force by 1·2 percentage points, while at \$1500 (near the top of the range) an extra \$100 decreases LPAGED by only 0·2 percentage points. This provides a basis for estimating the indirect effect of income on saving, as mentioned in section V. Equation 1.1 of Table 8.1 indicates that a 1 per cent increase in *LPAGED* causes the saving rate (S/Y) to fall by 0·25. Combining this with the result of equation 3.1 implies that a \$100 increase in income at $Y = \$600$ will increase S/Y by 0·30. Similarly, equation 3.1 implies that an increase in income from $Y = \$500$ to $Y = \$1000$ reduces *LPAGED* by 4·4 per cent and thus raises S/Y by 1·1 percentage points, or by nearly 10 per cent of its mean. This indirect effect may account for the positive effect that earlier international studies have found income to have on the saving rate.

An increase in social security benefits as a percentage of disposable income (B/Y) substantially reduces *LPAGED.* Since the value of B/Y has a sample standard deviation of 18, the coefficient of B/Y in equation 3.1 (i.e. −0·29) implies that an increase in B/Y from one standard deviation below the average to one standard deviation above it reduces *LPAGED* by nearly 10 points. The effect of B/Y depends, of course, on the extent of coverage of the social security programme; the specification of equation 3.1 must be regarded as a linear approximation similar to the savings equations. The coefficient of *SSPA* (−0·17) indicates that an increase in the extent of coverage also induces increased retirement. The elasticity of *LPAGED* with respect to B/Y (evaluated

[34] Of course, both compulsory retirement rules and the retirement provisions of private pensions will be influenced by the social insurance programmes, but other factors (including seniority systems and government rules) also will have an impact.

TABLE 8.3

LABOUR-FORCE PARTICIPATION OF MEN OVER 65 YEARS OLD

Equation	100/*Y*	*Y*/100	*B*/*Y*	*SSPA*	*SSPARA*	*RT*	*LE*65	*START*	$\bar{R}^2$	*SE*
3.1	43·7 (13·9)		–0·29 (0·15)	–0·17 (0·06)		–2·86 (5·24)			0·69	5·62
3.2	42·3 (17·6)		–0·18 (0·19)		–0·08 (0·06)	5·97 (4·40)			0·53	6·86
3.3	122·1 (19·6)	1·91 (0·43)	–0·25 (0·09)	–0·10 (0·04)		–8·17 (3·33)			0·89	3·33
3.4	175·4 (38·3)	3·15 (0·88)	–0·37 (0·12)	–0·20 (0·07)		–9·30 (3·90)	3·57 (3·23)	–0·39 (0·24)	0·90	3·21
3.5	134·9 (24·2)	2·22 (0·52)	–0·16 (0·11)		–0·03 (0·04)	–4·17 (3·58)			0·83	4·17
3.6	102·6 (71·5)	1·41 (1·78)	–0·06 (0·24)		0·02 (0·11)	–5·52 (5·63)	–2·02 (5·23)	0·24 (0·49)	0·79	4·64

Note: The dependent variable is *LPAGED*, expressed as a percentage. All equations contain a constant term, which is not shown. Standard errors are shown in parentheses. Equations are estimated by ordinary least square with 15 observations. See text for definitions and data.

at the means of both variables) is −0·41, while the corresponding elasticity with respect to *SSPA* is −0·32. This supports the view that in the current range there is less scope for greater coverage to induce retirement than there is for increased benefits to do so. The retirement-test variable (*RT*) has the correct sign (i.e. the existence of a retirement test reduces labour-force participation) but is small and completely insignificant. Omitting the *RT* variable results in little change in the other coefficients but does reduce their standard errors to a noticeable extent.

Equation 3.2 shows that similar results are obtained when the extent-of-coverage variable is adjusted for the retirement test (*SSPARA*), but the equation has lower overall explanatory power and the standard error of (B/Y) is substantially increased.

The implication that the retirement test has no effect on retirement is particularly puzzling and suggests that the equation may be misspecified. Equation 3.3 shows that a more general specification of the impact of the per capita income alters the estimated effect of the retirement test. The new specification includes the level of income as well as its inverse. Both of the income variables are very much larger than their standard errors. Although the coefficient of B/Y falls to −0·25 and the coefficient of *SSPA* to −0·10, both coefficients are more than twice their standard errors. The coefficient of the *RT* variable now implies that the existence of a retirement test decreases *LPAGED* by 8·2 percentage points, or by about 20 per cent of the sample mean; the coefficient is more than 2·5 times its standard error. The simple equation explains almost all of the variation in *LPAGED* among the 15 sample countries; the corrected $\bar{R}^2$ is 0·89.

The implied effect of income on retirement is now more complex. At low and moderate income levels, an increase in per capita income increases retirement (reduces *LPAGED*). But, when income exceeds \$800, higher per capita income appears to be associated with a lower retirement rate (higher *LPAGED*). It is not clear whether this reversal is a real phenomenon or simply a reflection of the particular form of nonlinearity in the specification; the parameter values imply almost no change in the retirement rate between income levels of \$600 and \$1000, and the sample contains only two countries with income over \$1000. It will be interesting to examine other nonlinear specifications and to return to this question with data for a more recent period in which incomes are generally higher.

Equation 3.4 shows that neither the life expectancy at age 65 (*LE*65) nor the age of the programme (*START*) has a statistically significant effect or alters the other coefficients. The sign of the coefficient of *LE*65 implies that greater life expectancy reduces the retirement rate as expected. The negative coefficient of *START* is also the more likely sign; an older programme implies a lower rate of labour-force participation.

The results with the social security coverage variable adjusted for the retirement test (*SSPARA*) are less clear because of relatively large standard errors. Equation 3.5 adds the income level to the specification of equation 3.2. The new variable is quite significant and this retirement test variable now has the anticipated sign. The coefficient of B/Y is approximately the same as before, but its standard error is reduced and the coefficient of the coverage variable (*SSPARA*) is much lower and smaller than its standard error. When *LE*65 and *START* are added to this specification (equation 3.6), all of the standard errors become so large relative to the coefficients that no meaningful inferences can be drawn.

Despite the ambiguity of this last case, the evidence supports the conclusion that higher retirement rates are induced by higher benefit levels, by a retirement test and, over a broad range, by a higher level of per capita income. These are, of course, average tendencies over the full range of sample values. It seem reasonable to believe that, as the retirement rate is increased by higher social security benefits, the effect of further increases in those benefits will be smaller. Although the current sample is not large enough to assess this non-linearity, a larger sample of international data or an aggregate time-series of cross-sections within a single country should be able to shed light on this important question.

VII. THE NET EFFECT OF INTERNATIONAL DIFFERENCES IN SOCIAL SECURITY ON PRIVATE SAVING

It is now time to combine the private saving function of section V and the retirement function of section VI, so as to assess the total net impact that international differences in social security have on rates of private saving. More specifically, I shall examine the effect on the private saving rate (S/Y) of a 25 percentage point difference in the relative benefit level (B/Y) and in the extent of coverage (*SSPA*).[35]

Equation 3.3 of Table 8.3 will be used to describe the induced retirement behaviour. The key coefficients of this equation are the effect of B/Y (i.e. −0·25) and the effect of *SSPA* (i.e. −0·10). The corresponding equation for the saving rate is equation 1.2 (Table 8.1). Here the key coefficients are the effect of *LPAGED* (−0·25), the effect of B/Y (−0·108) and the effect of *SSPA* (−0·083).

Consider first the effect of an increase in the relative benefit level (B/Y) by 25 percentage points. Equation 1.2 implies a pure wealth replacement effect that decreases the saving rate by 2·70 percentage points, about one-fifth of the sample average rate of saving (12·7 per cent).[36] The extent of the offsetting effect of induced retirement on saving will depend on the initial level of retirement behaviour. An increase in B/Y will have a greater effect when *LPAGED* is high than when it is low. Equation 3.3 indicates that, on average for the

[35] In the sample, (B/Y) varies from 35 per cent to 86 per cent, and *SSPA* effectively varies from nearly no pensions to complete coverage.

[36] As pointed out in section V, this is likely to underestimate the pure wealth replacement effect, because the *LPAGED* variable does not fully adjust for the induced retirement effect until the social security system has fully matured.

sample, an increase in *B/Y* of 25 per cent would decrease *LPAGED* by 6·2 percentage points; the pure induced retirement effect is thus an increase in the saving range of 0·24 (6·2) = 1·49.[37] Combining the wealth replacement effect and the induced retirement effect implies than an increase in *B/Y* of 25 per cent would reduce the private saving rate by about 1·21 percent.

The effect of increasing the fraction of the aged covered (*SSPA*) by 25 percentage points would be somewhat larger. The direct wealth replacement effect would be a reduction in the saving rate of 2·08 percentage points. The indirect induced retirement effect would be a 2·5 per cent increase in the retirement of men over 65 and, thus, an increase in saving of 0·60 percentage points. The net effect thus is a reduction in the saving rate of 1·48 percentage points.

The net effect of social security on private saving can also be estimated directly by excluding the retirement behaviour variable (*LPAGED*) from the savings equation, but including those other variables that indirectly affect saving through their impact on retirement. This generalised savings equation may be regarded as a reduced form of the two-equation behavioural model. Alternatively, the new equation may be considered the basic behaviour function, and the previous decomposition – into an effect of social security conditional on retirement, and an effect of social security on retirement itself – may be considered to be only an analytic convenience. The choice of interpretation depends on whether we regard the individual as simultaneously choosing a retirement and savings plan (as in the model of section II) or as making savings decisions conditional on a retirement plan. In either interpretation, the generalised savings function provides a direct estimate of the net effect that social security and other variables have on savings. The difficulties in estimating the retirement-behaviour equations (Table 8.3) and the problems of using two-stage least squares in small samples suggests that it is worthwhile to examine these direct estimates.

The results presented in Table 8.4 provide further confirmation of the extended life-cycle model and imply a somewhat stronger net effect of changes in social security. Comparing equation 4.1 with the equations of Table 8.1 shows the effect of estimating an *unconditional* savings function, i.e. of excluding *LPAGED*. The income variables and retirement-test variable are quite significant and the life-expectancy variable has a substantially larger effect. The two income variables imply that the saving rate rises with per capita income until income exceeds $750; the apparent reversal above this level may (as in the retirement equations of Table 8.3) reflect only the particular nonlinear specification. The simpler specification of the income effect in equation 4.2 also implies that the saving rate rises with income, but the coefficient is not statistically significant. These estimates may be contrasted with equation 1.3 of Table 8.1, in which income appears to have a negative effect

[37] Because the effect of *B/Y* on *LPAGED* is underestimated until the system has fully matured, the value of 1·49 may also be an underestimate.

TABLE 8.4

GENERALISED PRIVATE SAVINGS FUNCTION

Equation	*G*	*AGE*	*DEP*	*BPA/Y*	*B/Y*	*SSPA*	*BPARA/Y*	100/*Y*	*Y*/100	*LE*65	*RT*	$\bar{R}^2$	*SE*
4.1	1·93	–0·94	–0·22	–0·086				–37·9	–0·58	2·22	2·84	0·95	1·43
	(0·41)	(0·46)	(0·13)	(0·038)				(18·4)	(0·30)	(1·22)	(1·48)		
4.2	1·88	–0·54	–0·24	–0·071				– 7·1		2·64	1·64	0·92	1·67
	(0·48)	(0·48)	(0·15)	(0·044)				(10·0)		(1·41)	(1·55)		
4.3	1·61	–1·03	–0·14	–0·061				–41·9	–0·68		2·16	0·92	1·65
	(0·43)	(0·53)	(0·14)	(0·042)				(21·1)	(0·35)		(1·64)		
4.4	1·93	–0·92	–0·20		–0·077	–0·065		–39·2	–0·65	2·08	2·53	0·94	1·74
	(0·72)	(0·71)	(0·16)		(0·092)	(0·043)		(26·1)	(0·44)	(1·54)	(2·26)		
4.5	1·63	–0·86	–0·23				–0·070	–25·4	–0·38	2·31	3·81	0·97	1·06
	(0·26)	(0·31)	(0·08)				(0·018)	(12·1)	(0·22)	(0·90)	1·08		
4.6	1·66	–0·67	–0·27				–0·072	– 6·7		2·74	2·89	0·96	1·20
	(0·30)	(0·33)	(0·09)				(0·021)	(6·1)		(0·98)	(1·06)		

Note: The dependent variable is *S*/*Y*. All equations contain a constant term, which is not shown. Standard errors appear in parentheses. Equations are estimated by ordinary least squares with 15 observations. All ratio variables are measured as percentages. See text for definitions and data sources.

on the saving rate when retirement behaviour is held constant.[38] The implication is quite clear: a higher level of income raises the rate of saving (at least over some part of the income range) because it induces a higher rate of retirement. The positive effect that previous international studies (Houthakker, 1961 and 1965; Modigliani, 1970) found the income level to have on the saving rate[39] is therefore not inconsistent with the traditional model of homothetic consumption indifference curves. The stronger effect of the life expectancy at age 65 (compare equation 1.7) also shows that these variables indirectly affect savings by influencing the labour-force participation of the aged.

The net effect on the savings rate of an increase in social security benefits per aged person as a percentage of per capita income (BPA/Y) is −0·086. An increase in BPA/Y by 25 decreases the savings rate by 2·15 per cent, or by about 17 per cent of the average savings rate of 12·7 per cent. The effect here is larger than the net effect estimated by combining equations 1.2 and 3.3. When the life expectancy variable is omitted (equation 4.3), the coefficient of BPA/Y drops to −0·061 and the effect of a 25-point increase falls to a decrease of 1·53 per cent. The statistical significance of the *LE*65 variable and its potential indirect, as well as direct, effect suggest that relatively more weight should be given to the higher estimate.

If the social security benefit variable is divided into its two components (B/Y and *SSPA*), the separate coefficients (presented in equation 4.4) are quite similar to the coefficient of the composite BPA/Y variable in equation 4.1. Adjusting the social security eligibility variable for the effect of the retirement test (equations 4.5 and 4.6) changes the coefficients slightly but does not alter any of the qualitative results.

Although it is tempting to estimate the total impact of introducing the 'average' social security programme, it would be unwise to do so on the basis of the current equations. The specifications induce linear approximations that are likely to be quite misleading for analysing such gross changes.

VIII. CONCLUSION

This paper has provided international evidence to support the extended life-cycle model of household saving behaviour. The key characteristic of the model is the simultaneous determination of a retirement plan and a savings plan. The model thus emphasises that there are two important ways in which a social security programme influences individual saving: a wealth replacement effect and an induced retirement effect.

I regard the current parameter estimates as quite preliminary. A richer set of international data would permit more refined models and more precise estimates. A more specifically dynamic model using a longer time-series for

[38] When the income-level variable ($Y/100$) is added to the specification of Table 8.1 it is not significant.

[39] The stronger positive relation between S/Y and Y in previous studies probably reflects the larger number of low-income countries.

each country would be a vast improvement in dealing with the disequilibrium nature of the international observations. An analysis of micro-economic data would provide reassuring support for this international evidence and for the earlier aggregate time-series estimates for the United States.

No attempt has been made here to discuss the welfare implications of alternative social security programmes. It is clear that these programmes have substantial effects on retirement behaviour and on personal saving. They correct for imperfect private insurance markets but introduce inefficient distortions of their own. They affect the distribution of income, both directly and indirectly, through changes in the supplies of capital and labour. A thorough analysis of these welfare effects is a necessary first step for designing changes that will strengthen the social security programmes.

Finally, if social security programmes are to play a growing role in providing economic support for an increasingly aged population, it is important to develop policies that will offset the undesirable effects on aggregate capital accumulation. In the United States today, more than 75 per cent of men over 65 are now retired. Further increases in the provision of social security benefits are likely to decrease saving by substituting for private wealth without any substantial offsetting effect of additional retirement. An examination of the possible alternative policies to deal with this potential fall in capital accumulation lies beyond the scope of this paper.

REFERENCES

Aaron, Henry J., 'International Comparisons', Appendix D, in J. A. Pechman, H. J. Aaron and M. K. Taussig, *Social Security: Perspectives for Reform* (Washington, DC: The Brookings Institution, 1968).

Aaron, Henry J., 'Social Security: International Comparisons', in *Studies in the Economics of Income Maintenance,* ed. O. Eckstein (Washington, DC: The Brookings Institution, 1967), pp. 13–48.

Ando, Albert, and Modigliani, F., 'The "Life Cycle" Hypothesis of Saving: Aggregate Implications and Tests', *American Economic Review,* LIII (Mar 1963), pp. 55–84.

Brittain, John A., *Corporate Dividend Policy* (Washington, DC: The Brookings Institution, 1966).

Cagan, Philip, *The Effect of Pension Plans as Aggregate Savings* (New York: National Bureau of Economic Research, 1965).

Feldstein, Martin S., 'Corporate Taxation and Dividend Behavior', *Review of Economic Studies,* XXXVII (Jan 1970), pp. 57–72.

Feldstein, Martin S., 'Lowering the Permanent Rate of Unemployment', a study prepared for the use of the Joint Economic Committee, Congress of the United States (Washington, DC: US Government Printing Office, 1973).

Feldstein, Martin S., 'Tax Incentives, Corporate Saving, and Capital Accumulation in the United States', *Journal of Public Economics,* II (1973), pp. 159–71.

Feldstein, Martin S., 'Social Security, Induced Retirement and Aggregate Capital Accumulation', *Journal of Political Economy*, LXXXII (1974), pp. 905–26.

Feldstein, Martin S., and Fane, George, 'Taxes, Corporate Dividend Policy and Personal Savings: The British Postwar Experience', *Review of Economics and Statistics,* LV (Nov 1973), pp. 399–411.

Fisher, I., *The Theory of Interest* (New York: Macmillan, 1930).

Harrod, R. F., *Towards a Dynamic Economics* (London: Macmillan, 1948).

Houthakker, H. S., 'An International Comparison of Personal Saving', *Bulletin of the International Statistical Institute,* XXXVIII, (1961), pp. 56–9.

Houthakker, H. S., 'On Some Determinants of Saving in Developed and Underdeveloped Countries', in *Problems of Economic Development,* ed. E. A. G. Robinson (London: Macmillan, 1965), chapter 10.

International Labour Organisation, *Cost of Social Security* (Geneva).

International Labour Organisation, *Yearbook of Labor Statistics* (Geneva).

Katona, George, *Private Pensions and Individual Saving* (Survey Research Center, Institute for Social Research, The University of Michigan, 1965).

Leff, N. H., 'Dependency Rates and Savings Rates', *American Economic Review,* LIX (Dec 1969), pp. 886–96.

Mikesell, Raymond F., and Zinser, James E., 'The Nature of the Savings Function in Developing Countries: A Survey of the Theoretical and Empirical Literature', *Journal of Economic Literature,* XI, no 1 (Mar 1973), pp. 1–26.

Modigliani, Franco, 'The Life Cycle Hypothesis of Saving and Intercountry Differences in the Saving Ratio', in *Induction, Growth and Trade. Essays in Honour of Sir Roy Harrod,* ed. W. A. Eltis et al. (Oxford: The Clarendon Press, 1970).

Modigliani, F., and Brumberg, R., 'Utility Analysis and the Consumption Function: An Interpretation of Cross-Section Data', in *Post Keynesian Economics,* ed. K. Kurihara, (New Brunswick, NJ: Rutgers University Press, 1954), p. 430.

Munnell, Alicia, 'The Effect of Social Security on Personal Savings', PhD dissertation (Harvard University, 1974).

Tobin, James, 'Life Cycle Saving and Balanced Growth', in *Ten Economic Studies in the Tradition of Irving Fisher,* ed. W. Fellner et al. (New York: John Wiley and Sons, 1967).

Social Security Administration, US Department of Health, Education and Welfare, *Social Security Programs Throughout the World,* Research Report no. 40 (Washington, DC: US Government Printing Office, 1971).

United Nations, *Demographic Circular no. 24* (New York, 1958).

United Nations, *Demographic Yearbook* (New York).

United Nations Department of Economic and Social Affairs, *Yearbook of National Account Statistics* (New York).

9 A Social Security System and Short-Term Economic Policy

Patrick P. Jeanjean[1]
MINISTÈRE DE LA SANTÉ PUBLIQUE ET DE LA SECURITÉ SOCIALE, PARIS

The objective of this paper is to reach a better understanding of the way in which the social security system and macro-economic activity react upon each other. The particular example of France is studied. The first part of the paper presents the consequences for social security of a change in some aggregate variables, in particular in the inflation rate. In the second part, there is an analysis of the way in which the effectiveness of public expenditure stabilisation policies is affected by the social security system.

I. INTRODUCTION

The French social security budget reached 154·5 billion francs in 1973, while the State budget was 201 billion. The share of household income provided under the various social security schemes is one-fifth currently, and is getting larger. The importance and rapid development of social insurance can be observed everywhere in the Western world.

Not surprisingly, the principal motivations underlying the construction and improvement of the social security system were political or social. The system was designed to be self-supporting, and the main financial concern was to fulfil this objective. The magnitude of the social security budget suggests, nevertheless, that it may have important economic consequences at the aggregate level. However, in Europe, very little attention has been paid to the relationships between social security systems and economic behaviour or economic policies. To my knowledge, the only comprehensive study in this domain has been the one commissioned in 1968 and published by the EEC (1970). It was ambitious, but, because it lacked relevant data, the many problems with which it concerns itself are carefully stated rather than solved. Weitenberg (1968), using an econometric model that would be suitable for broader studies, examined, with specific reference to the Netherlands, the short-term and long-term incidences of an increase in social security contributions. In a simple way,

[1] The author is grateful to Professor Reviglio for helpful discussions and references.

Snyder (1970) tried to compare the macro-economic stabilising effects that social policy had, in several countries, during the years 1955–65.

In this paper, using France as an example, I shall investigate the reciprocal ways by which an economy, at the aggregate level, and its social security system react upon each other in the short term. There are two types of questions.

(1) How do economic fluctuations affect the social security budget? The problem is, indeed, to provide a huge public budget with adequate financing. Social security managers have intuitive answers to this question, but only one, very recent paper has been published on this topic, by Launay and Worms (1974). They used a simulation model much simpler than mine, but their conclusions are not very different.

(2) How does the social security system modify economic situations? More precisely, the social security system is built in such a way that its budget balance is very sensitive to economic fluctuations; therefore, it increases or decreases private disposable income and has a stabilising or destabilising effect that may reinforce or counteract traditional stabilisation policies. I shall describe those effects and try to estimate some orders of magnitude with a simplified version (Malgrange, 1972) of the economic model used by the Ministry of Finance for making short-term forecastings. Snyder (1970), using a simple model, also studied the stabilising effects of social security (for France and six other countries over the period 1955–65); however, his model treats benefits and contributions in a completely symmetrical way, a treatment that is questionable. Moreover, he was unable to distinguish between the automatic stabilising effects of the social security system as it is, which is the relevant point, and the effects of voluntary changes in social legislation.

First, since the reader may not be quite familiar with the French social security system, I must sketch its main features and emphasise points relevant for a dynamic analysis. More complete description can, of course, be found in specialised treatises (for example, Dupeynoux, 1971).

II. THE FRENCH SOCIAL SECURITY SYSTEM

GENERAL SET-UP

About 98 per cent of the French population is covered by the social security system. There are four types of benefits: health insurance benefits (which include maternity benefits and disability pensions), occupational disease and injury insurance, retirement pensions, and family benefits. In France, unemployment insurance is not considered part of the social security system. Public assistance programmes that provide special aid for only the poorest people also are independent of social security.

The social security programmes are organised on an occupational basis and are administered by different institutions. The most important scheme is the 'Régime Général', which covers about 60 per cent of the French population.

The different regulations obey the same general principles, but may vary widely on specific points.

Every employed or self-employed worker is covered by a *compulsory* health insurance programme and retirement plan, and receives family allowances. Only employed persons have an occupational disease and injury insurance. Compulsory health insurance generally does not provide 100 per cent coverage (except for very expensive treatments) and there are many private, complementary insurance plans. Pensions deriving from the compulsory public retirement schemes are proportional to earned income, but rather low; quite often they are supplemented by private, complementary pensions. A minimum complementary private programme is compulsory for those who are employed. With the exception of those who are retired and those who have lost their job and are registered at the National Unemployment Agency, inactive people are not as a rule, covered by any social security programme, other than on a voluntary basis.

Table 9.1 presents some data about the relative importance of different benefits. It is important to remember that in 1972 the State budget was 180 billion francs and gross national product 890 billion.

TABLE 9.1

Type of benefit		*Year 1972*		*Average growth rate 1973/1970 in real terms (per cent)*
		Billions francs	*Percentage*	
Health insurance		49·3	32·9	10·3
Occupational disease insurance		7·6	5·0	6·8
Retirement				
Basic schemes	58·0			
Complementary schemes	12·3			
Total		70·3	47·0	10·0
Family allowances		21·1	14·1	3·1
Unemployment		1·4	1·0	3·7
Total		149·7	100·0	8·1

Social benefits are financed mainly through the contributions of the people who are insured. These contributions are proportional to total income (for the self-employed, wages or taxable income) up to a certain limit; in addition, there is a health insurance contribution proportional to total earnings. For example, under the 'Régime Général', contribution rates are as follows.

(1) On earnings up to a ceiling: health insurance, 12·95 per cent; basic retirement pension, 10·25 per cent; family benefits, 9 per cent, occupational disease and injury insurance, 3·6 per cent.

(2) On total earnings: health insurance, 3 per cent.

For contributions of the first type, the ceiling was 27,820 francs per year in 1974; it is revised every year with reference to average wage increases during the previous year. I shall call an individual's income up to this ceiling his 'insured earnings'.

For employed people, contributions are paid monthly or quarterly by the employer; part of the payment is charged to the employee. Certain parts of the social security system, especially the farmers' schemes and the schemes for the self-employed, are financed also by particular taxes and government subsidies. Table 9.2 shows how the system was financed in 1972.

TABLE 9.2

Source of finance	*Structure of financing (year 1972)*	
	Billion francs	*Percentage*
Contributions	150·7	90·7
Taxes	3·9	2·4
Government subsidies	10·1	6·1
Other (interest, etc)	1·3	0·8
Total	166·0	100·0

In order to make clear the dynamics of the French social security system, it is necessary to describe the way benefits are computed. This task is tackled below.

HEALTH INSURANCE BENEFITS

The extent to which medical treatment expenditures are covered by health insurance depends on the circumstances. For long or expensive sicknesses the coverage rate is 100 per cent; in other cases, depending on the programme and the type of treatment, it may vary between 50 and 100 per cent. On average, it is about 80 per cent.

Compensation for loss of wages applies to wages earners only. A person who because of sickness is prevented from workings receives, depending on conditions, between 50 and 66·6 per cent of his insured income.

Maternity insurance and occupational disease and injury insurance are organised in the same way, but with better coverage. Health insurance coverage is limited to three years. If, after three years of sickness, a person still suffers a major loss of his earning capacity, he is eligible for a disability pension 30–50 per cent of previous insured income). These pensions are reassessed every year in the same way as old-age pensions are (see below).

The cost of health insurance has been growing steadily for many years. It is easy to see why this is so.

(1) The number of persons covered is increasing (slowly).
(2) The average per capita consumption of health services is growing.
(3) The cost of treatments is increasing. This cost can be broken down into three main components:

(i) Medical fees: about 95 per cent of French doctors have signed an agreement with the Health Insurance System; their fees are fixed by negotiations between the insurance authorities and the doctors' unions, and are revised (i.e. raised) every year.

(ii) Hospital cost: hospital prices must be approved by government agencies. They are increased at least once a year. Wages represent about two-thirds of total hospital costs.

(iii) Drugs: private companies manufacturing drugs have to justify their production costs and are not free to determine their selling prices, which are fixed or revised by a public commission.

OLD-AGE PENSIONS

Under the general schemes, workers are entitled to a pension from the age of 60. The pension is equal to a percentage of average insured earnings during the 10 best years before retirement. This percentage increases with the age of retirement and is proportional to the number of years during which a contribution was paid to the programme.

The pension cannot be less than a certain minimum. Every employed person is also entitled to supplementary pensions, provided under collective agreement, which are computed by analogous rules and are equal about to half of the basic pension.

The system is such that the normal retirement age is, in fact, 65. However, people unable to work can receive a full pension from the age of 60. Normal pensions are reassessed annually by statutory instrument, with reference to changes in average wage levels during the previous year.

The minimum pension can be revised only by a government decision and, thus, is not constrained by any specific rules. In the last few years, the minimum pension (now 2,450 francs per year) has been increasing faster than normal pensions have. For people with a very low personal income, the minimum pension is supplemented by a state solidarity pension in such a way that their total income does not exceed some upper limit (now 6,200 francs per year for single person 10,400 francs for a couple). This limit is raised with the minimum pension.

Retirement programmes for public-service and public-enterprise employees are more favourable than is this general scheme, since they provide for earlier retirement and feature higher pension rates. By contrast, programmes for the self-employed are less favourable.

FAMILY BENEFITS

There are three main types of family benefits.

(1) Family allowances (about 56 per cent of total family benefits) are paid to almost every French family with at least two children. The allowance is equal to a percentage of a basic monthly amount, and the percentage increases more than proportionally with the family size. The monthly figure that serves as the basis of calculation is readjusted every year on 1 August, with reference to the increase in consumer prices during the previous year.

(2) Single-wage allowances (about 19 per cent of total family benefits) are paid to families in which (a) there are one or more children, (b) only one of the parents is working, and (c) total income does not exceed a certain upper limit. There are two different single-wage allowances: one is fixed and the income exclusion ceiling is not increased over the course of time; the other is reassessed every year, with the exclusion ceiling reactivated with reference to the increase in the minimum wage (in France, wages cannot be lower than a minimum fixed by the government).

(3) Rent subsidies (about 14 per cent of total family benefits) are paid to families, young couples, and persons over 65. Subsidies are a function of the family income and size and the actual rent; the computation rules are rather complicated and are revised from time to time by an independent government decision.

Other benefits represent only 11 per cent of the total cost of family benefit, and will not be described here.

It is noteworthy that there is only one general family-benefit scheme, although allowances are served by different institutions.

UNEMPLOYMENT INSURANCE

In France, unemployment insurance is provided under collective agreement. Benefits are, then, proportional to previous wages.

This insurance supplements the public unemployment allowance, which is, in fact, a minimum income. It is paid to an unemployed worker only if his family's total income does not exceed a certain limit, and it is independent of his previous wages. This benefit is low (about 11 francs per day) and is supported by the State budget.

II. ECONOMIC CYCLES AND SOCIAL SECURITY BUDGET

The description presented in the previous section shows that social benefits and contributions depend heavily on a few economic parameters: the number of contributors (i.e. of working people), and the past and present wage and price levels. In different economic environments, the social security budget will exhibit different characteristics and will raise quite different financing problems.

This problem is interesting for its own sake. From the administrative point of view, social institutions must be able to find adequate financing. From the social point of view, financial concern is one of the most relevant points when planning improvements in a social security system that already constitutes a heavy burden on the economy. Besides, such a study will show whether the social security system reduces (or increases) disposable income in the face of developing inflation (or deflation), and, thus, whether it has a stabilising or a destabilising effect.

Of course, the evolution of the social security budget will also depend on demographic factors, economic behaviour (for example, retirement age or consumption of medical services) and government decisions. There is no easy direct way of acting on the first two factors, at least in the short run, and we shall consider them as given data. As for government decisions, some of them – for example, major reforms of the system, or the creation of new benefits or reassessment of others (for instance, rent subsidies) – are completely free of economic constraints (though not necessarily of political or social pressures); such decisions are beyond the scope of this paper. The degree of freedom in other decisions is limited; for example, if the decision results from negotiations (doctor's fees), from habit, or from facts (hospital costs). Such decisions can be fairly accurately forecast with reference to the past. Finally, some decisions are formal and completely determined by statutory instruments (as is the case with pension reassessment) or by policy that has already been publicly announced (minimum pension increases).

This description of the social security system is sufficient to reach some qualitative conclusions about its dynamics. However, results will be made more precise by the use of a simulation model.

MODEL AND HYPOTHESIS

The simulation model was built for making budget forecasts for social security over five-year periods. It is too long to present here, and its principal features are given in appendix A below. Although every benefit and contribution is forecast independently, only aggregated results will be used.

The model represents only the 'Regime Général', i.e. about two-thirds of the French population. This is not a severe drawback from the present point of view: although different schemes may cover populations with quite different demographic characteristics, and may show, therefore, quite different behaviour in a given economic history, the rules they obey are similar, as are the differential effects caused by changes in economic situations (which are the points studied). Moreover, the 'Regime Général' is apart from the programmes for the nonfarm self-employed) the only scheme that has potential financial problems. Other schemes cover public servants, public-enterprise employees, and farmers, and receive subsidies that automatically prevent them from running into deficit.

Simulations will be carried out on the basis of the following four economic 'histories' for the period 1973–7.

Hypothesis 1: deflation, Wage, price, and employment increases are steadily reduced from 1973 on.

Hypothesis 2: rising inflation. Wage, price and employment increases are steadily raised over the period.

These two hypotheses are connected to the real situation at the end of 1972, and lagged variables in 1973 were taken equal to their historical value. In this connection it is useful to recall that, between 1970 and 1972, inflation in France gradually rose. Consumer prices rose by 5 per cent in 1970, 5·7 per cent in 1971, and 6·6 per cent in 1972; the average wage rose by 9 per cent in 1970, 10 per cent in 1971, and 10·4 per cent in 1972; and the number of wage earners rose by 2·9 per cent in 1970, but by only 1·5 per cent in 1971 and 1·6 per cent in 1972.

Hypothesis 3: steady low inflation rate. Prices rise by 4 per cent every year, and wages by 8 per cent.

Hypothesis 4: steady high inflation rate. Prices rise by 7·2 per cent a year, and wages by 13 per cent (these parameters are close to their real values in 1973).

Lagged variables in 1973 are taken equal to their steady value in those last two hypotheses, and, thus, simulation results *cannot* be compared to the actual year 1972.

These hypotheses are not meant to be realistic, but, rather, are characteristic situations necessary to amplify observations. They are presented in detail, with simulation results, in appendix B.

Simulations were computed assuming that social legislation and regulation were identical to what they were at the *end* of 1972, i.e. slightly different from what they were at the beginning of the year. Actual results in 1972 are *not,* therefore, quite comparable to simulated results. Benefits were reassessed when reassessment was statutory, or when a particular policy was announced, or when a particular practice could be recognised from the past. Otherwise, benefits and computational rules were kept constant whatever the economic situation. This is not quite realistic, but it was impossible to make any other assumption. We shall not consider occupational disease and injury insurance, which is statutorily balanced, the contribution rate being readjusted, to this end, every year (actually, the rate is almost constant over time).

RESULTS

Simulation results are presented in appendix B below. One notices first that the balance of social security as a whole always improves over time. This is due only to the hypothesis of constant legislation for family benefits: family allowances are reassessed with prices; other benefits taking into account beneficiaries' incomes are likely to decrease over time; and contributions increase with wages, faster than do the allowances. Therefore, this branch will produce larger and larger surpluses, unless benefits are raised by some reform, which indeed happens quite often. To give an example, the cost of reforms in family benefits between 1970 and 1973 was equivalent to 16 per cent of the total benefits paid out in 1973. The hypothesis of constant legislation in this field is, thus, highly unrealistic. This phenomenon gives the government an important degree of freedom in deciding social expenditures.

It is interesting to compare health insurance budget balances in 1977 in the four situations studied:

	Deflation	*Rising inflation*	*Steady low inflation*	*Steady high inflation*
Billion francs	−3·2	−2·1	−3·3	−0·8
Percentage of contributions	4·0	2·1	4·6	0·9

The health insurance balance appears to be not very sensitive to economic fluctuations, which, indeed, is not surprising. Contributions rise with wages, and so do expenditures. Consumption of medical services was found to be independent of economic environment (except, perhaps, in extreme situations) but not of the treatment costs. Hospital costs will depend, obviously on wage and price levels; medical fees or drug prices are negotiated, but the economic situation is the basic factor in the negotiation.

It is clear that health insurance is better off in inflationary periods. By comparing hypotheses 3 and 4, it appears that an equilibrium, in the sense that the deficit is a constant percentage of contributions, is possible with a steady rate of inflation somewhere between these two hypotheses. The deficit *increases* if inflation rate gets *larger* or *smaller* than this equilibrium value; this means that expenditures are more sensitive to wage fluctuations than contributions are.

To understand what happens when a change in economic evolution occurs, look at hypothesis 1 for the period 1975–7: the wage increase rate is reduced by 1·5 per cent every year and employment is deteriorating. Health insurance costs rise more slowly as soon as the economic slowdown occurs: 15 per cent in 1974, 13·8 in 1975, 12·1 in 1976, and 11 in 1977. By contrast, contributions are still increased by 12·2 per cent in 1975, as against 12·5 per cent in 1974; but they rise by only 10·8 per cent in 1976 and 9·8 per cent in 1977. In effect, the contribution ceiling is raised every 1 January with reference to the previous year's hourly wage increase. If, in a particular year, this increase is larger than the average wage increase, then insured income and, therefore, contributions will grow faster than do wages, thus partially offsetting the consequences of a wage slowdown. In the present example, this difference is 2 per cent in 1975, raising contributions by 0·9 per cent. Such a smoothing phenomenon will go on as long as the slowdown is accelerating. The opposite would hold, of course, if inflation were rising faster and faster. It takes *two years* for health insurance to adjust fully to an economic change, the first-year effects being strongly attenuated.

Pension funds cannot be balanced, for two reasons. First, the French population is getting older, and this demographic factor will raise difficult financing problems in the near future. Second, these funds were created after 1930, and many people could not get a full pension when retiring because they had not contributed during all of their working life; new pensions thus are higher than the average pension is. As a result, pension funds exhibit a deficit in 1977 that depends very much on economic assumptions: only 7·9 per cent of their total income in hypothesis 2 (rising inflation), but 19·5 per cent in hypothesis 1 (deflation). Notice that the minimum pension is readjusted, from time to time, by a government decision, without explicit reference to the economic situation (in fact there exists a link, but a rather loose one). It was assumed to be raised by 15 per cent every year in the four hypotheses tested. This is a reason (but not the only one) why pension funds are better off in an inflationary period.

Our analysis of the progressive adjustment of health insurance contributions to economic changes holds also for pension funds, and for the same reasons. Since pensions are readjusted with reference to the previous year's wages, benefits for a given year mainly depend on the past economic situation (actually, since reassessments are implemented on 1 April, two years of history are relevant). For example, under hypotheses 1 and 2, pensions are increased by 12·5 per cent on 1 April 1974, although the economic situations are quite different; and by 12·2 and 13·8 per cent, respectively, on 1 April 1975. In the latter case, the rates of increase differ by 1·6 per cent, while the rates of increase for wages differ by 4·5 per cent. If, in a given year, the economy jumps from a steady inflation state to another one, then, in the first year following the change, pensions are unchanged and contributions are partially affected; in the second year, contributions reach their new level, and the pension rate of increase partially adjusts to its new value; and in the third year the transition is complete. It thus takes three years to adjust fully.

Except for the trend, exactly the same analysis holds for family benefits. It must be noted that the existence of benefits depending on family income prevents family benefits from increasing as fast as consumer prices do. One conclusion is that the financial equilibrium of old-age pension institutions or of the family allowance system will *improve* if inflation is going *faster* and *faster,* and will *deteriorate* when price and wage increases are getting *slower* and *slower.*

With all of its parts behaving in the same way, the dynamics of the social security system as a whole do not differ much from what has already been said. To eliminate the trend over time, it is useful to consider differences between the tested hypotheses and a reference one. I took the fourth hypothesis as a reference, and computed the results in constant 1973 francs:

Hypothesis	Differential balance (billion francs)					
	1972	*1973*	*1974*	*1975*	*1976*	*1977*
1. Deflation	0	0	–0·2	–1·9	–3·6	–5·4
2. Rising inflation	0	0	+0·3	+0·8	+1·3	+1·9
3. Steady low inflation	0	0	–1·5	–3·1	–5·9	–7·4

Although hypotheses 1 and 2 are almost symmetrical with respect to the reference hypothesis, the social security system loses more in deflationary periods than it gains in inflationary ones.

Reaction lags appear clearly. In the case of hypothesis 1, the effect of the deflationary trend beginning in 1974 does not become noticeable until 1975; and the same (except that the trend in this case is inflationary) is true for hypothesis 2. Balance in constant francs varies quite smoothly over time, depending on the hypothesis; in the case of hypothesis 1, it falls 1·7 billion francs per year, as compared with an annual rise of 0·5 billion under the second hypothesis. Globally, full adjustment seems almost completely achieved with a one-year lag.

One notices that the changes in balance depending on economic situation are large enough to be of some importance at the aggregate economic level. This is illustrated by the fact that policy intervention funds in France are about 2–3 billion francs.

IV. ECONOMIC STABILISATION AND THE SOCIAL SECURITY SYSTEM

The previous analysis showed that, with constant social legislation, a sudden rise in wages leads to an improvement in the social security budget balance and a reduction in private disposable income, thus having a deflationary effect on demand. Conversely, if the wage level is lowered (or grows more slowly), the social security balance deteriorates, increasing disposable income and stimulating demand. In this section, I shall try to evaluate the order of magnitude of some of these automatic stabilising effects. Moreover, one must wonder how the efficiency of classifical policy tools is changed by the actual social security system.

Notice that an increase in benefits, matched by a corresponding increase in contributions, may have macro-economic effects on demand if it transfers income from one social group to another. In particular, increases in different benefits may have different effects. Because of the lack of relevant data, this phenomenon cannot be studied for France, and will not be treated here.

This study is a short-term one, and the effects that I describe might be quite different from those appearing when full adjustment has been achieved. This short-term nature of the study also enables us to disregard regulatory reforms, which we showed to be unavoidable (especially in the field of family allowances), and changes in agents' behaviour. (For example, it is likely that the retirement age will drop if unemployment is high for a long time.)

Notice that the economic incidences of the social security system cannot be considered only from the point of view of demand analysis. The way in which social security reserves are invested may have huge effects on the financial markets or on liquidity of the economy. In France, however, reserves are small, since benefits during one period are financed by that period's contributions. Moreover, the reserves are deposited in an account at the Caisse des Depôts et Consignations (a state bank), and very little of it is invested. This bank is completely controlled by the government, and social security reserves may be considered as a negligible part of its funds. Analysis of the monetary effects of social security will not be pursued here.

THE MODEL

Rather than running simulations with a huge econometric model for exploring particular policies, I shall use a simplified model known as DECA, which is used by the Ministry of Finance for making short-term forecasts. The particular version of it employed here (see appendix C) was elaborated by Malgrange (1972), is small enough to be manageable by hand, and will give us a very precise understanding of what is happening. However, such an approach will not enable us to trace reactions over several years, and it should be noted that numerical applications concern the year 1972.

The stabilising effects of the social security system are mainly due to the fact that, for a given year, contributions vary with wages, while income transfers are almost independent of economic fluctuations. I therefore shall compare two situations: (1) the actual one, and (2) a neutral one where the contributions paid during a year are fixed (for example, with reference to previous earnings) and are independent of wage fluctuations during that year. This would be the case if social security were financed by income tax, which in France is computed from the previous year's income. Social security has, then, almost no stabilising effects. Of course, in numerical applications, contributions were taken equal to their real value in 1972, and we shall study the way in which different economic parameters vary around their 1972 value in reaction to various small shocks.

The model (see appendix C) distinguishes nine aggregates: gross national product, x_1; imports, x_2; exports, x_9; household consumption, x_3; productive investment, x_4; inventories, x_5; households' housing investment, x_8; corporations' housing investment, x_6; and public expenditures, x_7. A lower-case x represents a quantity; for instance, x_i represents the quantity of the ith aggregate, and, if p_i is its price, its value is, by definition, $X_i = p_i x_i$.

The consumption function is

$$X_3 = \alpha W + \beta Y + \gamma p_3 x_3^{-1} + \bar{X}_3 \tag{9.1}$$

where W is the total wage income, Y is the total nonwage income, x_3^{-1} is the one-year lagged real consumption, and $\bar{X}_3$ is exogenous. Other equations of the model are such that (9.1) can be written (see Malgrange, 1972)

$$X_3 = a_3S_1 + b_3S_2 + c_3X_1 + d_3p_3x_3^{-1} + e_3(S_1^{-1} + S_2^{-1} + S_a^{-1}) + \bar{X}_3 \quad (9.2)$$

where S_1 represents wages paid by nonfinancial corporations; S_2, wages paid by public services and financial corporations; S_a, wages paid by households; and S_1^{-1}, S_2^{-1}, S_a^{-1}, the same lagged variables.

The coefficients in equation (9.2) depend on the social security contribution rates and do not necessarily have the same value in both situations:

	a_3	b_3	c_3	d_3	e_3
Actual situation	0·64	1·216	0·1	0·26	–0·05
Neutral situation	0·738	1·284	0·1	0·20	–0·05

Not surprisingly, apparent marginal propensities to consume are, larger in the neutral situation, since increases in wages are not partially offset by increases in social contributions.

When one studies a particular year, lagged variables are constant. Moreover, we are interested in small changes around the 1972 solution. We can therefore linearise the equation system, as is done in Appendix C, and solve it. We obtain

$$dx_1 = \frac{k_1}{1 + k_1\mu_1'\epsilon_1}\left[(1 - V_3)\{d\bar{x}_3 + \frac{1}{p_3^*}(\beta d\bar{B} + a_3S_1^{-1}\,d\bar{s}_1 + b_3S_2^{-1}\,d\bar{s}_2)\}\right.$$
$$\left. + \sum_4^9 (1 - V_i)d\bar{x}_i - d\bar{x}_2 - \epsilon_1 d\bar{p}_1 - \epsilon_2 d\bar{p}_2\right] \quad (9.3)$$

where $d\bar{z}$ represents an exogenous change in variable z, B is the social benefits; and the V_is are import deperdition coefficients (see equations in appendix C). If the demand for the ith aggregate is increased by 1, only $1 - V_i$ is produced in the home country and V_i is imported. The model is such that an increase in income tax *IRPP* can be analysed as a negative social benefit.

The coefficient k_1 is

$$k_1 = \frac{1}{1 + \sum_3^9 \alpha_i(1 - V_i)}$$

where the *i*s are the marginal propensity of *i*th aggregate demand with respect to national product. If there are no imports, k_1 is equal to the familiar

$$\frac{1}{1 - \sum_3^9 \alpha_i}$$

ϵ_1 and ϵ_2 represent the effect of home price and import price increases. ϵ_1 and ϵ_2 are the sum of four terms (see Malgrange, 1972), one of them representing the loss of competitivity when prices increase, and the others the price effects on demand.

μ_1' represents the inflationary effects of an increase in national product (see Appendix C).

Denote

$$k' = \frac{k_1}{1 + k_1 \mu_1' \epsilon_1}$$

The coefficients can be readily computed from Malgrange (1970), and we simply state the results:

	k_1	ϵ_1	ϵ_2	k'
Actual situation	2·128	0·896	−1·053	2·055
Neutral situation	2·219	0·84	−1·053	2·144

Notice that k_1 is larger in the neutral situation. This is quite natural, as, in this situation, the apparent marginal propensity to consume national product is larger, because incomes are not reduced by social contributions. By contrast, ϵ_1 is larger in the actual situation. A price increase lowers the purchasing power of incomes, which reduces demand and the output. This output decrease pushes down wages, but this phenomenon will be smaller when the propensity to consume is larger.

Other coefficients are the same in both situations.

INFLATIONARY PERTURBATIONS

An *import price increase* $d\bar{p}_2$ stimulates the home economy ($-\epsilon_2 > 0$). Home manufactured goods become cheaper than imported ones and this substitution effect is larger than the income effect. The induced home price change is

$$dp_1 = \mu_1' \frac{\partial x_1}{\partial p_2} d\bar{p}_2 = 0{\cdot}26\, d\bar{p}_2$$

in the actual situation, and

$$dp_1 = 0{\cdot}27\, d\bar{p}_2$$

in the neutral situation. In the model, home economic reactions are not supposed to affect the import price level.

If there is an exogenous *home price increase* $d\bar{p}_1$, one easily computes from equation (9.3) and from equation 2.8 of Appendix C that

$$dp_1 = \frac{1}{1 + k_1 \mu_1' \epsilon_1} d\bar{p}_1$$

which is equal to $0{\cdot}965\ d\bar{p}_1$ in the actual situation and to $0{\cdot}966\ d\bar{p}_1$ in the neutral one.

If there is an *exogenous change* $d\bar{s}_1$ in the *rate of increase of wages* S_1, one obtains from equation (9.3) and from equation 1.14 of appendix C that

$$\frac{dS_1}{S_1^{-1}} = \left[1 + \frac{k_1(1 - V_3)a_3 S_1^{-1}}{1 + k_1 \mu_1' \epsilon_1}\left(-\sigma_1\mu_1 + \frac{\sigma_2}{x_1} + \frac{\sigma_3}{x_1^{-1}}\right)\right] d\bar{s}_1$$

One easily computes that $\dfrac{dS_1}{S_1^{-1}}$ is equal to $1{\cdot}221\ d\bar{s}_1$ in the actual situation and to $1{\cdot}266\ d\bar{s}_1$ in the neutral one. An increase in wages is amplified by the economy: it raises purchasing power and, thus, output, which in turn increases wages and prices. The wage effect happens to be larger than the price effect. The wage effect obviously is larger in the neutral situation, since the marginal propensities to consume are higher and, therefore, the output increase induced by a wage raise is larger. This wage destabilising effect is more important in the neutral situation.

The same conclusion holds with an exogenous increase $S_2^{-1}\,d\bar{s}_2$ in wages S_2, but the multiplier effect is negligible (the multiplier is about 1·01).

MULTIPLIERS AND STABILISATION POLICIES

For both situations, one easily computes multipliers representing the effect on national product of a 'shock' from a few variables:

	X_2	X_3	X_4	X_5	X_6	X_7	X_8	X_9	B/p^*	$\frac{IRPP}{p^*}$
Actual situation	−2·05	1·48	0·9	1·72	1·95	1·27	1·52	1·23	0·59	−0·59
Neutral situation	−2·14	1·54	0·94	1·79	2·03	1·33	1·59	1·28	0·61	−0·61

Multipliers are all about 5 per cent higher in the neutral situation. (This is explained by the different values of k'_1.) Policies acting upon demand are, therefore, 5 per cent more efficient in this situation.

Public expenditure policy is reasonably efficient (the multiplier is close to 1·3, which implies an elasticity of national product equal to 0·33). Increase in housing demand by corporations (x_6) or by households (x_8) is more efficient. Import controls are the most efficient policy.

On the other hand, a policy acting upon private disposable income by a change in social benefits *B* has a rather weak effect; it has a multiplier of 0·6, which implies a national product elasticity of 0·15. This is explained by the fact that consumption function (9.1) distinguishes two types of incomes: wages and nonwage income, including social benefits, the propensity to consume nonwage income being only $\beta = 0{\cdot}4$. Such a low figure can be justified by the idea that nonwage income is more stable than wages are, and that consumption does not depend on it much in the short run. However, one must be cautious in accepting this result. To my knowledge, no particular study of the marginal propensity of consumption by type and level of income or by social factors of households has yet been done in France. Actually, the propensity to consume different types of benefits must differ, but it is impossible to say precisely how.

In the model, income tax is equivalent to a negative social benefit. The same conclusion therefore applies. It was shown in Malgrange (1972) that the aggregate effect on the aggregate quantities (but not on their nominal values) is completely negligible when value-added tax rates are changed.

It is important to note that social benefits can be used as economic policy tools only in one way: if it is easy to increase benefits, it is politically almost impossible to reduce or suppress some of them. It therefore is possible to increase social benefits in order to stimulate the economy, but virtually impossible to reduce them in order to control inflation.

V. CONCLUSION

I have shown how balancing the social security budget depends on the economic situation. Generally speaking, it appears that social security is better off during inflationary periods and that its budget balance is very sensitive to a few economic parameters. Full adjustment to a new situation is carried out with about a one-year lag. Therefore, during cycles that are five to six years long, social security will have a beneficial stabilising effect at the downturn and at the upturn.

The stabilising effects were shown to be caused by differences between the adjustment lags of contributions and those of benefits. In order to evaluate the order of magnitude of these effects in the short run, we compared the actual situation with a 'neutral' one where social income transfers are independent of the economic environment in a given year. It appeared that the economy reacts to exogenous price changes in about the same way in both situations, but that it is more sensitive to wage increases in the neutral situation. By contrast, traditional demand-control policies are more effective in the neutral situation. Effects are small (they are, in a sense, second-order effects), but are not negligible.

These conclusions do, however, rely upon an econometric model that was not explicitly built to study the incidence of social benefits and contributions, and analysis should be pursued in this area of public finance before any definitive statement is made. In particular, it would be interesting to compare the effects of changes in different benefits (or contributions). Unintended economic consequences of social policies and inequitable consequences of economic policies could then be avoided, allowing for a more controlled development of society.

REFERENCES

Ackley, G., *Macroeconomic Theory*; (New York: Macmillan, 1961).

Billaudot, B., 'Le Modèle DECA', *Statistiques et Études Financières,* série orange, no. 1 (1971).

Dupeyroux, J. J., *Sécurité Sociale;* (Paris: Dalloz, 1971).
EEC Commission, 'Les Incidences Économiques de la Sécurité Sociale', *Études,* no. 21 (1970).
Launay, J. P., and Worms, G., 'Influence de la Croissance sur la Sécurité Sociale', *Statistiques et Études Financières,* série orange, no. 13 (1974).
Malgrange, P., 'Etude Analytique du Modèle DECA', *Annales de l'Institut National de la Statistique et des Études Économiques,* no. 11 (1972), pp. 85–139.
Snyder, W. W., 'Measuring the Stabilizing Effects of Social Security Programs in Seven Countries', *National Tax Journal,* XXIII (1970), pp. 263–72.
Weitenberg, J., 'The Incidence of Social Security Taxes', in International Public Finance Association, *Proceedings of the 1968 Turin Conference,* pp. 93–108.

APPENDIX A: SOCIAL SECURITY SIMULATION MODEL

This model was built for making financial forecasts for the 'Régime Général' over five-year periods. Only its main principles, which are simple, will be presented here. The 'Régime Général' provides private-company employees with health insurance, occupational disease and retirement benefits, and provides all employed workers with family benefits.

Forecasts are computed from very few economic parameters that are exogenous. These are: the increase in the number of employed people; the average and minimum wage increases; and the increase in consumer prices. Econometric adjustments have been made during the 1962–72 period.

Every particular benefit is forecast independently. When a benefit must be revised by statutory rules, these rules are built into the model, with the corresponding lag structure. Other benefits or rules are kept constant, unless a particular procedure for readjusting them can be clearly discovered from past practice, or unless some special policy objectives have been stated by the government.

All health insurance benefits are computed in the same way: the number of beneficiaries, the average consumption per capita, the average cost per unit, and the average rate of coverage are all forecast independently. For example, hospital expenditures are the product of the number of people covered, times the average number of hospital days per person, times the average price of treatment per day in hospital, times the average rate of coverage. It is noteworthy that the number of persons covered was found to be independent of economic cycles (the explanation being that unemployed registered people are covered) and that no economic parameter (for instance, total consumption or income) was found to be significant in explaining consumption of medical services. By contrast, the level of medical fees, treatment costs per day in hospital, and drug prices are very well explained by average wage and consumer price indexes.

As regards, family benefits and pensions, the model computes demographic forecasts for every type of population concerned (for example, the number of families with a certain number of children). For every population, it then computes the benefits according to existing rules. The model can therefore easily be used to explore the consequences of a change in those rules. The computation is simple when benefits are provided on a demographic basis, but when a beneficiary's income also is taken into account, the model must also compute the income distribution. Of course, benefits, like rent subsidies, which depend on the beneficiary's income and for which the computation rules are not often revised, are becoming less and less costly over time. One notices that new pensions are, on average, higher than existing pensions. This is because pension schemes have not been in existence long enough for everyone to have contributed throughout his working life and so be entitled to a full pension.

The percentage increase in contributions is computed as the product of the increase in the average wage, times the increase in the number of working contributors, times a residual. The residual is explained by the fact that, for a given year, the contribution ceiling does not increase exactly like the average wage and by other, less definite factors; it was estimated by regression.

APPENDIX B

HYPOTHESIS 1

(a) *Economic parameters (percentages)*

	1972	*1973*	*1974*	*1975*	*1976*	*1977*
Number of employees	+1·6	+2·1	+1·9	+1·7	+1·5	+1·3
Prices	+6·6	+7·5	+7·0	+6·5	+6·0	+5·5
Wages	+10·4	+13·0	+12·0	+10·5	+9·0	+7·5
Minimum wage	+11·4	+17·9	+14·0	+12·0	+10·0	+8·0
Contribution ceiling	+10·9	+11·5	+13·5	+12·5	+11·0	+9·5

(b) *Results (billion francs)*

	1972	*1973*	*1974*	*1975*	*1976*	*1977*
Health insurance						
Contributions	42·3	48·8	56·5	64·4	72·2	79·7
Total income	43·3	50·0	57·9	65·9	73·9	81·5
Benefits	41·3	47·6	54·8	62·3	69·9	77·5
Total expenditures	45·1	52·0	59·9	68·1	76·5	84·7
Balance	−1·8	−2·0	−2·0	−2·2	−2·6	−3·2
Family benefits						
Contributions	28·2	32·5	37·5	42·8	48·1	53·2
Total income	28·5	32·6	37·6	42·9	48·2	53·3
Benefits	22·5	26·0	27·8	29·6	30·8	32·2
Total expenditures	24·9	28·8	30·9	33·2	34·9	36·6
Balance	+3·6	+3·8	+6·7	+9·7	+13·3	+16·7
Pensions						
Contributions	18·75	21·7	25·1	28·6	32·2	35·6
Total income	19·6	22·2	25·7	29·2	32·9	36·4
Benefits	17·35	21·3	25·4	30·0	34·9	39·7
Total expenditures	19·5	23·5	27·9	33·0	38·2	43·5
Balance	+0·1	−1·3	−2·2	−3·8	−5·3	−7·1
General balance	+1·6	+0·5	+2·5	+3·7	+5·4	+6·4

HYPOTHESIS 2

(a) *Economic parameters (percentages)*

	1972	*1973*	*1974*	*1975*	*1976*	*1977*
Number of employees	+1·6	+2·1	+2·2	+2·3	+2·4	+2·5
Prices	+6·6	+7·5	+8·5	+9·5	+10·5	+11·5
Wages	+10·4	+13·0	+14·0	+15·0	+16·0	+17·0
Minimum wage	+11·4	+17·5	+16·0	+17·0	+18·0	+19·0
Contribution ceiling	+10·9	+11·5	+13·5	+14·5	+15·5	+16·5

(b) *Results (billion francs)*

	1972	*1973*	*1974*	*1975*	*1976*	*1977*
Health insurance						
Contributions	42·3	48·8	57·4	68·1	81·5	98·4
Total income	43·3	50·0	58·8	69·7	83·4	100·6
Benefits	41·3	47·6	55·8	65·9	78·4	93·9
Total expenditures	45·1	52·0	60·9	72·0	85·7	102·7
Balance	–1·8	–2·0	–2·1	–2·3	–2·3	–2·1
Family benefits						
Contributions	28·2	32·5	38·0	44·9	53·5	64·5
Total income	28·5	32·6	38·1	45·0	53·6	64·6
Benefits	22·5	26·0	28·0	29·3	31·3	34·2
Total expenditures	24·9	28·8	31·1	33·1	35·8	39·6
Balance	+3·6	+3·8	+7·0	+11·9	+17·8	+25·0
Pensions						
Contributions	18·75	21·7	25·5	30·2	36·1	43·7
Total income	19·6	22·2	26·0	30·8	36·8	44·4
Benefits	17·35	21·3	25·4	30·4	36·5	43·7
Total expenditures	19·5	23·5	27·9	33·4	40·0	47·9
Balance	+0·1	–1·3	–1·9	–2·6	–3·2	–3·5
General balance	+1·6	+0·5	+3·0	+7·0	+12·3	+19·4

HYPOTHESIS 3

(a) *Economic parameters (percentages)*

	1973	*1974*	*1975*	*1976*	*1977*
Number of employees	+1·9	+1·9	+1·9	+1·9	+1·9
Prices	+4·0	+4·0	+4·0	+4·0	+4·0
Wages	+8·0	+8·0	+8·0	+8·0	+8·0
Minimum wage	+9·0	+9·0	+9·0	+9·0	+9·0
Contribution ceiling	+8·5	+8·5	+8·5	+8·5	+8·5

(b) *Results (billion francs)*

	1973	*1974*	*1975*	*1976*	*1977*
Health insurance					
Contributions	46·7	51·9	57·7	64·1	71·2
Total income	47·8	53·2	59·0	65·6	72·8
Benefits	45·7	50·9	56·6	62·8	69·6
Total expenditures	50·0	55·6	61·8	68·7	76·1
Balance	−2·2	−2·4	−2·8	−3·1	−3·3
Family benefits					
Contributions	31·3	34·7	38·6	42·8	47·6
Total income	31·4	34·8	38·7	42·9	47·7
Benefits	25·7	27·2	28·4	29·5	30·6
Total expenditures	28·3	30·2	31·6	33·1	34·6
Balance	+3·0	+4·6	+7·1	+10·2	+13·1
Pensions					
Contributions	20·9	23·2	25·8	28·8	32·0
Total income	21·3	23·7	26·5	29·4	32·7
Benefits	20·9	24·1	37·6	31·3	35·3
Total expenditures	23·1	26·5	30·4	34·5	38·9
Balance	−1·8	−2·8	−3·9	−5·1	−6·2
General balance	−1·0	−0·6	+0·5	+2·0	+3·6

HYPOTHESIS 4

(a) *Economic parameters (percentages)*

	1973	*1974*	*1975*	*1976*	*1977*
Number of employees	+1·9	+1·9	+1·9	+1·9	+1·9
Prices	+7·2	+7·2	+7·2	+7·2	+7·2
Wages	+13·0	+13·0	+13·0	+13·0	+13·0
Minimum wage	+15·0	+15·0	+15·0	+15·0	+15·0
Contribution ceiling	+13·5	+13·5	+13·5	+13·5	+13·5

(b) *Results (billion francs)*

	1973	*1974*	*1975*	*1976*	*1977*
Health insurance					
Contributions	49·0	57·0	66·4	73·3	89·8
Total income	50·2	58·4	68·0	79·0	91·8
Benefits	47·3	55·0	63·6	73·3	84·4
Total expenditures	51·9	60·2	69·6	80·3	92·6
Balance	–1·7	–1·8	–1·6	–1·3	–0·8
Family benefits					
Contributions	32·6	37·9	44·0	51·1	59·4
Total income	32·7	38·0	44·1	51·2	59·5
Benefits	26·2	27·9	29·4	31·0	32·8
Total expenditures	29·0	31·1	33·1	35·3	37·8
Balance	+3·7	+6·9	+11·0	+15·9	+21·7
Pensions					
Contributions	21·8	25·4	29·6	34·4	40·0
Total income	22·3	25·9	30·2	35·1	40·8
Benefits	21·5	25·7	30·7	36·3	42·6
Total expenditures	23·8	28·3	33·7	39·7	46·6
Balance	–1·5	–2·4	–3·5	–4·6	–5·8
General balance	+0·5	+2·7	+5·9	+10·0	15·1

APPENDIX C: ECONOMIC MODEL

This model is a simplified version, developed by Malgrange (1972), of the DECA model used by the Ministry of Finance for making short-term forecasts.

EQUATIONS

(1.1) $$x_1 + x_2 = \sum_{3}^{9} x_i$$

(1.2) $$X_1 + X_2 = \sum_{3}^{9} X_i$$

(1.3) $$X_2 = (\mu_2'(p_1 - p_2 + p_1^{-1} - p_2^{-1}) + v_2') \sum_{3}^{9} X_i(m_i + m_1' \, t + n_1 \tilde{x}_i) + \underline{X}_2$$

(1.4) $$X_3 = a_3 S_1 + b_3 S_2 + c_3 X_1 + d_3 X_3^{-1} p_3 + e_3 (S_1^{-1} + S_2^{-1} + \underline{S}_a^{-1}) + \underline{\underline{X}}_3$$

(1.5) $$x_4 = (a_4 \hat{x}_1 + APF + b_4 \, APF^{-1} + c_4)(X_4^{-1} - p_4^{-1} \underline{x}_4^{-1}) + \underline{x}_4$$

(1.6) $$X_5 = a_5 (X_1 - X_1^{-1}) + \underline{X}_5$$

(1.7) $$x_i = \underline{x}_i \qquad i = 6, 7, 8$$

(1.8) $$x_9 = (a_9 (TF^{-1} + TF^{-2} - TF^{-3} - TF^{-4}) + b_9)(X_9^{-1} - p_9^{-1} \underline{x}_9^{-1}) + \underline{x}_9$$

(1.9) $$p_1 = \mu_1 \tilde{x}_1 + v_1 \, [TF^{-1} - TF^{-3} + v_1'(TF^{-1} - TFT^{-1})] + p_1$$

(1.10) $$p_2 = v_2 + \underline{p}_2$$

(1.11) $$p_i = \mu_i p_1 + v_i + \xi_i p_2 \frac{X_2^{-1}}{X_1^{-1} + X_2^{-1}} \quad i = 4, 6, 7, 8$$

(1.12) $$p_5 = \mu_5 p_1 + \mu_5' p_1^{-1} + \xi_5 \underline{p}_2 \frac{X_2^{-1}}{X_1^{-1} + X_2^{-1}}$$

(1.13) $$p_9 = \mu_9 (TF^{-1} + TF^{-2} - TF^{-3} - TF^{-4}) + v_9$$

(1.14) $$S_1 = (\sigma_1 p_1 + \sigma_2 \frac{x_1}{x_1^*} + \sigma_3 \hat{x}_1 + \sigma_4 APF + \underline{\underline{s}}_1) S_1^{-1}$$

(1.15) $$S_2 = (\sigma_1 p_1 + \sigma_2 \frac{x_1}{x_1^*} + \underline{\underline{s}}_2) S_2^{-1}$$

(1.16) $$APF = \sum_{1}^{5} \theta_i'(TF^{-i} - TFT^{-i})$$

(1.17) $TFT \quad = TFT^{-1} + \theta_2 + \theta_3(\tilde{X}_4^{-1} + \tilde{X}_4^{-2} - \tilde{X}_4^{-6} - \tilde{X}_4^{-7})$

(1.18) $TF \quad = \frac{1}{X_4}\ [\theta_4 X_1 + \theta_5(X_3 + X_6 + X_7) + \theta_6 X_5 + \theta_7 S_1 + \theta_8 S_2 + \underline{\underline{E}}_p]$

with $\underline{\underline{X}}_3 = \underline{X}_3 + f_3 S_a + c_3 \underline{GP} + g_3 \underline{B} + g_3 \underline{Y}$

Other variables are introduced in the model, but are of no use in the present study (for example: duration of work).

An underlined variable is *exogenous*; z^{-n} means the n-year lagged variable z, and z^* means the value of variable z on a reference path (the year 1972 in numerical applications).

x_i represents the quantity of the ith aggregate, i.e. its value at previous year prices. X_i is its value, and $p_i = \frac{X_i}{x_i}$ is its price. Therefore,

$\hat{x}_i = \frac{x_i}{X_i^{-1}} - 1$ is the quantity growth rate of the ith aggregate; and

$X_i = \frac{X_i}{X_i^{-1}} - 1$ is the nominal growth rate of the ith aggregate.

We denote:

$$\tilde{x}_i = 1 + \hat{x}_i$$

$$\tilde{X}_i = 1 + \hat{X}_i$$

The index 1 corresponds to the gross national product; 2 to imports; 3 to household consumption; 4 to productive investment; 5 to inventories; 6 to corporations' housing investment; 7 to public expenditures; 8 to households' housing investment; and 9 to exports.

S_1 represents wages paid by nonfinancial corporations; S_2, wages paid by financial corporations and public services; and S_a, wages paid by households.

TF, TFT, and *APF* characterise corporations' behaviour when financing investments. Since they are lagged variables only, they are constant in the present applications.

GP represents gross profits; *B*, social security benefits; and *Y*, nonwage income.

LINEARISATION

The previous model is nonlinear, but it will be used to explore economic responses to small shocks, in the neighbourhood of a reference situation. It is possible to keep lagged variables constant and to linearise the model. One obtains (computations are detailed Malgrange, 1972):

(2.1) $x_1 + x_2 = \sum_{3}^{9} x_i$

(2.2) $p_1 x_1 + p_2 x_2 = \sum_{3}^{9} p_i x_i$

(2.3) $p_2 x_2 = [\mu'_2(p_1 - p_2) + 1] \sum_{3}^{9} (p_i p_i x_i + r'_i x_i) + \underline{X}_2$

(2.4) $p_3 x_3 = \alpha'_3 p_1 x_1 + \beta_3 x_1 + \gamma_3 p_1 + \delta_3 p_3 + a_3 \underline{S}_1 + b_3 \underline{S}_2 + \underline{X}_3$

(2.5) $p_5 x_5 = \alpha_5 p_1 x_1 + \underline{X}_5$

(2.6) $x_i = \alpha_i x_1 + x_i \qquad i = 4, 6, 7, 8, 9$

(2.7) $p_1 = \mu'_1 x_1 + \underline{p}_1$

(2.8) $p_2 = \mu_2 p_1 + (1 - \mu_2) p_2^* + \underline{p}_2$

(2.9) $p_i = \mu_i p_1 + (1 - \mu_i) p_i^* + \xi'_i \underline{p}_2 \qquad i = 4, 5, 6, 7, 8, 9$

We denote:

$$V_i = r_i + r'_i / p_i$$

VALUE OF THE PARAMETERS

a_3	b_3	α'_3	β_3	γ_3	δ_3
0·3	1·22	0·1	0·2	1·29	0·05

Some of those parameters may take different numerical values when the method of financing social expenditures is changed.

$i =$	1	2	3	4	5	6	7	8	9
α_i	–	–	–	0·16	0·26	0	0	0	0
μ_i	–	0	–	1	7	1	0·92	1	0
μ'_i	0·02	0·25	–	–	–	–	–	–	–
ξ'_i	–	–	–	0·15	0·14	0·11	0·11	0·11	–
σ_i	0·7	0·23	0·64	0·05	–	–	–	–	–
V_i	–	–	0·28	0·56	0·16	0·05	0·38	0·26	0·4

10 Redistribution through Social Security: A Lesson from Italy

Franco Reviglio
UNIVERSITY OF TURIN

The aim of this paper is to show that social security in Italy is marked by large inefficiencies in resource distribution and allocation. Vertical redistribution is quite limited, mainly because of, first, the regressive effects of financing based on salary-geared contributions, and, second, the fact that pensions and family allowances are exempt from personal income tax. Most redistribution is horizontal, but there are also serious maldistributions, which go against vertical and horizontal equity. On the whole, the amount and the direction of redistribution seems often to have been determined by chance or by pressure groups. Inefficiency in allocation is serious in the health sector, where there is waste and where there are privileges for certain groups of citizens. Maldistribution, waste and privileges use up a considerable amount of social security finance. This amount could be used to meet the community's strong and growing demand for more benefits for the poorer groups, especially for increases in the currently insufficient minimum pensions, and for better and more complete health services.

I. INTRODUCTION

Originally social security programmes were seen as a means of promoting social welfare through collective action, i.e. of satisfying certain specific individual and family needs of that the market did not meet in an efficient way. Resources for these programmes were drawn from 'parafiscal' receipts (social security contributions). Social security therefore had a reallocative and not a redistributive role. A redistributive function was added only later, initially in a very limited fashion and then in a more extensive way. There is nowadays a widely held belief that social security achieves important redistribution. Indeed, according to widespread opinion, social security is above all aimed at redistribution. Often, the amount of money transfers, which accounts for the larger part of social security expenditures, is taken as an indication of the redistributive role of the State. Sometimes the growth rate of social security transfers relative to family consumption (between 1961 and 1970, this amount went up from 13·2 to 17·0 per cent in Italy) is taken as a sign of the greater redistributive role of the State. In the same way, health expenditures are taken as another sign of the State's striving toward redistribution.

This opinion seems to be supported by the results of a number studies on redistribution through public policies. These show that in many countries the most effective way to change income distribution has been through social security expenditures, which make up for, and, in certain cases, more than make up for, the regressive action of the tax system in general and of social security contributions in particular.[1]

Sections II and III of this paper will attempt to show that, for several reasons, the theory according to which social security works towards redistribution ought to be approached with caution. First, there are logical and statistical difficulties that stand in the way of every empirical study of redistribution, particularly those concerned with social security. Second, there are indications that in countries like Italy a part of the money transferred by social security has doubtful vertical redistributive effects. Another part redistributes horizontally, i.e. within the same or similar income groups, or is given to certain privileged groups, thus going against both horizontal and vertical equity. Vertical redistribution produced on the expenditure side is, then, at least partly compensated for by the regressive action of financing through salary-geared contributions and by the fact that pensions and family allowances are exempt from income tax.[2] On the whole, the amount and the direction of redistribution seems often to have been determined by chance or by pressure groups.

Section IV of this paper considers the lesson that can be learned from the Italian experience. In order to find the answer, one must bear in mind that social security in Italy is marked not only by transfer maldistributions, but also by an allocative inefficiency in benefits in kind and in services in the health sector, this having been brought about by privileges and waste. Maldistribution, waste and privileges use up a considerable amount of social security finance that could be put to better use.

II. LOGICAL AND STATISTICAL DIFFICULTIES

Logical and statistical difficulties can be divided into two types: those met by anyone studying the redistributive effects of public receipts and expenditures, and those marking all investigation into the redistributive effects of social security. Let us look at some of the first kind.

Any attempt to identify redistribution must first compare income distribution with the results of production before tax revenues and expenditures. The concept of income is fundamental, because on it depend the redistributive effects implied by the analysis, and the part they play in plans to reform the present system. In line with the attitude taken by most of the literature today,

[1] For a good review of these studies, see United Nations (1967), part 2, chapter 6.
[2] The tax reform of 1 January 1974 abolished these exemptions.

we should refer to income as 'receipt', which Simons defines as 'net accretion to purchasing power'. It is well known, however, that this definition requires that a whole series of difficult adjustments be made and that a number of serious conceptual problems be solved. Income has to be adjusted to include undistributed company profits, unshifted company profit taxes, imputed incomes and benefits in kind, income from abroad, capital gains, and, in the opinion of some, gifts and inherited property.

We must decide whether capital gains should be calculated on the basis of when they are gained or of when they are realised. If we take the first approach, then the problem of calculating them is almost insoluble. If they are calculated at existing prices, their value will almost certainly be exaggerated, since these prices are likely to fall if the capital assets from which the gain is expected are sold in the market. We should also have to take leisure into account as a good that is a rival to income and, therefore, to all the goods and services that make up the 'income' of the persons involved. It has been correctly pointed out that, if the object of redistribution is to affect the citizen's level of wellbeing, then leisure should be included in income on the basis of its opportunity cost (the renunciation of income).[3]

The redistributive effects of each of the adjustments mentioned are quite important and, if the adjustments are not made, they seriously affect the meaning of the results obtained in the analysis. A decision on what adjustments are to be made must take into account the probability that each adjustment will cause different repercussions on the changes in distribution brought about by social security. As a rule, there are no statistics showing the distribution of income as 'net accretion to purchasing power'. Existing data refer to disposable income or to income as defined by the income-tax laws, and both of these concepts are very different from that of income as 'receipts', which is the concept that should be used. Disposable income does not take into account capital gains, and taxable income, as a rule, does not correspond to the theoretical concept of income as 'receipts'. Moreover, there is the problem of tax evasion and, thus, of the differences between effective income and income as specified in tax statistics.

Because of all this, an approach that takes the existing distribution of incomes as a basis for empirical research into the redistributive effects of tax revenues and expenditures, including social security, cannot lead to satisfactory results. Unfortunately, our knowledge of modifications in the distribution of incomes as 'receipts' is not adequate to let us accurately calculate the changes in distribution effected by social security.

A second problem is that of choosing the units the income of which to consider. The distribution of family income would seem to be more relevant than the distribution of individual incomes.[4] It must be borne in mind, how-

[3] For an attempt to assess leisure as part of family wellbeing, see Morgan and Smith (1969), p. 453.

[4] For the reason given by Bentzel (1970), pp. 25ff.

ever, that, if the size and age–sex composition of the family vary among different income groups, choosing the family as the economic unit may distort the picture of redistribution through social security. If family size and composition are not the same from group to group, there is a risk of over- or underestimating the extent of redistribution, especially in light of the fact that many social security benefits involve all of the members of the family.

It is a commonly held belief that in underdeveloped countries the family is smaller the higher its income, because, as a rule, poorer families initially tend to be bigger. If this is indeed true, the extent of redistribution in favour of the poorer classes will probably be underestimated. The opposite is true in developed countries where the size of the family group is a positive function of the level of income. It does not seem possible to say how the age–sex composition of the family changes with income.

Basically, the problem is one of finding a concept of vertical inequality, of eliminating income differences that are not a sign of inequality. A concept of family income distribution that does not take into account the higher costs connected with more dependants and their personal circumstances does not give a real idea of the actual vertical inequality, because the same income does not necessarily mean the same standard of living. A redistribution, through tax facilities or subsidies, granted to families according to size levels will be really vertical – that is, in favour of lower-income groups – only when the advantages more than make up for the greater cost of more dependants or of particular personal circumstances. A redistribution aimed only at bringing to equivalency incomes that are nominally different, without considering the size of the family and personal circumstances, has no effect on vertical inequality.

Therefore, the problem is to make income homogeneous, since a bigger income enjoyed by a bigger family *may not* be a measure of inequality, and equal incomes in families of different make-up and circumstances *may* mean inequality. Obviously, it is difficult to estimate an equivalent standard of living, since the kind of expenditures differs according to age and tastes. In this case, we could, for instance, estimate only an approximate equivalent standard according to the main items of expenditure. These kinds of adjustment are not normally made in the study of redistributive effects of government measures; their neglect causes disparity between what is being measured and actual redistribution from rich to poor, since the measurement may also contain possible adjustments to make incomes homogeneous.

The measures do not even indicate vertical inequality due to current differences in annual income attributable to short-term fluctuations and to age. Usually, when we measure the degree of inequality in a community, we use statistics on income for one year. This system means that natural differences in income are taken as evidence of inequality. The year under consideration may show that *X* has an income ten times greater than *Y*'s, but this fact does not mean that there is inequality between the two individuals if, over the course of their lifetime, income is equal. It may simply mean that *X* is coming to the end of his career while *Y* is only just beginning. *Y* too, by the time he finishes, will receive an income similar to X's in that year. Therefore, to measure 'real' inequality, one must put aside differences due to age; otherwise, the value obtained is not correct. But it is practically impossible to attain such a treatment, because future incomes should be discounted. The only way to get round the difficulties is to compare two personal income distributions in two different years while assuming that there has been no change in horizontal distribution; that is, while assuming that differences in incomes in different professions, in age groups and in age composition in the community and in each single group have remained the same. But these assumptions look quite unrealistic. Perhaps it would be best to admit that, because of the lack of statistical data, one cannot consider the time dimension in income distribution, and that, because of this, one must be cautious about accepting calculations of redistributive changes.

The difficulty in excluding from income statistics taxes and public expenditures not affecting vertical distribution can be clearly shown in the case of pension contributions and benefits. As a rule, studies of redistribution through social security treat both contributions to pensions and pensions themselves as, respectively, deductions from and additions to the salaries of those who pay out or receive them during the year. Thus, it is shown that the inequality gap has narrowed, because, as a rule, contributions are paid in proportion to salaries, while the principal recipients of pensions are people belonging to the poorer classes. However, all, or at least part, of this supposed narrowing of the inequality gap is illusory. It does not, in fact, indicate a relative improvement in the conditions of the lower classes if one considers a lifetime's income and not just one year's income.

If one wants to ascertain the extent of redistribution – effected by pensions, one must (a) put aside those benefits that are equivalent in value to amounts paid, and (b) measure redistribution not in the light of a single period, but over the long term. The question, therefore, is one of identifying the relation between adequacy and the redistributionally neutral standard scheme. Once this problem has been solved, the redistribution effected by the pension system in a single year should, in principle, be measured by attributing to each pensioner the value of the differences, whether negative or positive, between the increase of benefits due in that year according to the amounts contributed and the prechosen level of adequacy, and the value of benefits effectively allowed under existing laws. Naturally, for this calculation to be made, one would have to know the value of this difference for each income group, but this is not practicable. One might, however, try to determine the value of this difference for individuals who differ in income and in the length of time over which they have paid contributions.

One can give alternative definitions of the relation of adequacy between benefits and contributions and the distributionally neutral standard scheme.[5]

[5] For an explicit attempt to define the distributionally neutral standard scheme, see Castellino (1968), pp. 19ff., and (1971) pp. 461ff. Implicit definitions are given in Harvey (1965), pp. 408ff., and Deran (1966), pp. 276 ff.

Initially, one might consider as adequate the relation that, in a private insurance system, would equalise the value of contributions and benefits according to correct demographic and financial assumptions (the actuarial criteria of private insurance, with a charge for overhead expenditures, perhaps increased by a 'normal' profit calculated on the basis of direct costs). Alternatively, in order to exclude from the calculation of the extent of redistribution the effects of measures aimed at offsetting a decrease in the real value of money, contributions and benefits might be determined according to a constant purchasing power as established by the cost-of-living index.

The crucial problem is to decide on the interest rate to discount the contributions and benefit flows. Some prefer to use more than one value; others propose using the interest rate current on the State bondmarket, or the interest rate corresponding to either the annual rate of increase of average money salaries[6] or the annual growth rate in money terms of GNP.[7] Each of the rates proposed is acceptable from one point of view or the other. The annual average monetary increase in salaries seems the most attractive, because, if the working population is constant, the system would become self-sufficient after the statutory period. If, however, the GNP growth rate is used, then, so long as the relationship between the income of labour and GNP remains constant over time, the method is self-sufficient no matter which way the working population goes. Whatever the standard scheme used, the redistributive effects of inflation are excluded from a study of redistribution through a given pension programme. This is because the real value of benefits is supposed constant in the standard scheme.

But would such standard schemes be really 'neutral', or would their neutrality be only conventional? Since different rates may be used and neither has more to offer than the other as regards real neutrality, it may be supposed they are only conventionally neutral. This is said without considering that a rigorous treatment of neutrality would require different interest rates in accordance with the workers subjective rates, which may differ according to individual preferences and incomes.

Another serious conceptual difficulty is that of deciding which families should bear the burden of financing social security, and which should benefit from the various social security programmes. Allocating of the burden means solving the problem of incidence. As regards contributions, including those paid by employers, it seems quite reasonable to place the burden on wage earners, since we are investigating only the long-term redistributive effects of financing.[8] This assumes that wages are lower than they would have been

[6] See Castellino (1971), p. 461, and Prest (1970), p. 11.

[7] See Aaron (1966) and Buchanan (1968).

[8] However, this incidence assumption, resting on the recent empirical work by Brittain (1971) is not generally accepted. For instance, in a recent empirical study of the redistributive effects of special insurance programmes, Feldstein, Friedman and Luft (1972) have supposed a partial shift on prices, which means a burden on family incomes and not only on wages.

without the contributions. This procedure seems wrong if we want to determine the short-term redistributive effects of changes in employers' contributions, as these are likely to affect, at least in part, the companies themselves.

Government grants to social security institutions should be distributed to families according to reasonable assumptions on the incidence of the main taxes included in the tax system. Where financing is obtained through deficit, the burden should be distributed among families according to inflation costs, if inflation can be attributed to the deficit brought about by social security financing. The distribution of taxes among families is, in practice, very difficult, because of the weakness of the results given by the incidence theory. However, we must come to a decision on this; and, while our decision should be based on what is known as traditional good sense, we must also bear in mind that any changes in our assumptions about burdens will also change the results of our analysis. Where social security contributions make up almost the whole of financing, allocating the burden of financing through taxes may be ignored as a problem.

In the distribution of social security contributions to families, one is faced with the delicate problem of evasion. If contributions are measured according to the formal rates of charge on salaries, there is the risk of underestimating the net benefits as a whole and, perhaps, to the poorer classes in particular. The evasion of contributions occurs above all in backward sectors – in small and medium-sized companies where salaries are relatively lower; and it is difficult to take account of it in income-distribution statistics. It remains to be seen whether evasion favours the workers, in the form of higher salaries, or to some extent favours the companies themselves. Obviously, it works against the workers if it means that they lose their rights to insurance benefits.

The distribution of benefits to families raises other problems, as some benefits (for instance, pensions, family allowances and health services for dependants) are a function of the size, composition and income group of the family. Health services, above all, favour certain kinds of people – the old, the infirm and the very young – the majority of whom belong to the poorer classes. Therefore, it is not enough to have information about the size and the age composition of families in the different income groups: we must also know how expenditures for health varies according to age. If this is not known, we can only assume an equal expenditure for all members of the family.

Finally, we must bear in mind that the redistributive effects of the distribution of costs and benefits (based on their nominal value) to the different income groups can not be stated in utilitarian terms unless it is implicitly assumed that the marginal utility of income remains constant in the different income groups. Recently, the validity of this assumption has been called into question and there have been interesting attempts to give the costs and benefits of social security programmes, different weights, according to their inverse relations with family incomes.[9] Unless we have an acceptable assumption of

[9] See Aaron and McGuire (1970), pp. 907 ff., and Feldstein Friedman and Luft (1972), p. 500.

the value to give to such weights, the conventional treatment gives us an additional reason to be very cautious in appraising the results of investigations of the redistributive effects of social security programmes.

III. REDISTRIBUTION THROUGH SOCIAL SECURITY IN ITALY

In order accurately to examine redistribution through social security in Italy, it is necessary to distinguish between programmes offering so-called short-term benefits (for instance, family allowances, sickness and maternity grants, and disability, accident and unemployment benefits), and those offering long-term benefits (for instance, retirement pensions). The reason for this is that the connection between payment and benefit is almost immediate in the case of short-term benefits, while long-term benefits can be enjoyed only after contributions have been made for a certain number of years, the amounts received varying according to the contributions made. Among the short-term benefits, there are some, such as survivors' pensions and disability pensions for work accidents, that may be paid for an indefinite period and that strictly, therefore, may be considered long-term benefits. However, we call them short-term, because, as a rule, they are calculated according to salary at the time of accident and are granted to the worker after a short period of insurance.

Redistribution through short-term benefits should be measured by dividing the population into family income groups and calculating the amount of contributions paid and benefits received by each group.[10] But a calculation cannot be made in Italy at present, because of (a) the lack of information about income distribution among families, (b) the many different kinds of insurance offered to workers of different categories, and (c) the many rules governing these schemes. The only remaining way is to calculate redistribution through short-term benefits and their relative sources of financing; for example, taxes, and contributions paid by workers and employers on salary. These should be classified according to the workers' income groups and family circumstances. Calculations of this kind have already been made for a number of European countries, and have recently been developed also for Italy, considering only the industrial sector.[11] Four different income situations were defined (i.e. those where workers' salaries or wages in the year studied equalled 75, 100, 150 or 200 per cent of the national average annual wage, gross of taxes and social security contributions).and broken down into four employment situations for each income group (i.e. unmarried workers; worker with wife; worker with wife and two children; and married couple working in industry and belonging to the same income group). The distribution of contributions was decided by assuming that the amounts paid by employers are shifted to the worker and that they pay their own contributions. State payments to social

[10] For investigations of this type, see Peacock and Browning (1950), p. 153; Conrad (1950), pp. 236 ff.; T. Higuchi (1965), pp. 229 ff.; and Schmidt, Schwarz and Thiebach (1965).

[11] See Burkus (1968), and (for Italy) Reviglio (1972).

insurance institutions were not distributed to families, mainly on account of difficulties in ascertaining how they should be allocated to the different income groups; however, in the year examined, the amount paid by the State accounted for only about 5 per cent of expenditure, and therefore our treatment should not impair the significance of the results.

Family allowances were distributed to the various income groups according to family composition. Other benefits were allocated to insured and protected individuals according to the per capita average. Actually, every individual receives benefits different from the average, in relation to the distribution of realised risks. But this is not a redistributive phenomenon.[12] Another implicit hypothesis of the above treatment is that the mortality quotient and health services are equal for each income class. This might be an unrealistic assumption, because it is plausible that benefits improve with standard of living and because the highest salary groups live in cities, where medical expenditures are higher on account of the greater availability of equipment. However, it does not appear that this assumption is so severe as to weaken the meaning of the results obtained. Besides, it should be remembered that all of those insured, as well as their dependants, receive benefits in kind (i.e. hospital treatment, general medical services, and so on) at cost prices. This, as the extensive literature on the value of public services in the national accounting has shown, may mean an over- or an underestimation of the services as compared with the value that they would have in a competitive market.

The calculations were made for 1967; however, the redistributive effects as assessed for that year are largely valid also for the following years. In fact, there are indications that in the following period the extent of redistributive changes has been strongly reaffirmed. The investigation for 1967 shows that benefits bring about a strong horizontal redistribution in favour of families made up of man and wife or of man and wife with two children, and that at the same time they bring about a lesser, though still significant, vertical redistribution from the highest to the lowest income group considered (see Table 10.1). If, however, contributions too are taken into account, then, for all but three of the income – family groups considered (the exceptions being families consisting of a married couple and two children and with an income 75, 100 or 150 per cent of the average), the amount of benefits is less than the amount of contributions paid (see Table 10.2). The reason for this is that the groups for which this is so, finance the administration expenditures, and the benefits received by other groups (such as the two-children families mentioned above, pensioners, agricultural workers, and workers in the commerce and credit sectors). Pensioners receive health benefits without paying contributions, and agricultural, credit and commerce workers pay smaller contributions relative to their salaries than do workers in the industrial sectors. This involves an important sectoral redistribution that has a dubious solidaristic meaning, because the beneficiaries' salaries are not necessarily lower than the payers' are; this seems

[12] As has been well shown by Coppini (1967), p. 25.

TABLE 10.1

SHORT-TERM BENEFITS AS PERCENTAGE OF ANNUAL WAGE (ITALIAN INDUSTRY, 19

Income–family group	*Family allowances*	*Sickness and maternity*	*Accidents*	*Unemployment*	*Tota*
Income 75% of average annual wage					
Bachelor	–	7·22	3·59	0·88	11·6
Insured and wife	6·65	12·12	3·99	0·88	23·6
Couple and two children	24·97	21·95	3·99	0·88	51·8
Working couple	–	8·28	3·52	0·88	12·6
Income 100% of average annual wage					
Bachelor	–	5·94	3·00	0·66	9·6
Insured and wife	4·99	9·62	3·47	0·66	18·7
Couple and two children	18·73	18·99	3·47	0·66	39·8
Working couple	–	6·73	3·00	0·66	10·4
Income 150% of average annual wage					
Bachelor	–	4·65	2·49	0·44	7·5
Insured and wife	3·32	7·11	2·96	0·44	13·8
Couple and two children	12·48	12·02	2·96	0·44	27·9
Working couple	–	5·18	2·49	0·44	8·1
Income 200% of average annual wage					
Bachelor	–	4·01	2·23	0·33	6·5
Insured and wife	2·49	5·85	2·71	0·33	11·3
Couple and two children	9·36	9·54	2·71	0·33	21·9
Working couple	–	4·41	2·23	0·33	6·9

Source: Reviglio (1972).

plausible, *a priori,* at least for some pensioners and agricultural workers. In any case, redistribution favours some groups over others in the same economic situation, and, because of this, horizontal equity is prejudiced.

However, not all industrial workers have contributed to redistribution to the same extent. Some of them (for instance, the two-children families mentioned above) are given an advantage because of their family situation and may not contribute, while those who do contribute pay more as their income grows and less as family burdens grow.

It is not easy to calculate the amount redistributed to the various economic sectors. For example, we tried to calculate it by subtracting total benefits from total contributions, not including family allowances and unemployment and accident benefits, which could not be determined separately for the various sectors. About 16 per cent of contributions were used to finance benefits to other categories and to meet running costs. Since the running costs of the principal body involved, the INAM, amount to about 6 per cent of benefits granted, one may say that around 10 per cent of contributions are redistributed.

TABLE 10.2

SHORT-TERM BENEFITS AS PERCENTAGE OF CONTRIBUTIONS PAID BY EMPLOYERS AND WORKERS

Income–family group	*Family allowances*	*Sickness and maternity*	*Accidents*	*Unemployment*	*Total*
Income 75% of average annual wage					
Bachelor	–	51·47	176·07	38·48	32·45
Insured and wife	38·50	86·44	199·63	38·48	66·04
Couple and two children	142·70	156·43	199·63	38·48	144·58
Working couple	–	59·03	175·83	38·48	35·41
Income 100% of average annual wage					
Bachelor	–	42·34	150·43	28·86	30·05
Insured and wife	36·56	68·56	174·00	28·86	58·64
Couple and two children	137·14	121·09	174·00	28·86	124·62
Working couple	–	48·01	150·43	28·86	32·53
Income 150% of average annual wage					
Bachelor	–	33·21	124·79	19·24	27·69
Insured and wife	36·57	50·69	148·36	19·24	50·49
Couple and two children	137·14	85·71	148·36	19·24	101·77
Working couple	–	36·99	124·79	19·24	29·62
Income 200% of average annual wage					
Bachelor	–	28·64	111·97	14·43	26·19
Insured and wife	36·57	41·76	135·54	14·43	45·30
Couple and two children	137·14	68·02	135·54	14·43	87·25
Working couple	–	31·47	111·97	14·43	27·77

Source: Reviglio (1972).

In addition to redistributing among economic sectors, short-term social security benefits redistribute a considerable amount of money geographically, in favour of the less developed areas of Italy (i.e. the 'Mezzogiorno'). It has been possible to measure this redistribution only as regards family allowances, since statistics concerning geographical redistribution through other benefits are not published. However, bearing in mind that in less developed areas salaries are relatively lower (as, therefore, are contributions paid), nonagricultural sectors are less important, families are bigger and unemployment is higher, we may assume that the other short-term benefits are responsible for a certain amount of such redistribution. On the other hand, though, certain expenses, especially hospitals and economic benefits, are probably relatively lower in the South; but it would appear unlikely that they are low enough to offset the relatively higher contributions.

As Table 10.3 shows, geographical redistribution through family allowances is quite large; i.e. there is a considerable difference between the amounts con-

TABLE 10.3

REGIONAL REDISTRIBUTION THROUGH FAMILY ALLOWANCE (DIFFERENCE BETWEEN CONTRIBUTIONS AND BENEFITS IN 1967)

Region	*Value (thousand million lire)*	*Percentage of contributions*
Lombardia	–40·1	–26
Piemonte	–33·2	–35
Emilia-Romagna	–7·2	–14
Liguria	–6·9	–22
Toscana	–5·1	–11
Friuli-Venezia Giulia	–2·1	–13
Valle d'Aosta	–0·3	–13
Umbria	+0·8	+11
Trentino Alto Adige	+1·2	+11
Molise	+1·2	+123
Marche	+1·9	+19
Abruzzi	+3·1	+50
Lazio	+3·1	+8
Basilicata	+4·1	+186
Veneto	+5·0	+9
Sardegna	+11·3	+122
Calabria	+16·8	+243
Puglia	+29·9	+175
Campania	+35·8	+129
Sicilia	+36·5	+159
(Mezzogiorno)	+134·3	+155

Source: Reviglio (1972).

tributed through payroll taxes and the family allowances received in the various regions of Italy. In 1967, Lombardy and Piedmont paid to other regions about 40 and 30 thousand million lire, respectively, i.e. 26 and 30 per cent of the contributions paid. The South received from the other regions 134 thousand million lire, i.e. one and a half times the amount contributed. Thus, the levelling effect of family allowances functioned perfectly, even if it is true that in certain individual cases it may have worked in a perverse direction, favouring individuals who were not in worse economic conditions than those from whom contributions were being redistributed.

There is further geographical redistribution in the case of disability pensions. It is a well-known fact that there has been an excessive increase in disability pensions in Italy. In 1972 there were 4·6 million disability pensions out of a total of about 11·20 million pensions. Disability pensions cost about 2·5 per cent of the national income, as against 3 per cent in France and 1·4 per cent in Germany. However, these figures are not completely comparable, as in Italy a disability pension does not become an old-age pension at retirement age, as it does in France and Germany. Nevertheless, these pensions represent a massive transfer of funds (in 1972 more than 1·6 billion lire) to a particular group of citizens.[13]

Conditions governing disability pensions are not as strict as those governing old-age pensions; to qualify for one, one need only have contributed for five years (as against 15 for an old-age pension), and the pension may be enjoyed along with an income. Because of this, the financing even of the minimum pension requires a very large transfer of funds, and, thus, whoever obtains a disability pension receives a benefit for which he has paid only in part. Basically, the workers show, by this redistribution of money, their solidarity with the disabled, while the State contributes a lesser share. Of course, a redistribution on this scale would naturally require a painstaking assessment of the kinds of disability, but, in reality, discretion has a large part to play in deciding what is classed as disability. This may be seen from the relatively greater number of disabiltiy pensions granted in the South, as compared with the Centre and the North. In a recent year, the number of disability pensions granted per 100 old-age pensions was 61 and 60, respectively, in Piedmont and Lombardy, but as many as 183 and 300 in Basilicata and Calabria.[14]

The wide discretionary criteria prevailing in the South may be largely justified by the need to ensure that pensions are granted to workers who, in the normal way of things have no right to one, perhaps because they were employed by companies that did not pay contributions. However, it may also be that disability pensions are sometimes granted as a result of string-pulling or of favouritism of other kinds.

If the man receiving a disability pension is not in fact disabled, his right to receive money from the State and from active workers should be decided according to his needs and according to the State's attempts to help people in his economic situation. Otherwise it may happen that an undeserving case receives an income when others in greater need are prevented from benefiting from community help. But lack of data makes it impossible to judge the economic situations of those who enjoy a disability pension, and, hence, it is impossible to calculate separately the amount distributed vertically and the amount maldistributed.

Old-age pension programmes also cause large transfers that give rise to incorrect vertical and horizontal redistribution. Between 1957 and 1966 (i.e. before the March 1968–April 1969 reform), those people who did not qualify for the minimum pension on the basis of contributions paid benefited, along with certain other groups of workers, from considerable transfers of income, mainly from industrial and bank workers. Among the workers who were not charged for these transfers were public employees, whether in State, local government or autonomous enterprises; and others (such as company managers, journalists, agents, entertainment workers, and professional men) who did not

[13] For statistical data on disability pensions, see Ministero de Bilancio (various years), appendix II.

[14] As was originally shown in Bargoni (1969), pp. 4ff. and table 5.

come within the general scheme run by the INPS, and who contributed either to special funds set up by the INPS or to separate bodies. These groups, who often enjoyed an above-average income, were exempt from making contributions to raise the incomes of the poorer classes.

The formula determining the amount of the pension was aimed at redistributing through the use of a minimum pension, through the use of a benefit-to-person ratio declining with contributions, and through the use of monetary coefficients differing for the various professional groups.[15] It is possible to estimate the transfers involved in this mechanism, assuming a rough approximation of the ideal distributionally neutral standard scheme.[16]

As shown in Table 10.4, between 1957 and 1966 the amount transferred to those who received the minimum pension reached about 35 per cent of overall benefits. Not all of this money benefited low-income groups: among those who were covered by the general scheme, besides those who probably as a rule were in that situation (i.e., a large proportion of the disabled, survivors of deceased workers, agricultural workers and domestic staff), there were certainly individuals who benefited from the transfer simply because they had paid contributions for only a short period, having otherwise evaded them by working at jobs not declared for social security purposes, or by doing independent work not covered by special insurance. Other people who benefited were those, such as farmers, sharecroppers, agricultural tenants, and artisans (and, from 1966, shopkeepers), who were covered by certain special funds for independent workers. In accordance with the laws by which all old people covered by the above special funds could have a pension after contributing for only a very brief period (in certain cases only a year), practically all the pensions received by farmers and artisans benefited from the transfer in the years 1957–66.

These people were not necessarily in need, at least in relation to other citizens in the same economic situation who were not covered by the transfer. Therefore, transfers aimed at ensuring minimum pensions did not necessarily redistribute from rich to poor; probably, at least in part, they did exactly the opposite. In any case, it cannot be said that such redistribution respected the principle of horizontal equality.

[15] The mechanism to determine contributions and pensions for the general programme was quite complicated. Contributions to be paid were defined partly as *basic* contributions, computed in 1938 lires, and partly (mainly, in fact) as a percentage of wages, and were transferred to a special fund aimed at revaluating the pensions paid. In order to determine the pensions to be paid, it was necessary to calculate the so-called basic pensions on the basis of total paid basic contributions, using a declining coefficient for the first 3000 lire and a constant one (20 per cent) thereafter. Basic pensions were then revaluated (using different coefficients for the different professional groups) in order to obtain the pensions to be paid. The relation between basic and proportional contributions therefore was not constant but variable (for instance, in 1963 it was 170–90 for industrial and service workers, 110 for houseworkers, and 20 for agricultural workers). In any case, pensions so obtained were raised to a minimum level.

[16] As given when pensions computed at constant purchasing power amount to 20 per cent of total *basic* contributions paid. In its treatment of this matter, the text follows Castellino (1968).

TABLE 10.4

TRANSFERS OF PENSIONS IN ITALY, 1957–66 (VALUES IN THOUSAND MILLION LIRES)

			Transfers									
	Pensions paid	*Pensions before increase to minimum*	*To beneficiaries of minimum pensions*		*To beneficiaries of declining coefficients used to determine basic pensions*		*To beneficiaries of coefficients used to revaluate basic contributions*		*Paid by the insured*		*Paid by the State*	
	(1)	*(2)*	*Value (1) – (2)*	*% of (1)*	*Value*	*% of (1)*	*Value*	*% of (1)*	*Value*	*% of (1)*	*Value*	*% of (1)*
General scheme	8645	6070	2575	30	1260	15	364[a]	4	2451	29	1849	21
Special scheme												
Farmers, sharecroppers, agricultural, tenants	1115	255	860	77	105	10			–575	–52	946	91
Artisans	103	45	58	56	no data	no data			–334	–324	81	79
Total	9863	6370	3493	35							2876	30

[a]Divided as follows: 103 to agricultural workers, 193 to apprentices, 68 to domestic staff.

Sources and methodological notes:

The table elaborates on data calculated by Castellino (1968). *Pensions paid* are pensions actually paid. *Pensions before increase to minimum* are those obtained when monetary revaluation coefficients then in force are applied to *basic* contributions (see footnote 15). *Transfers to beneficiaries of minimum pensions* are obtained by subtracting 'pensions before increase to minimum' from 'paid pensions'. *Transfers to beneficiaries of declining coefficients used to determine basic pensions* are fixed by the rule according to which basic pensions were calculated using a declining coefficient. *Transfers to beneficiaries of coefficients used to revaluate basic contributions* are calculated according to the difference between total 'theoretical' and total 'actual' contributions, 'theoretical' contributions being those that some of the insured would have paid if the average revaluation coefficient were calculated on basic contributions. Not included are some transfers made to lesser categories for instance to apprentices, cottage-industry workers, freshwater and small sea fishermen, and people who work at home). *Transfers paid by the insured* are calculated by assuming a distributionally neutral standard scheme in which basic contributions and basic pensions are recalculated according to a revaluation coefficient geared to the cost of living by calculating the difference between total contributions actually paid and contributions that would have been paid had the revaluation coefficient defined above been used (see footnote 15). The implicit hypothesis was that in the future, too, pensions would be calculated according to the rules then in force; but, due to the new rules introduced in the 1968–9 pension reform, this assumption is no longer valid. Therefore, transfers paid by the insured are not the same as those shown in the table; probably they will disappear, as the new pension scheme basically favours all insured people. *Transfers paid by the State* are those provided for by the current laws on pension financing and also those aimed at making up deficits. Naturally, contributions paid by the State as an employer are not included.

A second type of transfer was aimed at benefiting those people whose overall basic contribution was low, since the criteria for determining basic pensions were not strictly proportional to basic contributions paid, discriminating in favour of people who had paid very low basic contributions. In the general scheme, pensions benefited from a transfer of this type that, between 1957 and 1966, amounted to about 15 per cent of total benefits. Thanks to this transfer, a vertical redistribution among the groups taking part in the programme was realised, but it may again have been the case that some of the beneficiaries were people who had worked independently for a part of their active lives. Another minor transfer, involving about 4 per cent of total benefits, favoured some categories included in the general scheme (for instance, agricultural workers, apprentices and domestic staff) for whom the mechanism determining pensions, through the revaluation coefficients applied to basic contributions, was particularly favourable.

Transfers were at the expense of the State and of the people insured. In the period 1957–66, the government (i.e. the taxpayer) paid to the general pensions scheme a sum amounting to almost 21 per cent of pensions; and the people insured (above all, industrial and service industry workers) transferred a large part of their contributions, amounting to almost 29 per cent of benefits, as a true tax (see Table 10.4).

Other transfers benefited, in particular, the special pension scheme for farmers, sharecroppers and agricultural tenants, and, to a lesser extent, that for artisans. In the period 1957–66, these transfers amounted to 91 and 79 per cent, respectively, of benefits accruing to these two categories. For these two schemes there was a redistribution, from the taxpayer to the insured, that was primarily of benefit to those who were made eligible to minimum pensions. A considerable transfer was made to tradespeople as well. This transfer is cause for serious concern (as are the transfers to farmers and artisans), because it seems difficult to justify transfers to people whose salaries are certainly not lower than the average.

No conclusions concerning the redistributive nature of State financing can be drawn, because of the uncertain indications revealed by studies on the incidence of taxation in Italy. However, taking into account the generally held opinion about the regressive nature of Italian tax revenues, we cannot rule out the possibility that the process of levelling income correctly through the mechanism for determining pensions has in some way been offset by the practice of financing through the tax system. The fact that pensions are practically exempt from the personal income tax works in the same direction.

The mechanism devised to determine pensions has led also to regional transfers. In fact, underdeveloped regions, where salaries are relatively lower and where most people work in agriculture, have been relatively well favoured, because lower-paid workers, farmers, sharecroppers and agricultural tenants have been more likely to benefit from the raising of pensions to the minimum and from the particularly favourable rules governing the determination of basic pensions.

An idea of the extent and direction of interregional old-age pension flows within the general system can be drawn by measuring the difference between theoretically adequate and actual contributions and pensions, defining as theoretically adequate those contributions that should have been paid, and pensions that should have been received, if both relations between paid and basic contributions and pensions were the same as the national average. If we measure the difference for the years 1960–5 (Table 10.5), we see that five regions (Piedmont, Valle d'Aosta, Lombardy, Liguria and Lazio) transferred outward sums varying from 3 to 13 per cent of the total contributions. The payment of pensions involved relatively greater transfers. All of the Northern and Central Italian regions, except Emilia-Romagna and Abruzzi-Molise, sent money outwards; on the whole, transfers from the North were of the order of 14 per cent of actual pensions. The South and the islands were the main beneficiaries, and their gain was relatively high (i.e. almost a third of total pensions).

To the transfers shown in Table 10.5 must be added the ones effected by the special pension schemes for self-employed workers (farmers, sharecroppers, agricultural tenants, artisans and small traders). It is not possible to determine the level of these transfers, but as we have already seen, the pensions enjoyed by these workers are considerably higher than those determined through the standard scheme, and are paid for largely by the State and, thus, the taxpayer. Since, in the Central and Southern regions, agricultural workers, artisans and shopkeepers constitute the majority of wage earners, it is safe to assume that money transferred by the community as a whole mainly benefited people living in those regions.

IV. THE LESSON OF THE ITALIAN EXPERIENCE

What is the lesson to be learned from the Italian experience as described above? To understand it, one must bear in mind that social security in Italy is marked not only by maldistribution, but also by allocative inefficiency in providing benefits in kind in the health sector, thus causing serious waste and allowing privileges to certain groups of citizens.

The existence of waste and privileges is well known and we do not intend to go into detail here. Waste is due, above all, to the excessive use of medicines (in Italy, the percentage of total health service costs given over to medicines is almost three times greater than it is in England) and to inefficiency in hospital management, mainly because there is no incentive to keep costs down. Privileges are given to some groups of citizens (for instance, the medical profession and manufacturers of pharmaceutical products) who supply goods and services in the health sector. Waste and privileges account for a large share of the rocketing expenditure on health services and, therefore, for much of the related deficit (which rose from 6·4 per cent of overall expenditure in 1965 to 10·9 per cent in 1972).

Maldistribution, waste and privileges take a large slice out of social security resources that could be used to meet the community's urgent demand for

TABLE 10.5

INTERREGIONAL TRANSFERS WITHIN THE GENERAL PENSION SCHEME IN 1960–5 (AMOUNTS IN THOUSAND MILLION LIRE)

Region	*Total Contributions (1)*		*Pensions (2)*		*Transfers of contributions*				*Transfers of pensions*			
					Amounts		*% of (1)*		*Amounts*		*% of (2)*	
Piemonte	784·4		662·5		−34·4		−4		−108·0		−16	
Valle d'Aosta	19·9		14·4		−2·3		−13		−2·8		−19	
Lombardia	1775·6		1285·5		−77·3		−4		−219·8		−17	
Trentino Alto Adige	76·7	3462·2	68·4	2826·5	4·0	86·7	5	−3	1·4	−400·5	2	−14
Veneto	359·7		366·4		26·2		7		−2·1		−0·6	
Friuli-Venezia Giulia	142·3		151·7		17·3		12		−16·1		−11	
Liguria	305·6		277·6		−20·2		7		−53·1		−19	
Emilia-Romagna	383·1		459·1		20·4		5		−55·2		12	
Toscana	372·3		377·6		13·3		5		−35·4		−9	
Umbria	55·0		74·8		1·7		3		−5·1		−7	
Marche	70·9		97·4		9·1		13		−0·2		−0·2	
Lazio	546·9		358·6		−15·0		−3		−11·3		−3	
Abruzzi-Molise	49·3		82·7		5·4		1		19·9		24	
Campania	344·6		306·0		13·7		4		34·3		11	
Puglia	122·5		300·5		14·1		12		103·0		34	
Basilicata	17·5	772·8	44·9	1283·9	0·4	51·3	2	7	19·9	374·5	44	29
Calabria	49·2		149·6		6·4		13		74·7		50	
Sicilia	171·3		362·2		14·3		8		115·9		32	
Sardegna	67·7		120·7		2·9		4		26·7		22	
Total	5712·5		5560·6									

Sources and methodological notes: The contributions were obtained from the *Notizic statistiche* of the INPS (various years). Transfers of contributions are calculated according to the difference between 'theoretical' and 'actual' contributions, where 'theoretical' contributions are the basic contributions received multiplied by the relationship between basic contributions and total national contributions paid to the revaluation fund. These transfers were calculated for the years 1960–5 on data given in Bargoni (1969), table 2. Transfers of pensions are measured according to the difference between 'theoretical' and 'actual' pensions, defining 'theoretical' pensions as the basic pensions per region multiplied by the national relationship between actual and basic pensions. This difference is calculated in Bargoni (1969), table 3. The data given in the present table are not comparable to the data in Table 10.4, both because the periods in question are different and because of the different methods employed. (In particular, Bargoni's data do not take into account redistribution through transfers to the beneficiaries that result from the declining coefficients used to determine pensions.)

better benefits for the poorer groups (especially pensioners receiving the inadequate minimum pension), and for better and more efficient health services. To satisfy this demand for social reform, tax revenues or social security contributions should be increased; but, because of the inefficiency of the tax system, income from taxes does not affect the richer groups. Recently, by means of a reform that is more extensive than any yet tried in other Western countries, an attempt has been made to weed out such inefficiency; but it is expected that it will be a few years before the reform brings about any real changes, as it will take some while to alter habits and customs in the way required. In the meantime, the government has promised, tax rates will not be increased.

One alternative – that of raising social security contributions – does not seem feasible, as these contributions are already very high (i.e. more than 50 per cent of wages). Thus, the only course left is to resort to deficit financing; but many argue that this runs the risk of being inflationary, given the present serious state of the public budget, which already (1973) has a deficit of more than 10 per cent of GNP.

It follows that social security reforms requiring greater expenditures cannot be carried out. The same is true for reforms that the community is demanding in order to protect it more effectively against the inadequacies of the present economic and social system. Sufficient funds to finance free or low-cost housing for the poorer groups, cheap public transport, anti-pollution investments, and better education for the children of needy families cannot yet be found.

Since social reform is a *sine qua non* of stability and of the ordered development of the economic system, the distributive and allocative inefficiencies of social security are among the causes of the crisis of government as manifest in social dissatisfaction and unrest.

REFERENCES

Aaron, H. J., 'The Social Insurance Paradox', *Canadian Journal of Economics and Political Science,* Aug 1966.

Aaron, H. J., and McGuire, M., 'Public Goods and Income Distribution', *Econometrica,* Nov 1970.

Bargoni, A., 'Trasferimenti nel sistema pensionistico', *Note econometriche,* Jan–Mar 1969.

Bentzel, R., 'The Significance of Income Distribution Statistics', *The Review of Income and Wealth,* Sep 1970.

Brittain, J. A., 'The Incidence of Social Security Payroll Taxes', *American Economic Review,* Apr 1971.

Buchanan, J. M., 'Social Insurance in a Growing Economy: A Proposal for Radical Reform', *National Tax Journal,* Dec 1968.

Burkus, J., 'Some Aspects of Income Redistribution through Social Security in Four Western Countries', *International Labour Review,* Feb 1968.

Castellino, O., 'Incomes Redistribution through Old-Age Pensions: A Note on its Definition and Measurement', *Public Finance,* no. 3, 1971.

Castellino, O., 'Previdenza sociale e redistribuzione del reddito', *Saggi sull'economica della sicurezza sociale* (Turin: Giappichelli, 1968).

Conrad, A. C., 'Redistribution through Government Budget in the United States', in *Income Redistribution and Social Policy,* ed. A. T. Peacock (London, 1950).

Coppini, M. A., *Aspetti economici della sicurezza sociale* (Milan, 1967).

Deran, E., 'Income Redistribution under the Social Security System', *National Tax Journal,* Sep 1966.

Feldstein, M., Friedman, B., and Luft, H., 'Distributional Aspects of National Health Insurance Benefits and Finance', *National Tax Journal,* Dec 1972.

Harvey, E. V., 'Social Security Taxes – Regressive or Progressive?', *National Tax Journal,* Dec 1965.

Higuchi, T., 'La Redistribution du Revenu et la Securité Sociale: Interpretation d'une Enquête Menée au Japon', *Revue Internationale du Travail,* Sep 1965.

INPS, *Notizie statistiche* (various years).

Ministero del Bilancio, *Relazione generale sulla situazione economica del paese* (various years).

Morgan, J. N., and Smith, J. D., 'Measures of Economic Well-Offness and their Correlates', *American Economic Review,* May 1969.

Peacock, A. T., and Browning, P. R., 'The Social Services in Great Britain and the Redistribution of Income', in *Income Redistribution and Social Policy* (London, 1950).

Prest, A. R., 'Some Redistributional Aspects of the National Superannuation Fund', *Three Banks Review,* June 1970.

Reviglio, F., 'Bilancio pubblico e redistribuzione del reddito, con particolare riferimento alle assicurazioni sociali di breve periodo', in *Lezioni sulla politica economica in Italia* (Milan: Comunità, 1972).

Schmidt, K. D., Schwarz, U., and Thiebach, G., *Die Umverteilung des Volkseinkommens in der Bundesrepublik Deutschland 1955 und 1960* (Tübingen: Mohr, 1965).

United Nations, 'Incomes in Postwar Europe', in *Economic Survey of Europe in 1962* (Geneva, 1967).

Part V
Decentralised Provision of Public Services

11 The Supply of Communal Goods and Revenue Sharing

Eytan Sheshinski
THE HEBREW UNIVERSITY OF JERUSALEM

I. INTRODUCTION

The use of intergovernmental grants is found in most countries. Governments (especially central governments) that encompass relatively large jurisdictions frequently supplement with grants of funds the revenues of public units at more decentralised levels. These grants are of two basic types: conditional and unconditional ('lump-sum'). Among the former, a common type is the matching grant, where the recipient government is required to allocate funds from its own sources, in a specified ratio to the grant.

An extensive literature deals with the likely effects of intergovernmental matching and lump-sum grants, mostly in terms of the standard theory of individual choice (see, for example, Barlow, 1970; Boskin, 1973; Brainard and Dolbear, 1967; Oates, 1972; Thurow, 1966; and Wilde, 1968). The grant recipient has been viewed as an individual decision-maker whose preferences are defined over public ('communal') and private goods, and with this model it has been established that a matching grant has a stimulative impact on public expenditure relative to a lump-sum grant of equal size. The reason for this result is that a matching grant has an *income effect* and a *substitution effect,* while a lump-sum grant has only the former, working in favour of public expenditure.

The existing theory suffers from some serious deficiencies. One is that intergovernmental grants are grants to groups of people, not to individuals, and that, as such, their effects depend on the political process by which the group makes its collective decisions. A theoretical framework in which this process is treated explicitly has recently been analysed by Bradford and Oates (1971, 1971).

A second deficiency concerns the problem of 'adverse selection' and taxation by the recipient government units. The tax and revenue system of these governments may itself be influenced by the level and composition of grants from the central government, and because of this it is important to incorporate these interactions in the analysis of the effects of these grants.

State and local governments commonly choose to finance their expenditures on public goods through the imposition of income and property taxes. Such taxes are inefficient, introducing distortions that stem from the wedge that these taxes insert between supply and demand prices. The decision on the size of public expenditures undertaken by a decentralised government must, therefore, take into account two major, opposite considerations. One is the distortive effect that local taxes may have on, say, property size. The other is the size of the available lump-sum and matching grants.

In this paper is developed a model designed to analyse this problem. Given a system of federal income tax and local property taxes, individual taxpayers choose their optimum consumption pattern.

The local government's budget is financed from two sources: local property-tax revenue and federal lump-sum and matching grants. Given the terms of the federal grants, plus information on individual demand functions, the local government chooses the budget that maximises the welfare of the community. When all of the community members have equal tastes and incomes, there is no ambiguity in this process. If, however, the community is composed of heterogeneous income groups, each group may have a preference for a different size of budget. Public expenditures are used to purchase communal goods, supplied equally to all. Assuming these goods to be normal, high-income individuals will, other things being equal, prefer a relatively high level of consumption of these goods. On the other hand, knowing that the public finances draw on revenues from taxes on property, of which they own a relatively high proportion, they may prefer lower taxes and lower public expenditures. These elements, as well as the *substitution* and *complementarity* effects of the public goods on the demand for property, are explicitly considered here, employing the concept of 'voting equilibrium', in which the voter with median income is decisive.

Budgetary effects on the 'distribution of welfare' in the community are quite intricate. Increased progressivity of the tax system (federal or local) may have a negative effect on the equilibrium budget of the community. Public expenditures, providing equal benefits to everybody, are an important element in reducing inequality. Thus, the outcome of such a progressive redistribution may actually be an increase in inequality, when this concept properly includes the benefits from public expenditures. An example to this effect is presented below.

The goods and services provided by decentralised governments are, for the most part, not 'pure public goods' in the Samuelsonian sense of providing the same quantity to any number of individuals. The level of educational services per pupil, for example, varies with the number of pupils; more students mean fewer teachers per pupil. The present study therefore distinguishes the concept of a *communal good*, by which is meant a good that is collectively supplied in equal amount to all members of the community. The size of this amount is defined as the ratio of public expenditure to the number of members times unit price.

All persons in a nation consume whatever units of public goods the national government provides, with no range of choice for the individual. At the local level, however, the individual has some choice among levels of consumption of communal goods. First, he may select a community of residence that provides the public good at a level suited to his preferences. This is Tiebout's analysis (Tiebout, 1956). Second, in some instances (for example, as regards educational services), the individual may, of his own volition and despite the fact that he pays local taxes, purchase the good privately, giving up the opportunity of benefiting from the collectively supplied amount. We briefly discuss this possibility (which is examined in greater detail in Sheshinki, 1974) in the final section of this paper.

II. THE MODEL

Consider a local government that levies property taxes on its contituents and supplies services that are consumed in equal amount by all. We call such services 'pure communal goods', in contrast to the Samuelsonian 'pure public goods', and assume that the amount received by each user is equal to the total budget, divided by the population served, times unit cost. Since the good involves no economies of scale or externalities, efficiency considerations clearly favour individual rather than collective purchase. Initially, however, we shall disregard equity considerations and concentrate on the efficiency aspect.

In particular, we shall study the effects of the community of intergovernmental grants ('revenue-sharing') in the form of lump-sum and matching grants, taking explicitly into account the process through which the collectivity determines the levels of taxes and spending it applies to the communal good.

The representative taxpaying individual consumes three goods: a consumption good, $x (x \geqslant 0)$; housing property, $y (y \geqslant 0)$; and a communal good, $z (z \geqslant 0)$. The units of x and y are chosen so that their prices are unity. There is a property tax fixed at a rate of t per unit. The individual's budget constraint is, thus,

$$x + (1 + t)y = m - T \tag{11.1}$$

where $m (m \geqslant 0)$ is his (given) before-tax income, and $T (T \geqslant 0)$ is the (federal) income tax. The individual determines the amounts of x and y so as to maximise his utility

$$u = u(x, y, z) \tag{11.2}$$

for a given amount of z. The first-order conditions for a maximum are

$$\frac{u_2}{u_1} = 1 + t \tag{11.3}$$

and the budget constraint (11.1), where $u_2 = \dfrac{\partial u}{\partial x}$ and $u_1 = \dfrac{\partial u}{\partial y}$. We assume that $u(\cdot)$ is strictly quasi-concave in x and y, so that (11.1) and (11.3) uniquely determine the individual's demands:

$$x = x(t, z, m - T)$$

and $$y = y(t, z, m - T) \tag{11.4}$$

Substitution of (11.1) into (11.2) gives the representative individual's *indirect utility:*

$$u(x, y, z) = u[x(t, z, m - T), y(t, z, m - T), z] = v(t, z, m - T) \tag{11.5}$$

The communal budget contains property tax revenue, lump-sum grants from the federal government, and expenditures on the communal good. Let the unit price of the communal good be p. Then, assuming that the federal grants are equal to taxes collected from the community,

$$T + ty(t, z, m - T) = pz \tag{11.6}$$

Given its budget constraint, (11.6), and information on individual demands, y, the community's goal is to determine the tax rate t and the amount z so as to maximise utility (equation 11.5). With identical individuals there is no difficulty in assuming that the political process brings the best outcome to the community.

The first-order conditions for a maximum are

$$v_1 - \mu a = 0,\ v_2 - \mu b = 0\ (\mu > 0) \tag{11.7}$$

where μ is a Lagrange multiplier; or

$$\frac{v_2}{v_1} = \frac{b}{a}\ (a \neq 0) \tag{11.8}$$

where $$a = a(t, z, m, p, T) = y + ty_1 = y(1 - \eta) \tag{11.9}$$

and $$b = b(t, z, m, p, T) = ty_2 - p = -\left[p(1 - \lambda) + \frac{T}{z}\lambda\right] \tag{11.10}$$

$\eta = -ty_1/y$ is the own price elasticity, and $\lambda = zy_2/y$ is the elasticity of y with respect to z. We usually say that y and z are *complements (substitutes)* when $\lambda > 0$ (< 0). This effect should not be confused with the effect on property prices that is commonly associated with an increase in, say, neighbourhood schools. The sign of λ clearly depends on the nature of the communal good. On the other hand, it is safe to assume that $\eta > 0$. For (11.8) to be well defined, we assume that $\eta \neq 1$.

Condition (11.8) can be expressed in terms of direct utility. Using (11.1), (11.3) and (11.5),

$$v_1 = u_1x_1 + u_2y_1 = u_1[x_1 + (1 + t)y_1] = -u_1y$$

and $$v_2 = u_1x_2 + u_2y_2 + u_3 = u_1[x_2 + (1 + t)y_2] + u_3 = u_3 \tag{11.11}$$

Hence, (11.8) may be written

$$\frac{u_3}{u_1} = \frac{p(1-\lambda) + \frac{T}{z}\lambda}{1-\eta} \tag{11.8$'$}$$

The second-order conditions for a maximum is assumed to hold

$$\begin{vmatrix} v_{11} - \mu a_1 & v_{12} - \mu a_2 & a \\ v_{21} - \mu b_1 & v_{22} - \mu b_2 & b \\ a & b & \end{vmatrix} > 0 \tag{11.12}$$

(where $a_1 = \partial a/\partial t$, $a_2 = \partial a/\partial z$, and so on). We now define two functions, g and h:

$$g = g(t, z, m, p, T) \equiv \frac{v_2}{v_1} - \frac{b}{a} \tag{11.13}$$

$$h = h(t, z, m, p, T) \equiv T + ty - pz \tag{11.14}$$

For given m, p and T, the optimum of t and z, denoted t^* and z^*, respectively, are determined by the twin conditions

$$g(t, z, m, p, T) = 0 \tag{11.15}$$

and

$$h(t, z, m, p, T) = 0 \tag{11.16}$$

From (11.13) we calculate that

$$\begin{aligned} g_1 &= \frac{1}{v_1^2}(v_1 v_{21} - v_2 v_{11}) - \frac{1}{a^2}(ab_1 - ba_1) \\ &= \frac{\mu}{v_1^2}[av_{21} - bv_{11} - \mu(ab_1 - ba_1)] \end{aligned} \tag{11.17}$$

and

$$\begin{aligned} g_2 &= \frac{1}{v_1^2}(v_1 v_{22} - v_2 v_{12}) - \frac{1}{a^2}(ab_2 - ba_2) \\ &= \frac{\mu}{v_1^2}[av_{22} - bv_{12} - \mu(ab_2 - ba_2)] \end{aligned} \tag{11.18}$$

having used that $\mu = v_1/a = v_2/b$. Similarly,

$$\begin{aligned} h_1 &= a \\ h_2 &= b \end{aligned} \tag{11.19}$$

Implicitly differentiating (11.15), using (11.17) and (11.18), we find that

$$\left.\frac{dt}{dz}\right|_{g=0} = -\frac{g_2}{g_1} = -\frac{av_{22} - bv_{12} - \mu(ab_2 - ba_2)}{av_{21} - bv_{11} - \mu(ab_1 - ba_1)} \tag{11.20}$$

and

$$\left.\frac{dt}{dz}\right|_{h=0} = -\frac{h_2}{h_1} = -\frac{b}{a} \tag{11.21}$$

By (11.8′), b/a must be negative, at least around the optima t^*, z^*. I shall assume that for all t and z, $b/a < 0$. Thus, in the (z, t) plane of figure 11.1, the

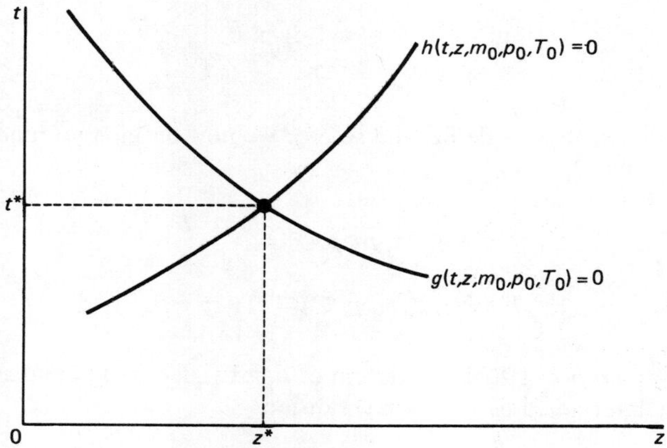

Fig. 11.1

slope of the curve $h = 0$ is positive. The slope of the curve $g = 0$ is ambiguous, but around the equilibrium point it must be smaller than the slope of the $h = 0$ curve. The condition

$$\left.\frac{dt}{dz}\right|_{g=0} < \left.\frac{dt}{dz}\right|_{h=0} \tag{11.22}$$

at (t^*, z^*) can be seen, using (11.20) and (11.21), to be *identical* to the second-order condition (11.12).

Under some conditions, it is reasonable to assume that $g_1 > 0$ and $g_2 > 0$, and, hence, that the slope of the curve $g = 0$ is negative. Having no notion of how the elasticities η and λ may depend on t and z, we assume these to be constant. Then, from (11.13) and (11.11) it is seen that, at $g = 0$, $Sgn[g_1] = -Sgn[\partial(u_3/u_1)/\partial t]$. Now, an increase in t, raising the relative price of y, decreases y, and, if $\eta < 1$, also decreases x. If z is a normal good, this must decrease (for z held constant) the marginal rate of substitution of x to z, u_3/u_1. Thus, we expect that $g_1 \gtreqless 0$ as $\eta \lesseqgtr 1$.

Similarly, when η and λ are constant, $Sgn[g_2] = -Sgn[\partial(u_3/u_1)/\partial z]$. An increase in z increases (decreases) y when these goods are complements (substitutes), i.e. when $\lambda > 0$ (< 0). By (11.1), $x_2 = -(1+t)y_2$. Thus, when $\lambda > 0$ (< 0), $x_2 < 0$ (> 0). An increase in z followed by a decrease in x must, under the normality of z assumption, decrease the marginal rate of substitution between x and z, u_3/u_1. Thus, when $\lambda > 0$, we expect $g_2 > 0$.

When these conditions hold, (11.15) and (11.16) determine a unique optimum solution (t^*, z^*). We shall now study the effects of changes in federal policy, in terms of the lump-sum and matching grants, on these solutions.

III. EFFECTS OF AN INCREASE IN MATCHING GRANTS

From the community's point of view, a federal matching grant is equivalent to a reduction in the supply price of the communal good. Suppose that the community faces the price $\pi(< p)$ for z. The matching grant is therefore equal to $(p - \pi)z$, and the community faces the budget

$$T' + ty = \pi z \tag{11.23}$$

where T' is a lump-sum grant, which is assumed to be fixed. The first-order condition for the community's optimum t and z is still (11.8), but the definition of b (previously (11.9)) now becomes

$$b \equiv ty_2 - \pi \tag{11.24}$$

The federal government's budget is assumed to be balanced, i.e. lump-sum plus matching grants are equal to tax revenue:

$$T' + (p - \pi)z = T \tag{11.25}$$

Substitution of (11.25) into (11.23) yields the previous condition (11.6). Also, using (11.23) and (11.25), (11.24) can be written

$$b = -\left[p(1-\lambda) + \frac{T}{z}\lambda\right] + (p - \pi) \tag{11.24$'$}$$

which reduces to (11.9) when $p = \pi$.

The definition of $g(\cdot)$, (11.13), now becomes

$$g = g(t, z, m, p, T, \pi) = \frac{v_2}{v_1} - \frac{b}{a} \tag{11.13$'$}$$

with b given by (11.24′).

The optimum (t^*, z^*) is determined by setting (11.13′) and (11.14) equal to zero. The equation $b = 0$ is independent of π. Along the curve $g = 0$, for a given z, an increase in π requires t to change by

$$\left.\frac{dt}{d\pi}\right|_{g=0,\,z} = -\frac{g_6}{g_1} = \frac{-1}{y(1-\eta)g_1} < 0 \tag{11.26}$$

As argued previously, it is reasonable to expect that $g_1(1-\eta) > 0$, which entails that (11.26) is negative. Thus, if $g_1(1-\eta) > 0$, *a decrease in* π *will increase the optimum amount of the communal good and will bring a further increase in the optimum local tax rate.* In Figure 11.2, the decrease in π changes the optimum configuration from (z^*, t^*) to (z^{**}, t^{**}).

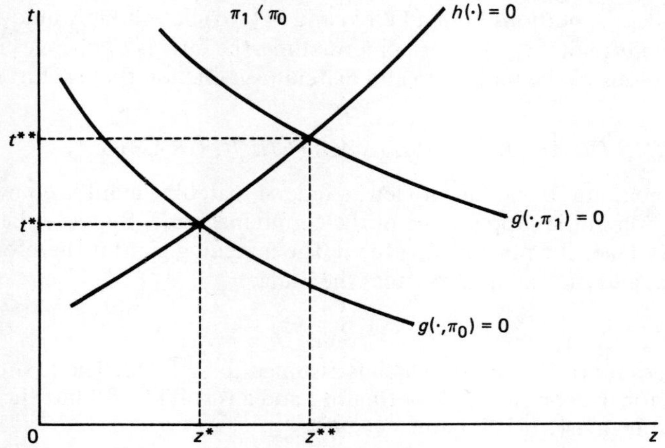

Fig. 11.2

On the other hand, if $g_1(1-\eta) < 0$, an increase in the matching grant will have a negative effect on the optimum amount of the communal good and on the optimum local tax rate.

Notice the kind of experiment that has been considered here. The increase in the matching grant (decrease in π) did not involve a change in federal tax (T) and, consequently, involved a decrease in the lump-sum grant to the community (T'). This is clearly seen from the federal government's budget constraint, (11.25). The foregoing conclusion with respect to changes in the optima of z and t should thus be interpreted as *net* changes, due to an increase in matching grants *combined* with an equivalent decrease in lump-sum grants.

IV. EFFECTS OF AN INCREASE IN LUMP-SUM GRANTS

Consider now the effect of an increase in lump-sum grants financed by an increase in federal taxes.

Assume that the elasticities η and λ are independent of income effects. Then, from (11.8′) and (11.13′), at $g = 0$,

$$g_5 = \frac{\partial g}{\partial T} = \frac{1}{y}\left[\frac{\lambda}{zy(1-\eta)} - \frac{1}{y}\frac{\partial}{\partial T}\left(\frac{u_3}{u_1}\right)\right] \tag{11.27}$$

An increase in T, decreasing net income, decreases x (if a normal good) and, for a given z, will (if z too is a normal good) decrease the marginal rate of substitution of x for z: $(\partial/\partial T)(u_3/u_1) < 0$. Hence, if $\eta < 1$ and $\lambda > 0$, $g_5 > 0$.

In the (z, t) plane, the shift in the curve $g = 0$ due to an increase in T (see Figure 11.3) is, under the previous assumptions,

$$\left.\frac{dt}{dT}\right|_{g=0,z} = -\frac{g_5}{g_1} < 0 \tag{11.28}$$

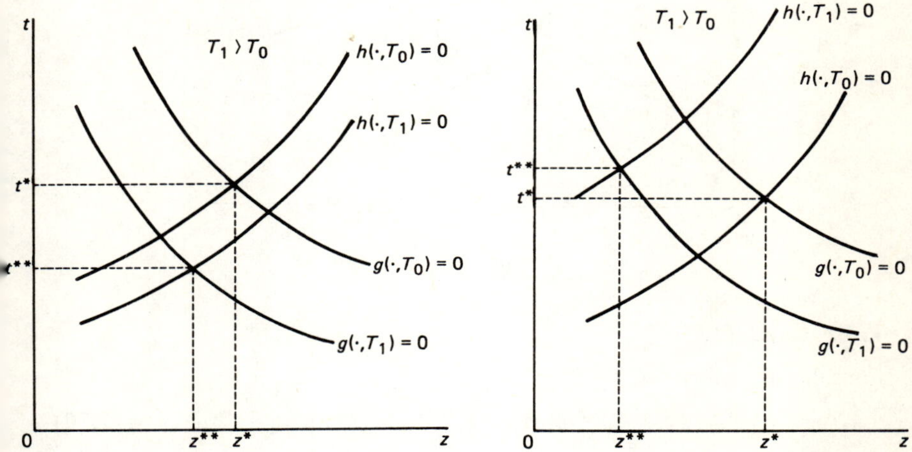

Fig. 11.3(a) Fig. 11.3(b)

The shift in the curve defined by $h = 0$, is given by

$$\left.\frac{dt}{dt}\right|_{h=0,z} = -\frac{h_5}{h_1} = -\frac{1 - ty_3}{y(1-\eta)} \tag{11.29}$$

Now, $y_3 = \partial y/\partial m$ is expected to be positive. If, however, the income effect can be assumed to be small, so that $1 - ty_3 > 0$, then, with $\eta < 1$, (11.29) is negative (see Figure 11.3). In this case, *an increase in lump-sum grants may increase or decrease the optimum amount of the communal good, and will decrease the optimum local tax rate.*

If, on the other hand, the income effect (of increased taxes) is large, so that $h_5 = 1 - ty_3 < 0$, then the outcome is as depicted in Fig. 11.3(b): the optimum amount of z decreases and the optimum local tax rate may increase or decrease.

The only case in which an increase in lump-sum grant will induce an unambiguous increase in the optimum z is in the present of a strong *substitution effect* between y and z, $\lambda < 0$. As seen from (11.27), a negatively large λ may yield $g_5 < 0$, in which case (11.28) becomes positive. The final outcome (see Figure 11.4) is an increase in the optimum amount of z.

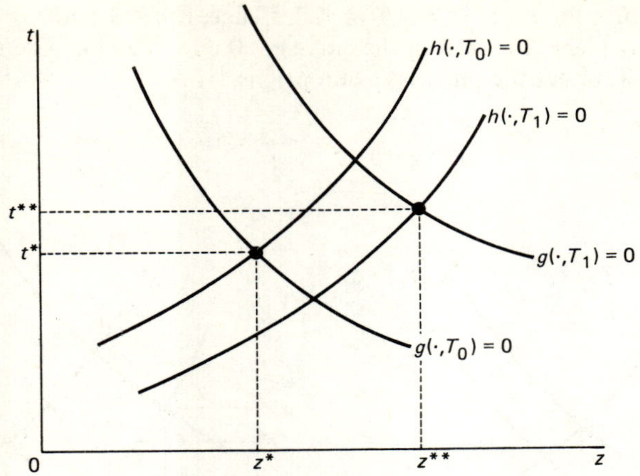

Fig. 11.4

V. AN EXAMPLE

Consider the utility function

$$u(x, y, z) = \alpha \log x + (1 - \alpha) \log y + \beta \log z \tag{11.30}$$

Maximising (11.30) subject to the budget constraint (11.1) yields the demand functions

$$x = \alpha(m - T)$$

and
$$y = \frac{(1 - \alpha)(m - T)}{1 + t} \tag{11.31}$$

Clearly, $\eta = -ty_1/y = t/(1 + t)$ and $\lambda = zy_2/y = 0$[1]. Condition (11.8) now becomes

$$\frac{\beta(m - T)}{z} = \pi(1 + t) \tag{11.32}$$

The functions g and h, defined in (11.13′) and (11.14), are given by

$$g(t, z, m, p, T, \pi) = \frac{1}{y}\left[\pi(1 + t) - \frac{\beta(m - T)}{z}\right] \tag{11.33}$$

and
$$h(t, z, m, p, T) = T + \frac{t(1 - \alpha)(m - T)}{1 + t} - pz \tag{11.34}$$

[1] If the marginal rate of substitution between x and y, u_2/u_1 is independent of z, then the otpimum x and y are clearly independent of z. This is the case if, and only if, utility is additively or multiplicatively separable, i.e. if $u = U(x, y) + V(z)$ or $u = U(x, y)V(z)$.

The optimum conditions $g = 0$ and $h = 0$, are (11.32) and

$$T + \frac{t(1-\alpha)(m-T)}{1+t} = pz \tag{11.35}$$

In the (z, t) plane, the curves $g = 0$ and $h = 0$ have the properties previously analysed. In a different representation, substituting (11.32) in (11.35) yields, after some manipulation,

$$\frac{T}{m} = \frac{\beta p - \pi(1-\alpha)t}{\beta p + \pi + \pi\alpha t} \tag{11.36}$$

Define

$$\phi(t, \pi) \equiv \frac{\beta p - \pi(1-\alpha)t}{\beta p + \pi + \pi\alpha t} \tag{11.37}$$

The function ϕ is seen (Fig. 11.5) to decrease with t, starting at $\phi = \beta p/(\beta p + \pi) \equiv \gamma$ at $t = 0$, and reaches zero, $\phi = 0$, at $\hat{t} = \beta p/\pi(1-\alpha)$.

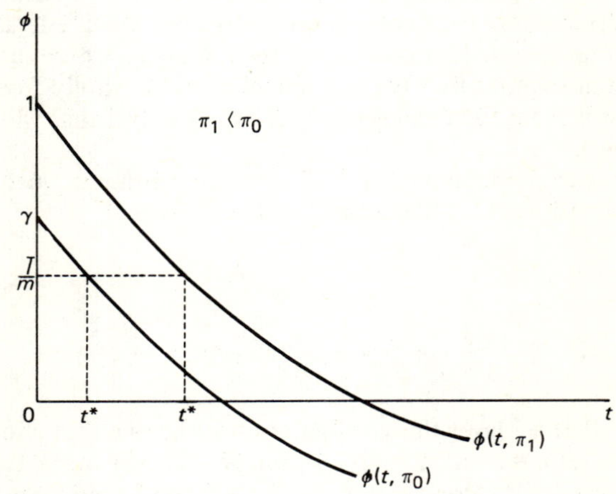

Fig. 11.5

By (11.36), a necessary condition for the existence of a solution $t^* > 0$ is that $T/m < \gamma$. Since $p \geqslant \pi$, $\gamma \geqslant \beta/\beta + 1$. Hence, it is sufficient to assume that

$$\frac{T}{m} < \frac{\beta}{1+\beta} \tag{11.38}$$

It is now easily seen that a decrease in π increases the optimum t and, by (11.35), the optimum z. Actually, implicit differentiation of (11.32) and (11.35) yields

$$\frac{dt^*}{d\pi} = -\frac{1}{\Delta}\frac{z^*(1+t^*)p}{\pi} < 0 \tag{11.39}$$

and
$$\frac{dz^*}{d\pi} = -\frac{1}{\Delta}\frac{(1-\alpha)z^*(m-T)}{\pi(1+t^*)} < 0 \tag{11.40}$$

where $\Delta = (1-\alpha)\,m + \alpha T > 0$. With respect to changes in T,

$$\frac{dt^*}{dT} = -\frac{1}{\Delta\pi}(\beta p + \pi + \alpha\pi t) < 0 \tag{11.41}$$

and
$$\frac{dz^*}{dT} = \frac{1}{\Delta}\alpha\beta\pi(1+t^*)(m-T) > 0 \tag{11.42}$$

These results are in conformity with previous conclusions, which were based on a general analysis.

VI. PARETO OPTIMUM

In the model under analysis, local taxes that are levied on housing property at a level determined by the taxpayer are distortive, while federal taxes are regarded as lump-sum deductions from a given income. Consequently, the Pareto optimum requires that the communal good be wholly financed by lump-sum grants from the federal government, at a level that will induce local taxes to be zero.

Consider the example in section V. The Pareto optimum quantities $(\hat{x}, \hat{y}, \hat{z})$ that maximises utility, (11.30), subject to the constraint

$$x + y + pz = m \tag{11.43}$$

are
$$\hat{x} = \frac{\alpha}{1+\beta}m,\ \hat{y} = \frac{1-\alpha}{1+\beta}m,\ \text{and}\ \hat{z} = \frac{\beta}{1+\beta}m \tag{11.44}$$

The policy that achieves this configuration is the one that allows federal government to set $p = \pi$ and $T = (\beta/1+\beta)m$. By (11.32) and (11.35) it is seen that it is optimal for the community to set $t = 0$ and to purchase an amount $\hat{z}$ of the communal good.

As has been seen from (11.41) and (11.42), in moving from a non-Pareto-optimal situation, with a positive local tax rate ($t > 0$), to the Pareto optimum, through increases in federal taxes and in lump-sum grants, the equilibrium amount of z is increased. Hence, in this example, *any non-Pareto-optimal equilibrium involves less of the communal good than does the Pareto optimum.* However, in view of our previous analysis (Fig. 11.3a), it is an open question how general this result is.

As has already been pointed out, the foregoing analysis is based on the assumption that federal taxes, unlike local taxes, entail no efficiency loss. Incorporating the disincentive effects of federal income taxes (on, say, working effort) is expected to yield an overall ('second-best') optimum, based on a combination of local taxes and revenue sharing.

VII. INCOME DISTRIBUTION AND A VOTING EQUILIBRIUM

Suppose, now, that incomes in the community are not equal but are distributed according to a density function $f(m)$:

$$f(m) \geqslant 0, \int_0^\infty f(m)dm = 1 \tag{11.45}$$

For simplicity, set federal taxes and grants at zero. The community's budget constraint is then

$$t \int y(t, z, m)f(m)dm = pz \tag{11.46}$$

Consider a taxpayer with an income m_0. The most desirable combination of tax rate and quantity of z is the one that maximises his utility, $v(t; z, m_0)$, subject to (11.46). The first-order conditions for a maximum may be written

$$\begin{aligned} &g(t, z, m_0, p) = 0 \\ \text{and} \quad &h(t, z, p) = 0 \end{aligned} \tag{11.47}$$

where
$$g(t, z, m_0, p) \equiv \frac{v_2(t, z, m_0)}{v_1(t, z, m_0)} + \frac{t}{z} \frac{\int y(1-\lambda)f(m)dm}{\int y(1-\eta)f(m)dm} \tag{11.48}$$

and
$$h(t, z, p) \equiv t \int y\, f(m)dm - pz \tag{11.49}$$

Denote the solution to (11.47) by $t^*(m_0)$ and $z^*(m_0)$. Since the function h is independent of m_0, it is seen (Fig. 11.6) that the change in z^* as m_0 increases depends on the direction of change of the curve $g = 0$. Now,

$$\left.\frac{dt}{dm_0}\right|_{g=0,z} = -\frac{g_3}{g_1} = -\frac{1}{g_1}\frac{\partial}{\partial m_0}\left(\frac{v_2}{v_1}\right) = \frac{1}{g_1}\frac{\partial}{\partial m_0}\left(\frac{u_3}{u_1 y}\right) \tag{11.50}$$

We have previously argued that $g_1 > 0$. If x and z are normal goods, an increase in income increases x and, thus, for a given z, the marginal rate of substitution of x for z. Hence, $(\partial(u_3/u_1)/\partial m_0) > 0$. On the other hand, if y is a normal good, $\partial y/\partial m_0 > 0$. Consequently, the sign of $(v_2/v_1)(\partial/\partial m_0)$ is, in general, ambiguous. We shall assume that $(\partial(v_2/v_1)/\partial m_0) \geqslant 0$. The sign of (11.50) is then positive, and, consequently,

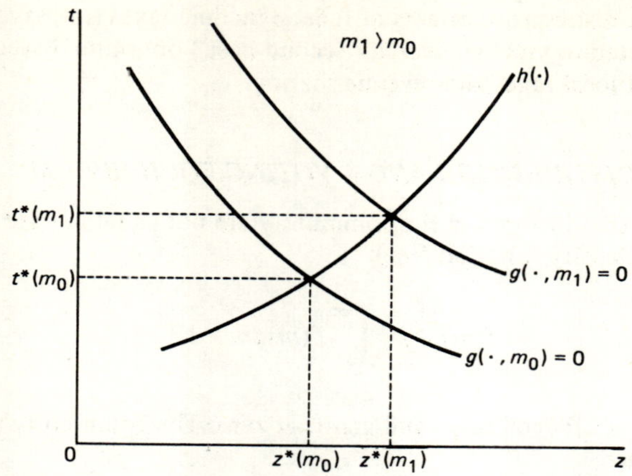

Fig. 11.6

$$\frac{dt^*}{dm_0} \geqslant 0$$

and
$$\frac{dz^*}{dm_0} \geqslant 0 \qquad (11.51)$$

Suppose that the size of the community's budget is determined by 'sincere' majority voting: each voter proposes the budget that his own preferences lead him to favour most. Under (11.51), voters can be ordered by income, and a voting equilibrium occurs at a budget level where more than 50 per cent of the voters oppose any further increase. This means that the preferences of the median voter are decisive, where the identity of that voter is determined by the distribution of incomes.[2] If the median income is $\hat{m}$, then the optimum tax rate and the amount of z are $t^*(\hat{m})$ and $z^*(\hat{m})$, respectively.

For the example examined in section V, one may calculate that the equilibrium equations (11.47) are

$$t^* = \frac{\beta}{1-\alpha}$$

and
$$pz = \frac{\beta(1-\alpha)\overline{m}}{1-\alpha+\beta} \qquad (11.52)$$

where $\overline{m} = \int mf(m)dm$ is the mean income. In this case, the optimum budget does not depend on the median income,[3] nor on the variation in incomes.

[2] There is no need for an actual referendum if decisions are made by elected officials responsive to majority rule (for instance, school boards).

[3] Since the sign of (11.50) in this case is zero.

Redistribution of incomes therefore would have no effect on the equilibrium budget. This result hinges on the fact that demand functions have *unitary* income elasticities, as will be seen below.

Consider a progressive redistribution of incomes such that each income changes from m to $m - \Delta(m)$, and

$$\Delta'(m) > 0, \int \Delta(m) f(m) dm = 0 \tag{11.53}$$

For a small Δ, the change in the function h is

$$h_\Delta = \frac{\partial h}{\partial \Delta} = -t \int y_3(t, z, m) \Delta(m) f(m) dm \tag{11.54}$$

Assume that the marginal propensity to spend on y, y_3 increases with income:

$$y_{33} = \frac{\partial^2 y}{\partial m^2} > 0 \tag{11.55}$$

(If $y_3(t, z, 0) = 0$, then (11.55) implies that the income elasticity of y is larger than unity.)

By (11.53), let $\tilde{m}$ be such that $\Delta(\tilde{m}) = 0$. Then, by (11.55),

$$y_3(t, z, m)\Delta(m) \geqslant y_3(t, z, \tilde{m})\Delta(m) \tag{11.56}$$

with strict inequality for $m \neq \tilde{m}$. Multiplying by $f(m)$ and integrating on both sides of (11.56),

$$\int y_3 \Delta(m) f(m) dm > y_3(t, z, \tilde{m}) \int \Delta(m) f(m) dm = 0 \tag{11.57}$$

by (11.53). Hence, $h_\Delta < 0$. By (11.19) and (11.9), if $\eta < 1$ then $h_1 > 0$. In such a case,

$$\left.\frac{dt}{d\Delta}\right|_{h = 0, z} = -\frac{h_\Delta}{h_1} > 0 \tag{11.58}$$

i.e. in the (z, t) plane, the curve $h = 0$ shifts upwards.

Assuming that the elasticities λ and η are constant, the shift of the $g = 0$ curve is given by the expression

$$\left.\frac{dt}{d\Delta}\right|_{g = 0, z} = -\frac{g_\Delta}{g_1} = \frac{1}{g_1} \frac{\partial}{\partial m} \frac{v_2(t, z, \tilde{m})}{v_1(t, z, \tilde{m})} \Delta(\tilde{m}) \tag{11.59}$$

which is non-negative if $\Delta(\tilde{m}) \geqslant 0$.[4] Another case in which the $h = 0$ curve shifts upwards is that in which $\eta > 1$ and the marginal propensity to spend decreases with income. If $\eta > 1$ then, by (11.19) and (11.9), $h_1 < 0$; and, when the marginal propensity to spend decreases with income ($y_{33} < 0$), we can prove, using an argument similar to that of (11.55)–(11.57), that $h_\Delta > 0$. This leads to the conclusion that, *if* (a) $\eta < 1$ *and the marginal propensity to spend on y increases with income,* or (b) $\eta > 1$ *and the marginal propensity to spend on y decreases with income, then a progressive redistribution of income increases the optimum tax rate and may increase or decrease the optimum amount of the communal good.*

In the next section is presented an example of case (b) in which the optimum z^* decreases due to a progressive redistribution.

VIII. AN EXAMPLE USING THE PARETO DISTRIBUTION

Let the indirect utility, (11.5), be given by

$$v = v(t, z, m) = (1 + t)^{1-\alpha} z^\beta + m^{1-\gamma} \tag{11.60}$$

We assume that

$$\alpha > 1, \beta > 0 \text{ and } 1 > \gamma > 0 \tag{11.61}$$

By (11.3) and (11.5) we have

$$v_1 = -u_1 y = (1 - \alpha)(1 + t)^{-\alpha} z^\beta$$

$$v_2 = u_3 = \beta(1 + t)^{1-\alpha} z^{\beta-1}$$

and

$$v_3 = u_1 = (1 - \gamma) m^{-\gamma}$$

from which it follows that

$$y = -\frac{v_1}{v_3} = a(1 + t)^{-\alpha} z^\beta m^\gamma \tag{11.62}$$

where $a = (\alpha - 1)/(1 - y) > 0$ by (11.61).

We find that $\lambda = y_2 z/y = \beta$, $\eta = -y_1 t/y = \alpha t/(1 + t)$ and $v_2/v_1 = \beta(1 + t)/(1 - \alpha)z$. The equilibrium equations (11.47) now become

$$t^* = \frac{\beta}{\alpha - 1} > 0 \tag{11.63}$$

and

$$pz^{*1-\beta} = at^*(1 + t^*)^{-\alpha} \int m^\gamma f(m) dm \tag{11.64}$$

[4] For example, a *linear* redistribution $\Delta(m) = -a + bm$, which satisfies (11.53), has $-a + b\bar{m} = 0$, and, thus, $\Delta(\tilde{m}) = b(\tilde{m} - \bar{m})$, which is negative for a *positively skewed* distribution.

In Fig. 11.7, (11.63) is a horizontal line. Differentiating (11.64) at (11.63),

$$\frac{dt^*}{dz^*} = \frac{(1-\beta)t^*(1+t^*)}{z[1+t^*(1-\alpha)]} = \frac{\beta(\beta+\alpha-1)}{z(\alpha-1)^2} > 0 \tag{11.65}$$

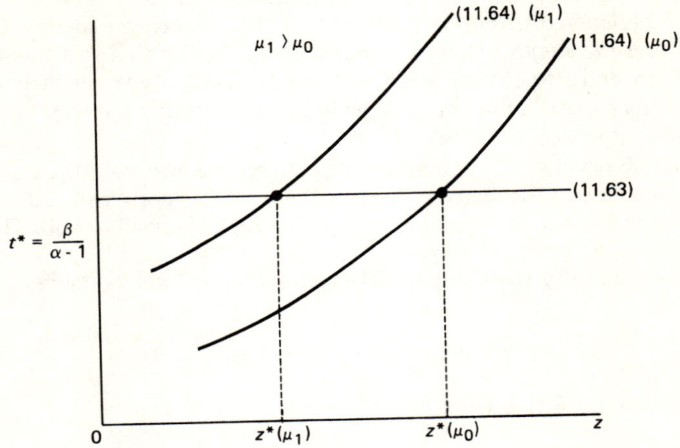

Fig. 11.7

by (11.61). Thus, there exists a unique optimum solution, (z^*, t^*), to (11.63) and (11.64).

Assume that incomes follow the Pareto distribution

$$f(m) = \mu \underline{m}^{\mu} m^{-\mu-1}, \; m \geqslant \underline{m} \tag{11.66}$$

with parameters $\underline{m} > 0$ and $\mu > 1$. Mean income, $\overline{m}$, is known to be

$$\overline{m} = \frac{\mu}{\mu - 1}\underline{m} \tag{11.67}$$

Equation (11.64) is now

$$pz^{*1-\beta} = at^*(1+t^*)^{-\alpha}\frac{\mu}{\mu-\gamma}\underline{m}^{\gamma} \tag{11.64$'$}$$

assuming $\mu - \gamma > 0$. A progressive redistribution that preserves the form (11.66) means an increase in μ and in $\underline{m}$, so as to keep $\overline{m}$ constant. The latter implies, by (11.67), that

$$\frac{d\mu}{d\underline{m}} = \frac{\mu(\mu-1)}{\underline{m}} \tag{11.68}$$

Differentiating (11.64′), using (11.68), yields

$$\left.\frac{dz^*}{d\underline{m}}\right|_{\bar{m}} = \frac{\gamma(1-\gamma)z}{(1-\beta)(\mu-\gamma)\underline{m}}\ (\beta \neq 1) \tag{11.69}$$

Clearly, in view of (11.61), (11.69) is negative if $\beta > 1$. This is a case where *progressive income redistribution* (by means of, say, progressive income taxation) *decreases the amount of the communal good.* Notice that this example requires that y and z be *complements,* with a cross-elasticity larger than unity.

Does such a redistribution and change in the amount of z improve or worsen the welfare of low-income taxpayers?

For such taxpayers, a redistribution of this kind has two opposite effects: a positive one, due to the increase in net income, and a negative one, due to the decrease in the amount of communal good supplied equally to all. The final outcome may go either way.

Consider the utility (equation 11.60) of the worst-off individual in equilibrium

$$v(t^*, z^*, \underline{m}) = (1+t)^{1-\alpha} z^{*\beta} + \underline{m}^{1-\gamma} \tag{11.70}$$

The change in his utility is given by

$$\begin{aligned}\frac{dv}{d\underline{m}} &= \beta(1+t^*)^{1-\alpha} z^{*\beta-1}\, \frac{dz^*}{d\underline{m}} + (1-\gamma)\underline{m}^{-\gamma} \\ &= \frac{1-\gamma}{m}\left[\beta(1+t^*)^{1-\alpha} z^{*\beta}\, \frac{\gamma}{(1-\beta)(\mu-\gamma)} + m^{1-\gamma}\right]\end{aligned} \tag{11.71}$$

Since $\gamma < 1$, the sign of (11.71) is negative if the term in brackets is negative. Take, for example, $\mu = 3/2\ \gamma = 1/2\ \beta = -2$, $\alpha = 2$ and $\underline{m} = 1$. Then (11.71) is negative if $z^{*2} > 3$. From (11.63), this inequality is seen to be satisfied when $p^2 > 4/3$.

The implications of this discussion in terms of a conventional summary measure of inequality can be seen as follows. The Lorenz curve, $\theta_\omega(x)$, for some (monotonically increasing) function $\omega(m)$, which shows the proportion of the total ω received by the bottom x per cent of income recipients, is implicitly defined by

$$\theta_\omega(x) = \frac{1}{\bar{\omega}} \int_0^{\hat{m}} \omega(m) f(m)dm, \qquad x = \int_{\bar{0}}^{\hat{m}} f(m)dm \tag{11.72}$$

where $\bar{\omega} = \int_0^\infty \omega(m)f(m)dm.$ The Lorenz curve of the *income distribution* is given by $\omega(m) = m$, and for the Pareto distribution (11.66) it can be shown that

$$\theta_m(x) = 1 - (1-x)^{\frac{\mu-1}{\mu}}, \qquad (0 \leqslant x \leqslant 1) \tag{11.73}$$

The Lorenz curve of the *utility distribution* is given when $\omega(m) = v = v(t^*, z^*, m)$. For the utility function (11.60) and the distribution (11.66), it can be shown that

$$\theta_v(x) = \frac{kx + \dfrac{\mu}{\mu+\gamma-1}\underline{m}^{1-\gamma}\left[1-(1-x)^{\frac{\mu+\gamma-1}{\mu}}\right]}{k + \dfrac{\mu}{\mu+\gamma-1}\underline{m}^{1-\gamma}}, \; (0 \leqslant x \leqslant 1) \tag{11.74}$$

where $k = (1+t^*)^{1-\alpha}z^{*\beta}$. It is not difficult to show that, for some values of the parameters, a progressive redistribution, increasing $\underline{m}$ and μ constrained by (11.68), and a consequent decrease in k, as shown in (11.69), will shift the Lorenz curve away from the line of complete equality at low x and towards the corresponding line for high x. The choice between these distributions depends, of course, on the weights attached to welfare at different points of the income distribution.

IX. EQUILIBRIUM WHEN SOME TAXPAYERS ARE NONUSERS

The voting equilibrium, by constraining everyone to consume the same amount of the communal good, introduces allocative inefficiencies if individuals can purchase z at the same price as the community does. Taxpayers with incomes above and below the median receive, in general, an amount that is different from the amounts they would like, given the price and their income. Collective consumption can be justified on resource-allocation grounds only if the group can purchase the communal good (say, educational services) at a lower price than individual voters can. Disregarding such economies, the justification for collective supply must rely on equity considerations, such as, in the case of education, the provision of 'equal opportunity' to all.

Consider the case where individuals are able to purchase z privately at a price of q. The individual who chooses to buy z privately faces the budget constraint

$$x + (1+t)y + qz = m \tag{11.75}$$

The first-order conditions for a maximum of (11.2) subject to (11.75) are

$$\frac{u_2}{u_1} = 1 + t$$

$$\text{and} \qquad \frac{u_3}{u_1} = q \tag{11.76}$$

Equations (11.75) and (11.76) yield optimum solutions $\hat{x} = \hat{x}(t, q, m)$, $\hat{y} = \hat{y}(t, q, m)$, and $\hat{z} = \hat{z}(t, q, m)$, which, upon substitution in (11.2), yield the indirect utility

$$\hat{v} = \hat{v}(t, q, m) \equiv u[\hat{x}(t, q, m), \hat{y}(t, q, m), \hat{z}(t, q, m)) \tag{11.77}$$

Whether an individual with a given income chooses to use the collectively supplied amount z or to purchase privately a quantity $\hat{z}$ depends on whether $v(t, z, m) - \hat{v}(t, q, m)$ is positive or negative. Expanding v around $\hat{v}$, using the first two terms,

$$v(t, z, m) = u(x, y, z) = u(\hat{x}, \hat{y}, \hat{z}) + u_1(x - \hat{x}) + u_2(y - \hat{y}) + u_3(z - \hat{z}) + dUd' \tag{11.78}$$

where u_1, u_2 and u_3 are evaluated at $(\hat{x}, \hat{y}, \hat{z})$; d is a vector $d = (x - \hat{x}, y - \hat{y}, z - \hat{z})$; and $U = [u_{ij}]$ is a 3 x 3 matrix.

Using the budget constraints (11.1) and (11.75), we simplify (11.78):

$$v(t, z, m) = \hat{v}(t, q, m) + u_1 [x - \hat{x} + (1 + t)(y - \hat{y}) + q(z - \hat{z})] + dUd' = \hat{v}(t, q, m) + u_1 qz + dUd' \tag{11.79}$$

Since u is concave, $dUd' \leqslant 0$. For a small m, u_1 may be sufficiently high to make $v > \hat{v}$, while at high incomes (small u_1) probably $v < \hat{v}$. This is borne out by the example in section V.

We calculate from (11.30) and (11.31) that

$$v(t, z, m) = a + \log m + \beta \log z \tag{11.80}$$

where $a = \alpha \log \alpha + (1 - \alpha) \log (1 - \alpha/1 + t)$. Using (11.76) we find that

$$\hat{v}(t, q, m) = a + b + (1 + \beta) \log m \tag{11.81}$$

where $b = \beta \log (\beta/q) - (1 + \beta) \log (1 + \beta)$. Let $\hat{m} = z^* e^{-\frac{b}{\beta}}$. Then, from (11.80) and (11.81) (see Fig. 11.8),

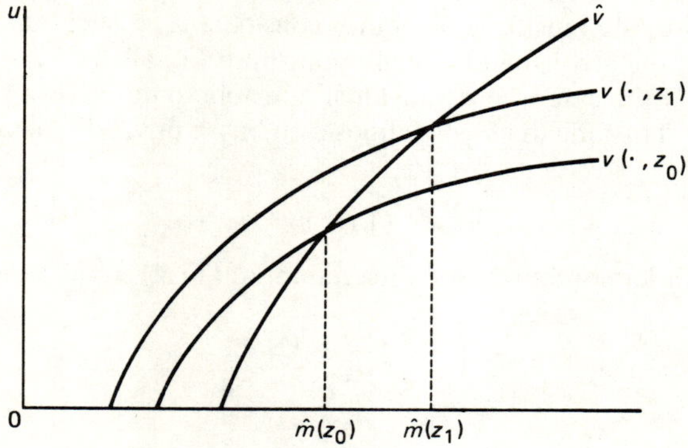

Fig. 11.8

$$v \gtreqless \hat{v}, \text{ as } m \lesseqgtr \hat{m} \tag{11.82}$$

Individuals with incomes above $\hat{m}$ find it worthwhile to substitute the collectively supplied amount z for a larger, privately purchased quantity. An increase in the collectively supplied amount will shift $\hat{m}$ upwards, thus increasing the number of users. It would be interesting to investigate how the community determines its optimum budget under these circumstances, and what the effects of revenue sharing are on the distribution of users and on the community's size, but this would carry us too far.

REFERENCES

Barlow, R., 'Efficiency Aspects of Local School Finance', *Journal of Political Economy,* LXXVIII (1970), pp. 1028–40.

Boskin, M., 'Local Government Tax and Product Competition and the Optimal Provision of Public Goods', *Journal of Political Economy,* LXXXI (1973), pp. 203–10.

Bradford, D., and Oates, W. E., 'Towards a Predictive Theory of Intergovernmental Grants', *American Economic Review, Papers and Proceedings,* May 1971, pp. 440–8.

Bradford, D., and Oates, W. E., 'The Analysis of Revenue-Sharing in a New Approach to Collective Fiscal Decisions', *Quarterly Journal of Economics,* LXXXV (1971), pp. 416–39.

Brainard, W., and Dolbear, F. T., 'The Possibility of Oversupply of Local Public Goods: A Critical Note', *Journal of Political Economy,* LXXV (1967), pp. 86–90.

Edelson, N., *Budgetary Outcomes in a Referendum Setting,* Discussion Paper no. 244, Department of Economics, University of Pennsylvania (Philadelphia, Oct 1972).

Oates, W. E., *Fiscal Federalism* (New York: Harcourt, Brace, Jovanovich, 1972).

Sheshinski, E., 'The Supply of Communal Goods and Community Size', Department of Economics, The Hebrew University of Jerusalem (Mar 1974).

Thurow, L., 'The Theory of Grants in Aid', *National Tax Journal,* XIX (1966), pp. 373–7.

Tiebout, C., 'The Pure Theory of Local Expenditures', *Journal of Political Economy,* LXIV (1956), pp. 416–24.

Wilde, J., 'The Expenditure Effects of Grants in Aid Programs', *National Tax Journal,* XXI (1968), pp. 340–8.

12 The Theory of Local Public Goods

Joseph E. Stiglitz [1]
STANFORD UNIVERSITY

I. INTRODUCTION

The purpose of this paper is to develop the broad outlines of the general theory of local public goods. The theory of local public goods is differentiated from the conventional theory of public goods in one important respect: in the latter, the population of each community is assumed fixed, while the theory of local public goods is concerned with the determination of the allocation of the population among the different communities.

One of the central questions of conventional public-goods theory has been the problem of preference revelation: if the amount that the individual pays in taxes is related to his revealed preferences for public goods, the individual will have an incentive to underestimate his true evaluation of public goods (the 'free rider' problem). Interest in local public goods was originally stimulated by the intriguing suggestion of Tiebout that, if there were enough communities, individuals would reveal their true preferences for public goods by the choice of community in which to live (in much the same way as individuals reveal their preferences for private goods by their choices). The implication of this suggestion is that, with local public goods, not only is the problem of revelation of preferences resolved, but also, since all of those choosing to live in the same community have essentially the same tastes, there is no voting problem; the allocation of resources will be Pareto optimal just as the allocation of resources with private goods is known to be Pareto optimal. But between public goods

[1] I am indebted to P. Mieszkowski, who, when we jointly taught the Public Finance Course at Yale in 1970–1, first stirred my interest in the topics discussed in this paper. In a joint paper with Flatters and Henderson (1974), he has done much to clarify the issues originally discussed by Buchanan and Goetz (1972). Several of the results of sections II–III, although independently arrived at, are similar to the results obtained by Flatters, Henderson and Mieszkowski. I have also benefited greatly from discussions with Frank Westhoff, whose doctoral dissertation develops the model that is discussed briefly in section IV. An earlier version of this paper was presented at the IEA Conference at Turin, and, in revising the paper, I have been greatly assisted by the discussion of it at the conference, and, especially, by the perspicacious comments of my discussant, J. Milleron. The exposition of section II.1, in particular, has benefited from his detailed comments. Research support from the Ford Foundation and the National Science Foundation is gratefully acknowledged.

and private goods there are certain important differences that make the analogy at least open to question.

(1) There is an essential nonconvexity associated with public goods when the population is endogenous.[2] Important nonconvexities in market economies are often associated with various kinds of noncompetitive behaviour. Here, because of the nonconvexity, there are likely to be fewer communities than there are individuals; the individual may not be able to find a community of individuals who are 'essentially identical' to him in tastes; and, if communities consist of individuals differing in tastes, we may again obtain those problems, associated with determining the level of public goods, that the model was intended to resolve.

(2) In a market equilibrium, there are prices to guide the decision-making of the individual and of the firm; because public goods cannot be bought or sold, it is not apparent, at least not immediately, what prices the 'city manager' is to use as the basis of his decision-making. As will be shown later, the problems associated with the incompleteness of markets for public goods bear some resemblance to those associated with the absence of a complete set of markets for private goods. In particular, the problems associated with tax capitalisation in the theory of local public goods are closely analogous to those associated with value maximisation in the theory of the firm.

(3) The problem of exclusion – of the rich attempting to keep the poor out of their community – has no obvious parallel in market economies. Yet it would appear that the pattern of local-community formation in the United States has much to do with the rich attempting to segregate themselves from the poor, in part because, even with proportional wealth taxation, there is a large element of redistribution involved in the provision of education and other services to the local community. By moving to their own communities, the rich can avoid this redistribution.[3]

This paper analyses the market equilibria and Pareto-optimal allocations; compares the two; and asks what kinds of taxes and subsidies can restore Pareto optimality. The analysis of the market equilibrium, in particular, turns out to be fairly complex; the nature of the solution depends on a number of specific assumptions. We need to specify:

(a) Whether migration is restricted or unrestricted. If there are restrictions, they may be outright bans, or they may be imposed through zoning laws. For most of the analysis, it will be assumed that there are no restrictions on migration.

(b) Whether immigrants can be treated differently from the original residents;

[2] It is important to emphasise that this is not necessarily the case when the population of the community is fixed.

[3] As we shall see below, it is of critical importanct to this argument that the marginal cost of providing the goods to an extra person be non-zero (either because of congestion costs or because, like education, it is a publicly provided private good). For a discussion of the notion of publicly provided private goods, see, for instance, Stiglitz (1974).

for example, whether it is possible to impose an immigration tax (effectively a higher wage tax than on the original residents), or to restrict the amount of government services provided to the immigrants. Throughout the analysis it is assumed that immigrants cannot be treated differently.

(c) How the level of public goods supply is determined within a community. For most of the analysis, a majority-voting equilibrium is assumed.

(d) What the decision-makers (voters) in each community take as given in deciding on the level of government expenditures; for example, whether they take into account the effects of different policies on migration or on land values.

The analysis is divided into four main parts, corresponding to sections II–V. In section II, it is assumed that individuals and 'islands' are identical; in section III, it is assumed that individuals are identical but that islands differ; and in section IV it is assumed that individuals are different but that islands are identical. Finally, in section V, it is assumed that both islands and individuals may differ.

This paper does not present a sequential development of a single model; rather, its object is to survey the most important problems associated with the theory of local public goods, and to develop the simplest model illustrating each of these problems.

II. IDENTICAL INDIVIDUALS AND ISLANDS

II.1 THE BASIC MODEL

Consider an islands with a fixed land supply. Then, output (Q) is an increasing, concave function of the number of workers (N):[4]

$$Q = f(N), f' \geqslant 0, f'' < 0 \tag{12.1}$$

There are two commodities, a private good and a public good. For simplicity, it is assumed that they are produced by the same technology:[5]

$$Q = cN + G \tag{12.2}$$

where c is per capita consumption of the private good, and G is consumption of the public good.

For any fixed N, (12.1) and (12.2) define the opportunity set, as illustrated in Fig. 12.1. Since, by assumption, all individuals are the same, the point chosen is the one that maximises utility, $U(c, G)$ where U is assumed to be quasi-concave; i.e. using (12.1) and (12.2), we wish to maximise $U[c, f(N) - cN]$.

[4] Implicitly, it is assumed that each labourer supplies one unit of labour. Later it will be shown that this assumption is not essential.

[5] Again, this is an inessential assumption. In an open economy, (12.2) essentially says that the island is a price-taker.

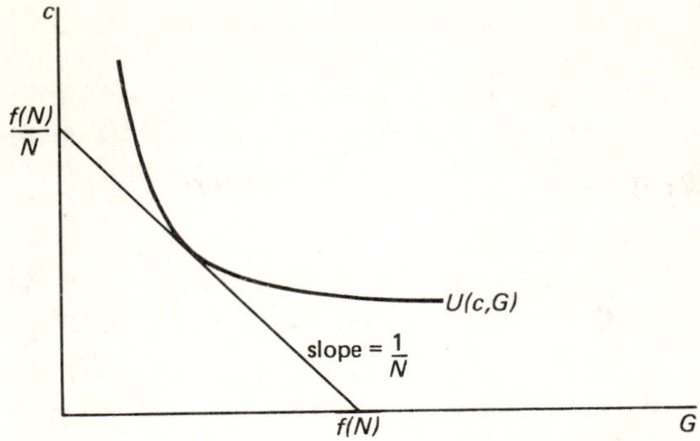

Fig. 12.1 Opportunity Set and Equilibrium for Fixed Population

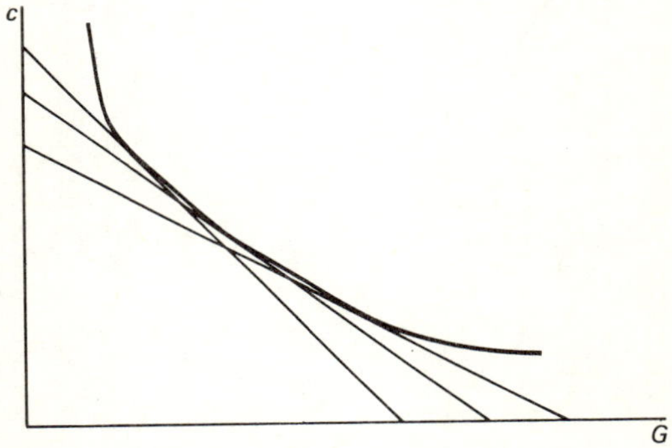

Fig. 12.2 Opportunity Set for Variable Population

Hence, $U_1 = U_2 N$, or

$$\frac{NU_2}{U_1} = 1 \tag{12.3}$$

which is the conventional result that the sum of the marginal rates of substitution equals the marginal rate of transformation.

As we increase N, the maximum level of public goods that we can obtain increases (since $f'(N) > 0$), but the maximum level of consumption per capita ($f(N)/N$) decreases. The variable-N opportunity locus is the outer envelope of the fixed-N opportunity loci. For each value of G we wish to maximise

$$c = \frac{f(N) - G}{N}$$

so that

$$\begin{cases} G = f(N) - f'(N)N & \text{(12.4a)} \\ c = f'(N) & \text{(12.4b)} \end{cases}$$

(12.4a) has an interesting interpretation. $f'(N)$ is the marginal productivity of a labourer; hence, $f(N) - f'(N)N$ is output minus wage payments – rents – if workers are paid their marginal product; thus, if the level of public-goods expenditure is fixed, but the size of population is variable, *the population that maximises consumption per capita is such that rents equal public-goods expenditure.*

The locus defined parametrically by (12.4) is convex.[6] Thus, the population that maximises (per capita) utility may be zero, infinite, or finite, as illustrated by Figs. 12.3(a)–(c). If the indifference curve is more 'curved' than the oppor-

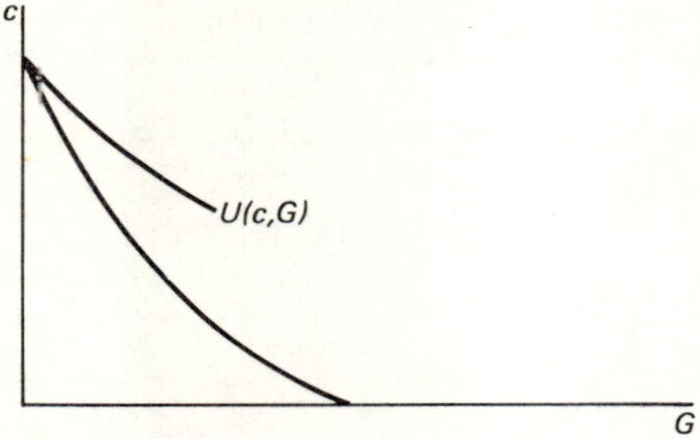

Fig. 12.3(a) Optimal Population is Zero

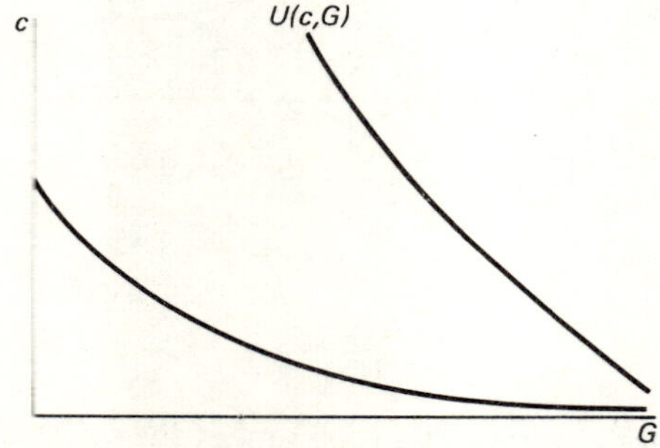

Fig. 12.3(b) Optimal Population is Infinite

tunity locus, then there is an 'interior' solution. This is likely to be the case if public and private goods are strong complements, so that the indifference curve is very curved. Otherwise, utility is maximised with only private goods being produced and a 'zero' population, or with only public goods being produced and an infinite population.

[6] If the production functions for the two commodities differ, the only effect is that the variable-N opportunity locus will not be strictly convex. This can be seen by considering the opportunity locus for two different values of N. The envelope will then consist of two concave segments. See Fig. 12.4.

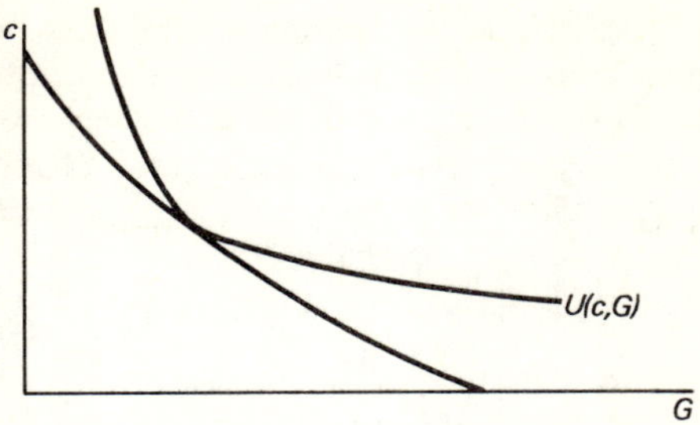

Fig. 12.3(c) Finite Optimal Population: Single Optimal N

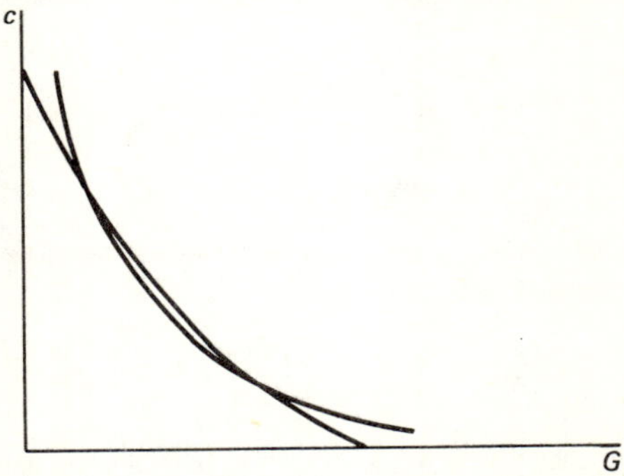

Fig. 12.3(d) Finite Optimal Population: Multiple Optimal N

These results should be contrasted with the comparable standard results in optimal population theory. If our objective is to maximise per capita utility, then, if there are only private goods, clearly consumption is maximised with an infinitesimal population, i.e.

$$\frac{df/N}{dN} < 0$$

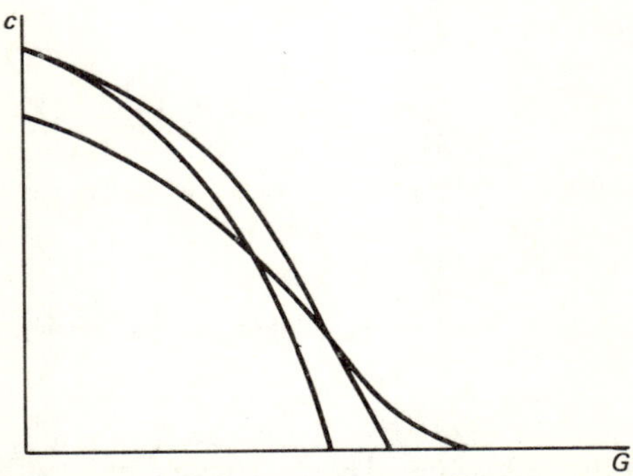

Fig. 12.4 Different Production Functions for Public and Private Goods

On the other hand, if there are only public goods, utility will be maximised with an infinite population, if $df/dN > 0$. Thus, if individuals value both private and public goods, there is a 'balancing' of these two effects.

Each point on the opportunity locus represents a different population size; larger values of G correspond to larger populations. For each level of population, we can solve for the maximum attainable level of utility:

$$v(N) \equiv \max_{\{c,\, G\}} U(c, G) \tag{12.5}$$

subject to $\quad cN + G = f(N)$

It should be clear from Fig. 12.3(d) that $v(N)$ need not have a single peak. More generally,

$$v'(N) = U_2(f' - c) = \frac{U_1}{N^2}\,[G - (f - f'N)] \gtrless 0 \tag{12.6}$$

as $\quad f' \gtrless c \text{ (or } f - f'N \lessgtr G)$

i.e. as the wage is greater or less than private consumption, or government expenditure is greater or less than rents.

$$v''(\mathrm{N})\,_{|v' = 0} = \left(\frac{dG}{dN} + f''N\right)\frac{U_1}{N^2} \tag{12.7}$$

As the population increases, we would normally expect both rents and government expenditures to rise; concavity of v requires the latter to rise more slowly than the former.

Sufficient conditions for v'' to be one-signed may be derived. Assume a homothetic indifference map and a constant returns-to-scale technology. Then,

$$\left.\frac{dG}{dN}\right|_{v' = 0} = f'(1 - a)\sigma_c \tag{12.8}$$

where σ_c is the elasticity of substitution along an indifference curve.[7] Substituting into (12.7), we obtain

$$v''(N)._{|v' = 0} = -f''N\{\sigma_c\sigma_p - 1\}\frac{U_1}{N^2} \tag{12.9}$$

[7] Let $1 - a$ represent the share of government expenditure in national output. Then,

$$G = f(1 - a)$$

$$\frac{dG}{dN} = f'(1 - a) - f\frac{da}{dN}$$

But, from the homotheticity assumption, recalling that the slope of the opportunity locus equals $1/N$, we obtain

$$\frac{d\ln c/G}{d\ln N} = \frac{d\ln a/(1 - a)}{d\ln N} - 1 = -\sigma_c$$

where σ_c is the elasticity of substitution in consumption. At $v' = 0$, $a = f'N/f$, so that $dG/dN - f'(1 - a)\sigma_c$.

where σ_p is the elasticity of substitution of the production function. This confirms our earlier remark that strong complements in consumption (low values of σ_c) will lead to a unique interior solution; but it also shows that strong complementarity in production leads to a flat opportunity locus.[8]

These properties of the $v(N)$ function will play an important role in the subsequent analysis.

Variable labour supply, or Henry George vindicated

If labour is elastically supplied, it is still true that, if there exists a finite optimal population size, it entails rents equal to government expenditure.

Let the 'modified' indirect utility function be written

$$\mathscr{W} = \mathscr{W}\left(w, \frac{R-G}{N}, G\right)$$

where w is the wage rate; $R = f - f'N$ = rents; $(R-G)/N$ is the individual's income from rents minus taxes to finance government expenditures; and G is the supply of public goods. Then,[9]

$$\frac{d\mathscr{W}}{dN} = \mathscr{W}_1 \frac{dw}{dN} + \mathscr{W}_2 \left(\frac{dR}{dN}\frac{1}{N} - \frac{R-G}{N^2}\right) = -\frac{\mathscr{W}_2(R-G)}{N^2} = 0 \qquad (12.10)$$

when $R = G$.[10]

[8] Along the variable-N opportunity locus,

$$\frac{dc}{dG} = -\frac{1}{N}, \frac{c}{G} = \frac{f'}{f - f'N}$$

Hence,
$$-\frac{d\ln c/G}{d\ln(-dc/dG)} = \frac{d\ln f'/f - f'N}{d\ln N} = \frac{ff''N}{f'(f - f'N)} = \frac{1}{\sigma_p}$$

[9] Here, as earlier, it is assumed that individuals are identical and are treated identically. If individuals differ with respect to their consumption-leisure trade-off, then, for the ith individual, if L_i is his supply of labour and $\bar{L}$ the average amount of labour supplied,

$$\left(\frac{d\mathscr{W}^i}{dN}\right)_{R=G} \gtreqless 0$$

as

$$L_i \lesseqgtr \bar{L}$$

i.e. whether he supplies more or less labour than the average supplied.

If rents are allocated in proportion to the contribution to labour supply, then, for all individuals, $d\mathscr{W}/dN = 0$, when $R = G$. (The 'effective' wage is then $w + (R-G)/LN = (Q-G)/LN$, which is clearly maximised when $R = G$.)

[10] $R = G$ gives the optimal population if our objective function is maximising per capita income. If we take a utilitarian approach, we maximise

$$N\mathscr{W}\left(w, \frac{R-G}{N}, G\right)$$

which implies (letting R^* and G^* denote the optimal values of R and G) that $R^* \gtrsim G^*$, as $\mathscr{W}(w, 0, G) \gtrsim 0$ when $R = G$.

This is a remarkable result. Not only was Henry George correct that a tax on land is nondistortionary, but, in an equilitarian society, in which we could choose our population optimally, the tax on land raises just enough revenue to finance the (optimally chosen) level of government expenditures.

II.2 DIVISION OF THE POPULATION BETWEEN TWO IDENTICAL ISLANDS

We now consider the division of a fixed population, $2\overline{N}$, between two islands that are identical. We shall consider a number of alternative equilibrium concepts.

We consider first the set of Pareto-optimal allocations that are within-island egalitarian, i.e. all individuals on a given island are treated identically. We then consider a market equilibrium where, in voting for a level of public expenditure and taxation, individuals ignore any effects on land values or immigration. Following this, we examine two nonmyopic equilibria, in the first of which individuals are aware of the effect on immigration but pay no attention to the effect of immigration on land values, and in the second of which they do pay attention to land values. Finally, we consider the core of this economy and show that it may be empty.

In the analysis described below we shall focus on the case where there exists a unique optimal population level, denoted by N^*. Much of our discussion will be concerned with the special case where $\overline{N} < N^* < 2\overline{N}$.

In the following discussion, we shall arbitrarily refer to one of the islands as island 1, and to the other as island 2. Variables pertaining to each will be denoted by appropriate subscripts.

Pareto-optimal allocations

If we restrict ourselves to allocations that are within-island egalitarian, the set of Pareto-optimal allocations may easily be described: Let $v(N_1)$ be the utility level on island 1 with population N_1. Pareto optimality requires that we maximise

$$v(N_2) \tag{12.11}$$

subject to
$$v(N_1) \geqslant \bar{v}(N_1) \tag{12.12}$$

and
$$N_1 + N_2 = 2\overline{N} \tag{12.13}$$

where $2\overline{N}$ is the total population. The opportunity locus is depicted in Fig. 12.5.

$$\frac{dv(N_1)}{dv(N_2)} = -\frac{U_c^1(G_1 - R_1)/N_1^2}{U_c^2(G_2 - R_2)/N_2^2} \tag{12.14}$$

from which it immediately follows that *Pareto optimality requires that both islands be below, or both above, optimal population size* (N^*).

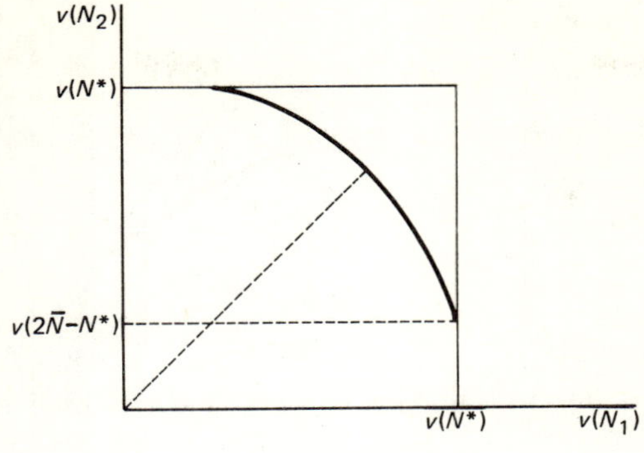

Fig. 12.5(a)

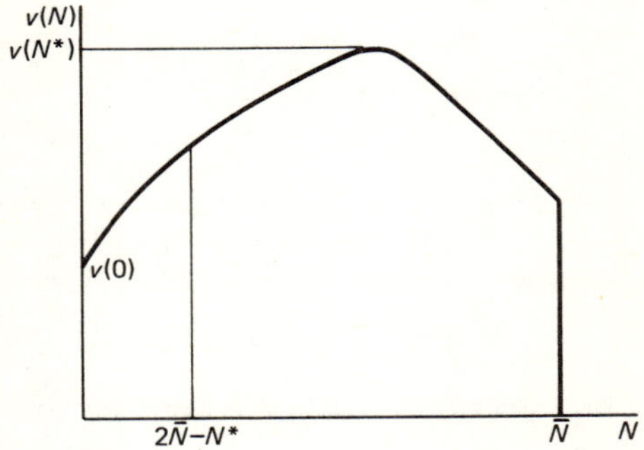

Fig. 12.5(b) Two-Island Opportunity Locus: No Subsidy

We now show that *Pareto optimality requires a lump-sum subsidy from one island to another,* if such subsidies are feasible, *except at the point where* $N_1 = \bar{N} = N_2$. We reformulate our maximisation problem as

$$\max U\left(\frac{[f(N_2) + s - G_2]}{N_2}, G_2\right) \tag{12.15}$$

subject to
$$\max U\left(\frac{[f(N_1) - s - G_1]}{N_1}, G_1\right) \geqslant \bar{U}_1 \tag{12.16}$$

and
$$N_1 + N_2 = 2\bar{N} \tag{12.17}$$

where s is the lump-sum transfer from island 1 to island 2. Thus, we require that

$$\frac{U_c^1}{N_1} = \lambda \frac{U_c^2}{N_2} \tag{12.18a}$$

$$\frac{U_c^1}{N_1} \frac{G_1 + s - R_1}{N_1} = \lambda \frac{U_c^2}{N_2} \frac{G_2 - s - R_2}{N_2} \tag{12.18b}$$

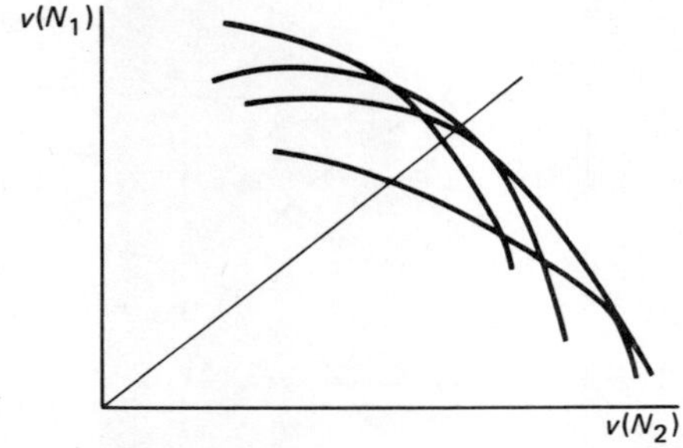

Fig. 12.6 Opportunity Locus with Subsidies

where λ is the Lagrange multiplier on a constraint (12.16). Thus, $s = 0$ if, and only if,

$$\frac{G_1 - R_1}{N_1} = \frac{G_2 - R_2}{N_2}$$

which will be the case at $N_1 = N_2$, but, in general, not otherwise.

Finally, we show that *social welfare maximisation may entail inequality.* Assume that we have a social welfare function of the form

$$\mathscr{W} = v(N_1)N_1 + v(N_2)N_2$$

Then, for equality to be locally optimal,[11] at $N_1 = N_2 = \bar{N}$,

$$\frac{\partial^2 \mathscr{W}}{\partial N^2} = 2[2v' + Nv''] < 0$$

Obviously, when $\bar{N} = N^*$, it follows that $v' = 0$ and $v'' < 0$, so that equality is desirable; but, when $\bar{N} < N^*$, it follows that $v' > 0$, and that v'', as we noted earlier, can be of either sign. Even if $v'' < 0$ when $v' = 0$, so that there is a unique optimal population, v'' need not be negative when $v' \neq 0$.[12]

Allocation of population with myopic voting

If there is free migration, and within each island all individuals are treated identically,[13] then equilibrium will entail that all individuals have the same

[11] The analysis taking into account optimal transfer is identical, since $(ds/dN)_{N_1 = N} = 0$.

[12] The result that social welfare maximisation may entail inequality is similar to that of Mirrlees (1972); other examples where nonconvexities have generated inequality in social welfare maximisation problems have been noted by Stiglitz (1973b, 1974b).

[13] That is, it is assumed that there is no differential taxation of immigrants and original occupants of each island. The analysis can be viewed as applying either to a 'socialist economy' in which all residents are treated identically, or to a private-ownership economy in which all individuals have identical endowments, i.e. own one plot of land on *each* island.

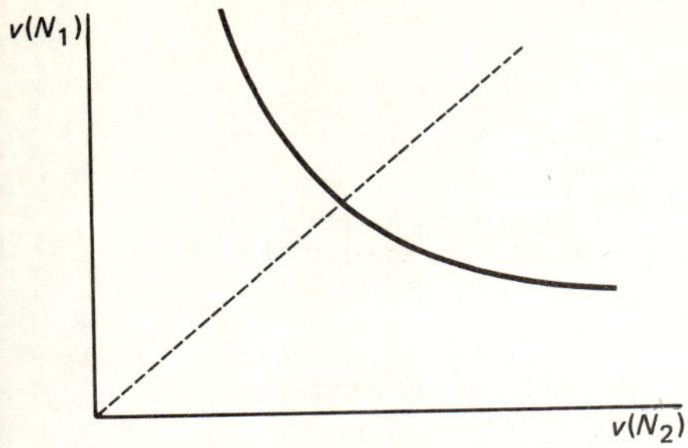

Fig. 12.7(a) Social Welfare Function

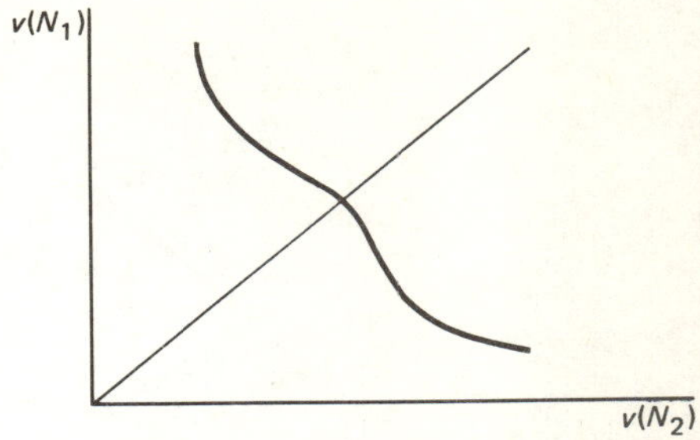

Fig. 12.7(b) Social Welfare Function

level of utility. If, in addition, we assume that within each island the level of public-goods expenditure is chosen to maximise utility, ignoring the effects of land values and migration, we obtain as our basic equilibrium conditions

$$v(N_1) = v(N_2) \tag{12.19a}$$

if both islands are occupied, and

$$v(2\overline{N}) \geqq v(0) \tag{12.19b}$$

if only one island is occupied. Any allocation satisfying (12.19) is a (Nash) equilibrium. We shall now show that there are *Pareto inferior equilibria that are stable, and that the Pareto efficient equilibrium may be unstable.*

The various possibilities are illustrated in Fig. 12.8, where N_1 is measured from the left axis and $N_2 = 2\overline{N} - N_1$ is measured from the right axis. Clearly, the allocation $N_1 = N_2 = \overline{N}$ is a Nash equilibrium, but it may be unstable.

Figure 12.8(a) illustrates the case where $N^* > \overline{N}$. As individuals leave island 2 and migrate to island 1, utility on island 1 increases and utility on island 2 decreases; thus, the equilibrium in which half the population is on each island is unstable. The equilibrium in which all individuals are on one island is stable,

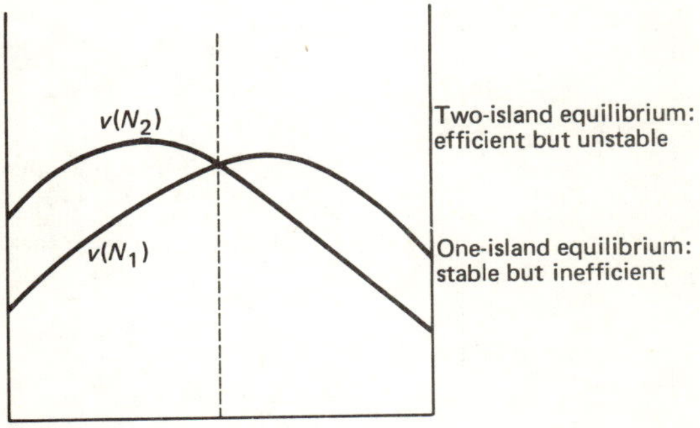

Fig. 12.8(a)

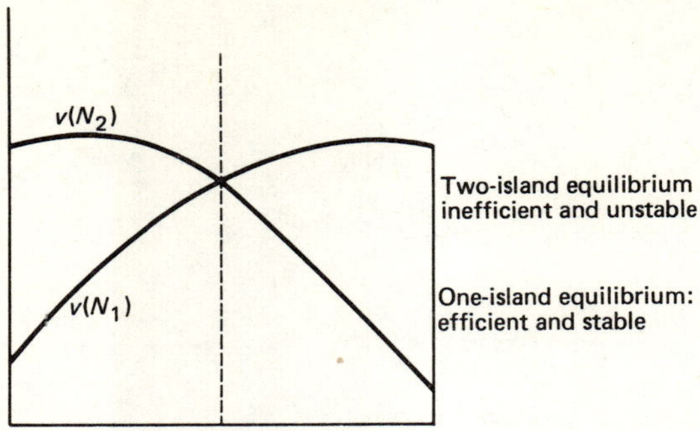

Fig. 12.8(b)

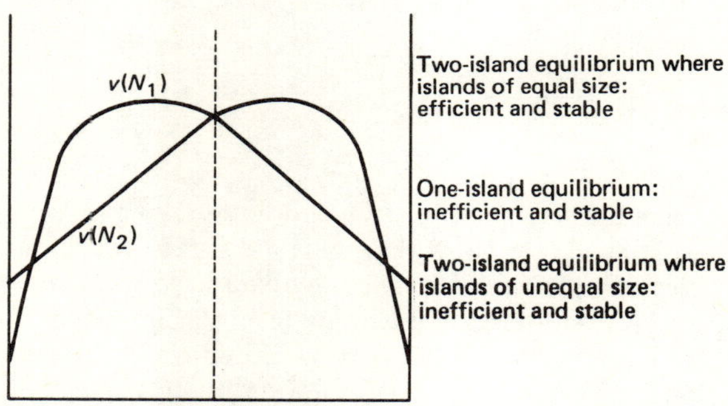

Fig. 12.8(c)

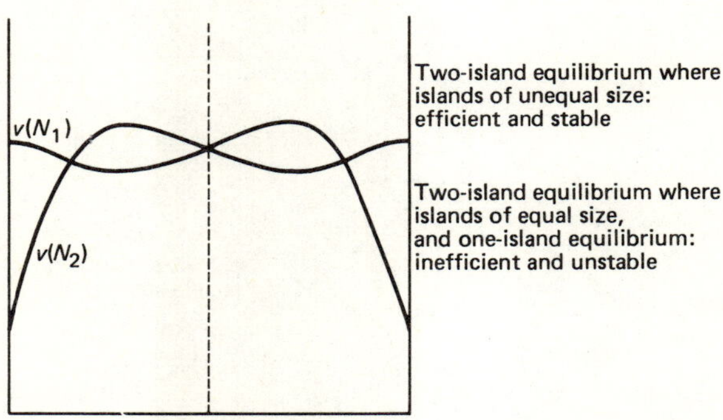

Fig. 12.8(d)

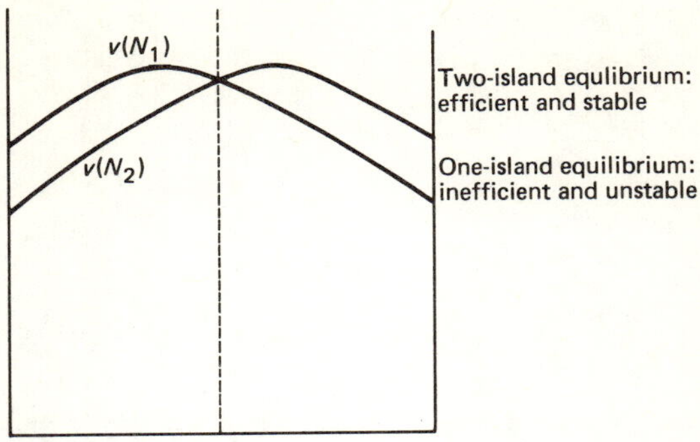

Fig. 12.8(e)

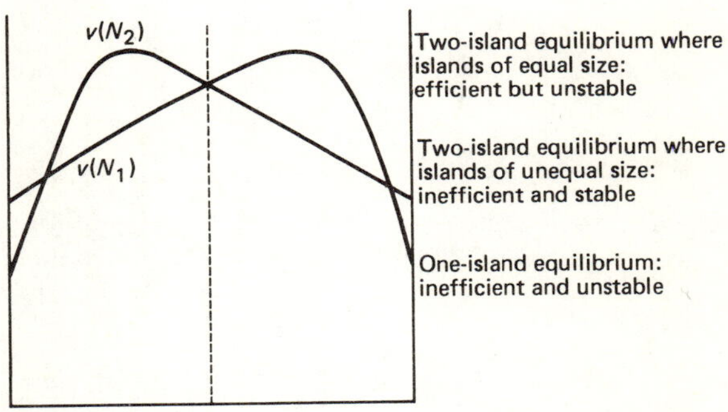

Fig. 12.8(f)

but has a lower level of utility than the unstable equilibrium with equal population on each island. The other possible cases include those in which the only stable equilibrium involves unequal-sized islands, and those in which the equilibrium of two equal-sized islands is stable but inefficient.

Nonmyopic voting: no land ownership

Let us now assume that the voters become aware that by changing the level of public-goods expenditure they can attract new immigrants. The legal and ethical structures of the two islands are such that they still insist on treating everyone within the island in the same way.[14]

[14] Although their ethics requires them to treat fellow islanders in the same way, they have no concern over the welfare of individuals who do not live on their island. One might argue that this is a peculiar set of ethical views; nevertheless, it does seem to represent the views of a large proportion of the population.

Given the levels of expenditure on public goods in each island, the population will divide itself to ensure equal utility on the two islands:

$$U\left(\frac{f(N_1)-G_1}{N_1}, G_1\right) = U\left(\frac{f(N_2)-G_2}{N_2}, G_2\right) \tag{12.20}$$

where, as usual, $N_1 + N_2 = 2\bar{N}$. Let

$$N_1 = \mathcal{N}_1(G_1, G_2)$$

$$N_2 = 2\bar{N} - N_1 = \mathcal{N}_2(G_1, G_2)$$

be the solution to (12.20).[15]

Let $\mathcal{N}_1^p(G_1, G_2)$ be the *perceived* relationship between expenditures and the allocation of the population. Then, the community that takes G_2 as given will choose G_1 to maximise

$$U\left(\frac{f[\mathcal{N}_1^p(G_1, G_2)] - G_1}{\mathcal{N}_1^p(G_1, G_2)}, G_1\right)$$

$$U_2 - \frac{U_1}{N_1} + \frac{G_1 - R_1}{N_1^2}\frac{\partial N_1^p}{\partial G_1} = 0$$

For any given allocation of population, the nonmyopic equilibrium will entail either greater or less expenditure on public goods than does the myopic equilibrium, as

$$\frac{G_1 - R_1}{N_1^2}\frac{\partial \mathcal{N}_1^p}{\partial G_1} \gtrless 0$$

A central case of interest is where $\mathcal{N}^p \equiv \mathcal{N}$, the perceived relationship is the actual relationship. Then,

$$\frac{\partial \mathcal{N}_1^p}{\partial G_1} = -(U_2 - U_1 N_1) \bigg/ \frac{U_1^1(G_1 - R_1)}{(N_1)^2} + U_1^2\frac{G_2 - R_2}{N_2^2}$$

from which it immediately follows that the allocations of public goods with myopic voting and nonmyopic voting are identical when $N_1 = N_2$ and $G_1 = G_2$. The Nash equilibrium in which the two islands have the same size is unaffected.

The analysis of stability is, however, altered. There are two aspects to this analysis.

(1) At any given level of G_1 and G_2, does migration equilibrate utility differences?

[15] There may be more than one solution to (12.20) but only one efficient solution, since

$$\frac{dU^1 - U^2}{dN_1} = U_c^1\frac{G_1 - R_1}{(N_1)^2} + U_c^2\frac{(G_2 - R_2)}{(N_2)^2}$$

If the utility functions are additive, what we may call *short-run stability* requires that

$$\frac{\partial w_1(1-\tau_1)}{\partial N_1} - \frac{\partial w_2(1-\tau_2)}{\partial N_1} > 0$$

i.e. $$\frac{\tau_1 f'(N_1)^2}{f(N_1)} + f''(N_1)(1-\tau_1) + \frac{\tau_2 f'(N_2)^2}{f(N_2)} + f''(N_2)(1-\tau_2) < 0$$

For G_1 near G_2 (N_1 near N_2), stability is ensured if

$$\tau - \frac{1-\alpha}{\alpha\sigma_p}(1-\tau) < 0 \qquad (12.21)$$

where σ_p is the elasticity of substitution of the production function. Thus, if $\bar{N} < N^*$, $\tau/(1-\tau) > (1-\alpha)/\alpha$, so that stability requires σ_p to be small (in particular, less than unity). Since, as $\bar{N}$ increases, $\dfrac{\tau/(1-\tau)}{(1-\alpha)/\alpha}$ decreases, stability is more likely for larger populations.

(2) Assuming that the population has allocated itself so that the marginal migrant is indifferent about which island he is on, do the reactions of the two communities' expenditure levels to each other lead to a stable equilibrium?

The answer to this question, for the equilibrium with $N_1 = \bar{N} = N_2$, is unambiguously 'yes'. Indeed, as we have drawn the reaction curves, not only is the two equal-sized islands equilibrium stable, but, in addition, it is the only equilibrium (see Fig. 12.9).[16]

The difference in stability should not be surprising, for the adjustment mechanisms are different. Whereas in the previous subsection we changed the population allocation, and government expenditures responded passively, in this subsection it is the government expenditures that have been changed and the population allocation that has responded.

Nonmyopic voting: land ownership

Migration has three effects: by increasing the labour-land ratio, it increases rents and decreases wages, and, as a result of the larger number of individuals

[16] If $\mathcal{N}_1^p \equiv \mathcal{N}_1$,

$$\frac{dG_1}{dG_2} \simeq \frac{\partial\left[U_2 - \frac{U_1}{N_1} + \frac{G_1 - R_1}{N_1^2}\frac{\partial \mathcal{N}_1^p}{\partial G_1}\right]\frac{\partial \mathcal{N}_1}{\partial G_2}}{\partial N_1}$$

$$\simeq \left[\left(U_{21} - \frac{U_{11}}{N_1}\right)\left(\frac{G_1 - R_1}{N_1^2}\right) + \frac{U_1}{N_1^2}\right]\frac{\partial \mathcal{N}_1}{\partial G_2} = 0$$

at $G_1^* = G_2^*$. The general shape of the reaction curves is based on the following considerations. If $G_1 = 0$, and everyone 'needs' some public goods, they will all live on island 2. Hence G_2 will be high – although not as high as it would be if they ignored the immigration effect. Similarly, if G_1 is very high, island 1 is unattractive and, thus, G_2 again is relatively high. Since $G_1 \leqq f(N_1) \leqq f(2\bar{N})$, there is a maximum feasible G_1.

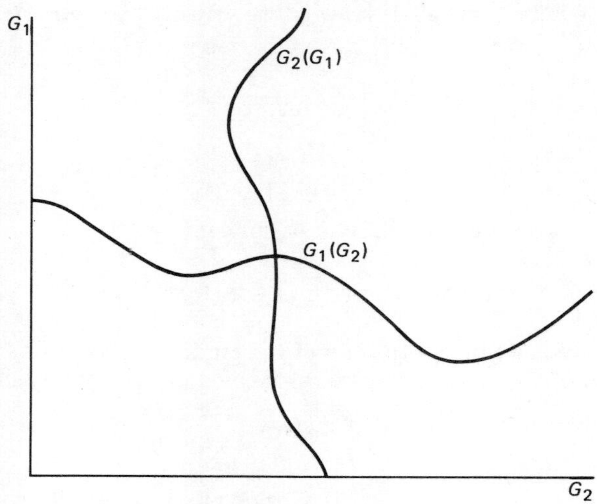

Fig. 12.9

among whom the taxes for the supply of the public good can be divided, it decreases the tax burden on each individual. In the previous subsection we focused on the last of these effects; here we consider the effects on the value of land and wages. Both of these effects have played a prominent role in discussions of migration. Workers may be worried that allowing migration will reduce their wages. Owners of land may favour high levels of public expenditure because of the migration it induces, which, in turn, increases the value of their land. The model presented in this subsection is the simplest that captures the effects of 'capitalisation' of taxes and government expenditures in the value of land. (Later a more complicated model entailing capitalisation will be examined.)

The consequences of different levels of expenditure on, say, land values depends on how the expenditures are financed. Obviously, if all expenditures were financed by land taxes, then, beyond a certain point, rents after taxes would fall, even if increased expenditures increased gross rents. The simplest case to investigate – and a realistic one – is that where there is a proportional income tax. The tax is paid in the country where the income is earned.

For simplicity, it is again assumed that everyone initially has the same total amount of land, but part of it is on one island and part of it is on the other. Initially, we assume that half the population lives on each island, and that the fraction of their land holdings that is on the other island (γ) is less than a half. We then denote by Y^{ij} the income of an individual who is born on island i but lives on island j:

$$Y^{ij} = (1-\gamma)R_i(1-\tau_i) + \gamma R_j(1-\tau_j) + w_j(1-\tau_j)$$

$$Y^{ii} = (1-\gamma)R_i(1-\tau_i) + \gamma R_j(1-\tau_j) + w_i(1-\tau_i)$$

where

$$w_i = f'(N_i) \qquad \text{(wages)}$$

$$R_i = (f - N_i f')/\overline{N} \qquad \text{(rents per capita)}$$

$$\tau_i = \frac{G_i}{f(N_i)} \qquad \text{(tax rate)}$$

We denote the utility level of an individual born and living on island j by

$$U^{ij} = U(Y^{ij}, G_j)$$

$$U^{ii} = U(Y^{ii}, G_i)$$

With expenditure levels (G_1, G_2), the population allocates itself so that the marginal migrant is indifferent to migrating. Without loss of generality, let $N_1 \geqq \overline{N}$, i.e. island 1 is the island to which individuals migrate. Then,

$$U^{21} = U^{22} \tag{12.22}$$

Let N_{ij} be the number of individuals born on island i and living on island j. If there is no cross-migration, $N_{21} < N_{11}$, so G_1 is chosen to maximise U^{11}:

$$\frac{\partial U^{11}}{\partial G_1} = U_2^{11} - \frac{U_1^{11}}{N_1}\Bigg[1 - \overbrace{\frac{N_1}{\overline{N}}\gamma(1-\alpha_1)}^{\text{(A)}} - \overbrace{\tau_1 \alpha_1 f\left(\frac{(1-\gamma)(1-\alpha_1)}{\overline{N}} + \frac{\alpha_1}{N_1}\right)}^{\text{(B)}} + \overbrace{\frac{\tau_2\alpha_2\gamma(1-\alpha_2)f}{\overline{N}}}^{\text{(C)}} - \overset{\text{(D)}}{N_1 f''(N_1)(1-\tau_1)}\left(1 - \overbrace{\frac{(1-\gamma)N_1}{\overline{N}}}^{\text{(E)}}\right) - (1-\tau_2)\cdot \overbrace{\gamma N_2 f''(N_2)\frac{N_1}{\overline{N}}}^{\text{(F)}}\Bigg]\frac{dN_1}{dG_1} = 0 \tag{12.23}$$

where $\alpha = f'N/f$ = share of wages.

In equation (12.23) are identified six distortions from Pareto optimality.

(A) Because part of the tax burden is imposed on nonresident landowners, the resident voters vote for excessive public expenditures. This term is zero only if $\gamma = 0$, i.e. land ownership is concentrated on a single island. The remaining distortions are associated with migration. The effects depend on whether increased expenditure on public goods induces in- or out-migration. The effects of migration can be broken into the following parts. If we assume that increased expenditure induces migration, then,

(B) the increased output resulting from migration reduces the tax burden, but

(C) it increases the tax burden on the other island. If the individual owns land on the other island, he will take this into account; this term is zero if, and only if, $\gamma = 0$. But so long as $\gamma < 1/2$ – i.e. the original residents own more land on the island on which they reside – (B) exceeds (C) for N_1 near N_2, so that, again, there is a tendency to vote for excessive expenditure on public goods.

(D) The migration reduces the wages on the island. Workers, in particular, will wish to limit public expenditure (below the Pareto-optimal level) so as to discourage migration.

(E) However, migration increases land values.

(F) Offsetting the increase in land values on one island are decreases in land values on the other island. To the extent that individuals on one island own land on the other, this will be taken into account. This term is zero if, and only if, $\gamma = 0$. In our formulation with equal initial endowments, the wage effect is larger than the land-capitalisation effect, at the point where $N_1 = \bar{N}$. However, when $\gamma = 0$, they exactly offset each other. On the other hand, when $N_1 > \bar{N}$ and $\gamma = 0$, the land-capitalisation effect always exceeds the wage effect. Thus, in equilibria in which the islands differ in size, the larger island is likely to have a larger than Pareto-optimal allocation of the public good. The smaller island may have a larger, or a smaller, than pareto-optimal allocation.

This analysis is entirely contigent upon increased expenditure inducing migration. That, in turn, depends on whether the migrants at the margin favour increased government expenditure.[17]

We assume that the equilibrium is stable in the usual sense that migration from the island with lower utility to that with higher utility reduces the difference in utility level. The effect of increased government expenditure on migration is given by

$$\frac{dN_1}{dG_1} = \frac{U_2^{21} - \dfrac{U_1^{21}}{N_1}\left(\alpha_1 + \dfrac{\gamma(1-\alpha_1)N_1}{\bar{N}}\right) + \dfrac{U_1^{22}}{N_1}\,\dfrac{\gamma(1-\alpha_1)N_1}{\bar{N}}}{U_1^{22}\,\dfrac{\partial Y^{22}}{\partial N_1} - U_1^{21}\,\dfrac{\partial Y^{21}}{\partial N_1}} \tag{12.24}$$

Stability ensures that the denominator is positive. At the point where

$$U_2 - \frac{U_1}{N_1} = 0$$

the numerator is unambiguously positive. This in turn implies that, if migration is desirable from the point of view of the original inhabitants of the island, the

[17] We assume that the migrants take the level of government expenditures, wages and taxes as given when they migrate; they ignore any effects they may have on these variables. This is not an unreasonable assumption.

equilibrium allocation will entail greater expenditure on public goods than it would have if they had ignored the migration effect. The equilibrium allocation will be a compromise between what the immigrants and what the original inhabitants would vote for (if they ignored migration effects). The compromise solution results not from a direct political process of compromise, but from the majority's taking into account the minority's option to leave.[18]

One of the interesting implications of the analysis is that, even when no migration occurs, taking into account the possibility of migration and its effects on land values will, in general, result in a Pareto-inferior allocation. To see this, consider (12.23) at the point where $N_1 = \bar{N}$, $G_1 = G_2$. We then obtain (since $U_2^{11} = U_2^{22} = U_2^{21}$, and $U_1^{11} = U_1^{21} = U_1^{22}$, we can drop the superscripts):

$$\frac{\partial U^{11}}{\partial G_1} = U_2 - \frac{U_1}{\bar{N}_1}\left[1 - \gamma(1-\alpha) - \frac{\tau f \alpha[(1-\alpha)(1-2\gamma)+\alpha] + 2N_1^2 f''(1-\tau)\gamma}{-2U_1(f''N_1(1-\tau)+\tau\alpha f')} \cdot \left(U_2 - \frac{U_1}{N_1}\alpha\right)\right] \tag{12.25}$$

$$= \left(U_2 - \frac{U_1}{N}\right)\left(1 + \frac{ZN_1}{U_1}\right) + \frac{U_1}{N_1}(1-\alpha)(\gamma + Z)$$

where $Z = \left[\tau\sigma_p\left(\frac{\alpha}{1-\alpha} + (1-2\gamma)\right) - 2\gamma(1-\tau)\right] \Big/ \left[2\ \ (1-\tau) - \frac{\tau\alpha}{1-\alpha}\sigma_p\right]$

where $\sigma_p = -\frac{f'(f-f'N)}{ff''N}$ = elasticity of substitution

Thus, there is no distortion if,[19] and only if, $\gamma + Z = 0$. But

$$\gamma + Z = \frac{\frac{\tau\sigma_p}{1-\alpha}(1-2\gamma)}{2\left[(1-\tau) - \frac{\tau\alpha}{1-\alpha}\sigma_p\right]} \quad \begin{array}{l} = 0 \text{ if } \gamma = 1/2 \\ > 0 \text{ if } \gamma < 1/2 \end{array}$$

[18] In section IV.1 a similar result is obtained, where the minority interests are reflected in the majority decision.

[19] At $G_1 = G_2$, $\mathcal{N}_1(G_1, G_2)$ may not be a differentiable function of G_1. Increments in G_1 induce in-migration, so that $\mathcal{N}_1$ is given by the solution to $U^{12} = U^{22}$, while decreases in G_1 may induce out-migration, so that $\mathcal{N}_1$ is given by $U^{11} = U^{12}$. Instead of (12.24) we have

$$\frac{dN_1}{dG_1} = \frac{U_2^{11} - \frac{U_1^{11}}{N_1}\left[\alpha_1 + (1-\gamma)\frac{N_1}{\bar{N}}(1-\alpha_1)\right] + \frac{U^{12}}{N_1}(1-\gamma)\frac{(1-\alpha)N_1}{\bar{N}}}{U_1^{12}\frac{\partial Y^{12}}{\partial N_1} - U_1^{11}\frac{\partial Y^{11}}{\partial N_1}}$$

But at $N_1 = N_2 = \bar{N}$, $G_1 = G_2$, $(\partial N_1/\partial G_1)^+ = (\partial N_1/\partial G_1)^-$.

(assuming that the equilibrium possesses the property of short-run stability described above, p. 289). Thus, if $\gamma = 1/2$ (i.e. each individual owns an equal amount of land on each island), the equilibrium is Pareto optimal; otherwise, there is an excessive expenditure on public goods.

Equilibria with land developers

We shall now show that there may exist no competitive equilibrium with 'developers'. A competitive equilibrium is defined as an allocation of individuals between islands, a level of public expenditure on each island, and a corresponding set of taxes such that

(a) no individual wishes to move from one island to the other;
(b) given the set of individuals on each island, the level of public expenditure (*cum* taxes) is preferred, by a majority, over any other level of public expenditure; and
(c) no 'developer' can buy an island, running it as a 'club' in which he offers a level of wages and government services, and by so doing make a profit.

Since all individuals were assumed to be identical, with the exception of a possible equilibrium with no migration, we can identify one of the islands as the emigrant island (the one that will have a smaller population in equilibrium) and the other as the immigrant island. The first condition assures us that, if anyone lives on the emigrant island, his level of utility must be the same as that of the immigrant on the immigrant island. The third condition assures us that rents on the two islands must be the same. For, if they were different, an individual could purchase the lower-rent island, promise slightly more government services on that island than is provided on the high-rent island at the same wages, and (by restricting migration to the same number of individuals as had previously lived on the high-rent island) make a pure capital gain by 'auctioning off' jobs on the island.

Consider the case where $\bar{N} < N^*$. First assume that all expenditures are financed by rent taxes, and that any excess of expenditures over rents is financed by wage taxes. Then, in the emigrant community, rents are zero (from condition (b) and the results derived earlier). If there is to be an equilibrium, rents in the immigrant community must be zero. If $N_1 \neq N^*$,

$$U < v^* = \max_{\{N,\, G\}} U\left(\frac{F(N, T) - G}{N}, G\right)$$

A 'developer' could purchase the first island and make a pure profit. Hence, if there is to be an equilibrium, the immigrant community must have a population of N^* and utility of v^*. But, then, the residents of the other island must have a lower level of utility, so condition (a) cannot be satisfied. Thus, there exists no equilibrium. An essentially identical argument will hold if government expenditures are financed by wage taxes.

On the other hand, if an equilibrium exists (in this formulation) it must be Pareto optimal. For, if it were not, a developer could purchase both islands, offer a slightly higher utility level to each individual, and make a pure capital gain.

The 'developer' plays a central role in this formulation. Essentially, the private developer can do anything that a centralised government can do, and, hence, if there are 'inefficiencies' he can eliminate them.

The core of the economy

The possibility of the nonexistence of equilibrium with land developers suggests that the core of this economy may be empty, which, in fact, turns out to be the case when $\bar{N} < N^*$. To discuss the core, we need to specify what a 'blocking coalition' is assumed capable of doing. In the following analysis it is assumed that it cannot expropriate land or extract revenues from individuals who are not in the coalition. We consider a case where N^* is uniquely defined, and where $\bar{N} < N^* < 2\bar{N}$, and $v(2\bar{N}) < v(\bar{N})$. Each individual is endowed with one unit of labour and with $1/N$ of the land of one of the islands. In addition, we assume that both goods are normal.

An allocation is described as follows. We partition the population into four sets, letting $\mathcal{N}^{ij}$ be the set of individuals owning land on island i and living on island j. We let $\{N^j\}$ be the set of individuals living on island j; then

$$\mathcal{N}^{1j} \cap \mathcal{N}^{2j} = \{N^j\} \qquad j = 1, 2$$

We require that

$$\{N^1\} \cap \{N^2\} = \{N\}$$

(the set of all individuals), and that individuals live on only one island.

$$\{\mathcal{N}^{i1}\} \cap \{\mathcal{N}^{i2}\} = \phi \qquad i = 1, 2$$

N^i will denote the number of individuals on island i. Each individual can supply one unit of labour and one unit of land. c^j denotes the consumption of the jth individual, and G_i the expenditure on private goods on the ith island.

An allocation is feasible if

$$G_i + \sum_{i \in \{N^j\}} c^i \leqq N_j F(1, 1) \qquad j = 1, 2$$

where F is a constant returns-to-scale concave production function giving output as a function of the input of labour, L, and land, T.[20]

Our proof has a simple structure. Clearly, an allocation in the core must have either $N_1 = N_2$ (the islands have the same population) or $N_1 > N_2$ (one of the islands, denoted for simplicity as the first, has a larger population than the other has). We show that the first alternative is not possible. This implies that on island 1 there must be some individuals who own land on island 2. The worst-off of these individuals must be worse off than the worst-off individual who owns land on island 2 and remains there; for, if that were not the case, one of the individuals living on island 2 could form a coalition with all of the other individuals living on island 1, which would improve the utility of everyone in the coalition.

On the other hand, the worse-off individual on island 1 must have a sufficiently high utility to ensure that island 2 cannot induce him to move by paying him slightly less than his marginal product. But, if $\bar{N} < N^*$, we show that the worse-off individual on island 2 must consume less than his marginal product in any allocation that is in the core; and, since we have already argued that the worse-off individual on island 1 has a lower utility than the worse-off individual on island 2, it immediately follows that island 2 can induce the worse-off individual on island 1 to migrate. Hence, the core must be empty.

More formally, we proceed by steps.

Lemma 1: In any imputation, within each island there must be production efficiency.

Although lemma 1 is obvious, it has an important implication: since the land on any island is fixed, the output on an island is simply a function of the number of individuals living on the island. Thus, we take it that

$$f(N_1) = F(N_1, \bar{N})$$

Lemma 2: In any imputation, if $N_i < N^*$, $\min_{\in \{jN_i\}} \{c^j\} < f'(N_i)$

Proof: If an allocation is in the core, clearly, it must be Pareto optimal; this requires, for each island, that

$$\sum_j \frac{U_2(c^j, G)}{U_1(c^j, G)} = \sum_i \frac{U_2\left[c^i, f(N) - \sum_j c^j\right]}{U_1\left[c^i, f(N) - \sum_j c^j\right]} = 1$$

[20] The characteristic equation for this game is given by

$$\mathscr{V}(\mathscr{S}) \equiv \{U^j \mid \max_{\{\mathscr{P}\}} \max_{\{\mathscr{A} \mid \mathscr{P}\}} U^j\}$$

when $\mathscr{P}$ is the set of feasible partitions and $\mathscr{A} \mid \mathscr{P}$ is the set of feasible allocations for a given partition.

But we know that there exists a $\hat{c} < f'(N)$ for $N < N^*$ such that

$$\sum \frac{U_2(\hat{c}, f - N\hat{c})}{U_1(\hat{c}, f - N\hat{c})} = 1 \tag{12.26}$$

Clearly, given the assumptions on normality and quasi-concavity of indifference curves, if $c_{\min} > \hat{c}$, then the left-handside of (12.26) would exceed unity.

Lemma 3: In an imputation, $\mathcal{N}_{12} \neq \phi$ or $\mathcal{N}_{21} \neq \phi$, if $\bar{N} < N^*$. There must be at least one landless worker on one of the islands.

Assume not. Assume that $G_1 \geqq G_2$. Then, a coalition consisting of $\{N_1\}$ and the individual with minimum consumption from island 2 can block the allocation, since by moving to island 2 he increases output by $f'(\bar{N})$ but requires consumption $\tilde{\bar{c}} \leqq c_{\min} < f'(\bar{N})$ to keep him on the same indifference curve.

Without loss of generality, we take it that $N_1 > N_2$.

Lemma 4: $\min_{j \in N_{21}} U(c^j, G_1) < \min_{\in \{jN_2\}} U(c^j, G_2)$

Otherwise, a coalition consisting of all but the worst-off person from island 1 and the worst-off person from island 2 could block the allocation.

Theorem: The core is empty.

Since $N_2 < N^*$, from lemma 2 and lemma 4,

$$U[f'(N_2), G_2] > \min_{j \in N_2} U(c^j, G_2) \geqq \min_{j \in \{N_{12}\}} U(c^j, G_1) \geqq \min_{j \in \{N_1\}} U(c^j, G_1)$$

But if

$$U[f'(N_2), G_2] > \min_{j \in \{N_1\}} U(c^j, G_1)$$

then, by offering the worse-off individual on island 1 an amount slightly less than his marginal product, the coalition consisting of $\{N_2\}$ and this individual can block the allocation. QED.

Although this proves that the core may be empty, it need not be. Assume, initially, that individuals are endowed with $1/2\bar{N}$ of each of the islands. Then the core is not empty if there are constant returns to scale. Consider the allocation $N_1 = \bar{N} = N_2$, $c^j = \hat{c}$, $G_1 = G_2 = \hat{G}$, where $\hat{c}\bar{N} + \hat{G} = f(\bar{N})$ and $\hat{c}$ maximises $U[c, f(\bar{N}) - N\hat{c}]$. To block this allocation, a coalition of a fraction of the individuals must be able to guarantee to the worse-off member of the coalition a utility of $U[\hat{c}, f(\bar{N}) - \bar{N}\hat{c}]$.

Let us define

$$V(N, T) \equiv \max_{\{c\}} U[c, F(N, T) - Nc]$$

Thus, a coalition of N individuals can decide either to divide itself between two islands or to stay on one island; if they were egalitarian, this would depend simply on whether

$$V\left(\frac{N}{2}, N\right) \gtrless V(N, N)$$

We assume that

$$V\left(\frac{\bar{N}}{2}, \bar{N}\right) > V(\bar{N}, \bar{N})$$

i.e. that it is Pareto optimal to have both islands inhabited.

The worse-off individual in a coalition consisting of $\tilde{N}$ individuals will have a utility less than, or equal to (choosing our units so that each individual owns one unit of land on each island),

$$\max\left\{V\left(\frac{\tilde{N}}{2}, \tilde{N}\right), V(\tilde{N}, \tilde{N})\right\}$$

But

$$\frac{dV\left(\frac{\tilde{N}}{2}, \tilde{N}\right)}{d\tilde{N}} = U_2\{F(\tfrac{1}{2}, 1) - c\} > 0$$

and

$$\frac{dV(\tilde{N}, \tilde{N})}{d\tilde{N}} = U_2\{F(1, 1) - c\} > 0$$

Thus, for all $\tilde{N} < 2\bar{N}$,

$$\max\left\{V\left(\frac{\tilde{N}}{2}, \tilde{N}\right), V(\tilde{N}, \tilde{N})\right\} \leqq V(\bar{N}, \bar{N})$$

the utility of the original allocation.

Large number of islands

In the previous subsections, the case of two islands was considered. We now consider what happens when we increase the number of islands and the number of individuals in such a way that the ratio of individuals to islands remains constant. Under these circumstances, the assumption that the behaviour of the other islands is unaffected by what any single island does is reasonable; moreover, each island can view itself as facing a horizontal supply schedule of labour at a given 'utility level' (when all individuals are identical), i.e. any combination of after-tax wages and provision of government services that leaves the individual at the same level of utility.

If $N/\bar{N} < 1$, then competitive equilibrium will be characterised by zero rents, with only a fraction of $N^*/\bar{N}$ of the islands inhabited. Rents are totally expended on public goods. If $N^*/\bar{N} > 1$, there is a land scarcity. And it is easy to show that at least one of the equilibria will be characterised by an equal population on all islands. The possibility of inefficient Nash equilibria arising from the misallocation of individuals among islands remains.

III. IDENTICAL INDIVIDUALS AND ISLANDS OF DIFFERENT SIZES

III.1 TWO ISLANDS

Now, assume that there are two islands, but this time of different size. Again, we first consider the case of publicly owned land. We now show that it is in the interests of one of the islands to subsidise the other, if there are no restrictions placed on immigration, but that the subsidy may be from the island with lower per capita income to the island with higher per capita income.

Fig. 12.10 may give some idea of why a subsidy may be desirable. The subsidy raises the level of utility obtainable at each level of population on one island, but lowers it in the other; however, the *equilibrium* may be either increased or decreased.

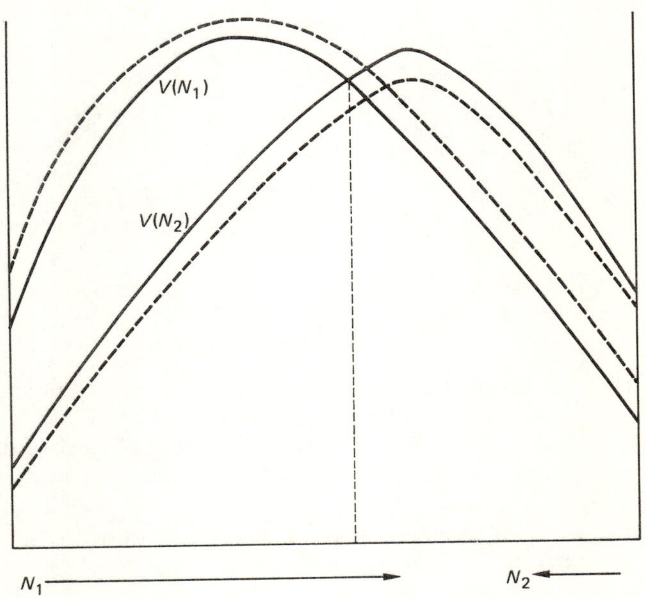

Fig. 12.10

To find the subsidy, we maximise

$$U\left(\frac{F(N_1, T_1) - G - SN_2}{N_1}, G\right) \tag{12.27}$$

subject to

$$U\left(\frac{F(N_2, T_2) - G_2}{N_1} + S, G_2\right) = U\left(\frac{F(N_1, T_1) - G_1 - SN_2}{N_1}, G_1\right) \tag{12.28}$$

and $\quad N_1 + N_2 = 2\bar{N}$ (12.29)

where S is the lump-sum subsidy paid to (received from) residents of island 1. Thus, optimality requires that[21]

$$S = \frac{N_1}{2\bar{N}}\left\{\frac{G_2 - R_2}{N_2} - \frac{G_1 - R_1}{N_1}\right\} \tag{12.30}$$

The nature of the inefficiency without subsidies is seen most clearly in the case depicted in Fig. 12.11. Let N_1^* be the optimal population for island 1, and let $2\bar{N}$ be the total population. In Fig. 12.10,

$$N_1^* + N_2^* = 2\bar{N}$$

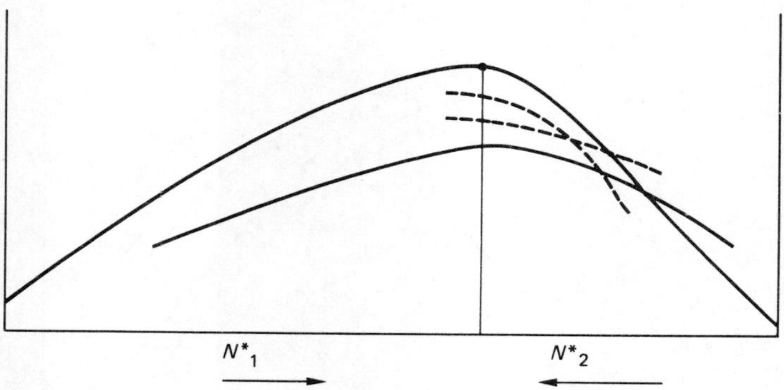

Fig. 12.11 Island 2 Subsidises Island 1

i.e. there are just enough people to give each island its optimal population. But the larger island will then have a higher level of utility (at the same land–labour ratio, it can provide the same level of per capita private consumption but a higher level of government expenditure). This induces immigration to

[21] Let λ be the Lagrange multiplier associated with (12.28). Then

$$U_1^1 \frac{N_2}{N_1}(1 - \lambda) - U_1^2 \lambda = 0$$

$$U_1^1\left(\frac{G_1 - R_1 + 2S\bar{N}}{N_1^2}\right)(1 - \lambda) - \lambda U_1^2\left(\frac{G_2 - R_2}{N_2^2}\right) = 0$$

the larger island from the smaller. The equilibrium is clearly Pareto inferior to the allocation where each island has its optimal population size. The large island, by giving a subsidy to the smaller one, is able to make individuals in both islands better off.

It is clear that if one island is above its optimal population size and the other island below it, it pays the larger (more populous) island to subsidise the smaller. But, as Fig. 12.12 makes clear, if individuals on the two islands are to have the same utility, the larger island must have a lower per capita income: the poor (on a per capita income basis) subsidise the rich.[22]

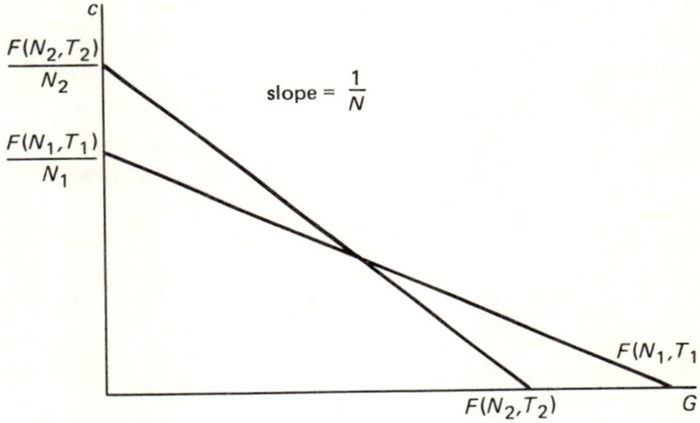

Fig. 12.12

Moreover, from (12.30) we obtain

$$c_i = w_i - [G_1 + G_2 - (R_1 + R_2)]/2\bar{N}$$

with optimal subsidies. Individuals in *both* islands always consume more or less than their marginal product, depending on whether total government expenditures are less or are greater than total rents.

The direction of subsidy becomes less clear when both islands are above or below their optimal size. Clearly $S = 0$ when $T_1 = T_2$.[23] We wish to know what happens to the subsidy as the amount of land on one of the island increases. An increase in land, at a fixed population, will normally increase both G and R, as will an increase in population at a fixed land size. But S depends on the relative changes in G and R, and to ascertain this requires detailed calculations.

[22] The larger island must have the larger G, and, hence, the low c; but the lower c is associated with the lower w, and the lower marginal product of labour with the lower average product of labour.

[23] Actually, $S = 0$, when $T_1 = T_2$ and $N_1 = N_2$ only ensures a critical point. Maximisation of U may entail a subsidy even with *ex ante* identical island, as noted earlier.

We can show that, if the islands are near each other in size, then whether the large island subsidises the smaller depends, in part, on whether $\bar{N} \gtrless N^*$.[24]

Social welfare maximisation

On the other hand, maximisation of social welfare (say, by a federal authority embracing both islands) will, in general, entail restricted migration and inequality of utility. Consider a Benthamite social welfare function. We wish to

[24] Let it be assumed that

$$X_i = \frac{G_i - R_i}{N_i}$$

so that

$$\left.\frac{dS}{dT_1}\right|_{T_1 = T_0} = \frac{1}{2}\left[\frac{dX_2}{dT_1} - \frac{dX_1}{dT_1}\right]$$

To calculate dX_1/dT_1, we totally differentiate the first-order conditions

$$\frac{U_1^1}{N_1} = U_2^1,\ \frac{U_1^2}{N_2} = U_2^2,\ U^1 = U^2$$

where, using (12.30)

$$c_i = w_i - (X_1N_1 + X_2N_2)/2\bar{N} \qquad i = 1, 2$$

$$G_i = R_i + X_iN_i \qquad i = 1, 2$$

At $T_1 = T_2$, $N_1 = N_2 = \bar{N}$, we obtain

$$\begin{bmatrix} a+b & b & \frac{X}{N}a - f''(a+2b) - \frac{U_1}{\bar{N}^2} \\ b & a+b & -\left(\frac{X_1}{N}a - f''(a+2b)\right) + \frac{U_1}{\bar{N}^2} \\ U_1 & -U_1 & 2U_2X_1 \end{bmatrix} \begin{bmatrix} dX_1 \\ dX_2 \\ dN_1 \end{bmatrix} = \begin{bmatrix} -\frac{f''N}{T^2}(a+2b) \\ 0 \\ 0 \end{bmatrix} dT_1$$

where, if both goods are normal,

$$\frac{a}{N_1} = \frac{d\frac{U_1^1}{N_1} - U_2^1}{dG_1} > 0$$

$$2b = -\frac{d\frac{U_1^1}{N_1} - U_2^1}{dc_1} > 0$$

Thus

$$\frac{d(X_2 - X_1)}{dT_1} = \frac{\frac{X_1}{N}(a+2b)\frac{f''N}{T^2}}{\left(\frac{U_1}{\bar{N}^2} + f''(a+2b)\right)}$$

If f'' is small, or if $\frac{(a+2b)}{U_1}$ is small, then this takes on the sign of $-X_1$, i.e. the sign of $R - G$.

$$\max_{\{N_1, c_1, c_2, G_1, G_2\}} \quad U(c_1, G_1)N_1 + U_2(c_2, G_2)N_2 \tag{12.31}$$

We obtain, in addition to the usual conditions on the optimality of the allocation within an island between private and public goods,

$$\frac{U_1^1}{N_1} = U_2^1, \frac{U_1^2}{N_2} = U_2^2 \tag{12.32}$$

Conditions for the optimal subsidy and optimal population allocation are

$$U_1^1 = U_1^2 \tag{12.33}$$

$$U^1 - U^2 + U_1^1\left(\frac{G_1 + 2S\bar{N} - R_1}{N_1}\right) - U_1^2\left(\frac{G_2 - R_2}{N_2}\right) = 0 \tag{12.34}$$

(12.33) is the not very surprising condition that the marginal utility of private consumption goods should be the same for all individuals. With an additive utility function, this implies the same level of private consumption for everyone. (12.32) and (12.33) together have one very striking implication: the island with the larger population must have the larger expenditure on public goods, and, hence, the higher level of utility. (12.34) may be rewritten using (12.32) and the fact that

$$c_1 = \frac{w_1 N_1 + R_1 - G_1 - SN_2}{N_1}$$

$$c_2 = \frac{w_2 N_2 + R_2 - G_2 + S}{N_2}$$

when $w_1 \equiv f_N(N_1, T_1)$. Thus,

$$U^1 - U^2 + U_1^1[(w_1 - c_1) - (w_2 - c_2)] = 0 \tag{12.35'}$$

For an additive utility function the implications of (12.35′) are immediate: since $c_1 = c_2$ but $U^1 > U^2$, $w^1 < w^2$. The larger island has a larger population – indeed, sufficiently larger to reduce the marginal product of labour to less than that on the smaller island. Individuals from the smaller island would like to migrate to the larger island, but are prohibited from doing so.

III.2 MANY ISLANDS

When there are only two islands, the fact that Pareto-optimal allocation cannot be attained in the absence of subsidies is not particularly serious. Since it is in the interests of both islands for the subsidy to be given, no central authority is required to ensure that it is.

Now, let us increase the number of islands and the population in proportion. As before, the maximisation of utility subject to the constraint that all individuals have the same utility involves a subsidy from one set of islands to the other. But now, without a federal authority to compel the transfer, no transfer will be made. If, say, all the large islands are providing subsidies to the small islands, it pays any single large island not to provide the subsidy.

However, if there is a federal authority to compel the transfer, there is no reason why it should be constrained to attempt equalising utility (assuming that it can impose migration taxes), and, in general, unless it has extremely strong egalitarian ethics (for instance, maximises the utility of the worst-off individual), it will not do so.

IV. IDENTICAL ISLANDS, DIFFERENCES IN INDIVIDUALS

In the following subsections we analyse the equilibrium in economies in which the islands are identical but individuals differ, with respect to either their wealth or their tastes. Again, the structure of the equilibrium critically depends on a number of fairly specific assumptions, as the following discussion should make clear. In each of the models presented below, the aim is to illustrate one important aspect of the problems arising out of individual differences.

The first model illustrates the consequences of an inability to identify which individuals are low demanders. As a result, the government does not, in the taxes it imposes, discriminate between high demanders and low demanders. The consequence of this is that there may then be an equilibrium with more than one community; this is clearly inefficient, relative to what could have been obtained were high and low demanders identifiable. On the other hand, there may be an equilibrium with a single community; in this case, the allocation to public goods is shown to represent a compromise between the high and the low demanders.

The next model illustrates the problems associated with matching individuals to form communities. An example with very diverse preferences is constructed where no equilibrium exists; another example, where an equilibrium exists but is inefficient, is also presented.

The next set of models attempts to describe the equilibrium when there is a large number of islands. Depending on whether there are more island than types of individuals, or the converse, the equilibrium that emerges may be thought of as a purely competitive or as a monopolistically competitive equilibrium. The surprising result is that even the monopolistically competitive equilibrium may be efficient – or, perhaps more accurately, the monopolistically competitive aspects of the analysis do not seem to introduce any distortions additional to those presented earlier.

The final set of models analyses problems associated with the rich attempting to exclude the poor from their communities. Equilibria with zoning and without zoning are analysed, and, as one might expect, zoning leads individuals to consume more 'housing' than they would otherwise do. On the other hand, the abolition of zoning may lead to a Pareto-inferior equilibrium. Again, there may be no equilibrium.

IV.1 DIVERSE PREFERENCES: INABILITY TO IDENTIFY HIGH AND LOW DEMANDERS

The basic point that we wish to establish can be developed without reference to production. Accordingly, assume that we have an economy in which each individual has an endowment of one unit of 'manna' that can be either converted (collectively) into public goods or consumed directly as a private good. Clearly, it pays all individuals of a given type to band together to provide the public good. The question is, does it pay individuals with different tastes to join together? We consider here the case where there are only two groups. Assume, for simplicity, that both groups are large, and differ in population by only one person (so that voting ties will not occur). Then there are only two possible equilibria: with two separate communities, or with a single merged community. Because it is assumed that the government cannot distinguish low demanders from high demanders, they must be taxed equally. Thus, in Fig. 12.13 the opportunity set facing individuals if two communities are formed is the line $\overline{GC}$, and, if a single community is formed, the line $2\overline{GC}$.

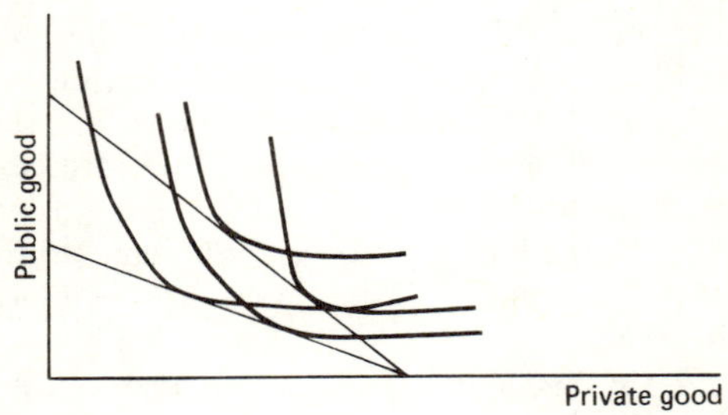

Fig. 12.13(a)

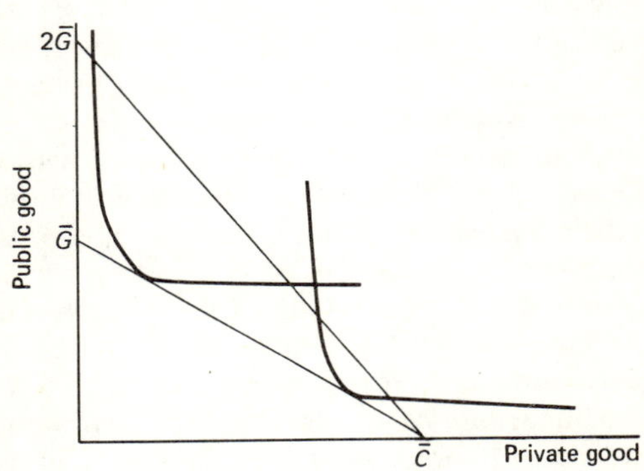

Fig. 12.13(b)

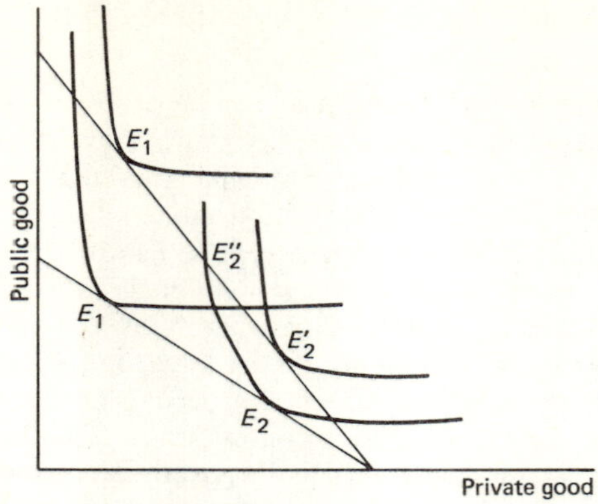

Fig. 12.13(c)

We assume that, when there is a single community, the equilibrium level is the one voted for by the majority (say group 1). Fig. 12.13 illustrates the three different possibilities. In Fig. 12.13(a) both groups are better off in the merged community than in the two separate communities, regardless of which group is in the majority. Fig. 12.13(b) considers the other polar case, where both groups are better off if two separate communities are formed. There will then be two communities in equilibrium. Of course, if we could identify the high demanders and tax them at a higher rate, we could make both groups better off by forming a single community. In this case, the 'cost' of the absence of information may be large.

Finally, in Fig. 12.13(c) is depicted a situation where both groups *could be* better off with a single community. But if each individual votes his true preferences, assuming that the other group will not leave and set up independently, the equilibrium will be, say, at point E_1', where the minority group is actually worse off than it was in isolation. Thus, with voting behaviour of this sort, there will be no equilibrium: if the communities merge, it pays for the minority community to separate and to form its own group; with the communities separated, it pays them to merge.

The absence of equilibrium in this case is associated with the extreme myopia of the individuals. When they are separated, they fail to observe that, once they are joined, the equilibrium will not be Pareto superior to their present position; they observe only that there exists a Pareto-superior allocation. The situation may be thought of as one where a private individual organises the 'joint' club and offers a level of dues in combination with a level of services; eventually, the determination of the equilibrium level of dues and services is to be left to the membership. An equilibrium is a situation in which (a) it cannot pay an individual to organise such a joint club, and (b) the level of dues and services is determined by majority voting by the members of the club. What we have established is that there is no equilibrium of this sort.

There is, however, an equilibrium if the majority take into account the possibility of a minority forming its own community. In that case, the equilibrium will be the point E_2'': the preferences of the minority act essentially as a veto over the wishes of the majority and are taken into account in the equilibrium.

IV.2 PROBLEMS OF MATCHING

Here we present two examples to illustrate the problems of matching individuals to form communities. The first illustrates the possibility of nonexistence, the second that of inefficiency.

Nonexistence

Suppose that there are many of different kinds of public goods. First consider the case where there are four groups of individuals. Individual 1 is indifferent about public goods A, B and C but receives a large negative utility from all other public goods. Individual 2 is indifferent about B, C and D and receives a large negative utility from all other public goods; similarly, individual 3 receives utility only from C, D and A, and individual 4 receives utility only from D, A and B. For simplicity, however, it is assumed that the indifference curve between public and private goods is the same for all individuals. Then, it is clear that the core of this economy is empty. The only possible allocations involve either two communities of two groups each, or one community with three groups and one with one. The latter can be blocked by the isolated group bribing the lowest utility group in the larger community (or any group, if they receive the same level of utility). The former can be blocked by one of the two communities bribing one of the groups in the other community so that it changes sides. A similar analysis leads to the conclusion that there is no market equilibrium in this example.

The introduction of production leaves the analysis essentially unaffected. Assume that the individuals are perfect substitutes in production and that all island are of identical size. Assume, moreover, that the number of individuals of any type is less than or equal to $(1/3)N^*$. Then, if, as the number of islands increases, the number of types of individuals increases in such a way that each individual likes exactly three goods, and each good is liked by exactly three types of individuals, there will exist no equilibrium even with an infinite number of islands.

Inefficient Matching Equilibrium

Even when equilibrium exists, it may not be efficient. People of different tastes may be matched in the wrong way, so that in each community the choice of public goods is Pareto optimal. Moreover, it does not pay any individual to migrate. However, there is one arrangement of individuals within communities that can make everyone better off.

Consider the following simple example. There are four groups within the population, and these have utility functions as follows.

A: $u(c) + v(G_1 + 2G_2 - G_3 - G_4)$
B: $u(c) + v(G_1 - G_2 + G_3 - G_4)$
C: $u(c) + v(-G_1 + G_2 + G_3 - G_4)$
D: $u(c) + v(-G_1 - G_2 + G_3 + G_4)$

Let N be the number of individuals of type i. Assume that $N_A = N_D = N/2$, and that $N_C = N_B = (N/2)\mu + 1$ (this is just to avoid ties in voting). Thus, each island will be inhabited by two groups. There are two possible equilibria: (1) A and B form a community, supplying public good G_1 at a level unanimously agreed upon, and C and D form a community, supplying public good C_3 at a level unanimously agreed upon; or (2) A and C form a community, supplying public good G_2 at a level desired by group C, and B and D form a community, supplying public good G_3 at a level unanimously agreed upon. Note that from the point of view of B, C and D the two equilibria are equivalent; A, however, is unambiguously better off in the second equilibrium than in the first.

Other, somewhat more elaborate examples of inefficient Nash equilibria are presented in section V.1. One way of understanding these results is to observe that here, unlike in the conventional competitive equilibrium model, there are no prices to guide the efficient allocation of individuals among communities or the choice of goods to be produced by communities.

IV.3 COMPETITIVE MODELS OF LOCAL PUBLIC GOODS

The basic result of this section is that, if there are more islands than there are types of individuals, the equilibrium may be Pareto optimal. This is, I suspect, the basic result intuited by Tiebout in his classic paper. To obtain this result, we have to ignore some of the difficulties encountered in the analysis presented in section II; there, it will be recalled, we established that, even with identical individuals, the equilibrium allocation may not be Pareto optimal. Thus, to isolate the effects of individual-preference heterogeneity, we assume that there is an allocation of individuals by types among islands, with an *equal number* of individuals on each island, that is Pareto optimal. We simply ask, can this allocation be sustained as a Nash equilibrium?

Assume, first, that the individuals are perfect substitutes in production. Then, in equilibrium, each island will have only one kind of individual; the analysis of the equilibrium population on each island is the same as in section II.

On the other hand, when the two kinds of individuals supply, say, complementary labour, there is unanimity concerning the optimal number of individuals and the supply of public goods on each island. Consider the interests of group A. To obtain labour of type B, it must pay a wage w^i as a function of the level of public goods supplied:

$$w^i = w^i(G), \text{ with } w^i = -\frac{dU^i/dG}{dU^i/dc} \qquad i = A, B$$

(the marginal rate of substitution of the *i*th type of individual.) Consider an island that is owned by $\bar{N}^A$ individuals of type A, and $\bar{N}^B$ individuals of type B, each of whom has an equal ownership share. Then, individuals of type A wish to

$$\max_{\{G, N^A, N^B\}} \quad U^A\left(\frac{Y(N^A, N^B) - w^A N^A - w^B N^B - G}{\bar{N}^A + \bar{N}^B} + w^A, G\right) \tag{12.36}$$

where $Y(N^A, N^B)$ is the production function and superscripts refer to the type of labour. Thus,

$$Y_{N^A} = w^A \tag{12.37}$$

$$Y_{N^B} = w^B \tag{12.38}$$

$$\frac{\partial U^A}{\partial G} + \frac{\partial U^A}{\partial c}\left[\frac{\partial U^B/\partial G}{\partial U^B/\partial c}\frac{N^B}{\bar{N}^A + \bar{N}^B} - \frac{1}{\bar{N}^A + \bar{N}^B} - \left(1 - \frac{N^A}{\bar{N}^A + \bar{N}^B}\right)\frac{\partial U^A/\partial G}{\partial U^B/\partial G}\right] = 0$$

or

$$\frac{\partial U^A/\partial G}{\partial U^A/\partial c}N^A + \frac{\partial U^B/\partial G}{\partial U^B/\partial c}N^B = 1 \tag{12.39}$$

(12.39) is simply the conventional result for Pareto optimality: the sum of the marginal rates of substitution equals the marginal rate of transformation. But exactly the same conditions are obtained for individuals of type B. Thus, as long as the voters correctly perceive the supply functions of the various types of labour, there is unanimity concerning the supply of public goods, even though the tastes of the individuals differ.

IV.4 MONOPOLISTICALLY COMPETITIVE MODELS OF LOCAL PUBLIC GOODS

The previous section considered a case where there were more islands than there were types of individuals, so the result that preference diversity did not present a serious problem was not surprising. Here we examine a case where there is a continuum of types of individuals, and far fewer communities than types of individuals. The canonical representation of preference diversity in the literature is the Hotelling linear spatial model, and the model presented here is an adaptation of that model to the analysis of local public goods.

Each individual is located at a point on the line. The public goods (swimming pool, club rooms, and so on) are located at certain points. The individual must travel to the public good; travel costs are a function of distance, and we shall assume that they are simply proportional. Clubs will be formed at different points on the line. We wish to know how 'far apart' the different clubs will be.

There is an obvious slight modification to the analysis in which the differences are not with respect to location but with respect to preferences for different public goods. Each public good is represented by a point on a line (of possibly infinite length), and each individual has a most desired public good. Other public goods have less value and can be converted, by a simple transformation, into equivalent units of the 'most-desired' public good. Thus, if G^* is the most-desired public good, the equivalent consumption of good G, which, on our linear scale, is at a 'distance' t from G^*, is $\psi(t)G$, where $\psi' < 0$, $0 < \psi \leqq 1$.]

Equilibrium with compensation

First we consider the case where the club has strong egalitarian ethics and, like the Yale Club in New York, which charges individuals who live outside New York a lower fee than it charges those who live in the city, compensates individuals who live further away by setting their dues lower. Thus, in equilibrium, all individuals are assumed to have the same utility. For simplicity, we assume that individuals are uniformly distributed along the line, with a density of 1 per unit length. Each individual has a unit of wealth. Travel costs are d per unit length. Since all individuals have the same utility, optimality clearly requires choosing the size of club, N (equivalently, the distance between clubs), to

$$\max_{\{d,\, G\}} U\left(1 - \frac{dN}{4} - \frac{G}{N}, G\right) \tag{12.40}$$

i.e.

$$N = \sqrt{4G/d} \tag{12.41a}$$

and

$$U_1 = \frac{U_2}{N} \tag{12.41b}$$

On the other hand, consider a representative club. It is a 'utility taker', i.e. it believes that it can get new members by offering them a slightly higher level of utility than they receive at present. Thus, the fee that it charges to attract residents is a function of the level of public goods that it provides:

$$\tau = \tau(G, U) \tag{12.42}$$

The club chooses τ and N to maximise

$$U\left(\frac{\tau(N - N^*)}{N} - \frac{(dN^2 - dN^{*2})}{4N} + 1 - \frac{dN^*}{4} - \frac{G}{N^*}, G\right) \tag{12.43}$$

In equilibrium, $N^* = N$, i.e. no club attempts to recruit members from other clubs. Hence, in equilibrium,

$$\tau = \frac{Nd}{2} \tag{12.44a}$$

and

$$U_1 = \frac{U_2}{N} \tag{12.44b}$$

Since

$$G = \tau N - \frac{dN^2}{4} \tag{12.45}$$

(12.44a) can be written as

$$G = \frac{N^2 d}{4}$$

or

$$N = \sqrt{4G/d} \tag{12.44a'}$$

The equilibrium is identical to the Pareto-optimal allocation.

Equilibrium with no compensation

More generally, however, it will be difficult, if not impossible, for clubs to pay perfect compensation for differential travel costs.[25] (This is particularly true in the interpretation of the model where different locations represent different 'preferred' public goods.) Then, the level of utility of an individual will depend on whether he is lucky and lives near a club or is unlucky and lives far away. Because they have different real incomes, the demands for public goods will differ among individuals. We assume that the actual level is determined by a majority vote. Now, the club charges a fixed fee for membership. By lowering this or by increasing the level of its provision of the public good, it can attract members from neighbouring clubs. We require that all of the revenue raised by the club be spent on public goods (and that all members of the club be treated the same, i.e. face the same dues). Then, the median individual votes for the level of dues, which maximises

$$U\left(1 - \tau - \frac{dN^*}{4}, \tau N\right)$$

i.e.

$$\frac{dU}{d\tau} = U_2\left(1 - \tau - \frac{dN^*}{4}, \tau N\right)N - U_1\left(1 - \tau - \frac{dN^*}{4}, \tau N\right) + U_2 \tau \frac{dN}{d\tau} = 0 \tag{12.46}$$

To calculate $dN/d\tau$, we have to consider the consequences of individuals leaving neighbouring clubs to come to the given club. For simplicity, let us assume that neighbouring clubs fix τ in the short run and adjust government expenditure. Thus, let $\Delta = N - N^*$; then

$$U\left[1 - \tau^* - d\left(\frac{N^*}{2} - \frac{\Delta}{2}\right), \tau^*\left(N^* - \frac{\Delta}{2}\right)\right] = U\left[1 - \tau - d\left(\frac{N^*}{2} + \frac{\Delta}{2}\right), \tau(N^* + \Delta)\right] \tag{12.47}$$

[25] This is not quite correct; if there is a competitive land market, rent differentials will exactly compensate for travel-cost differentials.

so that

$$\left.\frac{dN}{d\tau}\right|_{\Delta=0} = \frac{U_2 N^* - U_1}{U_1 d - \frac{3}{2} U_2 \tau^*} \tag{12.48}$$

If population adjustments are to be equilibrating, the denominator of (12.48) is positive. Hence, from (12.46), the equilibrium expenditure on public goods represents a 'compromise' between what the median individuals would have chosen, had they ignored the migration effect, and what the marginal individual would have chosen.

By contrast, maximisation of the average level of utility requires that

$$\frac{\int U}{N} = \frac{G \int U_2}{N} + U\left(1 - \tau - \frac{Nd}{2}, \tau N\right). \tag{12.49}$$

and

$$\int (U_2 N - U_1) = 0 \tag{12.50}$$

The first condition simply says that optimality requires that the average value of utility equal the utility of the worse-off person plus the marginal utility of his extra tax contributions. The second condition is similar to the familiar condition that the sum of the marginal rates of substitution should equal the marginal rate of transformation. By contrast to (12.46), where the marginal rates of substitution of the median and marginal individuals were crucial in determining the allocation to public goods, (12.50) treats all individuals symmetrically, as one would expect in social welfare maximisation.

The relationship between the two is not obvious. The following example shows that there may be either too many or too few clubs. Let it be assumed that $U = c + V(G)$. Then, $U_2/U_1 = V'$ for all individuals in a club. Substituting (12.48) into (12.46), we immediately obtain the result that $dU/d\tau = 0$ whenever $U_2/U_1)N = 1$, i.e. $V'(G)N = 1$. From (12.50) this is also a condition for Pareto optimality, but (12.49) imposes the further condition that $(G/N)V'(G) = dN/4$. Thus, in this example, one of the possible equilibria is social-welfare maximising, but there do exist some equilibria with too many communities and some with too few.

IV.5 WEALTH INEQUALITY

One of the most striking aspects of local communities in the United States (and, I suspect, in many other countries as well) is the marked differences in wealth among them. Of course, one expects the wealthy to live near each other, to live in the same neighbourhood; but what we are concerned with here is not the tendency to separate into neighbourhoods, but to separate into different governmental units. This might, of course, be because differences in tastes with respect to public goods are systematically associated with differences in income. But, although there is, undoubtedly, some correlation, there are other factors (such as education) that are equally strong in determining preferences.

In fact, if the goods that were publicly provided were true public goods without congestion effects, then the reason why the rich would be interested in excluding the poor would be the difference in levels of demand for the public goods. The fact that the poor may be 'free riders' may be ethically objectionable, but does not detract from the consumption of the rich. But, because they are (at least in a relative sense) free riders, they may well demand an excessive amount of public goods (essentially using public goods as an 'admissible' method of redistribution).

However, probably more important than this effect is the fact that education, the main publicly provided good at the local level, is not a pure public good; on the contrary, the marginal cost of educating an additional child is close to average cost. Thus, the provision of a uniform level of education to all children, regardless of the wealth of their parents (and perhaps even financed by even a proportional wealth tax), involves, in effect, considerable redistribution. By forming communities of individuals of identical wealth, this redistribution can be avoided.

It is not surprising, then, that wealthy communities attempt to exclude poorer inhabitants. The methods of exclusion are indirect; zoning restrictions have perhaps been the main method of restriction. (Some recent court cases have suggested that this may not be as effective a method of restriction in the future as it has been in the past.) The consequence of this is that wealthier communities are induced to consume more housing than they otherwise would have consumed. We shall show, moreover, that (a) allowing direct restrictions to be imposed may be a Pareto-superior improvement to forcing communities to rely on indirect (zoning) restrictions; (b) not allowing zoning restrictions may result in an equilibrium with zoning restrictions; and (c) allowing votes to be cast in proportion to wealth may result in a Pareto-superior improvement.

It should be emphasises that in this analysis we take a completely individualistic approach; we ignore, for instance, any social value (positive or negative) associated with having 'mixed' communites.[26] As a consequence, these results should be considered to be of only limited normative value.

The analysis will consider the equilibrium under three different regimes. In the first, it is assumed that complete exclusion is possible. In the second, it is assumed that zoning is not possible, but that the rich communities may still find exclusion possible – either by having a very high tax rate or a very low level of expenditure on public goods – and, under some circumstances, even desirable. In the final subsection, zoning is allowed.

Complete exclusion feasible

We assume, for simplicity, that there are only two groups in the population. The rich, who will be referred to by a superscript R, have a wealth per capita

[26] These returns have been particularly emphasised in the context of education. For a discussion of the economic costs and benefits of heterogeneity, see Stiglitz (1973a).

of W^R while the poor (who will be referred to by a superscript L, for 'lower class') have a wealth per capita of W^L: $W^R \geqq W^L$. We let g be the publicly provided private good; i.e. the good is supplied in equal quantity to each individual, but the marginal cost of supplying it to one extra person is equal to the average cost of supplying it. The (privately provided) private good will be denoted by c. The utility functions are given by $U^L(c, g)$ and $U^R(c, g)$ (the functions may be the same). Later, we shall consider a special case where the utility functions are identical and additive.

$$U = u(c) + v(g)$$

With complete exclusion, the equilibrium for each group is given by the solution to

$$\max U(c^i, g^i) \tag{12.51}$$

subject to

$$c^i + g^i \leqslant W^i \qquad i = L, R \tag{12.52}$$

The solution values will be denoted by an asterisk, and are shown diagrammatically in Fig. 12.14.

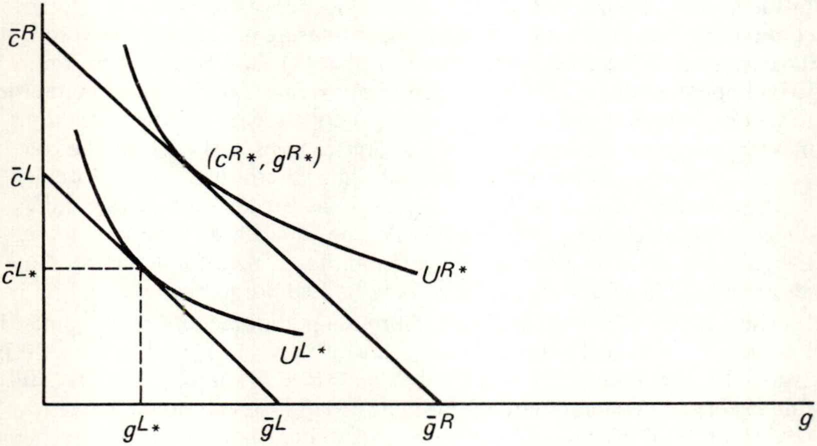

Fig. 12.14

No zoning

When direct exclusion is not feasible, the rich community must resort to indirect methods of exclusion if it is to exclude at all. There are two possible situations: one where the rich and the poor form separate communities, and one where the rich and the poor form a single community.

With separate communities, the poor can guarantee themselves a level of utility U^{L*} (the level of utility that they obtain in the complete-exclusion equilibrium), but no more. The rich, on the other hand, are restricted to choosing a tax rate and a level of public expenditure that does not attract the poor.

We assume that the public expenditure is financed by a proportional wealth tax. (This assumption is vital to much of the subsequent analysis.) We can then put the problem of the rich community as

$$\max U^R(c^R, g^R) \tag{12.53}$$

subject to
$$c^R + g^R \leqq W^R \tag{12.54}$$

and
$$U^L(W^L(1-\tau^R), g^R) \leqq U^{L*} \tag{12.55}$$

where τ is the tax rate required to finance the given level of expenditure

$$\tau = \frac{G^R}{W^R} \tag{12.56}$$

Figure 12.15 shows the solution to this problem diagrammatically. The lines $\bar{c}^R\bar{g}^R$ and $\bar{c}^L\bar{g}^L$ give the opportunity sets for the two communities separately. The line $\bar{g}^R\bar{c}^L$ gives the opportunity set for a single individual of the lower group who chooses to live in a 'rich community'; i.e. if the rich community provides a level of public goods g^R, then the corresponding point on $\bar{g}^R\bar{c}^L$ gives a poor individual's consumption of private goods in that community. The

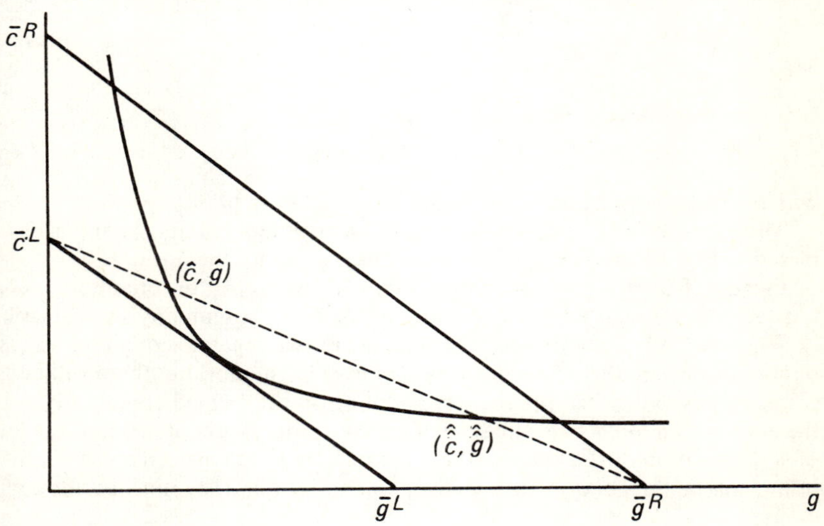

Fig. 12.15

indifference curve of the poor individual, $U^L(c, g) = U^{L*}$, cuts the curve $\bar{g}^R \bar{c}^L$ at two points, denoted $(\hat{c}, \hat{g})$ and $(\hat{\hat{c}}, \hat{\hat{g}})$; these are the two *exclusionary* points. For levels of g^R below $\hat{g}$ or above $\hat{\hat{g}}$, the poor individual will not be attracted to the rich community; for other levels of g, he will be. In general, the exclusionary constraint will be binding, so that the rich community will choose either $\hat{g}$ or $\hat{\hat{g}}$, depending on which yields a higher utility. We take it that

$$\max \{U^R(\hat{c}^R, \hat{g}), U^R(\hat{\hat{c}}^R \hat{\hat{g}})\} = \hat{U}^R$$

where $\hat{c}^R \equiv W^R - \hat{g}, \hat{\hat{c}}^R \equiv W^r - \hat{\hat{g}}$

Let us interpret this result: in order to exclude the poor, the rich community, chooses either a higher or a lower level of public expenditure than it would have chosen in the equilibrium where direct exclusion was feasible. Essentially, the tax rate in the higher equilibrium is so high that the poor cannot afford to live in the community; the amount of private consumption that they are left with is 'inadequate'. In the lower equilibrium, government expenditure is very low. The rich can purchase private goods that are 'substitutes' for the public good; the poor, however, cannot do this, and thus prefer to remain in their own communities. One can observe both extremes of behaviour in rich communities in the United States.

But the rich community need not exclude the poor. It must compare the level of utility obtained in the exclusionary equilibrium with the best that it can obtain if they merge; i.e. it solves

$$\max_{\{g^R\}} U^R[(1-\tau)W^R, g^R] \tag{12.57}$$

where $\tau = g^R/\overline{W}$

$\overline{W}$ is the mean wealth of the community,

$$\overline{W} = \lambda W^R + (1-\lambda)W^L \tag{12.58}$$

where λ is the proportion of the population that is 'rich'.

The solution to (12.57) will be denoted with a double asterisk, and is depicted in Fig. 12.16. The opportunity locus is given by the line $(\bar{c}^R, \bar{g})$.

Clearly, if $U^{R**} > \hat{U}^R$, an equilibrium with two separate communities is not feasible; while, if $U^{R**} < \hat{U}^R$, one with a single community is not feasible.

When the rich are better off where there are two separate communities (as opposed to where there is a single community) in equilibrium, there will be two communities; but, when the rich are better off in the merged community, what the equilibrium looks like will depend on the voting procedure and on the level of sophistication of the voters. Where the rich are in the majority, the equilibrium will be the point of the merged community that they most preferred;[27]

[27] It can be shown that, if the rich prefer this point to the best of the exclusion points, the poor will have a higher level of utility at this point than at U^{L*}.

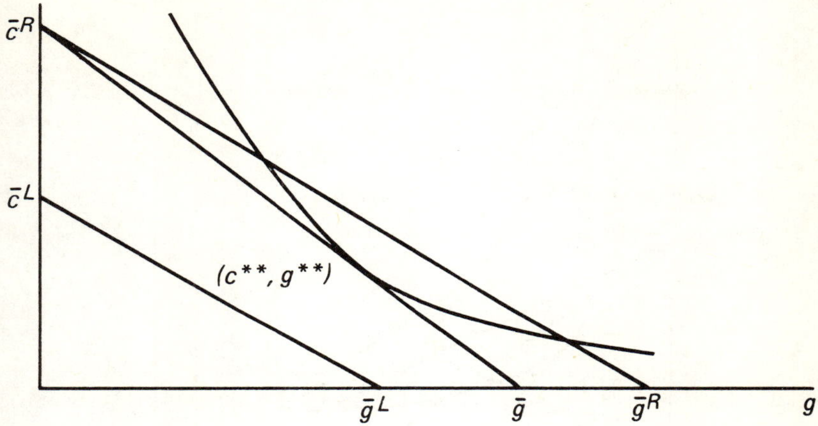

Fig. 12.16

but, where the rich are in the minority, several possibilities arise. Let $\{\tau^{L**}, g^{L**}\}$ be the tax rate of government expenditure that maximises U^L subject to $c + g \leqq \overline{W}$. Then, $U^R[(1-\tau^{L**})W^R, g^{L**}] \gtrless \widehat{U}^R$.

If the poor vote myopically and $U^R[(1-\tau^{L**})W^R, g^{L**}] < \widehat{U}^R$, then the rich observe that by forming their own community they can be better off, even if they have to restrict themselves to policies that exclude the poor. This is a case where the non-Pareto optimality of the equilibrium is clear: two communities are formed when a single merged community would be preferred by both groups. Note that, if votes were allocated in proportion to wealth, then, provided $W^R\lambda > (1-\lambda)W^L$, the equilibrium that emerges will be the one, described above, where the rich are in the majority; the poor will be no worse off and the rich will be better off. (See Fig. 12.17).

If the poor vote myopically and $U^R[(1-\tau^{L**})W^R, g^{L**}] > \widehat{U}^R$, there are three possibilities. Let $\{\tilde{\tau}, \tilde{g}\}$ be the solution to

$$\max U^R$$

subject to $\quad g = \tau W^R$

and $\quad U^L[(1-\tau)W^L, g] \leqq U^L[(1-\tau^{L**})W^L, g^{L**}]$

Then, if $\widetilde{U}^R \equiv U^R[(1-\tilde{\tau})W^R, \tilde{g}] < U^R[(1-\tau^{L**})W^R, g^{L**}]$, the equilibrium will consist of a single community. On the other hand, if $U^R[(1-\tilde{\tau})W^R, \tilde{g}] > U^R(1-\tau^{L**})W^R, g^{L**}]$ and the rich are myopic and noncollusive in their behaviour, then some of them will form a community consisting only of rich

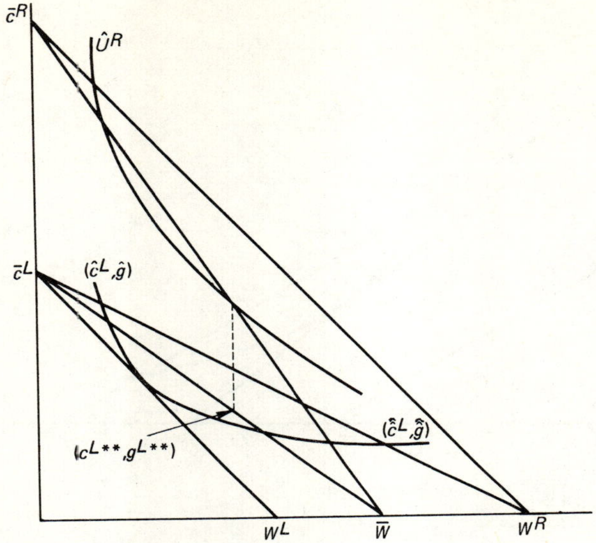

Fig. 12.17

individuals. (See Fig. 12.18). Since such a community is more attractive to the rich than the mixed community is, they leave the mixed community; but, when this happens, the poor all prefer to live in the rich community and the rich who have left the mixed community lose the advantage they originally

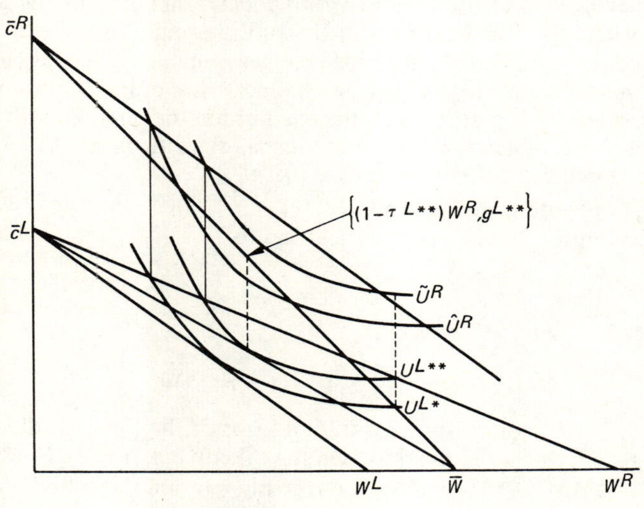

Fig. 12.18

sought in moving away. With both the poor and the rich voting myopically, there is no equilibrium.

The point of this is that, to any small group of rich people, there appear to be strong returns from forming a separate community with other rich individuals: they can evade the redistribution that living in a mixed community imposes on them. But the rich are worse off in the equilibrium where the rich and poor live in separate communities.

Finally, there is the possibility that the rich do not vote myopically and do act collusively; then the mixed community could be sustained.

If the poor do not vote myopically, they are aware that the rich might leave their community. If the rich are known not to act collusively, then the poor maximise U^L subject to $c + g \leqq \overline{W}$ and $U^R \geqq \widehat{U}^R$. Thus, by the veto power of emigration, the rich affect the equilibrium allocation.

So far, it has been assumed that the rich can either mix with the poor or attempt to exclude them, by choosing a level of public goods expenditure and taxation that they find unattractive. There is, however, a third possibility: the rich can give lump-sum subsidies to the poor. We now show that, if feasible, a lump-sum subsidy is preferable to forming a mixed community; and, even if it does not pay the two communities to merge, it may pay the richer community to give a subsidy to the poorer one.

The basic reason for the desirability of the lump-sum subsidy is the following. As noted earlier, in a mixed community the rich are implicity subsidising the poor, but it is an inefficient subsidy. In order to obtain the subsidy, the poor must accept a level of public goods that is different from the one they would have chosen. Figure 12.19 shows how a lump-sum subsidy could leave the poor on the same indifference curve but increase the utility of the rich.

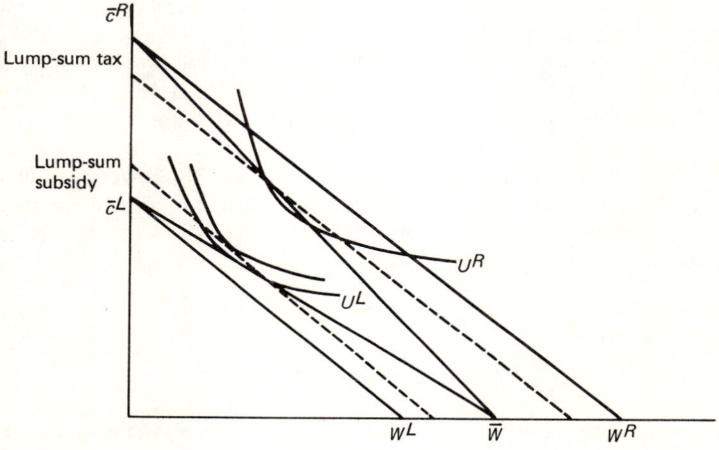

Fig. 12.19

Let $U^{L*}(a)$ be the solution to

$$\max U^L$$

subject to $$g + c = W^L + a$$

and let $\hat{U}^R(a)$ be the solution to

$$\max U^R$$

subject to $$g + c = W^R - \frac{a\lambda}{1+\lambda}$$

and $$U^L(c, g) \leqq U^{L*}(a)$$

Then, if

$$\max_a \hat{U}^R(a)$$

subject to $$0 \leqq a \leqq W^R - W^L$$

occurs at an interior value of a, the equilibrium will entail a subsidy, if this is feasible. If $\lambda/(1 + \lambda)$ is small, i.e. there are relatively few poor, this will always be the case.[28]

Zoning

Introducing the possibility of zoning means that an additional instrument for exclusion is now possible: the rich can exclude the poor not only by choosing a very high or a very low level of government expenditure, but also by requiring a high expenditure on housing.

If the equilibrium that emerged from the earlier analysis were one in which there were two separate communities, then with zoning there would still be two separate communities. The poor would be at the same level of utility as they were before, but, since the rich can avail themselves of less costly methods of exclusion, they would be better off. Thus, allowing zoning may be a Pareto improvement.

On the other hand, the equilibrium when zoning is not allowed may entail a single mixed community, while the equilibrium with zoning may entail two separate communities. In that case, allowing zoning increases the welfare of the rich but decreases that of the poor.

[28] We have not found any simple, more complete characterisation of the circumstances in which that will occur.

$$\left.\frac{d\hat{U}^R(a)}{da}\right|_{a=0} = \frac{-U_c^R\lambda}{1+\lambda} + \left(U_g^R - U_c^R\right)\frac{dg}{da}$$

The second term is positive: if $U_g^R > U_c^R$, an increase in the lump-sum subsidy allows an increase in g and exclusion still obtains. It can be shown that, $\lambda/(1 + \lambda)$ is sufficiently small, the second term dominates the first.

We shall now show that, if zoning is allowed and utility functions are additive, then zoning will, in fact, always be used as a method of exclusion.

We use h to denote expenditure on housing; o to denote expenditure on other goods; and g to denote expenditure on the publicly provided good. The utility functions are assumed additive:

$$U(h, o, g) = u_h(h) + u_o(o) + v(g) \tag{12.59}$$

(As before, we have chosen units so that the price of each of the goods is unity.)

First we consider the equilibrium with two separate communities, (assuming that such an equilibrium exists). The poorer community simply chooses g, h, and o to maximise U, subject to the budget constraint

$$g + h + o = W^L \tag{12.60}$$

Let U^{L*} be the resulting value of utility.

The wealthier community must choose a tax rate and a zoning restriction to maximise its utility while excluding the poorer individuals, i.e.

$$\max_{\{g,\, h^R\}} \; v(g) + u_h(h^R) + u_o(W^R - h^R - g) \tag{12.61}$$

subject to $\quad \tilde{u}^L \leqslant u^{L*}$

where $\tilde{u}^L$ is defined by

$$\tilde{u}^L \equiv \max v(g) + u_h(h^L) + u_o\left(W^L\left(1 - \frac{g}{W^R}\right) - h^L\right) \tag{12.62}$$

subject to $\quad h^L \geqq h^R$

Exclusion is guaranteed if

$$h^R \geqq \left(1 - \frac{g}{W^R}\right) W^L \tag{12.63}$$

and it immediately follows from (12.61) that the zoning restrictions (in this model) will be chosen to make living in the rich community infeasible for the poor.[29] Then g is chosen so as to maximise

$$v(g) + u_h\left[\left(1 - \frac{g}{W^R}\right) W^L\right] + u_o\left[\left(W^R - W^L\right)\left(1 - \frac{g}{W^R}\right)\right] \tag{12.64}$$

i.e. $$v' - u_o' = (u_h' - u_o')\frac{W^L}{W^R} \tag{12.65}$$

[29] If the wealth of the two communities differs greatly, then the unconstrained maximisation problem may entail

$$h^R \geqq \left(1 - \frac{g^R}{W^R}\right) W^L$$

in which case the equilibrium is identical to that with perfect exclusion, described earlier.

Thus, the richer community undertakes more housing and more government expenditure than it would in the absence of the poorer communities.

Whether this is an equilibrium depends on whether the level of utility attainable by the richer community could be increased by subsidising the poorer community; i.e. if the richer community transferred wealth per capita of a to the poorer community, the latter's level of utility would be $U^{*L}(W^L + a)$ and the level of utility attainable by the richer community would be given by the solution to[30]

$$\max v(g) + u_h\left[\left(1 - \frac{g + \frac{\lambda a}{1-\lambda}}{W^R}\right)W^L\right] + u_o\ (W^R - W^L)\left(1 - \frac{g + \frac{\lambda a}{1+\lambda}}{W^R}\right)$$

Since

$$\frac{dU^{R*}(a)}{da} = \frac{-\lambda}{1+\lambda}\left[u_o' \frac{(W^R - W^L)}{W^R} + \frac{u_h' W^L}{W^R}\right] < 0$$

it never pays to give a direct subsidy. (This result should be contrasted with that obtained in the previous subsection, in the case where there is no zoning. There it was found that such subsidies are often desirable.)

If a subsidy is to occur, it must be 'indirect', through merging the two communities; i.e. we must compare the solution to (12.64) with the value of utility attained by the upper group in a merged community. If the poor are in a majority and are myopic (i.e. ignore the possibility of the rich leaving their community) they would maximise

$$v(\tau\overline{W}) + u_h(h) + u_o[W^L(1-\tau) - h] \tag{12.66}$$

i.e.

$$v' = u_o' \frac{W^L}{\overline{W}} \tag{12.66a}$$

and

$$v_h' = u_o' \tag{12.66b}$$

This may entail either a higher or lower level of per capita government expenditure than the rich would vote for; the poor pay less than their proportionate share of costs ($W^L/\overline{W} < 1$), but have a higher marginal utility of private goods. Let τ^{**} be the solution to (12.66). Then we must compare $U^{R**} \equiv v(\tau^{**}\overline{W}) + \max\{u_h(h) + u_o[W^R(1-\tau^{**}) - h]\}$ with the solution to (12.64), which we denote by $\hat{U}^R$. If $\hat{U}^R$ is larger, there is a single community; otherwise there are two.

An example may be illuminating. Let it be assumed that

$$U = \alpha_1 \ln g + \alpha_2 \ln h + (1 - \alpha_1 - \alpha_2) \ln o$$

[30] Implicitly, this formulation assumes that the subsidy is financed by proportional taxation of those living in the rich community and is paid only to those living in the poor one.

Then (12.65) implies that

$$\frac{(1-\alpha_1-\alpha_2)W^R}{(W^R-W^L)(1-\tau)} - \frac{\alpha_1}{\tau} = \frac{W^L(1-\alpha_1-\alpha_2)}{(W^R-W^L)(1-\tau)} - \frac{\alpha_2}{1-\tau}$$

or that $\alpha_1 = \tau$

so that $$\hat{U}^R = \alpha_1 \ln \alpha_1 + \alpha_2 \ln (1-\alpha_1) + (1-\alpha_1-\alpha_2) \ln (1-\alpha_1) + \alpha_1 \ln W^R + \alpha_2 \ln W^L + (1-\alpha_1-\alpha_2) \ln (W^R - W^L)$$

This must be compared with[31]

$$U^{R**} = \alpha_1 \ln \alpha_1 + \alpha_2 \ln \alpha_2 + (1-\alpha_1-\alpha_2) \ln (1-\alpha_1-\alpha_2) + \alpha_1 \ln \overline{W} + (1-\alpha_1) \ln W^R$$

Thus, letting α_3 equal $1-\alpha_1-\alpha_2$,

$$\hat{U}^R - U^{R**} = \alpha_2 [\ln (\alpha_2 + \alpha_3/\alpha_2)] + (1-\alpha_1-\alpha_2)[\ln (\alpha_2+\alpha_3)/\alpha_3] + \alpha_1 \ln W^R/\overline{W} + \alpha_2 \ln W^L/W^R + \alpha_3 \ln (W^R - W^L)/W^R$$

Note that (a),

as $$W^R \to W^L$$
$$\hat{U}^R - U^{R**} \to -\infty$$

i.e. it always pays to merge; and (b),

if $$\frac{W^L}{W^R} \to 0$$

then $$\frac{W^R}{\overline{W}} \to \frac{1}{\lambda}, \frac{W^R - W^L}{W^R} \to 1, \text{ and } \hat{U}^{R*} - U^{R**} \to -\infty$$

i.e. it always pays to merge; and (c)

$$\frac{d\hat{U}^R - U^{R**}}{d\lambda} = -\frac{\alpha_1 W^R}{\overline{W}} < 0$$

Hence, for every value of (W^L, W^R) there exists a critical value of λ, λ^*, such that, for $\lambda < \lambda^*$, it does not pay to merge; for $\lambda > \lambda^*$ it does.

Thus, *it pays to merge if the rich are much richer than the poor, if the rich and the poor are not much different, and if there are relatively few poor.*

This subsection and the previous one have considered two methods of exclusion: an attractive fiscal package and zoning. There are, of course, numerous other exclusionary devices, imposing varying costs on the rich and the poor. For instance, a school may be located in a neighbourhood that is not easily

[31] The tax rate in the merged community will, in fact, be unanimously agreed upon as α_1.

accessible by public transportation; or a school may develop programmes that make it more attractive to one group than to the other. The important point to observe is that eliminating the more direct exclusionary devices (such as zoning) may not eliminate exclusionary practices; to achieve 'mixing' may require more direct intervention.

Many islands

So far, we have couched our analysis in terms of two isolated islands (or communities), the one inhabited by the rich and the other by the poor, but with free migration between them. We now wish to consider what difference it makes if there is a large number of islands.

(a) If an equilibrium exists in which poor and rich live in communities together, then the equilibrium must be at the point that maximises the utility of the rich. Otherwise, the rich can choose a level of public services and taxes that attracts them but does not attract the poor – at least, not in the proportion that it previously did.[32] Thus, in Fig. 12.20, g^{**} may be considered an

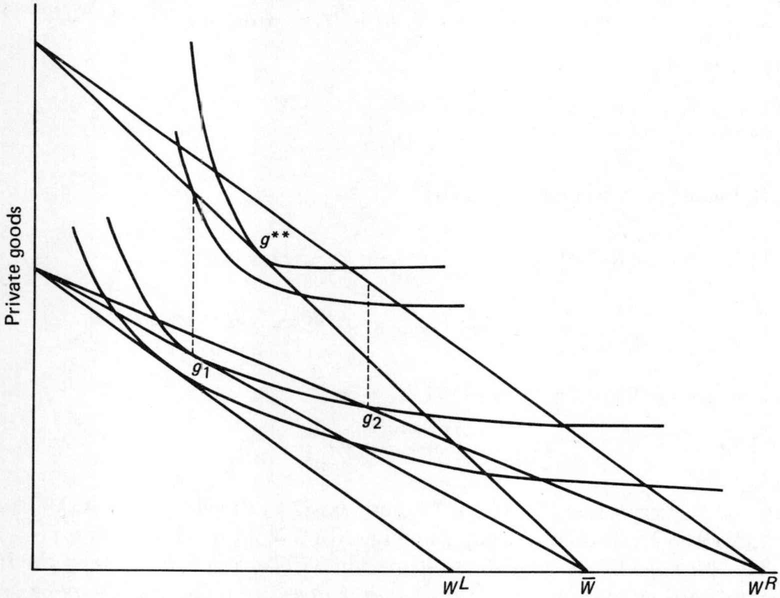

Fig. 12.20

[32] That is, for any level of g, as the ratio of poor to rich increases, the utility of both the poor and the rich decreases. Consider Fig. 12.20. Assume, initially, that all communities are identical and provide public goods at level g_1. If there are only two potential islands, g_1 will be an equilibrium. Note, however, that, if the rich form a community in which they are in the majority, they may choose a level of public goods g_2 and a tax rate that would make the poor indifferent to migrating; alternatively, the poor may 'bid' for the rich, thereby lowering their taxes.

equilibrium. There is no variation in g that will not inundate the community with poor *and* raise the level of utility of the rich.

(b) If an equilibrium exists, it cannot involve the kinds of lump-sum subsidies discussed above, for it would be in the interests of each rich community not to give the subsidies. A federal authority that could compel transfer of the desired sort may be a Pareto improvement.

(c) There may exist no equilibrium. With many communities it is reasonable for the rich to take as given the utility of the poor; and, if the indifference curves are as in Fig. 12.18, there will exist no equilibrium. If an equilibrium does exist, then, clearly, all the rich must have the same utility, and all the poor must have the same utility. Thus, if an equilibrium exists, it consists either of two kinds of communities or of one kind of community; in the latter case, the ratio of poor to rich in each community must be that of the population as a whole. But, in Fig. 12.18 there clearly exists no 'mixed' community equilibrium, for it would then pay the rich to isolate themselves; and there exists no two-community equilibrium, for it does not then pay any rich community to attempt to keep out the poor.

Pure public goods

The analysis for pure public goods follows very much the same course. For simplicity, consider the case with a single private good. Then the merged communities' possibility curve actually lies above the nonmerged possibility curve for both communities for high levels of g. On the other hand, it is possible, as depicted in Fig. 12.21, for the vote of the poor to entail so much (or so little) public expenditure as to make the rich individuals prefer living in their own community. If the poor voters behave in a sophisticated manner,

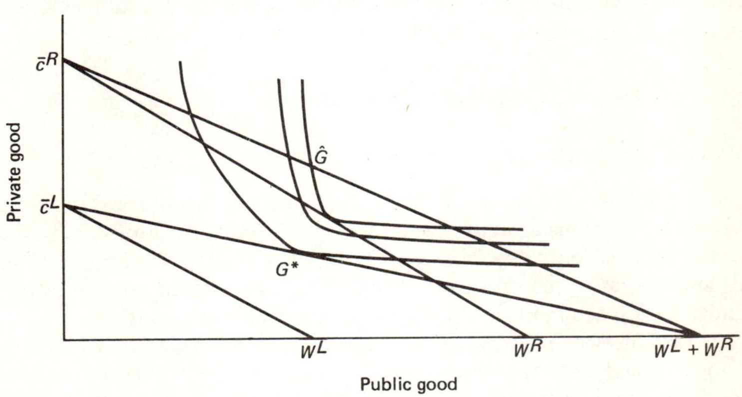

G^*: level of G voted by naîve poor voters
$\hat{G}$: level of G voted by 'sophisticated' poor voters

Fig. 12.21

the equilibrium will entail the level of public expenditure that just makes the rich individuals indifferent about whether they remain in the merged community or opt out. The rich exert a kind of 'veto' power.

Figure 12.22 illustrates the possibility, where there are large differences in tastes, that even the poor would prefer to form separate communities were

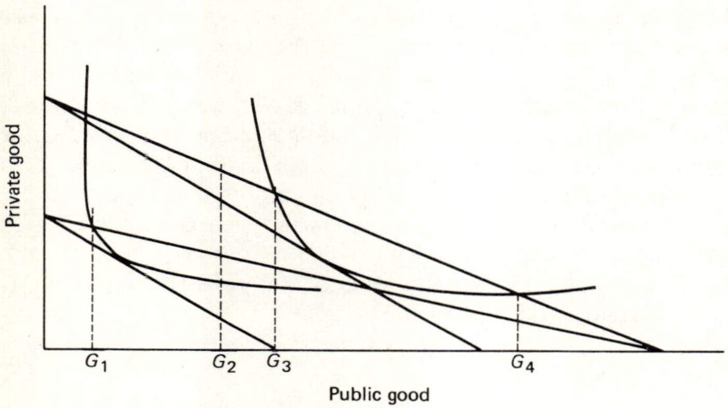

Between G_1 and G_2, poor prefer merged community

Between G_3 and G_4, rich prefer merged community

Fig. 12.22

they in the minority. Obviously, in that case, differential taxation of the two groups could result in a Pareto-optimal improvement; this would generally entail a lower tax rate on the rich than on the poor.

V. ISLAND AND INDIVIDUALS DIFFER

V.1 LAND VALUES AND PUBLIC GOODS

One of the extensively discussed topics in the economics of local public goods concerns the 'capitalisation' of public services: if one community supplies a greater number of public goods, or, at least, a more desirable bundle of public goods and tax rates, than does another community, should not the differences be capitalised in the land (house) values in the two communities?

There are obvious problems in attempting to verify whether such capitalisation does, in fact, occur. One needs to separate out the differences in land value arising from other sources (for instance, locational advantages) from those arising simply from the public policy. Moreover, it is not just the level of public expenditures that is capitalised, but the total 'public policy', and there is no immediate way of quantifying this.

From the theoretical point of view, there is a more fundamental problem with analysing capitalisation within an equilibrium model in which individuals are identical and communities differ only with respect to their public policies. For, if the value of land in the two communities were to differ, a 'smart' developer would buy the land, form a community, announce a new public policy and make a pure capital gain (as we noticed in our earlier discussions). Thus, in the long run, capitalisation would be unobservable.

However, individuals are not identical and this has one important implication. The value of land is determined so as to make the marginal individual indifferent about which of the two communities he lives in, but the inframarginal individuals are not indifferent. Thus, a land developer would find, as he attempted to purchase more and more of the land of a given community, that he would have to pay higher and higher prices. Thus, even if the market value of the land of two otherwise identical islands differed, if the public goods offered on the two islands also differed and the individuals believed that those differences would persist, the inframarginal individuals would require higher compensation to sell their land. In short, the amount required to take over a community is greater than the market value of the land.

Moreover, even if, in the long run, the 'capitalisation effect' disappeared, as the relative size of different communities adjusted, there is little doubt that public policy would affect land values in the short run.

In the subsequent analysis it will be assumed that voters are aware of these effects when deciding which public policy the community should pursue. The result, as we shall now show, is that the equilibrium is likely not to be Pareto-optimal.

We begin our analysis with the simplest possible model: there are two islands, and these differ in their production-possibilities schedule. Island A has a comparative advantage in transforming private goods, while island B has a comparative advantage in public goods. We assume, moreover, that individuals can move only at the beginning of their life, and that it is prohibitively expensive to transport public goods.

Everyone has the same endowment of the factor L; although individuals differ in their relative evaluation of public and private goods, the public authorities have no way of distinguishing among individuals and, hence, finance all public expenditures with a uniform lump-sum tax. Everyone requires a fixed-size plot of land to live on; and the population is equally divided between the two islands.[33]

Each individual lives for only two periods. During the first period, the public good is relatively important; during the second, the private good is. For simplicity, we take the extreme case where the individual receives utility from public goods in both periods and from the private good only in the second. There is a perfect capital market with equilibrium interest rate r^*. Finally, the technology of public goods production involves a one-period gestation, so that

[33] These assumptions are made to capture the 'short-run' nature of the adjustments.

the level of public goods enjoyed today depends on the expenditure on public goods in the previous period.

Clearly, equilibrium will entail that all those with higher preferences for public goods live on the island with a comparative advantage for public goods. The individual who least prefers living on, say, island B must be just indifferent to moving.[34] Let the supply of public goods be G_1^A in the first period and G_2^A in the second (and similarly for island B). The utility functions are of the form

$$v(G_1) + v(G_2) + u(c)\alpha \tag{12.67}$$

(where α will differ across individuals). The production possibilities schedules on the two island are of the form

$$2G^A + c^A N = LN \tag{12.68}$$

for island A, and

$$G^B + 2c^B N = LN \tag{12.69}$$

for island B. Then, in equilibrium, for the marginal individual $\tilde{\alpha}$,

$$\begin{aligned} &v(G_1^A) + v(G_2^A) + u\left[\left(L - \frac{2G^A}{N} - V_A\right)(1+r) + V_A\right]\tilde{\alpha} \\ &= v(G_1^B) + v(G_2^B) + u\left[\left(\frac{L}{2} - \frac{G^B}{2N} - V_B\right)(1+r) + V_B\right]\tilde{\alpha} \end{aligned} \tag{12.70}$$

where V_i is the value of a plot of land on island i. In deciding on the level of public expenditure, the median voter in each community is concerned not only with the utility that he receives from the public goods, but also with the effect of the public policy on what he can get if he sells his plot of land. Thus, the median voter in A, whose $\alpha = \hat{\alpha}^A$, chooses G_A so that

$$\left(\frac{dV_A}{dG_A} - \frac{2(1+r)}{N}\right) = \frac{V'(G^A)}{u'\hat{\alpha}^A} \tag{12.71}$$

Likewise, for the median voter in B,

$$\left(\frac{dV_B}{dG_B} - \frac{(1+r)}{2N}\right) = \frac{V'(G^B)}{u'\hat{\alpha}^B} \tag{12.72}$$

Note that, if individuals, say in A, do not value public goods in the second period, even though voters have different preferences, they agree that $dV_A/dG_A = 2(1+r)/N$ gives the appropriate rule to follow. But note that the equilibrium market values are determined not by the median, but by the marginal, individual, who is just indifferent about moving. On the other hand, given our assumptions, the marginal individual cannot move: each of the islands must have just half of the population. Thus, equilibrium is consistent with one of

[34] For simplicity, we assume that each individual pays taxes and votes only the first period of his life.

the two islands having a zero valuation. For that island, the determination of the level of public goods is the same as in the conventional analysis. Assume that the island with a positive value is B, the island with the comparative advantage in public goods. Then, lowering the level of public expenditure from the level that would be desired by the median voter, were he to ignore valuation effects, would increase the desirability of the island from the point of view of the marginal individual in A. Thus, the market value of B would increase. Clearly, the market-valuation effect induces the island with a comparative advantage in public goods to reduce its expenditure from what it would otherwise have been (just as, if $V_B = 0$ and $V_A > 0$, the effect would be to increase the expenditure on public goods in the island with a comparative advantage in private goods).

To see that this may not be Pareto optimal, consider the case where the populations on each island are homogeneous, and assume that each island starts with the supply of public goods that maximises the steady-state utility, i.e.

$$v'^A + \frac{\alpha^A u'(1+r)}{N} = 0 \tag{12.73a}$$

and

$$4v'^B + \frac{\alpha^B u'(1+r)}{N} = 0 \tag{12.73b}$$

There would then be an incentive, on island B, for the next generation to lower the supply of public goods, and the reverse on island A; in effect, by getting the individuals from the other island to bid up the price, there is an intertemporal transfer from the next generation to the present one. But this is an inefficient transfer. Everyone could be made better off by having a direct transfer and choosing some other level of expenditure for public goods. For instance, assume that it is the island with a comparative advantage in private goods that has a positive valuation; in the new equilibrium, it is spending too much on public goods. If each generation could commit itself to buying land from its grandparents at the same price as they had paid, and, if government expenditures were lowered to the value satisfying (12.73), then every generation would be better off.

V.2 MATCHING OF COMMUNITIES WITH INDIVIDUALS

When island and individuals differ, there is a problem, similar to that discussed above in section IV.2, of matching islands and people. The market equilibrium may not be Pareto optimal.

Assume that there are two islands. One of them has a comparative advantage in the provision of public good G_1 (say, swimming, since the island's shores are sandy beaches) while the other has a comparative advantage in G_2 (say, skiing, since there are mountains on the island). Some individuals have a relatively high preference for G_1, others for G_2. For simplicity, assume that there are only two groups, and that the number in each group equals N^*, the optimal number of individuals on an island. Also, for the moment, assume that the first group have no desire for G_2, and that the second group have no desire for G_1. It is clear, then, that each island will provide, in equilibrium, only one public good. The problem is that there are two equilibria, in one of which the island with the comparative advantage in G_1 produces G_2, and conversely. This equilibrium is Pareto inferior to the equilibrium in which each island produces the good for which it has a comparative advantage. For, given the selection of public goods that is produced, no individual has an incentive to move, and the public goods produced in each island are (both in amount and in type) the ones unanimously preferred by those living on the island.

This problem can arise under much weaker conditions. In Fig. 12.23, we

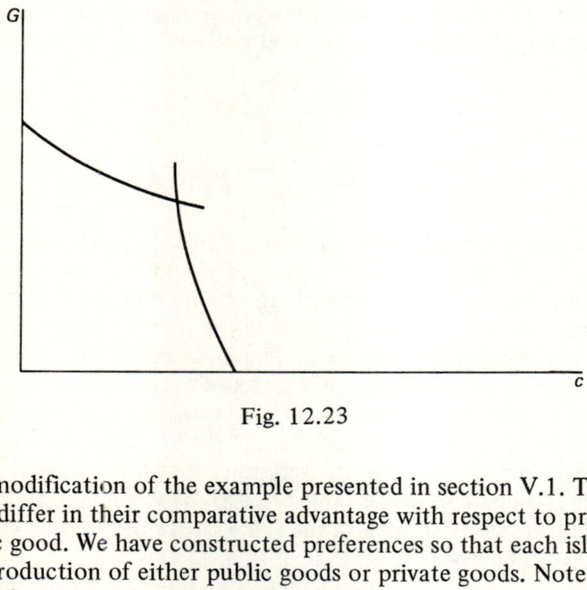

Fig. 12.23

illustrate a modification of the example presented in section V.1. There, the two islands differ in their comparative advantage with respect to producing the single public good. We have constructed preferences so that each island specialises in the production of either public goods or private goods. Note that it is possible for the wrong island to specialise in the production of public goods.

This model has certain similarities to – and some important differences from – the stock-market models analysed by Stiglitz (1972a, b) and Dreze. They both involve a mixture of a political model with an economic model: in the absence of a full set of Arrow Debreu securities, the shareholders generally will not be unanimous about what the correct course for the firm would be. As a consequence, the decision about what production plan should be pursued must be resolved by a political mechanism. However, who the voters in any 'community' are is decided, by an economic mechanism: in the case of local public goods, by migration; in the case of the stock market, by choosing a portfolio. The decision about what production plan should be pursued involves direct consumption and valuation effects – just as with the local public-goods model presented in section V.1.

There are, however, some important differences. First, it is natural to assume that the individual lives in only one community, but there is a natural presumption that individuals mix their portfolios. Second, if firms do not maximise their stock-market value, there is always the possibility of a takeover. For much of the earlier part of this discussion, the role of the 'developer' was portrayed in much the same way; yet there can be little doubt that, in practice, developers are far less important within local public goods than are takeovers within the stock market. (One reason for this may be that, whereas individuals have the right to sell their vote on the stock market, in local communities this action is frowned upon.) Finally, prices play a less natural role in local public goods than they do in the stock market. In the stock market, if we had two firms and two states of nature, we should have a Pareto-optimal situation. Since public goods cannot be bought and sold by individuals, the fact that the marginal rate of transformation between public and private goods on one island differs from that on another does not imply that there are 'pure profits' to be made by arbitrage.

VI. CONCLUDING COMMENTS

Though both perspicacious and suggestive, Tiebout's argument that the local provision of public goods resolves the problem of revealing preferences for public goods is clearly incorrect. For true public goods, without strong congestion effects, efficient size groupings will entail sufficient diversity within the community for the problem of preference revelation to remain.

The analysis presented in this paper has shown that the economics of local public goods entails a number of problems not encountered in the analysis of public goods in a 'closed' economy. These problems are as follows.

(1) *Existence.* One of the sources of interest in local public goods involves the problem of the appropriate equilibrium notion. In this paper several alternative notions have been investigated. In four cases, we encountered problems of nonexistence: (i) with a homogeneous population that exceeds the efficient size for two islands when there are 'land developers'; (ii) where there are preference matching problems; (iii) where the majority of voters act myopically; and (iv) where the poor attempt to join communities of the rich, and the rich attempt to form communities without the poor. The first existence problem disappears when there is a large number of islands – which, by contrast, is when the fourth problem appears. The third disappears when voters do not act myopically and do take into account migration behaviour.

(2) *Inefficiency.* Six sources of inefficiency were delineated: (i) in the number of islands inhabited; (ii) in the allocation of individuals between islands of different size (productivity); (iii) in the matching of individuals who have different tastes; (iv) in circumstances where the rich attempt to escape from the poor and the poor attempt to attract the rich (by altering the level of

expenditure on public goods; and, where there are zoning requirements, by purchasing a different type of housing from that that they would normally purchase were direct restrictions on migration available); (v) in choosing a public policy on the basis of its effect on land values, as well as its effect on direct consumption; and (vi) in matching individuals with islands (communities).

(3) *Public policy implications.* At a number of points attention has been drawn to the public policy implications of these inefficiencies. In particular, some of the inefficiencies may be alleviated by a federal authority requiring that one of the communities (one of the groups of individuals) transfer payments to the other. Such transfers have been shown to be Pareto improvements when the source of the inefficiency is the allocation of individuals between islands of different productivity, and, in some cases, when the source of the inefficiency is the attempt of the rich to separate themselves from the poor.

In some cases where the source of the inefficiency is the rich attempting to separate themselves from the poor, direct wealth tests for settling in a community may be a Pareto improvement. In cases where zoning requirements are effective, the elimination of tests may lead to a Pareto-inferior equilibrium.

Nationalisation of the land, with the government competitively renting it out, would eliminate the inefficiency resulting from individuals worrying about the effect of policy on market valuation; but, in a broader context, it probably would introduce far more problems than it would resolve. The 'land developers' were the source of the nonexistence problem encountered in section II.1; but, on the other hand, they ensured the optimality of the equilibrium where one existed.

For the other sources of inefficiency, there appears to be no simple remedy.

Even when the equilibrium is not inefficient, it may not maximise social welfare; in particular, social welfare maximisation was shown to entail inequality unless the social welfare function maximised the welfare of the worst-off individuals.

REFERENCES

Buchanan, J. M., and Goetz, C., 'Efficiency Limits of Fiscal Mobility: An Assessment of the Tiebout Model', *Journal of Public Economics,* I (Mar 1972), pp. 25–45.

Dreze, J., 'Investment under Private Ownership; Optimality, Equilibrium, and Stability', CORE Discussion Paper.

Flatters, Frank, Henderson V., and Mieszkowski P., 'Public Goods, Efficiency, and Regional Fiscal Equalization', *Journal of Public Economics,* 1974.

Hotelling, H., 'Stability in Competition', *Economics Journal,* XXXIX (Mar 1929), pp. 41–57.

McGuire, M. C., 'Private Good Clubs and Public Good Clubs', *Swedish Journal of Economics,* 1972.

Mirrlees, J., 'The Optimum Town', *Swedish Journal of Economics,* 1972.

Oates, W. E., *Fiscal Federalism* (New York: Harcourt, Brace, Jovanovich, 1972).

Pauly, M. V., 'Optimality, "Public Goods", and Local Governments: A General Theoretical Analysis', *Journal of Political Economy,* LXXVIII, no. 3 (May/June 1970), pp. 572.

Pauly, M. V., 'Cores and Clubs', *Public Choice,* IX (Fall, 1970), pp. 53–65.

Polinsky, A. M., 'Collective Consumption Goods and Local Public Finance Theory: A Suggested Analytic Framework', in *Issues in Urban Public Finance,* papers and proceedings of the 28th Conference of the International Institute of Public Finance (Saarbrucken, Sep 1973), pp. 166–81.

Stern, N., 'The Optimal Size of Market Areas', *Journal of Economic Theory,* IV, no. 2 (Apr 1972).

Stiglitz, J., 'On the Optimality of the Stock Market Allocation of Investment', *Quarterly Journal of Economics,* LXXXVI (Feb 1972), pp. 25–60.

Stiglitz, J., 'Some Aspects of the Pure Theory of Corporate Finance: Bankruptcies and Take-overs', *Bell Journal of Economics and Management Science,* 1972, pp. 458–82.

Stiglitz, J., 'Education and Inequality', *Annals of the American Academy of Political and Social Sciences,* Sep 1973.

Stiglitz, J., 'Incentives, Risk, and Information: Notes Toward a Theory of Hierarchy', paper presented to the Berlin Symposium on Planning, 1973.

Stiglitz, J., 'Demand for Education in Public and Private School Systems', *Journal of Public Economics*, III (1974), pp. 349–85.

Stiglitz, J., 'The Efficiency Wage Hypothesis, Surplus Labor, and the Distribution of Income in L.D.C.s', *Oxford Economic Papers,* 1974.

Tiebout, C. M., 'A Pure Theory of Local Expenditures', *Journal of Political Economy,* LXIV (Oct 1956), pp. 416–24.

13 The City as a Firm

William Vickrey
COLUMBIA UNIVERSITY

A simplified model is produced to illustrate the proposition that, where efficiently operating cities compete on a world market, land rents representing the social opportunity costs of land occupancy will in each city aggregate to the sum of the intramarginal residues that reflect the economies of scale of the activities the existence of which within the city account for its optimal size being as large as it is. Full efficiency thus requires that all such land rents be devoted to the subsidy of these decreasing-cost industries, and the appropriation of these rents by landlords for other purposes precludes the achievement of full efficiency. Where such appropriation precludes efficiency elsewhere, and world prices are thus not at the efficiency level, it will be to the general long-run advantage of landlords in a particular city, as well as to locally constrained labour, for rents to be used for such subsidy, even though initially they may be inadequate to do the full job.

I. INTRODUCTION

The purpose of this paper is to develop a rigorously optimisable model of a city, incorporating in this model two elements that seem to be vital to the development of large modern cities: transportation costs and economies of scale in the activities carried on within the city. If there were no transportation costs, so that goods and persons could be moved anywhere instantly and at no cost, and if there were no positive neighbourhood effects, then activity could be indiscriminately scattered over the landscape instead of being concentrated in large urban complexes. Again, if there were no economies of scale, so that each activity could be carried on efficiently on as minute a scale as would be desired, activity could be organised in hamlets or small towns, each with a suitable complex of activities carried out on a small scale, with no need for the costly infrastructure characteristic of our large cities. Some degree of concentration into small cities might be accounted for by positive neighbourhood effects of the kind that involves direct influence not mediated through a market transaction. The forces that bring our large cities into being are, however, predominantly those mediated through the purchase and sale of goods and services, so that the important positive externalities are of the market type, involving, in general, substantial economies of scale in at least some of the activities involved. Again, while some cities owe their location to an economically important natural feature of their site, such as a harbour or a mineral deposit, the size of the city that would coalesce around such a natural feature would, in the absence of economies of scale, be far smaller than those we actually observe.

The existence of economies of scale within the activities involved immediately precludes an analysis based on perfect competition. On the other hand, none of the manifold models of imperfect competition readily lends itself to incorporation in a precise model; and all of these models lack the optimising properties that are being sought here. We shall, therefore, examine the problem of the optimal organisation of a city in terms of some form of overall management structure, in effect regarding the city as a firm attempting to maximise some objective function. Even so, the inherent complexity of the situation dictates that, on the one hand, we keep the model stripped down to its barest essentials, and, on the other, that even then we stop somewhat short of full rigour of analysis, relying to a considerable extent on heuristics derived from classical models of perfect competition, or, perhaps, of a type of decentralised management derived from the analyses of Walras, Lange and Lerner.

II. LITTORAL CITY

To construct a model stripped of all but the barest essentials while still retaining the essential elements of transportation cost and economies of scale, we consider a city laid out on a strip of land of uniform width along a shore. This strip will be considered to be long enough to contain all the activities to be carried out in the city, while leaving a vacant margin at either end, yet not long enough to enable a second city to be established on the adjacent portion of the strip. The sections of the strip not occupied by the city have no alternative use, while the land, if any, behind the strip is unusable for any purpose. Imports from, and exports to, other cities can be landed or loaded indifferently at any point along the strip at a uniform, delivered or free-on-board price, while coastal ('intra-city') transportation is handled at a constant cost per mile per unit of output of the *i*th commodity, t_i.

The character of the city is determined by the selection of a set of n activities to be carried on within the city, designated $i = 1, \ldots, n$. The level at which each activity is carried on is defined in terms of the volume of its single output, q_i. Economies of scale are represented by the fact that each activity requires a fixed quantum of imports f_i, measured in terms of aggregate delivered cost, in addition to a variable quantum of imports $m_i q_i$ proportional to the output q_i. The fixed element f_i is assumed to be large enough to assure that it will be nonoptimal to establish a second unit of activity i within the city. The extra fixed cost of setting up a second establishment would outweigh any saving that might be made in transportation costs within the city if a second and, possibly, closer source of supply for some users were provided. Each activity further requires the occupancy of $a_i q_i$ units of land, which, if the width of the strip is taken as unity, also implies the occupancy of a frontage equal to a_iq_i. In addition, each activity i may require as inputs amounts of the outputs of other activities, j, given by $b_{ji}q_i$. Inputs must be transported to, and outputs must be available at, the midpoint of the stretch of coastline occupied by each activity. The complication of the transportation cost of the inputs to the transportation process is avoided by stipulating that all of these inputs be imported. Finally, some or all of the output of an activity q_i may be exported at a net realisation of x_ip_i, x_i being the amount exported and p_i the net price.

The optimisation problem may be defined as one of maximising

$$S = \sum p_i x_i - \sum f_i - \sum m_i q_i - T \tag{13.1}$$

where

$$T = \sum_i \sum_j (t_i\, d_{ij}\, b_{ij}\, q_j) \tag{13.2}$$

is the total transportation cost, and

$$d_{ij} = (a_i q_i + a_j q_j)/2 + \sum_{s_i \lessgtr s_k \lessgtr s_j} (a_k q_k) \qquad i \neq j,\ d_{ii} = 0 \tag{13.3}$$

is the distance between the centre of activity i and the centre of activity j, with s_i representing the sequence order of the ith activity along the strip, subject to

$$x_i + \sum_j b_{ij} q_j \leqslant q_i \qquad q_i > 0,\ x_i \geqslant 0 \tag{13.4}$$

$s_1, s_2, \ldots, s_n$ is a permutation of $1, 2, \ldots, n$.

Mathematically, the solution of this problem for any given permutation of the activities along the strip is a fairly straightforward quadratic programming problem. Determining which of the permutations is the optimal one presents more of a problem, although, since the number of permutations is finite, the problem is, in mathematical principle, solvable, even though carrying out a solution by examining all permutations would very rapidly become infeasible for any large number of activities. The problem of developing an algorithm that would shorten the process is an interesting one, but is not the main concern here. In any case, sufficiently close results could probably be obtained by testing interchanges of each pair of adjacent activities, performing the interchange where an improvement is noted, and proceeding until further interchanges show no gain. If, when this stage is reached, further tests are made for the interchange of any two nonadjacent activities, and, then, possibly for the removal of an activity from one place in the order to another, one might be fairly confident of being close to the optimum; but, unless some rather difficult theorem to this effect can be demonstrated, one could not be absolutely sure of a full optimum.

III. DECENTRALISED SOLUTION

For the present, more interest attaches to a solution by *tâtonnements* along the lines of a Lange–Lerner decentralised socialist state, in which each activity is in the hands of a manager instructed to behave in a pseudo-competitive manner, and in which the role of the city manager is limited to the determination of the sequence in which the activities will be located and of the rents that the activities will be required to pay for the space they occupy. Rents will be set equal to the marginal social cost of land occupancy, which in this case consists of the increase in transportation costs involved in the occupancy of more land. Indeed, if a given activity manager wishes to occupy more land, the consequence will be that all traffic that formerly traversed his frontage will now have to go that much further, assuming that, in effect, all facilities used by an activity can be freely shifted along the strip. The land rent of each activity will then be equal to the cost of the transportation carried out in front of the area that it occupies, and total transportation costs will be equal to total land rents. (This compares with the more familiar result for the two-dimensional case that transportation costs are twice land rents). Determination of the proper sequence for the activities is a less automatic process, but we shall assume that by some means it is satisfactorily accomplished. Starting from some arbitrary set of prices, rents, land-occupancy levels and output levels, each manager will determine his own marginal cost on the basis of these prices, rents, and the costs of transportation over the distances indicated by the intervening levels of land occupancy; add to his output for export if this cost is below the world price; determine his demand for the outputs of other activities; and report the results. These are fed into a second round, in which each manager aggregates the demands made by other managers, so as to determine his own level of output for domestic consumption; adds, where appropriate, an amount for export, to get his new level of output; and recomputes his marginal cost. This is repeated until an equilibrium is reached in which the price of each output is equal to its marginal cost, and is either equal to the world price (where the item is being exported) or equal to or greater than the world price (where it is not being exported). The city manager can then test whether an interchange is desirable by examining the total per-mile freight costs of the items of input into two adjacent activities, i and j. If the costs for the inputs that are brought to i past j and to j past i are more than half of the total per-mile freight costs of all inputs to these activities (other than between i and j), the exchange should be made, but otherwise it should not.

IV. COMPETITION BETWEEN CITIES

Although not all cities are of the same type (i.e. carry on the same mix of activities), it would seem reasonable to assume that there is a sufficiently large number of cities of each type, equally advantageously located with respect to world markets, and with no lack of additional vacant strips of land on which other cities might be established, to allow us to subject the city to the analysis developed for the firm in perfect competition. If, for simplicity, we assume that each city type exports only one commodity, we can represent the situation as in Fig. 13.1, in which the volume of the exported commodity is on the

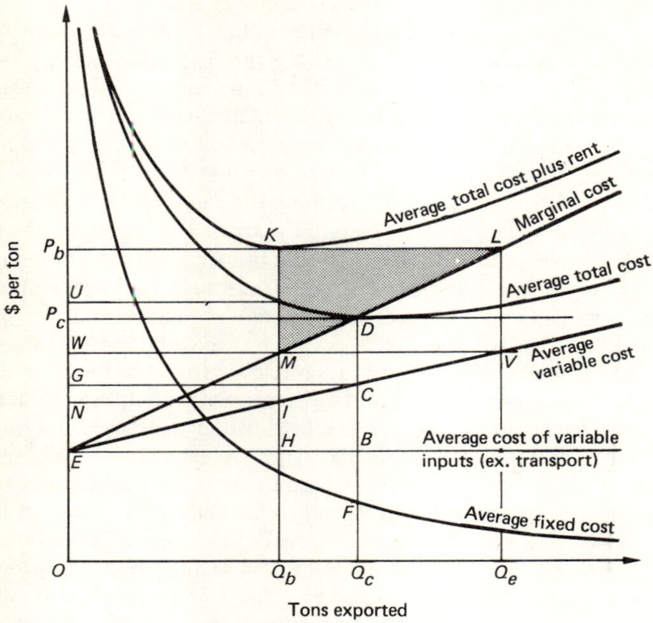

Fig. 13.1

horizontal axis and costs per unit are measured vertically. The total average cost is made up of three components, corresponding to the last three terms of equation (13.1). We have, first, the constant variable cost other than transportation, represented by $\Sigma\, m_i q_i$ in the equation and shown as *OE* in Fig. 13.1, and the horizontal line *EHB*.

The transportation-cost term, *T*, is homogeneous of second degree in the q_i, so that the average transportation cost is proportional to the level of activity and to the level of export x_1, and can be represented by the difference between the straight lines *EHB* and *EICV*. *EICV* is then the average variable cost including transportation. The corresponding marginal cost is *EMDL*, with $BC = CD$, and so on. The fixed-cost term yields the equilaterial hyperbola through *F* as the average fixed cost. When added to the average variable cost, this yields the average total cost curve *JD*, intersecting the marginal-cost curve at its minimum point, *D*.

Then, if we have an unlimited number of cities of each type, with free entry for new cities and perfect competition operating among the various cities, equilibrium should establish itself with the price of the exported commodity settling down to the level P_c relative to the cost structure, with price equal to marginal cost equal to average cost, from the standpoint of the city as a whole. However, from the standpoint of the individual firm within the city, the picture will look slightly different. The price that it will be quoting (calculated at marginal cost, other prices being considered fixed) will cover the delivered cost of the variable inputs plus the rental charged for the land it occupies, but will not cover the fixed costs, f_i. For this the firm will need a subsidy from the city manager. For any individual activity, there need not be a relation between the amount of land rent paid to the city manager and the amount of the subsidy needed to cover the fixed costs.

However, for the city as a whole, rents will just balance the subsidy, as can be seen from Fig. 13.1, where the transportation costs given by the rectangle *EBCG* are equal to the fixed costs represented by *GCDU,* by virtue of the fact that $BC = CD$. But we have seen that the rents on each piece of land are equal to the marginal social opportunity cost represented by the transportation costs incurred in front of the property; hence, total land rents are equal to total transportation costs. In the aggregate, then, aggregate land rents at rates representing the marginal social cost of land occupancy will be just sufficient, and no more, to pay the subsidies required to permit the individual activities to lower their prices to marginal cost. Thus, to the proposition of Henry George that, as a matter of justice, the land rents that have arisen through no effort on the part of any individual land-owner should be appropriated for public purposes, and the suggestion of Harold Hotelling that taxes on land rents would be an appropriate means of financing the intramarginal cost residues of increasing-return industries pricing their output at marginal cost, we add the following theorem, which we call the 'GHV' theorem.

In an economy of efficiently organised cities in a state of perfect competition with each other, the aggregate of the land rents (calculated as the marginal social cost of holding land) generated by the urban agglomeration produced by the existence of activities with economies of scale within the city will equal the subsidies required to enable these activities to sell their output at prices equal to their respective marginal costs.

In other words, if a perfectly efficient world is to be organised on a classical decentralised basis, it is necessary that all of the land rent generated by the presence of the city be appropriated to the subsidy of the decreasing-cost industries within the city. If any of these land rents are appropriated by private landlords for their own purposes, this action will preclude the achievement of complete efficiency.

V. THE SCOPE OF THE GHV THEOREM

Thus far, this theorem has been illustrated rather than proved, but there is reason to believe that it is valid well beyond the rather oversimplified example given above. For example, it would seem that going from a one-dimensional to a two-dimensional, or even a three-dimensional, model would not destroy the validity of the theorem. In a two-dimensional model, transportation costs per unit of output would tend to vary as the square root of the volume of output, and marginal transportation costs would then be 3/2 of average transportation costs. In terms of Fig. 13.1, we would replace the line *EIC* with a parabola with axis *EB*, and *EDL* would be another parabola, with $BD = 3/2\ BC$. At the minimum cost point *D*, the fixed cost would thus be equal to half the transportation cost. There are also a number of models that, for a two-dimensional case, produce an equality between transportation cost and twice the total land rents. Thus, again, we have land rents equal to the fixed costs. If we allow for the possibility of expanding vertically, say by thinking of the city as being, in effect, constructed in a k-dimensional space, with $2 < k < 3$, then we can have $T = kR = kF$, with, again, $R = F$, though in this case T may have to be thought of as including the cost of lifts, stairs and the like.

Again, the assumption of a linear production function with a constant term does not appear to be critical, since any production function can be approximated, in the neighbourhood of the optimal point, by a linear function tangent to the actual function at the equilibrium point, with a constant term that can be taken as the effective intramarginal residue. Similarly, the fact that transportation costs do not vary simply in proportion to distance, but vary in a curvilinear fashion, may be allowed for by replacing the actual transportation-cost function with one that is a linear function tangent to the actual one at the equilibrium point, and by taking the element of cost represented by the intercept and incorporating it, as packing or loading costs, in the costs of the shipping activity. Among the matters that are not so simple to deal with, but that probably can be handled along analogous lines, is the possibility that part of the fixed costs of activities may take the form of a fixed land requirement, or that inputs to the transportation service are locally produced.

An element that may be more likely to disable the theorem is the fact that, in practice, much transportation does not take the form of a direct origin-to-destination shipment, but is multipurpose in character, as when an individual stops at the barber on his way to work, or, more importantly, when a delivery truck drops off or picks up shipments at various points along a route. Computing a relevant marginal cost under these circumstances is difficult, and it is not even clear that there will be any simple algorithm for determining the optimum pattern on a decentralised basis (consider the travelling-salesman problem).

Another caveat to be kept in mind is that the theorem applies only to the intramarginal residues occurring in those industries that are either entirely local in their markets or are replicated in similar cities. A local newspaper or a television station, for example, is a factor in the agglomerative power of a given city, and the land rents generated by this agglomerative power will cover the intramarginal costs of these activities. On the other hand, whereas publication in a given city of a unique book with a worldwide distribution may add, in some degree, to the agglomerative power of the city, it is unlikely to do so to a degree that would cause land rents to rise sufficiently to cover the writing, typesetting and preparation costs involved. In effect, the theorem applies to local economies of scale, not to global ones. However, the economies of scale involved are not necessarily manifested in large organisations: the factory that makes buttons of a given model more cheaply in lots of 600 than in lots of 500 is operating under conditions of economies of scale, even though there would be no reduction in average cost if it produced 500 buttons in each of 200, instead of 100, models.

VI. OPTIMISING IN AN ENVIRONMENT OF NONOPTIMISING CITIES

A more immediate question, given the remoteness of a fully optimised situation, is how a city might optimise in a context in which other cities are behaving in a nonoptimal manner, and what the consequences of such action might be. This involves, first, defining a specific nonoptimal type of behaviour that is to be ascribed to the outer universe of cities. Given the possibilities for various varieties of imperfect competition inherent in the prevalence of economies of scale, this is a wide-open opportunity for variation. Since we are concerned with the relation of land rents to city efficiency, let us assume that the one constraint against optimality is that land rents, instead of being used to subsidise the decreasing-cost activities so as to permit marginal cost pricing, are used by landlords for their own private purposes (for instance, consumption of additional imports). This will mean that individual activities will have to be financed from their own receipts without subsidy, and that prices must cover the full average cost, inclusive of purchased inputs, land rents, and fixed costs. Let us assume, further, that land rents are optimally set so as to reflect the marginal cost of land occupancy, as determined by the cost of transportation. The average variable cost will then be *OE* plus twice the transportation cost, or *EMDL*, and the average total cost, inclusive of rent, will be indicated by the curve through *K*. We may then suppose the world price relationships to be set at the level represented by P_b, the output being at the level represented by Q_b. Of the total proceeds OP_bKQ_b, $OENQ_b$ represents variable direct imports, *NIHE* the imports for transportation, *NIMW* is the rents consumed by landlords, and WP_bKM the fixed costs.

If, now, in the context of such inefficient cities, a given city wishes to optimise its own operations, it should operate at the point where marginal cost, net, equals the world price, or at *L*. Expansion from *K* to *L* produces additional revenues of KLQ_bQ_e against additional costs of MLQ_eQ_b, leaving a net gain of *MKL*. This gain, in the linear case, is equal to the former level of rents, with $Q_e = 2\,Q_b = 1{\cdot}414\,Q_c$. For the *k*-dimensional case, the corresponding results are

$$Q_c = \left(\frac{kF}{t}\right)^{k/(k+1)}$$

where t is the transportation cost involved in a city producing one unit of output,

$$Q_b = Q_c\left(\frac{k}{k+1}\right)^{k/(k+1)}$$

and

$$Q_e = \left(\frac{k+1}{k}\right)^k Q_b = Q_c\left(\frac{1+k}{k+1}\right)^{k^2/(k+1)}$$

The land rents to be collected at K will be

$$L_b = F\frac{k}{k+1}$$

and the total surplus available at L will be

$$S_e = F\left[\left(\frac{k+1}{k}\right)^k - 1\right]$$

At L, however, land rents at the social opportunity cost would be

$$F\left(\frac{k+1}{k}\right)^k$$

so that the surplus is insufficient, by the amount F of the fixed costs, to cover these rents.

In effect, if the landlords constitute the ruling class of the city, it would be in their own long-run interests, with world prices at P_b, to levy against their rents to subsidise to the extent of F, inducing in the long run (assuming that no other cities do likewise) an expansion to L and an increase in the gross land rents by more than the subsidy F. Of course, this process would take time. Indeed, at the initial point K, land rents are less than F, and would be insufficient at that point to do the whole job. It is only as the city expands beyond the output Q_c that land rents become sufficient to cover the entire intramarginal costs of the decreasing-cost industries.

VII. SURPLUS AND EFFICIENCY

Of course, if all cities started to do this simultaneously, one might ask in what sense a shift from K to D is an increase in efficiency, since it eliminates surplus. The answer is to be found in what happens to the returns available to whatever are, ultimately, the scarce resources in the universe under discussion. An overall shortage of suitable sites for cities would lead, of course, to a surplus rent. A more interesting concept would be that of a limited labour force, freely mobile among cities. Expansion of the scale of cities, and, possibly, the establishment of new cities, would lead to an increase in the demand for labour, and an increase in its wages, represented in this model by the level of the input coefficients to the labour supply activity, representing an increase in the supply of consumer goods necessary to produce a unit of labour for use in the other activities in the city. Full competition among cities would, in this instance, lead (a) to the elimination of any new land rents to landlords, over and above the amounts taken to finance the fixed costs; and (b) to the transfer of this surplus, plus the additional surplus generated from the increase in efficiency to labour, at least in the case where there is no shortage of city sites and, hence, conceptually free entry for additional cities.

VIII. SUMMARY

While it is dangerous to extrapolate too freely from admittedly oversimplified and even caricatured models (such as the above) to the complexities of the real world, it seems not too rash to draw the conclusion that urban land rents are, fundamentally, a reflection of the economies of scale of the activities that are carried on within the city, and that efficient organisation of a city, or even of the urban life of a nation as a whole, requires that these land rents, or their equivalent, be devoted primarily to the financing of the intramarginal residues that represent the difference between revenues derived from prices set at marginal cost and the total cost of the activities characterised by increasing returns. This means that revenues derived from these rents must defray not only those overhead costs of government and public services that are not marginally attributable to specific outputs, but also the intramarginal elements of most public utility costs, as well as those of a considerable range of activities ordinarily thought of as belonging to the private sector. Such a subsidy is especially crucial for mass transit and for other forms of transportation where economies of scale are significant, given the special relationship existing between transportation and land values.

Use of land rents, or, at least, of a major fraction of them, for public purposes is therefore not merely an ethical imperative, derived from categorisation of these rents as an unearned income derived from private appropriation of publicly created values, but is, even more importantly, a fundamental requirement for economic efficiency. Cities that take the lead in such public use of land rents may find that in the long run the subsidy is self-financing through the enhancement in land values that results, while cities that lag may find that in the long run they are unable to compete in national or world markets with the cities that manage to organise themselves more efficiently through the use of land rents to cover intramarginal residues. There will, of course, be many an agonising slip between abstract economic analysis and cold political and economic reality. Lack of comprehension, political intervention, strategic recalcitrance, and the inertia associated with heavy commitments of fixed capital in what the French so aptly term *immeubles* may slow the processes involved to a glacial pace. But the fundamental tendencies and requirements inherent in the very nature of the city can be ignored only at great peril to its economic health.

14 The Assignment Problem in Federal Structures[1]

Albert Breton* and Anthony Scott†
*UNIVERSITY OF TORONTO
†UNIVERSITY OF BRITISH COLUMBIA

This paper contains a simple model of the assignment of functions among the jurisdictional levels that make up the public sector. The model rests on the notion that it is possible to classify the activities of individuals and governments who participate in the public sector and to impute costs – sometimes called transaction costs – to these activities. Following a description of the nature of these activities and costs, it is argued that an equilibrium assignment table, i.e. a cross-classification of functions on jurisdictional levels, can be determined. The paper then notes how misassignment problems can be dealt with by the use of interjurisdictional grants.

I. INTRODUCTION

The traditional theory that one finds in the literature dealing explicitly with the assignment of supply and regulatory functions to the various levels of government of a federal country, and that can be interpreted as contributing to the solution of the problem, is usually formulated in terms of the non-exclusion properties of public and nonprivate goods and of interjurisdictional spillovers, and/or in terms of economies of scale in the production and provision of certain goods.[2] Although that theory, under plausible (but seldom,

[1] This paper is part of an ongoing research project and was written in January 1974. A number of the more restrictive assumptions that were criticised by the official discussant and others at the IEA Conference in Turin had already been removed by that date; still others were removed when the text was revised; and, we hope, still others will be abandoned before our grant runs out. Apart from certain clarifications, this final draft is the paper that was presented in Turin.

[2] The relevant literature is voluminous. A partial list (in alphabetical order) will suffice: Y. Barzel, 'Two Propositions on the Optimum Level of Producing Collective Goods', *Public Choice,* Spring 1969; A. Breton, 'A Theory of Government Grants', *The Canadian Journal of Economics and Political Science,* May 1965; J. M. Buchanan and G. Tullock, *The Calculus of Consent,* (Ann Arbor, Mich., 1962); J. M. Buchanan, 'Notes for an Economic Theory of Socialism', *Public Choice,* Spring 1970; W. E. Oates, *Fiscal Federalism,* (New York: Harcourt, Brace, Jovanovich, 1972); M. Olson Jr, 'The Principle of

if ever, explicitly stated) assumptions about the behaviour of spillovers and economies of scale, yields an equilibrium assignment of functions, it is an empirically uninteresting theory because, in equilibrium, the number of government levels and units can be as large as the number of public goods supplied by the public sector. That theory usually predicts that there is one optimal currency area, one optimal national defence area, one optimal police protection area, and so on, all of different sizes and each 'administered' by a government.

While the empirical emptiness of that theory was becoming recognised, it was also realised, initially as a by-product of empirical work on the supply of certain goods at the local-government level, that the economies of scale in the production and supply half (or third) of the traditional theory was a weak and largely unnecessary part, since the opportunity it afforded to suppliers for profitably purchasing the particular service that they had been elected to provide could be bought from specialised producers, private or public, and the available economies of scale could thus be exhausted.[3]

The economies of scale in the production part of the traditional theory were replaced, as it were, by a mixed bag of variables that we can label the costs of collective decision-making. These include the costs of setting up and operating governments and governmental bodies, the costs to individual citizens of bunching government services in bundles or packages that would be nonoptimal from the citizen's own point of view, and the costs that result from the loss of control over governments as their numbers shrink and, consequently, their size increases.[4]

The currently accepted theory of the assignment of functions in a federation is, then, based on these two building blocks: public goods and spillovers, and the costs of collective decision-making. As it stands, this new version is only slightly more empirically interesting than the older version of the traditional theory, since it does not appear capable of producing comparative-static predictions. In addition, the new theory, like the older version, suffers from what seems to us a fatal flaw. This, simply stated, is that, in the various versions of the theory, a function that has been assigned to a given level of government will have to be reassigned when there is a change in the amount demanded or supplied, per unit of time, of the good provided under the authority (function) assigned by the constitution. Or, to put it differently, a decision by a government, at a given level, to increase the supply of public good X_1 – a responsibility assigned to it by the constitution – from a quantity x_1 to a quantity $x_1 + \Delta x_1$ per unit of time may alter the flow of spillovers generated by that

---

"Fiscal Equivalence": The Division of Responsibilties among Different Levels of Government', *American Economic Review*, May 1969; and G. Tullock, 'Social Cost and Government Action', *American Economic Review*, May 1969.

[3] W. Ostrom, C. M. Tiebout, and R. Warren, 'The Organization of Government in Metropolitan Areas: A Theoretical Inquiry', *American Political Science Review*, Dec 1961; and W. Hirsch, 'The Supply of Urban Public Service', in *Issues in Urban Economics*, ed. H. Perloff and L. Wingo (Baltimore: Johns Hopkins Press, 1968).

[4] G. Tullock, 'Federalism: Problems of Scale', *Public Choice*, Spring 1969.

good, as well as the costs of collective decisions (recall how these are defined). Hence, it may make it necessary to reassign the function that authorises the supply of X_1 to a different level of government.

Further, since the problem of assigning functions is intimately related to that of defining the size of jurisdictions to which functions are assigned, changes in the flow of public goods should, according to the new version of the traditional theory of assignment, lead us to observe a greater number of changes, both in the assignment of functions and in the size and composition of jurisdictions, than we do, in fact, observe.

One can go a step further in criticising the currently dominant theory by noting that the fact that at least two of the three components of collective decision-making costs (namely, the cost of being forced to accept full lines of public policies, and the cost of losing control over the apparatus of government) – are largely individualised and, consequently, can be expected to vary from individual to individual – so much so, in fact, that, if there were only the two components of collective decision-making costs, the number of government units and the number of government levels could be expected to vary with changes in the variance and, possibly, in the skewness of the distributions of preferences, of income, and of wealth in the population. This kind of model does not seem able to account for many of the differences that we observe among federal structures.[5] Nor, for that matter, does it seem that the costs of setting up and of operating governments can do so.

We recognise, however, that the historical substitution of the costs of collective decision-making for the economies-of-scale argument in the theory of federalism does go in the right direction. Indeed, it is consistent with much of the modern research on externalities.[6] In the remainder of this paper, we hope to push the substitution further and to provide a theory of the assignment of functions in federal structures that not only possesses an equilibrium solution, but also is capable of shedding light on the empirical configurations that the world of experience throws up for our consideration.

With that purpose in mind, we introduce in the next section the concepts and assumptions that are needed for the model developed in section III. In sections IV and V we examine a few of the predictions that can be derived from the model, and in section VI we begin the discussion of the problem that the misassignment of functions may give rise to in the real world.

We wish to stress that this paper is exclusively concerned with the assignment problem related to expenditure and regulatory functions. We do not in any way consider the assignment problem pertaining to tax bases or to distri-

[5] A good survey of these differences and of changes therein can be found in C. J. Friedrich, *Trends of Federalism in Theory and Practice* (New York: Praeger, 1968).

[6] R. H. Coase, 'The Problem of Social Cost', *Journal of Law and Economics*, Oct 1960; and K. J. Arrow, 'Political and Economic Evaluation of Social Effects and Externalities', in *The Analysis of Public Output*, ed. J. Margolis (National Bureau of Economic Research, Columbia University Press, 1970).

bution and stabilisation functions. That task will be undertaken in the larger project of which this paper forms a part.

II. A FEW PRELIMINARY CONCEPTS

To be in a position to formulate a theory of federalism, we need to make explicit a number of concepts that have either been left in implicit form in the existing literature or have not been incorporated in the theory. In this section, we shall define three of these concepts. They are: (a) the assignment table; (b) the constitutional instruments; and (c) the constituent assembly.

To define the concept of the assignment table, we must be clear on two other concepts: those of function and of jurisdiction. A function must be distinguished sharply from a policy or a set of policies. The former refers to the class of variables over which a jurisdiction has authority and responsibility, while the latter refers to the level at which the variables are set. For example, currency, international trade, immigration, and weights and measures are *functions*, which are assigned to jurisdictional levels, while decisions about whether a currency should be decimalised or not, the rate of increase in the money supply, the level of tariffs and the goods to which they should apply, the flow of immigrants and the use of the metric system are all *policies.* The subject matter of this paper is the assignment of functions and not the determination of the level at which policies should be fixed.

The above definition accords fairly well with everyday usage. This is not quite the case with our definition of 'jurisdiction', which is often used as a synonym for 'government'. Our use of the word will cover that usage, but we shall also use the word to refer to any institution to which a function has been assigned or to which one could be assigned. For example, the Canadian provinces of Prince Edward Island, Nova Scotia and New Brunswick are all jurisdictions in the usual sense of the word, but the 'Maritime Provinces' are not. They would, however, be a jurisdiction in our sense, since some functions could, in principle, be assigned to a body with responsibility for these functions over the whole population of the area. In fact, we extend the concept of jurisdictions beyond that usage to include electorally nonresponsible administrative bodies such as the International Joint Commission.

Given these definitions, it is possible to make a list of all possible functions and of all possible jurisdictions and to bring these together in the form of a table such as that portrayed in Fig. 14.1. The rows of the table refer to the various functions (f_i), while the columns depict the jurisdictions (j_k). For example, f_1 could be water; f_2, ice; f_3, education; f_4, police; f_5, weights and measures; f_6, currency; and so on. Reading in the other direction, j_1 could be Canada, j_2, British Columbia; j_3, Alberta; j_4, Saskatchewan; j_{12}, British Columbia and Alberta; j_{13}, British Columbia and Saskatchewan; and j_{n-1}, a jurisdiction made up of all bar one of the municipalities in Canada. In addition, j_{m-a} could be a jurisdiction made up of part of Quebec (for example, the

	i_1	i_2	i_3			i_k			i_m
f_1	0	0	1	0	0	0	1	1	0
f_2			1			0			0
f_3	1	0	0	0	0	0	0	0	0
						1			0
	0	0	0	0	0	0	0	0	0
f_i						1			0
						1			0
						1			0
						1			0
f_n						1			0

Fig. 14.1

The Assignment Table

lower St Lawrence region) and part of New Brunswick (for instance, Restigouche and Madawaska counties).

This general table, then, provides us with a framework to describe the assignment of functions between jurisdictions in any given country. To do this we need two symbols to fill out the cells of the table: we shall use 0 to indicate that a function is not under the responsibility of a given jurisdiction, and 1 to indicate that it is. Note should be taken of the fact that in any row there may be more than one 1, since the same function can be assigned to more than one jurisdiction. This is known as the phenomenon of 'joint authority'.

Furthermore, one expects that a number of columns of the table will be made up only of zeros, since generally there will be potential jurisdictions that do not exist at a specified point of time. Similarly, a row could be made up exclusively of zeros, if a function has not been assigned to any jurisdictions. The concept of an assignment table is, therefore, independent of whether an equilibrium assignment can be defined and of whether an optimal assignment exists.

All changes in the assignment table are carried out by using one or more of the available constitutional instruments. It is not possible to enumerate all of these instruments, except in a purely formal way, because, as with commodities, new ones are invented regularly and old ones disappear. It will help, however, if we take some space to illustrate what it is that we mean by constitutional instruments.

One way of changing the assignment table is to amend the constitution. This is an instrument that is used more often than it may appear to be, since changing the constitution is not limited to a fundamental redrafting of the basic constitutional document, but is defined to encompass amendments of specific clauses related to limited issues, as well as the reinterpretation of a clause directly by the parties involved or by appeal to the courts.

Another way of altering the assignment table is to modify the jurisdictional boundaries. If a territory is already completely mapped out, a change in jurisdictional boundaries can be achieved only by enlarging one jurisdiction at the expense of another. Since jurisdictional boundaries are defined for functions, it is possible to extend the boundaries of one jurisdiction for one function, while curtailing them for another. This is an instrument that is often used, especially at the local and municipal level.

A third constitutional instrument is the delegation of a function by one level of government to another. Such delegation can be upwards, downwards or even sideways, and is not restricted to federal, provincial and municipal governments. On the contrary, it must be seen to extend to governing bodies such as metropolitan governments, school boards, regional administrations, and so on. Other instruments that can be used are the formation of function-specific political or quasi-political jurisdictions such as school boards, metropolitan governments, district governments, and so on, or the formation of function-specific nonpolitical – i.e. administrative or bureaucratic – units such as the International Joint Commission or the Tennessee Valley Authority. The major difference between these two types of units is that the first is responsible directly to an electorate, while the second is not.

Our last illustration of constitutional instruments is the exercise of power by a given level of government for the purpose of 'occupying' a field in which another level of goverment has not yet legislated. Alternatively, the one level may legislate on issues related to a function that has been assigned to a different level of government, hoping that simply by doing so it will create a situation of fact that will eventually come to be accepted as the legal one. Whether such exercises are successful will depend on whether the level of government whose authority is thus eroded will choose not to react, or, instead, will decide to act so as to restore, safeguard and/or strengthen its authority in the particular field. This instrument is often used. As examples may be cited a regulation that the government of Saskatchewan introduced with regard to the export of potash; the 'upgrading', by the governments of Ontario and British Columbia, of exports of natural resources; and the protection that practically all provincial administrations in Canada have given, through discriminatory pricing practices, to domestic producers of wine and liquor. In all of these cases power has been used with respect to a function that is assigned to the central government.

Throughout this paper it will be assumed that the constitutional instruments are used and operated by a constituent assembly. Depending on the assumption that we make about the behaviour of the individuals who compose the assembly, that body can be thought of as being real or fictitious. To put it differently, the extent to which the constituent assembly will correspond to real-world constituent assemblies – such as the Philadelphia and the Charlottetown assemblies – will depend on the assumptions that are made about the motivation and behaviour of the participants.

For most of this paper, it is assumed that the constituent assembly acts in such a way as to minimise total social costs, and that the resulting assignment of functions reflects this fact. In addition, however, a brief examination will be made of the situation that arises when the behaviour of members of the constituent assembly is such that a wedge is introduced between social and private costs.

III. THE MODEL

As stated above, we assume that the constituent assembly acts so as to minimise total social costs. We shall devote more space in the next section to a definition of these costs, but for present purposes we shall call them transaction costs. Since the substance of the hypothesis is completely dependent on exactly what definition of transaction cost is adopted, the most that we can do in this section is to develop the model at a very formal level and to display its skeleton.

Consider, therefore, a particular function f_i. Assume that initially the constituent assembly tries to assign it to the lowest possible level of government, a level that we shall call the 'local' level. Assume, further, that, if assigned at that level, the level of output that the constituent assembly can expect will be provided by local governments over what it takes to be the relevant time horizon,[7] will generate interjurisdictional spillovers, and/or will fall short of exploiting all available economies of scale.

Given the existence of these spillovers and/or economies of scale, and given the assumptions that it makes about the degree of responsiveness of local and other governments to the presence of these spillovers and economies, the constituent assembly will estimate the various transaction costs that must be met in order to internalise both spillovers and economies. In other words, it will estimate the costs of acquiring information about the ways and means of dealing with the spillovers and economies; the costs of negotiation and bargaining between government units; the costs of drafting and enforcing contracts; the costs of operating local governments with f_i located there; the mobility costs that may arise as a result of the fact that citizens may be induced to move from one jurisdiction so as to benefit from the larger spillovers and economies in another; and so on. Having made that estimate, the assembly will calculate the cost of assigning the function to a higher level of government, including the cost of frustrating the preferences of a number of citizens.

Given these estimates, it will locate the function f_i at the level that will minimise the sum of these costs. Having done this for all functions, it will have achieved an equilibrium that, it should be noted, will be independent of the

[7] We do not discuss here the problem of defining the time horizon. Suffice it to mention that it is related, among other things, to the behaviour of transaction costs.

level of output of any particular good in the public sector. Indeed, even though the level of spillovers and the extent of scale economies can be expected to vary with the level of output, the various components of transaction costs can generally be assumed to be independent of the level of output.

In addition, the equilibrium reached is not one that implies one government per public good or per citizen or group of homogeneous citizens, since the costs of setting up and operating so many governments, as well as the costs of negotiation and of enforcing contracts between them, are taken into account and act as a deterrent to increasing the number of governments.

Recall, also, that in this paper the term 'jurisdiction' includes not only what in everyday language is called a 'government', but also the many and various other administrative units. These may be created because their costs of operation are lower than those of *bona fide* governments would be, were they to serve the same function. However, another reason for the creation of these specialised administrative units may be that they enjoy a similar advantage with regard to the costs of negotiation between units and of enforcement, as well as of searching for and accumulating information.

In addition, it is important to stress that the equilibrium assignment table that we obtain in this way will correspond to what we observe in the real world only to the extent that constituent assemblies, or their counterpart, can be assumed to be minimising transaction costs. Similarly, differences between federal structures may be imputable to differences in transaction costs, but only to the extent that in various jurisdictions the constituent assemblies, or their counterparts, all minimise total transaction costs.

Finally, we should like to insist that the equilibrium assignment table obtained by minimising total transaction costs may, or may not, be an optimum, even within the limited context resulting from the elimination of stabilisation and distribution considerations. Indeed, to be certain that the equilibrium assignment table is an optimum one, we must be certain that the 'technology' used to produce the various transactions displays properties that are conducive to optimality: properties that correspond to the convexity of the production set in the theory of production of private goods. We do not discuss this question in any detail in this paper.

IV. SOME TRANSACTION COSTS

In this section, we wish to illustrate, by looking at more-or-less hypothetical cases, what we mean by transaction costs, and in this way give more substance to our hypothesis. It should be emphasised that the discussion in this section is still more tentative than that in the other sections of this paper – largely because our work in this area is now only beginning – and, in consequence, the discussion is limited largely to illustrations. We hope, however, that these illustrations will provide the reader with a good idea of the kind of analysis that we hope ultimately to provide.

Let us focus initially on what we mean by the costs of moving. These include, of course, the costs of the actual move, the costs of relocation in a new area, and the costs of dislocation and uprooting (both psychological and physical) involved in leaving one area and going to another. They include, also, the loss in human capital that occurs as a result of the fact that information that had been accumulated about minimum prices, quality and other characteristics of products, as well as about other magnitudes that contribute to a higher real income, is now lost.

Let us now assume, for purposes of illustration, that the only component of transaction costs on which the constituent assembly focuses its attention, in seeking to determine the equilibrium assignment table, is the cost of mobility. Let us assume that the constituent assembly, acting somewhat like a Walrasian *crieur*, assigns to a junior level of government a function such as the responsibility for regulating natural resources. The constituent assembly seeking to minimise the costs of mobility will reason that, if, perhaps, one particular type of natural resource (say, crude oil) turned out to be located in only one or two of the junior jurisdictions that make up the country, while another type of resource was located in some other limited number of jurisdictions, and a third type in still other jurisdictions, large variations in world demand for these resources would lead to large variations in the rents generated in the different jurisdictions.

The constituent assembly would further reason that, if some of the jurisdictions levied royalties on the extraction of some of the resources, large variations in world demand would lead to substantial variations in the revenues of the governments of the jurisdictions that charged royalties and would, therefore, induce some people to move into the jurisdictions that gained and away from those that lost. Since this mobility would generate costs that could be avoided by assigning the function to a more senior level of government, thereby 'equalising' and 'stabilising' the royalties from the rents for the various resources, the constituent assembly would ensure, by so assigning the function, that these costs were not incurred.

We leave to the next section the question of how the constituent assembly or its counterpart will deal with the problem of a function that is misassigned (for whatever reason) and has to be reassigned. However, we pause to note that the Canadian provincial governments, to which the constituent assembly had assigned the responsibility for natural resources, have, until very recently, shied away from levying royalties on the exploitation of these resources, even though various groups in the country have often exerted pressure on them to do so. In consequence, the mechanism described above has, until recently, remained inoperative, so much so that it was possible to say that the function was not misassigned. It would be interesting, but beyond the scope of this paper, to discover why the provincial governments did not collect any royalties and, in particular, whether that decision was related in any way to a knowledge, however intuitive and inchoate, that the levy of such royalties would probably lead to a reassignment of the function and that this was not desired. In addition, and for the same reason, one would like to know why, in recent years, some provinces have decided to levy royalties on some natural resources.

Another component of transaction costs that is important to an understanding of the assignment problem is the cost of ascertaining the preferences of citizens. In making decisions relating to this component, the constituent assembly will take into account the fact that the government to which a function is assigned will use up resources in searching for information on the effective preferences of citizens regarding the provision of public goods and of regulatory activities that are authorised by that function. Further, the assembly will take account of the fact that citizens will allocate resources to the matter of signalling their preferences with regard to these policies.

In estimating search costs, the constituent assembly will keep in mind that it is not the preferences of all citizens that have to be ascertained, but only those of that fraction of the population that the various jurisdictions' electoral decision rules (defined to include the extent of enfranchisement) dictate should be satisfied if governing parties seeking re-election are to be re-elected. In addition, the constituent assembly will take into account the fact that search costs are dependent on the particular characteristics of the frequency distribution of preferences over the population. If the distribution is unimodal, the preferences of the population can be ascertained by searching for the preferences of the median citizen; but, if the frequency distribution is bimodal, or displays other, more complex features, the measurement of preferences will be more difficult. The difficulty can, however, be reduced if functions are reassigned so as to make the frequency distribution of preferences unimodal.

Consider the simple case of the overall maintenance of residential and arterial streets in cities. If the responsibility for that task is assigned to the national jurisdiction, there is no doubt that the distribution of preferences for this overall maintenance will, in a country like Canada or the United States, be multimodal, even if only because snow accumulation is zero in some areas, moderate in others, and large in still others, and because the terrain of cities may be flat or hilly and so raise different problems with regard to road construction, the properties of rights of way for public transportation, and so on.

The costs of searching for what citizens desire in terms of street maintenance will be high for the national government. Assigning the function to a more junior level of government will break up the global frequency distribution, make the problems of searching for the representative preferences simpler, and raise the likelihood that the median effective preferences will be found and satisfied.

A third component of transaction costs is the cost of setting up and operating governmental and administrative units. For the particular problem that concerns us – namely, the problem of assigning functions in federal structures – operating costs will primarily be the costs of negotiation and co-ordination between units, and the costs of acquiring the general capability and the information necessary for these activities. In addition, one should include in these costs the costs of concluding and of enforcing proper contracts.

Consider the cases of water supply and sewage disposal, which have attracted much attention in recent years. As has been pointed out by many observers, these functions can be assigned to some very junior level of government – for instance, municipal governments. These will then negotiate with each other about the amounts of water and the sewage disposal capacity to be supplied, as well as about the prices to be charged for these services. Alternatively, if the cost of negotiation, contracting and enforcement are high relative to the cost of searching for the preferences of consumer-citizens, the constituent assembly may decide to assign the function to a less junior level of government – for instance, a metropolitan government – including in its calculations the cost, in terms of personnel, space, paper, and so on, of that additional level.

Following Pennock,[8] we call the fourth and last component of transaction costs 'frustration' costs. These are defined and measured in the following way: given the collective-decision rule in force in society, frustration costs will fall when the organisation of the public sector is such that the fraction of the population casting negative votes for the implementation of a given programme or proposal also falls. The best way to illustrate these costs is by reference to Pennock's own discussion. Suppose that, in a society made up of 100 individuals, 60 favour a given policy while 40 oppose it and favour another. If the decision rule is that of a simple majority, the policy implemented will be the one supported by 60 per cent of the people. Call that policy X_1. Suppose that the society, instead of being just one jurisdiction, is broken into two, equal-sized jurisdictions. In one of these, say J_1, 30 people favour X_2 (the other policy) and 20 support X_1. Since, in the other jurisdiction (J_2), the population is unchanged, 40 people in J_2 must want X_1 and 10 X_2. Therefore, the policy implemented will be X_1 in J_2, and X_2 in J_1. Whereas, under the unitary structure, 40 per cent of the citizens would be frustrated – frustration costs, we say, are equal to 40 – in the federal structure only 30 per cent would be.

It should be noted that our measure of frustration cost does not take into account the intensity of frustration; it deals only with its presence or absence, individual by individual. It is our contention that only frustration as here defined is relevant to the assignment problem. Intensity of frustration, which we may call coercion, is relevant to the day-to-day operations of governments, not to constitutional issues.[9]

The central hypothesis of this paper can now be stated more explicitly. The problem of the assignment of expenditure and regulatory functions to various levels of governments in a federal structure is the problem of minimising total transaction costs. For that specific problem, transaction costs can be viewed as made up of four components: mobility costs, search costs, co-ordination costs and frustration costs. An equilibrium assignment table is one that minimises these costs.

[8] J. R. Pennock, 'Federal and Unitary Government: Disharmony and Frustration', *Behavioral Science*, Apr 1959.

[9] On a definition of coercion and its use in a model of day-to-day decisions, see A. Breton, *The Economics Theory of Representative Government* (Chicago: Aldine, 1974).

V. DISPLACING THE EQUILIBRIUM

Changes in any of the four components of transaction costs may be brought about by changes in these costs themselves or by changes in the factors that affect them, and, along with changes in the number, nature and characteristics of functions, will require a cost-minimising constituent assembly to find a new equilibrium assignment table by reassigning functions between existing and, possibly, new jurisdictions.

At present, it is difficult (and will remain so until more work has been done on the factors governing transaction costs) to make very definite predictions about the new assignment table relative to the old. Nevertheless, the nature of the comparative-static exercise can be illustrated. Suppose that the cost of searching for the preferences of the population (or, where these preferences are known to display a unimodal distribution, the cost of searching for the median preference) falls as a result of some exogenous technological change. One would then expect that, *ceteris paribus,* a number of functions would be reassigned to more senior levels of government, since these would be able to ascertain the preferences of the electorate more effectively than previously, and would not have become less effective on other counts.

In a similar fashion, if the costs of moving fall, a cost-minimising constituent assembly will, *ceteris paribus,* reassign functions to more junior governments, because the resources used up by individuals moving from one jurisdiction to another will be less than they were. Similar reasoning can be applied to all of the components of transaction costs, and can thus be used to generate predictions about the assignment problem.

In doing so, one should take note of the fact that the various components of transaction costs display different characteristics for each and every component, so that, when one talks about changes in the costs of search or the costs of mobility, one talks about changes in these costs as they pertain to a specific function. It is not impossible to imagine a situation where changes in the components of transaction costs operate across the full range of functions, but observation seems to indicate that such changes usually affect a very small number of functions.

The reassignment of functions by the constituent assembly is always effected by the use of one or more of the constitutional instruments. Indeed, there is no other way in which it can be done. Which one of these instruments is used will depend on their relative costs. While one expects that certain constitutional instruments will be used more frequently in reassigning certain classes of functions, it is impossible, *a priori*, to attach the use of particular instruments to the task of reassigning particular functions.

It is important to insist that functions are often reassigned in federal structures. Indeed, it is one of the virtues of the present model, in which all reassignments require the use of constitutional instruments, that, by alerting us to the use of constitutional instruments by the real-world counterparts of constituent assemblies, it can help us recognise, in the first instance at least, where reassignment is taking place. One of the difficulties often experienced in the observation and ascertainment of reassignment comes from the implicit requirement that we impose on ourselves that these changes be accompanied by constitutional reforms. Constitutional change is only one way of reassigning functions: there are many other methods that can be, and are in fact, used.

VI. MISASSIGNMENT OF FUNCTIONS

In concluding this paper we should like to point to circumstances that could lead to a misassignment of functions by the constituent assembly. We shall indicate two such circumstances.

First of all, it should be noticed that there are no forces (competition, for instance) that operate to require the constituent assembly, or any of its many historical counterparts, to minimise total social transaction costs. Indeed, the most easily observable forces acting on the constituent assembly do not seem to be of that nature. Constituent assemblies seem to be made up of individuals whose position in life would lead them to pursue such objectives as the maximisation of the probability of their re-election; or, perhaps equivalently, the maximisation of the jurisdictional sovereignty of the political unit that they represent; or, simply, the minimisation of administrative costs. However, we wish to stress that we are unable to assert at this stage that the pursuit of alternative objectives is not, in some way, equivalent to the minimisation of transaction costs. Furthermore, it is difficult to infer from casual observation that the historical counterparts of our constituent assembly, which appear to be preoccupied with a host of more or less important issues, are not minimising transaction costs. For these reasons, we prefer to focus on the next source of misassignment as the more important one, and to stay with the assumption that transaction costs are minimised.

Misassignment would also result (regardless of whether or not constituent assembly acts to minimise total transaction costs) if, as a result of nonconvexities or interdependencies in the 'technologies' underlying the various components of transaction costs, there exist discrepancies between private (to the constituent assembly) and social magnitudes. Misassignment in this case would be of the same variety as the ordinary production externalities that are so common in the literature of welfare economics.

This kind of misassignment may be more easily corrected than the first through a recognition that it exists, and through the use of Pigouvian taxes and subsidies (or interjurisdictional grants, as they are usually called in this case). Indeed, the presence of this kind of misassignment may be the main reason for the existence of allocative grants between jurisdictions. (Remember that distributive and stabilisation functions and, hence, grants related to these functions are not considered here.) Furthermore, it is easy to imagine that the discrepancies between private and social costs may be such as to require more than unconditional grants; that is, conditional grants, whether matching or nonmatching, and according to alternative formulae, may be required to eliminate the discrepancies. Space and the preliminary nature of our work do not allow us to go into these questions in more detail here. That will be attempted in the larger project.

VII. CONCLUDING NOTE

We wish to re-emphasise that many of the ideas put forward in this paper are still preliminary and that a number will certainly be modified as we progress and seek to incorporate new phenomena in the analysis. We are aware, also, that there may well be a number of assumptions underlying our model that are implicit and will, therefore, have to be brought into the open. Nevertheless, we are fairly confident that, however we modify it, the central part of the model will remain pretty much as it is.

Part VI
Public Production and Finance

15 Optimal Taxation and Public Production with Budget Constraints

Alain Bernard

COMMISSARIAT GÉNÉRAL DU PLAN, PARIS

This paper proposes a formulation of problems of public economics – taxation, public production – within the framework of one-kind allocation models. It differs from the similar approaches by Boiteux and by Diamond and Mirrlees in that the (second-best) models are written in primal language – specifically without the use of indirect utility functions – and, thus, are nearer to usual Paretian formulations. The main topics are the conditions of production efficiency in the case of profit taxation, marketable public goods, and proportional indirect taxation with sectoral budget constraints.

I. INSTRUMENTS AND CONSTRAINTS OF GOVERNMENT IN A MIXED ECONOMY

Recent developments in public economics tend to examine the main problems with models of allocation where the government – or the public sector at large – is an economic agent endowed with *instruments* and subject to *constraints.*

INSTRUMENTS

Leaving aside any regulative consideration, we can discern two categories: provision of commodities to private agents – directly or through the market – and taxation. What is each aiming at?

Provision of commodities

With regard to the first kind of instruments, the question is, 'Why should the public sector provide any commodity?', or, more generally, 'Which commodities should be provided by the private sector and which by the public sector?'

Though much economic thinking has been devoted to these problems, models of allocation do not present a formalised answer. They consider public enterprises as given and attempt to determine which price system – real prices or shadow prices – is relevant for the production decisions made by these enterprises. In particular, the question most often raised is that of whether production efficiency – i.e. using the same price system as the private production sector uses – is desirable or not. However, models of allocation do give some insight into the desirability of taking private firms into the public sector.

Taxation

Taxation serves three purposes. These are: raising money to finance public outlays; redistributing income among households; and guiding the behaviour of private agents.

Putting aside lump-sum transfers, a tax system is defined by two essential features: the flows (possibly the stocks) that are taxed; and the degree of discrimination (between agents and/or between commodities) that is allowed (or feasible). There is complete discrimination when the rates of taxation of two flows are independent; no discrimination when they are equal. Partial discrimination arises when there is a more-or-less direct relationship; for instance, if the rates of taxation are constrained to the same upper (or lower) limit or if the rate of taxation of any flow of one kind is a function of another's magnitude and of one (or several) shift parameter(s).

There are two main types of taxation: indirect and direct. With indirect taxation, the flows concerned are the transactions between economic agents, usually the sales of the productive sector to households. Indirect taxation is, then, a tax on consumption: if there is discrimination among commodities, indirect taxation results in different price vectors for producers, on the one hand, and for households, on the other.

With direct taxation, the flows concerned are the profits of producers and rents on scarce resources.

Wage taxation raises a special problem: if labour is considered as a negative consumption, then wage taxation belongs to the first category. If, on the other hand, time for labour (and, eventually, leisure) appears as a scarce resource, then wage taxation belongs to the second category.

Before closing generalities about the instruments available to the government, it is well worth being precise about terminology. First, note that the problem of determining the relevent price vector for the public sector is also a problem of taxation. Then, in the most general situation, we are faced with three price vectors: (1) consumer prices (for households), (2) producer prices (for private producers), and (3) shadow prices (for public enterprises); and taxes may be defined by reference to any one of them. Actually, there is also a fourth price vector, based on the social values of commodities; i.e. for each good, the increase in social welfare that would arise from one extra unit of endowment. According to the situation, this last vector might be represented by one of the first three, but this is not necessary. Taking the social values of goods as a referential system, we define:

consumer tax rates: 1–4;
producer tax rates: 2–4;
shadow tax rates: 3–4;

We reserve the term 'indirect taxation' for 1–2.

CONSTRAINTS

Leaving aside physical constraints, such as those that public-enterprise production sets and limits on the availability of instruments, the main constraints to which the public sector at large is subject are budget constraints. Of course, the public sector is not unique in this, since other agents' decisions are constrained within the limits of a budget.

Overall budget constraint

A decentralised economy cannot be at equilibrium if this constraint is not satisfied, for, if it is not, either one market (at least) would not clear, or for one household (at least) the value of consumption would not equalise income. Equilibrium in all markets and budget balance for all households are, then, sufficient to insure aggregate balance for the public sector.

It is important to note that, in an equilibrium with taxes (both direct and indirect), the tax system is not uniquely defined, i.e. the same allocation can be arrived at with different sets of taxes. This is related to the fact that the consumer price vector need not be normalised with respect to producer prices.

Let q, p be consumer and producer vectors, and x, y, z be consumption, private-production and public-production vectors. For households – assuming, for simplicity of exposition, that there is a unique rate of profit taxation $(1 - \tau)$ – we have

$$qx = \tau py \tag{15.1}$$

and, since

$$x - y - z = 0$$

we obtain

$$(q - p)x + (1 - \tau)py + pz = 0 \tag{15.2}$$

which represents the aggregate balance for the public sector. If we change q to λq, and τ to $\lambda\tau$, it is easy to check that the overall budget of the public sector is still balanced.

We can conclude that taking into account constraints on tax rates, for instance $\tau \leqslant k$, has meaning only if the consumer and producer price vectors are normalised relative to each other. Otherwise, the constraints could be met merely by changing the level of one price system.

Sectoral budget constraints

The first to use this kind of constraint in the framework of a general equilibrium model was Boiteux, who introduced it to deal with the problem of public utilities, subject to a break-even constraint. Sectoral budget constraints can be contemplated in the case of public administrations that are endowed with 'public investment envelopes' – either a yearly envelope within the national budget or pluri-annual envelopes within the framework of a planning process.

Unlike the case with the aggregate constraint, the reality and significance of sectoral budget constraints are a matter of controversy. One may wonder why the government should assign itself such limitations.

In the case of publicly owned enterprises, the underlying idea is that the nonallowance of deficits – even when there are economies of scale – is an efficient incentive for better management. Such a justification is not entirely convincing.

As for public administrations, which provide commodities to private agents without charge and, thus, cannot use the market to reveal preferences, the setting of budget constraints seems a powerful instrument of decentralisation inside the public sector. It makes it possible to choose between sectors by choosing between marginal projects. In theory, such a process should be iterative and converge towards an optimum where budget constraints vanish. However, this is not true in practice, for the following reasons.

(a) planning processes stop before convergence is reached;
(b) arbitrations between sectors occur at a relatively high degree of aggregation, involving 'functions' rather than well defined projects;
(c) there may be a divergence between individual preferences and their evaluation by the political authority. Also, the latter is often less able to give information about its own scale of values than about its willingness to spend in the related sector.

FOCUS OF THE PAPER

The purpose of the paper is to present a general framework for the major problems of taxation and public production within budget constraints. These problems have been the subject of many contributions in the economic literature, the foremost being the studies by Boiteux (1956), and Diamond and Mirrlees (1971). Other valuable contributions are those of Kolm (1970), who was concerned with the theory of value constraints; Atkinson and Stiglitz (1972), who looked at indirect taxation; and Stiglitz and Dasgupta (1971), Dasgupta and Stiglitz (1972), Hahn (1973), and Mirrlees (1972), all of whom were concerned mainly with the problem of profit taxation and efficiency.

The present paper's originality lies in the fact that it formulates second-best models in primal language – specifically without use of indirect utility functions – and, thus, comes closer to the usual Paretian formulations. It leads to results – especially tax formulas – framed in terms of utility functions instead of demand functions, thus generalising the one-consumer approach of Atkinson and Stiglitz.

Though it is heavier in money, the solution appears advantageous whenever *compensated* demand derivatives are involved; whenever price normalisations are taken into consideration; and whenever household demands are not unique functions of consumer prices (marketable public goods) or when household incomes depend on variables (production prices, rates of taxation, and so on).

Section II recalls formulas linking up supply and demand (compensated or noncompensated) derivatives to first- and second-order derivatives of production and utility functions.

Section III is concerned with overall budget constraints. It focuses on three problems: profit taxation (with a restatement of more precise conditions for efficiency), marketable public goods, and optimal choice of managerial activity in an economy with taxes.

Section IV deals with sectoral budget constraints – with or without lump-sum transfers, and with or without indirect taxation. We arrive at a model generalising the Boiteux and the Diamond and Mirrlees models. We shall focus more specifically on the problem of proportional taxation – not so much with regard to consumer taxation as with regard to producer taxation.

Above all, we want to stress, in the present paper, the profound unity of all the results that have been obtained in taxation theory in the framework of a general equilibrium model.

General notations used throughout the paper

In the economy there are n commodities (index i, j), $\hat{h}$ households (index h), $\hat{k}$ public enterprises (index k) and $\hat{l}$ private firms (index l).

$f^l(y^l)$ is the production function of the lth firm $\left(f_1^l = \dfrac{\partial f^l}{\partial y_i} \geqslant 0\right)$. We suppose, as needed, that it is once or twice differentiable and has the usual convex properties.

$g^k(z^k)$ is the production function of the kth public enterprise ($g_i^k \geqslant 0$).

$U^h(x^h)$ is the utility function of household h, twice differentiable and with the usual convex properties.

W is the social welfare function, which we write $W(U^k)$, since we assume that it respects household preferences.

$(1 - \tau^l)$ is the rate of taxation of gross profit applied to the lth firm ($\tau^l \leqslant 1$).

θ_h^l is the share of household h in the net profit of firm $l \left(\sum_h \theta_h^l = 1\right)$.

$q = (q_1, q_2, \ldots, q_n)$ is the consumer price vector.
$p = (p_1, p_2, \ldots, p_n)$ is the producer price vector.
$u = (u_1, u_2, \ldots, u_n)$ is the vector of social values of commodities.
$t = q - u$ is the consumer tax vector.
$t' = u - p$ is the producer tax vector.

$T^h = \sum_h t_i x_i^h$ is the total amount of taxes paid by household h.

$T'^{l} = \sum_i t'_i y_i^l$ is the total amount of indirect taxes paid by firm l.

$D^l = (1 - \tau^l) \sum_l p_i y_i^p$ is the total amount of direct taxes paid by firm l.

II. DEMAND AND SUPPLY DERIVATIVES – SOME FORMULAS

Let $U(x_1, \ldots, x_n)$ be the twice-differentiable utility function of a consumer; I, his income; and $q = (q_1, q_2, \ldots, q_n)$, the price vector. Differentiating the equilibrium conditions,

$$U_i = \alpha q_i \text{ (with } \alpha = \text{marginal utility of income)}$$

and

$$\sum_i q_i x_i = I$$

we get (see, for instance Malinvaud, 1969, p. 56)

$$\begin{bmatrix} U'' & -q \\ -\tilde{q} & 0 \end{bmatrix} \begin{bmatrix} dx \\ d\alpha \end{bmatrix} = \begin{bmatrix} \alpha I & 0 \\ \tilde{x} & 1 \end{bmatrix} \begin{bmatrix} dq \\ -dI \end{bmatrix}$$

where U'' is the (n, n) matrix of second-order derivatives of U. Setting

$$dq = (0, \ldots, dq_j, \ldots, 0)$$

$$dI = x_j dq_j$$

and substituting U/α to q, we arrive at the well-known relationships between compensated demand derivatives $[(i, j) = (\partial x_i/\partial q_j)_u]$ and first- and second-order derivatives of the utility function:

$$\begin{bmatrix} U'' & -U' \\ -\tilde{U}' & 0 \end{bmatrix} \begin{bmatrix} q_j & (i, j) \\ q_j & h \end{bmatrix} = \begin{bmatrix} U_j & \delta_j \\ & 0 \end{bmatrix} \tag{15.3}$$

where δ_{ij} is the Kronecker symbol.

It is easy to demonstrate that $h = -(\partial x_j/\partial I)$. From the previous equations,

$$h = \left(\frac{\partial \log \alpha}{\partial q_j}\right)_U.$$

We have to show that

$$\left(\frac{\partial \log \alpha}{\partial q_j}\right)_U = -\frac{\partial x_j}{\partial I}$$

or, equivalently,

$$\frac{\partial \alpha}{\partial q_j} = -\frac{\partial \alpha x_j}{\partial I}$$

This results from the fact that

$$-\alpha x_j = \frac{\partial V}{\partial q_j}$$

and

$$\alpha = \frac{\partial V}{\partial I}$$

where $V(q_1, q_2, \ldots, q_n, I)$ is the indirect utility function.

Suppose that an $(n + 1)$ vector v, λ satisfies

$$\begin{bmatrix} U'' & -U' \\ -\widetilde{U}' & 0 \end{bmatrix} \begin{bmatrix} v \\ \lambda \end{bmatrix} = \begin{bmatrix} u \\ 0 \end{bmatrix}$$

where the first-hand coefficients matrix is regular. From the above results, we can infer that

$$v_j = \frac{1}{\alpha} \sum_j u_i(i, j)$$

and that

$$\lambda = -\frac{1}{\alpha} \sum_j u_i \frac{\partial x_i}{\partial I}$$

Suppose now that, in addition to the consumption vector x, U depends on a parameter x_0. We can show that

$$\sum_j U_{oj}(i, j) = -\alpha \frac{\partial x_i}{\partial x_o}$$

Starting from

$$\sum_j U_j(i, j) \equiv 0$$

and taking derivatives with respect to x_o, we get

$$\sum_j U_{oj}(i, j) + \sum_j U_j \frac{\partial}{\partial x_o} \left[\frac{\partial x_j}{\partial q_i} + x_i \frac{dx_j}{dI} \right] = 0$$

and
$$-\sum_j U_{oj}(i, j) = \alpha \frac{\partial x_i}{\partial x_o} \underbrace{\sum_j q_j \frac{\partial x_j}{\partial I}}_{=1} + \alpha \underbrace{\sum_j q_j \left[\frac{\partial}{q_i} \left(\frac{\partial x_j}{\partial x_o} \right) + x_i \frac{\partial}{\partial I} \left(\frac{\partial x_j}{\partial x_o} \right) \right]}_{=0}$$

$= 0$, since the price vector q and income I are the same when the demand is x and when it is $x + (\partial x / \partial x_0) dx_0$.

Let us now turn to supply derivatives. It can easily be checked that supply derivatives of a firm can be expressed in terms of first- and second-order derivatives of the production function, using exactly the same formulas as the ones giving compensated demand derivatives in terms of first- and second-order derivatives of the utility function:

$$\begin{bmatrix} f'' & -f' \\ -\tilde{f}' & 0 \end{bmatrix} \begin{bmatrix} p_j & \dfrac{\partial y}{\partial p_j} \\ p_j & h \end{bmatrix} = \begin{bmatrix} f_j & \partial_j \\ 0 & \end{bmatrix} \tag{15.4}$$

The h variable cannot in this case be given a straightforward interpretation. Suppose, however, that the production function depends on a parameter m – say, the managerial activity by the firm's owner. (Without loss of generality, one can write $f(x) - m = 0$.)
By analogy with the consumer case,

$$h = -\frac{\partial y_j}{\partial B}$$

at constant prices, where B is the profit of the firm. Since $dm = dB$ (at constant prices),

$$h = -\delta \frac{\partial y_j}{\partial m}$$

where δ is the marginal productivity of money.

III. AGGREGATE BUDGET CONSTRAINT FOR THE PUBLIC SECTOR

The general theorem first outlined by Diamond and Mirrlees (1971) and subsequently made more accurate in works by Stiglitz and Dasgupta (1971), Dasgupta and Stiglitz (1972), Mirrlees (1972), and Hahn (1973) can be stated as follows:

Production efficiency is desirable in so far as a minimum degree of discrimination is allowed in the tax system:

– complete discrimination in commodity taxation (among commodities, but not necessarily among households or firms); and
– complete discrimination in profit taxation among private firms.

Leaving aside technical conditions, this result holds if, and only if, an optimum exists. If it does not, this is due to one of two main causes: either the attainable set is empty, or it is unfounded.

When there are no profits in the private sector (constant returns to scale), or when profits are fully taxed, an optimum exists under quite reasonable assumptions (see Diamond and Mirrlees, 1971). When profits are not constrained to 100 per cent taxation, there may exist no optimum. Since the attainable set is larger, this is due not to emptiness but to unboundedness. Let us be more precise.

THE MODEL

We have to maximise $W(U^h)$ under the following constraints:

$$(u_i) \quad \sum_n x_i^h - \sum_l y_i^l - \sum_k z_i^k = 0$$

$$(v_i^h) \quad U_i^h - \alpha^h q_i = 0 \qquad \text{with } q_1 = 1$$

$$(r^h) \quad \sum_j q_j x_j^h - \sum_l \theta_h^l R^l = 0$$

$$(S^l) \quad R^l \geqslant 0$$

$$(\lambda^l) \quad f^l(y_i^l) = 0$$

$$(\mu^k) \quad g^k(z_i^k) = 0$$

$$(\phi^l) \quad R^l - \tau^l \sum_l y_i^k p_i^l = 0 \qquad \text{with } p_i^l = \delta^l f_i^l \text{ and } p_1^l = 1 \ \forall l$$

This formulation raises no special problem but we must make two remarks. First, we did not write that all private firms are faced with the same price vector; this will result from the optimality conditions. Second, the (θ^l) constraints do not play any role in the determination of the optimal allocation, since each τ^l variable occurs in only one equation. Once R^l and $\sum_i y_i^l p_i^l$ are known, τ^l can be calculated by the (θ^l) equation. Of course, what may arise is that, at the optimum of the problem without the (θ^l) equations, R^l is strictly positive while $\sum_i y_i^l p_i^l = 0$, so that there should be an infinite rate of subsidy for the shareholders of the lth firm. Here lies, as has already been pointed out (see Dasgupta and Stiglitz, 1972; and Mirrlees, 1972), the cause of nonexistence. In such circumstances, the general problem we are dealing with can make sense only if a maximum rate of subsidy is fixed, i.e. if τ^l is given an upper limit.

Let us start with the model without any constraint on the τ^l variables (and without the θ^l equations). This model is the equivalent of the 'less constrained model' used by Mirrlees (1972, p. 106, equation 5). In the special case where all θ_h^l are set to zero, we have the original Diamond and Mirrlees model.

NO CONSTRAINT ON PROFIT TAXATION RATES

Optimality conditions can be written:

$$(x_i^h)\quad u_i = \left(W^h - \frac{r^h}{\alpha^h}\right) U_i^h - \sum_j v_j^h\, U_{ij}^h$$

$$(\alpha^h)\quad \sum_j v_j^h U_j^h = 0$$

$$(q_j)\quad \sum_h \alpha^h v_j^h = \sum_h r^h x_j^h \;{}^{1}$$

$$(R^l)\quad \sum_h \theta_h^l\, r^h = s^l$$

$$(y_i^l)\quad u_i = \lambda^l f_i^l$$

$$(z_i^k)\quad u_i = \mu^k g_i^k$$

The two last equations illustrate the classical production efficiency theorem. The others permit the quantification of the optimal tax system.

From (x^h) and (α^h), we get, as has been shown in section II,

$$v_j^h = -\frac{1}{\alpha^h}\sum_i u_i\,(i, j)$$

and

$$W^h - \frac{r^h}{\alpha^h} = \frac{1}{\alpha^h}\sum_i u_i \frac{\partial x_i^h}{\partial I^h}$$

which can be written

$$r^h = \beta^h - \sum_i u_i \frac{\partial x_i^h}{\partial I^h}$$

where $\beta^h = \alpha^h W^h$ = marginal social utility of income to household h.

Reporting in (q_j), we can then write optimal tax formulas[2] in two ways:

(1) with compensated demand derivatives:

$$\sum_h r^h x_j^h = \sum_{th} t_i (i, j)^h \tag{15.5}$$

[1] Since q_1 is exogeneous, the (q_1) relation does not come from maximisation of the Lagrangian. It can be obtained by summing up the (r^h) equations (after multiplying each by r^h) and subtracting the (R^l) and $[(q_j), j \neq 1]$ relations (each being multiplied by the corresponding primal variable).

[2] The complete summary relative to commodities shows that any of these can be taken as an untaxed good in the implementation of tax formulas. This is related to the fact that the two price vectors need not be normalised relative to each other.

(2) with noncompensated demand derivatives:

$$\sum_h \beta^h x_j^h = -\sum_{ih} u_i \frac{\partial x_i^h}{\partial q_j}$$

or

$$\sum_h \beta^h x_j^h = \sum_h \frac{\partial T^h}{\partial t_j} \tag{15.6}$$

When there are many – and nonidentical – consumers, the second formula is more manageable, or at least more suggestive, since the weights β^h have an intrinsic meaning, while the r^h depend on optimal taxes. In the case of one consumer or identical consumers, and especially when we are interested in proportional taxation, the first formula is more useful, since compensated demand derivatives have 'nicer' properties than noncompensated derivatives have.

We may also note that, if lump-sum transfers were possible between households, we should have obtained tax formulas with compensated demand derivatives:

$$r\sum_h x^h = \sum_{ih} t_i(i, j)^h$$

CONSTRAINTS ON PROFIT TAX RATES

The reason that induces one to take into account constraints on profit taxation rates is the possible unboundedness of the attainable set and, thus, the possible nonexistence of an optimum. However, the appeal for less discrimination in profit taxation seems to have a wider justification.

In fact, complete discrimination in profit taxation appears to be more or less a substitute for lump-sum transfers. Take, for instance, an economy where each household owns at least one firm – albeit very small – where production sets are such that, for every frontier point on the global production set, each firm produces and makes a profit.[3] Let us go further and suppose that there is no negative consumption (time for labour and leisure being a scarce resource); then, with discriminatory profit (and rent) taxation the optimum that is obtained is not second-best but Pareto optimal. Of course, there is nothing wrong in obtaining Pareto optima, but here it shows clearly that the problem has been evaded. Actually, there seem to be as many difficulties in determining and enforcing discriminatory profit taxes as in determining and enforcing lump-sum transfers. We shall consider the case where minima $1 - \tau_{\max}^h$ and maxima $1 - \tau_{\min}^h$ are set for the possible rates of profit taxation.[4]

[3] For instance, Inada conditions are satisfied and each set is strictly convex.

[4] Note that the unconstrained case corresponds to $\tau_{\min}^h = 0$ (100 per cent taxation) and $\tau_{\max}^h = +\infty$ (infinite subsidy).

With such constraints, and assuming, for simplicity (as did Mirrlees, 1972), that each firm is owned by one household, so that we are dealing with household-firms, we can write the model as follows:

max $W(U^h)$

subject to the constraints

$(u_i)\quad \sum_h x_i^h - \sum_h y_i^h - \sum_k z_i^k = 0$

$(V_i^h)\quad U_i^h - \alpha^h q_i = 0$ with $q_1 = 1$

$(r^h)\quad \sum_j q_j x_j^h - \tau^h \sum_j p_j y_j^l = 0$

$(\lambda^h)\quad f^h(y_i^h) = 0$

$(w_i^h)\quad f_i^h - \delta^h p_i = 0$ with $p_1 = 1$

$(\mu^k)\quad g^k(z_i^k) = 0$

$(s^h)\quad \tau^h \leqslant \tau_{\max}^h$

$(s'^h)\quad -\tau^h \leqslant -\tau_{\min}^h$

The optimality conditions are[5]

$$(x_i^h)\quad u_i = \left(W^h - \frac{r^h}{\alpha^h}\right) U_i^h - \sum_j v_j^h U_{ij}^h$$

$$(\alpha^h)\quad \sum_j v_j^h U_j^h = 0$$

$$(\tau^h)\quad s^h - s'^h = r^h \sum_j p_j y_j^h$$

$$(y_i^h)\quad u_i = -\frac{r^h \tau^h f_i^h}{\delta^h} + \lambda^h f_i^h + \sum_j w_j^h f_{ij}^h$$

[5] Constraints of non-negativity or nonpositivity for the y_i^h variables are not explicitly taken into account here. To deal with such constraints (for instance $y_i^h \geqslant 0$), we would have to modify (w_i^h) in

$$(w_i^h)\; f_i^h - \delta^h p_i \leqslant 0$$

with equality if $y_i^h > 0$. We can check that this is equivalent to writing

$$(w_i^h)\; y_i^h (f_i^h - \delta^h p_i) = 0$$

which does not change tax formulas.

$(\delta^h)\quad \sum_j w_j^h f_j^h = 0$

$(q_j)\quad \sum_h \alpha^h v_j^h = \sum_h r^h x_j^h \qquad j \neq 1$

$(p_j)\quad \sum_h r^h \tau^h y_j^h + \sum_h w_j^h \delta^h = 0 \qquad j \neq 1$

$(z_i^k)\quad u_i = \mu^k g_i^k$

OPTIMAL TAXATION

When constraints are set on profit-tax rates, production efficiency does not hold any longer, as we can see. We must then determine both consumer and producer tax rates. We have also to determine the optimal rates of taxation on profits.

Profit taxation

As previously, we obtain from the (x_i^h) and (α^h) equations

$$r^h = \beta^h - \sum_i u_i \frac{\partial x_i^h}{\partial I^h}$$

or

$$r^h = \beta^h - 1 + T_m^h$$

with $T_m^h = \partial \sum t_i x_i^h / \partial I^h$ = the marginal rate of consumer taxation.

From the (τ^h) equations we infer that

$$\begin{aligned} \tau^h &= \tau_{\max}^h && \text{if } r^h > 0 \\ \tau^h &= \tau_{\min}^k && \text{if } r^h < 0 \\ \tau_{\min}^h \leqslant \tau^h &\leqslant \tau_{\max}^h && \text{if } r^h = 0 \end{aligned}$$

Thus, *the profit-tax rate for a household is a maximum (minimum) if the sum of the marginal rate of consumer taxation (i.e. the increase in consumer taxes for a unit increase in income) and the marginal social utility of income is greater (less) than one.*

Consumer taxation

Reporting the value of r^h in (q_j), we have

$$\sum_h \beta^h x_j^h = -\sum_{ih} u_i \frac{\partial x_i^h}{\partial q_j} \qquad j \neq 1 \qquad (15.7)$$

which can be written

$$\sum_h \beta^h x_j^h = \frac{\partial \sum T^h}{\partial t_j} \qquad j \neq 1 \quad (15.7')$$

Consumer tax formulas are the same as those in the case of unconstrained profit taxation. The only difference is that we can take only the commodity (or bundle of commodities) on the price normalisation as the untaxed goods instead of any commodity.

Producer taxation

From (y_i^h) and (δ^h), we obtain

$$w_j^h = \frac{1}{\delta^h} \sum_i u_i \frac{\partial y_i^h}{\partial p_j}$$

Reporting the values of r^h and w_j^h in (p_j), we have

$$\sum_h \beta^h \tau^h y_j^h = -\sum_{ih} u_i \frac{\partial y_i^h}{\partial p_j} - \tau^h y_j^h \frac{\partial x_i^h}{\partial I^h} \qquad j \neq 1$$

or, since $\tau^h y_j^h (\partial x_i^h / \partial I^h)$ represents the effect on consumption x_i^h of a change in price p_j (through the income of household h),

$$\sum_h \beta^h \tau^h y_j^h = -\sum_{ih} u_i \left(\frac{\partial y_i^h}{\partial p_j} - \frac{\partial x_i^h}{\partial p_j} \right) \qquad j \neq 1 \quad (15.8)$$

which can be written

$$\sum_h (\beta^h \tau^h + 1 - \tau^h) y_i^h = - \frac{\partial \sum_h (T^h + T'^h)}{\partial t'_j} \qquad j \neq 1 \quad (15.8')$$

This formula generalises the one obtained by Mirrlees (1972) in the case of $\tau^h = 1$.

Here again, there is no symmetry relative to commodities. However, consumer and producer taxation can be given a more symmetrical form. Summing up the (r^h) equations (each multiplied by the corresponding dual variable) and subtracting the (q_j) and (p_j) equations (each multiplied by the corresponding primal variable), we obtain, all calculations made,

$$\sum_h r^h x_1^h - \sum_h \alpha^h v_1^h = \sum_h r^h \tau^h y_1^h + \sum_h w_1^h \delta^h$$

or

$$\sum_h \beta^h (x_1^h - \tau^h y_1^h) = \sum_{ih} u_i \left(\frac{\partial y_1^h}{\partial \pi_1} - \frac{\partial x_1^h}{\partial \pi_1} \right) \qquad (15.9)$$

with $\pi_1 = p_1 = q_1$. Rewriting the budget constraint of each household-firm:

$$\pi_1(x_1^h - \tau^h y_1^h) + \sum_{j \neq 1} q_j x_j^h + \sum_{j \neq 1} p_j(-\tau^h y_j^h) = 0$$

or, if we give a different index for each 'commodity' the 'net demand' for which is evaluated at a different price in the budget constraint,

$$\sum_{i=1}^{2n-1} \pi_i d_i^h = 0$$

(where d_i^h = 'net demand' for the 'commodity' i by household-firm h), we can gather all tax formulas into one:

$$\sum_h \beta^h d_j^h = -\sum_{ih} u_i\left(\frac{\partial y_i^h}{\partial \pi_j} - \frac{\partial x_i^h}{\partial \pi_j}\right) \qquad j = 1, \ldots, 2n-1 \qquad (15.10)$$

or, equivalently,

$$\sum \beta^h d_j^h = \frac{\partial \sum u_i z_i}{\partial \pi_j} \qquad j = 1, \ldots, 2n-1 \quad (15.10')$$

where $z = \sum_h z^l$ (net supply by the public sector).

This formula holds more generally when constraints other than the one related to price normalisation are set on indirect taxation, and, in particular, when the indirect tax rates are set equal to zero, the 'net demands' are then

$$d_j^h = x_j^h - \tau^h y_j^h \qquad j = 1, \ldots, n$$

PRODUCTION EFFICIENCY

As we have seen, constraints on profit-taxation *generally* lead to *production inefficiency.* This runs counter to a theorem formulated by Hahn, according to which the setting of maximum rates of profit taxation – i.e. a lower limit for the τ^h – does not prevent production efficiency. The reason is that Hahn does not normalise the consumer price vector relative to the producer price vector. Suppose that, without constraints on tax rates, there exists an optimum such that no firm is fully taxed (i.e. in the notations of the previous subsection, $R = 0$ and $\sum_i p_i y_i > 0$). We can then adjust the consumer price vector in such a way that, for the firm which has the highest such vector, the tax rates equalises any given number: *the maximum-tax-rates constraints are satisfied though nothing has changed in the allocation of goods to households and to producers.*

If, on the other hand, there exists in the unconstrained problem at least one firm (with nonzero profit) that is fully taxed, obviously the constrained problem has no optimum (since we can get as close as we want to the unconstrained optimum by increasing the consumer price level).

Are there, however, situations where production efficiency holds, and can we characterise such situations? A necessary and sufficient condition for efficiency is

$$W_j^h \delta^h = 0 \qquad \forall j, \forall h$$

After the optimality relation (p_j), a necessary condition is

$$\sum_h r^h \tau^h y_j^h = 0 \qquad \forall j \neq 1$$

which is met, in particular, when, for each firm, either $r^h \tau^h = 0$: the optimal profit-tax rate is not bounded by the lower or the upper limit (unless the latter is 100 per cent taxation); or $y_j^h = 0 \, \forall j$: the firm does not produce.

Clearly, this condition is sufficient for production efficiency. We then have to know whether it is also necessary; i.e. whether it is possible to have

$$\sum_h r^h \tau^h y_j^h = 0 \qquad \forall j \neq 1$$

without $r^h \tau^h$ for all the firms that produce.

This would not be possible, for instance, if one commodity – other than commodity 1 – is, for the private productive sector, only an input (labour) or only on output (final good), and if all the r^h have the same sign (i.e. there is not one firm for which the rate of taxation is bound by the lower limit, and another for which it is bound by the upper limit). It would not be possible, either, if, for any price vector, the production plans[6] of the private firms were independent.

In fact, though it is possible to provide examples where production efficiency holds without $r^h \tau^h = 0$ for all the firms that produce, such a situation appears very exceptional. Without much loss of accuracy, we can then say that *the necessary and sufficient condition for production efficiency is that, for all the firms that produce, the optimal profit-tax rate should not be bounded by the lower or the upper limit (unless the latter is 100 per cent taxation).*

Let us turn back to the problem dealt with in the previous subsection, where no constraint was set on profit-tax rates, and suppose a situation where no optimum exists, due to the need for an infinite rate of subsidy for a certain firm h. Suppose that an upper bound is set on the rate of subsidy. Will efficiency hold?

We must distinguish two cases.

[6] In fact, the $(2, 3, \ldots, n)$ composite of the production plans.

First, *if firm h is dominated by a private firm* – and under the reasonable assumption that, as was pointed out by Hahn, it is not possible to prevent a private firm from producing if it is profitable – then the optimum solution would be no production for firm h and production efficiency would then hold. *In the conflict between equity and efficiency, the functioning of the model favours the latter.*

Second, *if firm h is dominated by a public firm,* then, in most circumstances, the optimum would be some production for firm h – depending, of course, on the maximum rate of subsidy that is allowed – and production efficiency would no longer hold (though it would hold separately in the private and in the public sectors). *Here the arbitration between efficiency and equity appears more balanced.*

These results differ from those obtained by Dasgupta and Stiglitz (1972) and Diamond and Mirrlees (1971), who did not take into account constraints on profit-tax rates and made the assumption that it was possible to forbid a private firm to produce. There remains, however, the fact that it may be desirable to nationalise a private firm – not to make production more efficient, but, exactly the opposite, to make it less efficient.

MANAGERIAL ACTIVITY BY HOUSEHOLDS

Managerial activity has been introduced by Mirrlees (1972) in response to the problem raised by the possible lack of incentive to producers when profits can be fully taxed. Managerial activity in an optimal taxation model does itself raise an interesting and unusual problem of externality, since, in this instance, taxation is not the remedy but the cause of the phenomenon.

Mirrlees (1972) assumes that each household-firm chooses managerial activity m so as to maximise utility subject to household budget and production function constraints:

$$\max U(x, m)$$

subject to

$$(\alpha) \quad \sum_j q_j x_j - \tau \sum_j p_j y_j = 0$$

$$(\phi) \quad f(y_j) - m = 0$$

Optimality conditions show that the level of managerial activity chosen by the household is such that $U'_m = \alpha\tau/\delta$, where α is the marginal utility of income, and δ is the marginal productivity of money.

Should the 'planner' determine the optimum level of managerial activity by household h, what would it be? The model of the penultimate subsection, where U^h and f^h are supposed to be functions of m^h, gives, in deriving the Lagrangian with respect to m^h,

$$W^h U_m^h = \sum_j v_j^h U_{jm}^h - \lambda^h$$

But
$$\sum_j v_j^h U_{jm}^h = -\frac{1}{\alpha^h}\sum_{ij} u_i(i, j) U_{jm}^h = \sum_i u_i \frac{\partial x_i^h}{\partial m}$$

(cf. p. 367 above) and

$$\lambda^h - \frac{r^h \tau^h}{\delta^h} = \sum_i u_i \frac{\partial y_i^h}{\partial m}$$

(cf. p. 368 above). Then,

$$W^h U_m^h = W^h \frac{\alpha^h \tau^h}{\delta^h} + \sum_i \frac{\partial t_i' y_i^h}{\partial m} + \sum_i \frac{\partial t_i x_i^h}{\partial m} + \frac{\tau^h}{\delta^h} \sum_i \frac{\partial t_i x_i^h}{\partial I^h} - \frac{\tau^h}{\delta^h}$$

The four last terms represent, respectively, for a unit change in managerial activity:

(1) the change in producer taxes;
(2) the change in consumer taxes (at constant income; i.e. through the change in the demand functions);
(3) the change in consumer taxes (through the change of $\frac{\tau^h}{\delta^h}$ in net income); and
(4) the change in profit taxes.

Thus, it appears that the choice of managerial activity by any household-firm will, if a change in this activity would induce a nonzero change in the total amount of taxes – direct and indirect – paid by this household, deviate from the level that is optimal for society as a whole. More precisely, it will be lower (higher) if an increase in managerial activity would induce an increase (decrease) in total taxes.

We can say that, in determining its managerial activity, each household-firm should take into account the effect of its decision on the other households. What is particularly simple in the previous result is that *this externality is measured by the marginal change in total taxes paid by the household-firm.*

We can also note that this externality still exists when there is no commodity taxation and only profit taxation. This clearly shows, contrary to what is usually said to be the case, that profit taxation is not neutral: *a positive rate of profit taxation induces households to provide less managerial activity than would be optimal for society as a whole.*

MARKETABLE PUBLIC GOODS

In their treatment of the subject, Diamond and Mirrlees (1971) and Stiglitz and Dasgupta (1971) considered public goods to be nonpriced goods. Though in real life most public goods are free – or are priced after conventional rules – we are, in fact, faced with two different problems. On the one hand, it is interesting to see how optimal tax formulas stand when there are priced public goods. On the other hand, there is the problem of determining, for nonpriced goods – be they public or private – the 'shadow' demand, which can be expressed by the relationship between marginal cost of production and households' willingness to pay. This, essentially, was the problem studied by the above-mentioned authors; and, though they looked at it in relation to public goods, their results can easily be adapted for private goods (see section IV below).

Let us, then, focus on the first problem. Commodity n is a public good that can be priced according to willingness to pay (q_n^h). The constraints (v_i^h) and (r^h) are replaced by

$$(v_n^h) \quad U_n^h - \alpha^h q_n^h = 0$$

$$(v_i^h) \quad U_i^h - \alpha^h q_i = 0 \qquad i \neq n$$

$$(r^h) \quad q_n^h x_n + \sum_{j \neq n} q_j x_j^h = 0$$

and the optimality conditions by:

$$(x_n) \quad u_n = \sum_h \left(W^h - \frac{r^h}{\alpha^h} \right) U_n^h - \sum_{jn} v_j^h U_{nj}^h$$

$$(x_i^h) \quad u_i = \left(W^h - \frac{r^h}{\alpha^h} \right) U_i^h - \sum_j v_j^h U_{ij}^h \qquad i \neq n$$

$$(q_n^h) \quad \alpha^h v_n^h = r^h x_n$$

$$(q_j) \quad \sum_h \alpha^h v_j^h = \sum_h r^h x_j^h \qquad j \neq n$$

Before resolving this general system, two points must be made.

First, whether pricing a given public good is desirable or not depends on the sign of $\sum_h r^h q_n^h$. *If there is no lower limit on rates of profit taxation* (i.e. it is possible to increase the net income of any household-firm by changing direct fiscality), then $r^h \leqslant 0, \forall h$, and *pricing leads, in any case, to higher social welfare.* If, on the other hand, there are household-firms whose profit tax is bounded lower, and for whom a given public good has a great utility (relative to other households), then it may be desirable to provide the good freely.

Second, if utility functions are separable with respect to public consumption ($U_{in}^h = 0, i \neq n$), then optimal consumer taxes can be derived with the same formulas as would apply were only private goods (public consumption and personalised prices being held constant).

Resolution in the general case

Since there is only one consumption decision for commodity n, there corresponds to it just one dual equation; we cannot, as in the second subsection of section III, obtain the v_j^h variables in terms of the u_i. But this becomes possible if we split (x_n) into $\hat{h}$ relations by setting

$$u_n^h = \left(W^h - \frac{r^h}{\alpha^h}\right)U_n^h - \sum_j v_j^h U_{nj}^h$$

where $u_n = \sum_h u_n^h$. We can then resolve (writing, for simplicity, u_i^h instead of u_i, even for $i \neq n$)

$$v_j^h = -\frac{1}{\alpha^h}\sum_i u_i^h (i, j)^h$$

and

$$W^h - \frac{r^h}{\alpha^h} = \frac{1}{\alpha^h}\sum_i u_i^h \frac{\partial x_i^h}{\partial I^h}$$

Reporting in (q_n^h) and (q_j), we obtain the formulas

$$\beta^h x_n = -\sum_i u_i^h \frac{\partial x_i^h}{\partial q_n^h}$$

and

$$\sum_h \beta^h x_j^h = -\sum_{ih} u_i^h \frac{\partial x_i^h}{\partial q_j} \tag{15.11}$$

where $\sum_h u_n^h = u_n$ and $u_i^h = u_i \; i \neq n$.

The emergence of personalised prices u_i^h at the production and at the consumption level can be readily interpreted: it is as if the demand for the public good by each household were taxed at discriminatory rates.

The optimal tax rates – both uniform taxes on private goods and personalised taxes on public goods – obey the general logic of taxation: *a change in each tax rate would produce a change in tax revenue proportionate to the actual total demand for the related good by households (weighted by their marginal social utilities of income).*

IV. SECTORAL BUDGET CONSTRAINTS

The Boiteux model

Let us start by transcribing into our language the Boiteux model. The only difference is that, instead of choosing a particular commodity to express the right-hand side of budget constraints, we allow for the choice (*ex ante*) of any bundle of commodities, and, eventually, for different bundles for different public enterprises.

Using the general notation given in section I, the Boiteux model can be written:

$$\max W(U^h)$$

subject to the constraints

$$(u_i) \quad \sum_h x_i^h - \sum_f y_i^l - \sum_h z_i^k = 0$$

$$(v_i^h) \quad U_i^h - \alpha^h q_i = 0 \qquad \text{with } q_1 = 1$$

$$(\lambda^l) \quad f^l(y_i^l) = 0$$

$$(w_i^l) \quad f_i^l - \delta^l q_i = 0$$

$$(\mu^k) \quad g^k(z_i^k) = 0$$

$$(\gamma^k) \quad \sum_j z_j^k q_j = b^k \sum_j v_j^k q_j \qquad \text{with } \sum_j v_j^k = 1$$

The optimality conditions are

$$(x_i^h) \quad u_i = W^h U_i^h - \sum_j v_j^h U_{ij}^h$$

$$(\alpha^h) \quad \sum_j v_j^h U_j^h = 0$$

$$(q_j) \quad \sum_h \gamma^k (z_j^k - b^k v_j^k) = \sum_h \alpha^h v_j^h + \sum_l w_j^l \delta^l$$

$$(y_i^l) \quad u_i = \lambda^l f_i^l + \sum_j w_j^l f_{ij}^l$$

$$(\delta^l) \quad \sum_j w_j^l q_j = 0$$

$$(z_j^k) \quad u_i = \mu^k g_i^k + \gamma^k q_i$$

Shadow prices are no longer equal to marginal social values of commodities (u_i). Shadow taxes, for every public enterprise, are proportional to market prices, the level for each one being such that the related budget constraint is exactly met. In particular, shadow taxes are zero for an unconstrained public enterprise.[7]

The determination of the tax system is straightforward; from (x_i^h) and (α^h) we obtain

$$\alpha^h v_j^h = -\sum_i u_i (i, j)^h$$

Similarly, from (y_i^l) and (δ^l),

$$\delta^l w_j^l = \sum_i u_i \frac{\partial y_i^l}{\partial q_i}$$

Reporting in (q_j), we obtain

$$\sum_k \gamma^k (z_j^k - b^k v_j^k) = -\sum_i t_i e_{ij} \tag{15.12}$$

where $t_i = q_i - u_i$

and $$e_{ij} = \sum_l \frac{\partial y_i^l}{\partial q_i} - \sum_h (i, j)^h$$

The matrix e_{ij} is singular, since $\sum_j q_j e_{ij} = 0, \forall i$. But we can also check that $\sum_j q_j \left[\sum_k \gamma^k (z_j^k - b^k v_j^k) \right] = 0, \forall i$, given which the system of equations (15.12) has a solution that is defined mod. vector q_j. A particular solution can be obtained by setting $t_1 = 0$, and $(t_2, t_3, \ldots, t_n)$ is determined by

$$\sum_k \gamma^k (z_j^k - b^k v_j^k) = -\sum_{j \neq 1} t_i e_{ij} \qquad j \neq 1$$

This, in the case where $v^k = (1, 0, \ldots, 0)$, corresponds to the formulas given in Boiteux (1956). We may note, once again, that, if lump-sum transfers from one household to another are allowed, it is compensated demand derivatives that come across in tax formulas.

[7] Nationalising any private firm would then improve the aggregate welfare.

AGGREGATE BALANCE FOR THE PUBLIC SECTOR

Do sectoral budget constraints induce aggregate balance for the public sector? If strict budget balance is required of each public enterprise, then aggregate balance results, without any (real) tax. If this is not the case, we may think that aggregate balance could be obtained by means of proportional indirect taxation, i.e. by adjusting the level of consumer prices with respect to producer prices. Actually, nothing in the model as it is written in the previous subsection requires the two levels to be equal. χ being the level of producer prices with respect to consumer prices, aggregate balance means

$$\sum_{jh}(1-\chi)q_j x_j^h = \chi \sum_k b^k \left[\sum_j v_j^k q_j\right]$$

or, taking into account (u_i) and (γ^k),

$$\sum_{jh} q_j x_j^h = \chi \sum_{jl} q_j y_j^l \tag{15.13}$$

Two conclusions can be drawn from the above relationship.

First, we should have arrived at the same formula if, instead of using proportional indirect taxation, we had tried to obtain an aggregate balance with a uniform profit tax.

Second, an acceptable value of χ is obtained only if the value of private consumption is non-negative. This condition is always satisfied (under regular properties of the utility functions) when there is no negative consumption – time for labour being a scarce resource. If this is not the case, then aggregate balance makes it necessary to add to the model the constraint

$$(r) \sum_{jh} q_j x_j^h \geqslant 0$$

i.e. the kind of constraint that was taken into account in the models of the Diamond and Mirrlees type.

Clearly, then, sectoral budget constraints – even if there is only one for the whole public sector – appear to be of a quite different nature from the overall budget constraint that we were dealing with in section III. They express the limited availability of public funds for the different public purposes, and, thus, the corresponding dual variables can be viewed as 'opportunity costs of public funds' (relative to each purpose).

BOITEUX MODEL WITHOUT LUMP-SUM TRANSFERS

Instead of considering a single budget constraint for households as a whole, let us consider separate budget constraints, so as to see what happens in the Boiteux model when lump-sum transfers are not feasible. We examine first the case for proportional, then that for differential, indirect taxation.

Proportional indirect taxation

Adding into the model presented in the penultimate subsection the following constraints,

$$(r^h)\quad \sum_j q_j x_j^h - \sum_l \theta_h^l R^l = 0$$

$$(s^l)\quad R^l \geqslant 0$$

leads to the replacement of the (x_i^h) and (q_j) optimality conditions by

$$(x_i^h)\quad u_i = \left(W^h - \frac{r^h}{\alpha^h}\right)U_l^h - \sum_j v_j^h U_{ij}^h$$

$$(q_j)\quad \sum_k \gamma^k(z_j^k - b^k v_j^k) = \sum_h \alpha^h v_j^h + \sum_l w_j^l \delta^l - \sum_h r^h x_j^h$$

Thus, the optimal tax formulas become

$$\sum_h \beta^h x_j^h + \sum_k \gamma^k(z_j^k - b^k v_j^k) = \sum_i u_i\left[\sum_l \frac{\partial y_i^l}{\partial q_j} - \sum_h \frac{\partial x_i^h}{\partial q_j}\right] \tag{15.14}$$

Differential indirect taxation

If we want to allow differential indirect taxation, we are faced with the following problem: should the sectoral budget constraints of public enterprises be written with consumer or with producer prices? Of course, one is free to choose either possibility, but it is interesting to discuss which is the more meaningful – and the easier to handle.

Stiglitz and Dasgupta have looked at the first possibility; we shall examine the second. We can argue that producers – public and private – are more accustomed to dealing with producer prices (i.e. 'before tax' prices) than with consumer prices ('after tax' prices). Writing sectoral budget constraints with producer prices also leads to simpler results. Actually, the above tax formulas are of two kinds:

(1) consumer tax formulas (which are the usual Diamond and Mirrlees type):

$$\sum_h \beta^h x_j^h = -\sum_{ih} u_i \frac{\partial x_i^h}{\partial q_j} \tag{15.15}$$

(2) producer tax formulas:

$$\sum_k \gamma^k(z_j^k - b^k v_j^k) = \sum_{il} u_i \frac{\partial y_i^l}{\partial p_j} \tag{15.16}$$

Public-enterprise shadow taxes are proportional to producer prices.

NONMARKET GOODS

Thus far, we have been dealing with public enterprises providing commodities to private agents through the market. Budget constraints have meant the limitation of deficit – eventually profit – to a given figure. What if, among the sectors under consideration, there are administrations that provide commodities to households without charge? For such goods, there exist neither consumer nor producer prices. Budget constraints, then, have a more traditional content, i.e. the endowment of funds to be spent in the purchase of commodities for a given activity.

We can check first that both consumer and producer tax formulas that involve only market commodities are unchanged. Then, as regards the optimal production and allocation of nonmarket goods, there are two separate problems:

(1) that of determining the 'shadow' demand, i.e. the relationship between social value (u'_j) and willingness to pay (q'^h_j). Formulas analogous to those of Diamond and Mirrlees (1971, p. 271) obtain

$$u'_j = \beta^h q'^h_j - \sum_i u_i \frac{\partial x_i^h}{\partial x'^h_j}$$

in the case of private goods, and

$$u'_j = \sum_h \beta^h q'^h_j - \sum_{ih} u_i \frac{\partial x_i^h}{\partial x'_j}$$

in the case of public goods.

(2) that of determining the shadow prices for public enterprises and administrations. While shadow taxes are proportional to producer prices for market commodities, they are null for nonmarket goods:

$$\mu^k \frac{\partial g^k}{\partial z_i^k} = u_i - \gamma^k p_i$$

$$\mu^k \frac{\partial g^k}{\partial x_j} = u_i$$

When proportionality obtains for producer taxation, then the rule, in terms of prices, that each administration must follow in evaluating public projects becomes very simple: use social values for outputs, use producer prices for inputs, and apply to outlays an 'opportunity cost' such that the budget constraint set for the administration is exactly met. In particular, this rule involves different discount rates for, on the one hand, commodities provided to households, and, on the other, commodities purchased in the market.

PROPORTIONAL TAXATION

Proportional consumer taxation – for all commodities, bar one considered nontaxable – has been much studied in the economic literature. Conditions for proportionality obtain with enough generality only in the case of a single household or, which is almost the same, in the case of identical households. Proportionality, then, results from an *intrinsic property of the utility function,* which is the equicompensated demand elasticity of taxable commodities with respect to the nontaxed commodity price. The only separable utility function to possess this property is the direct addilog function (see Diamond and Mirrlees, 1971; and Atkinson and Stiglitz, 1972).

Let us now turn to *producer taxation* as it appears in the present context. Full proportionality (i.e. for all market commodities) cannot be contemplated when sectoral budget constraints involve only public enterprises, for it would then mean production efficiency. We shall consider, for the sake of simplicity, that there is a single administration (and, thus, a single budget constraint). Clearly, as in the case of consumer taxation, proportional taxation cannot result from an intrinsic property of production functions. Moreover, producer taxes are heavily dependent on the *numéraire* that is used for writing the budget constraint.

Since taking one *numéraire* rather than another has no specific meaning, we can put the problem in the following terms: is there, among all possible *numéraires,* one for which proportionality occurs?

Actually, parametrisation of the *numéraire* raises a difficulty: as producer prices are endogenous variables in the model, two budget constraints written with different *numéraires* are hardly comparable with each other; and this situation is inconsistent with the requirement that the budget constraint have an intrinsic content.

We can, however, cope with the difficulty by referring to the situation that would obtain were the budget constraint not taken into account. Let $\bar{u}$ and $\bar{z}$ be the values of vectors u (social values of market commodities) and z (net supply of market commodities by the public sector) in this less constrained situation – where, it should be noted, production efficiency holds. Considering the constrained situation 'close' to the unconstrained one (and especially u 'close' to $\bar{u}$), we can write the budget constraint in the following way:

$$\sum_j p_j z_j = (1-\eta)\sum_j \bar{u}_i \bar{z}_i \left(\frac{v_1}{\bar{u}_1}p_1 + \frac{v_2}{\bar{u}_2}p_2 + \ldots + \frac{v_n}{\bar{u}_n}p_n\right)$$

where $v_j \geqslant 0$ and $\sum_j v_j = 1$. This permits the selection of any possible *numéraire* and, at the same time, ensures that, whatever the choice, the budget constraint has the same content (i.e. cuts the endowment of the sector by a percentage of η under what would have been 'optimal').

Applying tax formulas (15.16) now gives

$$\gamma\left[z_j - (1-\eta)\frac{v_j}{u_j}\sum_i \bar{u}_i\bar{z}_i\right] = \sum_{il} u_i \frac{\partial y_i^l}{\partial p_j} \qquad \forall_j \qquad (15.17)$$

and, since we want proportionality to hold,

$$\sum_{il} u_i \frac{\partial y_i^l}{\partial p_j} = 0 \qquad \forall j$$

Moreover,

$$z_j \sim \bar{z}_j - \gamma \sum_i \xi_{ij} u_i \quad {}^{8}$$

where ξ_{ij} is the supply derivative of market commodity i with respect to the price of market commodity j for the public sector.

Reporting in (15.17), we obtain

$$\bar{u}_j\bar{z}_j = \gamma\bar{u}_j \sum_i \xi_{ij}\bar{u}_i + (1-\eta)v_j \sum_i \bar{u}_i\bar{z}_i \qquad (15.18)$$

which, together with

$$\sum_j v_j = 1$$

forms an $n + 1$ equations system determining γ and the *numéraire* v.

Summing up (15.18) gives

$$\gamma \sum_j \bar{u}_j \left[\sum_i \xi_{ij}\bar{u}_i\right] = \eta \sum_i \bar{u}_i\bar{z}_i$$

If η is sufficiently close to zero, i.e. *if the budget constraint is not too stringent,* then γ is sufficiently close to zero and all v_j are positive: *there exists a numéraire such that proportional producer taxation holds.*

We can ask whether this result holds also in the case of a public enterprise (not for all commodities, since, as we have said, this would mean production efficiency, but for all bar one – for example, the commodity that is produced by this enterprise). Proportionality would then be equivalent to *average cost pricing* (only for final demand).

[8] Shadow prices for the public sector are $\bar{u}_1, \bar{u}_2, \ldots, \bar{u}_n, \bar{u}_1, \bar{u}'_2, \ldots, \bar{u}'_n$ in the unconstrained situation, and $(1-\gamma)u_1, (1-\gamma)u_2, \ldots, (1-\gamma)u_n, u'_1, \ldots, u'_n$ in the constrained situation. Assuming u close to $\bar{u}$ and u' close to $\bar{u}'$ leads, thus, to the written formula. It is to be noted that $\sum_i \xi_{ij}\bar{u}_i \neq 0$ since the production function of the public sector also involves nonmarket commodities.

Following the same approach as in the case of a public administration, we can demonstrate that proportional producer taxation (for all commodities bar one) is not optimal, whatever the *numéraire.* Indeed, it would require:

$$\gamma\left[z_j - (1-\eta)\frac{v_j}{\bar{u}_j}\sum_i \bar{u}_i\bar{z}_i\right] = \sum_{il} u_i \frac{\partial y_i^l}{\partial p_j} \qquad \forall j \quad (15.19)$$

the price vectors being

$$(1-\lambda)u_1, u_2, \ldots, u_n$$

for producer prices, and

$$\left(1 + \frac{\gamma\lambda}{1-\gamma}\right)u_1, u_2, \ldots, u_n$$

for shadow prices, with λ being some nonzero parameter. Then,

$$\sum_{il} u_i \frac{\partial y_i^l}{\partial p_j} = \lambda u_1 \sum_l \frac{\partial y_1^l}{\partial p_j}$$

and

$$z_j = \bar{z}_j + \frac{\gamma\lambda}{1-\gamma}\xi_{1j}u_1$$

where ξ_{1j} is the supply derivative of commodity 1 with respect to the price of commodity j for the public enterprise.

Reporting in (15.19), and assuming u is close to $\bar{u}$:

$$\gamma\bar{z}_j + \gamma^2\frac{\lambda}{1-\gamma}\xi_{1j}\bar{u}_1 - \gamma(1-\eta)\frac{v_j}{\bar{u}_j}\sum_i \bar{u}_i\bar{z}_i = \lambda\bar{u}_1\sum_l \frac{\partial y_1^l}{\partial p_j} \qquad j = 1, n$$

Multiplying by $\bar{u}_j$ and summing up:

$$\gamma\eta\sum_i \bar{u}_i\bar{z}_i = \lambda^2(u_1)^2\sum_l \frac{\partial y_1^l}{\partial p_1} \quad (15.20)$$

since $\sum_j \xi_{1j}\bar{u}_j = 0$.

The right-hand side of (15.20) obviously is negative, while the left-hand side is positive (γ and $\sum_i \bar{u}_i\bar{z}_i$ being of opposite signs). QED.

V. CONCLUDING COMMENTS

What conclusions can we draw from this survey of problems of taxation and public production within budget constraints? At the beginning of this paper we said that taxation serves three purposes: raising money to finance public outlays; redistributing income among households; and guiding the behaviour of private (and also, if we consider shadow taxation, public) decision-makers. How do the fiscal instruments perform these tasks, and – more fundamentally – are they really consistent with a decentralised operation of the economy? Surely fiscal instruments are not specific to a single purpose, and this makes the question more intricate. However, we cannot fail to remark that, so long as redistributive purposes are not taken into consideration,[9] the Pareto-like framework performs fairly well. Enforcement of optimal indirect taxation requires a limited amount of information, and decentralisation can take place through market prices in the private sector and through market prices and budget constraints in the public sector.

Taking into account redistributive targets changes the matter to a considerable extent. Determining the optimal fiscal structure, and, especially, taxes on profits, requires a considerable amount of information – theoretically, knowledge of every flow in the economy.

Finally, we wish to stress a point that, in our opinion, underlines the special nature of economies with taxation. As the example of managerial activity shows, private decisions that would adjust to optimality in classical Paretian economies may deviate from the optimum when there is taxation, and even only taxation on profits and scarce resources – *As soon as it enforces taxation, the government becomes involved in every economic activity – whether the latter is connected with the market directly or indirectly.*

REFERENCES

Atkinson, A. B., and Stiglitz, J. E., 'The Structure of Indirect Taxation and Economic Efficiency', *Journal of Public Economics,* no. 1 (1972).

Boiteux, M., 'Sur la Gestion des Monopoles Astreints à l'Equilibre Budgétaire', *Econometrica,* XXIV (1956).

Dasgupta, P., and Stiglitz, J., 'On Optimum Taxation and Public Production', *Review of Economic Studies,* Jan 1972.

Diamond, P. A., and Mirrlees, J. A., 'Optimal Taxation and Public Production', *American Economic Review,* LXI (1971).

Hahn, F. H., 'On Optimum Taxation', *Journal of Economic Theory,* Feb 1973.

Kolm, S. C., *Théorie des Contraintes de Valeur* (DUNOD, 1970).

Malinvaud, E., *Lecons de Théorie Microéconomique* (DUNOD, 1969).

Mirrlees, J. A., 'On Producer Taxation', *Review of Economic Studies,* Jan 1972.

Stiglitz, J., and Dasgupta, P., 'Differential Taxation, Public Goods and Economic Efficiency', *Review of Economic Studies,* Apr 1971.

[9] As in the case of identical households, or when lump-sum transfers are possible from one household to another.

16 A Challenge to the Monopoly of the Rate of Discount in Investment Choices[1]

Jacques Thédié

MINISTÈRE DE L'ÉQUIPEMENT, PARIS

Economic decisions almost always require intertemporal arbitrage. These arbitrage calculations are performed with the aid of a discount rate. In the classical theory of discounting, this rate is such that, for the marginal investments, the aggregated value of the benefit is equal to the invested capital. The thesis of the present author is that the capital itself, independent of all intertemporal arbitrage, has an opportunity cost. The investment equilibrium depends not only on the discount rate, but also on the opportunity cost, which is as important as the rate of discount. The determination of the discount rate therefore is modified, as, of course, are all of the resulting choices.

I. INTRODUCTION

The rate of discount by which to reduce future to present values has given rise to a lot of theorising – or perhaps it was the other way round. It certainly is a most useful concept, but I am inclined to think that more is being expected of it than it can do. If we are not to stray too far from 'reality' (I shall explain presently what sort of reality I mean) we need to introduce a competitor to contest the monopoly of the rate of discount in intertemporal choices. But this competitor has to express so many options and constraints that it is difficult to find a suitable name for it. For lack of a better idea I shall call it the coefficient β or, sometimes, the 'scarcity-of-funds' coefficient. It is my purpose in this paper to mark out for this coefficient a place alongside its elder brother, the discount rate.

It may be useful to begin with a very brief summary of the classical theory of present value – not in order to add anything to it, but, on the contrary, to reduce it to its essentials and to strip it of a number of notions generally associated with it on the basis of more or less implicit assumptions that are not fundamental to the theory. I shall talk in terms of a single decision-maker.

[1] This paper was translated by Elizabeth Henderson.

II. DEFINITION AND PROPERTIES OF PRESENT VALUE

ASSUMPTIONS

Consider a decision-maker whose choices are guided by a set of values for expenditure, revenue, benefits and disadvantages entailed by his choices. The future is assumed to be wholly certain (uncertainty would not affect the concept of present value, but would introduce difficulties that have nothing to do with my purpose).

The decision-maker has an initial capital K_o and prior annual revenues K_1, $K_2, \ldots K_n$. He also has open to him a set of opportunities meaning that he is free to exchange an expenditure schedule (I_i) against a revenue schedule or, more generally, a schedule of monetary or nonmonetary benefits (A_i).

Our decision-maker will then settle on a programme that he considers optimal in the light of his own value system. It does not matter, for the moment, how he arrives at this programme. It may well be that our comments on his optimal programme, which he is assumed to have worked out, will have helped him. But this is not the point; we assume, for the time being, that this optimal programme does actually exist. In time it will lead to a redistribution of disposable benefits such that the new distribution is considered preferable to the initial set (K_i).

In the course of year i, this optimal programme entails an amount of consumption, C_i, and of investment, I_i. This amount of investment generates a schedule of benefits additional to those pertinent to all other investments. These benefits, in their turn, are either consumed or invested each year.

One more assumption has to be made. This is the more restrictive one that, close to the optimum, there exist small opportunities (which, logically, should be infinitely small) that would enable the benefits of any year i to be exchanged indirectly for those of any year j, in accordance with a rate of exchange offering a continuous range of possibilities in the neighbourhood of the chosen limiting rate. The last acceptable exchanges between year i and year j occur at the rate λ_{ij}.

DISCOUNT FACTORS

From these assumptions it is clear that the coefficients λ_{ij} are consistent only when $\lambda_{ij} = \lambda_{ik}\lambda_{kj}$. It is then possible to define coefficients a_i such that $a_j = \lambda_{ij}a_i$, at whatever i and j. If this set of proportional coefficients is so chosen that a_o equals unity, they are called discount factors. They have, by definition, the property that one dollar of year i is exchanged indifferently against a_i dollars of year zero.

THE MEANING OF THE ASSUMPTIONS

Capital–revenue–benefits

The assumptions imply the existence of a common unit of measurement for the present and the future value of money, goods and all other benefits. In a more refined analysis, a different time schedule of successive values has to be assigned to each good. The concept of present value is workable only if all of these schedules are assumed to diverge only slightly from one central reference schedule.

The divergences of each separate schedule from the reference schedule are then considered as divergences of the value of each good from the value of the reference money unit – say, one dollar. In what follows I shall not enter into this problem of different goods, but argue simply in terms of dollars of constant value.

The decision-maker

The assumptions say nothing about the subjective preferences of the decision-maker, except that it can be taken for granted that they are consistent. Nothing more need be assumed for the existence of discount factors. Nevertheless, in certain cases, or as a help in following certain lines of thought, one may wish to make additional assumptions about what guides a decision-maker's choices. To this end, his preferences may be expressed by an intertemporal utility function $U(t, C_t)$, which is the value that he attributes today to his consumption of a quantity C_t in the course of year t.

The derivative $\partial U/\partial C = V$ is the value of one additional dollar in year t at the consumption level C_t. The decision-maker works out his programme in the light of the function U and of all the opportunities open to him. If his programme is optimal, the level of consumption is situated at a certain value C_t, and the discount factor a_t then equals $V(t, C_t)$.

Note that the discount factor a_t does not, and cannot, depend solely on year t. It depends also on the level of consumption C_t resulting from the optimal programme.

It follows that, if one speaks of a psychological rate of interest ψ (in analogy to a rate of discount), one implicitly takes as known the consumption levels of different years. If this is overlooked and such a psychological rate of interest is assigned a permanent value independent of the C_t levels, one inevitably runs into a number of paradoxes. (In addition, one supposes, *ex posteriori,* that the function U brings t into play in the form $(1 + \psi)^{-t}$.)

Actually, the function U depends not only on C_t, but also on all prior and subsequent consumption levels. Quite definitely, changes in consumption make at least as strong an impact as does the level of consumption as such. These changes can easily be accounted for in the above definitions as functions of $t, C_1, C_2, \ldots$. But this does not alter the discount factor a_t, which still remains equal to $\partial U/\partial C$.

Initial capital

The data must obviously include the decision-maker's present and future resources in the form of money or goods (producer or consumer goods). Here, it is implicitly assumed that, at the decision-maker's discretion, any sum of money can be used for consumption or investment. The contrary case will be discussed later.

Given opportunities

Discount factors depend not only on the decision-maker, but also on the schedule of consumption at which he arrives; and this, in turn, depends on his opportunities. Once again, we find that the discount factors are not purely psychological.

Anybody can have reasonable knowledge about present opportunities. As regards future opportunities, all one has to go by is informed guesses about such things as returns, lifetime, and type of schedule. But these guesses are good enough if they convey some knowledge of the prospective schedule of consumption $C_1, \ldots, C_n$.

Of course, even that knowledge can refer only to probabilities. But our argument here assumes that the future is certain.

Small investments in the neighbourhood of the optimum

A set of opportunities in which there is room each year for only a small number of major units precludes the determination of discount factors. The consistency and optimisation of decisions can be discussed only if the shape of the decision-maker's utility function is known.

To introduce discount factors is tantamount to recognising that, in the neighbourhood of a point, the utility function can, at a first approximation, be regarded as linear (ΔU is proportional to ΔC_t). If every decision causes a major displacement of C_t, no discount factors can be determined.

A 'small' opportunity, therefore, can be defined as one that causes no appreciable change in the marginal value of the consumption dollar. In this sense, a motorway is a small investment from the point of view of the nation.

THE ROLE OF DISCOUNT FACTORS

Discount factors, as defined above, seem to be pretty useless, since we have assumed that the optimal programme has already been established and have merely verified it. But our very knowledge that these factors exist (supposing that all of the conditions are met) enables us to do three things: we can verify that a programme really is optimal; we can improve a near-optimal programme; and we can appraise additional (small) opportunities.

By definition, the better of two marginal variants is the one that maximises

$$\sum a_i(A_i - I_i).$$

This last paragraph is so short that it fails to do justice to what it says. Let us put it in different words. It follows from the definition of discount factors that, provided the choices to be made do not fundamentally alter the levels of consumption and, hence, the discount factors themselves, the best choice is always the one that maximises the sum of benefits at present value less expenditure (also at present value).

THE RATE OF DISCOUNT

Definition

So far we have spoken only of discount factors. In our deliberately very general exposition these factors may form any sequence of numbers whatever. However, uncertainty about future opportunities and about the results of present opportunities, as well as the subjective nature of preferences, lead us, in practice, to assume a certain continuity of the values of successive discount factors.

In particular, we may assume a constant ratio between the discount factors of successive years. We can then write $a_n = (1 + \alpha)^{-n}$, where α is the rate of discount.

The term 'discount rate' is applicable also when the ratio remains constant for several years and then changes. For instance, we can say that the discount rate is 10 per cent until 1980, and 8 per cent thereafter. But it is better not to use the term 'discount rate' for the rate that is defined solely by the coefficient a_{t+1} in relation to a_t, writing $a_{t+1} = \dfrac{a_t}{1+\alpha}$. This may sometimes be a convenient rate to use, but in order to avoid ambiguities it is better to call it the instantaneous rate of discount.

Rate of discount and market rate of interest

It is often assumed that the opportunities include the possibility of lending or borrowing, at a fixed rate, an unlimited amount of money. In such a case, that double possibility is one of the marginal and small opportunities mentioned above, in the first part of section II. It therefore governs the discount factors, all by itself. The instantaneous discount rate then equals the loan rate, and, so long as the loan rate is assumed to be constant, the discount factors are so ordered that they make up a discount rate equal to the market rate of interest.

Rate of discount and rate of subjective preference

The rate of subjective preference ψ equals the discount rate α, just as subjective marginal utility each year equals the discount factor. But this does not mean that ψ is to be taken as given, and α as a consequence of that datum. Both depend on the distribution of the incomes obtained, and this distribution is optimal precisely when it equalises the values of α and ψ, due account being taken of the whole set of data and constraints.

Perhaps, indeed, the introduction of ψ in this form amounts to a tautology, which may turn out to be dangerous. To introduce ψ can be useful only if the utility function $U(t, C_t)$ is made explicit – for instance, in such a form as $e^{-\psi t} f(C_t)$. But, then, ψ assumes a different meaning: it represents intertemporal preference at *constant* consumption, rather than at expected consumption (which comes to the same as the rate of discount).

PRESENT CONSUMPTION VERSUS FUTURE RETURNS

Compatibility of the two aspects

Do the discount factors indicate a preference for consumption today rather than tomorrow, or for transforming present resources, via investment, into future, larger ones? The answer, in the context of our problem, is: both. The decision-maker is free to transform one marginal consumption dollar into one marginal investment dollar. The value of the two is the same. To look for an optimal programme is, precisely, to look for a programme in which the two alternatives merge into one.

The internal rate of return of the marginal investment

The internal rate of return of a project is the rate of discount that reduces the project to indifference:

$$\sum \frac{A_i}{(I+r)^i} = \sum \frac{I_i}{(I+r)^i}$$

If the discount factors form a rate of discount i, then:

(1) if $r < i$, the project should be discarded (it is better to do nothing than to carry out the project);
(2) if $r > i$ and the project has no influence on other opportunities, it should be selected;
(3) if $r > i$ and the project does affect other opportunities (for instance, belongs to a set of exclusive projects), then, without examining the whole set of exclusive opportunities, it is impossible to say whether the project should be selected or not.

The existence of this third case is sometimes forgotten, and, thus, one may hear it said that all projects the internal rate of return of which exceeds the rate of discount should be selected. More often still, it is said that, because of the preceding assertion, the rate of discount (supposing that it exists) is equal to the internal rate of return of the least profitable projects of the optimal programme.

This is true only if the optimum has in its neighbourhood *independent*[2] (and *small*) projects. But this does not often happen. Provided only that every profitable project has at least one profitable variant (size, starting date, and so on), the internal rate of return of all selected projects will exceed the rate of discount, and never equal it. In this case, the small opportunities mentioned earlier consist of the transition from one variant to another, rather than of the best variant as such. The rate of return of one additional dollar is then defined not in terms of financing one additional (one-dollar) project, but of replacing an n-dollar project by another costing $(n + 1)$ dollars.

The internal rate of return is a tricky concept, and, except after considering the three cases listed above, is best not used.

INTRODUCING ADDITIONAL ASSUMPTIONS

Everything that has been said so far leaves intact the omnipotence of the discount rate, or, at least, of the discount factors. We now turn to matters where present value is inadequate for expressing choices between investment and consumption. Without abandoning the highly theoretical character of the discussion, we shall introduce a few additional assumptions and examine their consequences. We shall see later that there are real cases of which these additional assumptions constitute a reasonable model.

An investment ceiling

Let us add to the data of our original problem (beginning of section II) the following constraint: the amount of investment in year i must not exceed a fixed amount J_i (or, the amount of borrowing in year i must not exceed E_i).

If this constraint is effective, the marginal values of the consumption dollar and the investment dollar cease to be equal, since the investment dollar is bound to be worth more for the decision-maker. This means that, instead of there being just one sequence of discount factors, $1, a_1, a_2, \ldots, a_n$, there are now two sequences – the first pertinent to consumption dollars (say, $1, a_1, a_2, \ldots, a_n$) and the second to investment dollars (say, $b_o, b_i, \ldots, b_n - b_o$ being different from the marginal value of the immediate consumption dollar, which is taken as unity).

This is an important point. For some, including myself, it is self-evident that two different goods have two different values, and two dollars definitely are two different goods if one of them is subject to a constraint on its use (it must not be invested). Others may prefer to speak of dual value linked to a constraint.

In these circumstances, can there exist a *rate* of discount? There can be a rate of discount for sequence (a_i), or one for sequence (b_i), or one for both. The simplest case would be for the b factors to have a constant ratio to the a

[2] An independent project is a project that is not exclusive of any other one, or, more generally, has no influence on any other opportunity.

factors, and for both to follow a rate of discount (which would then be the same for both). Such a constant ratio a_i/b_i could be taken to signify fairly constant intensity of the constraint on annual investment.

Of course, in the presence of such an investment ceiling, the optimal programme is not the same as it would be without it (unless the constraint is inoperative). The discount factors, or the discount rate, are altered (increased). Thus, the introduction of the b factors cannot be interpreted as meaning that the rate of discount remains the same as it would be without the constraint, and that the b factors re-establish equality of marginal values. The rate of discount itself is altered by the investment constraint.

But this change in the discount rate does not have the effect of equalising the marginal values of the investment dollar and the consumption dollar. If it did, it would mean that the investment ceiling could be abolished without altering the optimal programme. The investment ceiling is held up in some way, both by an increase in the rate of discount and by a value difference between a current and an investment dollar.

Let $U(C_1, C_2, \ldots, C_t)$ be a utility function to be maximised; (E_i), a set of opportunities enabling investments $I_1, I_2, \ldots,$ to be substituted for consumptions $C_1, C_2, \ldots,$ such that there is scope, in the neighbourhood of the optimum, for infinitely small substitutions between all the I_i and all the C_i; $K_1, K_2, \ldots, K_i$, investable funds available initially; and, J_n, the upper limit imposed on total investment I_i during each year i.

For the rest, I say simply that, in the neighbourhood of the optimum, maximisation of the function U is equivalent to maximisation of a function $\sum a_iC_i - \sum b_iI_i$, or else $\sum a_i(C_i - \beta_iI_i)$, where a_i is the discount factor of year i, and β_i is the 'scarcity of funds'[3] coefficient of year i. No set of factors a' can be equivalent, for investment choices, to the double sequence of coefficients a_i, β_i^i.[4]

Investment charges as indirect cost

Let us return to the data of our original problem and assume that if the decision-maker wants to invest one dollar he has to pay a charge h. We can say simply that the investment now costs him $(1 + h)$, and then we are back at the original problem. Alternatively (should it prove more convenient), we can say that there are two kinds of dollars, consumption dollars and investment dollars,

[3] Meaning scarcity of funds available for investment purposes.

[4] In this mathematical problem, the factors a_i, b_i and β_i can take any value, and there is absolutely no reason why these values should present any character of fixity or regularity from year to year. In real cases, factors a_i will generally make a regular progression and factors β_i will generally be constant or change very slowly from year to year (except where one knows or can forecast that one particular year will be subject to exceptional constraints); this is because of the continuity of economic data, and uncertainty about the future.

and that it costs a sum h to shift one dollar from the first into the second group. The coefficient $(1 + h)$ then has the same formal effect as the β coefficients have. If the assumptions of this and the previous subsection are made simultaneously, they lead to a unique series of coefficients that combines the incidence of the two constraints. The effect of h on the discount factors would be the same if not all investments were subject to the charge, but provided the marginal ones were.

There are other assumptions that might have the same effect as the charge h. Basically, this will follow whenever an investment decision itself occasions a cost – direct, indirect or psychological – that, for marginal investments, can be considered proportional to the amount of investment (it is enough that this proportionality holds for marginal investments). We are then up against the same barrier between consumption dollars and investment dollars, and there is the same marginal cost of breaking through the barrier.

In all these cases, of course, the introduction of the charge h has the same sort of effect on the choice of the optimum investment programme as has the introduction of the scarcity-of-funds coefficient β, which here is equal to $1 + h$.

CONSEQUENCES FOR THE FIRST-YEAR INVESTMENT PROGRAMME

First-year investment is, rightly, the aspect of the problem that arouses the most interest. From what has been said above, we can draw the following conclusions.

(1) On rather broad assumptions, we can say that there exist discount factors a_i such that the best choice among projects is the one that maximises $\sum a_i(A_i - I_i)$ (present value of benefits less present value of costs).

(2) If there exists a rate of discount, it can be written

$$\sum \frac{(A_i - I_i)}{(1 + \alpha)^i} \qquad \text{(discounted profits)}$$

(3) Both the discount factors and the discount rate depend not only on subjective preferences, but also on the whole set of opportunities.

(4) In a perfect capital market the rate of discount equals the market rate of interest.

(5) Any project the internal rate of return of which is less than the rate of discount is to be discarded.

(6) Any *independent* project the internal rate of return of which is higher than the rate of discount should be selected.

(7) The internal rate of return is no guide for choosing between incompatible projects (especially variants).

(8) A limitation on the volume of investment, or a charge on investment, leads to different values being assigned to investment dollars and to consump-

tion dollars (which is not tantamount to altering the rate of discount in the choice between variants).

(9) This value difference is expressed by a series of marginal costs of investment dollars differing from the series of discount factors. Alternatively, it may be expressed by a series of scarcity of funds coefficients.

(10) The expression to be maximised then takes the form

$$\sum(a_i A_i - b_i I_i)$$

or

$$\sum a_i(A_i - \beta_i I_i)$$

(11) If there exists a rate of discount, the expression can be written

$$\frac{A_i - \beta_i I_i}{(1+\alpha)^i} \text{ (generalised discounted net value)}$$

(12) If the coefficients β_i are equal, we have

$$\sum \frac{A_i - \beta I_i}{(1+\alpha)^i}$$

(13) The choices resulting from these expressions will obviously not be the same as those that would be made without the introduction of the β coefficients, even if the rate of discount were altered. In particular, choices among incompatible variants will be different, because these involve a complete calculation of discounted net values.

III. APPLICATION TO REAL CASES OF INVESTMENT

The rate of discount, then, is a criterion of investment choice in the context of a set of rather broad assumptions, but it needs to be supplemented by a coefficient β as soon as one goes beyond these assumptions for some reason or other. I shall now try to show that, in the real world, we do in fact encounter a number of circumstances that require the introduction of a β coefficient. Some of these circumstances are peculiar to the public sector and some to the private sector, while some are common to both.

LEVELS OF DECISION-MAKING

The process of decision-making often involves several successive levels. Some top-level authority appropriates certain funds and lays down general targets, and it is then up to the lower levels to use these resources as best they can, with a view to achieving the targets. It is these lower levels who are responsible for the calculation of the optimum. If the targets are fairly well defined – for instance, if values are attached to all of the prospective benefits – then the lower levels have no active part to play. All they have to do is work out the calculations.

However, it is often the case that the top and the lower levels do not view with the same terms the benefits of possible investments. Top-level decision-makers certainly do take account of direct benefits, but in less detail than is ultimately necessary. On the other hand, they also think in terms of broader[5] or indirect[6] benefits that have no place in the calculation of the optimum.

The lower levels will then have to calculate a sub-optimum, and in so doing will take account

(a) of a fixed investment maximum (one of the main reasons for introducing the β coefficient; see section II, subsection entitled 'An investment ceiling');
(b) of the existence of indirect benefits that defy calculation but can, at best, be supposed to be proportional to the direct benefits of each project. The least-inadequate way of dealing with them is to attach a constant coefficient to the benefits, and this amounts to altering the β coefficient.

It follows that the existence of successive levels of decision-making creates circumstances that justify the introduction of a β coefficient alongside the rate of discount.

EXTERNAL LIMITATION OF FUNDS

The amount a private firm can invest depends on how much it can borrow. Its borrowing capacity may be limited by banks or other lends, in the light not only of the benefits from the proposed investment, but also (and perhaps mainly) of the firm's present financial strength. As often as not, therefore, a private firm has to make do with loans of a smaller amount than it feels it could invest profitably. Once again, it finds itself in the sort of situation described earlier (under the heading 'An investment ceiling'), with an *a priori* limit to the volume of investment. It has to reckon with a scarcity of funds coefficient.

[5] It is important to have some idea of what these broader benefits might be. The following are some examples.

In the private sector, the most typical case is the introduction of the risk of bankruptcy, or the firm may wish to change its general orientation in years to come. In the public sector, the government may wish to guide the country's economy in certain directions (for instance, industrialisation in France under the Sixth Plan). Similarly, continuity of budget allocations to each separate sector may be regarded as a broad objective that runs counter to micro-optimisation at the margin.

[6] For example, prestige may be an indirect benefit for a private firm. For the government, indirect benefits may result from the wish to favour certain population groups; to promote exports; or to combat unemployment. Clearly, every different kind of investment will bring a different amount and a different sort of indirect benefit.

Similar situations may arise in the public sector in so far as government is regarded as external to certain public corporations, or if a country has to raise capital abroad and finds it impossible to do so to the desired extent.

THE DISUTILITY OF TAXATION

At the level of government choices, levying one additional dollar in taxes (or raising it by a public loan issue) entails economic and political disadvantages, even though the extra tax is, by itself, a mere transfer and, as such, neutral from the point of view of the community. The disutility of the additional tax dollar no doubt has a heavy weight in the government's choice of the total amount of taxation. Formally, this marginal disutility is expressed by the coefficient h discussed earlier (under the heading 'Investment charges as indirect cost') and it calls for the introduction of a β coefficient.

A similar disutility affects each additional dollar of public loans. The mere fact that the choice of how to finance public expenditure is not a matter of indifference to government proves the existence of these disutilities.

In the absence of any constraint, the disutility of taxation and public borrowing should be equal in the equilibrium situation. But constraints do exist (social and legislative constraints, constraints of continuity, and so on) and, consequently, one of the two methods of raising funds may in certain cases be considered 'easier' (i.e. to entail less disutility) than the other.

CONCLUSION

We see that, both for the private and for the public sector, there are a number of reasons why it would be unrealistic to make assumptions that exclude a scarcity-of-funds coefficient (β). Real conditions suggest a model like that described in section II (under the headings 'An investment ceiling' and 'Investment charges as indirect cost'), where we were led to introduce such a coefficient.

IV. CONSEQUENCES OF THE INTRODUCTION OF A SCARCITY-OF-FUNDS COEFFICIENT

First let us see how the β coefficient affects the manner of determining the rate of discount at different levels of decision-making.

GENERAL OBSERVATIONS

In the classical theory, where intertemporal choices rest on the discount rate alone, there must be close consistency between the discount rate and the volume of investment funds, so that marginal investments are 'explained' by the level of the discount rate. Given knowledge of the volume of investment and of the investment programme, the rate of discount can be deduced; and, given knowledge of the discount rate and of the investment opportunities, the volume of investment can be deduced. At the cost of repeated trial and error, every single decision-making unit can thus determine both its best investment volume and its appropriate discount rate.

The introduction of a β coefficient alters this situation. Things may become more complicated or simpler, depending on the level of decision-making.

THE NATIONAL RATE OF DISCOUNT

At the national level – say, of the planning board – the β coefficient introduces an additional element of complexity. Without it, the nation's overall choices between investment and consumption can, in principle, be expressed by a discount rate α. With it, they are consistent with an infinite number of possible pairs (α, β). More thought and investigation will be needed for choosing the best of these pairs. In consequence, the discount rate will be lower at an unchanged volume of funds, or, in other words, more room will be made for long-run, as opposed to short-run, investments.

THE SECTORAL ALLOCATION OF NATIONAL INVESTMENT FUNDS

Once a national discount rate has been determined, the allocation of investment funds to separate sectors (roads, telecommunications, schools, and so on) brings to light β coefficients $(\beta_1, \beta_2, \ldots)$ peculiar to each sector. Consequently, before finally determining these sectoral allocations, the relevant government authorities can easily gain from these coefficients an idea of the importance, in each sector, of motivations other than profitability, and so obtain some guidance on the best choice to make. Not only is this way of looking at the problem more realistic; it also is clearer for those authorities than is the method that confines itself to intersectoral differences in the rate of discount or even the rate of return.

In addition, these β coefficients provide *a posteriori* justification for any overall allocation. This is not likely to please economists, but it happens to be how things really are. The economist produces figures; the politician amends them in the light of nonmeasurable elements; and it is these that, in large part, are reflected in the sectoral coefficients $\beta_1, \beta_2, \ldots$.

SECTORAL DECISION-MAKING

Each investment sector receives from the government (or from some intermediary authority) two binding directives: the value of the discount rate and the volume of investment. For each sector, things are then both clearer and simpler. The rate of discount is fixed, and the resources constraint entails a β coefficient, which can easily be determined by comparison with possible opportunities. This coefficient may result from the national β, or from the sectoral or even a subsectoral β, but the sectoral decision-maker need not know that in order to optimise the use of resources.

PRIVATE ENTERPRISE

Probably the best advice for private firms, is to adopt one single rate of discount, barring some special reason or particular investigation. The adjustment of resources to opportunities is then governed solely by the β coefficient. This would have the advantage of making calculations easier for small and medium-sized firms; furthermore, the result would be consistent with each firm's own real interests, and also closer to the national interest (but I am not suggesting that this single rate of discount should be the same as that applicable to national investment).

CONSEQUENCES OF THE β COEFFICIENT FOR THE NATURE OF INVESTMENT

One final interesting question is when, and how, the introduction of a β coefficient alters investment choices. The introduction of the scarcity of funds coefficient affects investment choices only if (a) one considers costs and benefits over several years and not merely substitutions as between two successive years; and (b) one has to choose among exclusive investment opportunities (variants of one project, different scales, and so on).

The chief effect of the β coefficient is to set a lower value for the discount rate than it would have according to the rules of classical theory. In other words, investment choices will give more weight to long-term than to short-term benefits.

In conclusion, I would venture the following statements.

(1) A good investment choice should be guided by a discount rate (or by discount factors).

(2) The discount rate should not be the sole guide for the choice of marginal investments, but should be supplemented by the opportunity cost of capital, to be calculated by multiplying capital by a coefficient that might conveniently be called the 'scarcity of funds' coefficient.

(3) This approach should lead to lower discount rates than are generally used.

(4) The joint use of these two coefficients, rather than of a single one, is more realistic and, in effect, simplifies application.

(5) This approach should alter the choice among investment variants in the direction of giving more weight to the future than classical theory does.

17 Transportation as a Public Service in the USSR

T. S. Khatchaturov
ACADEMY OF SCIENCES OF THE USSR

This paper contains a description of the Soviet transport system, with its different kinds of services, and an analysis of transportation facts and figures. There is a high effectiveness of the system, with its large capacity to meet the people's needs, its comparatively low fares and, at the same time, its satisfactory profits. These features of Soviet transport are related to the integration of all forms of transportation, to centralised management and planning, and to the system's high technical level. A very effective solution to the density problem of intra-city traffic is provided by public transportation, in particular the underground, in combination with other forms of transport. The paper also includes information on the planning and co-ordination of transport and on problems of its further development.

I. INTRODUCTION

Transportation is one of the oldest public services in the Soviet Union. Railway and river transportation networks were already in existence before the 1917 revolution. Transportation accounted for about one-third of the total capital stock of the nation's economy, and the development and expansion of the transport network played an important role in the economic growth of the country at the end of the 19th and beginning of the 20th century.

The importance of transportation in the USSR is also very largely due to the huge area of the world's largest country, to the size of its population, and to its vast volumes of output. Hence, the development of a transportation system was essential in order to meet social needs for the relocation of passengers and freight.

One can quote several figures proving the high level of transport development in the USSR. The railway system,which accounts for somewhat more than 10 per cent of the world's railways, carries one-half of the world's railway freight traffic. The USSR possesses the world's longest commercial river-navigation network, and its river-borne freight exceeds in volume that of any other country. The carrying capacity of USSR's commercial fleet, which used to rank very low in the world table, has now moved up to sixth place. Aeroflot is the largest airline in the world, both in the length of its routes and in the volume of freight carried.

An important feature of the Soviet transportation system is its integration, which is based on the socialist ownership of all the major means of transportation: railways, sea and river vessels, aeroplanes, pipelines, trucks and highways. This allows for centralized planning of the whole transport system as part of the planned national economy, thus providing for the efficient and all-round development of all the means of transportation.

The large size of the transport enterprises makes centralised planning easier. A network of railways with a track length of nearly 140 thousand kilometres is controlled by 26 State railway companies under the direction of the Ministry of Communications. Management of river and sea transport is organised in a similar way. There are 16 State steamship companies responsible to the Ministry of Merchant Marine, and 28 State river steamship companies responsible to the river transport ministries of the various Soviet republics.

Civil airlines are run by Aeroflot under the auspices of the Ministry of Civil Aviation. Pipelines are controlled by the oil and gas industry ministries. Public automobile transport and highways are centrally managed by the ministries of the various Soviet republics and by their departments. Trucks belong either to public automobile enterprises or to industrial, agricultural and other enterprises. Buses, taxis, trams and underground railways are controlled by the municipal transport organisations. Finally, there are private cars and motor boats.

In general, this paper deals only with public transportation, although it does take account of pipelines and private cars. Specialised transport systems operated by industrial and other enterprises (conveyors, carriers, elevators, railways, and so on) will not be considered here.

In spite of considerable development and the great distances covered, the share of public transportation in the gross national product and national income is not significant, amounting to about 4 and 5 per cent, respectively. Thus, in 1972, transportation and communications accounted for only 29 thousand million roubles out of a gross national product of 717 thousand million, and for 18 thousand million roubles out of a national income of 313 thousand million. Thus, in general, transportation costs increase the costs of products only insignificantly. Of course, the share of transportation cost varies for different kinds of products. For bulk cargoes such as coal or iron ore, the cost of transportation is about 30–50 per cent of the price at the place of consumption; while, for expensive manufactured products such as equipment or textiles, the share of transportation cost is very small, even if the highest tariffs are applied.

The major reasons for the low share of transportation in the cost of manufactured products are the high efficiency of transportation, its mass nature, and the full utilisation of available transport capacities as a result of planning. Suffice it to mention that, in 1972, the average load per kilometre of railway track was 20·3 million tonnokilometres a year, or six times higher than in the United States. At the same time, the railways are technologically very advanced. 36 thousand kilometres of rail are electrified, which is more than in any other country of the world, while, with rare exceptions, diesel traction is used elsewhere on the system.

The productivity of labour in transport is very high. Thus, the number of people employed in the railways has not increased since the mid-1950s, while the volume of transportation has increased threefold. That means that the productivity of labour also has increased threefold. The growth of labour productivity has been even more substantial in the merchant marine, and it has been quite high in relation to the other means of transportation.

The rising efficiency of the major means of transportation can be illustrated by the fact that the increase in the railway capital stock has been less than the growth in the volume of transportation: in the past decade, they were 60 and 65 per cent, respectively. However, the reverse is the case in other rapidly developing means of transportation (merchant marine, pipelines, air and road transport). In general, the use of the basic transport stocks has somewhat improved, and at present these stocks account for 12·3 per cent of the national capital funds.

One should mention another reason for transportation's relatively low share (compared to, say, that of industry) in the gross national product and the national income. It should be remembered that transportation costs do not include the price of the freight carried, while, in industry, the prices of raw and other materials make up a major part of the cost of production.

Coming closer to our topic, let us begin by considering passenger transportation, for this is the most 'public' function of transport, in the narrow sense of the word. Of course, freight carriage (which we shall consider in section III) is also of public significance, for it serves production, the final aim of which is to satisfy public needs.

II. PASSENGER TRANSPORTATION

Passenger transportation can be classified as long-distance (inter-city), suburban, and intra-city. In passenger kilometres (that is, by volume of passenger traffic) long-distance transport occupies the first place, with (in 1971) a total of 335 thousand million passenger kilometres, of which railways accounted for 193 thousand million, air transport for 89 thousand million, and inter-city bus services for 49 thousand million. Thus, of these three, first place goes to the railways, which carry long-distance passengers for an average of 610 kilometres each. Air transportation is growing rapidly (it has grown sevenfold within the last ten years), with the average haul being of 1250 kilometres. Bus transportation has increased threefold in the last decade, but the average distance per passenger is short – about 33 kilometres.

The composition of long-distance traffic is as follows. First of all, there is the very large amount of traffic resulting from people going on holiday. The high share of this category accounts for a sharp increase in passenger traffic in the warm months. Also substantial is the share of business trips. Next comes the planned migration of workers contracted for construction, agriculture and new industrial enterprises. Finally, a large number of passengers travel for various private reasons.

Long-distance railway tariffs are relatively lower in the USSR than in Western countries. Thus, a ticket for a sleeper from Moscow to Leningrad, a distance of 650 kilometres, costs 12 roubles; and a similar journey from Moscow to Sochi on the Black Sea, a distance of 2000 kilometres, costs 25 roubles. Profits earned by the railway average 0·87 kopecks per passenger kilometre, while the average cost is 0·55 kopecks. These figures refer to all passenger railway traffic and are somewhat higher for long-distance and somewhat lower for suburban communications. Passengers travelling for long distances can obtain a sleeping berth for a relatively small extra fee.

Because of the rapid growth of passenger transportation, and in order to provide for greater comfort and safety, all rolling stock was replaced, following the Second World War, with newer and more comfortable all-metal carriages. Electrification of the main railways and the introduction of diesel traction on all other lines allowed for faster trains. Large passenger railway stations were built in many cities.

The rapid increase of long-distance air traffic has been stimulated by low tariffs and by the speed of this form of transportation. The price of an air ticket is roughly equal to the price of a berth in an express train. For distances of over 300 kilometres, the tourist class fare is only 1·5 kopecks per passenger kilometre.

That is why the air communications network is expanding. The total length of the domestic air-service network exceeds 600 thousand kilometres, including 260 thousand kilometres of major national air routes. Civil airlines are equipped with large modern aircraft capable of cruising at speeds of up to 1000 kilometres an hour, while supersonic passenger planes capable of doing up to 2500 kilometres an hour are being tested. Such planes will be especially efficient for flights of 5–8 thousand and more kilometres, such as from Moscow to the Far East.

Long-distance passenger transportation by sea and river is much less important, in terms of volume, than that by rail, air or bus. Suburban trips by water transport are not of great significance, since, generally speaking, the people who make them are on vacation. Business trips by sea or river vessels are rare, since slow, and are usually undertaken only in those parts of the country – mostly in the east and in the north – where water transport is the main kind of mass transportation. Even the use of the most up-to-date types of fast vessels does not increase the volume of passengers substantially, because, by comparison with air, and even rail, transport, water transport remains slow. Nevertheless, the sea and river fleets have been enlarged with fast, modern vessels allowing for greater comfort (for instance, ocean liners of the 'Alexander Pushkin' class), small ships for coastal navigation, and comfortable four-deck diesel river boats.

Because of the small volume of passenger traffic by water, the average cost, as compared with that of rail transport, is three times higher for river transport and eight times higher for sea transport. In spite of this, and in the interests of passengers, tariffs are kept below costs, and the losses sustained by passenger transportation are compensated for by profits from freight traffic.

Suburban passenger services are provided mostly by railways and buses, and only to a minor extent by water transport. Most of the passengers who use these services are commuters, who travel an average distance of 27 kilometres by rail and 10 by bus. Major citites such as Moscow (population 7·4 million), Leningrad (4·1 million) and Kiev (1·8 million) have the most substantial local traffic.

Suburban lines within the large urban areas are electrified. Local tariffs are much lower than are long-distance ones, and a journey of 30–40 kilometres costs only 20–25 kopecks (28–35 United States cents).

Intra-city passenger transportation, which, due the growth of urban population, is increasing rapidly (by 40 per cent during the 1960s), is undertaken mostly by public transport belonging to the municipalities. City transport is developing rapidly. During the 1960s, the total kilometres of tramways increased by 30 per cent, of trolley-bus lines by 150 per cent, of underground railways by 100 per cent, and of bus routes by 300 per cent. There are now underground railways in five cities – Moscow, Leningrad, Kiev, Tbilisi and Baku. The high share of public transportation in total urban passenger traffic results in less air pollution and in a more rational use of street space than is possible where private cars predominate. The total national volume of urban passenger traffic is as high as 200 thousand million passenger kilometers per annum, which is equivalent to about three-quarters of the total volume of railway passenger transportation.

Each branch of transport has its own plan of passenger transportation. The nature of these plans is, naturally, different from that of production plans, because it is up to the passenger whether to travel or not and what means of transport to use. These plans cannot be compulsory for the passenger, yet they must be fulfilled by the transport organisations, which have to back them with rolling stock and provide for greater comfort, so as to attract passengers.

A variety of data are used to construct a passenger transportation plan. To begin with, it is essential for a long-term plan to have advance knowledge of the mobility of the population in general, as well as in specific areas, and to take into account the expected migration of population. Such data are produced by the State's statistics and planning organs. It is then possible to calculate potential population growth for the country as a whole, for specific republics and areas, and for the big cities. On the basis of this information, future passenger flows can be calculated.

This can be done with the help of population-mobility coefficients, i.e. the number of trips per person for all means of transportation, and for each of them separately. These coefficients are calculated not only for the country as a whole, but also for specific republics, areas and cities.

It is obvious that population-mobility coefficients calculated on the basis of past activities cannot be used in predictive calculations, but should be adjusted. Each adjustment can be based on a number of data, of which the most important is the rise in the material welfare and the income of the population. The increase in the number of trips per person depends on that growth, although the degree of dependence varies. In addition, some indirect data are considered. These include data relating to the potential number of students; the development of resorts and of other tourist and recreational areas; and so forth.

Of great significance in planning passenger flows are the planned data on the development of industry, agriculture and capital construction in different areas, especially with respect to the newly developed industrial centres and their needs for manpower. The same applies to the construction of new (and expansion of existing) enterprises and social and cultural establishments, especially when this is connected with developing a new suburb, or the like.

Periodically, passenger opinion is surveyed, so producing extensive information for use in the analysis of passenger flows by composition, direction, and so on, and for consideration in planning.

Finally, passenger-transportation statistics relating to past years are studied in terms of mode of transportation, direction of flow, and seasonality. These statistics can provide useful data and reveal patterns to be taken into account when assessing future prospects.

On the basis of all this information, the plan of passenger transportation is designed and measures for technological backing and the development of passenger services (for instance, by provision of new rolling stock, cars, buses, vessels, aeroplanes, roads, airports, river and sea ports, railways and railway stations) are suggested.

III. FREIGHT TRANSPORTATION

The first thing that should be noted about freight transportation is that it belongs to the sphere of material production. Raw materials, fuel, semi-manufactured goods and other materials are taken to industrial enterprises, and the transportation involved should be considered as part of the production process. Delivering the finished goods to the consumer is also, in essence, a continuation of the process of material production.

It has already been noted that, because of the high level of production and the great distances involved, freight transportation in the USSR is operated on a huge scale. All means of transport are utilised, and the planned division of functions among them is as follows.

The most important means of mass freight transportation is the railways, which account for more than two-thirds of the national freight traffic. For decades, the railways have proved the most convenient form of transport in the USSR, especially as regards bulk transport (of coal, ores, construction materials, and so on) across great distances (for rail freight transport, the average haul is about 900 kilometres). Sea transport carries foreign trade goods and is of particular importance in the north and the Far East, where other means of mass transportation are not yet sufficiently developed. River transport is used for carrying timber and liquid cargo (oil, etc.) in those areas where there are convenient river routes. Automobile transport is used for short hauls, the average haul in this case being about 16 kilometres. Air transport is used for carrying some especially valuable goods demanding urgent delivery, as well as mail. Finally, large quantities of oil and gas are delivered by pipeline.

Various means of transportation co-operate in the work of carrying cargo. In the USSR, great attention is paid to co-ordinating the operations of different means of transport, thereby ensuring that freight can be passed from one means to another without having to be stored in between. This demands the co-ordination of schedules and attention to the carrying capacities of the ships or vehicles being employed.

Freight transportation is planned in advance for periods of five years, one year, three months and a month. Five- and one-year plans are made on the basis of production and consumption plans for different types of products, and with regard to the direction of travel. Transportation–economic balances are used for each of the republics and areas comprising the USSR. Production and consumption, or, to be more precise, resources and their distribution, are compared in these balances for each type of freight and with respect to every region. With the help of such balances, the areas that have a surplus of a given product are 'tied' to the areas lacking it, thus making it possible to create a national plan of transportation.

Operational quarterly and monthly plans are made on the basis of the annual plan and senders' claims for the necessary rolling stock. These claims are placed with the railways, steamship companies, or other mass transportation organisations. These then consider the claims and reject those that, in their opinion, are not rational or do not fit into the annual plan. An adopted operational transportation plan has the force of a contract between the sender and the carrier.

Mass transportation in the USSR is legally regulated as a public service, and relations between the sender and the carrier are subject to special regulations, such as the 'Railways Statute'. This statute determines the rights and commitments of both sides with respect to passenger and freight transportation in accordance with plans.

Rooted in the plans of passenger and freight transportation are the maintenance plans for each of the means of transportation, and capital investment plans governing the introduction of new technology and the construction of new (and reconstruction of existing) railways, ports, and so on.

IV. CONCLUSION

In spite of low tariffs, all of the means of transportation in the USSR are highly profitable, as can be seen from Table 17.1. The sum of the profits earned in 1972 by the four means of transport listed in the table amounts to

TABLE 17.1

Means of transportation	*Profits (million roubles)*		*Profits as a percentage of the cost of the funds*	
	1965	1972	1965	1972
Railway transport	4414	5803	13·3	12·7
Sea	247	1227	6·3	17·0
River	196	445	8·5	12·2
Automobile	990	2410	24·6	31·5

about 10 thousand million roubles. In all cases, the profits exceeded capital investment, which in the same year totalled about 8 thousand million roubles. Thus, although all capital investments in the major means of transportation are made in a centralised way and from the State budget, they are far surpassed by the profits earned.

Transport in the USSR has reached a high level of development and satisfies the demands for passenger and freight movement in the Soviet socialist society. The future rapid growth of the economy in the USSR will demand considerable further development of all of the means of transportation.

The basic tasks of that development are, in outline, the following.

(1) Rail transport: a number of railways are to be built in the east and the north, where the existing network is still not sufficient; second tracks should be constructed where major lines are at present only single track.

(2) The road network is to be considerably expanded, in order to meet the prospect of a multi-million automobile fleet. An important task is to design motors (probably electric) that would allow for a sharp decrease in, or the elimination of, air pollution.

(3) Seaports are to be reconstructed and deepened, and the merchant-marine tonnage will increase considerably.

(4) After the construction of canals providing water for the Caspian and Aral Seas and for irrigation in Central Asia, the inland waterway network will become more extensive.

(5) Oil and gas pipelines will be extended and new ones built.

(6) Air transport will be improved by the addition to the air fleet of planes capable of carrying up to 500 passengers or more, and of flying at supersonic speeds.

Transport in the USSR is a very important public service, providing travel facilities for the public and acting as a link between producers and consumers. Further development of transport will result in its gaining even greater significance as a public service.

Part VII
Macro-Economic Aspects of Public Services

18 On the Political Economy of Public Service

Bruno S. Frey [1]
UNIVERSITIES OF KONSTANZ AND BASEL

A positive study of the intertemporal variation of public services and investment is undertaken, with special emphasis on the electoral period. The government is assumed to undertake public investments in order to maximise its utility over the current election period, subject to the constraint that such policy assures re-election. Government utility depends on various elements, to which the various parties assign different weights according to their ideology. Alternatively, it is assumed that governments want to maximise the time period during which they are in power. A major influence on public expenditures is exerted by bureaucracy, which is assumed to act incrementally and tends to maximise budgets.

These behavioural assumptions are studied within a macro-economic framework by simulating the effects of various exogenous shocks upon the system. It is shown how well the government fares under various environments of voters' preferences, and when there is a change of party in power. The model serves as a step towards the development of empirically estimated politico-economic models.

I. INTRODUCTION

Public expenditures and the supply of public services show considerable variation over time; in particular, there is a close connection with the legislative term. Such variations in public expenditures (and other government actions) may lead to 'political business cycles', though a more appropriate name would be 'politico-economic cycles'.[2] These have recently received attention from theoreticians, especially in Europe.[3]

[1] The author is grateful to Friedrich Schneider for performing the computations and for helpful comments.

[2] For empirical evidence, see, for example, Lindbeck (1970), and Snyder (1970). For England in particular, see Dow (1964), esp. p. 384, and Prest (1968).

[3] The forerunner is Kalecki (1943). Goodhart and Bhansali (1970), and Nordhaus (1972) analyse the phenomenon in the Phillips-curve context. Special emphasis is put on the time perspective by Frey and Lau (1968) and Liefmann-Keil (1970). A simple simulation model of the politico-economic system without public services and bureaucracy, and with no explicit optimising behaviour of the government, is presented in Frey (1974).

The approach taken in the present paper can be characterised as having three main aspects:

(1) The study is *positive,* i.e. sets out to be explicative and concerns itself with *intertemporal variations* of public services;
(2) the analysis is in an explicit *macro-economic* framework, which seems appropriate because of the quantitative importance of public services in a modern society;
(3) the theoretical background is given by the *new political economy* or *public choice.* However, the restrictive setup of, for instance, Downs (1957) is abandoned: the government is assumed to maximise its own utility;[4] elections are discontinuous; and the emphasis lies on the disequilibrium dynamics.

The government is not the only politically relevant decision-maker that will be taken into account: public bureaucracy will also be considered.

Section II presents the basic model. In section III it is assumed that the government maximises its utility; and, in section IV, that it maximises the length of its stay in power. In section V bureaucratic behaviour is added, and some concluding remarks are made in section VI.

II. THE BASIC MODEL

The model developed is kept as simple as possible. It is composed of four parts, among which are three sectors:

(1) the economy,
(2) public services, and
(3) the polity

The fourth part consists of the interaction equations connecting these sectors, and is itself made up of two parts:

(a) the popularity function transmitting economic impulses into the political sector; and
(b) the reaction functions showing how the government uses the various instruments to reach its goals.

The economy is pictured as a real one-good model. The emphasis lies on intertemporal aspects introduced through investment equations and various

[4] Note that it is only under four very strong conditions that utility maximisation non-trivially boils down to vote maximisation by the government: (1) a two-party system, (2) perfect political competition, (3) continuous elections, and (4) full equilibrium.

time lags. Full employment of capital and labour is assumed. The time periods can be interpreted as each covering half a year, with elections taking place each fourth year (i.e. at $t = 8, 16, 24, 32, \ldots$).

The basic model consists of the following equations.

THE ECONOMY

Real national income Y depends on the real capital stock K by means of a linear-limitational production function

$$Y(t) = k(t) \cdot K(t) \tag{18.1}$$

Capital productivity k rises as public services (PS) increase their share of national income (i.e. more are offered), and falls as the share of current public expenditures (PEC) increases. This last effect is due to the anti-productive effect of much *current* public expenditure.[5]

$$k(t) = k_o + k_{PS}\left[\frac{PS(t)}{Y(t)}\right] - k_{PEC}\left[\frac{PEC(t)}{Y(t)}\right] \tag{18.2}$$

where k_o = const.

Real capital stock is increased by 'private' investment I and 'political' investment PI, and decreased by depreciation D.

$$K(t+1) = K(t) + I(t) + PI(t) - D(t) \tag{18.3}$$

The terms 'private' and 'political' investment refer to the *controlling* entity. A considerable part of the investment undertaken for private profit reasons can be controlled by government intervention. Thus, 'political' investment covers not only infrastructural investments in the widest sense, but also part of investment in the private sector. It is undertaken by government for political reasons. To minimise the fluctuations originating from privately controlled investment, it is simply taken to be a constant fraction of income.

$$I(t) = v \cdot Y(t) \tag{18.4}$$

Capital depreciation is proportional to capital stock:

$$D(t) = d \cdot K(t) \tag{18.5}$$

Private consumption goods are simply assumed to be a constant fraction of income:

$$C(t) = c \cdot Y(t) \tag{18.6}$$

The government politicians receive an 'income' in the form of consumption goods. This 'political' consumption, PC, is residually determined by

[5] Current public expenditures often impede growth by subsidising inefficient sectors such as agriculture. For a theoretical discussion see Bernholz (1966).

$$PC(t) = Y(t) - I(t) - D(t) - C(t) - PT(t) \tag{18.7}$$

where *PT* represents government expenditures for investment and public services.

PUBLIC SERVICES

Government expenditures can be used for investment into real capital ('political investment', *PI*) or for the production of public services. The latter expenditures must be split up into those immediately increasing the output of public services (current public expenditure, *PEC*), those increasing it only after a time lag of two periods (medium-run public expenditure, *PEM*), and those increasing it only after a lag of four periods (long-run public expenditure, *PEL*). Total government expenditures (*PT*) are

$$PT(t) = PI(t) + PEC(t) + PEM(t) + PEL(t) \tag{18.8}$$

The production function for the output of public services is

$$PS(t) = PEC(t) + \beta_{PEM} \cdot PEM(t-2) + \beta_{PEL} \cdot PEL(t-4) \tag{18.9}$$

It is reasonable to assume that $1 < \beta_{PEM} < \beta_{PEL}$, i.e. that expenditures with a lagged effect have a higher productivity.

THE POLITY

Using the analogy of real capital, we introduce the concept of a *political capital stock,* which reflects the *long-run* or *basic* evaluation of the government's performance from the voters' point of view. A similar concept is used by some empirically-oriented political scientists (for instance, Campbell, Converse, Miller and Stokes, 1960) and corresponds to the stock of 'goodwill' as estimated in econometric studies of advertising (for instance, Peles, 1971, and Tsurumi, 1973).

Political capital stock *PK* is increased by popularity *POP* and decreased by political depreciation *PD*:

$$PK(t+1) = PK(t) + POP(t) - PD(t) \tag{18.10}$$

The depreciation of political capital is due to voters forgetting past government achievements. It is assumed to be proportional to the stock:

$$PD(t) = \delta \cdot PK(t) \tag{18.11}$$

Popularity, on the other hand, refers to the consumer–voters' *short-run* or *current* evaluation of the government's behaviour.

In each time period t, the politicians in power estimate their likely vote share, $S(t)$, at the next election. They base this estimate upon the stock of political capital accumulated. They know that the (reasonably rational) voters base their judgement of the government's expected performance over the next electoral period not upon short-lived impressions reflected in popularity ratings, but, rather, upon their more basic evaluation reflected in political capital. Thus, government politicans expect their electoral vote share to rise if political capital is increased.

$$S(t) = S(t-1) + \gamma[PK(t) - PK(t-1)] \tag{18.12}$$

The vote share received by the government is measured in percentage points such that $0 \leqslant S(t) \leqslant 100$. *Before* the elections, it indicates the *vote share expected by the government if it does not undertake any action* to influence popularity ratings. *At election time, S* indicates the *actual* vote share received by the government. If S is lower than a given minimum share, $SMIN$, the government changes and is taken over by the former opposition party (or by a coalition of former opposition parties). The size of $SMIN$ depends on a great many factors, such as the number of competing parties and their coalition possibilities; institutional factors (for instance, the number of seats that, on the basis of S, are obtained in parliament); and so on. In the present model, $SMIN$ is taken to be exogenously determined and is fixed at 50 per cent; and the opposition is assumed to comprise only one party and not to compete *strategically* with the party in power (which would involve the construction of a differential game).

Similarly to the government, the opposition party builds up a stock of political capital (in this case, PKO):

$$PKO(t+1) = PKO(t) + POPO(t) - PDO(t) \tag{18.13}$$

$$PDO(t) = \delta o \cdot PKO(t) \tag{18.14}$$

where the opposition's popularity and depreciation are $POPO$ and PDO, respectively.

The consumer–voters have expectations concerning the provision of private consumption and public services. These expectations are formed on the basis of discounted past experience. The consumption expectation EC is

$$EC(t) = (1 - \lambda_c) \sum_{i=0}^{\infty} \lambda_c^i C(t-i)$$

and the expectation about public services EPS is

$$EPS(t) = (1 - \lambda_{PS}) \sum_{i=0}^{\infty} \lambda^i{}_{PS} C(t-i)$$

Using Koyck transformations, this simplifies to

$$EC(t) = (1 - \lambda_c)C(t) + \lambda_c EC(t-1) \tag{18.15}$$

and

$$EPS(t) = (1 - \lambda_{PS})PS(t) + \lambda_{PS} EPS(t-1) \tag{18.16}$$

[6]

INTERACTION EQUATIONS

In this simple model, government popularity *POP* is influenced only by the level of private consumption and the supply of public services, as compared with voters' expectations.

$$POP(t) = POP(t-1) + \pi_c\,[C(t) - EC(t)] + \pi_{PS}\,[PS(t) - EPS(t)] \tag{18.17}$$

Popularity is also measured in percentage points; hence, $0 \leqslant POP(t) \leqslant 100$.

Popularity functions have recently received much attention from mathematical political scientists and economists. A connection between economic conditions (mainly inflation, unemployment and growth of income) and party popularity has been conjectured for a long time – for instance, by Åkerman (1947) for various European countries, and by Bean (1940) for the United States. The Nazi takeover in Germany has been shown to have been closely related to the failing economic situation in the Weimar Republic (Kaltefleiter, 1966).

These studies, however, used inadequate statistical methods. Of great interest are the recent studies by Goodhart and Bhansali (1970) and Kramer (1971), which use regression and spectral analysis for Great Britain and the United States, respectively. Frey and Garbers (1972) have produced a corresponding study for Germany. Though there is some criticism of these approaches,[7] it seems reasonable to assume (a) that popularity functions reflect a relationship existing in reality, and (b) that public services are a significant determinant (a proposition that is so far untested).

The second type of interaction equations, the *action and reaction functions* of political decision-makers, is discussed below.

III. A UTILITY-MAXIMISING GOVERNMENT

THE MAXIMISATION PROBLEM IN THE POLITICO-ECONOMIC SYSTEM AS PERCEIVED BY THE GOVERNMENT

It seems that, for most governments, the relevant time horizon is confined to one term and the next election. Such a government is not concerned with any

[6] The parameter values used in the simulation runs discussed later in this paper were chosen with a view to realism: $K_0 = 0{\cdot}125$, $K_{PS} = 0.18$, $K_{PEC} = 0{\cdot}07$, $V = 0{\cdot}08$, $d = 0{\cdot}05$, $c = 0{\cdot}50$, $\beta_{PEM} = 1{\cdot}15$, $\beta_{PEL} = 1{\cdot}40$, $\delta = 0{\cdot}20$, $\delta o = 0{\cdot}20$, $\gamma = 0{\cdot}50$, $\lambda c = 0{\cdot}68$, $\lambda_{PS} = 0{\cdot}70$. For reasons of capacity, *PI* can be changed only to the extent of five units per period.

[7] See, in particular, the discussion between Stigler (1973) and Okun (1973).

election farther in the future. It seeks to maximise the utility of being in power (PU) over the election term $T_{i+1} - T_i$ (where T_i indicates election dates occurring at $t = 8, 16, 24, \ldots$) subject to the condition of re-election at the end of the term. The maximisation problem is

$$\max_{\text{(policy instruments)}} \sum_{t=T_i}^{t=T_{i+1}} PU(t)$$

subject to $S(T_{i+1}) \geqslant SMIN$

(the Lagrangian multiplier corresponding to this constraint will be denoted by Λ, with $\Lambda = 0$ indicating that it is nonbinding, $\Lambda > 0$ that it is binding).

Government utility depends on the government's ideological views about the levels of consumption and public services available to the population, and on its own consumption:

$$PU(t) = i_c \cdot C(t) + i_{PS} \cdot PS(t) + \epsilon \cdot PC(t) \tag{18.18}$$

The government does not have full information about the politico-economic system in which it is acting. It is forced to perform the above maximisation problem within the system as it *perceives* it, which is certainly *simplified* as compared with the 'true' structure developed in section II. Thus, the (small) effect of public expenditures on capacity output is disregarded ($k'_{PS} = 0$, $k'_{PEC} = 0$).[8] Due to incomplete information, the government finds it particularly difficult to make an estimate of the popularity function (18.17). It has only a vague notion of how consumption and public services affect its popularity and feels unable to separate the *direct* effect of $C(t)$ and $PS(t)$ from the *indirect* effect through the induced change in voters' expectation.[9] To reduce complexity, the government takes the popularity function to be

$$POP(t) = \Pi'_c C(t) + \Pi'_{PS} PS(t) \tag{18.17'}$$

but makes a conservative estimate of Π'_c and Π'_{PS} to take account of the changes in voters' expectations (Π'_c and Π'_{PS} will be taken to be much smaller than Π_c and Π_{PS}, respectively).

The maximisation problem that the government perceives is solved here by dynamic programming. However, a solution can be found, or, at least suitably approximated by means of intuitive reasoning of a sort that may well be within the capabilities of government politicians.

[8] Primed parameters indicate the values as perceived by the government.

[9] Note from (18.15), (18.16), and (18.17) that the *total* effect is

$$\partial POP(t)/\partial C(t) = \Pi_c - \Pi_c(1 - \lambda_c) = \Pi_c \lambda_c$$

and

$$\partial POP(t)/\partial PS(t) = \Pi_{PS} - \Pi_{PS}(1 - \lambda_{PS}) = \Pi_{PS} \lambda_{PS}$$

The *optimal* (starred) values for the policy instruments available to the government have the following properties.

(1) Due to a four-period lag, long-run public expenditures PEL^* can have no effect on the current election term during the last four periods before an election, and, thus, are always reduced to zero for these four periods.

(2) For a similar reason, political investment PI^* is always reduced to zero in the last period before an election.

Particularly interesting results can be presented for the case of governments with special ideological views. For the purpose of exposition, three 'ideal' types of government ideology ('ideal' in Max Weber's sense) are assumed.

(1) An 'extreme left-wing' government that puts no value at all on private consumption and on its own political consumption. It is interested only in providing the population with public services.

$$PU_{LW}(t) = i_{PS} \cdot PS(t) \qquad (18.18a)$$

$$i_c = \epsilon = 0$$

(2) An 'extreme right-wing' government that is interested only in the population's consumption level.

$$\begin{aligned} PU_{RW}(t) &= i_c \cdot C(t) \\ i_{PS} &= \epsilon = 0 \end{aligned} \qquad (18.18b)$$

(3) An 'extreme exploitative' government whose only desire is to consume as much as possible during the period in power.

$$\begin{aligned} PU_{EX}(t) &= \epsilon \cdot PC(t) \\ i_c &= i_{PS} = 0 \end{aligned} \qquad (18.18c)$$

Moreover, a complete set of optimal policies can be specified only if the many degrees of freedom due to the linearity of the conceived (and 'true') politico-economic model are removed. It is realistic to assume that the government solves the problem by a rule of thumb, i.e. by allocating *equal amounts* to each 'free' instrument within the limits set on public expenditures and 'political' consumption, as given by

$$PT(t) + PC(t) = Y(t) - C(t) - I(t) = m \cdot Y(t) \qquad (18.19)$$

where $m = 1 - c - v$.

If the re-election constraint is nonbinding, the extreme left-wing government allocates its expenditures solely for the production of public services and completely disregards political investments. Long-run public expenditures having no effect in the current election period are discontinued in the four last periods before the election; all outlays are then devoted to current public expenditures.

The extreme right-wing and extreme exploitative governments have the same optimal policy, as, in order to achieve, in the last period, the highest attainable level of private and political consumption (a 'consumption orgy'), they are both concerned to increase capital accumulation as much as possible.

If the governments have to use their instruments in order to achieve re-election, the optimal policies of the various types of government become much more similar. Ideological values must be sacrificed in order that power be retained, which means that the government now has to take into account voters' opinions as reflected in the parameters of the popularity function. The extreme left-wing and right-wing governments pursue practically identical policies, with the obvious difference that, shortly before elections, the left-wing government switches to current public expenditures. The right-wing government's behaviour during the election period is to increase its 'political' consumption to its maximum $mY(t)$, as given in equation (18.19). The exploitative government's policy depends on the strength of the re-election constraint; no general description can be given. As before, of course, no type of government undertakes any investments *PI* in the election period, since these would have no effect on output in the current election term.

In order to obtain more definitive results, it is interesting to see how the three types of government fare with their optimal strategies under alternatively perceived 'environments'. These environments are characterised by the voters' preferences with respect to public services and private consumption as they materialise in the popularity function. Two basic environmental conditions are discussed here: one in which the voters have a bias for public services ($\Pi'_C = 0{\cdot}05$, $\Pi'_{PS} = 0{\cdot}1364$; the population is 'left'); and one in which the voters have a bias for private consumption ($\Pi'_C = 0{\cdot}1$, $\Pi'_{PS} = 0{\cdot}05$; the population is 'right'). On these assumptions, it can be shown by simulation (though, to save space, the exact figures are not reproduced here) that only a right-wing or exploitative party in power in a right-wing environment can simply maximise its own utility without regard to elections. In all other cases, the government must make a compromise in order to stay in power. Under this proviso, the extreme right-wing and exploitative governments expect to stay in power indefinitely. This is due to the fact that their own goals – the maximisation of private or 'political' consumption – involves building up the real capital stock, which is, at the same time, a prerequisite for political survival in the long run. Under the simplified politico-economic structure that is assumed, the left-wing government is in a much more difficult situation. Even when environmental conditions are favourable (i.e. if the voters also are 'left'), it can expect to survive only for three legislative periods. At the fourth election it is defeated, even if in the preceding electoral period it takes voters' wishes into account as much as possible. With a right-wing population, the left-wing government can expect to hold power for only two periods; a defeat at the third election is unavoidable.

APPLICATION OF THE 'OPTIMAL POLICY' AS PERCEIVED BY THE GOVERNMENT

The government, having no knowledge of the 'true' structure of the politico-economic system, is forced to apply the policy that it finds optimal within the system as it *perceives* it. Thus, it sets the instruments available (*PI, PEL* and *PEC*) as in the previous section. The simulation results (again, the figures are not given here) show that the choice of that policy is not very advantageous for any type of government; at best, the government is re-elected for another term. This result, of course, is not surprising, as the structure of the two systems is different. The government's lack of knowledge, especially about the influence of voter's expectations on popularity, is a major reason for its poor performance. It is interesting to note that expectations have the same importance in quite different fields of disequilibrium economics (see, for instance, Stiglitz, 1973).

IV. A GOVERNMENT MAXIMISING THE LENGTH OF ITS STAY IN POWER

THE THEORY

A Government that considers not only the current election term, but, in addition, the periods thereafter, will, if it expects to receive *more* than the necessary vote share (*SMIN*) in the next election,[10] take any opportunity that it can to shift the *current* re-election potential – given by $S(t)$ into the future. This can be achieved by (a) building up the real capital stock by *increasing* political investment, (b) *increasing* public expenditures designed to push up the supply of public services in *future* periods (*PEM, PEL*), and (c) *decreasing* current public expenditures (*PEC*).

The corresponding simple linear reaction functions are

$$PI(t+1) = PI(t) + \rho_{PI} \cdot [S(t) - SMIN] \qquad (18.19a)$$

$$PEL(t+1) = PEL(t) + \rho_{PEL} \cdot [S(t) - SMIN] \qquad (18.19b)$$

$$PEM(t+1) = PEM(t) + \rho_{PEM} \cdot [S(t) - SMIN] \qquad (18.19c)$$

and

$$PEC(t+1) = PEC(t) - \rho_{PEC} \cdot [S(t) - SMIN] \qquad (18.19d)$$

If $S(t) < SMIN$, public expenditures with an immediate popularity effect (*PEC*) are increased, and all other expenditures (*PI, PEM, PEL*) are decreased. Such behaviour corresponds to discounting the future, with the *rate of time discount* equal to one minus the *re-election probability*: a government absolutely certain to win the next election has no need to discount over the respective election term;[11] but, when the re-election is uncertain, the next term is 'worth'

[10] For the study of long-run behaviour, *PC* is assumed to be zero and private consumption is a residual: $C(t) = Y(t) - I(t) - PT(t)$. See equation (18.6).

[11] Assuming that the government is composed of politicians of different ages, and that prospective government members also have some influence, the *subjective* discounting government politicians can be neglected.

less to the government than is the current one, and so on. If P_n is the probability of being (re-)elected in period n, the probability of being continually in power over period n and of being thrown out of power in period $n + 1$ is

$$(1 - P_{n+1}) \prod_{t=1}^{n} P_t$$

A government interested in staying in power for as long a time as possible has to maximise the sum of the different periods of uninterrupted government, $t = 1, 2, \ldots$, weighted by the above probability. Realistically assuming that the government is never absolutely sure of being re-elected ($0 \leqslant P_n < 1$), this reduces to

$$\sum_{t=1}^{\infty} \prod_{\tau=1}^{t} P_\tau$$

Putting

$$\prod_{\tau=1}^{t} P_\tau = Z_t$$

it follows that

$$Z_t = P_t Z_{t-1}$$

from which it is easy to see that $P_t = 1 + \rho_t$, with ρ_t the rate of time discount of period t.[12]

THE SIMULATION RUNS

The politico-economic system as developed in equations (18.1)–(18.17),[13] combined with the government's behavioural equations (18.19),[14] is in stationary equilibrium if all expectations are fulfilled ($EC = C$, $EPS = PS$) and if the government has been elected with the minimum share of votes ($S = SMIN$). This stationary equilibrium serves as a starting point for the application of exogenous shocks to the popularity function. These exogenous shifts may be due to *external* developments (for instance, international crises) or to *internal* noneconomic shocks (such as political scandals).

Table 18.1 shows the effects of positive popularity shocks of +20 and +5 percentage points, and negative popularity shocks of −5 and −20 percentage points. For simplicity, the table shows only the two variables entering the popularity function – consumption $C(t)$ and public services $PS(t)$ – and the government's vote share in the election periods – $S(t)$.

[12] See Frey and Ramser (1974). Compare the present approach to that of Inagaki (1970), who, simply and quite untheoretically, stipulates an 'instaneous government'.

[13] It is assumed that consumption has a somewhat larger weight in the popularity function than public services have: $\Pi_C = 0{\cdot}30$, $\Pi_{PS} = 0{\cdot}20$.

[14] The assumed parameter values are: $\rho_{PI} = 0{\cdot}95$, $\rho_{PEL} = 0{\cdot}10$, $\rho_{PEM} = 0{\cdot}10$, $\rho_{PEC} = 0{\cdot}35$.

TABLE 18.1

SIMULATION RUNS FOR POSITIVE AND NEGATIVE SHOCKS: CONSUMPTION (*C*), PUBLIC SERVICES (*PS*), AND THE GOVERNMENT'S VOTE SHARE (*S*) IN ELECTION PERIODS

Run	*Exogenous popularity shock*	*Variable*	*Initial equilibrium*	*Election period*					
				8	16	24	32	40	48
1	+20%	*C*	250	247	232	234	233	260	309
		PS	178	146	189	231	324	426	528
		S	50	73·54	66·51	94·48	100	100	100
2	+5%	*C*	250	242	246	283	276	276	302
		PS	178	174	167	153	203	302	404
		S	50	50·02	56·50	67·95	100	100	100
3	−5%	*C*	250	259	252	237	209	177	156
		PS	178	181	186	191	188	171	162
		S P_1	50	50·06	(42·39)	63·89	(34·16)	56·79	59·74
		S P_2			57·61	(36·11)	65·84	(43·21)	
4	−20%	*C*	250	256	190	165	171	125	108
		PS	178	197	219	164	185	204	168
		S P_1	50	(41·19)	86·93	51·27	(48·14)	75·75	(48·01)
		S P_2		58·81	(13·07)		51·86	(24·25)	51·99

Note: The figures for consumption and public services are rounded. In the rows for vote shares, the upper figure shows the election outcome for party 1, where the lower shows that for party 2. Figures in parentheses indicate an insufficient vote share ($S < SMIN$) and a change of government.

Because of the simultaneous interdependence of variables in the politico-economic system it is not easy to give a verbal account of the developments. However, an attempt is made, nevertheless, to give an intuitive explanation of them.

Run 1

A high exogenous popularity increase of 20 per cent enables the government to invest in the future by rapidly stepping up long-run expenditures (*PI* and *PEL*). As the government is very confident of its re-election, it reduces short-run public expenditures to zero up until the first election. The rapid increase of political investment and of total public expenditures leads, however, to a displacement of consumption. Though public services are rising all along, government popularity and, therefore, its expected vote share for the third election fall somewhat ($S(16) = 66$ per cent). The real capital stock and national income continually rise in all periods due to the heavy public investment. Between periods 12 and 32 this capacity effect is about as strong as the displacement effect: consumption fluctuates around 233. Thereafter, the capacity effect dominates, and the government's vote share reaches the upper limit of 100 per cent, the variables being connected in a 'virtuous' circle.

Run 2

With an exogenous popularity increase of only 5 per cent (see Figs. 18.1 a–c), the government just manages to win the first election, but can barely raise

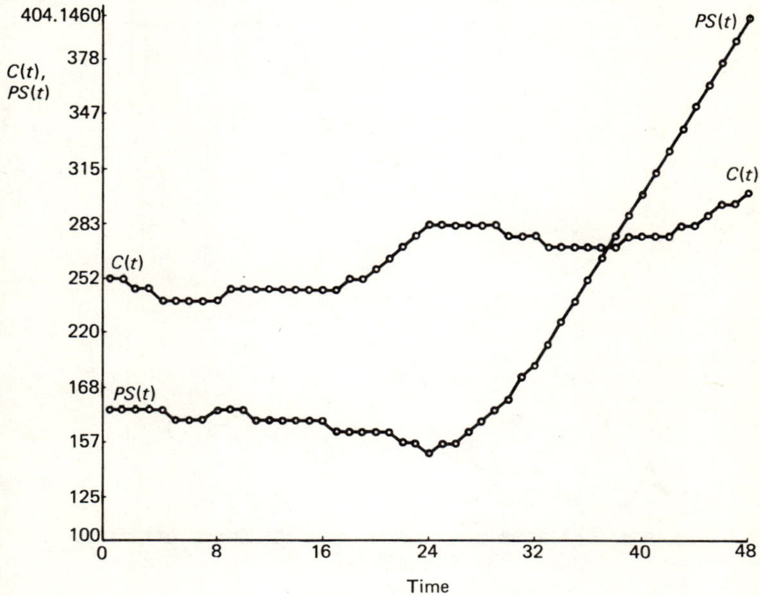

Fig. 18.1(a)

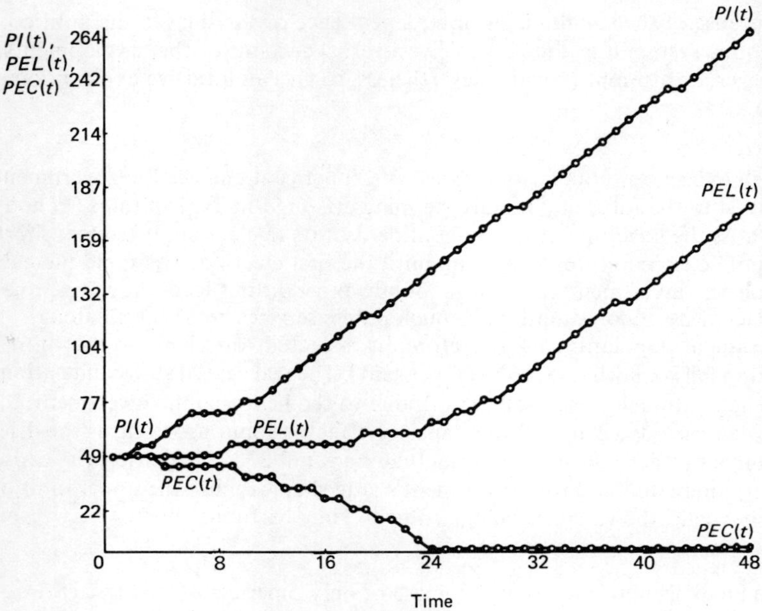

Fig. 18.1(b)

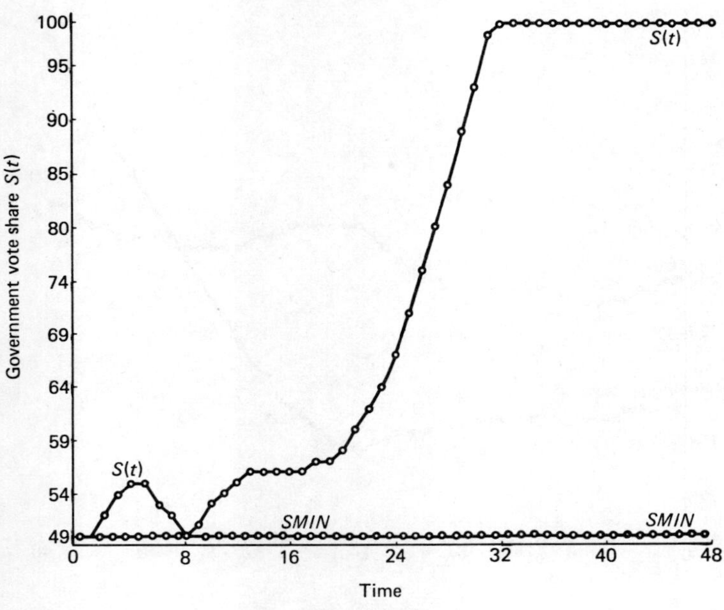

Fig. 18.1(c)

expenditures for future public services (*PEL, PEM*). The same holds true for the following election term, in which consumption and public services stay nearly constant. After the election victory, at $t = 16$, the capacity effect of the increase in political investment leads to a rise in consumption, while public services fall somewhat, mainly due to the now-possible reduction of current public expenditures. The effect is a more comfortable victory at the next election. Now the government is able to invest in future public services, which yield a maximum vote share at $t = 32$, despite a consumption setback due to displacement.

Run 3

The government's policy is quite different when it suffers an exogenous popularity decrease, even if only as small as 5 per cent (see Figs. 18.2a–c). Fearing that it will not be re-elected, the government reduces investment in real capital and (less severely) long- and medium-run public expenditures. At the same time, short-run public expenditures are somewhat increased. These drive up both consumption and the supply of public services, and the government is re-elected. In the new term, a long-run policy is pursued to begin with, but the concomitant decline in popularity forces the government to reduce long-run expenditures (*PI, PEL* and *PEM*) and strongly to step up expenditures with an immediate effect on public-services output. Though this reversal of policy

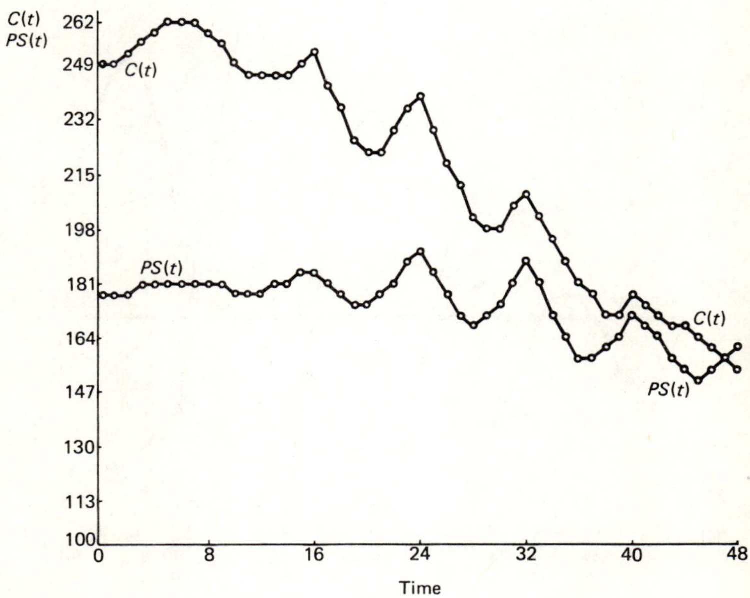

Fig. 18.2(a)

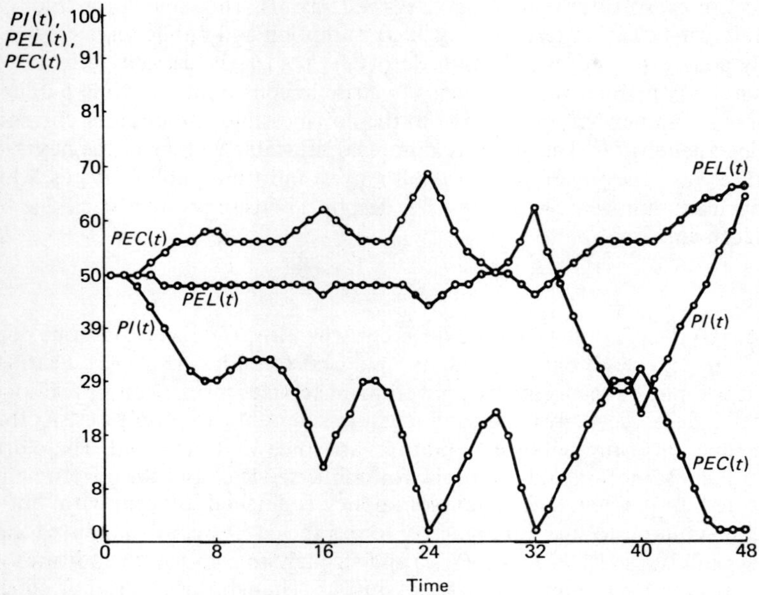

Fig. 18.2(b)

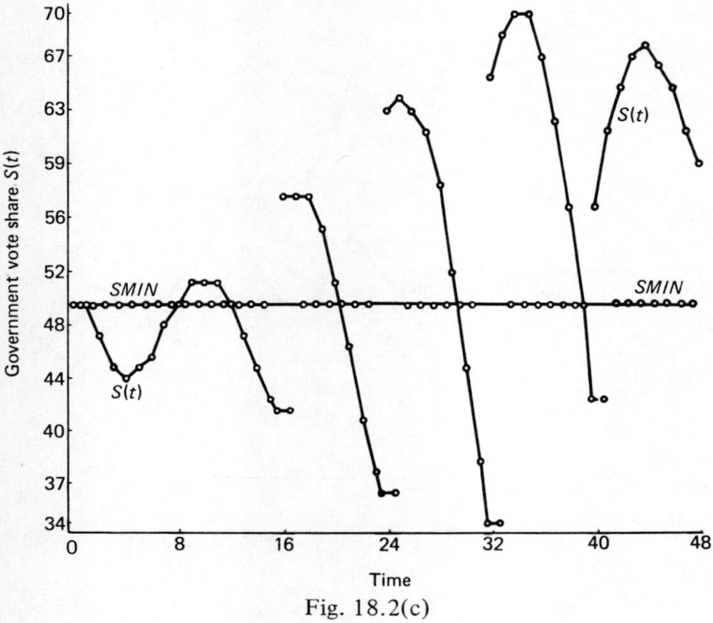

Fig. 18.2(c)

has a positive effect on both consumption and public services, the government receives only 42 per cent of the vote and, thus, is defeated.

The new government comes into power with a relatively small majority (58 per cent) and, therefore, is soon forced to pursue a short-run policy. It manages to increase public-expenditure output somewhat, but consumption steadily decreases. The real capital stock gradually falls as political investment is reduced to zero. The government stays in power for only one period, as its vote share does not go beyond 36 per cent in $t = 24$.

Succeeding governments are confronted with the same situation. The real capital stock and national income gradually fall, as no party in power can afford to undertake any significant investments. For the same reason, public-services output experiences a long-run fall. There are, however, some short-run fluctuations within this long-run trend, and in period 48 a government manages to be re-elected, partly because voters' expectations have been adjusted strongly downwards.

Run 4

With an exogenous popularity loss of 20 per cent, the real capital stock and consumption have a long-run falling trend. Public services show more marked short-run fluctuations than consumption does. There are many government changes, but after a large victory (i.e. a heavy defeat of the party in power) the new government is sometimes able to obtain re-election for another term (here at $t = 24$).

V. BUREAUCRATIC BEHAVIOUR

Governments have only partial control over policy instruments; bureaucracy also has an important say. Within the politico-economic model developed, this influence shows in two forms:

(1) Bureaucracies resist structural changes for various reasons (for example, established positions may be threatened, and lack of information may make it difficult to adapt quickly to changed circumstances). Empirical studies show that bureaucracies act 'incrementally' (Wildavsky, 1964). They are willing – or can be forced – to follow only *part* of the government's intentions regarding expenditure.

(2) The income, career and prestige of any bureaucrat are closely linked with the size of the entity in which he is acting. Each bureaucrat is interested in continually increasing the size of overall bureaucracy and, hence, of the budget. Bureaucrats are even described as 'budget maximisers' (Niskanen, 1971).

These two effects may be formalised as

$$PIB(t) = INC_{PI} \cdot PIB(t-1) + b_{PI} \cdot [PI(t) - PI(t-1)]$$
$$PELB(t) = INC_{PEL} \cdot PELB(t-1) + b_{PEL} \cdot [PEL(t) - PEL(t-1)]$$
$$PEMB(t) = INC_{PEM} \cdot PEMB(t-1) + b_{PEM} \cdot [PEM(t) - PEM(t-1)]$$
$$PECB(t) = INC_{PEC} \cdot PECB(t-1) + b_{PEC} \cdot [PEC(t) - PEC(t-1)]$$

The letter B after an expenditure category indicates the actual allocation undertaken by the bureaucracy. The first expression on the right-hand side shows the auto-dynamic effect of continually rising expenditures (all $INC > 1$); the second expression indicates that only fraction b of an expenditure change intended by the government actually materialises.

This bureaucratic behaviour is now introduced into the long-run maximisation model. It is assumed that the bureaucracy autonomously spends 1 per cent more per period in every sector, and that, in any period, only 95 per cent of the instrument changes intended by the government are actually effected.[15] For reasons of space, only a verbal account of the results is given. Table 18.2 gives the vote shares for the model with bureaucracy; it should be contrasted with Table 18.1. The interference of bureaucracy with the government's plans means that there no longer exists any equilibrium, and that there is a continuous tendency for any government to lose votes. While the government, taken

TABLE 18.2

SIMULATION RUNS FOR THE POLITICO-ECONOMIC MODEL WITH BUREAUCRACY

	Vote share	*Election period* 0	8	16	24	32	40	48
No exogenous shock	S P_1	50	(47·49)	54·11	(43·19)	58·43	(42·93)	
	S P_2		52·51	(45·45)	56·81	(41·57)	57·07	53·03
Exogenous popularity shock								
+20%	S	50	71·43	62·80	87·76	100	100	100
+5%	S P_1	50	(47·62)					
	S P_2		52·38	51·96	64·87	91·73	100	100
–5%	S P_1	50	(47·34)	63·70	(30·36)	51·74	63·47	69·08
	S P_2		52·66	(36·10)	69·64	(48·26)		
–20%	S P_1	50	(35·64)	81·86	55·82	(42·78)	72·28	(47·22)
	S P_2		64·35	(18·14)		57·22	(27·72)	52·68

[15] $INC_{PI} = INC_{PEL} = INC_{PEM} = INC_{PEC} = 1{\cdot}01$
$b_{PI} = b_{PEL} = b_{PEM} = b_{PEC} = 0{\cdot}95$

alone, would be able to manage the politico-economic system such that it survives exogenous popularity falls of 5 per cent for one term (S = 50·06 per cent) as shown in Table 18.1), the lack of adaptability and the incremental behaviour of the bureaucracy prohibits this success (S = 47·34 per cent).

VI. CONCLUDING REMARKS

The model formulated and the various simulation runs discussed serve three main purposes.

(1) They should contribute to a better understanding of political–economic interaction, with special emphasis on the intertemporal fluctuations in the supply of public services.

(2) They serve as an initial step towards an endogenous treatment of the government sector in economic models. This applies particularly to macro-econometric models, the use of which for explanation and as a forecasting device is severely limited. The future course of the economy in a modern society depends, to a very large extent, on the government's actions, which, in all existing econometric models, are exogenous. Present econometric model-building suffers from a serious imbalance, since, whereas purely economic aspects are treated in a very refined way, nothing is said about government behaviour. The 'reaction functions' (see, for example, Friedlaender, 1973) serve only the purpose of revealing the government's preferences under the (completely unrealistic) assumption that there are *no* political influences. They represent 'measurement without theory' in political economy.

(3) Closely related is the fact that the model and simulation runs help towards a fuller understanding of the problems connected with the formal estimation of politico-economic relations ('politometrics') such as the popularity function or the determinants of the supply of public services (in the sense of, for example, Pryor, 1968).

No general discussion of the merits and demerits of simulations is intended here. It must be pointed out, however, that the simulation runs presented are *not* thought directly to represent reality; they should, rather, give a 'feeling' of how the interaction of political and economic systems may be modelled. Realism is approached only when the economic system is represented by a full-scale econometric model, the political and interacting equations are empirically estimated, and all are combined. Obviously, the analytic method is in some respects more powerful, but has a disadvantage in that it is difficult to deal with large models without having to deal almost exclusively with the mathematical instead of the material aspects. Here an attempt has been made to combine the analytic and simulation approaches.

REFERENCES

Åkerman, Johann, 'Political Economic Cycles', *Kyklos,* I (1947), pp. 107–17.

Bean, Louis H., *Ballot Behavior. A Study of Presidential Elections* (Washington, DC: American Council on Public Affairs, 1940).

Bernholz, Peter, 'Economic Policies in a Democracy', *Kyklos,* IX (1966), pp. 48–80.

Dow, J. C. R., *The Management of the British Economy 1945–1960* (Cambridge: Cambridge University Press, 1964).

Downs, Anthony, *An Economic Theory of Democracy* (New York: Harper and Row, 1957).

Frey, Bruno S., 'The Politico-Economic System: A Simulation Model', *Kyklos,* XXVII, (1974).

Frey, Bruno S., and Garbers, Hermann, 'Der Einfluss wirtschaftlicher Variablen auf die Popularität der Regierung', *Jahrbücher für Nationalökonomie und Statistik*, no. 186 (1972), pp. 281–95.

Frey, Bruno S., and Lau, Laurence J., 'Towards a Mathematical Model of Government Behaviour', *Zeitschrift für Nationalökonomie,* XXVIII (1968), pp. 335–80.

Frey, Bruno S., and Ramser, Hans-Jürgen, 'Eine Theorie der endogenen Zeitdiskontierung', *Zeitschrift für Wirtschafts- und Sozialwissenschaft* (1974).

Friedlaender, Ann, 'Macro-Policy Goals in the Postwar Period: A Study of Revealed Preference', *Quarterly Journal of Economics,* LXXXVII (1973).

Goodhart, C. A. E., and Bhansali, R. J., 'Political Economy', *Political Studies,* XVIII (1970), pp. 43–106.

Inagaki, K., *Optimal Economic Growth: Shifting Finite versus Infinite Time Horizon* (Amsterdam and London: North Holland, 1970).

Kalecki, Michael, 'Political Aspects of Full Employment', *Political Quarterly,* XIV (1943), pp. 322–31.

Kaltefleiter, Werner, *Wirtschaft und Politik in Deutschland* (Cologne: Westdeutscher Verlag, 1966).

Kramer, Gerald H., 'Short-run Fluctuation in U.S. Voting Behavior, 1896–1964', *American Political Science Review,* LXV (1971), pp. 131–43.

Liefmann-Keil, Elisabeth, 'Intertemporale Spillovereffekte und öffentlicher Haushalt', in *Theorie und Politik des finanzpolitischer Interventionismus*, ed. Haller et al. (Tübingen: Mohr Siebeck, 1970), pp. 61–76.

Lindbeck, Assar, 'Fiscal Policy as a Tool of Economic Stabilization', *Kyklos,* XXIII (1970).

Niskanen, William A., *Bureaucracy and Representative Government* (Chicago: Aldine, 1971).

Nordhaus, William B., 'The Political Business Cycle', *Cowles Foundation Discussion Paper no. 333* (1972).

Okun Arthur, M., 'Comments on Stigler's Paper', *American Economic Review, Papers and Proceedings,* LXIII (1973), pp. 172–7.

Prest, Alan R., 'Sense and Nonsense in Budgetary Policy', *Economic Journal,* LXXVIII (1968).

Pryor, Frederick L., *Public Expenditures in Communist and Capitalist Nations* (London: Allen and Unwin, 1968).

Snyder, Wayne M., 'Measuring Economic Stablization', *American Economic Review,* LX, (1970).

Stigler, George J., 'General Economic Conditions and National Elections', *American Economic Review, Papers and Proceedings,* LXIII (1973), pp. 160–7.

Stiglitz, Joseph, 'The Badly Behaved Economy with the Well Behaved Production Function', in *Models of Economic Growth,* ed. J. A. Mirrlees and N. H. Stern (London: Macmillan, 1973).

Wildavsky, Aaron, *The Politics of the Budgetary Process* (Boston: Little, Brown and Co., 1964).

19 Some Considerations on the Productive Capacity of Consumption Expenditures

Leo H. Klaassen* and Wietze Eizenga†
*UNIVERSITY OF ROTTERDAM
†UNIVERSITY OF MICHIGAN

This paper deals with the relation between the level and the structure of consumption and their influence on the labour productivity of the consumer. Assuming such a relationship, an optimal savings ratio will exist, below which savings are to be preferred over consumption and above which a consumption increase will contribute more to a rise in income than to higher savings. Empirical evidence is presented in so far as it was available to the authors.

I. INTRODUCTION

> The mathematically precise economic growth models that have been in vogue since the 1940's seldom take explicit account of the notion of investment in human beings. Increases in tomorrow's income are assumed to result primarily from today's additions to material capital, and since consumption displaces capital investment, it becomes an enemy of growth, not a handmaiden.[1]

In the existing economic literature a sharp difference is still made between consumption expenditures, on the one hand, and investments, on the other. This is done in spite of the fact that actual government policy often takes a different position, albeit implicitly.

The rationale of the distinction is that it is assumed that investments contribute to the increase of the capital stock and, therefore, via an increase in production, to a further increase in consumption potentials. With consumption, however, the end of the productive chain is reached. As Marshall has expressed it, 'consumption is the end of production'.

By putting the problem in this way, a number of important statements made

[1] Alan Berg, *The Nutrition Factor, its Role in Natural Development* (Washington, DC, 1973), p. 16.

by classical authors are being neglected. These authors repeatedly pointed out that the physical and psychical wellbeing of a human being is decisive for his productive capacity, and that this wellbeing is to a considerable extent influenced by the level of his consumption.

In the words of Adam Smith,

> A plentiful subsistence increases the bodily strength of the labourer, and the comfortable hope of bettering his condition, and of ending his days perhaps in ease and plenty, animates him to exert that strength to the utmost.[2]

Marshall indicates that the 'necessaries' of an ordinary agricultural, or unskilled town, labourer consist of

> . . . a well-drained dwelling with several rooms, warm clothing, with some changes of underclothing, pure water, a plentiful supply of cereal food, with moderate allowance of meat and milk, and a little tea, etc., some education and some recreation, and lastly, sufficient freedom for his wife from other work to enable her to perform properly her maternal and her household duties.[3]

Rothschild states that

> Only workers who can afford certain 'semi-luxuries', like better and quicker forms of transport, better housing, holidays and entertainment, will be able to stand up fully to the nerve-racking atmosphere of modern factory life.[4]

These statements indicate two important things. First, it is assumed that a certain level of consumption is needed to enable the worker to maintain a certain level of productivity; and, second, it is assumed that a higher level of productivity requires a higher level of consumption.

The last statement is particularly interesting, since the reasoning is usually the other way round; namely, that a higher level of consumption can be attained only through an increase in production or productivity. This is true, of course; but the point is that an increase in productivity can be maintained only if it is supported by a higher level of consumption. This means, in fact, that for any level of performance to be maintained in the long run, the person concerned requires certain inputs, be they physical or psychical.

The validity of this statement is evident in so far as physical labour and food are concerned. A certain amount of food is needed if a person is to maintain a given physical performance over an extended period of time. But it is no less

[2] Adam Smith, *The Wealth of Nations,* I (Oxford, 1869), p. 86.

[3] Alfred Marshall, *Principles of Economics. An Introduction,* 8th ed. (London, 1952), p. 58.

[4] K. W. Rothschild, *The Theory of Wages* (Oxford, 1954), p. 31.

acceptable to assume that, with increasing psychical tensions in an occupation, inputs of a higher order (such as recreation, proper medical care, and further training) will be needed in order to guarantee that the level of performance will not decline in the long run.

The foregoing would appear to justify an attempt to introduce the productive capacity of consumption expenditures into economic models. It may be assumed that such a procedure, particularly for growth models, could contribute to our insight into growth processes and into the effectiveness of government policy. This does not hold only for models of Western economics, and may be even more important for those relating to developing countries.

In the next section, an attempt is made to construct a very simple model of the type required.

II. A SIMPLE ALTERNATIVE GROWTH MODEL

Let us start from the usual simple Harrod–Domar model. The well-known principle of this model is

$$\Delta Y = \frac{1}{\kappa}(Y - C) = \frac{1 - \alpha}{\kappa} Y \tag{19.1}$$

resulting in

$$g = \frac{1 - \alpha}{\kappa} \tag{19.2}$$

where Y = income,
C = consumption,
κ = capital output ratio,
α = consumption quota,
g = rate of growth.

The most essential objection to this model is that income growth reaches a maximum if the savings quota is unity, which means that the consumption quota is zero. This evidently erroneous assumption stems from the more basic assumption that income can grow only as a result of net additions to the capital stock and, consequently, that consumption is unproductive. This latter assumption implies that consumption may be reduced to zero without influencing the productive capacity of labour.

If we drop this assumption, the model changes drastically and becomes, at the same time, considerably more realistic. We make two basic assumptions:

(1) that a certain level of consumption is needed to keep the productive capacity of labour just constant (to be indicated as *regenerative* consumption); and
(2) that a consumption higher than this level contributes positively to the growth of productivity (income), even if at a decreasing rate with growing income.

The first assumption is analogous to the one used concerning investments. In order to maintain the productive capacity of capital, reinvestments in capital goods have to take place. Thus, a certain level of investment is essential. Only in so far as gross investments exceed this level can we speak of an increase in the capital stock or, rather, of an increase in the productive capacity of the capital stock. I in equation (19.1) therefore represents the degree to which gross investments exceed the level of investment needed to maintain the productive capacity of the capital stock.

Is the assumption with regard to consumption completely analogous to this? If the productive capacity of labour depends on the level of training, physical health and nutrition, the quality of housing, and so on, then it is clear that a certain amount of all these things is needed in order to maintain at a given level the productivity of labour. Housing, nutrition and medical care are needed, and so, in a macro sense, is education, since elderly people leave the active population and are replaced in it by younger people. The latter need education in order to maintain the average education level of the active population as a whole.

It follows, furthermore, from this last example that the level of consumption that is needed is not independent of the income level. A higher level of income will necessarily be linked to a higher level of education of the population in general and of the active population in particular. In order to maintain this higher level of education, the expenditure for education will have to be higher than it would need be were the level of education lower. The other categories of consumption expenditures show a similar picture. The higher the strain on labour, the higher will be the need for medical care, for recreation, and so on; in other words, the level of consumption will have to be higher in order to prevent a decrease in productive performance.

The second assumption follows logically from the first one. This is that, if consumption exceeds the level required according to the first assumption, a positive contribution is made to labour productivity, albeit to a decreasing extent as consumption increases. As a matter of fact, the same elements play a role here. Better housing and nutrition, better medical and recreational possibilities, more education, and so on, all contribute, in principle, to an increase in the potential performance of the active population. The transportation to which individuals have access (from bicycles to automobiles) is another factor in raising the productivity of labour. This applies as much to developing countries as it does to industrialised ones.

If we incorporate both assumptions in a simple growth model, the result is as follows:

$$Y = C + I \tag{19.3}$$

$$C = \alpha Y \tag{19.4}$$

$$\Delta Y = \beta_0 (C - \bar{C})^{\beta_1} I^{\beta_2} \tag{19.5}$$

where I represents net investments, and $\overline{C}$ represents regenerative consumption.

It should be remarked here that equation (19.5) makes an additional assumption, this being that if $C = \overline{C}$, net investments do not contribute to an increase in income. This means that net investments are ineffective if the productive capacity of labour is not raised at the same time. This assumption expresses the idea that an intensified capital stock sets higher requirements for labour, and that, if these are not met, investments will show no return.

One more assumption should be made. It is assumed, as stated before, that the level of the regenerative consumption is a function of the existing level of income. The most simple hypothesis would be that

$$\overline{C} = \overline{\alpha} Y \tag{19.6}$$

which completes the model.

The solution of the model is

$$\Delta Y = \beta_0 (\alpha - \overline{\alpha})^{\beta_1} (1 - \alpha)^{\beta_2} Y^{\beta_1 + \beta_2} \tag{19.7}$$

or

$$g = \beta_0 (\alpha - \overline{\alpha})^{\beta_1} (1 - \alpha)^{\beta_2} Y^{\beta_1 + \beta_2 - 1} \tag{19.8}$$

The optimal value of α, i.e. the value of α that maximises g at any level of Y, can be derived from

$$\frac{\partial g}{\partial \alpha} = \left(\frac{\beta_1}{\alpha - \overline{\alpha}} - \frac{\beta_2}{1 - \alpha} \right) g = 0 \tag{19.9}$$

or

$$\alpha^{OPT} = \frac{\beta_1 + \beta_2 \overline{\alpha}}{\beta_1 + \beta_2} \tag{19.10}$$

If we write for the optimal savings quota

$$\sigma^{OPT} = 1 - \alpha^{OPT} \tag{19.11}$$

we then find that

$$\sigma^{OPT} = (1 - \overline{\alpha}) \frac{\beta_2}{\beta_1 + \beta_2} \tag{19.12}$$

If σ exceeds $(1 - \overline{\alpha})$, a decrease in income will result. $1 - \overline{\alpha}$ may therefore be defined as the maximum (and $\overline{\alpha}$ as the minimum) savings quota. We may thus write

$$\sigma^{OPT} = \frac{\beta_2}{\beta_1 + \beta_2} \sigma^{MAX} \tag{19.13}$$

The preceding equations express the importance of $C - \overline{C}$ and I (which, in fact, has been defined as $I^G - R$: gross investments minus the necessary replacements). The higher β_2 is in relation to the sum of β_1 and β_2, the higher the optimal savings quota (and, correspondingly, the lower the optimal consumption quota) will be.

III. THEORY AND POLICY

Contrary to the Harrod–Domar model, which concentrates solely on savings, the preceding model would indicate that an increase in the level of consumption, in so far as the optimum level of consumption has not yet been reached, contributes more to economic growth than savings (investments) could do. From this it follows that, for countries with a very low income level, aid in the form of stimulation of consumption may make much more sense than aid in the form of investments. In practice, this fact has been recognised, though not always explicitly, by many a government. Almost every government stresses the desirability of better training, improvement of medical care and recreational possibilities, better housing, and so on, and this certainly is not a recent phenomenon. In addition, it has to be recognised that a redistribution of income may increase the productivity of consumption. For different income groups, a higher level of consumption may have different effects on productivity. The significance of these objectives has no doubt always been that each of them is desirable as such, even without taking into account the consequences for productivity; but it has also implicitly been stated that they all are needed to meet the requirements of the development of society. It does not seem unrealistic to state that economists initiated the thinking in this direction and that afterwards (but not necessarily consequently) governments started to pursue a policy of stimulating certain consumption categories. In the meantime, economists ceased to consider these things important.

It is evident that governments have not been inclined to stimulate *all* sorts of consumption. They clearly discriminate between different groups of expenditures and promote consumption more strongly if the assumed influence on wellbeing (and, through this, on productivity) is supposed to be larger. The extremes run from compulsory consumption (primary education), via the subsidisation of secondary and higher education, medical care and recreation, to the taxation of alcoholic drinks and tobacco and even the prohibition of some sorts of consumption (certain drugs). This clearly means that governments intend to decrease the level of certain forms of consumption and increase others, according to their assumed influence on wellbeing. Implicitly, the effect of consumption on productivity is thereby maximised. It does not seem unlikely that governments, by behaving in this way, anticipated the development of economic theory.

This conclusion can be drawn not only with regard to the macro-level of government policy, but also with regard to the micro-level of business management. In recent years, the importance of the human factor in organisations has been increasingly emphasised by management. The willingness to incur costs for the acquisition and development of human resources is therefore understandable.

However, it seems that, in this field also, theory is lagging behind actual developments. This is particularly true for accountancy procedures as usually applied. According to conventional accountancy procedures, expenditures for the items mentioned above are registered as expenses. This implies that a relationship between expenditures and revenues is assumed only for the current year. Nevertheless, often a part, and sometimes even a large part, of such expenditures relates to returns in future years. In so far as this is the case, conventional accountancy theory cannot be regarded as a useful basis for the long-term management of human assets.

In so far as expenditures in favour of human resources are related to the current period only, a manager will find it more difficult to justify funds for building human assets than for building physical assets. According to conventional accountancy, operating expenses are overstated and net income is understated when an organisation is investing more in human capabilities than is being consumed.[5] On the other hand, conventional accountancy understates operating expenses and overstates net income when human capabilities are being liquidated faster than they are being created. One should keep in mind that write-offs of human resources are not recorded. Furthermore, investment in human resources is not included in the measurement of the net return for evaluating current and future projects.

In this framework it is very interesting to mention the human-resource accounting research project at the University of Michigan. This project, which has been undertaken in co-operation with business, is directed towards developing a human-resource accounting system. It deals with questions such as how expenditures for recruitment and training (both on and off the job) should show up on balance sheets in order to serve management, not only with regard to physical assets, but also with regard to human assets. As a result of such research, one can learn to what extent the costs of acquisition, recruitment, and on-the-job training are related to future years. Examples of investments in human resources recognised in one firm are found in William C. Pyle's 'An Accounting System for Human Resources' (*Innovation*, no. 10, 1970).

It has become evident in this section of the study dealing with government policy and business management that, at least with regard to the impact of certain types of consumption on productivity, theory is lagging behind reality. Similar remarks can be made concerning consumer behaviour. Certain types of consumer spending are regarded by the operating units themselves as being productive, i.e. as contributing to working capacity. An example is expenditure on further education, through tuition, books or study. In considering whether to use the evening for study or for leisure, one has to take into account future revenues. The same might apply to other expenditures; for instance, to those relating to medical treatment and housing. As Katona puts it, 'The sum total of skills and education . . ., as well of their health, represent economic assets.'[6]

[5] William C. Pyle, 'Monitoring Human Resources on Line', *Michigan Business Review*, July 1970.

[6] G. Katona, 'Consumer Investment and Business Investment', *Michigan Business Review*, July 1961.

And it really does not matter whether the government, business, or consumer units pay for them.

It will be clear that disregarding the impact of certain types of consumer expenditure on production can lead to miscalculation and may prevent us from making the right decision.

IV. A COST–BENEFIT APPROACH

The question arises of how far the foregoing considerations could contribute to more effective government spending. It seems that the answer is to be found in the application of a general cost–benefit approach in which all of the effects of different government expenditures are considered. Basically, cost–benefit analysis, though applying certain principles of economics, does not discriminate between consumption and investment expenditures. It is concerned solely with benefits, on the one hand, and costs (in whatever form), on the other. The formal procedure is as follows.

Write

$$\underline{x} = A\underline{x} + B\underline{z} \tag{19.14}$$

in which x is the vector of variables influenced, and $\underline{z}$ is the vector of the elements of a given project. The matrix B represents the primary effects of $\underline{z}$, and the matrix A the influences among the xs. The solution runs

$$\underline{x} = [I - A]^{-1} B\underline{z} \tag{19.15}$$

The total benefits of the project are

$$B = i' \hat{\lambda}\underline{x} = i'\hat{\lambda}[I - A]^{-1} B\underline{z} \tag{19.16}$$

in which i is the unit vector and $\hat{\lambda}$ is the diagonal matrix of the (money) weights to be attached to $\underline{x}$. Total costs equal

$$C = i'\hat{c}\underline{z} \tag{19.17}$$

in which $\hat{c}$ represents the diagonal matrix of the unit costs for $\underline{z}$. The project considered is to be carried out if $B > C$, or if

$$i'\{\hat{\lambda}[I - A]^{-1} B - \hat{c}\}\underline{z} > 0 \tag{19.18}$$

It appears that, in this procedure, all effects are taken into account regardless of the character of $\underline{z}$. This means that no distinction is made between the zs that represent investment costs and those that represent other costs. This is, in fact, in complete accord with reality. If the project is a road project, not only the investment costs, but also the maintenance and other costs, of the road are considered. If the procedure is applied to an educational project, higher incomes in the future belong to the x variables, since the interaction coefficients represent *all* the effects initiated by the project.

The foregoing means that the application of cost–benefit analysis forces us to consider not only the conventional effects of income creation by investments, but also the effects of all sorts of expenditures on any variable considered to be relevant in a societal context. This implies that the effects of consumption expenditures are explicitly taken into account.

Since cost–benefit analysis does not, *a priori,* exclude certain effects, it may be said that, in this sort of analysis a wider approach to expenditure problems is followed than is the case in conventional economic theory. The latter starts from an *a priori* structure of the A and B matrices, dictated by mere convention. Cost–benefit analysis, though not a theory and merely a method of estimating the effects of a given expenditure, does not exclude certain interactions and, consequently, considers all possible direct and indirect effects in order to facilitate the evaluation of the viability of the project.

Leaving aside the fact that conventional economic theory considers only the effects of investments on income and not the effects of so-called consumption expenditures on income, there is still another basic difference between the conventional theory and cost–benefit analysis. $\underline{x}$ represents *all* variables that are influenced by $\underline{z}$ – not only the economic, but also the environmental, social and other, variables. The theory that underlies cost–benefit analysis thus is considerably wider than economic theory. If properly applied, its application forces us to reconsider economic theory, to make it more general and to incorporate it into a much wider theoretical framework in which all elements that are relevant for human wellbeing are properly taken into account. It should be noted that all the studies that have been concerned with testing theories on the assumed interaction of the variables make use, in principle, of some sort of cost–benefit approach, though not always in the very general sense indicated above.

V. STATISTICAL EVIDENCE

From the foregoing it follows, as expected, that, apart from a number of cost–benefit analyses, not much research has been done to analyse the productive effect of certain kinds of consumption. Some studies have been mentioned in L. H. Klaassen, *Social Amenities in Area Economic Growth* (Paris: OECD, 1968). The most well-known study in this area is probably Leland S. Burns, *Cost–Benefit Analysis of Improved Housing, A Case Study*, (University of California at Los Angeles, 1965), in which, for a number of regions of the world, residential housing projects have been analysed with regard to their productivity effects. This study was a part of the International Housing Productivity Study, to which B. K. Tjioe of the Netherlands Economic Institute made important contributions. In this study was observed the net revenues of a subsidised residential housing project in the Indian Pine Ridge reservation in South Dakota. Two-thirds of these revenues consisted of indirect productivity effects and savings in the medical and educational field. 45 per cent total revenues were due to productivity effects. An interesting study by H. Correa,

The Economics of Human Resources, (The Hague, North Holland, 1962), must also be mentioned. Correa emphasises (p. 13) 'that labour is to some extent also subject to deliberate transformation and that it therefore makes sense to speak of a production function of labour'. The various inputs of this production function – man and the social-economic factors that affect his productive power – are the object of this examination.

In this framework, may also be mentioned several studies in the nutritional field. These are concerned with the way in which the relationship between calorie intake and physical and psychological conditions determines the capability to work. On this subject, it is useful to quote Harvey Leibenstein's *Economic Backwardness and Economic Growth* (New York and London, 1957, p. 63): 'The wage–productivity relationship can best be examined if it is broken up into two parts: (1) the relation between income (= wages) and nutrition and (2) the relation between nutrition and productivity.' A 1936 study by Lord Boyd Orr shows clearly that, in England, the value of the nutritive components of diet (that is, calories, proteins, fats, calcium, iron, and so on) are monotonically increasing functions of income. Similar studies reported by the League of Nations' Committee on Nutrition gave similar results for a number of other countries. It is also evidence from the United Nations Food and Agriculture Organisation estimates of calorie consumption in various countries that, generally speaking, low calorie consumption is found in the countries with a low income per capita and high calorie consumption is found in countries with a high income per capita. Also, it is clear from a number of detailed studies of workers in various underdeveloped countries that the calorie intake per man per day is, in these cases, considerably below that designated by nutrition authorities as adequate for the maintenance of health, of normal body weight, and for the carrying out of a full day's work at 'normal' speed.

The following are some further references to material in these fields.

Nutrition and Working Efficiency, no. 5 in the basic studies series 'Freedom from Hunger Campaign' (Rome: United Nations Food and Agriculture Organisation, 1962). No. 2 in the same series, *Relation between Diet and Working Capacity,* presents much evidence with regard to the positive relationship between dietary improvement and health and production in different countries. Similar evidence is to be found in: H. A. Kraut and E. A. Muller, 'Calorie Intake and Industrial Output', *Science,* CIV, no. 2709 (29 Nov, 1946).

H. Kraut, 'Über die Deckung des Nährstoffsbedarfs in West Deutschland', Bibl., *Nutricio et Diets* (Basel and New York, 1960). See, in particular, the graph on page 46, which clearly suggests a positive correlation between calorie intake and production in Germany during the period 1936–52.

Alan Berg, *The Nutrition Factor, Its Role in National Development,* (Washington, DC, 1973).

G. C. M. Gonigle and J. Kirby, *Poverty and Public Health* (London, 1936). Chapter 7 is of particular interest. On the basis of a nice piece of human field research, it shows that increased mortality is associated with dietary deficiencies. Because people moved to better housing with higher rentals, not enough money was left to buy the necessary calories in order to maintain health and working capacity. This study emphasises the importance of generating adequate quantities of housing within the financial reach of relocatees.

A similar conclusion can be drawn from Michael W. Pozen et al., 'Evaluation of Housing Standards of Families within Four Years of Relocation by Urban Renewal', *American Journal of Public Health and the Nation's Health,* LVIII, no. 7 (July 1968).

K. Rodahl et al., 'Physical Work Capacity', *Archives of Environmental Health*, II, no. 5 (May 1961). Although the physical characteristics of groups of school children in Philadelphia, Germany and Sweden were, in general, quite comparable, it was concluded 'that Swedish children were superior to both in work capacity, supposedly as a result of greater physical activity'. (See editorial by Oscar J. Balchum.)

James M. Hundley, et al., 'Height and Weight of First-Grade Children as a Potential Index of Nutritional Status', *American Journal of Public Health and the Nation's Health,* XLV, no. 11 (Nov 1955). On the basis of data concerning the height and weight (as indicators of health and working capacity) of first-grade children in Philadelphia public schools for the periods 1925–7, 1932–4, and 1947–9, it was concluded that

> The data indicate that children from economically favoured areas were taller and heavier than children from economically underprivileged areas. Both economic groups of children showed a secular increase in growth. During the depression years, 1932–34, children from the lower economic areas showed no interruption in their secular trend. On the other hand, children in the economically favoured areas during the depression did show a significant deviation from their secular trends. This deviation was statistically significant for height in boys and for stockiness in both boys and girls.

Evidence about a relationship between health and productivity is to be found in Wilfred Malenbaum, 'Health and Productivity in Poor Areas', in *Empirical Studies in Health Economics,* Proceedings of the Second Conference on the Economics of Health, Baltimore, ed. H. Klarman (London, 1970), in which it is said that

> The data for the developing areas as national units do seem to provide evidence of statistically significant relationships between production and health; moreover, the influence of health factors on output appears to be quantitatively large relative to the influence of other factors, including the familiar agricultural outputs.

In the educational field, see P. de Wolff and R. Ruiter's paper for the Vereniging voor de Staathuishoudkunde en De Economie van het Onderwijs, The Hague. In this study, a cost–benefit analysis was made of higher education.

The results of the methodology discussed have to be characterised in the author's own terms, as being meagre. At best, this study provided a minimum quantitative indication of the contribution that expenditure on education makes to economic growth.

M. Blaug, in *An Introduction to the Economics of Education* (London, 1970), derives similar conclusions.

Part VIII
Report on the Proceedings

Robert P. Inman

Discussion of Anthony Atkinson, 'Housing Allowances, Income Maintenance and Income Taxation'

Professor Bradford introduced the Atkinson paper, noting that it is a first attempt to analyse government public-service expenditure policy within a general equilibrium framework, subject to constraints on the available policy instruments. Such analysis requires a judicious mixing of sophisticated mathematical modelling with a clear understanding of the policy issues and institutional restrictions facing real governments. Professor Bradford praised Professor Atkinson's efforts at blending sound economic theory with institutional fact in his analysis of public housing policy, but felt that two extensions of the analysis would be in order. First, as the Atkinson analysis now stands, there is nothing to distinguish housing services from any other commodity. But the politics of government housing policy suggest that the commodity is, indeed, a 'special' or 'merit want' commodity. This should not lead to major revisions of the analytical structure of the problem, but the policy conclusions of analysis may be significantly altered in the direction of a housing subsidy. Second, Professor Bradford thought that it would be desirable to build into the analysis the fact that housing subsidies support expenditures on a *vector* of 'housing services' involving not only living space (which we may wish to subsidise), but also locational amenities such as clear air and beautiful views (which we may not want to subsidise). To treat housing as a simple commodity that is uniform from place to place and person to person may lead to very misleading policy conclusions.

Professor von Weizsäcker raised two points with regard to the Atkinson paper. First, Professor Atkinson assumes a perfectly elastic supply of housing in his model. While this assumption might be acceptable at the national level, it is certain that at the local or regional level the supply elasticity of housing is less than infinite. When one considers the welfare implications of a regional housing policy where the supply elasticity is less than infinite, the distribution of private land rents that such a housing policy generates will become a crucial element in our evaluation of that policy. The Atkinson analysis avoids this admittedly difficult problem. In the same spirit, with a regionalised housing policy there may be significant efficiency losses with mobile labour. A housing policy favourable to one region may act as a false signal for labour reallocation. Second, Professor von Weizsäcker wondered why families who are eligible for housing subsidies do not in fact make use of the available housing allowances. In Germany, for example, approximately 50 per cent of the eligible families elect to receive the subsidies. This 'fact' should be introduced into any analyses like Atkinson's, but the important question of how to model this problem of 'take-up' has not yet been explored, either theoretically or empirically. Is it simply a problem of insufficient information?

Professor Stiglitz noted that the problem that Professor Atkinson discussed is a special case of a larger class of policy problems on optimal taxes and subsidies. He felt that it would be helpful to place the Atkinson analysis in this perspective. As a result, it would be possible to give an intuitive interpretation to one of Professor Atkinson's main results and to suggest some limitations on his results.

Very generally, we could write an individual's taxes as a function of all the sales and purchases that he makes:

$$T = T(x_1, \ldots, x_n, L; y_1, \ldots, y_n)$$

where, say, $\underline{x}$ is the vector of purchases, L is the labour supplied, and y is a vector of economic and demographic characteristics such as age, sex, and family size.

Most tax structures impose a level of separability on T; for example,

$$T = \sum t_i(x_i, L, \underline{y})$$

Special cases include an excise tax structure with an income tax:

$$T = \sum_i t_i x_i + t_L(wL)$$

where w is a wage rate with a wage tax subsidy structure of

$$T_L = t_L(w) \cdot L$$

The particular problem upon which Atkinson focused is a special case of the following problem. Assume that all costs of production are constant and unity. Define the cost functions:

$$c_i(x_i) = 1 + t_i(x_i)$$

Assume that wages are the only source of inequality. Let $Y = Y(wL)$ be after-tax income as a function of before-tax income. Then, individuals face budget constraints of the form

$$\sum_i C_i(X_i) = Y(wL)$$

Assume that we maximise a social welfare function of the form

$$W = \int U(\underline{x}, L) f(w) dw$$

where $f(w)$ is the distribution of individuals by before-tax wages. The optimal solution to this problem when $U(\cdot)$ is separable between labour and all other goods, i.e. $U(\cdot) = u(\underline{x}) + v(L)$, entails the condition

$$c_i(x_i) = 1$$

That is, *only an income tax is imposed.* The intuition for this is that, since labour is the only source of inequality, it is natural to attack inequality by an income tax. Under the circumstances, an optimal income tax comes as close as we can get to a lump-sum tax. The above result shows that the separability of utility functions gives income taxation with no commodity taxation (or subsidies).

The above model can also be used to show the sensitivity of our policy conclusions to changes in the available set of tax instruments. For example, by substituting a wage tax for an income tax, we can show that it will be optimal to have taxes or subsidies on specific commodities such as food or housing. The exact structure of taxes or subsidies will depend on the particular parameters of the commodity demand functions.

Finally, Professor Stiglitz stressed that one important limitation of the above model and of Professor Atkinson's is the assumption of identical preferences. If, for example, there is a correlation between tastes for housing and 'ability', but a low correlation between working hours and 'ability', then housing taxes and subsidies may provide a better instrument for welfare redistribution than do income taxation and subsidisation.

Dr Jeanjean raised the following question. While Atkinson's results suggest that, under the conditions of his model, there may be no need for a direct housing subsidy, this result would surely be lost if we introduced housing directly into the social welfare function. Perhaps a more reasonable characterisation of housing policy, particularly in France, is the requirement that all families receive a minimum level of housing services. Would the Atkinson results continue to hold if such a minimum housing constraint were imposed when maximising social welfare?

Professor Aaron wished to reinforce the importance of the comments of Dr Jeanjean and Professor Bradford on the need to introduce a social 'merit want' or 'consumption externality' preference for housing. On the question of the appropriate base for housing subsidies, Professor Aaron suggested that we may want to consider not only family income, but also, perhaps, family size, the age distribution of children, and other family characteristics. Finally, on the question of 'take-up', raised both in the Atkinson paper and in the comments of Professor von Weizsäcker, Professor Aaron stressed that any model of programme utilisation must consider both the demand and the supply sides. As a political strategy, governments are free to vary *de facto* barriers – as distinct from the *de jure* eligibility rules – limiting a family's participation in a public programme.

Professor Sheshinski offered two comments. First, Atkinson's final proposition is based on the assumption that housing prices and wages are independent. In housing markets with market imperfections this need not be true. Whether the correlation between family income and housing prices is positive or negative, however, is not obvious. In any case, the Atkinson results are limited by this special assumption. Sheshinski's second comment extended von Weizsäcker's earlier discussion of the elasticity of housing supply. Under Atkinson's assumption of a perfectly elastic housing supply, his analysis is correct in treating the price of housing as exogenous. However, in economies where the elasticity of supply of housing is not infinite, subsidies that alter the demand for housing will at the same time alter the equilibrium housing price. Therefore, housing prices are endogenous to the welfare optimising problem for this more realistic specification.

Professor Stern presented still another potential 'special characteristic' of housing, in addition to the consumption externality arguments mentioned earlier. There may be a relationship between housing and the quality of labour in the long run. The productivity of individuals may depend very much on their home background and on the quantity and quality of housing that is currently available to them. In this sense, housing might be considered a human capital investment analogous to health or education.

Professor Michael Bruno agreed with the earlier comments that, from a policy perspective, housing is indeed a special commodity. Quite apart from Dr Jeanjean's observation that societies often pursue a minimum housing standard (a reflection with which Professor Bruno agreed), the durable nature of the commodity, coupled with loan market imperfections, may be another reason for public policy intervention in the housing market. Subsidies related to income or, perhaps, to the age of the family might therefore be required to offset discriminatory loan policies.

Professor Feldstein made three points. First, since housing is a capital-intensive commodity, a useful extension of the Atkinson analysis would be to consider the effects of housing policy on the rate of return to capital. Such an extension would, of course, require a general equilibrium formulation of the problem. Second, in response to Dr Jeanjean's suggestion that housing policy may be directed at supplying a minimum level of housing, Professor Feldstein suggested that, in this case, a subsidy up to some expenditure limit would be preferable to the open-ended subsidies considered in the Atkinson paper. Finally, building on the comments of Professor Stiglitz, Professor Feldstein noted that, when income-tax reform is not politically possible, housing subsidies may be an important second-best, but politically feasible, policy instrument.

In response, *Professor Atkinson* thanked the discussants and noted his agreement with most of the comments that had been made. He did, however, elaborate on two of the points raised in the discussions. First, while agreeing with Professor Aaron that an analysis of programme utilisation or 'take-up' should, in principle, consider both supply and demand factors, he stressed his feeling that the major constraints are in encouraging family utilisation. In Britain, significant efforts at greatly expanding the utilisation of public programmes still showed that a sizable number of eligible participants did not participate in the programmes. Finally, in reply to the comments of Dr Jeanjean and others on the matter of a minimum housing standard, Professor Atkinson noted that his proposition 4 closely approximates such a policy recommendation. The validity of this proposition is, of course, dependent on the assumed independence of housing prices and income – an assumption for which empirical evidence is needed.

Discussion of Francesco Forte, 'Public Expenditures for Housing: The Italian Case'

Professor Pauly began the discussion of the Forte paper by thanking the author for an interesting if discouraging story of one country's efforts to increase the supply of housing services. Professor Forte's policy conclusion from his review of the Italian case is to stick with old methods of direct supply of low-rent housing, however imperfect and ineffective such strategies may have been. The rejected alternative is a policy of rent subsidies. Professor Pauly felt that such advice must be seriously questioned.

As Professor Forte's paper has shown, the policy of direct provision has been frustrated by red tape and a lack of supportive public utilities. The rent-subsidy approach turns the job of production over to the private market. Professor Pauly then asked whether private developers are likely to have less red tape to deal with, and to be more successful in dealing with what red tape they do encounter than the public authorities are. There is little doubt that there will be less red tape. Fewer requirements for the approval of 'planners', and fewer complexities in bidding are just two examples. In addition, the red tape that does remain is likely to be more efficiently handled by the private sector, as there is more incentive to get things done, perhaps to the point of using 'benevolent graft'.

Professor Pauly then explored the question of whether the rent-subsidy strategy to stimulate an increase in housing would do so only at much higher rents. Surely gross rents would be higher. But it is important to note that 'public housing' does not leave rents unchanged either. If the public sector must pay market prices for inputs (including land, if it is condemned at a fair market value), the provision of such housing will also raise gross rents. In general, because the 'public housing' supply curve is likely to be more inelastic, gross rents will rise by *more* if a given increment in housing is publicly produced. It is more difficult to say what will happen to net rents, since that depends on the rent-setting policy. But, more importantly, with the public production of housing, a rise in gross rents of low-income housing may be necessary if resources are to be lured away from currently more profitable luxury housing.

But what about the lack of public utilities? Can a rent-subsidy policy deal with this problem? Professor Pauly noted that a rent-subsidy policy cannot be any less successful than are the current efforts at public low-income housing. Indeed, rent subsidies may be a more suitable way of stimulating construction on isolated lots that already are supplied with utilities.

Professor Pauly concluded his discussion of the Forte paper by noting that, quite apart from administrative red-tape or lack of public utilities, a transfer of a large part of housing provision to the public sector may result in less, not more, housing. Figure A makes this point. Assume, for the sake of argument,

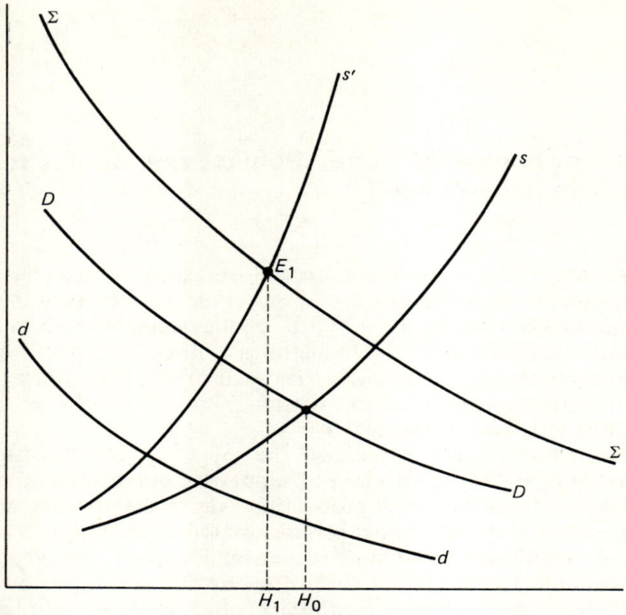

Fig. A

that the reason for public intervention in the housing market is the consumption externalities in housing consumption denoted by curve *dd* in Fig. A. This external demand is added vertically to the private demand for housing, denoted by curve *DD*. To satisfy this external demand, collectivisation is required. Collectivisation may, however, result in the recognition of monopsony power on the part of the now-unique provider of low-income housing. The result is housing supplied on a curve, denoted by s', marginal to the market supply curve s. This leads to an equilibrium level of housing at point E_1, with a *reduction,* from H_0 to H_1, in final housing services supplied.

Dr Kolm noted that the French experience is not unlike (though perhaps it is less extreme than) the Italian one. Like the Italian subsidy, the nominally proportional French subsidy is a transfer to upper-income groups. There are two reasons for this regressivity against income. First, the subsidy is proportional to housing expenditures, which rise as a share in income as income rises. Second, the wealthy understand the subtleties of the subsidy policy and are therefore able to take advantage of the complicated tax-deduction provisions favourable to housing.

Professor Vickrey stressed that housing construction is a long-run commitment. Thus, one of the difficulties in finding an effective instrument for increasing housing supply is in giving the private investor adequate assurance that the subsidy will be continued as planned (for a policy of rent subsidies) or that (for a policy of construction subsidies) the market conditions will not be altered. Professor Vickrey noted that a policy of subsidised public housing might actually decrease the total supply of housing by creating such uncertainty in the minds of those constructing private units that the supply of such units decreases by more than the public supply increases. Further, in the case of rent subsidies, it is virtually impossible for most democratic governments to guarantee that a rent subsidy will be continued for five, 10, or 15 years. The ideal form of subsidy might be a rent subsidy that is promised not to begin immediately, but to begin, perhaps, three years hence, and to be continued at an increasing rate according to a defined schedule for the next 20 years.

Professor Breton noted that governments often do intervene in markets without creating the kind of uncertainty that Professor Vickrey had in mind. This can be, and has been, effected by creating public bodies such as Crown Corporations or regulatory agencies that are at one remove from the political process and that develop a life of their own. Because they are largely removed from the political arena, these institutions are able to provide guarantees to operators in any market. Indeed, one is impressed not by the uncertainty created by such government agencies, but by the certainty that these public bodies often generate.

Professor Hochman noted that both the present discussion and the paper by Professor Forte stressed just two policy alternatives – rent subsidies on the demand side, and direct low-income housing construction on the supply side. A third policy alternative builds on what has come to be known as the 'trickle-down' model of the housing market. This model suggests that housing construction for upper- and middle-income families releases dwellings for inhabitation by lower-income families. Thus, subsidies for middle-class housing may eventually lead to benefits for low-income families.

In response to the discussants, *Professor Forte* argued that, by simplifying relations between the public administration and general contractors, the scheme suggested by him copes with the inefficiencies that result from fragmentation and disorganisation on the supply side. From a management point of view, this comes very close to a transfer expenditure, i.e. to a subsidy on the supply side. Unlike subsidies on the demand side, this is a highly concentrated set of operations, so that it requires much less bureaucratic activity. For Italy, at any rate, the lack of supportive public utilities simply makes a rent subsidy infeasible. To handle the perversities of Professor Pauly's counterexample in Fig. A, the public sector can simply alter the agency's terms of trade so as to offset the propensity of the collective to operate as a monopsony supplier. Professor Forte agreed with Professor Hochman on the need to consider additional policy alternatives. In addition, he stressed that we need to broaden our analytic vision and, instead of looking just at the national market, undertake a detailed examination of the effects of interregional variations in housing policies. Such variations may lead to sizable inefficiencies in the regional allocation of labour, which would be missed with an analysis based only on national data.

Discussion of Michael Bruno, 'Efficiency and Equity in Public Education Expenditures'

Opening the discussion of the Bruno paper, *Dr Kolm* made a number of observations about education as a vehicle for social justice. Both in the west and in the European socialist countries, education has been touted as the means to social equality. In fact, however, the record has been disappointing. Economies that have attempted to establish a strong negative correlation between a child's education and his parents' social class have generally not been successful. We must therefore conclude that, in order to achieve social justice by way of education, extreme inequities in the distribution of education are required. There is, however, a preferable solution – one that cuts the strong ties between education and income. This has been successful in several societies – China, Cuba and North Vietnam; but it has been argued that such a policy would have large efficiency losses. Dr Kolm doubted that such losses would, in fact, emerge. Individuals can continue to be strongly motivated towards their employment because of the intrinsic interest of their job, because of a sense of public obligation, or because of the nonmonetary rewards (power, prestige) of their employment.

On a more specific level, Dr Kolm raised two questions about the behavioural model presented in the Bruno paper. First, why do students select an additional year of education? Professor Bruno's model assumes that students adopt a lifetime approach and are predominately interested in the earnings derived from the additional education. Both assumptions seem in error as behavioural specifications. It is unlikely that a student now making a decision about his education will be very sensitive to tax rates on his income 30 years hence. Contrary to the Bruno model, tax rates simply are not known to the student. In addition, individuals make educational decisions on the basis of occupational prestige and not simply on the basis of potential earnings. A second element of the behavioural model that must be considered is who in fact chooses the child's educational level. Parents are the likely selectors until the child reaches the age of 18, and it is not clear that the decisions made by the parents are taken on the basis of the child's future earnings stream. On the normative structure of the Bruno model, Dr Kolm felt that there is a need, in Professor Bruno's analysis, to consider intergenerational equity along the lines of the Layard model, and not simply intragenerational equity, the central concern in the Bruno paper. Finally, Dr Kolm offered a comment on the form of the Bruno earnings function, which assumes that income is separable in intellectual abilities and schooling, where intellectual abilities and schooling are the only determinants of income. The function also assumes that, for two individuals with the same years of schooling, the ratio of their incomes will be equal to the ratio of their intellectual abilities. But many individuals may receive no years of formal schooling. If this is so, then, by the Bruno earnings function, income is simply a function of intellectual ability. This specification, however, is inconsistent with the facts. For example, untrained individuals largely perform physical work, which is not a function of an individual's intellectual ability. Therefore, the earnings function should be expanded, perhaps by simply including a constant term as an indication of 'other abilities'.

Professor Machlup offered five comments on the paper in question. The first refers to Professor Bruno's measure of education as the 'years of education completed'. The number of years of enrolment at a school (or university) is not the same as the number of years of attendance, which, in turn, is not the same as the number of years of real study, and none of these is the *same* as education or an appropriate *measure* of education or even a good *proxy* for it. In many countries you may be enrolled, registered, matriculated or otherwise certified as being in *statu pupilaris* without ever attending any lecture, class, seminar, or tutorial session. In many educational institutions you may physically attend without ever being tested for having paid attention or for having learned anything. How, then, can we reasonably accept enrolment or registration as a measure of education? And should we take attendance to be 'education', as if attending a nongraded course in art appreciation or sociology were the same 'educational input' as a concentrated study of electrical engineering or computer programming?

Second, the assumption that an increase in the number of years of education will always (or will as a rule) increase the productivity or the earnings of the graduate may be in error. The effect of longer education, compulsory or under pressure, may well be negative. Unwilling students are not good learners, and the longer they are kept at school against their will the less productive they may become.

Third, longer education for all will not necessarily tend to equalise incomes. If longer education helps the productivity of willing learners but reduces the productivity of the unwilling ones, compulsory extension of the school-leaving age for all can only increase the differences in earnings. If greater equality of incomes were the chief objective, there would be only one educational policy that could contribute to the attainment of that objective: to deny education to those willing and able to learn.

Fourth, Professor Machlup sought to explain why Professor Bruno, along with virtually all other writers on the economics of education, takes it for granted that education makes a positive contribution to the earnings, or lifetime earnings, of graduates. Most such writers were convinced by the findings of Theodore Schultz and Gary Becker, who obtained a satisfactory positive rate of return to additional years of schooling on the basis of positive income differentials earned by those who have completed more years of formal education. Professor Machlup now believes that the data do not support the hypothesis. Data showing the year-after-year incomes of a given cohort of persons who differ in the length of, but have all recently completed, their education are not, and cannot be, available. 'Cannot' because those who graduated from secondary school or from a university in, say, 1960 had been gainfully employed for nine years, at most, by the time the 1970 census figures were collected. Nine years do not give us data for the estimation of lifetime earnings. Hence, cross-sectional data are the only information on which estimates of these earnings and differential earnings can be based. Such data were, in fact, the bases of the Schultz and Becker studies. However, what can the income data from the 1960 census – the latest available for any studies that have so far been published – tell us about incomes earned by persons 30 or 40 years after their graduation? They would tell how much more the median college graduate earned as compared with the median high-school graduate, both of whom had graduated at a time *when few people completed high school* and a *relatively miniscule number of people completed college.* In the 1920s and 1930s the percentage of persons of the relevant school age who had more than secondary education was very small indeed, and, as a result, college graduates had a scarcity value. College graduates who are now in their fifties and sixties are still from this small group. Yet times have changed radically: now, more than 50 per cent of 18-year-olds enrol in college, and we cannot reasonably assume that college graduates will command a scarcity value 20 or 30 years from now and will earn much more than high-school graduates of equal ability. Thus, college graduates may no longer obtain a higher market value than do their colleagues without college education. Even now, construction workers and truck drivers earn more then school teachers and associate professors do, and we cannot expect that lifetime earnings for the mass of persons with higher education will be greater than for equally intelligent persons with less schooling.

As a final comment, Professor Machlup noted that Professor Bruno's formula for the determination of earnings omits the most important factors: industry, drive, and the input of sheer effort. Those who work harder (longer hours or with greater intensity or both) make more money per year and over their lifetime. Differences in ability may remain important, but it should be obvious that equally intelligent persons will earn more if they work 60 hours a week than if they work only 40 hours. Differences in labour input may be the most effective source of inequality of incomes.

Professor Stiglitz asked why, if there is an optimal income tax, we should want to interfere with productive efficiency in the education sector by putting a charge on tuition costing more than the marginal social cost of education. But, given the second-best character of the real-world policy problem, Professor Stiglitz felt that we might well find that, as a characteristic of the solution, it would prove desirable to impose an education tax as well as a general consumption tax. A tuition tax would, in effect, reduce the degree of inequality in incomes and reduce the burden on the consumption tax as the main redistributive instrument.

Following the lead provided by Professor Stiglitz's comment, *Professor Feldstein* noted that the policy conclusions of such an extended model could simply be reversed from those generated by the Bruno analysis. Specifically, we might choose to encourage the more able to seek high levels of education but then tax their subsequent higher earnings to support an income subsidy for the less able.

Professor Bradford offered a number of comments. First, he posed a question for clarification: are forgone earnings included in the cost of education? Second, he stated that, if, as a device for the redistribution of income, one is going to tax tuition costing more than the marginal cost, one must be in a position to control the individual's options to exit to a private school system. The Bruno policy prescriptions are viable only in a fully public educational system with no on-the-job training. There is a final difficulty in implementing policies such as those recommended by the Bruno analysis: how do we measure ability? If one is going to attempt to measure ability by individual testing, then there are clear incentives for individuals not to score well in examinations. The results are therefore biased. Attempts to measure ability by means that cannot be individually controlled – for example, by classifying individuals on the basis of the average performances of their ethnic or socio-economic groups – raise serious dangers of misclassification and of violation of individual rights.

Professor Pauly raised two points. First, when estimating the income or earnings function, should allowances be made for sex and racial discrimination? Clearly, in our pursuit of equity, such discrimination should not be allowed. However, an earnings function based on a discriminatory market may bias our results in that direction. In the same spirit, the returns from education may simply not be visible in terms of measurable income. For example, there is a growing literature that argues tht one of the main consequences of education is increased efficiency in the provision of 'home products' – that a more educated wife or a more educated husband is a more productive provider of family commodities such as home education, home environment, and home-produced health services. How would this fact affect the results of the Bruno analysis?

Professor Sandmo stressed that it is important to consider the effects of education on equity in the context of a growing economy. Too often, the analysis of such questions appears only in an analysis involving comparative statics. For example, in deciding between income taxes and an educational tax as a redistributive device, we should note the fact that certain members of the labour force (namely, the older workers) have already made an occupational choice to which they are firmly committed. An income tax on this group may have very small efficiency losses. However, an income tax imposed on younger workers about to make an occupational choice may have significant efficiency consequences. For this group, the prudent policy would be to use both income taxes and tuition taxes as redistributive instruments.

Professor Vickrey noted that a tuition subsidy may be effective for the poor only if this subsidy includes an income subsidy to replace forgone earnings. Such earnings by student-age members of poor families may be quite important sources of income. Professor Vickrey also noted that we may, in preference to direct tuition subsidies, wish to structure a loan programme for students. Such a step is at least a move away from the regressive structure of current United States subsidies for higher education, which often redistribute income from lower- and middle-income taxpayers to students who will become high-wage earners in the future.

In response to the discussants, *Professor Bruno* made two points. First, he noted that the word 'ability' is perhaps to narrow for what he had in mind. He wished to include not only intellectual ability, but also physical ability, home background, education of parents, and so forth. Second, in response to comments on the earnings function, he made the following points. Dr Kolm's criticism of the earnings function could be met by using a more symmetric specification. Adopting an earnings function where education and ability enter not in a multiplicative way, but just in a general form, one can show that many of the results remain the same. However, in one special case where there is a negative interaction between ability and education (the higher the ability, the less an increment of education adds to income), we obtain the result that, under either an efficiency or an equity criterion, the optimal policy will be to give less education to the more able. On the empirical analysis of the earnings function, two comments are in order. First, the population used in the statistical analysis was heterogeneous. The data base was composed of immigrants and immigrants' sons. For this group, clearly, a year of education for one individual is not equivalent to a year of education for another. The results should be repeated for a more homogeneous population, but the data are not available. Second, in the study from which the empirical results are taken, various interaction specifications were tried for the variables in the earnings function, and the 'ability' variable still had a positive effect. The exact magnitude of this effect must, however, still be considered uncertain. Professor Bruno agreed with the comments of Professors Feldstein and Stiglitz that income taxation and educational tuition should be considered as two instruments in the same policy package. One interesting twist in such a study would be to consider a small economy from which labour is free to migrate. In such a brain-drain economy, a high tax on education and a low tax on future earnings may be the preferable policy. Finally, Professor Bruno stressed that, though his analysis was couched primarily in terms of society's interest in the distribution of income, society may have direct preferences for the distribution of human capital as well. In fact, it seems that many societies provide their education policies with just such an objective in mind.

Discussion of Richard Layard, 'On Measuring the Redistribution of Lifetime Income'

Professor Sergio Bruno introduced the discussion of the Layard paper by complimenting the author on an interesting and useful piece of work. Particularly important is Professor Layard's attention to lifetime earnings as the basis of his analysis. It is important to note that a policy introduced today may have both equalising and unequalising effects, though at different points in the life-cycle. Granting educational aid to a poor child from a poor family may be equalising today, but such aid may prove unequalising in the long run if that child, through increased education, becomes a member of the wealthy class. Professor Layard's lifetime income approach allows one to handle such subtle considerations in educational policy. But, despite the overall quality of Professor Layard's paper, one is somewhat disappointed when comparing the careful theoretical exercise at the beginning of the paper with the concluding empirical implications of the analysis. Through no fault of his own, Professor Layard is forced to use annual – or, at least, short-period cross-sectional – data for his empirical analysis. Obviously, these data are bound to embody past history and past disequilibria occurring at different points in time and for different individuals. Such data will not allow one to draw truly equilibrium conclusions for a life-cycle model.

Professor Stern wished to raise questions about Professor Layard's rejection of utilitarianism on the basis of Professor Sen's arguments in *On Economic Inequality.* Sen's rejection of utilitarianism is not fully persuasive. The example that he uses to argue against utilitarianism is that of a cripple to whom one might wish to give a pound even though the cripple had a lower utility and even though he had a lower marginal utility. (All of these arguments assume, of course, a particular cardinalisation). But what of a man who is merely a grouser? Would we want to transfer income to an individual who claimed to be miserable (and we believed him) even though he had a high money income? To answer these questions, we must, of course, first decide what aspects of an individual's marginal utility are ethically relevant. One might wish to argue that the fact that an individual is crippled is ethically relevant, while the fact that he is a grouser is not. Clearly, before Sen's arguments can be accepted, there is a whole class of rather difficult philosophical questions that must be answered.

Professor von Weizsäcker wanted to encourage work such as Professor Layard's, which uses cross-sectional data to estimate life-cycle models of educational behaviour. Such data are clearly appropriate if the educational–labour market is experiencing steady-state equilibrium. But critics have often noted that such an equilibrium assumption is not justified. Professor von Weizsäcker, however, suggested that cross-sectional data may still be the relevant information. Disequilibrium is marked by uncertainty, which makes individual life-cycle planning difficult. The only references that individuals have in making their educational decisions are, in fact, incomes earned by other individuals in the current period – that is, cross-sectional information. Such information may be appropriate for behavioural analysis even in a disequilibrium economy.

Professor Atkinson raised the question of how important education is, as compared with ability and family environment, as a determinant of earnings. Is it possible for the independent effects of education on earnings to be isolated more carefully than they are in Layard's work?

Professor Stiglitz asked if it were not possible that including only income measures of inequality would lead to serious bias in our results in terms of our neglect of leisure and other sources of human satisfaction – for example, work quality or work environment. Professor Stiglitz also questioned the partial-equilibrium nature of Professor Layard's paper. First, the paper neglects the interaction between the public and private educational sectors. Increased aid to the public sector may lead to an expansion or to a decline in the private sector. How does this result fit into the Layard analysis? Second, if a programme of State aid to education is large, the rate of return to education need not be constant. Third, education is, in part, a screening process such that the social returns may be significantly less than the private returns. Finally, government participation in the education market need not be viewed as an exercise in income transfers, and may, in fact, be viewed as an effort to improve a capital market. Increased aid for children's education can be viewed as a loan to the child and as leading, via increased future earnings, to increased future taxes in repayment of the loan. For example, these future taxes may, in fact, pay the social security of today's adults. Thus, the loan is from today's adults to today's children. When one talks about policy changes of the order of magnitude discussed in the Layard paper, a general equilibrium framework is required.

Dr Kolm raised the following criticism of Professor Layard's objective function. Formally, the Layard utilitarian objective function assumes the form

$$W = F\left[\sum_{ij} f_j^i(C_j^i)\right]$$

where C_j^i is the consumption of the ith person in the jth time period. To this basic functional form, Professor Layard appends three additional assumptions: (1) no pure time preference ($f_j^i = f^i$), (2) homothetic preferences, and (3) all individuals are alike. Under these restrictions, the objective function reduces to $W = \sum_{ij} (C_j^i)^\alpha$. Dr Kolm rejects this form of W. The problems centre on the assumptions of homotheticity and no pure rate of the time preference, which together imply that social indifference curves between current and future consumption are homothetic and symmetric. Fig. B demonstrates the weakness of the homotheticity assumption. Point s in this graph corresponds to a point of satiation in consumption. All consumption bundles above the satiation point are points of indifference and are indicated by the shaded area. But the homotheticity assumption implies that all indifference curves must have a shape identical to the one at the satiation point. Therefore, the rate of time preference

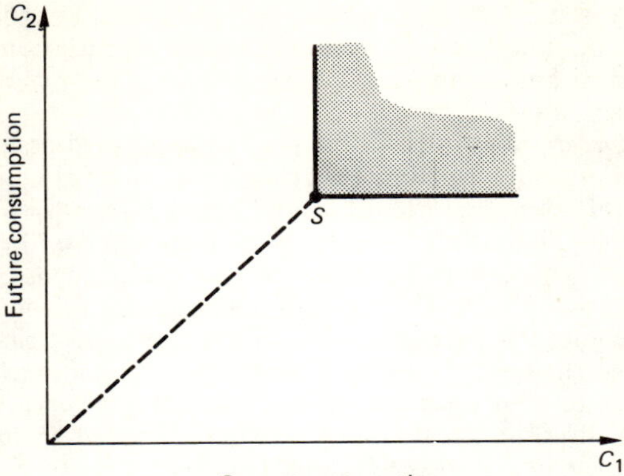

Fig. B

must be either zero, infinity, or undetermined. This is clearly an unacceptable conclusion and means that we must reject homothetic preferences.

Figure C illustrates the problems with the symmetry assumption. If consumption in period 1 falls below some critical minimum, C_1^*, the individual will die. In death, presumably, we are indifferent about different consumption levels in the future period. Therefore, the indifference curves from points less than C_1^* will be vertical lines. Clearly, such indifference curves are not symmetric between periods C_2 and C_1, and symmetry must be rejected. We can only conclude that the utilitarian structure that Professor Layard has chosen is incorrect, though convenient.

In an effort to defend Professor Layard against Dr Kolm's comments, *Professor Vickrey* said that we do not know very much about the shape of

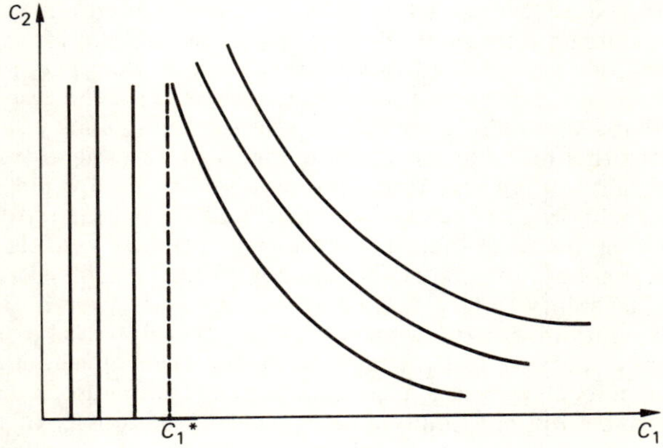

Fig. C

indifference curves at satiation. For example, one could imagine a satiation point where the amount of consumption required for satiation in period 2 is dependent on consumption in period 1. Such an indifference map is not necessarily at right angles.

Professor Feldstein began his comments on the Layard paper by raising questions on the estimated income function. First, there is an upward bias to the estimated coefficient on years of schooling, because the equation omits a measure of child ability. Ability and years of schooling are likely to be positively correlated. Thus, the coefficient on years of schooling is an overstatement of the pure education effect. This upward bias will lead to the conclusion that redistributive policies through education are more effective than they actually are. Second, given the imperfections in the human capital market, does it make any sense to use a present-value calculation? May it not be more informative simply to use the lifetime stream of an individual's consumption benefits? Third, as regards the use of cross-sectional results, Professor Feldstein said that he agreed with Professor von Weizsäcker that such information is probably the correct information to use when trying to draw inferences about individual behaviour in the human capital market. However, in the Layard paper this is not what is being estimated in the earnings function. What is being predicted is the actual earnings of individuals at future points in time, and the appropriateness of cross-sectional information for this type of analysis is less obvious.

Professor Feldstein concluded by supporting Professor Layard against the comments of Dr Kolm. While Dr Kolm has offered an interesting discussion of the individual utility functions in the extremes of satiation and death, it is not altogether obvious that the assumptions of homotheticity and symmetry do not provide reasonable approximations for social choice for the middle ranges of human existence.

Professor Klevorick suggested that one possible way of dealing with imperfect capital-market problems associated with the Layard analysis is to undertake sensitivity analyses assuming different discount rates for different individuals where the discount rates are functions of the individuals' abilities and parental incomes. Professor Klevorick also wondered whether alternative specifications and possible interaction were tried in estimating the earnings functions.

Professor Layard thanked the discussants for their useful comments. His reply was limited to three aspects of the discussion. First, he agreed with those comments that faulted his model for the omission of an ability variable. However, he stated that his earnings equation does include a selective-school dummy variable and that this is a very rough proxy for ability. In Britain, admission to the 'selective schools' has been by examination. (As an aside, Professor Layard noted that, even in studies that have more refined ability variables included in the earnings function, the ability measured is never the ability to earn income, but, rather, the ability to take examinations.) However, even if one does have appropriate ability information, there is yet another potential problem with such earnings equations. This is the problem that years of schooling may be used as a screening device, and, thus, that in earnings functions the years-of-schooling variable will not simply measure social productivity of education. Professor Stiglitz had emphasised this point, but Professor Layard cited one of his recent papers (mentioned in the references to his current paper) to indicate that screening may not be an important source of bias in estimates of the social returns to education.

Second, in response to Professor Klevorick's suggestion that we ought to use the individual's own discount rate, Professor Layard emphasised again (see section I of the paper) that this would not be the correct procedure. However, a calculation that he would not object to would be to compute the annuity that an individual would earn at his own discount rate out of his income.

Finally, Professor Layard responded to the two sets of comments on the construction of his objective function. First, in response to Professor Stern, he stated that you cannot argue against the Sen argument simply by saying that it is not clear what the relevant utilities should be. The issue is, for given utilities, whether one should add them up or take a concave function of them. Second, in response to Dr Kolm's comments, Professor Layard noted that homotheticity is not a crucial assumption for his analysis and that the basic structure of his argument would hold without it. The symmetry assumption struck him as perfectly consistent with his preference for an *ex post* perspective on individual situations. When looking back over life from a particular point in time, it seems perfectly reasonable to treat all earlier periods symmetrically.

Discussion of Alvin Klevorick, 'Jury Size and Composition: An Economic Approach'

Professor von Weizsäcker began the discussion of Professor Klevorick's paper by commending the author for pursuing in an illuminating and provocative way a subject of both intellectual and moral importance. However, he thought that the following extensions of the Klevorick analysis would be in order. First, strictly speaking, it is not appropriate to limit oneself to only the case where erroneous conviction matters. The best way to minimise erroneous convictions is simply to minimise convictions altogether. To appoint a jury under this criterion is really not the purpose of the judicial system. The interesting cases are those where both the errors of convicting an innocent person and the errors of releasing a guilty person are considered. Second, more attention should be given to the interesting causes of correlation between juror's decision probabilities. Even given the true state of innocence or guilt, the probability of conviction will strongly depend on the particulars of the trial – that is, the evidence. Therefore, it is likely that all of the decision probabilities of jurors will be highly positively correlated, even when they do not speak with each other. The case of stochastic independence is not an interesting case to examine.

Professor von Weizsäcker then presented a simple model of jury decision-making without assuming stochastic independence of juror decisions. Assume that the probability that jurors 1 and 2 come to a different decision is π. Given the likelihood that there will be a high positive correlation between juror decisions, π should be low – certainly less than one half. Assume also that π is the probability that jurors 1 and 3 will disagree. It is easy to see that, with this symmetric model, the probability that both juror 2 and juror 3 will disagree with juror 1 is $\pi/2$. Now, assume that the probability of a decision error by person 1 is p, where we assume that $p < 0{\cdot}5$. In a majority of cases, juror 1 is right in his judgement of guilt or innocence. Finally, let us assume that the majority's decision at the first ballot does in fact prove to be the jury's final, unanimous decision. (The Klevorick paper provides some evidence that this is a reasonable assumption.) We can, therefore, concentrate on the case of majority rule. Now, what is the probability of erroneous decision? (For convenience, let the social cost of type I and type II errors be equal to each other, so that we can talk about error without having to specify what kind of error.) With a three-person jury, the probability that juror 1 will commit an error is p, and the probability that jurors 2 and 3 will agree with his decision is $(1 - \pi/2)$. Thus, the probability that juror 1 is wrong and that the others go along with his decision is $p(1 - \pi/2)$. The probability that juror 1 is right is $(1 - p)$. The probability that jurors 2 and 3 will disagree with his decision and outvote juror 1 is $\pi/2$. Thus, the probability that juror 1 will be correct but outvoted is $(1 - p)\pi/2$. The total probability of error by a jury is equal to $(1 - p)(\pi/2) + p(1 - \pi/2)$. What is the probability that juror 1 acting alone will make an error? It is p.

Comparing p to the probability of error with a three-person jury, we see that the jury will be more likely to make an error when $(1-p)\pi/2 + p(1-\pi/2) > p$, or when $\pi(\frac{1}{2} - p) > 0$. Thus, when p is less than 0·5, individual decision-making is preferable. Against the criterion of minimising the probability of wrong decisions, juries are likely to be useful only if disagreement and decision-making error are positively correlated. What is needed for analysis of this kind is a more detailed model of the influence that the joint deliberations of a jury have on its final decisions. But the jury problem in this context is just a special case of a more general, and little understood, analytic problem in economic theory – the nature of interpersonal influences on probabilities.

Professor Aaron wished to stress that one of the essential characteristics of jury decision-making is the interaction among jurors. There is a strong presumption that the pooling of judgements associated with the jury process is preferable to individual decision-making. How to model this interaction process and, then, how to test empirically the models developed are two very large, but important, questions.

Professor Sandmo noted that jury decisions will often depend on the punishments associated with the crimes being considered by the jury. This suggests that decisions on the optimal jury size and on representativeness will not be independent of the level of fines and punishments.

Professor Pauly observed that the decisions by juries are, in effect, decisions on the level of a public good – here, the level of criminal activity. This observation leads to speculation about why the jury method – the random selection of a representative group of individuals whose decisions are binding on the larger community – has not been seriously considered as an alternative method for determining the level of other public services.

Professor Stiglitz suggested that, given our uncertainty regarding the correctness of a jury's decision, perhaps this uncertainty should be incorporated into our eventual decisions on punishment. Thus, fine schedules ought to be directly connected to the jury's decision on guilt or innocence and to their judgement on the certainty of their decision. Once we recognise an uncertainty, we ought to incorporate this information into our later decisions.

Professor Atkinson wondered whether we should agree with the implicit assumption in the Klevorick objective function involving the trade-off between vertical and horizontal equity in the criminal justice system. In defining our objective function for fact-finding in a criminal justice system, might not horizontal equity ('the equal treatment of equals') receive top priority in a lexicographic ranking of values?

Professor Inman noted that, in addition to Professor von Weizsäcker's requirement that group disagreement and individual error should be positively correlated, there may be another reason for large juries. The argument might be entitled 'the missing bullet motivation'. One of the main objectives in using a firing squad for execution is to ensure that no one person can be identified as he who killed the victim. This same motivation may be a very important argument for large juries, particularly in cases involving capital offences. Convicting an innocent person by error may be a burden that society does not wish to have shouldered by one person. The 'moral costs' of a wrong decision should be spread over many people, so that no one person need feel morally responsible for the error or can be identified by others as *the* person who in fact sentenced an innocent person to his death.

In an effort to integrate Professor von Weizsäcker's model with Professor Inman's comment, *Professor Feldstein* suggested that perhaps the optimal jury should consist of many individuals deciding independently, with the final decision drawn randomly from the set of individual decisions.

In response to Professor Feldstein's comment, *Professor von Weizsäcker* emphasised that he did not view his model as a case for individual decision-making in criminal cases. Group interaction is important. Indeed, one important source of the required positive correlation between group disagreement and individual error is the individual interactions that occur with multiperson juries.

Professor Aaron made the observation that Professor Feldstein's characterisation of the 'missing bullet motivation' was not quite correct. The analogue to Professor Feldstein's jury system is not a single missing bullet, but, rather, a single bullet in one gun. The essence of Professor Inman's point is that there is a reduction in the sense of involvement or responsibility by virtue of being part of a group that is jointly engaged in the decision. In the case that Professor Feldstein describes, an erroneous decision may mean that someone would always feel that he may have been solely responsible.

Dr Guesnerie offered an additional argument for multiperson, representative juries. To a large extent, the social costs associated with type I and type II errors in judgement of guilt are not unambiguously fixed and known, but are, in an important sense, similar to measuring social willingness to pay for public goods (or 'bads'). Being put in jail when an individual is not guilty involves not only individual, but also collective, damage. The amount of funds that a society is willing to spend to avoid such a situation must be estimated as with any public good. This 'public-choice' characteristic of jury decision-making pleads strongly for representativeness on juries. An evaluation of the social costs of wrong decisions may therefore require a representative jury.

In response to the comments of Professor von Weizsäcker and others, *Professor Klevorick* made the following points. Even in the case where only convicting an innocent person invokes social costs, there is the additional cost of reaching a nondecision if, in fact, the individual is innocent. In the context of the model, both of these outcomes have costs, and much of the question of whether one wants a representative or nonrepresentative jury would therefore depend on the levels of these costs. This special case was not meant to be a model of what the social loss function should in fact be. It was offered only as an example of the needed analysis for one polar case. Clearly, other possibilities should be explored, as was done by Professor von Weizsäcker.

Professor Klevorick agreed with Professor von Weizsäcker's point that the consideration of joint determination of individual probabilities is an extremely important matter, but with this generalisation the analysis proved initially too complicated for any useful conclusions to emerge. As an empirical matter, however, there is some indication that, in coming to a final, unanimous decision, a jury almost always reaches the verdict that the majority of jury members favoured at the start of their deliberations and before interaction. Evidence of this point is presented in the paper. In response to Professor Sandmo's point, Professor Klevorick stated his agreement and mentioned that his work is introduced explicitly as a partial-equilibrium exercise. The relationships between the Klevorick analysis and the work of Carr-Hill and Stern are obvious in this connection. The comments of Professors Stiglitz and Inman both suggest that the noneconomic costs in the social loss functions should not be independent of jury size. The connection between noneconomic costs and jury size is obvious in the case proposed by Professor Inman. The connection is somewhat indirect in the case of Professor Stiglitz's point. The probability of guilt – which determines the level of fines, which, in turn, determines the noneconomic costs of jury decisions – will initially depend on jury size. Finally, in response to Professor Atkinson's question on the role of horizontal equity in the objective function, Professor Klevorick noted that such considerations require an explicit definition of individuals who are similarly situated. The definitions of 'equals' may be extremely difficult in cases of criminal activity. Do we define horizontal equity as simply treating all innocent individuals equally and all guilty individuals equally? If so, then in the first instance we are interested in minimising the type I error and in the second case we are interested in minimising the type II error. Such considerations easily fit into the Klevorick analysis.

Discussion of R. A. Carr-Hill and N. H. Stern, 'The Theory and Estimation in Models of Crime and its Social Control and their Relations to the Concepts of Social Output'

Beginning the discussion of the Carr-Hill and Stern paper, *Professor Inman* made a number of observations on the econometric results presented in section III of the paper. He noted that this section offers one of the first serious attempts at directly estimating a public-service production function. The Carr-Hill and Stern paper deserves careful attention, not only for the information that it provides on the determinants of crime, but also as a general approach to public-service production studies. The basic equation of the production model, equation (6.1), adopts the crime rate as a measure of public-service output, or, more correctly, minus the public-service output. The dependent variable is defined as the probability that a particular average individual will suffer a crime over a given time period. The basic production model being proposed by Carr-Hill and Stern might be generalised as follows:

$$Y = \phi[X(C, E), N, T(P, F, A, S, \% \text{ urban})] \tag{1}$$

where Y is the crime rate; $X(C, E)$ is a quantity index of police protection *facilities* provided by the number of policemen (C) and supporting equipment (E); N is the population of the city; and $T(\cdot)$ describes the criminal 'threat' environment as a function of the probability of apprehension (P), fines (F), and assorted socio-economic variables (A, S, % urban). Generally, we would expect that a *ceteris paribus* increase in police facilities (X) would mean an increase in public services (reduce Y). Thus, C and E should be negatively related to Y. For all public services except Samuelsonian pure public goods, a *ceteris paribus* increase in population N should reduce public-service outputs. Thus, N should be positively related to Y. Finally, a reduction in the threat environment, holding X and N fixed, should reduce Y. Thus, P and F should be negatively related to Y. The Carr-Hill and Stern paper tests all of these relationships – except the relationship of population (congestion) to Y – and the results are generally consistent with our *a priori* expectations. The one surprising result is the significantly *positive* relationship between the number of policemen and the crime rate.

How might we explain this paradoxical result? Carr-Hill and Stern argue that the problem centres on errors in the reporting of criminal activity. They hypothesise that the more policemen there are, the higher the observed reporting rate will be. One might expect, however, that the crimes that policemen report are also the crimes that they are likely to clear up. Thus, if the 'reporting phenomenon' is the whole story, we should see a positive relationship between policemen and the clear-up rate. We do observe this in the 1971 results, but not in the 1966 results, where there is a quite strong negative relationship between policemen and clear-up. Perhaps an alternative explanation is required.

One alternative might be the following. Imagine a town with wealthy and poor families. Originally, the criminals attacked the wealthy and did quite well. In a utility maximising model of criminal behaviour with risk aversion, each criminal need commit only one or two crimes a month. However, in the town in question, the rich control the political process, and they demand an increase in police protection. The number of policemen is therefore increased and the extra protection services are directed at protecting the richer neighbourhoods. What happens now? The criminals find that the risks have substantially increased in the wealthy neighbourhoods, and so they turn to the relatively less risky middle-class and lower-income neighbourhoods. But the 'take' is not as great from each crime, and, consequently, more crimes are committed. Thus, in increasing the number of policemen in the town, the number of observed crimes has also been increased. There is an increase in crime in the poor and middle-income neighbourhoods, a reduced level of attack on the upper-income neighbourhoods, an increase in the number of crimes reported, and an increase in the number of policemen. Does this model also explain why there may be a negative relationship between the number of policemen and the clear-up rate? First, a *ceteris paribus* increase in the number of committed crimes reduces clear-up. Second, aggregate security in the community may decline as the rich substitute public protection for private protection. If some of the increased public protection in rich neighbourhoods comes at the expense of public protection in poor neighbourhoods, the security levels may actually decline in lower- and middle-class neighbourhoods. Crimes increase, as we have seen, but it is also possible that the lower level of security will now induce others to enter criminal activity. The number of criminals increases, and clear-up becomes much more difficult. No longer will catching one burglar necessarily clear-up 20 burglaries. This alternative model strongly suggests the need for disaggregated analysis, by geographical region or, in this case, by type of crime. Analysis at the aggregated level of the Carr-Hill and Stern paper may conceal more than it reveals.

Professor Inman offered one additional comment. The Carr-Hill and Stern specification of equation (1) above is a Cobb-Douglas form. With user population (N) included in the production model as it should be, the log–log form implies decreasing congestion ($\partial^2 Y/\partial N^2 > 0$) as N increases. An alternative specification with more reasonable congestion properties would be CES.

In support of the analysis presented in section II of the Carr-Hill and Stern paper, *Professor Frey* offered the following critique of the Becker model, which takes it to be self-evident that crime can be fought by increasing punishment. Professor Stern rightly observes that there are limits to the size of fines. In the context of a dynamic model of crime, it is possible to show that increasing fines would not necessarily reduce crime and may increase it cumulatively. Consider an economy with two sets of activities – a set of legal, and a set of illegal, activities. It is reasonable to assume that members of a society will consider past punishment to be an indication that the punished individual is likely to commit further crime in the future. Such a behavioural assumption would correspond to a minimisation of search costs when hiring new employees. As a consequence of such discrimination, there will be a change, in favour of the illegal sector, in the relevant rates of return to a punished individual. The consequences of applying a Becker crime-prevention policy, given the above behavioural assumption, can be developed with the help of two differential equations.

(1) According to the behavioural hypothesis, crime (C) will increase as the amount of punishment (P) increases. It is further assumed that the crime level already achieved has a negative effect on its further rate of increase. Therefore,

$$\dot{C} = \Psi(C, P)$$

where $$\dot{C} = \frac{dC}{Ct}, \frac{\partial \Psi}{\partial C} < 0, \frac{\partial \Psi}{\partial P} > 0$$

(2) If a Becker policy is followed, an increase in the level of crime will mean that punishment must be increased so as to fight this situation. It is again assumed that the level of punishment already achieved has a dampening effect on further punishments. Thus,

$$\dot{P} = \Phi(C, P)$$

where $$\dot{P} = \frac{dC}{dt}, \frac{\partial \Phi}{\partial C} > 0, \frac{\partial \Phi}{\partial P} < 0$$

The actual development of the detention system over time depends on the exact form of the differential equations. However, Fig. D may prove consistent with reality.

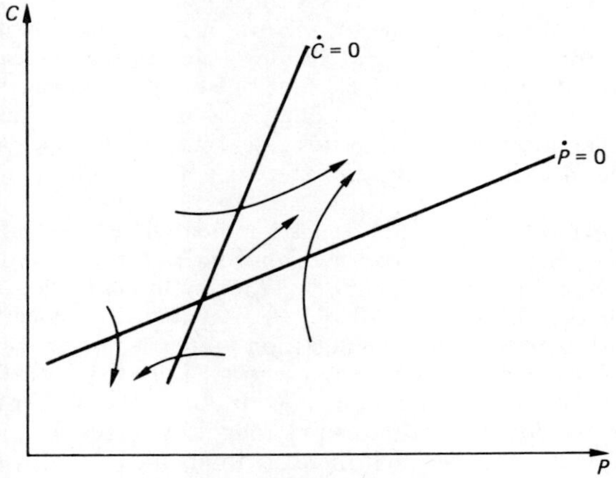

Fig. D

In the case above, if the initial values of punishment and crime are not too low, there is an explosive accumulation of crime and punishment. Eventually, all citizens are criminals. These considerations suggest that negative sanctions may have extreme welfare-minimising effects in the long run. Positive sanctions may therefore be the preferred policy alternative.

Professor Khachaturov felt that it was particularly important, when analysing the problem of controlling crime, to draw the relationship between the level of public wealth and the number of types of crimes committed. It was Professor Khachaturov's feeling that, as individual well-being increased, one would observe a decrease in crime against property.

Professor Breton emphasised the need to disaggregate not only by geographical size, as recommended by Inman, but also by type of crime. For example, the Inman model is likely to apply to crimes against property but not to crimes against persons. In addition, when specifying a supply schedule of criminal activity, one must keep in mind that, even though criminals define the schedules, legislators, who formulate the laws, may have a significant impact on the position and slope of that supply curve.

Professor Aaron made two comments. First, he found the theoretical discussion in section II a useful demolition of the Becker model's intuitively absurd policy deduction of infinite fines. Second, he doubted that the econometric work in section III could be usefully reproduced using cross-sectional United States data. The fundamental problem stems from the political nature of United States crime statistics. Changes in city or county administrations will often produce 100 per cent adjustments in reported criminal offences. Similarly, data on clear-up rates may be a function of the local political environment. Clear-up rates will often depend on the strategy an administration adopts with regard to the prosecution of offences – specifically, the use of plea bargaining. The susceptibility of criminal statistics to political manipulation raises serious questions as to their usefulness in studies such as Carr-Hill and Stern's. Do such problems afflict the British data?

Professor Layard offered the following comments. There are many crimes, such as motoring offences, for which the benefits to the criminal rise with his income. Optimal deterrence requires that the fine (cost) also rise with income. For crimes where the motivation is nonrational, it may also be just to let the fine vary with individual income, given the diminishing marginal utility of income. How, then, might we explain the observed fact that there is often no relationship between fine and the finee's income? The prevalence of the retribution motive, as pointed out by Carr-Hill and Stern, is clearly one explanation. An alternative explanation is society's need for a well-defined and understandable penalty schedule to be associated with the consequences of an individual's actions. Clearly, the simplest schedule is one that simply specifies a unique fine for each criminal activity.

Professor Feldstein began his comments by noting that Carr-Hill and Stern argue that, given a diminishing marginal utility of income schedule, there should be a smaller fine for a given crime if the offender is poor. But, in the case of economic crimes, such a rule may lead to situations where the value of the stolen goods would exceed the expected payment of the fine (the probability of having to pay a fine times the amount of the fine) for low-income individuals.

Such a fine schedule would, therefore, simply be encouraging the transfer of wealth from high- to low-income individuals by making the expected net gain of criminal activity positive for the poor. Even if you want to redistribute, this is a very inefficient way of transferring assets from high- to low-income persons. Why does the theory go wrong? Because Carr-Hill and Stern have not correctly valued the stolen assets. The value of \$100 in goods stolen by a criminal is going to be higher for low-income than for high-income individuals, so that whatever utility function you want to apply to the value of the fines you should apply also to the value of the stolen goods. Utility differences then are largely cancelled.

Professor Feldstein offered one additional comment on section II. We often talk of the 'deserving poor' ('poor but honest'), but poor criminals might reasonably be seen by the rest of society as less deserving. The weights given to poor criminals (and rich criminals as well) can clearly be affected by the fact that they have little concern for society. Might not society have less concern for them? These comments raise the question of the role of retribution in criminal justice, something for which democratic societies have often expressed a preference.

Professor Feldstein also discussed the empirical results. First, Carr-Hill and Stern express some surprise that their model explained the data better in 1971 than it did in earlier years. The reason for that could be aggregation. For 1971, they were dealing with 41 observations instead of 110; and, typically, as one deals with more aggregate data, there is just less noise and one therefore obtains a better explanation. Second, with regard to Table 6.4(b), which presents the 1971 restricted results, Professor Feldstein wondered whether the clear-up rate equation were really identified *vis à vis* the equation for policemen, the third equation. In this, the only exogenous variable that does not appear in the clear-up equation is M (percentage of population in the middle class), and it has a t statistic of 0·2.

Finally, Professor Feldstein noted that, contrary to the arguments of Professor Frey, the Carr-Hill and Stern results do indicate quite clearly that one can fight crime by increased punishment. It is certainly true that other things can be done and that one should extend to include other activities the maximand or minimand in the Carr-Hill and Stern paper. There is, obviously, an optimal mix of deterrents and positive inducements. But one certainly would not want to eliminate punishment completely.

Professor Sandmo observed that the probability of detection and the severity of punishment are, in fact, substitutes in the function that explains the level of criminal activity. Given this point, could one explain the historical decline in the severity of punishment by the historical rise in the probability of criminal detection? On Professor Frey's distinction between positive and negative sanctions, Professor Sandmo noted that the distinction is just that – one of sign. It is not clear that the distinction is a meaningful one in behavioural terms. If all individuals receive at birth a flat grant from which deductions will be extracted for criminal acts (the positive sanction), the behavioural effect is identical to a tax or fines (the negative sanction) on criminal activities.

Professor Vickrey noted that one reason why society does not move in the direction of Becker's recommendation of very high fines for the control of crime is that such a result offends our sense of justice. Indeed, justice may require that, instead of a very high fine being imposed on a few captured offenders, more moderate or low fines should be imposed on many captured offenders. When penalties are high, it may happen that juries, if they believe that the defendant is being unfairly singled out as an example for society, will not convict.

Professor Stern began his comments by thanking Professor Inman and the other contributors to the discussion for their helpful and constructive comments. He agreed with many of these, but discussed only those points where he felt that clarification or extension would be helpful.

Professor Inman had spent some time discussing the negative coefficient (in 1966) on the number of policemen per capita in the equation modelling the determination of the crime rate. The story he told was interesting, but Professor Stern believed that many of the effects that Professor Inman described were included in the simultaneous equations of the model – for example, the dependence, in the third equation, of the number of policemen on the number of offences and the class structure of an area. In their article in the November 1973 issue of the *Journal of Public Economics*, Carr-Hill and Stern suggested (p. 308) that part of the reason for the negative second-equation coefficient on *c* (for the 1966 data) may lie with the 'reporting effect'. More police in an area may imply that some minor crimes are reported (perhaps through a greater consciousness of the law) by individuals who would not otherwise have reported them. The clear-up rate for such marginal offences may be low and, thus, the clear-up rate would be depressed.

Professor Stern agrees with the suggestion that further disaggregation would be fruitful. However, the disaggregation of police time and the collection of information on the more specific variables supposed to determine the particular offences would raise formidable data problems. So far, Professor Stern noted, he and Carr-Hill had been working entirely with published data (apart from clear-up rates kindly made available by the Home Office) and the collection had involved a good deal of work. The disaggregation suggestion, were it to be pursued, would involve a research project lasting several years. We should be clear, however, on what kind of offence is being examined here. The definition is 'total indictable offences', about 90 per cent of which are either larcenies or breaking-and-entering offences, i.e. thefts involving no violence against the person. Crimes such as murder, rape and robbery with violence play an insignificant role.

The reason why Carr-Hill and Stern chose the log–log form for the equation is that it performed as well as did any other specification they tried, and is helpful in their discussion of the identification problems associated with the difference between 'true' and 'recorded' offences (see their discussion of these points in the November 1973 issue of the *Journal of Public Economics*).

Professor Stern said that he would like to share Professor Khatchaturov's optimistic belief that crimes decrease with wealth, but such evidence as there is points in the opposite direction. The Wilkins time-series study of car thefts in the United States showed that such thefts are highly correlated with the number of cars. Professor Sergio Bruno has already quoted Italian evidence to the effect that property offences increase with wealth. Finally, Carr-Hill and Stern's own work on the 1961 and 1966 data showed that, cross-sectionally for the towns of England and Wales, offences and wealth are positively related.

Professor Stern said that he had some sympathy with the approach taken in Professor Frey's model, but stated that he also had some reservations about it. We should be catholic in our approach to models of behaviour in this area. Many different models may shed some light. Further, Carr-Hill has produced a model of reconviction rates based on ideas similar to those advanced by Professor Frey, and has achieved good empirical results with its use.

In response to Professor Aaron, Professor Stern noted that police districts in England and Wales form a more homogeneous sample than areas covering the whole of the United States would be likely to form. Further, he and Carr-Hill had tried to take account of the way in which the authorities interact with the population to produce the recorded statistics. Indeed, this interaction is one of the central features in the model and in the interpretation of results (see, for example, the discussion, in the last part of section III of the paper, of the variance–covariance matrix of residuals).

Finally, Professor Stern responded to Professor Feldstein's points. He did not think that, in the discussion of why fines to poorer offenders should be lower, no account had been taken of the effects of the larger subjective value that stolen assets possess for poorer offenders. Indeed, it had been suggested, in section II, that, for a simple expected utility model, a poorer person would be less likely to commit an offence than would a rich person with a similar utility function, provided one adopts the (weak) assumption of decreasing absolute risk aversion. Further, Professor Feldstein's point that scaling fines according to wealth might lead to fines less than the money value of stolen property can be met by the design of a system in which fines increase with the wealth of an offender but are always higher than the value of the stolen goods. While accepting that there may be some identification problems, the models reported are the ones that, on the whole, performed best with regard to t values and chi-square values of the log-likelihood ratio. In the early stages of the work, an attempt had been made to specify two other variables as endogenous – the expenditure per officer and the severity of punishment – but these attempts did not yield good fits and raised further identification problems. Carr-Hill and Stern hope to do some further work in connection with the identification problems that seem to arise for the second and third equations when applied to the 1971 data.

Discussion of Henry Aaron, 'Demographic Effects on the Equity of Social Security Benefits'

Professor Atkinson introduced the discussion of the Aaron paper by complimenting the author on performing an interesting and useful exercise. However, he did have some reservations. First, as the results are presented, it is very difficult to see the quantitative importance of the various factors operating in the Aaron model. It would be more helpful to have a step-by-step analysis indicating the contribution of each of the central factors – differential mortality rates, variants in tax payments across income groups, and variations in benefit schedules across income groups. Moreover, there are a number of other factors, mentioned by the author in his paper, that should be included in the formal quantitative analysis. For example, retirement after the age of 65 by higher-income workers is common, and the analysis omits the inclusion of survivors' benefits. In this kind of work, sensitivity analysis is of great importance, and it is not adequately treated by the author in the results presented in Tables 7.1–7.3.

Second, the author gives only a very short and unsatisfactory treatment of the incidence of the social security tax. The only reference to this important issue is the bold statement that 'The worker is assumed to bear the payroll tax collected from employers on his earnings, as well as his own tax.' This view is based on the work of Brittain. However, the Brittain analysis has been questioned, and, in any event, Brittain did not attempt to distinguish between forward shifting of the tax through higher prices, and backward shifting through lower wages. The implications of tax shifting may well depend on the direction (whether backward or forward) as well as on the degree of shift. In a paper of this nature, shifting of the social security tax should be examined in much greater detail.

Finally, in comparing the time streams of benefits, the choice of discount rate is clearly an important matter. When faced with this choice, one is simultaneously faced with the problem of imperfections in the capital market. In this context it is necessary to distinguish between (a) different discount rates among individuals, and (b) different borrowing and lending rates for one person. For example, the rich may have more attractive investment opportunities than the poor have, and social security may therefore be a less attractive investment. For this reason, the discount rate should be higher for the rich. Working against this tendency, it may be the case that the pension scheme forces people in the low-income groups to save when they are, in fact, anxious to borrow at high rates of interest. If this is so, then the discount rate applied to the stream of net benefits should, perhaps, be higher for the lower-income groups. In any case, a more careful treatment of the discount rate to be used in the analysis is required.

Professor Hochman wanted to stress a point mentioned briefly by Professor

Atkinson. High-income individuals often remain in the labour force long after low-income individuals have left it. If this is so, then some high-income individuals may never collect social security benefits, and others would collect for a greatly shortened period. Thus, given this additional piece of information, Professor Aaron's conclusion that a progressive earnings tax is required to restore proportionality or progressitivity to the social security programme may not follow.

Professor Layard offered two comments on the Aaron paper. First, in his calculation, Professor Aaron does not take into account the fact that, for a person with a given income during his working life, an increase in longevity will reduce the level of annual consumption that it would be possible for that person to achieve. It would therefore be interesting if, for each group in the population, there were computed, over the expected length of life, the annuity having the same present value as the individual's earnings. This annuity could then be taken as a true measure of the person's underlying welfare. The social security system would be regressive only if this annuity were positively correlated with the distribution of net social security benefits. Second, the appropriate discount rate to use in the Aaron analysis is a weighted average of the individual discount rates. The growth rate, which Professor Aaron does use, is appropriate only when it equals this weighted average of individual time preferences.

Professor Sheshinski wondered what policy instruments Professor Aaron thought might be effective in altering a nonoptimal distribution of benefits to costs in the social security system.

Professor Klevorick noted that, before one draws conclusions about how progressive or regressive one would like the social security system to be, one must perform similar analyses for other public services. Our concern is the overall redistributive effect of the entire public budget. Policy conclusions for the social security system, or for any public sector, must be considered within this general equilibrium context.

Professor Stern noted that the social security system often is not completely self-financed but is financed, in part, through the general tax system. How would this fact alter Professor Aaron's conclusions?

Dr Jeanjean questioned whether redistribution should be the sole objective of the social security system. Though Professor Aaron's empirical analysis is interesting, his policy conclusions may be quite premature.

Professor Aaron offered the following comments in response to the discussants. First, in reply to Professor Klevorick, Dr Jeanjean and others on the important question of the objective of the social security system, he noted that his paper had been developed with a specific policy question in mind. In the debate about social security in the United States, the issue had been raised of whether low-income individuals should be relieved of the obligation to contribute to the social security system. The argument that had been offered to defend the current system was that, on a lifetime approach, the social security system is progressive and, therefore, a progressive tax schedule is not needed. The work in his paper was an effort to test the validity of this argument directly. On a more general level, however, Professor Aaron did agree with the comments of Professor Klevorick and Dr Jeanjean that, before analysing a specific public-service programme such as social security, one should first debate the more fundamental issues of policy objectives.

Second, in response to Professor Atkinson's request for sensitivity analysis, Professor Aaron said that some work in this direction had been performed. The analysis and preliminary results, with the inclusion of survivors' benefits, does suggest a weakening of the conclusion that the overall system is regressive, but the inclusion of survivors' benefits does not overturn the basic conclusion of regressivity. For the variables that are included in the analysis reported in Tables 7.1–7.3, the prime determinant of regressivity is the life-expectancy variable. Entry into the labour force is the second most important variable, while the lifetime profile of earnings is really rather insignificant in its impact on the regressivity of the overall system. Professor Aaron admitted that the question of incidence is not adequately treated in his paper. However, he did note that the question of whether the tax is shifted forward onto prices or backward into a wage reduction is of no importance in the long run, which is the basis of these calculations. In the long run, the supply of labour is a function of the real wage, and forward or backward shifting is not relevant.

Finally, in response to Professor Sheshinski's question as to what policy instruments one might adopt to alter the distributional effects of the social security system, Professor Aaron mentioned three: first, tax relief in the form of a more progressive tax schedule; second, a more progressive benefits schedule; and, third, setting the payroll tax from a certain age, and allowing people to defer payment if they are not actually in the labour force, or to recover additional taxes later, with interest, if they enter the labour force at an earlier date.

Discussion of Martin Feldstein, 'Social Security and Private Savings: International Evidence in an Extended Life-Cycle Model'

Professor Sandmo began the discussion of the Feldstein paper by noting that it was an interesting, important and stimulating piece of work. The problem area is a large one, and one where there remains much to be done both in theory and in measurement.

Professor Sandmo noted that there are three arguments for having a compulsory social security system. First, there are the imperfections of the private capital markets. Second, in contrast with private insurance, social security may have favourable redistributive effects. Third, people may be myopic and, therefore, unable to take care of their own future in a reliable way, even in the presence of perfect loan and insurance markets. Professor Sandmo's formal comments concentrated on the first two arguments for compulsory social insurance. Professor Feldstein's model assumes that income taken away from private individuals in the first period will earn the same rate of interest as would have been earned by private savings. If this were not true – if, for example, the public rate of interest were higher than the private rate of return – there would, as Professor Feldstein correctly notes, be an income effect on the consumption-saving decision with compulsory social security. Such an income effect would operate to increase consumption in the first period or to decrease private savings by more than the amount of social security taxes. Professor Sandmo wished to draw attention to another effect of social security on savings – namely, that with uncertainty there may be a similar, but additional, impact on savings, because the yield in social security taxes may be more certain than the yield on private savings. To see this, consider the following simple model of savings and portfolio choice.

The labour supply is taken as given. Individuals can invest their savings in money (m) where the rate of return is certain and equal to zero, or in a risky asset (a) with a stochastic gross rate of return R with $E(R) = \mu > 1$. The first-period budget constraint is

$$C_1 + a + m + B - Y_1 = 0$$

where B is social security payments. Future consumption is given by

$$C_2 = aR + m + B\mu$$

The implied rate of return on social security payments (B) is set equal to the *expected* rate of return in private capital markets. Underlying this is the assumption of larger, averaging opportunities for the public sector. With additive utility we can write expected utility as

$$U(C_1) + E[V\{Y_1 - C_1 + (R-1)a + (\mu - 1)B\}]$$

The first-order maximum conditions are

$$U'(C_1) - E[V'(C_2)] = 0$$

and

$$E[V'(C_2)(R-1)] = 0$$

One can now differentiate these equations with respect to B to obtain the partial derivatives $\partial C_1/\partial B$ and $\partial a/\partial B$. Provided that the appropriate second-order conditions are satisfied, and with some additional plausible assumptions (involving, in particular, the Arrow–Pratt risk-aversion functions) one can argue that $\partial C_1/\partial B$ is positive; private saving is more than displaced by social security. Here is an independent argument for the hypothesis that social security increases the private rate of consumption and reduces total saving. Interestingly, on the same set of assumptions, one can derive the result that $\partial a/\partial B$ is positive; the composition of the private-savings portfolio shifts in the direction of more risky assets.

Professor Sandmo's final comment had to do with the redistributive effects of social security. Most social security systems involve a considerable degree of redistribution, and, if the private savings ratio depends on the distribution of income, this may be a rather powerful effect neglected in the Feldstein analysis. (The Feldstein model takes into account only redistribution from the young to the old.) If the assumption of perfect loan markets does not hold, an effect by way of redistribution can no longer be ruled out, and the impact may well be quite significant. If the redistribution is mainly from the rich to the poor, we would expect the savings ratio to fall as a result.

Professor Pauly commented that it is rather difficult to argue with success, as Professor Feldstein's model seems to have predicted fairly well against the empirical facts in his sample. But these good results are somewhat surprising. Implicit within the Feldstein model is an assumption of a political equilibrium, so that savers can base their decisions on present social security benefits and taxes. This may well not be reasonable. At least in the United States, real social security benefits and taxes have been changing. Thus, in the econometric model, one would want to substitute *expected* benefits and taxes for present benefits and taxes. Expected benefits and taxes could be estimated either on the basis of the rate of change in real benefits and taxes in the recent past or, possibly, by using demographic projections to predict changes in real benefits (taxes held constant) given the rate of flow of workers into, and retirees out of, the system. Such considerations may improve the explanatory power of the model.

Professor Frey wanted to stress that Professor Sandmo's third reason for compulsory social security may in fact be the dominant political reason. Particularly in European countries, the argument for social security often proceeds on the basis of a 'merit–want' case against consumer myopia.

In response to this comment by Professor Frey, *Professor Sandmo* noted that, although myopia may be important as an explanation of the social security system, it may not be an important explanatory factor relative to the problem discussed by Professor Feldstein. In any case, it may be very difficult to introduce myopia as a separate explanatory factor.

Professor Sheshinski raised two points. First, are Professor Feldstein's assumptions of exogeneity sufficient to remove what appear to be potentially serious problems of simultaneity in his econometric analysis? Second, Professor

Sandmo's comments on the redistributive effects of social security as they affect savings deserve further emphasis. The degree of progressivity in net social security benefits clearly varies across the countries in Professor Feldstein's sample. From the theoretical analysis, it is clear that the various derivatives of individual behaviour with respect to the social security parameters change as income changes. Therefore, the redistributive effect should be considered, perhaps by including in the regressions such summary measures as the variance of net benefits.

Professor Klevorick stressed that much private saving is accounted for not by individuals acting on their own, but, rather, by individuals participating in group saving programmes such as private pension funds. How would this affect the Feldstein results, based as they are on a model of individual decision-making?

Dr Jeanjean wondered whether the rate of inflation should not be considered as an explicit variable. In Europe at least, an individual preparing for retirement, with a choice between private savings and a subscription to a public retirement plan, would be well advised to select the latter. Public retirement plans have much higher real rates of return, because pensions are reassessed according to a cost-of-living index. The steady inflation rate can be considered an important stimulant to the expansion of publicly funded old-age pension plans.

Professor Aaron raised several points about the empirical aspects of the Feldstein paper. First, the data are rather old, relating to the period 1954–60. In particular, growth rates and saving rates in that period still reflected residual effects from the Second World War. Would the results be different with more recent data? Second, how robust are the results if you exclude any one of the countries, in particular Japan? Japan is a real outlier, having a very high growth rate, very low incomes (relative to West European countries for the period in question), and extremely high saving rates. These facts may be due to the kind of relationship posited in the paper, but, more likely, they are due to some other special characteristics of Japan. Would the results have been the same without Japan? Third, as Professor Sheshinski noted, there may be serious simultaneity problems in the econometric results, particularly between savings and the rate of growth. The rate of growth really is driving the savings regressions very heavily when one looks at standard errors, yet simultaneity between these two variables may be quite important.

Professor Stiglitz further elaborated on potential simultaneity in the Feldstein model. Social security will affect not only the saving rate, but also its feedbacks into wage rates and the rate of interest. It may be reasonable to argue that these feedbacks can be neutralised by monetary policy, but, then, one ought explicitly to introduce into the analysis money (or, what is essentially the equivalent, nontax funding of the social security programme).

Professor Feldstein thanked Professor Sandmo and the other discussants for their useful and stimulating comments on his paper. In response to Professor Frey on the question of consumer myopia, Professor Feldstein noted that the empirical evidence presented in this and in another paper of his tends to support Professor Sandmo's suspicion that this factor may not be a very important determinant of changes in savings behaviour with social security. In a study of the United States data, there appears to be an almost dollar-for-dollar replacement of compulsory social security savings for private savings. Professor Feldstein noted that a number of people had emphasised the effect of redistribution on savings and said that the only defence he had for not trying to take this into account in the international work was the lack of available data. However, he noted that one would hope this to be a second-order effect. The fact that, across the sample of countries, saving rates vary from a low of 7 per cent to a high of 21 per cent gives some reason for believing that the redistributive effect may not be of very great importance.

Professor Feldstein agreed with Professor Pauly that it would be desirable to build expected payments and taxes into the analysis, and he agreed that simultaneous-equation bias may be a problem as well. In response to Professor Aaron, he too felt that Second World War effects might have biased his results. He did note that the bias due to Japan's atypical economic history might not have been too serious, as all observations were weighted by each country's population. On Professor Stiglitz's suggestion that interest rates ought to be included in the savings equation, Professor Feldstein wondered what interest rate one should use for international comparisons. And Dr Jeanjean's concern about inflation was directed, in part, to this question. Professor Feldstein argued that the only reason why inflation matters is, presumably, that interest rates do not sufficiently adjust to maintain real rates. To get real rates, one must specify anticipated inflation rates, and he conjectured that this may be the reason why, in most domestic studies of savings, interest-rate variables prove insignificant. As a final point of comparision, Professors Feldstein and Khachaturov exchanged social security and savings figures for the United States and the USSR. In the United States, private wealth is three times GNP, while, in the USSR, private wealth is about one-quarter of GNP. As a fraction of wages, old-age social security benefits in the USSR substantially exceed those in the United States. The two facts provide additional, though still tentative, evidence of the depressing effect of social security on private savings.

Discussion of Patrick Jeanjean, 'A Social Security System and Short-Term Economic Policy'

Professor Lengyel complimented Dr Jeanjean for exploring an important topic in a sophisticated, but clear, manner, and offered two general comments on the paper. First, current simulation models of social security systems are, at this point, apolitical. Random shocks to the economy are analysed within a given structure of social security taxes and benefits. But this is clearly unrealistic, as Dr Jeanjean recognises. Governments will respond to macro-economic forces that worsen the position of the insured by irreversibly improving the benefit package. How can these 'political' reactions be built into such simulation models? One alternative would be to develop predictions by iterative collaborations between economists and policy-makers. A prediction is made and policy-makers are asked to respond (or to 'guess' a response) to the economic change. The new social security policy specification is then fed into the economic model and new predictions are generated. A favoured policy or time-path of policies can then be specified. Clemenceau once said that war is too serious to be left to the generals. Perhaps, too, social security is too important to be left to either economists or politicians alone. Second, Professor Lengyel noted that Dr Jeanjean's model is a short-run macro model. However, social-security policy has important long-run policy implications, which also will require sophisticated analysis. Though our macro forecasting models may be less accurate for long-run projections, order-of-magnitude long-run predictions can, and should, be made.

Professor Reviglio noted that, in addition to those mentioned in Dr Jeanjean's study, there have recently been other studies of the relationship of social security to short-term economic fluctuations. Their main conclusion is that, for many European countries, social security taxes and benefit payments are the major stabilisation policy tool. In addition, Professor Reviglio asked why Dr Jeanjean did not use social security contributions as a policy instrument for stabilisation.

Dr Jeanjean agreed with Professor Lengyel that there is no effective 'recall' of benefit improvements in the social security system. However, it is important to know the 'pure economic effects' of government decisions on the financing and on the level and distribution of social security benefits. Second, in response to Professor Reviglio, Dr Jeanjean said that the intention of his paper was not to consider a full list of the stabilisation instruments available through the social security system, but, rather, to compare the actual social security system in France with a policy alternative that had no stabilising effect. The conclusion was that the system did not make a great deal of difference to the stability of the overall economy. Therefore, one cannot justify the present social security system in France on the basis of its stabilisation of macro-fluctuations.

Discussion of Franco Reviglio, 'Redistribution through Social Security: A Lesson From Italy'

Professor Hochman introduced the discussion of the Reviglio paper by thanking the author for providing a useful description of the Italian social security system. Professor Hochman then offered three comments. To begin with, in response to the results presented in section II of the paper, he stated that Professor Reviglio had done nothing to discuss the secondary distributional effects of the social security system – effects resulting from the fact that non-neutralities, relative to the appropriate incidence, have significant behavioural implications, particularly when the contribution rate is as high as it is in Italy. Because Professor Reviglio concentrates entirely on the primary distributional effects, he fails, in this section of the paper, to add significantly to what we already know.

In section III he presents his main results. One of the interesting conclusions is that, for a variety of reasons, there appears to be a substantial geographical redistribution from the North to the 'Mezzogiorno'. However, this redistribution may be spurious. The in-payments credited to the North may be derived from workers who have migrated from Southern Italy, workers who, upon retirement, will return to the South, which is then debited for the pensions that these workers receive. Professor Hochman's primary criticism of the Reviglio paper was that it contains no explicit normative model that allows us to evaluate separately the performance of the social security system in terms of its insurance and redistributive objectives. Depending on which of these objectives applies, the programme and the incidence patterns that would be optimal are clearly very different. One wishes, then, that Professor Reviglio had made some effort to distil from legislative debate, or from some other source, some concept of what the applicable objective function really is in the Italian context, and that he had then discussed the observed outcomes relative to this standard. The paper is descriptive, with little theoretical content, and therefore is less interesting to someone whose concern is with social security generally than it is to someone concerned with the Italian case in particular. Yet, even without any formal model, we can still observe from the Reviglio paper that the outcome of Italian social security is one that serves neither the principle of intertemporal or lifetime redistribution nor the usual principles of social justice implicit in the call for equalising redistribution. In this sense, the Italian situation does not seem to be very different from that prevailing elsewhere.

Professor Sergio Bruno commented on the apparently high rate of social security tax payrolls found in Italy. Three reasons can be given for this. First, social security payments include medical care, with almost everybody participating in the health services sector of the programme. Second, with so many public agencies involved in the programme, there are very high administrative costs. Finally, and perhaps most importantly, the Italian economy is marked by a very low participation rate of the population in the labour force. The reason why this participation rate is so low and continues to decline are not altogether clear, but consideration of the features of the Italian economy may shed some light on this issue. In general, Italy's economy does not seem able to supply a sufficient number of job opportunities. This tendency is particularly strong in the underdeveloped regions of the South. Occupational difficulties affect the more aged workers more strongly, and, as a result, lower the average age of retirement. This lack of job opportunities may also explain why the number of disabled persons per capita is so much higher in the South than it is in the North.

Professor Khachaturov offered some observations on the USSR social security system. There are no contributions from workers and the employees to the social security system. At the same time, the social security payments are rather high. In the USSR there are now more than 40 million pensioners, who receive, each year, about 20 thousand million roubles (1 rouble = US $1·25). Retirement benefits are available from the age of 60 for males and 55 for females. Workers also receive other benefits – for example, rent reductions and cheaper transportation. It is difficult to estimate the total value of the services involved. Payments for sick leave total about 7 thousand million roubles per year. One might also wish to add the social costs of health care and education, because they are free in the USSR. The payments for public health are about 13 thousand million roubles and twice that for education. The total cost of pensions and all social services comes to about 66 thousand million roubles a year – about 21 per cent of the national income. Payment for these social services comes from funds received by the State from industry, commerce, savings banks, and taxation. It may be concluded, then, that the system of social benefits is a good deal simpler in the USSR than in Western countries, and, therefore, that many of the problems that the Western economies experience as regards social security are absent from the USSR.

Professor Lengyel pursued the question of the role of social security as a determinant of the final distribution of income. His comments were restricted to the worker–employee population, whose income is almost entirely derived from wages and from social benefits. Our starting observation must be that wage incomes and social benefits are first aggregated and redistributed within the smallest income and consumption communities, i.e. in households. Thus, in deriving judgements on how well people live, we must, in the final analysis, consider not only wage incomes, but also (a) the number, and the total earnings of earners in the household, (b) the number of persons who have to live on those earnings, and (c) the redistributive effect of social benefits. It follows from the principle of distribution according to work that those who perform more successful, effective and useful activities and, thus, give more to society, should receive a greater share of the total sum of material goods and services. But it is possible that, in spite of relatively high wage earnings, members of families bearing a greater burden in the activity of labour-force reproduction and the maintenance of the aged have, as a rule, less purchasing power than others have. Social security payments can be an important force for correcting such inequities.

As an analytical base for such policies, the following formula is used in

Hungary for measuring the sources of income inequality and for reassuring the redistributive effects of social security:

$$\frac{I}{P} = \left(\frac{W}{a}\right)\left(\frac{a}{p}\right)\left(\frac{p}{P}\right)\left(\frac{W+S}{W}\right)\left(\frac{I}{W+S}\right)$$

where I = the total of disposable incomes,
P = the total number of persons (or consumption units),
W = wages and salaries (income and work),
a = economically active persons,
p = the number of persons able to work, irrespective of their age and of whether they are earners, and
S = social benefits in cash (pensions, sick pay, family allowances, scholarships, other grants, and subsidies).

All the key elements in the equation may be interpreted in economic terms.

The first term, W/a, computes the average level of wages and salaries; the second term, a/p, defines the 'economic' determinants of family employment, while the third term, p/P, describes the 'demographic' determinants of employment. The fourth term, $(W + S)/W$, describes the impact of social benefits in cash, and the fifth term, $I/(W + S)$, shows to what extent the total of disposable family incomes exceeds the sum of incomes from work and from social benefits. The formula may be used as a tool for static or for dynamic analysis. By taking the derivatives of the logarithms of the individual term in the equation, we can calculate the relative importance of each term on the overall change in I/P, either through time or across groups.

From the Hungarian perspective, changes in the third, fourth and fifth terms are the most interesting. These terms show what effects demographic changes, on the one hand, and the offsetting impact of social security payments, on the other, have on inequality. There are two points to be emphasised here. First, the greater the social benefits in cash and in kind, the smaller will be the inequality in incomes resulting from demographic differences (earners–dependents ratio) across families. Second, and consequently, social security plays an important role in protecting the income-distribution principle that the purchasing power of families should be determined by the differences in the quantity, quality and social importance of work performed.

In response to the comments, *Professor Reviglio* noted his agreement with Professor Hochman on the importance of considering the secondary redistribution effects of social security policies. However, the data in Italy are extremely poor and, thus, estimation of good behavioural models is virtually impossible. A sound analysis of the secondary redistributional effects that arise because of individual adjustments to social security and other public programmes is virtually impossible, given our data base. Moreover, it has to be recalled that, as Professor Beckerman has recently stressed in a paper prepared for the OECD, satisfactory analysis of the problem of feedback from the social security programmes has so far defied solution; it would require a difficult econometric analysis within the framework of a general equilibrium model.

On Professor Hochman's second point, Professor Reviglio stressed that his paper was not aimed at describing the objectives of social security policy, but at assessing its efficiency *vis-à-vis* certain objectives, such as vertical redistribution, horizontal equity, and redistribution to the South. The analysis showed that the amount and the direction of redistribution seems often to have been determined by chance or by pressure groups, because it violates both vertical and horizontal equity. The implicit normative model supposed in the paper was defined on an *a priori* basis: social security programmes should conform to horizontal equity and attain vertical redistribution in the correct direction (from the rich to the poor). The amount of vertical redistribution to be reached was not assumed on an *a priori* basis, but was assessed in the paper without implying that it complies with the applicable function in the Italian context. This function cannot be distilled from legislative debate or from official documents, but only from the direct observed outcome resulting from a very complex and heterogeneous legislation.

In response to the comments of Professor Bruno, Professor Reviglio disagreed with the speculation that administrative costs are a major reason why social security payments assume such a comparatively large portion of GNP for Italy. If we look at government budgets, we in fact find that administrative costs are not a significantly larger percentage of total social security expenditures in Italy than they are in other countries. Professor Reviglio did agree with Professor Bruno's comments on the likely source of the large disability payments in the South. Many workers in the South were not covered by the general pension programme. Thus, the disability pension programme was used, for these workers, as a substitute for the general programme. This fact largely explains why the rate of disability payments was much higher in the South than in the North.

Discussion of Eytan Sheshinski, 'The Supply of Communal Goods and Revenue Sharing'

Mr Bessière raised four questions on the Sheshinski analysis. First, how realistic is it to assume that the primary institutional difference between the central government and a local government is that the former has access to an income tax, while the latter is restricted to property taxation? Is this simply a statement about current practices, or is there an economic rationale for this division of tax instruments? Second, what exactly is the difference between Sheshinski's communal good and the more usual Samuelsonian public good? Third, can the model be extended to include an optimal determination of central government behaviour? In this extended framework, we could, perhaps, define an optimal mix of matching to lump-sum grants-in-aid. Fourth, is there a way of specifying in the model the often-observed decision by wealthy families to opt out of the public system and in favour of private provision – notably for education and recreation? If the consequence of such a process of abandonment is a decline in public services to the poor, as (perhaps most of) the rich prefer low public output and low taxes, does Sheshinski's model suggest any solution to this problem?

In an attempt to clarify the distinction between communal goods and Samuelsonian pure public goods, *Professor Vickrey* offered the following taxonomy of public services. Fig. E illustrates the two key dimensions for classifying public services. On the vertical axis we represent economies of

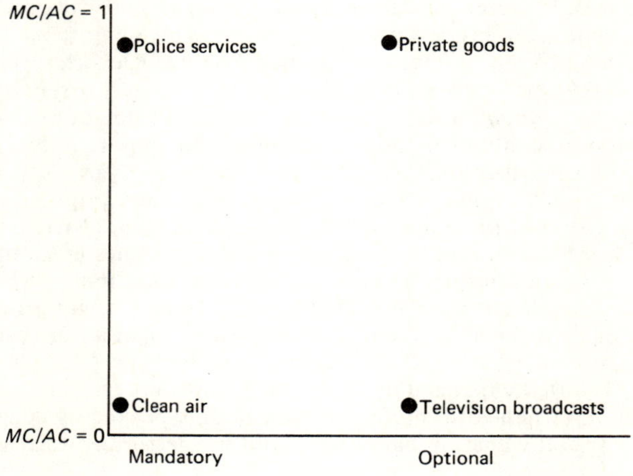

Fig. E

scale in service provision by the ratio of the marginal cost of one more user to the average cost of one more user (MC/AC), holding service quality (output per user) fixed. The horizontal axis represents the degree of 'option' that a user may have in consuming the good. A fully optional public service allows the consumer not to consume the good if he does not wish to do so. The other extreme is mandatory consumption, such as mosquito control or cleaner air. Examples of the important extremes in this taxonomy are private goods, clean air, television broadcasts, and, perhaps, police protection, which provides an example of a mandatory but congested public service.

Professor Stiglitz wondered if, in the Sheshinski construction of the problem, there were anything unique that characterised the key issues in fiscal decentralisation. Indeed, one is tempted to view this model as an exercise in choosing between an optimal lump-sum tax available at the 'federal' level and a distortionary property tax available at the 'local' level. There does not seem to be anything in the structure of the problem that assigns the nondistortionary tax to the federal level and the distortionary tax to the local level. If this presumption is correct, we can then draw on the work in the optimal-tax literature to derive Professor Sheshinski's basic conclusions. Clearly, there will be a role for federal aid as a mechanism for replacing the local distortionary tax by the nondistortionary federal lump-sum tax. What happens to the level of public output when nondistortionary taxes replace a distortionary tax is less clear. If the original distortion is small, or if the price elasticity of demand for public services is constant (as in Professor Sheshinski's analysis), then his conclusions hold. In any case, the point to be stressed is that the Sheshinski analysis concentrates on only one, though an important, role for grants-in-aid improving the overall tax structure of a federalist political economy.

Professor Stiglitz offered two additional comments. First, in a voting model where households retain the option of dropping out of the public systems, household preferences for *public* services may not be single-peaked. Households may prefer both very low and very high levels of public services to output in the middle ranges. If preferences for outputs are not single-peaked, then a majority voting decision process need not produce a stable outcome. In such cases we may have to talk of local voting equilibria *à la* Klevorick and Kramer (see their 'Social Choice on Pollution Management: The *Genossenschaften'*, *Journal of Public Economics,* II, Apr 1973). Second, Professor Sheshinski's distinction between communal goods and Samuelsonian pure public goods is, though important in other contexts, irrelevant for his analysis, as he assumes that community population is fixed. By fixing community population, the degree of congestion of the public service becomes exogenous to his problem.

Professor Aaron noted that the Sheshinski model assumes no capitalisation effects on the price of housing, or, equivalently, that the supply of housing is perfectly elastic within the community. This is an unusual assumption, given the empirical facts for most local communities. How might a less than perfectly elastic supply of housing affect the Sheshinski conclusions?

Professor Klevorick expanded on Professor Stiglitz's suggestion of searching for local equilibria when voter preferences are double-peaked by suggesting that comparative-static analysis can, and should be, performed relative to these local equilibria.

Professor Inman made two comments on the specification adopted in the

Sheshinski paper. First, by limiting the analysis to one local community, much of what is of interest in grants-in-aid policy planning is lost. Intercommunity spillovers are neglected, as is the use of aid as a substitute tax-transfer mechanism for redistribution from the rich to poor living in rich, and to poor living in poor, communities. Second, the simple median-voter model adopted by Professor Sheshinski is a naïve, behavioural specification of local politics. Imperfect information and the fact that political activity is itself a public good imply less than full voter participation. As a minimum, then, a model of who votes is needed, as well as a demand model, to define each voter's preferred output. More likely, however, is a breakdown of the median-voter (Downsian) model altogether. If information is imperfect, then those who control the information channels are in a strong position to control local public-service allocations. This suggests that oligopoly bargaining models of political entrepreneurship and bureaucracy behaviour may offer more accurate specifications of the local response to grants-in-aid.

Professor Feldstein also urged Professor Sheshinski to extend his analysis to the multicommunity framework, but said that in so doing one introduces the difficulty of trying to model by households the pattern and effects of intercommunity migration. Each round of relocation by households will lead to alterations in public outputs and taxes in each community, prompting, in turn, another series of relocations. Whether this process ever converges to a stable configuration of public services and local taxation is not clear. Professor Feldstein suggested that another extention might be introduced more easily. There is no compelling reason for believing that only income defines voter tastes for public outputs and that the median voter must necessarily be in the median position of the income distribution. The model might be extended to a bivariate distribution of voter preferences – for instance, over income and the number of school-age children. Finally, Professor Feldstein requested Professor Sheshinski to clarify the result in section VII where a progressive redistribution of income results in a reduction of public output.

In reply, *Professor Sheshinski* turned first to the questions posed by Mr Bessière. First, on the distinction between Samuelsonian pure public goods and communal goods, Professor Sheshinski stressed that pure public goods provide a flow of consumer services that is independent of the number of users, while communal goods provide a flow of services that is reduced as the number of users increases. Communal goods admit the possibility of congestion. Second, Mr Bessière's questions on the allocation of tax instruments between the central and local fiscs, and on the possibility of optimising the performance of the central government, are both, in part, related to the issue of an optimal federal structure. The grants-in-aid issue examined in the present paper is but a small part of this far broader and deeper question. Professor Sheshinski argued that, in facing this problem of an optimal federal structure, one might wish to frame the exercise as a question of optimal organisational design where preference information and resources must flow from constituents to decision-makers and service outputs must be moved from decision-makers to constituents. Decision-makers may be organised in a hierarchical fashion using a decentralised structure with rewards or punishments (grants-in-aid). Alternatively, services may be provided directly by the central body.

In response to Mr Bessière's fourth question – the problem of the rich leaving the local service sector – Professor Sheshinski argued that the final equilibrium position may fundamentally depend on the initial level of public services. If the initial level of output is high, public services are normal goods, and, if the tax schedule is not 'too progressive', then the rich will choose to use the public system and vote for continued or, perhaps, for increased public services. If the initial output is low, or if the tax schedule is strongly progressive, the rich may turn to private providers and vote for zero public outputs. As Professor Stiglitz pointed out with regard to the possibility that people will choose not to use the public-sector services, the median-voter model may admit only local equilibria.

Finally, in answer to Professor Feldstein's request for elaboration of the results in section VII, Professor Sheshinski explained that, with a progressive redistribution of income, voters whose incomes had declined would demand fewer local services, while those whose incomes had increased would demand more services. If the median income position experiences a decline in income, as is the case in the example in section VII, then the preferred level of public outputs will decline. We may therefore face an important policy trade-off not previously noticed in the literature. Local public services often have a 'merit–want' character, so that society values an increase in the provision of them to the poor. If so, then a progressive income redistribution favourable to the income position of the poor may also produce a socially undesirable change in local public output levels. Clearly, a closer examination of this trade-off is needed.

Discussion of Joseph Stiglitz, 'The Theory of Local Public Goods'

Professor Milleron began the discussion of the Stiglitz paper with a summary and an alternative formulation of the main results.

The point of departure of the Stiglitz analysis is the premise that, with sufficient mobility of the economic agents, the well-known difficulty of incorrect preference revelation for public goods might disappear. With local public goods, agents have the option of moving to communities that provide the level of public goods that is best suited to their own preferences. The main concern of Professor Stiglitz's paper is to examine the validity of this argument. To see whether such an argument is correct we must (a) try to define adequate concepts of equilibrium, (b) investigate whether these equilibria have optimality properties, and (c), if not, try to define policies to improve their quality.

Professor Milleron then examined Professor Stiglitz's one-community case in somewhat greater detail, so as to clarify the key role of nonconvexities in the analysis. For just *one island*, the problem of choosing an optimal level of population and a level of production of public good may be written:

$$\max U(c, G)$$

$$Nc + G = f(N) \tag{1}$$

(Since land is given, we have written: $f(N) = F(N, T)$.) Here the 'budgetary constraint' appears in the (c, G) space as a straight line, depending on the value of the parameter N. We can therefore find the envelope of this straight line.

The point of tangency is defined by the following equations:

$$c = f'(N) \tag{2}$$

and

$$G = f(N) - Nf'(N) \tag{1'}$$

Relation (2) is obtained by taking the derivative of (1) with respect to the parameter N. (1$'$) is obtained from (1), given (2). Equations (2) and (1$'$) define the equation of the envelope, where the co-ordinates of a point in the (c, G) space are defined as a function of N.

We can now examine the shape of the envelope. Suppose that f has the form shown in Fig. F. f' is a decreasing function (concavity of f); when $N \to 0$, $f' \to +\infty$; and, when $N \to +\infty$, $f \to +\infty$ and $f' \to 0$. These assumptions are implicit in the Stiglitz analysis. We see that, when $N \to 0$, $c \to +\infty$ and $G \to 0$; and that, when $N \to +\infty$, $c \to 0$ and $G \to +\infty$.

The function $G(c)$, just defined, is a convex function, since, from (2);

$$dc = f''(N)dN$$

and, from (1$'$)

$$dG = [f'(N) - f'(N) - Nf''(N)]\,dN$$

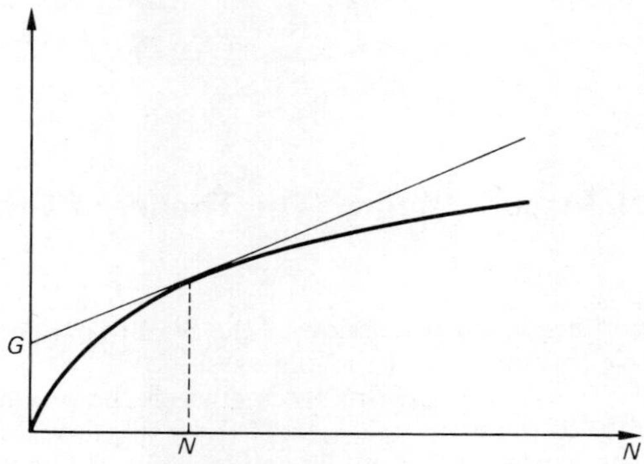

Fig. F

so that we have

$$\frac{dG}{dc} = -N$$

Thus, dG/dc is a decreasing function of N and an increasing function of c (since f' is decreasing). The envelope of the budgetary constraint therefore looks like the curve in Fig. G.

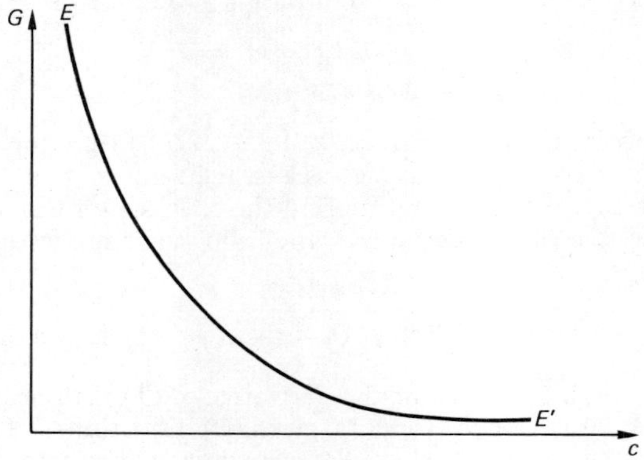

Fig. G

If, *given N*, we want to maximise U, we have to draw the straight line corresponding to the value of N (it is tangent to $E\,E'$) and maximise U along this line. This is a concave programming problem, as illustrated in Fig. H.

The solution is given by the equation

$$\frac{U_1}{N} = \frac{U_2}{1} \tag{3}$$

which is equation (12.3) of the Stiglitz paper.

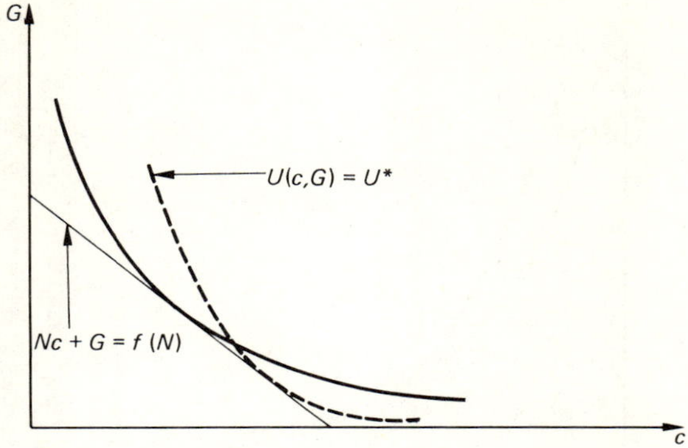

Fig. H

Alternatively, *given G*, maximising the utility function with respect to N is also a concave programming problem. The optimal solution is the point M, where the horizontal line corresponding to G intersects the curve $E\,E'$ (see Fig. I). Since M is a point of $E\,E'$, equation (1′) is satisfied, which is equation (12.2) of the Stiglitz paper.

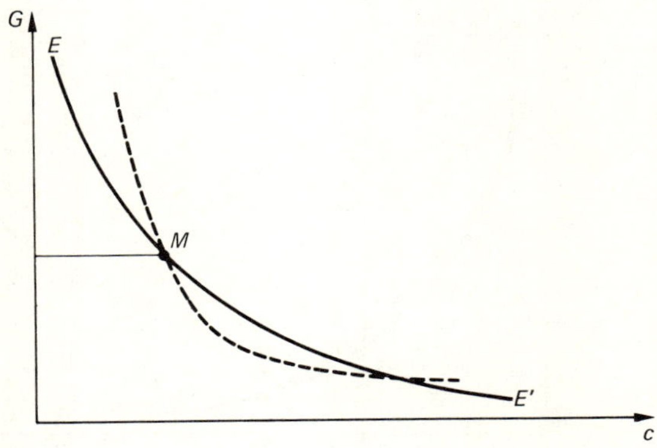

Fig. I

Note, however, that if we wish to find the *optimum optimorum* point – i.e. the maximum of U, given (1) – it is clear that this problem is not a concave programming problem. Four cases may be considered.

(i) There is only one maximum, defined by the condition that the indifference curve is tangent to the $E\,E'$ curve. Such a case may occur if there is a strong enough complementarity between c and G (see Fig. J). In such a case, the results of the paper are correct and the co-ordinates of M are defined by (2), (1′) and (3).

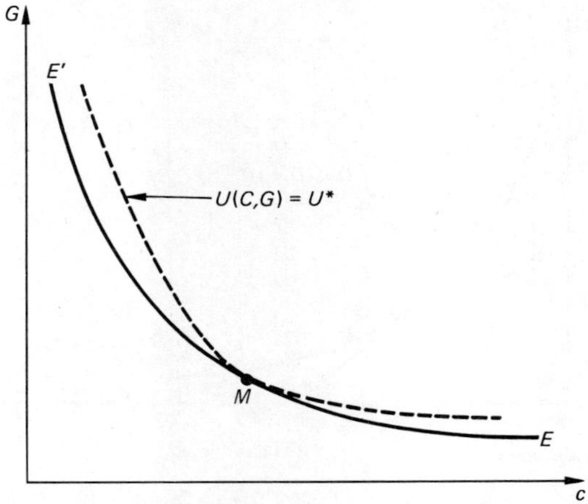

Fig. J

(ii) There may exist several maxima corresponding to the same level of utility (see Fig. K). This case has also been considered by Professor Stiglitz (see his Fig. 12.2).

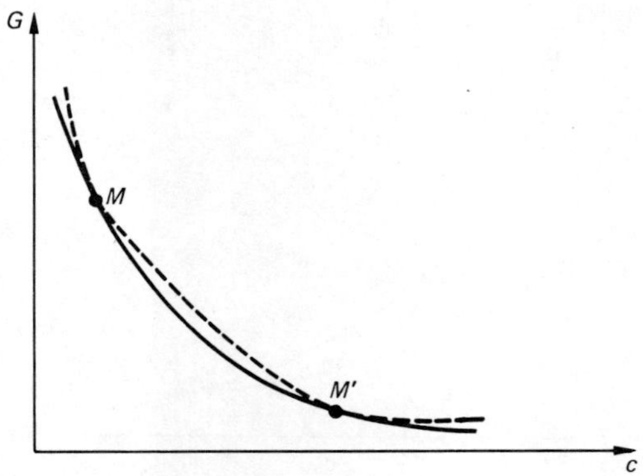

Fig. K

(iii) If there is a large degree of substitutability between c and G, such that the point of tangency is a *minimum* and not a maximum of U (see Fig. L). This result has a reasonably intuitive interpretation. Since there is a high degree of substitutability between c and G, it is always better to have a very low population (and a high c) or a large population (and a high G).

(iv) Finally, for some reasonable indifference curves there may be no tangency point at all. The optimal population may be zero (see Fig. M) or infinity (see Fig. N).

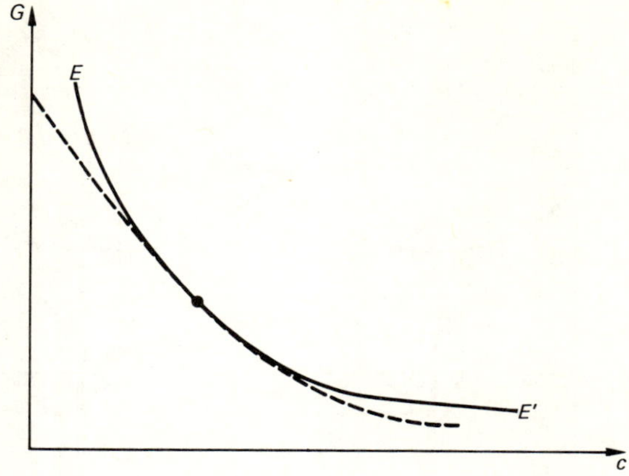

Fig. L

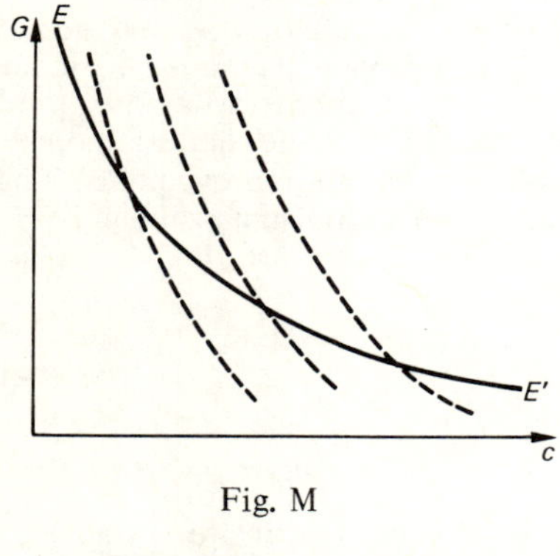

Fig. M

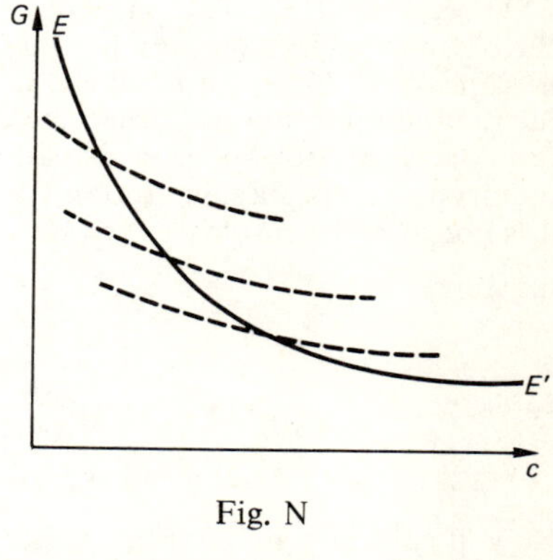

Fig. N

Cases (iii) and (iv) were not considered in detail in the Stiglitz paper but they remain very real and important possibilities. For example, using case (iii), one can describe a Pareto-inferior but locally stable equilibrium. If the N^o corresponds to the population at point M in Fig. L and $\overline{N}/2 < \overline{N}^o < \overline{N}$, ($N$ = total regional population), then one may achieve the Pareto-inferior equilibrium shown by point A in Fig. P.

Professor Milleron offered a number of other comments and questions on the Stiglitz paper. On section II of the paper, he commented that, the result that is given on the nonexistence of the core appears to be highly dependent on the choice of a 'nice case' corresponding to Fig. J above. Also, with regard to section II, he asked if there were any connection between Professor Stiglitz's concept of an 'equilibrium with land developers' and the concept of a 'public competitive equilibrium' such as defined by Foley (see D. Foley, 'Resource Allocation and the Public Sector', *Yale Economic Essays,* Spring 1967).

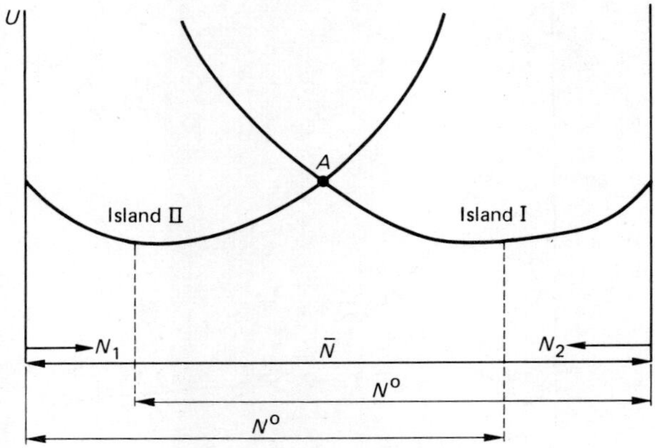

Fig. P

In section III, where community sizes are not given but are endogenous to the optimising problem, the Benthamite social welfare function W, may not be concave with respect to all the variables of the problem. There is no guarantee that an optimum will in fact be defined without further restrictions on the problem. Professor Milleron also attempted to clarify the role that intercommunity transfers play, in section III, in establishing Pareto improvements. When it is not feasible to transfer private commodities our optimising problem is:

$$\text{maximise} \quad U(c_1, G_1)$$
$$\text{subject to} \quad \begin{cases} U(c_2, G_2) = U_2^* \\ N_1 c_1 + G_1 = f_1(N_1) \\ N_2 c_2 + G_2 = f_2(N_2) \\ N_1 + N_2 = \overline{N} \end{cases} \tag{4}$$

Now, if subsidies are allowed, S being the (negative, zero or positive) transfer from island 1 to island 2, the optimising problem becomes:

$$\text{maximise} \quad U(c_1, G_1)$$
$$\text{subject to} \quad \begin{cases} U(c_2, G_2) = U_2^* \\ N_1 c_1 + G_1 + S = f_1(N_1) \\ N_2 c_2 + G_2 - S = f_2(N_2) \\ N_1 + N_2 = \overline{N} \end{cases} \tag{5}$$

It is clear that the set of feasible programmes defined by (5) contains the set of feasible programmes defined by (4), so that the introduction of transfers can lead to a Pareto improvement.

On the work in section IV, Professor Milleron noted that one aspect of the nonconvexity problem is removed by Professor Stiglitz's assumption (with respect to labour) of a constant returns to scale production function. Such an assumption is equivalent to saying that each individual is endowed with 'one unit of manna'. Professor Milleron then asked two questions about Professor Stiglitz's analysis in this section. First, in the case in which there are more kinds of individuals than there are islands, the result on emptiness of the core seems to be strongly dependent on the assumption that utility is a decreasing function of only some of its arguments. It is known, however, that when utility is not nondecreasing with respect to all of its arguments, difficulties appear in proving the nonemptiness of the core in an economy with public goods. Is this result, then, really specific to the studied problem? Second, in the case of a continuum of individuals, are the necessary conditions (12.6) correct once we take into account the difficulties mentioned above with regard to non-convexities?

In conclusion, Professor Milleron felt that, in section V, a more careful treatment of land ownership rights would have been helpful. Sometimes land is privately owned and sometimes it is publicly appropriated. In each case, it is difficult to see how the results are affected by the change from one case to the other. Professor Milleron ended his remarks by thanking the author for so thorough an introduction to such a difficult analytic problem. However, Professor Stiglitz's fine work notwithstanding, Professor Milleron felt that much work remains to be done in developing a general theory of local public goods.

Dr Kolm observed the conflict in the Stiglitz results between a just outcome where everyone has identical utilities, and the social-welfare maximising outcome where the optimal solution may require different utility levels on different islands. Free migration, while inefficient from a utilitarian point of view, may be optimal for a just society.

Professor Stern underlined an interesting point that had been made in Professor Stiglitz's analysis, but had perhaps not been emphasised enough. In the Stiglitz model, income segregated configurations are possible equilibria, but, depending on the parameters, so are integrated configurations. A further point, however, is that individuals may value the social integration of income classes. When would there be likely to arise a stable heterogeneous solution with this motivation included in the behavioural analysis? In those instances where segregated solutions are still the only stable outcomes, despite individual preferences for integration, how can society enforce or induce an optimum if this involves an integrated community?

Professor Klevorick explored in somewhat greater detail the result, in the Stiglitz paper, that without zoning we should observe a fall in the provision of public services in rich towns, thereby excluding the poor. This conclusion is not obvious. The actual outcome depends on a wider range of facts than are considered in the Stiglitz model. The Stiglitz result would lead me to expect that, the less the shift in local property taxation, the lower the poor's share of the fiscal base, and the greater the degree of substitutability between private consumption (for instance, private education, recreation, and protection) and public services.

Professor Inman extended Professor Klevorick's comment by noting that some communities may have locationally unique barriers to the entry of the poor, so that the loss of zoning as an exclusion device may have little effect on their provision of public output. For example, one would expect that rich communities far from the main employment centres for the poor (in regions with poor public transportation) would be less vocal in the fight for zoning than would rich communities near the main employment centres. Thus, the removal of zoning may permit a few (unemployed) poor to filter into the fringe rich towns without occasioning the fall in public output envisaged in the Stiglitz model. However, output may still fall in communities nearer the employment centre. For the 'lucky' poor who enter the fringe towns, a favourable redistribution occurs. Whether this gain is sufficient to justify the inefficiencies generated in the inner suburban ring remains to be seen.

Professor Pauly noted that, without the integration motive suggested by Professor Stern's comments, zoning for income (or taste) segregation will always promote an efficient outcome. The only consequence of abolishing zoning will be to permit an (efficiency costly) redistribution of income. It should be noted that, in the case of identical tastes, zoning is required for efficiency only when the local tax base is proportional to wealth. Were communities able to use head taxes, zoning would not be needed for efficiency.

On the existence of equilibria, Professor Pauly felt that even the pessimistic Stiglitz analysis may have understated the problem. In another paper, Professor Pauly has shown that, for identical individuals, when $\bar{N}$ is the total population and N_O is the optimal community size, the core will be empty if $\bar{N}/N_O$ is not an integer. The reason is quite simple. If some people are left out of optimally sized towns, utilities will not be same for both the excluded (in too-large or too-small towns) and the included. Such structurally required differences in utilities imply that no equilibrium can exist. In the case where tastes for public services differ, equilibrium again is unlikely to occur. Imagine that the distribution of tastes for public service has initially been satisfied, and that in each community – which initially satisfies a segment of this distribution – public output levels are set so as to maximise land rents. If this initial configuration is an equilibrium, rents must be equal across all communities. Will this supposed equilibrium be stable? The answer is no. Each community can initially increase its land rents by moving towards the mode of the distribution of preferred output levels. But will an allocation with all communities at the mode be a stable equilibrium? No, because then one community would be able to jump to a tail of the distribution of preferences, attract new residents from communities at the node, and, thereby, increase land rents. The process is a 'cobweb' spiralling about the mode, with no equilibrium provision of local public outputs.

Professor Feldstein introduced into the analysis of equilibrium for local public goods an additional element that may act as a stabilising force in the Stiglitz and Pauly models – the capitalisation of fiscal advantages into land prices. Such capitalisation acts as 'tax' for entry into fiscally advantaged towns or 'islands', or as a 'bribe' for entry into the fiscally less-favoured communities.

Professor Tulkens wondered whether the Stiglitz framework might usefully be interpreted as a search for a Lindahl equilibrium. Specifically, what is the relationship between land prices in the capitalisation model and the usual Lindahl tax prices?

In the same spirit, *Dr Guesnerie* felt that the theory of the core, particularly as it applies to Lindahl equilibria, might provide a useful framework for understanding some of Stiglitz's results. A departing member is one who, at the same time, has an incentive to block the particular allocation being proposed in his community.

Professor Michael Bruno suggested that the basic model and some of the nonconvexity problems could be further clarified by resorting to the concept of the 'factor-price frontier'. Using Professor Stiglitz's notation, Q = output, T = land, N = workers ($Q = F(N, T)$, a constant-returns production function), G = public good, and c = consumption per capita = $(Q - G)/N$.

Maximisation of c leads to $G = F_T T$ – see Stiglitz's equation (12.2). If we vary G and look for alternative values of max c, we obtain a transformation curve between G and c that is downward-sloping and concave. It gives the technologically optimal combinations of G and c. If we now add a concave utility maximand $U(c, G)$, we run into some of the multiple (or no) equilibria problems that Professor Stiglitz and Milleron have pointed out.

If we divide G by T, which is assumed fixed, and note that in the optimum $c = w = F_N$ (the marginal productivity of workers), it becomes clear that the $c - G$ curve is nothing but the factor-price frontier (FPF) in terms of the land rental rate $P = F_T$ and the wage rate $w = F_N$.

This formal identity can now be used to point out that the properties of the $c - G$ curve are those of the FPF and have nothing to do with G being a public good. In particular, there is nothing inherent that should make for a nonconvex curve. Its present shape comes from the one-sector production model used. Thus, suppose that G and c are produced by a two-sector technology with the G sector being less labour–land intensive in production than the c sector. In that case, the FPF (and, therefore, the $c - G$ curve) will be convex, and some of the above nonconvexity problems would presumably not arise.

For instance, in the special two-sector fixed-proportions case with coefficient matrix

$$\begin{bmatrix} n_c n_g \\ l_c \, l_g \end{bmatrix}$$

the curve will become $$c = \frac{T - l_g G}{T n_c - M_o G}$$

and its curvature $$\frac{d^2 c}{dG^2} = \frac{2 T l_c n_g}{(T n_c - M_o G)^3} \cdot M_o$$

where $M_o = \det M \gtrless 0$, according to the relative factor intensities.

Professor Stiglitz thanked the discussants for their elaborations of his analysis. He found all of their comments useful extensions of reinterpretations of his results. He concluded by responding directly to Professor Bruno's question. The nonconvexity described in the paper and so nicely in the Milleron diagrams is, indeed, an inherent characteristic of the problem. It arises from the fact that the marginal cost of providing the public good to one additional user is zero. There is no escaping the problems of nonconvexity with such a public-good technology.

Discussion of William Vickrey, 'The City as a Firm'

Dr Guesnerie began the discussion of the Vickrey paper by noting that the arguments that it presents are very much within the tradition of Walras, Hotelling and Alais. Professor Vickrey's theorem, as developed in his paper, goes further than the usual neoclassical arguments in that it argues that land-rent revenues are not only a convenient way of financing fixed costs, but, in addition, fit this task exactly. We must not, however, misinterpret this argument. The fact that the land rents equal the total intramarginal residuals is not a decisive argument on land taxes, independent of Hotelling's reasoning about them. On the other hand, the equality of land rents to the intramarginal residuals does assure the consistency of the first-best arguments for land taxes, as emphasised by Hotelling. If this equality is not true, the other, second-best means of financing fixed costs must be found – for example, income taxes. Such taxes will have incentive effects and will involve deadweight losses. In effect, then, the Vickrey argument completes the case for land taxes as a first-best policy prescription. This is the main interest of the paper.

The Vickrey analysis does, however, leave several questions open. In addition to the limitations mentioned by Professor Vickrey himself, Dr Guesnerie noted three points that, in his opinion, are not totally clarified by the analysis. First, does the Vickrey analysis (corresponding to that presented in the diagram) generalise to the multi-city case? Second, the analysis is not convincing in its attempt to transcribe the model of firm competition to the problem of competition among cities. It is not clear that the results of marginal costs equalling average costs would automatically prevail in the city-competition case. Third, the extension of the Vickrey argument to the k-dimension city is impressive. However, Dr Guesnerie felt that the conclusion was so general that it ought to be expressed and demonstrated through a more basic line of argument. Finally, Dr Guesnerie thought that it might be useful to contrast Professor Vickrey's approach with those adopted in recent papers on the 'optimal city'. The originality of the model built here is that it considered a city as a set of linear activities with a fixed cost. It turns out that there is no possibility of technological choice – though this may not matter a great deal – but the model also excludes the possibility of consumer choice. This omission may be much more serious. Indeed, the point of the optima-city models is to give full play to consumer choice on such central activities as housing and household location. Elaborations in this direction would be a useful extension of Professor Vickrey's interesting and important work on the 'city as a firm'.

Professor Rey wondered if Professor Vickrey would elaborate on the most effective means of extracting land rents from land-owners. Would there be any disincentive effects attached to such taxation?

Professor von Weizsäcker wondered whether the reason why Professor Vickrey felt that he could generalise his results was that we know from the theory of the firm that total cost is equal to total revenue, so that no rent remains. Therefore, something similar should exist here in the theory of the city as a firm. Is this correct? To reverse Professor Vickrey's theme, might not work on the theory of the firm gain substantially by viewing the firm as a city? The firm clearly faces many of the problems that a city such as Professor Vickrey's faces. There can be public goods, congestion, and economies of scale in organisational structures.

Professor Sheshinski raised an additional point for consideration in the Vickrey model – the question of congestion costs as the city's population grows. For small cities, the Vickrey economies of scale are likely to predominate, but, as city size increases to exhaust these 'private' economies of scale, we run into the problem of congestion and negative externalities in both the private and the public sector. This suggests that there may be an optimal city size in which these two factors balance each other so as to minimise the aggregate social cost per capita. This problem has been considered in recent papers by Mills and Solow, in which there is, in fact, found an optimal city size with these two effects balancing.

Professor Feldstein wondered whether horizontal inequities would result from the Vickrey proposals. One group of individuals may hold wealth in the form of land, while another group holds its wealth in non-land assets. While the Vickrey proposals may generate an efficient solution, they may, at the same time, generate a horizontal inequitable outcome by extracting the wealth of individuals who own land, but not of those who hold other assets.

In response to Professor Rey, *Professor Vickrey* said that the tax problem is, indeed, a delicate question of policy. As taxes begin to reach the full value of land rents, disincentive effects will appear. In the extreme case, in which taxes exceed the private entrepreneur's land rents, the State will find that the land will be abandoned. But there is a second problem associated with land-rent taxes, and that is the determination of the market value of the land. If property is not always sold on the open market, such calculations may be extremely difficult to make. An operative criterion is to determine the value in a way that will not be affected by the use to which the land is put. Ideally, one should establish market value in a 'standard state', defined, perhaps, as the state capable of supporting construction. In any case, the problem that Professor Rey has raised is a very difficult one, and Professor Vickrey doubted that policy would ever achieve the ideal state outlined for his optimal city.

On Professor Sheshinski's comment, Professor Vickrey noted that public goods and resident-related congestion could easily be incorporated into his model, as additional activities. However, for public goods to fit within the Vickrey framework they must be capable of being priced at marginal cost, and many public commodities simply cannot be priced, because exclusion is difficult.

In reply to Professor Feldstein, Professor Vickrey noted that his theorem is a timeless one. In the world of theory, the model applies *de novo*, so that the issue that Professor Feldstein raises is not applicable. In the real world of course, horizontal inequities may result as we move from our present tax system to a tax on land values. We should, therefore, make the transition as rapidly as possible, so as not to defer the efficiency impact. And, in principle, as we are making a change that increases efficiency, there is at least the theoretical possibility that the gainers will be able to compensate the losers completely. Moreover, in this case we can specifically identify the losers – a luxury not always available.

Professors Feldstein and *Klevorick* took exception to Professor Vickrey's response. First, Professor Klevorick doubted that the best policy was to move to land taxation as quickly as possible. A rapid move to land taxation may involve extraordinarily high transition costs, which a more moderate adjustment process phased over several years might avoid. Professor Feldstein questioned Professor Vickrey's compensation arguments. To be able to compensate the losers, you eventually have to buy the land from them, but the value of the land is the present value of the rents that you want to take away from them. In fact, therefore, if you buy the land, you have to give them back exactly what it is that you are trying not to let them have.

Professor Vickrey responded to Professor Klevorick by again emphasising his belief that, relative to efficiency gains, the transition costs of a rapid move to land taxation would be minimal. In response to Professor Feldstein, he replied that we are under no obligation to offer land-owners full compensation for their losses.

Discussion of Albert Breton and Anthony Scott, 'The Assignment Problem in Federal Structures'

Professor Pedone opened the discussion of the Breton and Scott paper and raised four questions about the analysis presented in it. First, are jurisdictions defined, in the assignment table, on the basis of historically given jurisdictions or do they comprise any institution to which a function can be potentially assigned? If the latter is the case (as it seems to be in the paper), then it is not clear (a) how one defines the set of possible jurisdictions, and (b) which criteria are used to select jurisdictions for inclusion in the assignment table. Second, even if we can compute the transactions associated with any particular assignment table, we may be faced with a table containing not a single equilibrium, but many equilibria. In such cases, how shall we choose among the different equilibria? Third, while it is true that allowing for multiple jurisdictions will always act to reduce the 'frustration costs' of political decision-making, the majority in the originally large jurisdiction may be so splintered in the multiple-jurisdiction case as never to see their policies adopted. Does Professor Breton see this as a problem? Finally, it is extraordinarily difficult to measure each of the transaction costs considered by the Breton and Scott analysis. What are the important determinants of the various costs of transactions? What is the relative importance of each of these costs in the assignment problem? How rapidly are the costs changing? And can the costs be defined without any reference to the revenue side, an aspect of the fiscal problem explicitly neglected in the Breton and Scott paper?

Professor Giardina also emphasised the need to integrate the revenue and expenditure sides of fiscal decisions when defining the assignment of fiscal functions. Indeed, how can one define citizen preferences for public services without expressing those preferences relative to some tax cost?

Professor Giardina was also sceptical of the assumption that the equilibrium assignment can be made independent of the levels of output of the assigned service. The various components of the transaction costs cannot generally be assumed to be independent of the level of output. Consider, for example, the costs of moving. One may reasonably suppose that, the greater the level of fiscal activity, the more people will be attracted or repelled by it. If so, then we shall observe increased mobility and greater costs of moving. Or consider negotiation costs. The evidence from the private sector leads us to expect negotiation costs to be an increasing function of the level of output – for example, legal costs rise as increased output requires more contracts. Search costs may also depend on output levels. Individual tax costs depend on the quantity (and/or quality) of public services. We may reasonably suppose, then, that, with the growth of the output level, it is increasingly to the individual's advantage to disguise his preferences. Therefore, the search costs to the government increase. Frustration costs or the costs of coercion are allowed to vary with output, but Breton and Scott assume that these costs are not relevant to the constitutional issue of assignment. Professor Giardina did not find this assumption acceptable. Constitutional decisions are not made at a simple point in time and valid for all time, but are, in fact, interlaced with the daily, operative decisions of government. Constitutional assignment decisions will involve frustration costs, just as output decisions do.

Professor Giardina found inadequate the Breton and Scott treatment of search costs. Their hypothesis that the assignment of a function to local governments may render the frequency distribution of preferences unimodal, and thus reduce the search costs, is valid only if the compatibility of public-goods preferences is the sole reason why families collect in particular communities. One may reasonably doubt, however, that this is the case.

Professor Giardina offered two final comments. First, it may be extremely difficult to define jurisdiction. The authors include in their definition all of the bodies that have responsibility for some function, a definition that includes electorally nonresponsible administrative bodies. But central governments often work through local administrative institutions with some responsibility to the local electorate. Are these agencies arms of the central jurisdiction or independent local jurisdictions? And how do we classify local agencies fully funded by central government grants-in-aid? Perhaps a good working criterion would be to define as independent jurisdictions only those agencies that have independent decision-making capacities. Second, Breton and Scott wish their model to be a positive one, but do not fully treat the problems of objectives and behaviour of the members of the constitutional assembly. Their paper may thus best be treated as an effort at a normative theory of federalism. As such, it is an important contribution.

Professor Frey suggested that, instead of minimising search costs, as the Breton and Scott analysis suggests, one ought perhaps to be interested in maximising these kinds of transactions. Economists tend to look at the process of political participation as a means to an end. In fact, it may be an end in itself. Thus, if one is interested in maximising such participation, one subsequently maximises the costs of such participation. In this same vein, we tend to view citizen political preferences as given, but it is more likely that these preferences are not well defined and given. Thus, the process of search – the process of political participation – becomes, in fact, the mechanism for defining tastes and preferences. Again, rather than minimise these costs, our interests here ought to be to provide information for preference formulation. This may be quite costly.

Professor Sergio Bruno raised two points. First, as Professor Giardina had pointed out, the assumption made by Breton and Scott that transaction costs are independent of the scale of output seems too restrictive. If one drops this assumption, then jurisdictional assignments will be a function of output levels. Second, the assignment of functions to a particular level may not be independent of the functions already handled by that level. There may be interdependencies and economies of agglomeration associated with the assignment of the function. This makes the problem a good deal more difficult. Rather than treating the assignment problem as simply a one-to-one matching of services to jurisdictions, we must now consider the matching of service combinations to jurisdictions. The number of policy alternatives increases tremendously.

Professor Inman offered the following comments on the Breton and Scott paper. The analysis is static and assumes a given technology and preferences. But the constitutional question of assignment cannot be treated as a timeless problem in a certain world. The assignment of functions will be designing governmental forms for 25 or 50 years from now. Uncertainties about technology and preferences over this time horizon should clearly be introduced into the formal analysis. If these uncertainties dominate the jurisdictional question, then we should have a high premium on flexibility, preferring the most decentralised structure possible, or a more centralised system with rules for facilitating changes in assignment. The central assignment problem in an uncertain world is to define the rules whereby jurisdictional functions can be smoothly altered as technologies and preferences change.

Professor Michael Bruno wondered about the predictive power of the Breton and Scott theory. Can the relevant transaction costs in fact be measured and incorporated into a behavioural specification? If one treats the Breton and Scott analysis as a behavioural specification, will not the noneconomic factors largely dominate the determination of government assignments? How do we specify such a model? And if one reads the Breton and Scott paper as a normative exercise, it is not at all clear that our objective should be one of minimising transaction costs.

Professor Sandmo said that he saw problems with the way the words 'equilibrium' and 'optimality' were used in the paper. Imagine a political system in which there are several electorally responsive decision-making bodies and a top constituent assembly that computes an optimum with respect to the minimisation of transactions costs. If there are interdependencies among the transaction costs of the various subgovernments, then an optimum would not necessarily be a political equilibrium, because the lower-level jurisdictions might try to change the allocation that the constituent assembly had determined.

In response to the various comments, *Professor Breton* first noted that it is quite easy to bring the tax function into the analytic framework of this paper. In the case of revenues, the assignment problem is to place tax bases at different jurisdictional levels. Such a model may also shed useful light on the design structure of grants-in-aids. Professor Breton agreed with Professor Frey that it would be useful to extend the analysis to consider levels of political participation as an additional objective in the model. But, for any given level of participation, it still makes sense to try to minimise the search costs associated with the extraction of voter preferences. Professor Breton again emphasised that the problem with which the paper was concerned was not the process of determining the level of public-goods outputs, but, rather, the question of what government jurisdiction should be *assigned* the problem of output determination. Thus, Professor Breton agreed with Professor Michael Bruno that the *overall* government objective should not be one of minimising costs (including transaction costs). But, for the assignment task, the minimisation of transaction costs can still be treated as a meaningful social objective.

For those who had criticised the assumption that transaction costs are independent of the level of output, Professor Breton mentioned that, in additional work being carried out by himself and Professor Scott, the conclusions do extend in a reasonably straightforward way to the more general case of transaction costs varying with public output. As has been pointed out, when transaction costs do vary with output, assignments will have to be adjusted when levels change. In response to Professor Sandmo's point, Professor Breton said that it is important to note that the transaction costs discussed in the paper are related to assignment tables. Since these tables are obviously not continuous, it is not clear that the discussion fits easily into the usual theory of equilibrium processes. This is a difficult problem, and the authors had not yet been able to tackle it.

In response to Professor Inman's question, Professor Breton said that he and Professor Scott were aware that their model is a timeless one. The applicability of the timeless model to a dynamic setting largely depends on the costs of assignment changes. If these costs are sizable, then Inman's objection is correct, and the analysis needs to be extended to handle such uncertainties. One possible extension along this line is the role that grants-in-aids can play in a second-best context to overcome any misassignment of functions. In a dynamic economy with high costs to reassignment, policy instruments such as grants may become the most viable policy alternative.

Discussion of Alain Bernard, 'Optimal Taxation and Public Production with Budget Constraints'

Professor Bradford introduced the Bernard paper by clarifying an important definitional difference between Dr Bernard's work and the usual optimal-tax literature. Of particular importance to him is the vector, denoted by u, of the social values of commodities. It is a concept new to this literature and deserves elaboration. Simply, u_i represents the increment to social welfare of adding one more unit of commodity i. All taxes are defined relative to this vector of social value of commodities. Dr Bernard also raises a subtle existence problem that to date has been neglected by the optimal-tax literature. Professor Bradford elaborated on it. From the optimisation of welfare we might well conclude that household 1 should have a positive income at an equilibrium welfare-maximising vector of prices. On the other hand, at this vector of prices, firm 1, which is owned by household 1, might produce a vector of outputs that causes it to earn a zero profit. At the optimum, therefore, household 1 is required to have a positive income, but firm 1 owned by household 1 must earn zero profits. These two characteristics of the optimum are incompatible and the problem has no solution. What can be done, however, is to get very 'close' to the solution (like trying to find the largest number less than 1) by selecting a production vector very close to the optimal production vector, such that the plane of the production frontier permits a positive profit for firm 1.

Professor Bradford concluded his comments by asking three questions for clarification. First, might Dr Bernard reinterpret those theorems where the operative price vector is the vector of social values of commodities? Second, in section III on marketable public goods, Dr Bernard assumes that individuals will be price-takers. But, if the commodities involved are Samuelsonian pure public goods, how can the government induce individuals to be price-takers when exclusion from consumption is not possible? Third, in the last part of section IV, Dr Bernard raises the question of when it will be appropriate to use as producer prices a vector of prices generated by a proportional tax on all commodities but the *numeraire* good. To answer this question, Dr Bernard applies a clever method involving changes in the *numéraire*. But could he give a more intuitive explanation of what is happening here? When you change the *numéraire* you change your problem and comparison becomes difficult.

Professor Stiglitz offered the following general comments on the Bernard analysis. First, analyses such as Dr Bernard's tend to produce policy conclusions that are often very sensitive to the specification of the problem, particularly the list of available tax instruments. An example of this sensitivity was provided in the discussion of the Atkinson paper (see the comments by Professor Stiglitz), where a mild amount of separability in the utility function, plus the availability of an income tax, gave zero commodity excise taxes as the optimal solution. Substituting a wage tax for an income tax completely reversed this conclusion. Given this sensitivity of the conclusions to the available set of tax instruments, it would be extraordinarily useful if this set could be defined as part of the optimising problem itself. One promising avenue for such an extension is that of explicitly allowing, in optimal tax models, for the costs of tax administration and tax avoidance. Some recent work has attempted to move in this direction.[1]

Professor Vickrey felt that models such as Dr Bernard's miss an important element in public tax policy – namely, the introduction of new taxes. New taxes may involve quantum jumps in administrative costs, but the efficiency gains may be quite impressive. The possibility of introducing new taxes will often arise with the development of new collection technologies. For example, it is now possible to monitor automobile travel in an administratively efficient way, thus permitting the use of automobile taxes. Also, the development of new commodities introduces the possibility of new taxes. How might these nonmarginal breaks in policy be introduced into an optimising model such as Bernard's?

Dr Guesnerie restated Professor Vickrey's point as a problem of nonconvexities. But this is a central problem to all second-best analysis. Studies of optimal taxation often have been quite negligent in their treatment of sufficient conditions. On the Bernard paper itself, Dr Guesnerie wished to stress that Dr Bernard makes clear a point that is often quite obscure in the literature concerning the difference between aggregate financial constraints and sectoral constraints. It has sometimes been argued that the Boiteux-type model and the Diamond–Mirrlees models are intimately related. Bernard's paper shows that this is true only to a limited extend, and that the mathematical structure and the results from the two types of models are, in fact, quite different.

Dr Bernard responded first to the request by Professor Bradford to clarify the optimal-tax formula that uses the vector of social value of goods, u. The optimal-tax formula in question appears in section III for noncompensated demand derivatives. Note, however, that $u_1 = q_i - t_i$. On substitution we obtain

$$\sum_h \beta^h x_j^h = -\sum (q_i - t_i)\frac{\partial x_i^h}{\partial q_j} = \sum q_i \frac{\partial x_i^h}{\partial q_j} + \sum t_i \frac{\partial x_i^h}{\partial q_j} \tag{1}$$

and

$$\sum_h \beta^h x_j^h = -\sum \frac{\partial (x_i^h q_i)}{\partial q_j} + \sum \frac{\partial (t_i x_i^h)}{\partial q_j} \tag{1'}$$

The first term on the right-hand side equals the change in income I as the price of good j changes, but $\partial I/\partial q_j = 0$. Thus, (1′) reduces to Dr Bernard's equation (15.6). However, this equation is the usual optimal-tax formula where an increment in the rate of taxation gives an increment in total taxes that is proportional to consumption (x_j^h) weighted by the marginal utility of income to

[1] W. P. Heller and Karl Shell, 'On Optimal Taxation with Costly Administration', *American Economic Review,* May 1974; M. G. Allingham and A. Sandmo, 'Income Tax Evasion: A Theoretical Analysis', *Journal of Public Economics,* Nov 1972; and T. N. Srinivasan, 'Tax Evasion: A Model', *Journal of Public Economics,* Nov 1973.

consumers (β^h). In reply to Professor Bradford's question on consumers as price-takers for marketable public goods, Dr Bernard noted that the intention of this section was simply to make the point that, when designing the tax system, we must also consider (a) the possibility of taxing marketed public services, and (b) that the optimal solution will require these taxes to be discriminatory. In conclusion, Dr Bernard noted his agreement with both Professor Stiglitz's comment on the sensitivity of the policy results to the set of available tax instruments, and Professor Vickrey's criticism that such optimal-tax studies neglect the possibility of introducing new tax instruments into the available set. This is clearly an area for future work, perhaps along the lines of administrative costs, as suggested by Professor Stiglitz.

Discussion of Jacques Thédié, 'A Challenge to the Monopoly of the Rate of Discount in Investment Choices'

Professor Paelinck introduced the discussion of the Thédié paper by noting that it would be useful to understand the institutional decision-making problem to which it is addressed. The paper is an exercise in decentralised planning in which a bureau-level decision-maker must make investment choices subject to a centrally defined and imposed budget constraint. The usual investment decision rule for selecting projects according to the project's discounted present value is computed as

$$PV = \sum_{t=0}^{\infty} a_t(A_t - I_t) > 0 \qquad (1)$$

where A_t and I_t are, respectively, the benefits and costs in period t, and a_t is the well-known Fisher–Malinvaud discount factor. The question raised by Dr Thédié is whether the same a_ts should be applied to the A_ts and I_ts when financial limits act as a constraint on the I_ts. In response, Dr Thédié argues that a set of dual variables (ρ_ts) defined by the constraints on I_t, should be applied to the discount factors for the I_ts. The series of ρ_ts will satisfy $\rho_t > a_t$ for all t. Dr Thedie's revised decision rule is given by

$$PV = \sum_{t=0}^{\infty} (a_t A_t - \rho_t I_t) \geqslant 0 \qquad (2)$$

Professor Paelinck sees the Thédié approach as the correct one and as formally equivalent to the mathematical programming problem analysed by Kornai and Liptak (see J. Kornai and T. Liptak, 'Two-Level Planning', *Econometrica,* XXXIII, 1963). Higher-level authorities set dual prices for the capital available to the various subsectors, and the subsector authorities then maximise their objective function, using these prices. The process converges, under certain assumptions, from the theory of differential games.

Professors Paelinck and *Klevorick* independently offered the following alternative formal derivation of the Thédié investment rule. Consider P alternative (but *not* mutually exclusive) investment projects indexed $p = 1, 2, \ldots, P$. Let $x_p = 1$ or 0 be a decision variable denoting that project p is decided ($x_p = 1$) or rejected ($x_p = 0$), and, finally, let J_t be the investment ceiling for year t. Then, the bureau's budgeting problem may be written as

$$\max_{\{x_p\}} \sum_p \sum_t a_t A_{pt} x_p \tag{3}$$

subject to

$$\sum_p I_{pt} \leqslant J_t$$

for all t, and $\quad x_p = 0 \text{ or } 1$

Now, let ρ_i be the dual variable (shadow price) associated with constraint J_i. Ignoring the integrality constraints on x_p, the duality properties of an optimal solution of the above linear programme imply that, for every p, $x_p > 0$ if, and only if

$$\sum_t (a_t A_{pt} - \rho_t I_{pt}) \geqslant 0$$

or

$$\sum_t a_t \left(A_{pt} - \frac{\rho_t}{a_t} I_{pt} \right) \geqslant 0$$

It can be seen that, if chosen appropriately, Dr Thédié's coefficients β_t play the role of the ratios ρ_t/a_t in the above formula.

Professor Tulkens commented that the elegant conciseness of Dr Thédié's paper makes its provocative thesis a convincing one at first reading; further readings, however, leave the following questions unanswered. First, at a theoretical level, what is the fundamental model of choice behind the Thédié conclusions? Professors Paelinck and Klevorick have offered a specification that appears to justify the Thédié rule, but is it the 'correct' specification of a bureau's budgeting problem? Professor Tulkens offered the following alternative formulation of the budgeting problem with constraints.

Let us define I_{ij} as the amount of investment, made in year i, that is apt to provide consumption services C in year j; and $f_{ij}(I_{ij})$ as the production function determining the amounts of consumption services available in year j for a given investment I_{ij} made in year i. Consider an arbitrary (but finite) time horizon T, with $i = 1, 2, \ldots, T$. The model may then be expressed as follows:

$$\max_{\{C_i, I_{ij}\}} U(C_1, C_2, \ldots, C_i, \ldots, C_j, \ldots, C_T)$$

subject to $T + (T-1)$ constraints of the form

$$\left.\begin{aligned} C_i + \sum_{j>i} I_{ij} - \sum_{h<i} f_{hi}(I_{hi}) &= K_i && i = 1, \ldots, T \\ \sum_{j>i} I_{ij} &\leqslant J_i && i = 1, \ldots, T-1 \\ C_i, I_{ij} &\geqslant 0 && i, j = 1, \ldots, T \end{aligned}\right\} \tag{4}$$

Using $\lambda_i \geqslant 0$ and $\mu_i \geqslant 0$ as Lagrange multipliers associated with the constraints in (4), the first-order conditions for a maximum are (ignoring corner solutions)

$$\frac{\partial U}{\partial C_i} - \lambda_i = 0 \qquad \forall i$$

$$-\lambda_i + \lambda_j \frac{df_{ij}}{dI_{ij}} - \mu_i = 0 \qquad \forall i \text{ and } \forall j, \text{ such that } j >$$

which imply that

$$\frac{\partial U}{\partial C_i} = \frac{\partial U}{\partial C_j}\frac{df_{ij}}{dI_{ij}} + \mu_i = 0 \qquad \forall i, j, \text{ with } j < i,$$

or

$$\frac{\partial U/\partial C_i}{\partial U/\partial C_j} = -\frac{dC_j}{dC_i} = \frac{df_{ij}}{dI_{ij}} + \frac{\mu_i}{\partial U/\partial C_j} \tag{5}$$

Note how this model is related to the classical case; namely, the one with no investment ceilings. If, for some i, $\mu_i = 0$ (i.e. if the corresponding budget constraint is not binding), the last expression may be rewritten as

$$-\frac{dC_i}{dC_j} = \left(\frac{df_{ij}}{dI_{ij}}\right)^{-1} \tag{6}$$

or

$$\left(\frac{df_{ij}}{dI_{ij}}\right)^{-1} dC_j + dC_i = 0 \tag{7}$$

This equation simply denotes the trade-off conditions, at an optimum, between consumptions at time j and consumptions at time i; it is easily related to the standard net-benefits formula $\sum_i a_i(A_i - I_i)$ (used by the author elsewhere in his paper) if one applies this formula to the particular project where there is invested, in year i, an amount $I_i = dI_{ij} > 0$ (implying, in view of (4), that $dC_i < 0$) which yields benefits only in year j (so that $A_j = dC_j > 0$). The ratio $[df_{ij}/dI_{ij}]^{-1}$ here plays, in an obvious way, the role of the discount factor a_i. If we now suppose that the budget constraint J_i is binding, we have $\mu_i > 0$ in (5), and (6) becomes

$$-\frac{dC_i}{dC_j} = \left(\frac{df_{ij}}{dI_{ij}}\right)^{-1} + \frac{\partial U/\partial C_j}{\mu_i}$$

or

$$\left[\left(\frac{\partial f_{ij}}{\partial I_{ij}}\right)^{-1} + \frac{\partial U/\partial C_j}{\mu_i}\right] dC_j + dC_i = 0 \tag{8}$$

Comparing this with (7), one observes that the result of the binding character of the budget constraint is to modify the value of the coefficient associated with future benefits; that is, in Dr Thédié's notation, the discount factor a_i. Now, apparently the author's claim is that the model sketched out in his paper should yield, as a result

$$\left(\frac{\partial f_{ij}}{\partial I_{ij}}\right)^{-1} dC_j + \beta_i dC_i = 0$$

instead of (8). Clearly, this result does not follow from the present model. Therefore, the validity of the Thédié specification of the constrained bureau's investment rule depends, fundamentally, on the validity of the underlying specification of the choice problem. Dr Thédié does not face this issue.

Professor Tulkens also took exception to Dr Thédié's claim that his rule should be applied by private firms facing a capital constraint. However, while it often happens that investment (or borrowing) ceilings are imposed on firms for a *given* interest rate, the firms in question usually can borrow more if they pay a *higher* interest rate. In that case, what, from the viewpoint of the private firm, is the exact meaning of using the β coefficient under such market circumstances?

Turning back to the public sector, Professor Tulkens noted that a major claim of the paper is that, if the various government agencies are making proper use of coefficients β, the 'national' discount rate α (which enters in the definition of the discount factors a_i) could be lower. But lower than what? And how low? More generally, if, given α, government agencies find profitable investment opportunities at some time i, but at the same time face budget constraint J_i, a natural question to ask is: which parameter has been incorrectly chosen, α or J_i? In other words, if J_i is binding, is this not an indication either that α has been chosen too low, or that the appropriation J_i has been incorrectly determined? Is there not a danger that the generalised use of coefficients β to 'make up' budget restrictions at all levels (and sublevels) of government would lead the higher authorities to dispense with the necessity of choosing the budgets J_i and the national discount rate α properly – that is, such that the supply of available funds effectively meets the demands corresponding to all profitable projects?

Dr Guesnerie wished to point the connection between Dr Thédié's analysis and earlier work by Martin Feldstein (see M. S. Feldstein, 'Net Social Benefit Calculations and Public Investment Decisions', *Oxford Economic Papers*, Mar 1964). Dr Thédié's β is very closely related to the concept, outlined by Feldstein, of the opportunity cost of expenditures. The rate of discount in both the Thédié and Feldstein analyses is the community's rate of time preference. Might we not observe, then, that, in some appropriate general equilibrium framework, the budget constraint of the State may appear as resulting from an arbitrage between the public and private sectors in the spirit of the opportunity-cost approach? In this way, the views of Dr Thédié and Professor Feldstein might be formally related.

In reply to the comments on his paper, *Dr Thédié* expressed his strong belief that, for formal economic analysis to be a useful tool for resource allocation, it must be sensitive to the institutional setting in which the analysis is to be used. As a person practically concerned with this problem, Dr Thédié had noted the future of cost–benefit algorithms to take into account the important fact that bureaux operate under rigid budget constraints; and it was this omission that his paper had sought to correct. The alternative algorithm that he had proposed is conceptually valid (as the comments of Professors Paelinck and Klevorick show) and administratively workable in a decentralised context. At the agency level, the budget and the rate of discount are given and one need only vary the βs until the budget is just exhausted by all favourable projects. The allocation task at the central level is, of course, more difficult. There, both the rate of discount and the agency budget levels must be set.

Discussion of T. S. Khachaturov, 'Transportation as a Public Service in the USSR'

Professor Vickrey began the discussion of the Khachaturov paper by thanking the author for a very interesting description of some rather surprising features of the Soviet railway transportation system. Professor Vickrey made two technical points about the statistical analysis in the Khachaturov paper. First, one must be extremely careful when interpreting traffic density figures. The startling contrast in density between the USSR and the United States is probably explained by the historical development of the two railway systems. The United States system was developed in a spirit of 'boosterism', in which a high premium was placed on the development of branch lines. These lines are now little used. By contrast, the Russian system was developed more rationally, so that excess capacity was likely to be minimised. This would explain the startling differences in the traffic density of the two systems. Second, do Professor Khachaturov's profit calculations for the Russian railway system make allowances for depreciation or for other capital expenses?

Professor Vickrey then raised three more general questions. First, the Russian system involves something of the order of 26 administrative agencies. How is administrative co-ordination achieved within this system? Second, would Professor Khachaturov please give a rationale for the pricing system described in his paper? It appears that, in the Russian pricing system, no particular attention is paid to problems of peak and off-speak pricing. Finally, has there been any attempt, in the planning of the USSR transportation system, to pursue a linear programming approach to the problem of freight backhaul?

Professor Milleron remarked that, about seven years ago, at a European Econometric Society meeting, a colleague of Professor Khachatuov's had mentioned that mathematical programming procedures were beginning to be applied to planning in the transportation sector. What was the present state of mathematical planning for the USSR transportation system?

Professor Feldstein commented that he could understand why the Russian transportation system had low costs, but why, then, are prices not lower? What is the point of making a profit in the transportation sector?

Professor Vickrey wished to pursue the point raised by Professor Feldstein. If the Russian transportation system does indeed exhibit economies of scale, this must mean that marginal costs are a good deal below the average prices charged to the users of the system. If so, there must then be misallocations of resources. Will not decision-makers making decisions on the basis of these profit-making prices use too little of the available transportation facilities?

In response to the questions of Professors Feldstein and Vickrey, *Professor Khachaturov* noted that, for current business, managers use the tariffs, while, for investment project planning, real costs are used. Inefficiencies (if any) generated by prices greater than marginal costs would be slight, because transport tariffs constitute only a very small percentage of industry costs. Profits earned from fixing prices at above the average costs are used to cover capital investments. While it is true that capital investment costs can be covered out of funds from general taxation, it had been decided to cover these costs through pricing in the transportation sector itself.

Discussion of Bruno Frey, 'On the Political Economy of Public Services'

Professor Pauly introduced the discussion of the paper by Professor Frey by complimenting the author for considering an important research area. Positive analysis of the public sector is of interest in its own right, but it is particularly important as a counterbalance to the implicit assumption, in much of the research that governments are social welfare optimisers simply waiting for the truth of economic analysis. It is far more reasonable to suppose, as Professor Frey does, that representatives are private maximisers worried about ideology, staying in office, and ensuring their private incomes. The best-intentioned politician may not be much helped, when advised to change taxes so as to achieve a welfare optimum, if the advice ignores his own political constraints. An 'optimal' policy will be more effective if the normative prescription is combined with an anaiysis of the political feasibility of that policy. The Frey paper is presented in this spirit, and the author is to be commended for undertaking such an analysis.

Professor Pauly offered three specific comments on the model itself. First, the model assumes totally myopic consumers. This seems unreasonable. It seems more likely that consumers do have some foresight and do take into account the future real income productivity of public expenditures. Second, the opposition party plays no explicit role in the Frey model. The government plays its political game against the world and not against a political opposition. If a party loses, it is not because it performs less well than the opposition, but because it does not generate enough pleasant surprises for the voters. This assumption also seems unrealistic. An expanded model should include an opposition party that also is able to make promises to the voters. The voters would then be forced to choose between two expected values of income based on party promises and on voter expectations about the fulfilment of these promises. Third, the model ignores inflation and unemployment – clearly, important issues in any Western political campaign.

On a more general level, Professor Pauly questioned the usefulness, for policy analysis, of simulations based on models with *ad hoc* parameter values. While we may have reasonable estimates of the saving rate, we at present have little idea of what the rate of depreciation of a politician's stock of political capital might be. If simulation models such as Professor Frey's are to be of any use, the key political parameter values must be estimated from econometric models of the political process. Such work remains to be done. Finally, Professor Pauly noted that, when the government sector becomes endogenous to our policy models, the policy-advising role of economists becomes endogenous as well. Instead of being impartial social-welfare optimisers, economists become, in these broader models, advisers to particular 'private interests'. The role of economists in such a social system is something we know very little about.

Professor von Weizsäcker commented that, though we may find it necessary to make specific criticisms of Professor Frey's paper, his efforts mark an important break with the economists's traditional approach to policy-making. Work such as Professor Frey's should become a number-one priority. We have prided ourselves on expanding our economic analysis into a general equilibrium framework, but, at the same time, we have narrowly restricted our work to economic parameters only. For a democracy certainly, politics are as much an endogenous element of the social system as is the economy. The economic approach to policy has been to assume a benevolent dictator with a benevolent social welfare function, where the economist's task is simply to advise such a dictator. It is naïve to assume that such a situation really exists.

Professor Stern began his comments by saying that he had enjoyed the paper very much and had a great deal of sympathy for the approach. But where is the class struggle in the Frey analysis? One can imagine a fairly simple extension of the model that would include party and class politics. Suppose that there are two groups with different preferences, and that parties are loosely connected with these groups. The enthusiasm of a group for its connected party is influenced by the performance of the party in power, and, if this is not its own party, by the memory of the most recent performance by its own party. Naturally, memories fade. Whether or not a particular party stays in power depends on the relative enthusiasm of groups for their own party.

Professor Stiglitz noted that, in a macro-economic political model such as Professor Frey's, the politically accurate specification of the model might stress the rates of change rather than the levels of the key variables. For example, voters seem more sensitive to the changes in the rate of unemployment than to the level of unemployment itself. Professor Stiglitz also wondered whether Professor Frey could give some intuitive interpretation of the observed patterns of political change. When is one likely to expect a high turnover among parties in office, and when is one likely to expect a stable political system – that is, one party in power for many years?

In defence of Professor Frey's model, with respect to the comments of Professors Pauly and Stern, *Professor Breton* argued that a noncompetitive model of party behaviour may be more realistic than a two-party competitive model. Certainly some competition among parties will exist, but it is unlikely that competition will assume the major motivating role that is given it by, for example, the Downsian models. As suggested by Professor Frey, people do forget past political errors, and parties often hold office for four or five years without any legal commitment to stand for election. Thus, there is considerable noncompetitive slack in a system of the type that the Frey model assumes.

In response to the discussants, *Professor Frey* said that he too was dissatisfied with a simulation model based on *ad hoc* parameters. However, he had found, in previous joint efforts with Professor Lau, that algebraic modelling is far too inconclusive to be useful on its own. Clearly, the next step is econometric estimation, and it was in that spirit that the present paper had been offered. The specifications can all be estimated, given an appropriate data base. Professor Frey welcomed Professor Breton's defence of his noncompetitive specification. Indeed, partly collusion against the voters may be more useful rather than party competition. In any case, the formal introduction of party competition over time into models such as the present one must be pursued as a differential game, the analysis of which is exceedingly complex and may not allow of a solution. Finally, Professor Frey agreed with the comments stressing the need to introduce into the model the macro-economic variables of unemployment and price inflation. The reason why they had not already been introduced was that such an extension would require a major macro-economic submodel appended to a political model that is already quite involved. Such an extension would be an important addition to the present analysis.

Discussion of Leo H. Klaassen and Wietze Eizenga, 'Some Considerations on the Productive Capacity of Consumption Expenditures'

Professor Martsinkevich opened the discussion by noting that Professor Klaassen's approach to public-expenditure theory – treating the investment as well as the consumption benefits of many social services – appears to be a very fruitful approach for analysis. Of course, this insight is not new. It has been developing steadily, particularly in the Marxist economies. In addition to Marshall's words cited by the author, Professor Martsinkevich presented the Marxian thesis that 'consumption is not only a final act due to which product transforms into product, but is also an act in which a producer becomes a producer'. In section II of their paper, the authors modify the simple Harrod–Domar model to include income as a function not only of net investments, but also of so-called 'regenerative consumption'. The authors assume that a certain level of consumption is needed to keep the productive capacity of labour just constant at a given level. At this point, problems begin to enter the analysis. The distinction between consumption and investment is not as simple as that outlined by the authors. Such important public services as health and education may be serving dual roles. For example, in the course of many decades, the educational sphere in the USSR has been undergoing growth in all respects. Growth has stimulated not only an improvement in human capital stock, but also a growth in the consumption of social and other cultural activities. Education is a key stimulus to growth in other sectors of the USSR economy. In order adequately to incorporate such dual growth effects of certain key public services, the model must be substantially changed – changed to the point of becoming so complex that it becomes less useful as a tool for analysis. The cost–benefit approach developed in section IV of the paper appears to be a more promising basis for analysis. It is regrettable that the presentation of this approach is so concise, since the topic deserves much more attention. In an effort to develop a sound theoretical grounding for such a complex planning and cost–benefit approach, economists and sociologists in the USSR are working to find better and more exact methods for measuring the social, economic and other benefits of health, education, and other public services. Such measures, it is hoped, will allow economically significant comparisons to be made between the social-service and manufacturing sectors of the economy. The development of such measures is a priority for sound economic and social planning.

Professor Breton commented on the Klaassen and Eizenga paper by noting that the private market may adequately internalise the investment returns from certain 'consumption' activities. If the private market really does operate perfectly for these services, then it should be possible to infer, from econometric analysis of individual market behaviour, a rate of return to the investment margin of such consumption activities. This comment has some relevance for the last two sections of the paper

Professor Paelinck, speaking on behalf of Professor Klaassen, who could not attend the discussion, agreed with the commentators that a distinction between the pure consumption and investment effects of commodities was particularly important for growth analysis. Previous growth analysis has not pursued this line, yet there is some tentative econometric evidence from the United States and the Netherlands to indicate that such effects may indeed be present.

Name Index

Subject Index